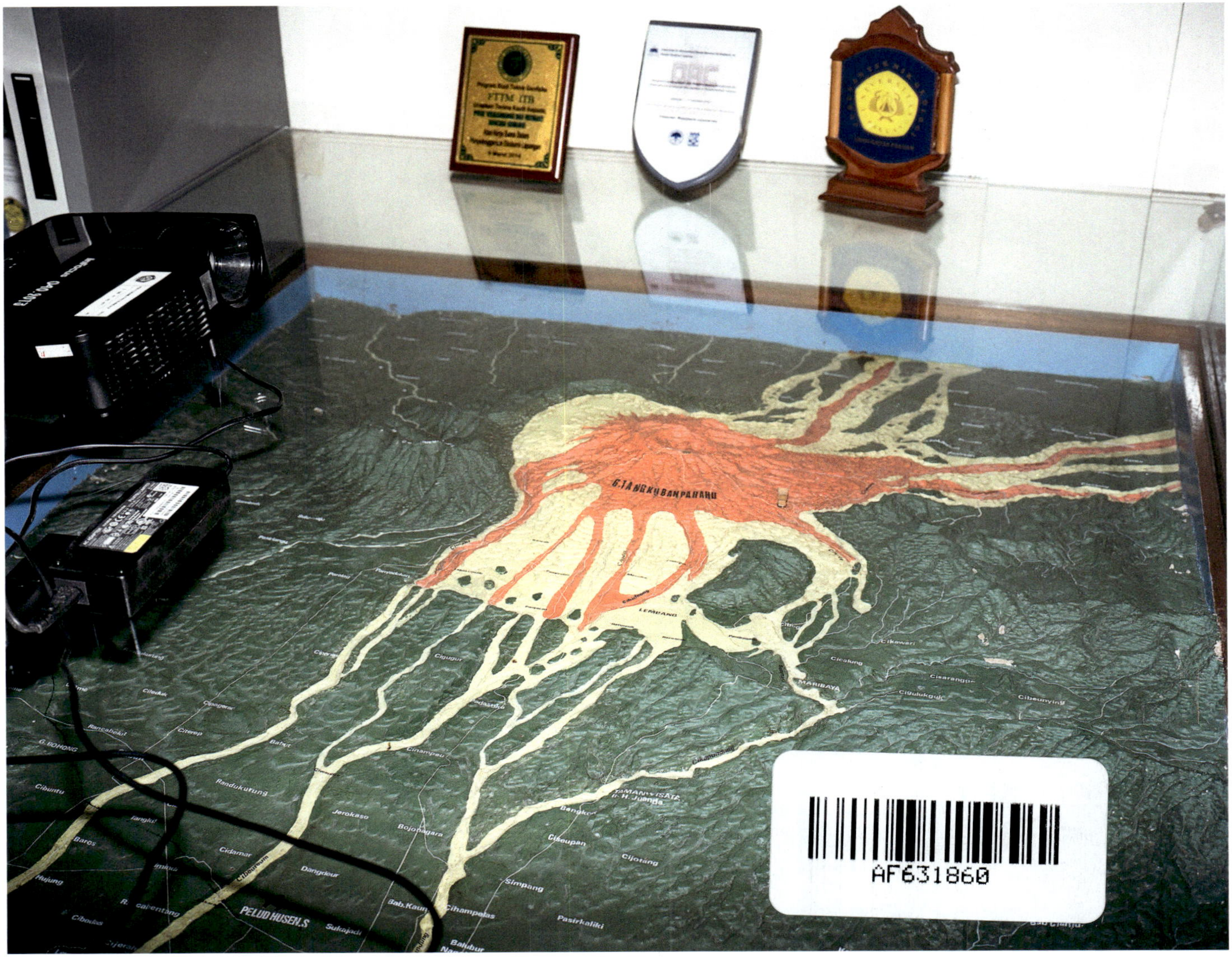

A 3D terrain model illustrates the potential directions of lava flow during a volcanic eruption.

Unselected

1–46

Tangkuban Perahu Volcano, local monitoring station, Bandung, Indonesia, 2015

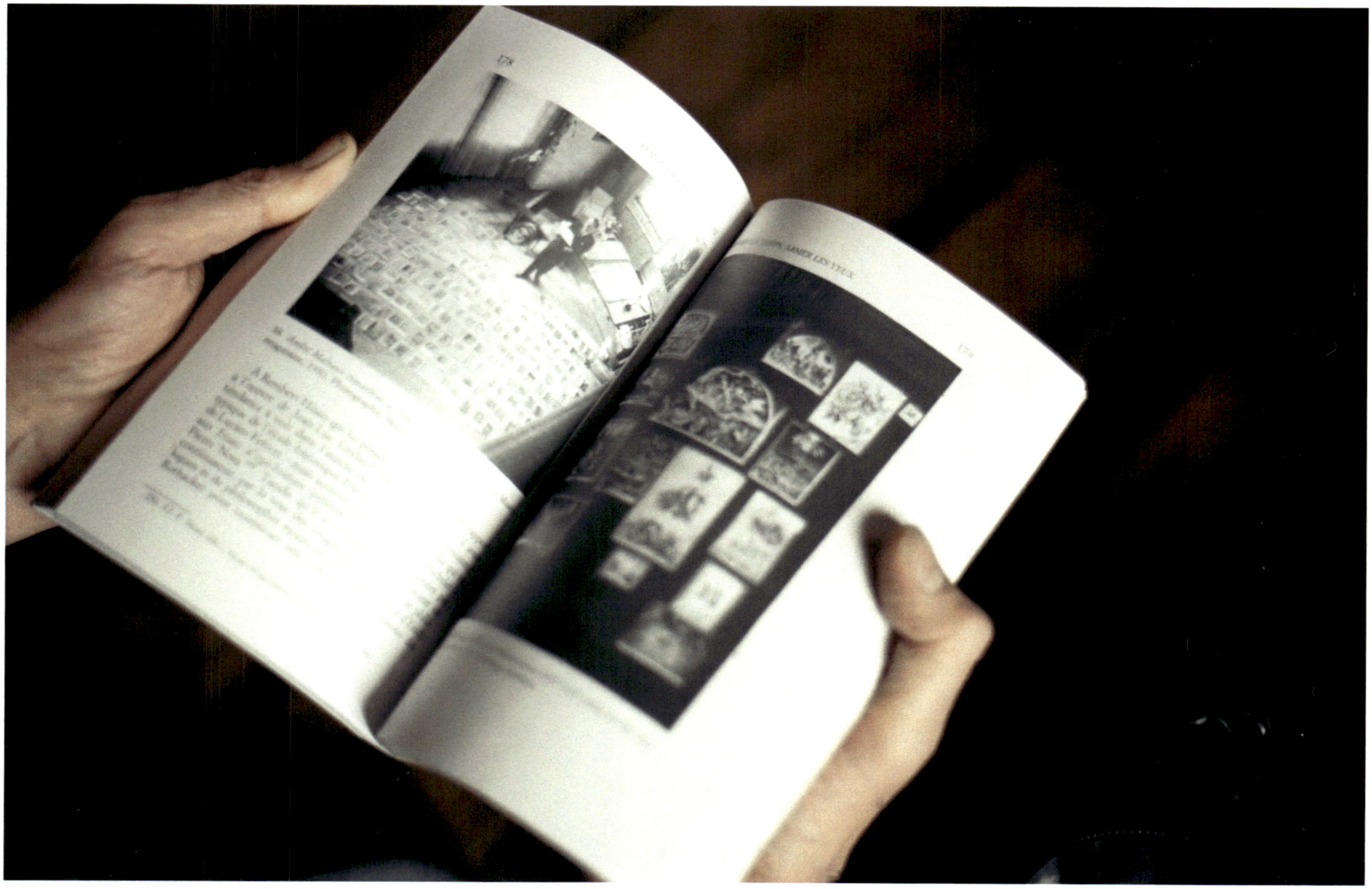

Harun Farocki, Berlin, Germany, 2011

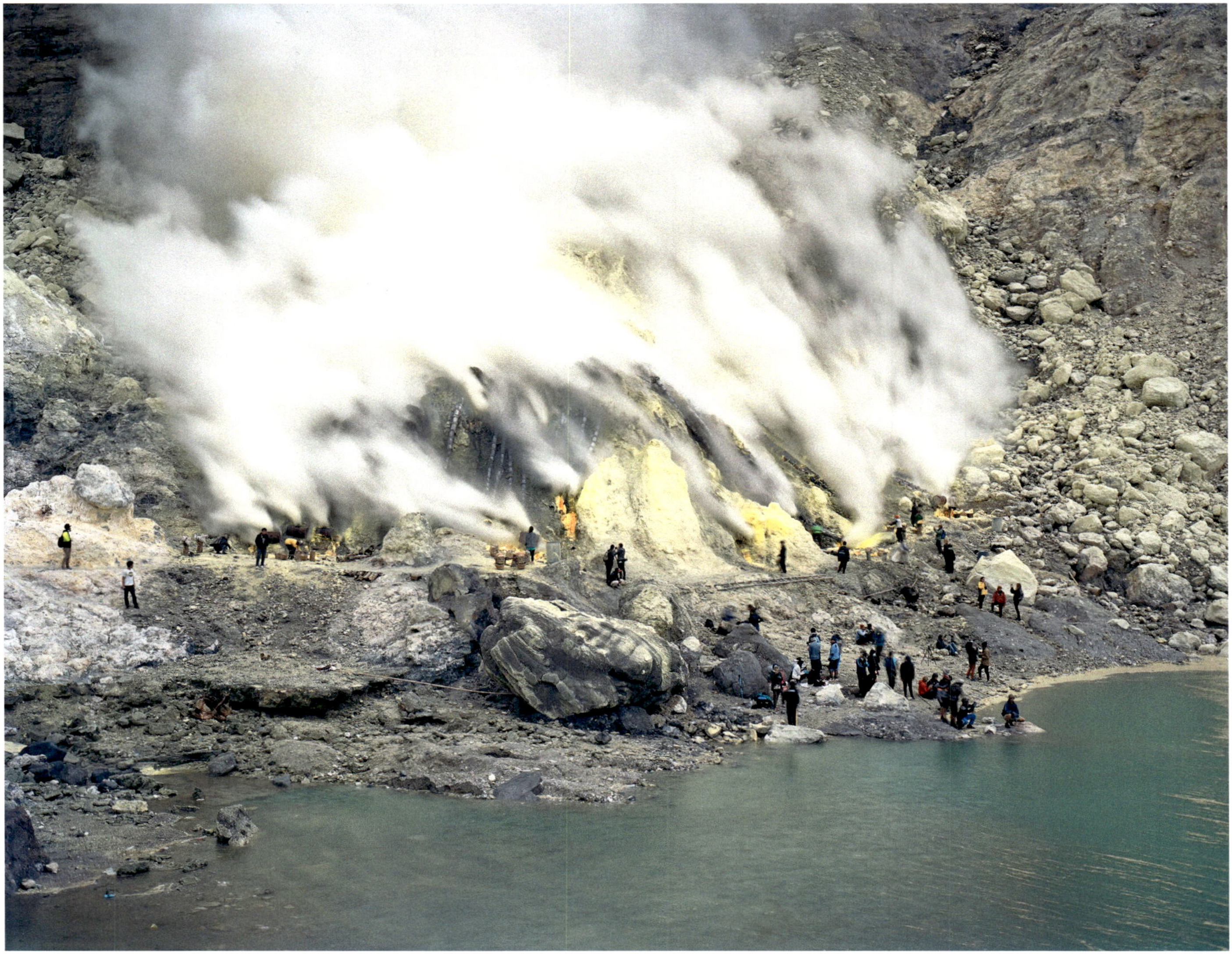

An active volcanic vent at the edge of this acid crater lake is a source of sulfur. The miners install long ceramic pipes into the fumaroles to collect the hot, liquid sulfur. As it drips out, it cools and solidifies. The workers break the bright yellow material into pieces and carry it away in baskets. They have to climb 3,000 ft. from the crater where the lake is situated and descend 9,000 ft. from the volcano's summit to the ground. They are paid according to the weight of the sulfur they extract.

Kawah Ijen Volcano, Biau, Jawa Timur, Indonesia, 2016

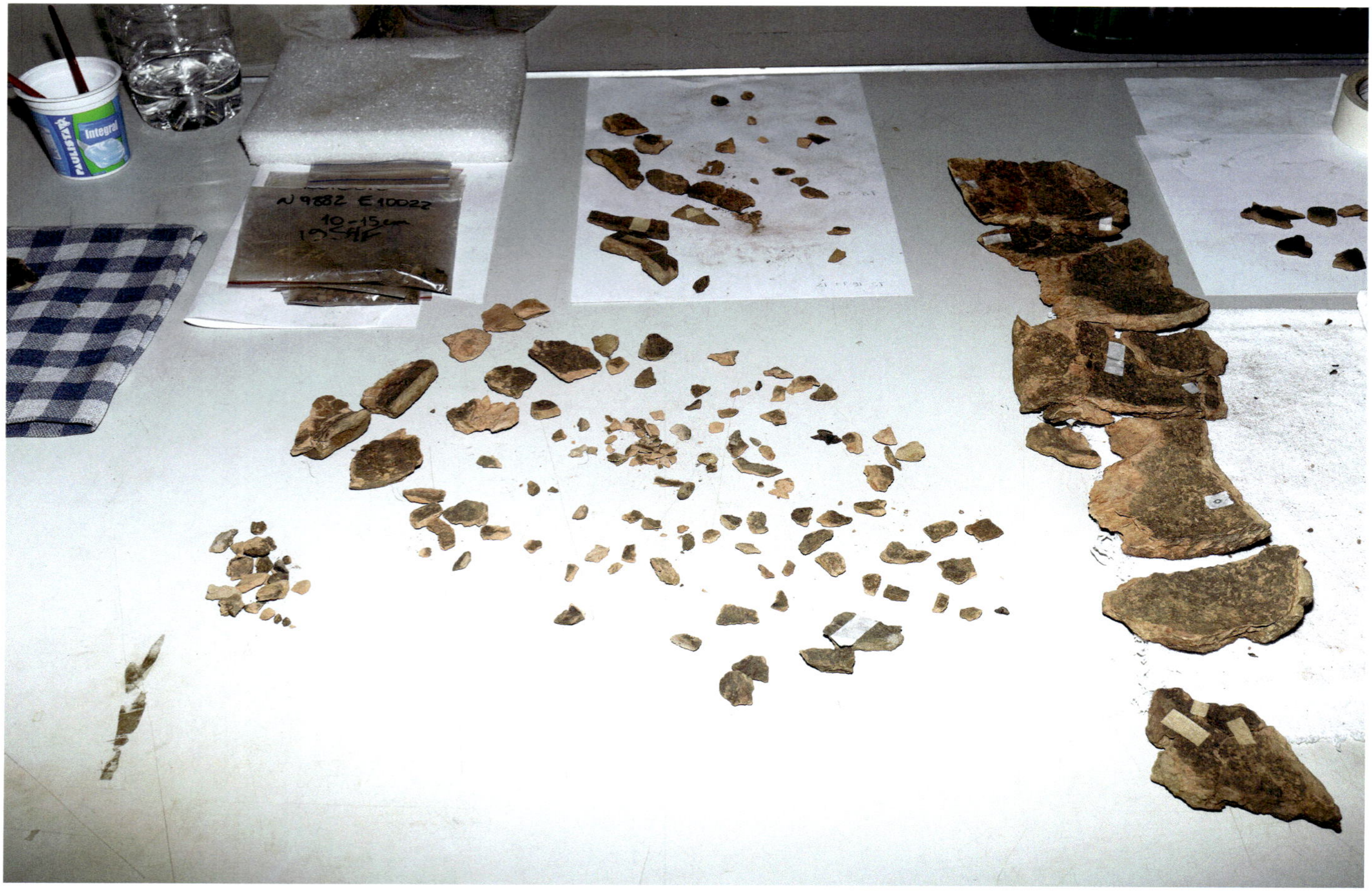

Paulo Nieves's working laboratory, Museum of Archaeology and Ethnology, São Paulo, Brazil, 2015

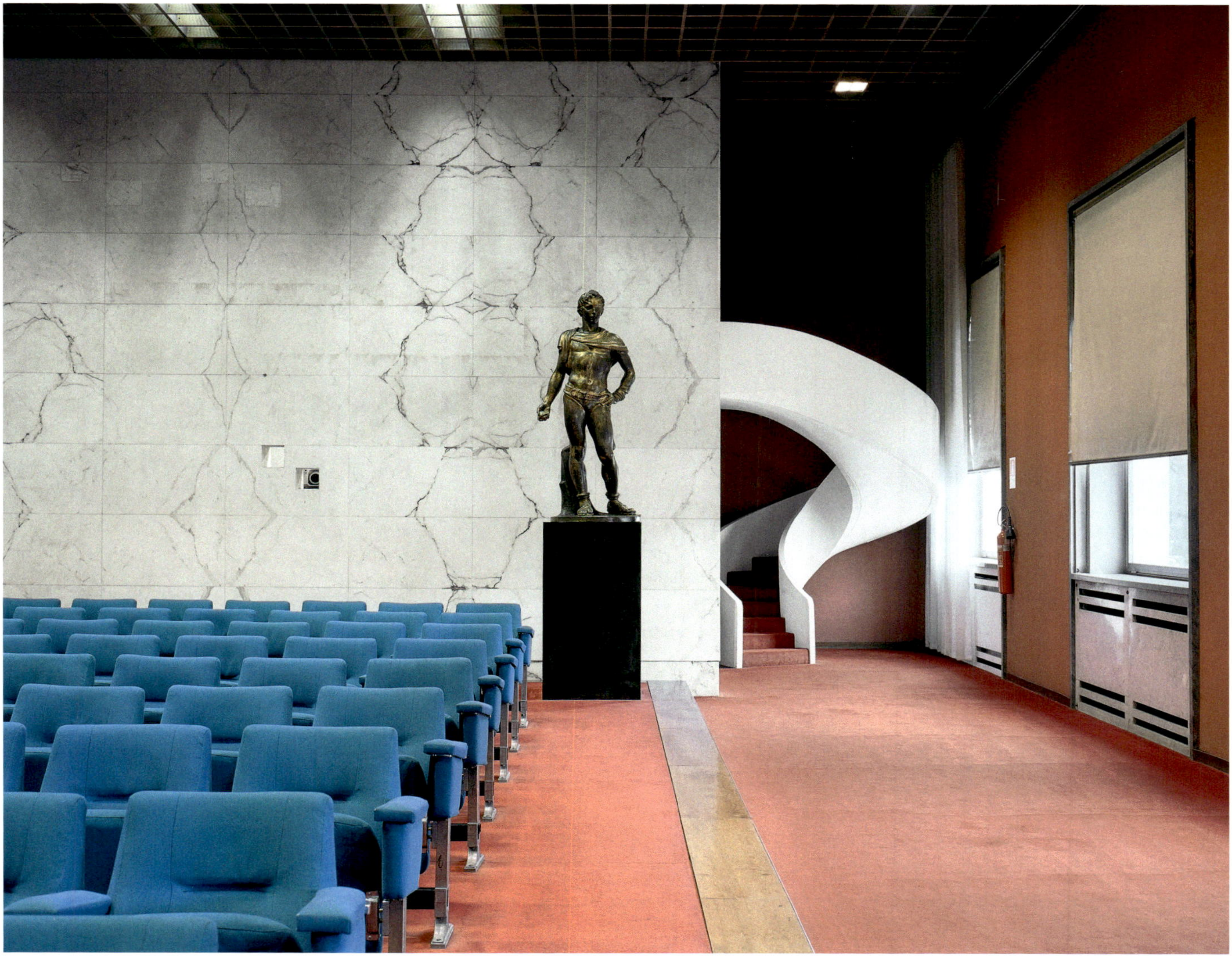

CONI, Foro Italico, Originally built as Benito Mussolini's gym, designed by Luigi Moretti, currently the conference hall of the Italian Swimming Federation, Rome, Italy, 2008

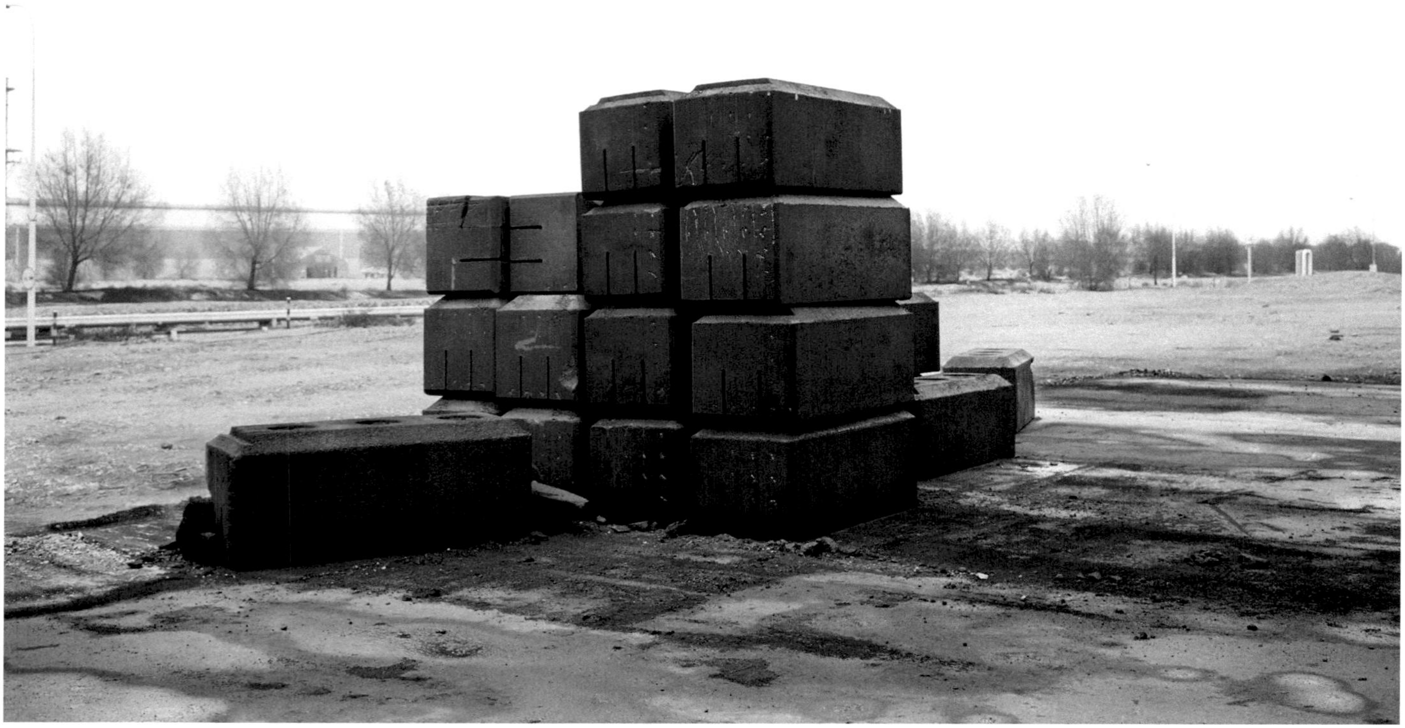

To produce anode carbon blocks, green petroleum coke, a byproduct of the coking process in oil refineries, is imported to Bahrain. In the smelting industry the anodes are needed for electrolysis to separate pure aluminum from its oxide form.

Anode carbon blocks, Manama, Bahrain, 2016

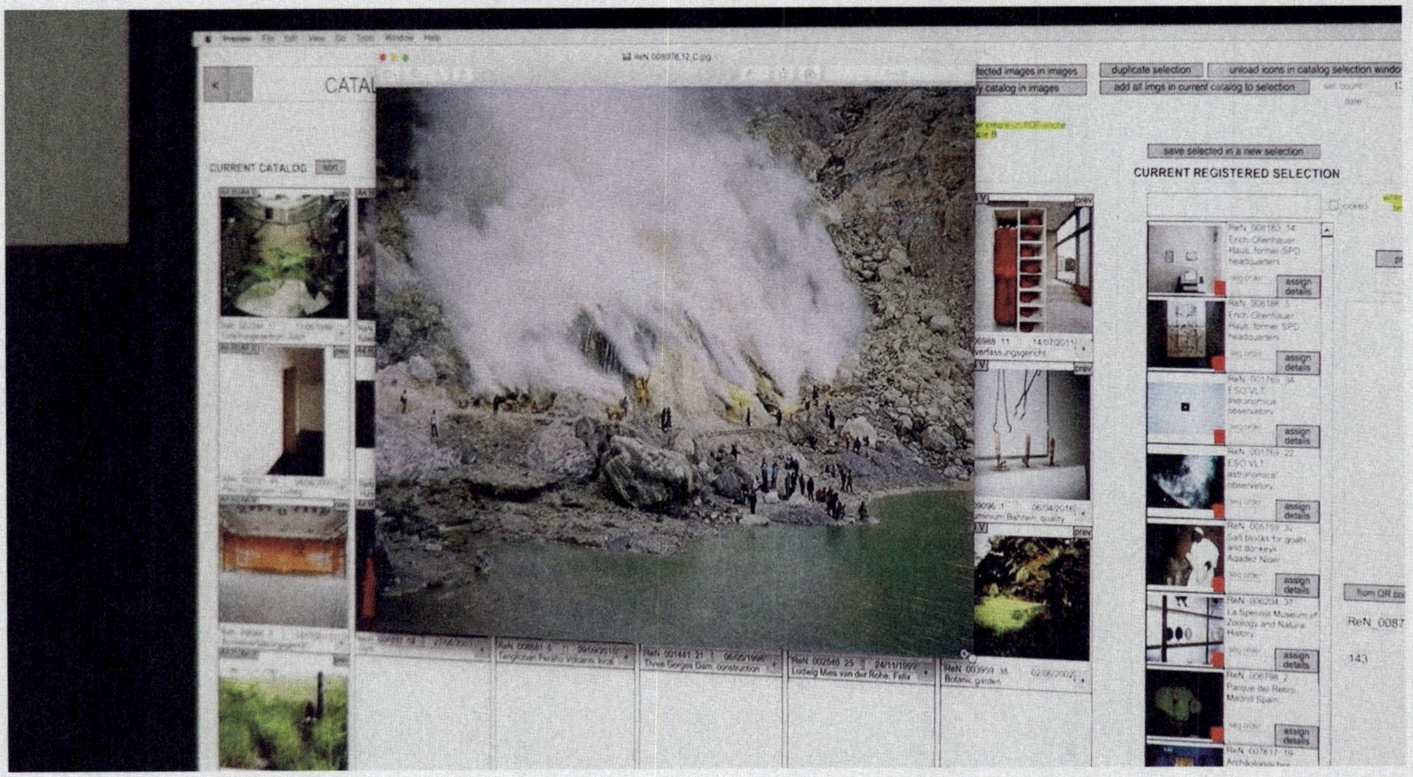

Armin Linke

Armin Linke at his studio, Berlin, November 2014

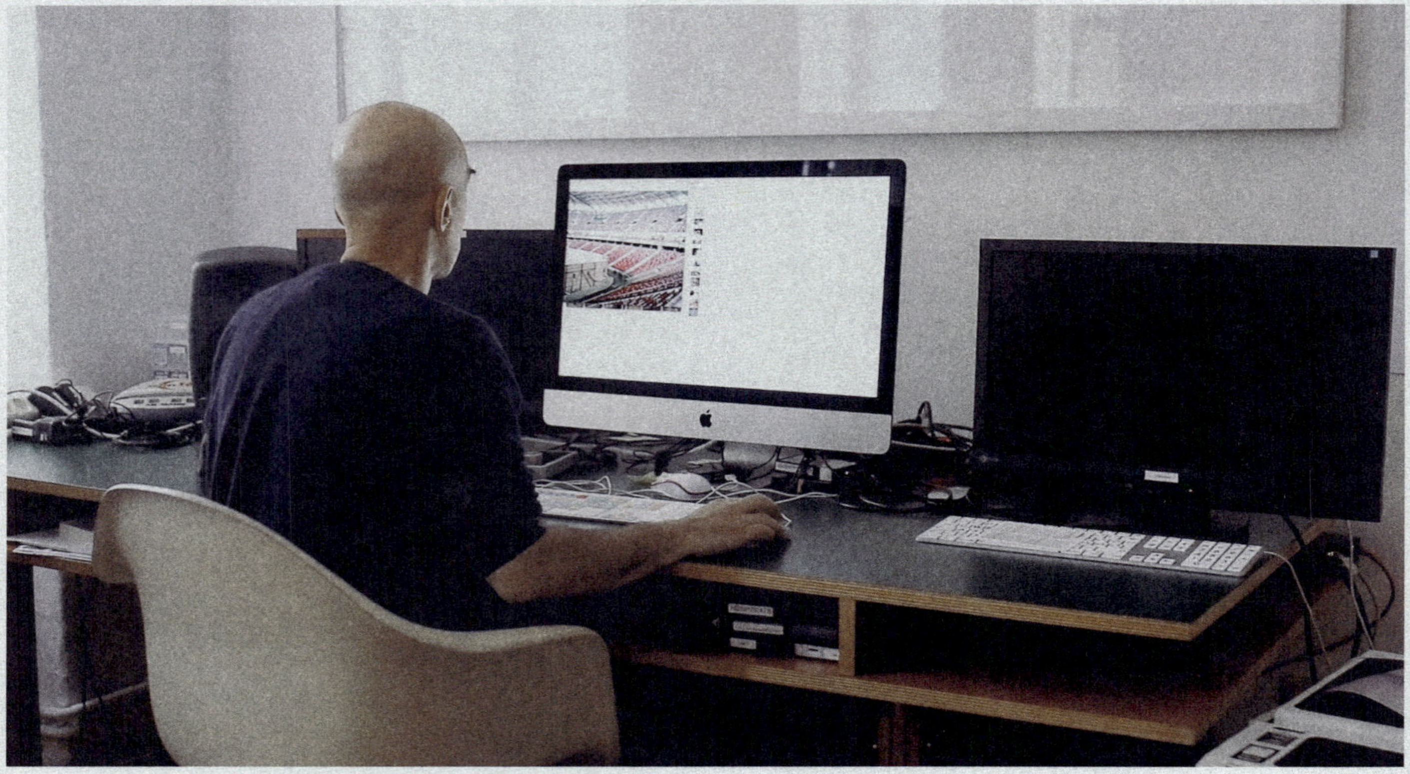

Armin Linke at his studio, Berlin, November 2014

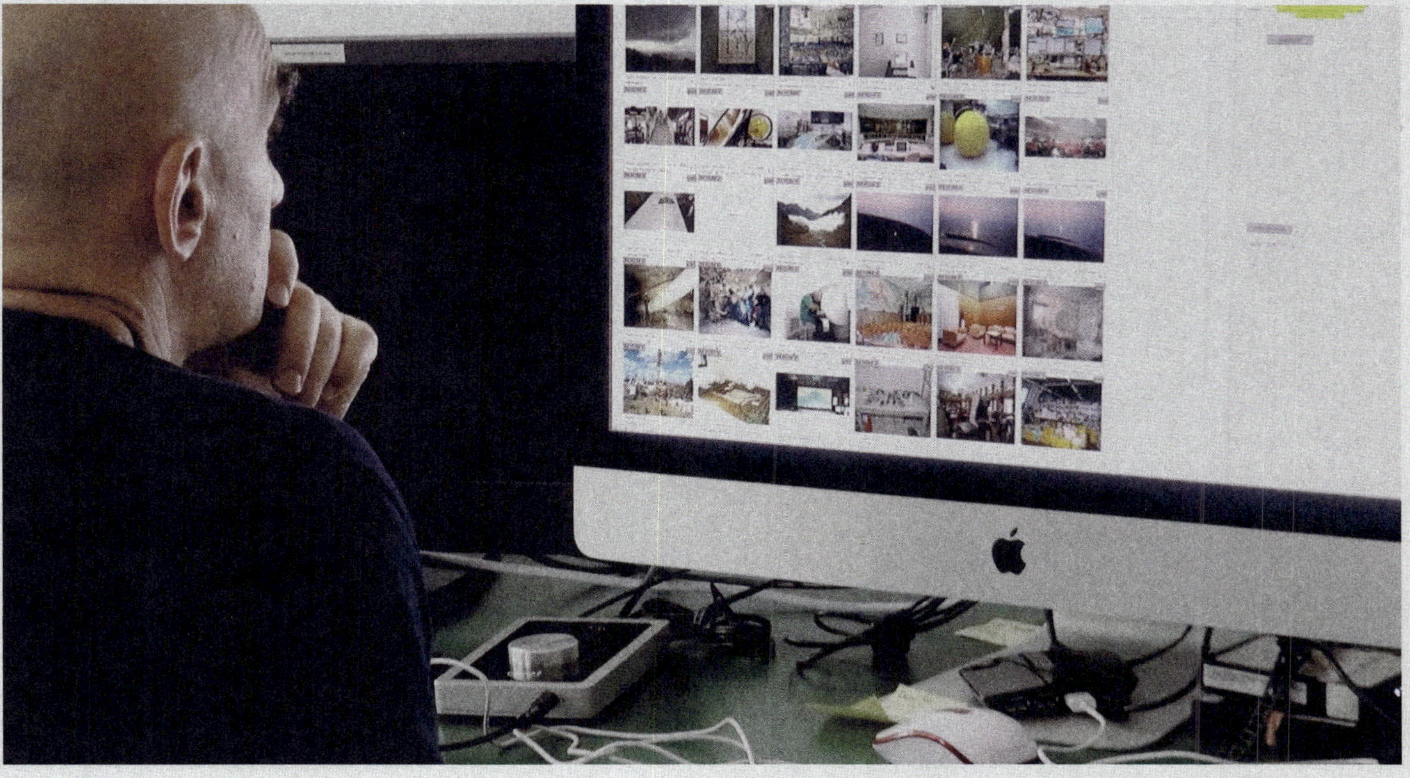

Armin Linke at his studio, Berlin, November 2014

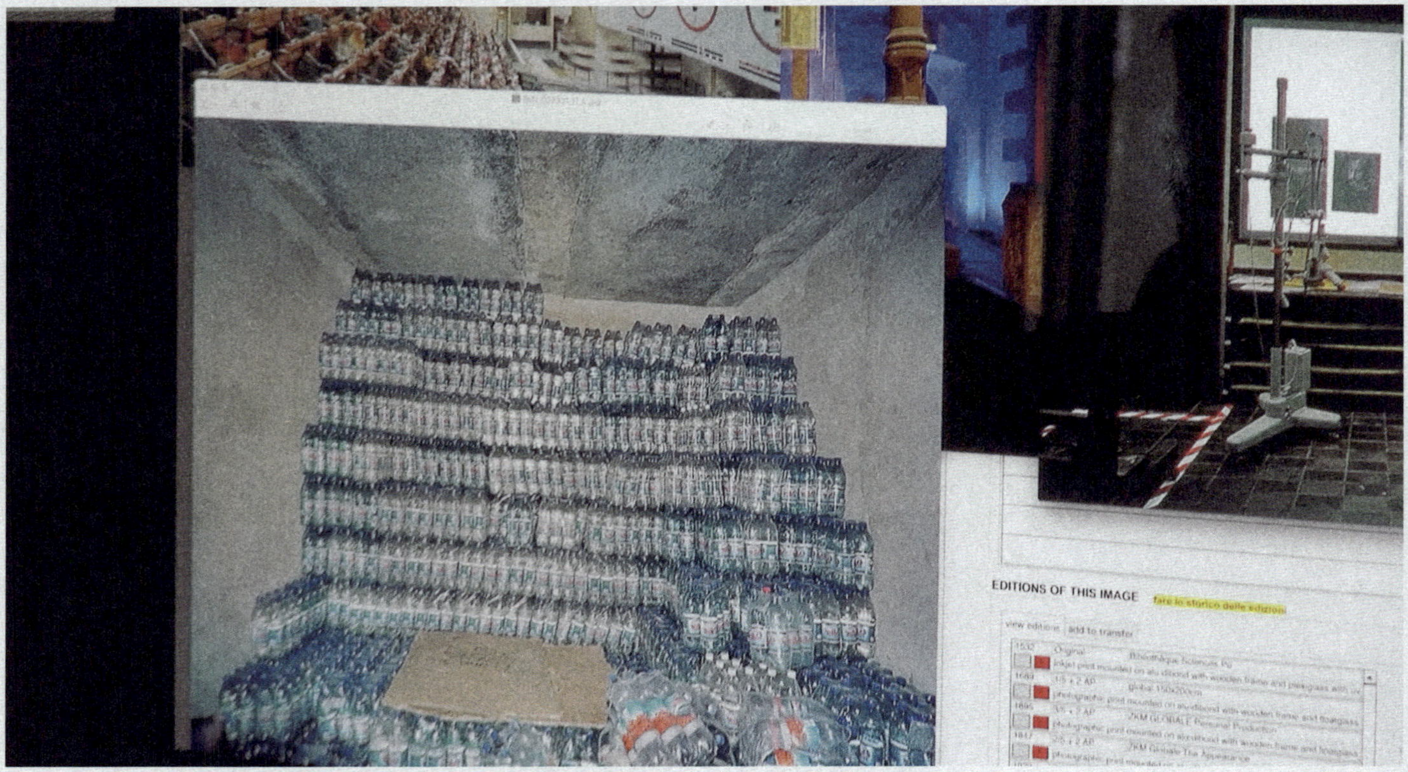

Armin Linke at his studio, Berlin, November 2014

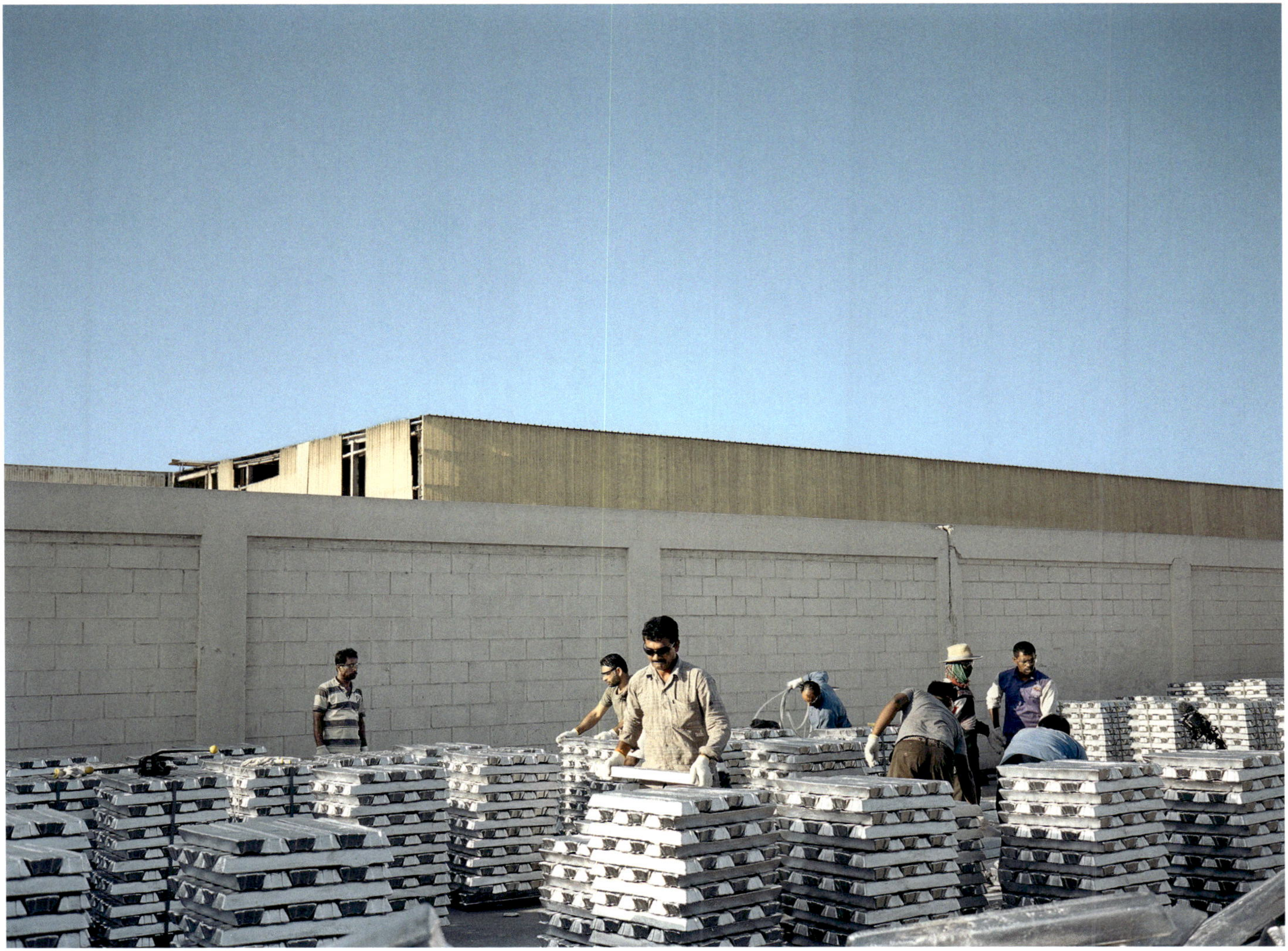

Aluminum alloy casting, Manama, Bahrain, 2016

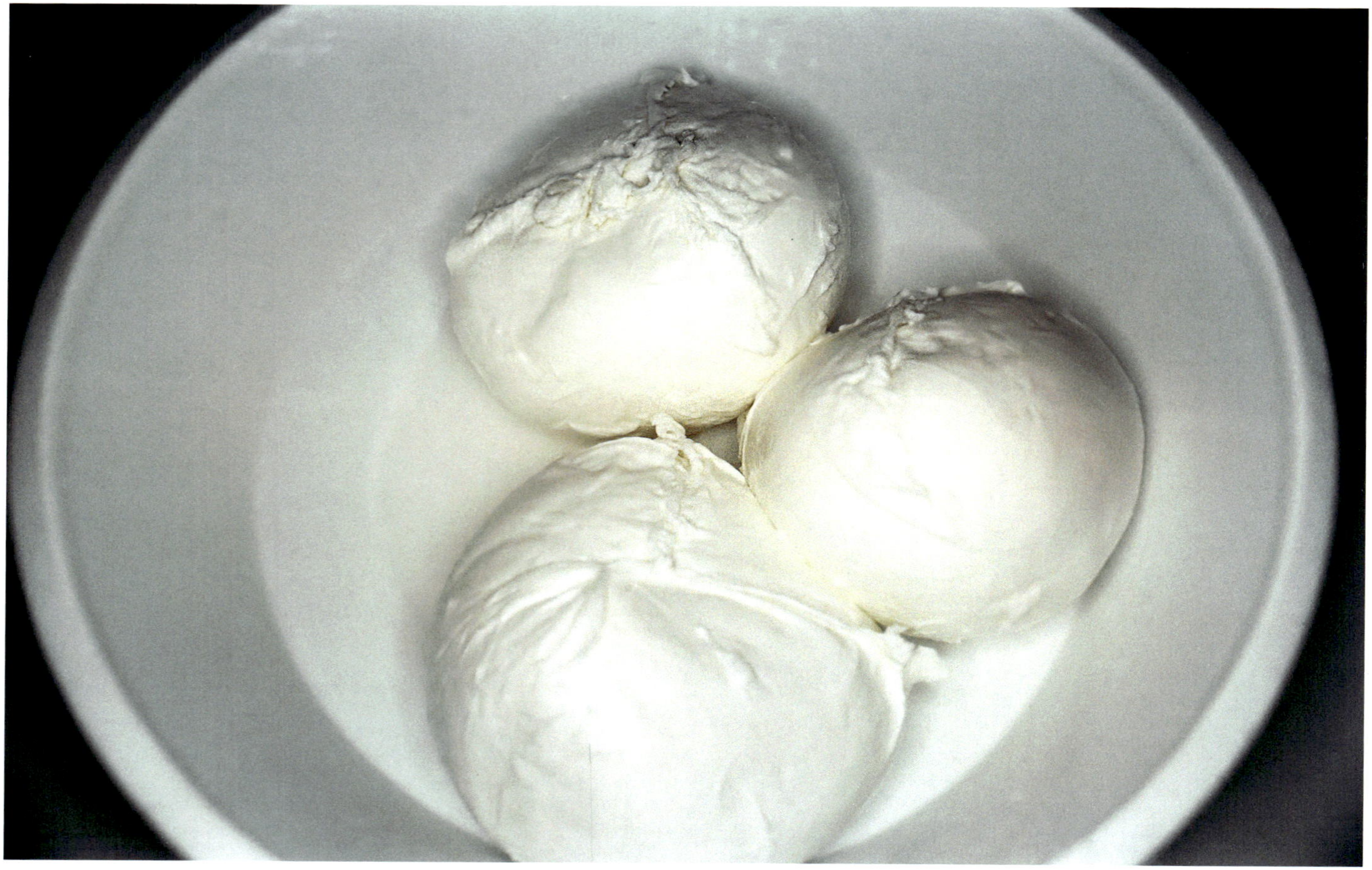

Mozzarella, Naples, Italy, 1997

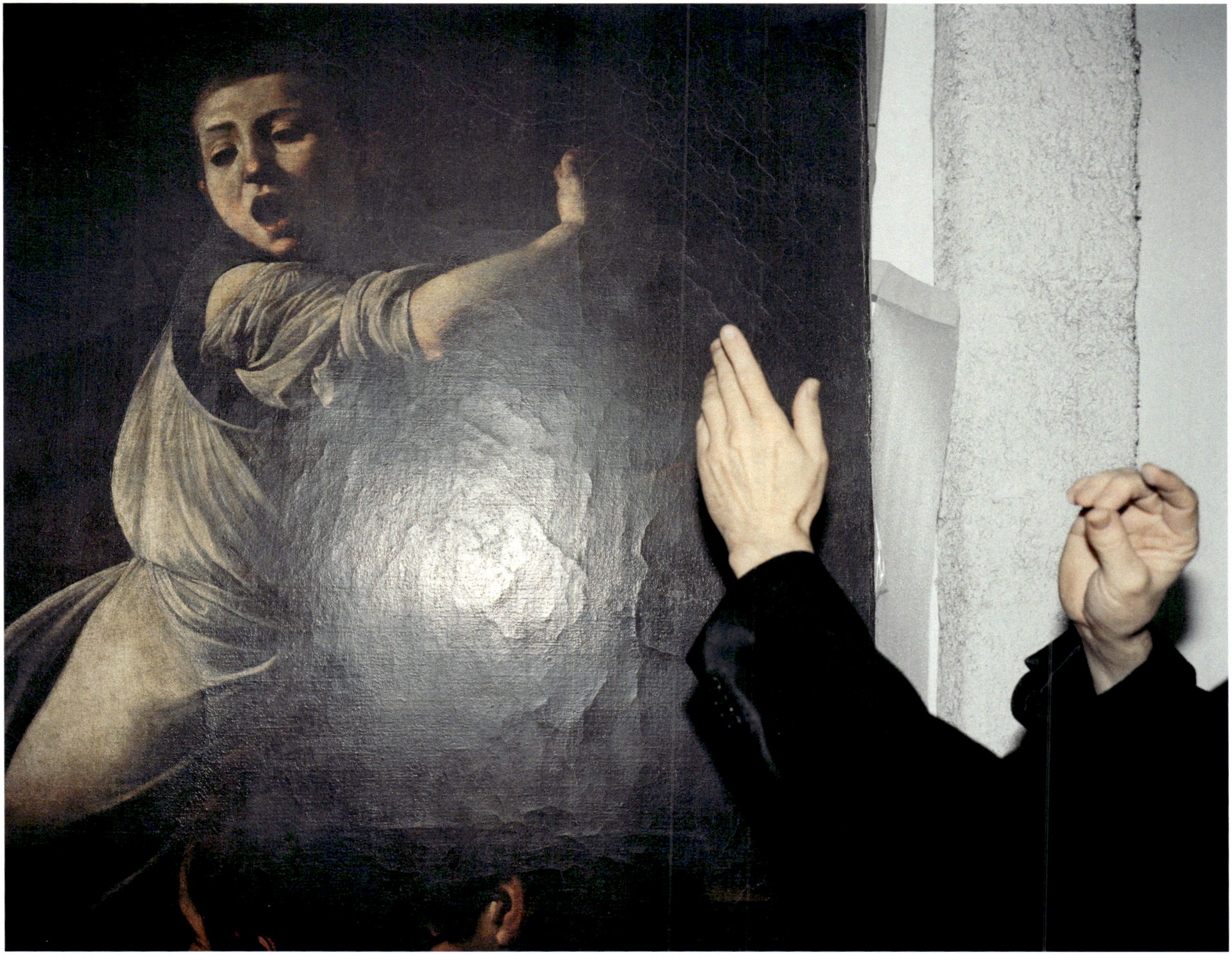

Adam Lowe and his team at Factum Arte develop new 3D scanning and printing technologies to create facsimiles of artworks. Using this technique, they are able to recreate the surface characteristics of the painting.

Adam Lowe, Caravaggio's *The Martyrdom of Saint Matthew*, Factum Arte, Madrid, Spain, 2011

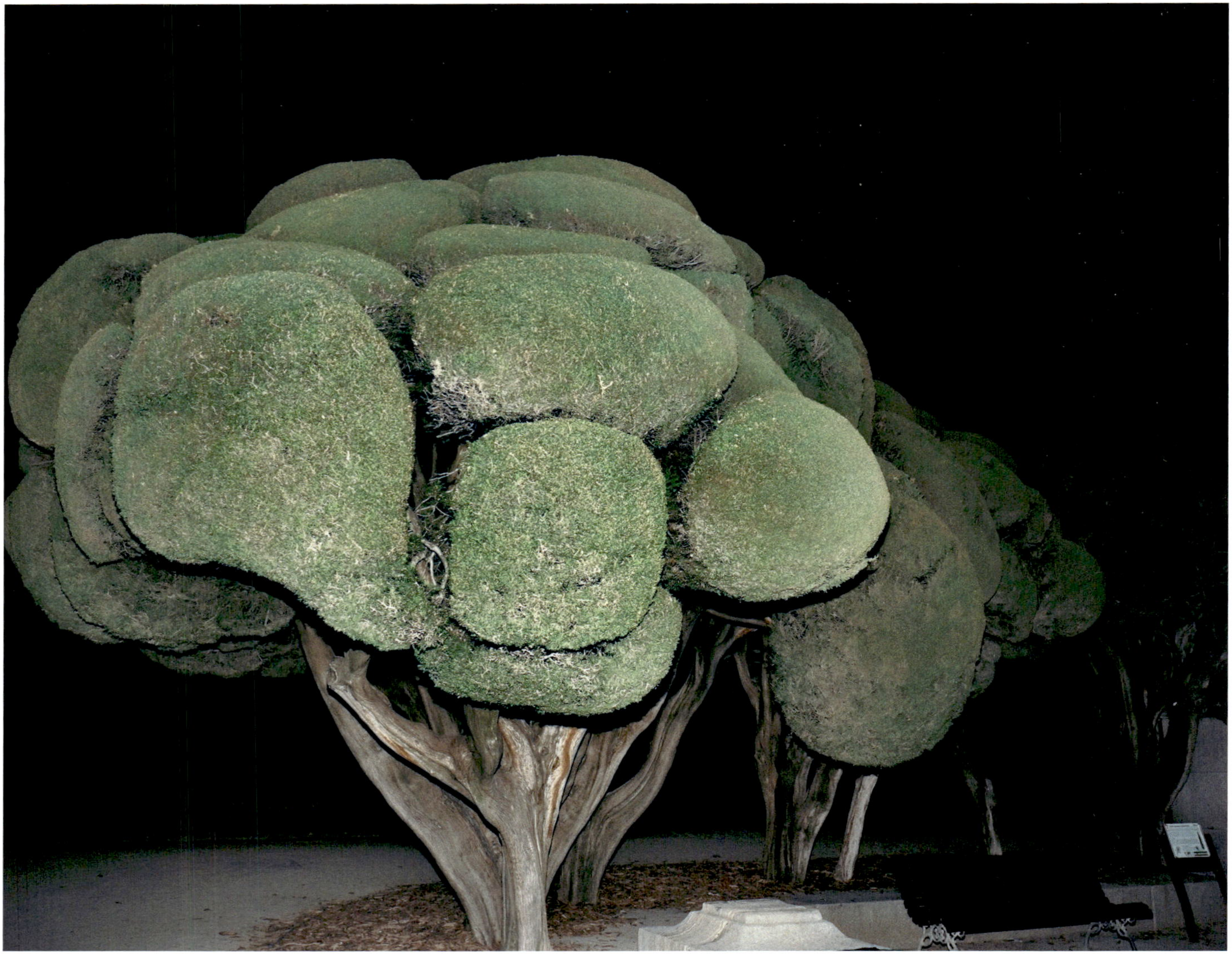

Parque del Retiro, Madrid, Spain, 2011

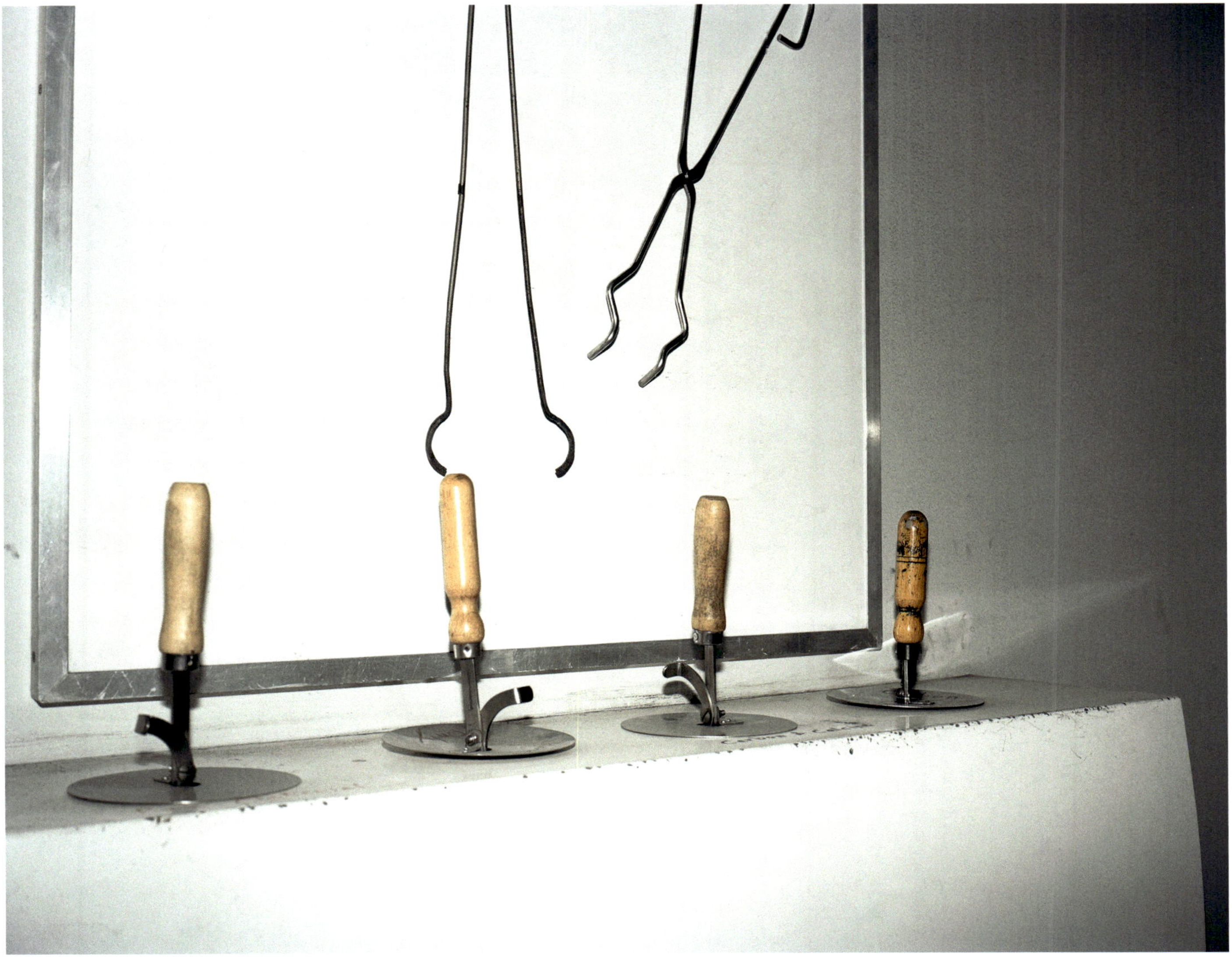

In the quality control laboratory, different chemical compositions of aluminum are tested in little furnaces. The test results are extracted with pliers.

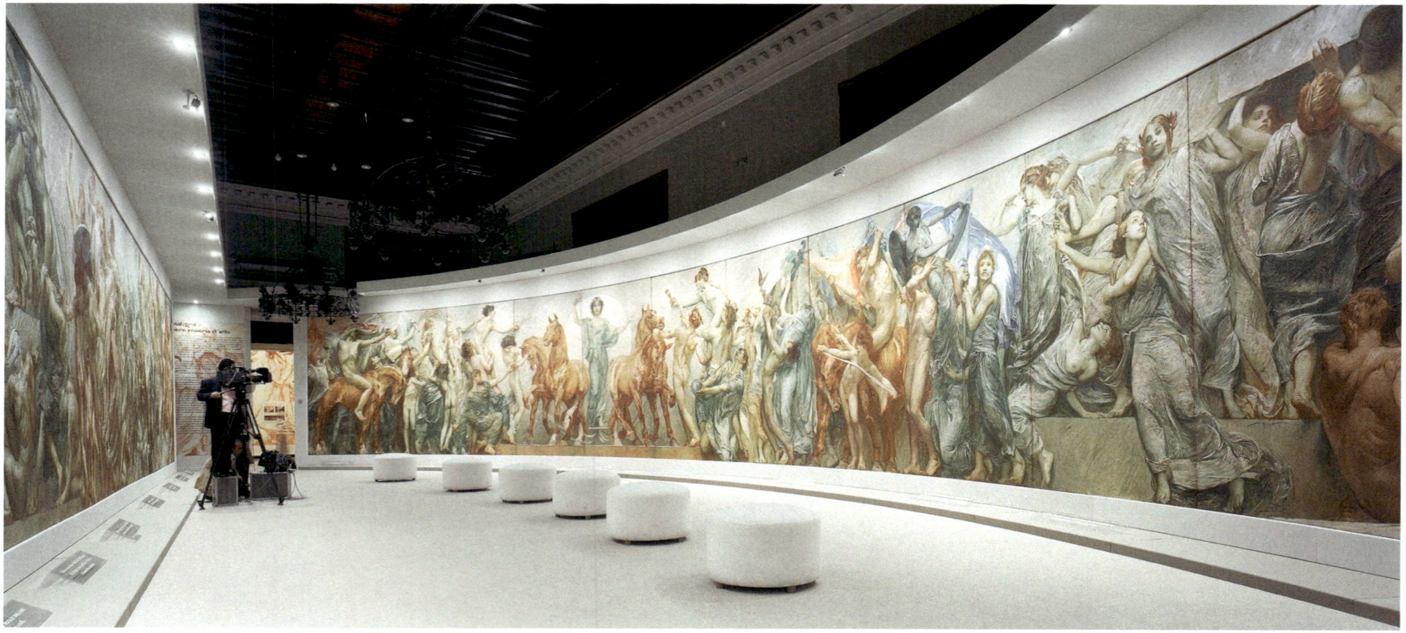

The wall painting by Giulio Aristide Sartorio depicts the Young Italy just before World War I. The painting hangs as a frieze in the Italian parliament. A TV team captures the scene shortly after it has been restored and re-installed.

Chamber of Deputies, Palazzo Montecitorio, Rome, Italy, 2007

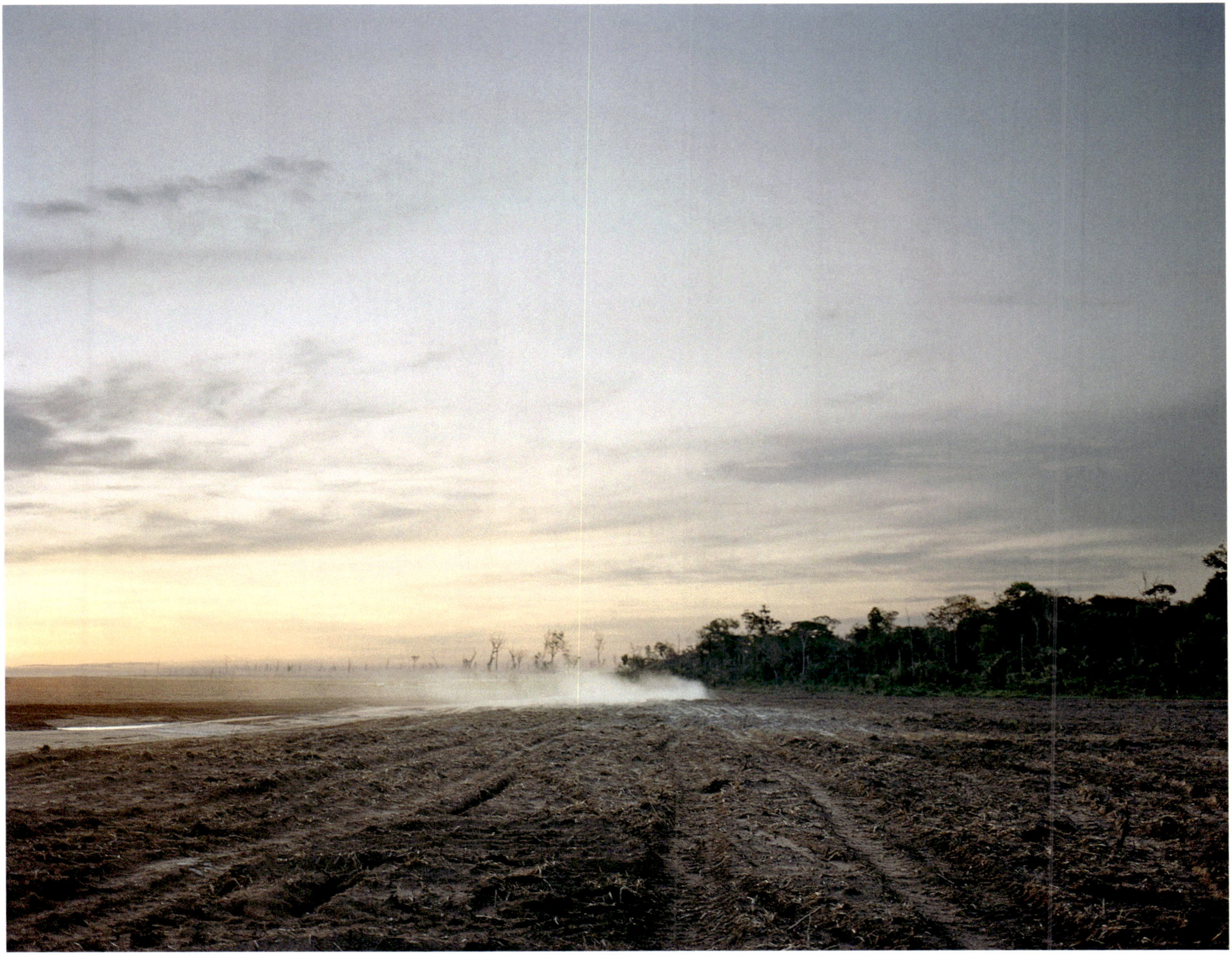

In the course of the deforestation along the edge of the Amazon rainforest, trees are cut and the remaining vegetation is set on fire. After preparation with lime and chemicals, the soil is used for soy monocultures.

A tractor sprays chemicals on a soybean plantation, Amazonias, Brazil, 2015

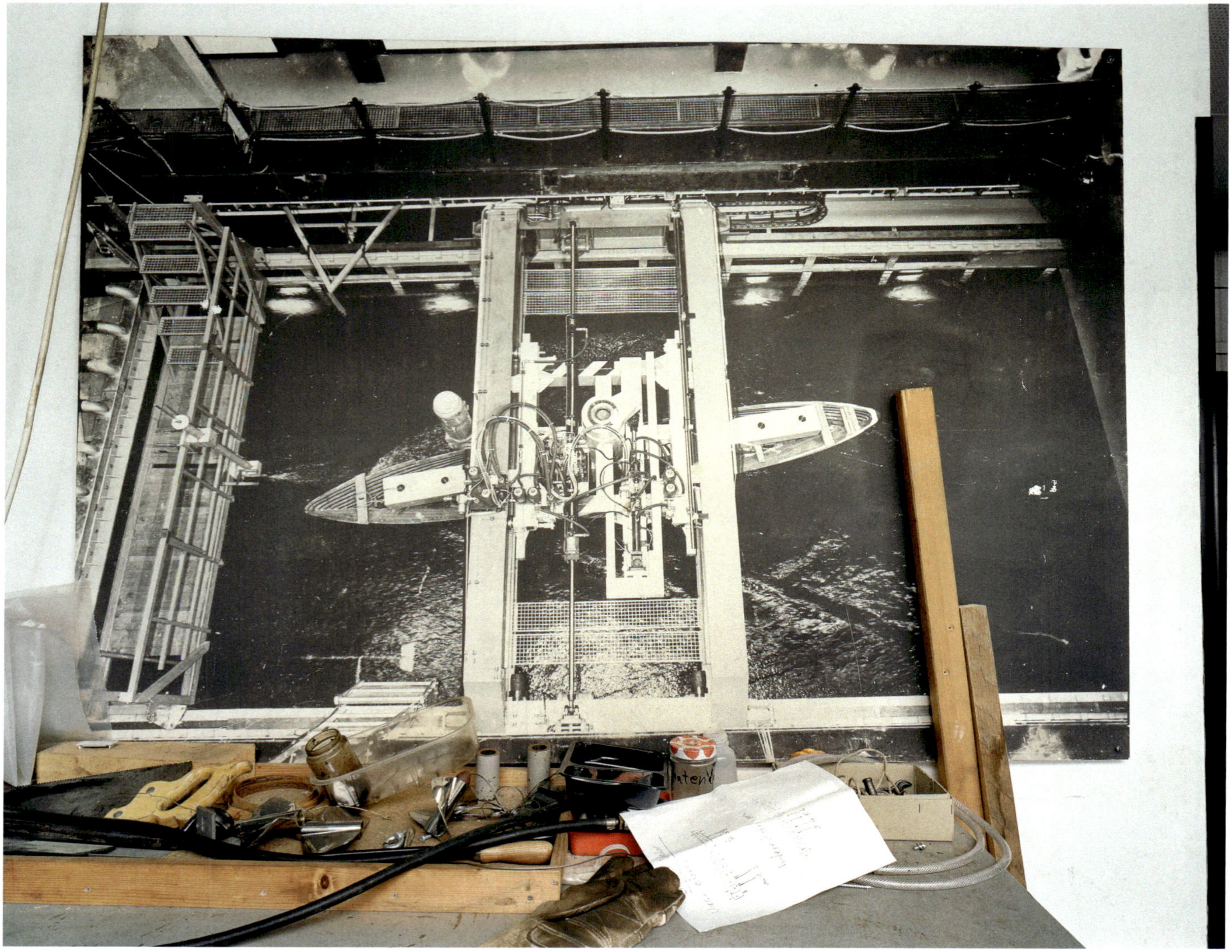

Research center for naval architecture and hydro engineering,
Berlin, Germany, 2012

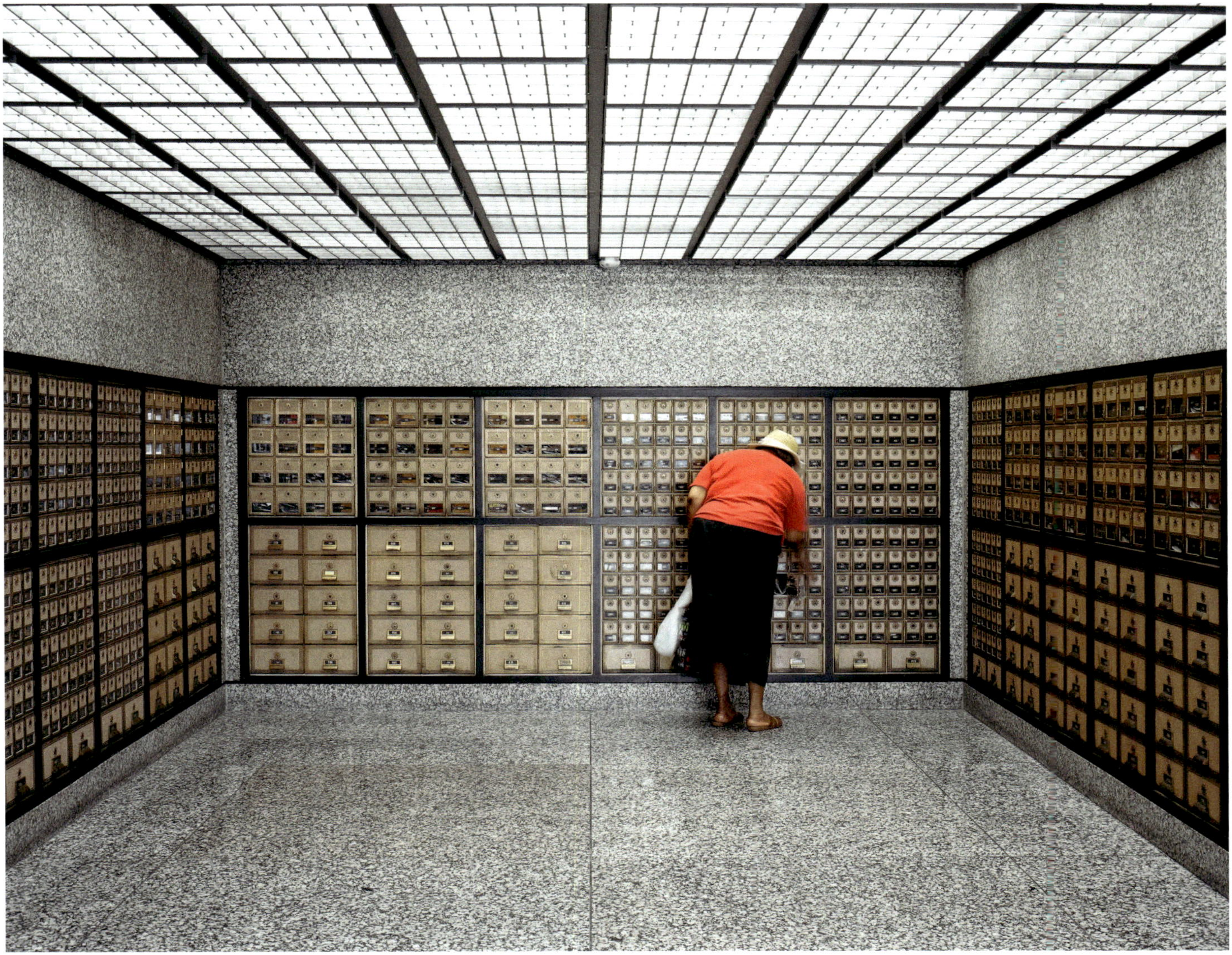

Mies van der Rohe, post office, Chicago, USA, 2011

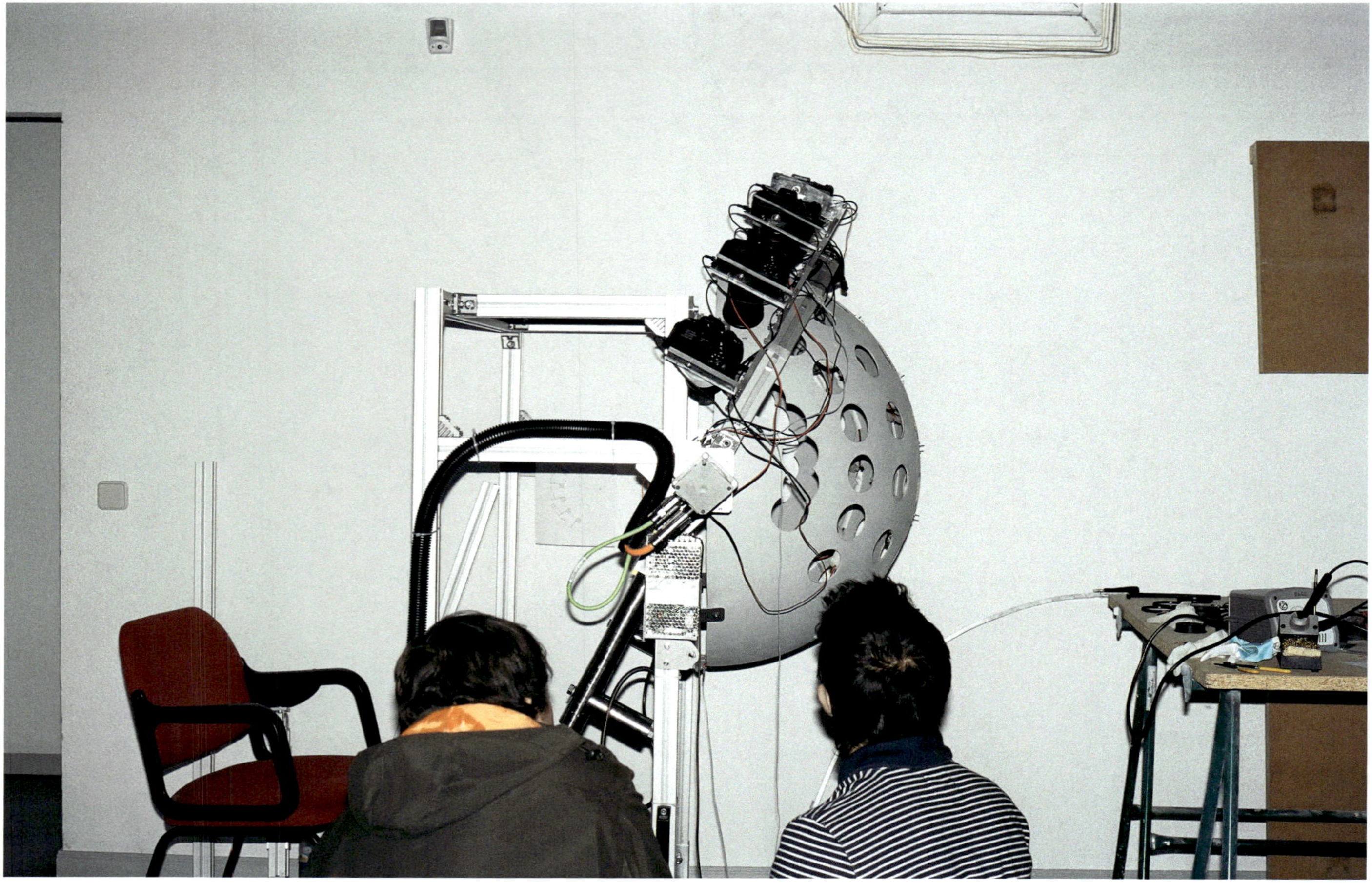

Manuel Franquelo testing a photographic 3D scanning machine for three-dimensional head scanning

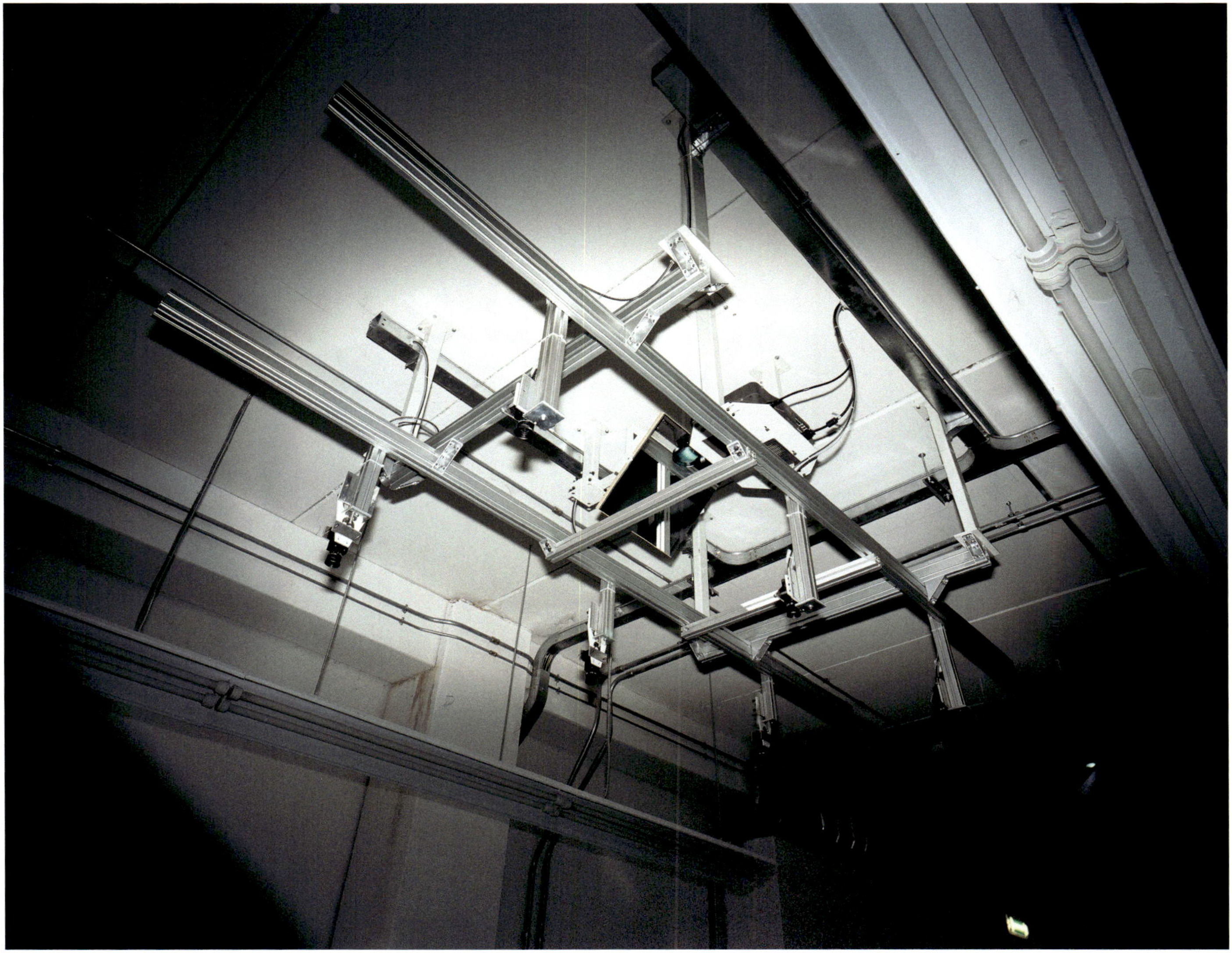

By means of a mirror construction on the ceiling, a projector maps different templates on a leather skin for the production of shoes.

Lamos Prada, Arezzo, Italy, 2001

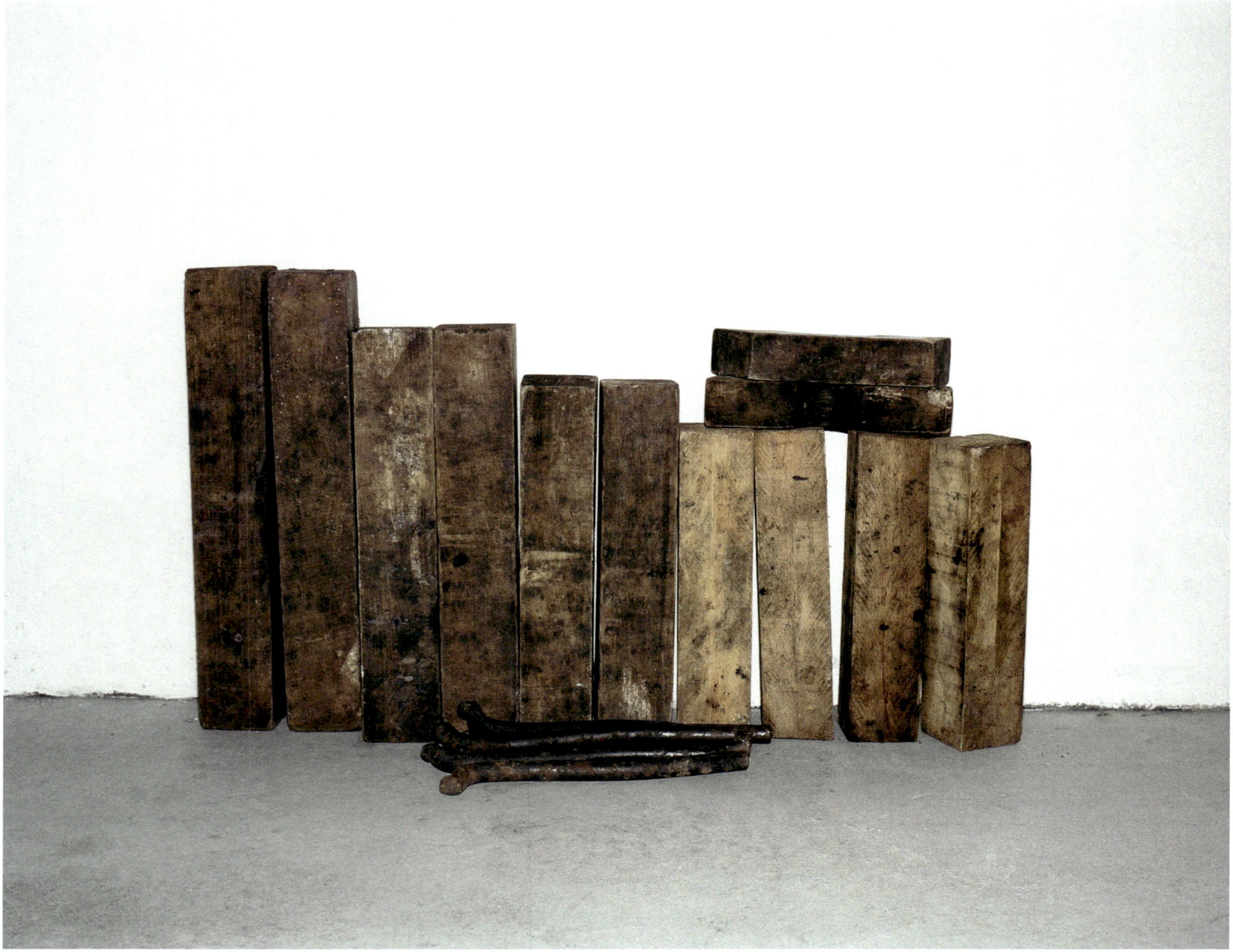

These wooden beams are used to keep barrels of olive oil or wine in place in the farm cellars.

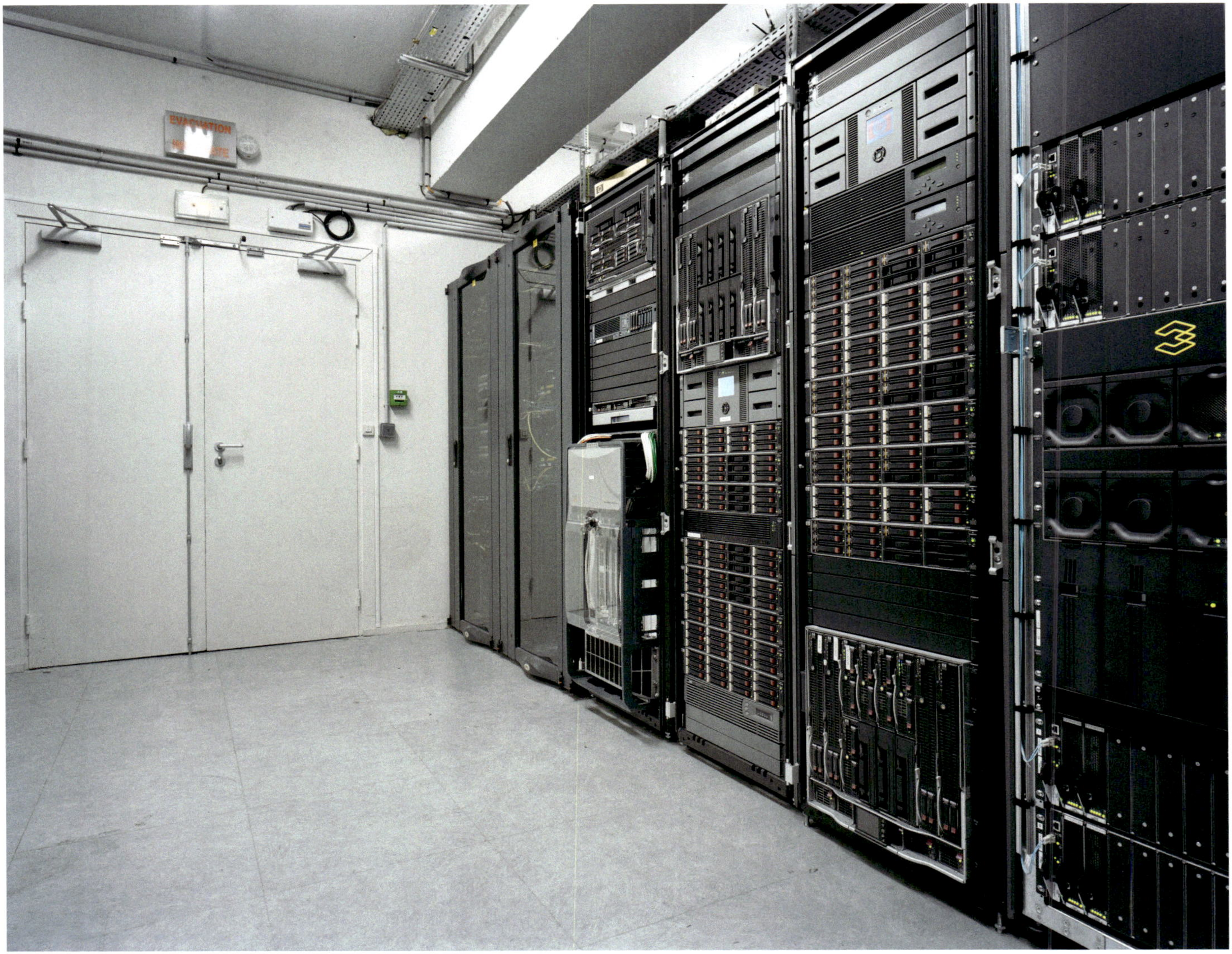

Bibliothèque, Sciences Po, server room, Paris, France, 2012

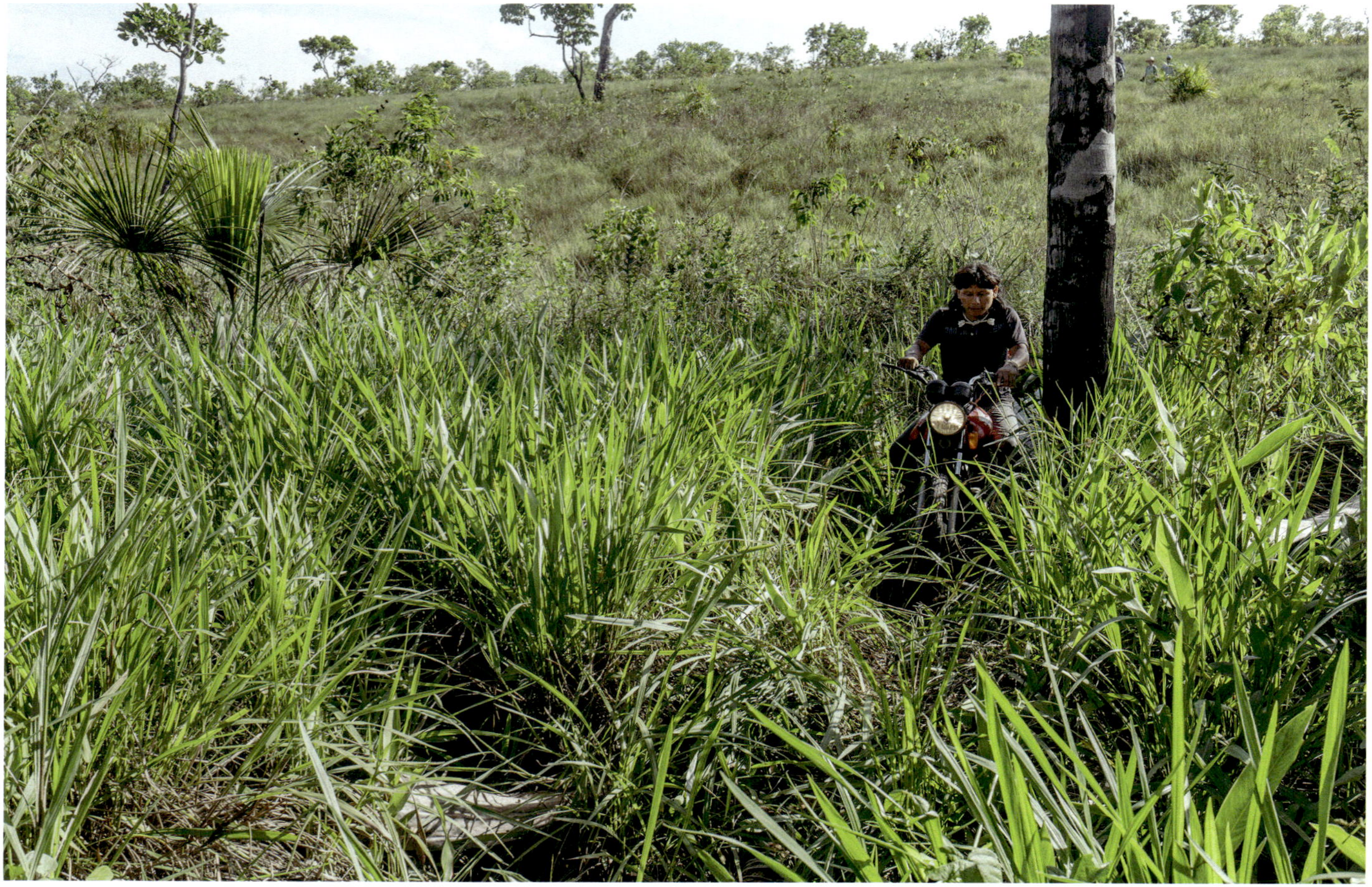

Riding on his motorbike, Leandro, the leader of the Wede'rã village, navigates his way through the Amazonian savanna to reach an abandoned village. As the area is deforested, the indigenous people are increasingly being displaced to accommodate expanding soy plantations.

Aldeia Wedera, Xavante Village, riding through the savanna to reach the border of the reservation, Terra Indigena Pimentel Barbosa, Municipio de Canarana, Mato Grosso, Brazil, 2015

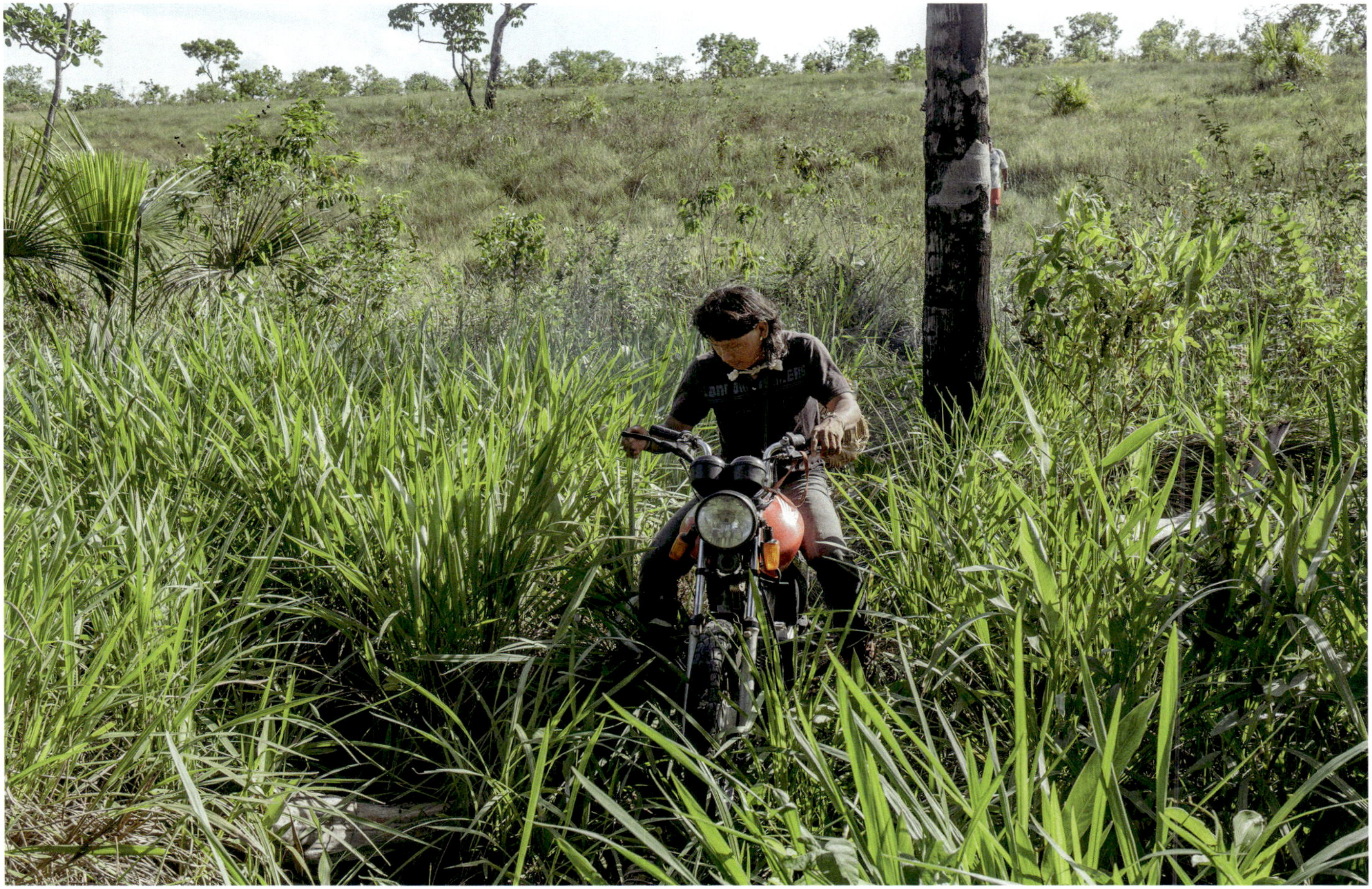

Aldeia Wedera, Xavante Village, riding through the savanna to reach the border of the reservation, Terra Indigena Pimentel Barbosa, Municipio de Canarana, Mato Grosso, Brazil, 2015

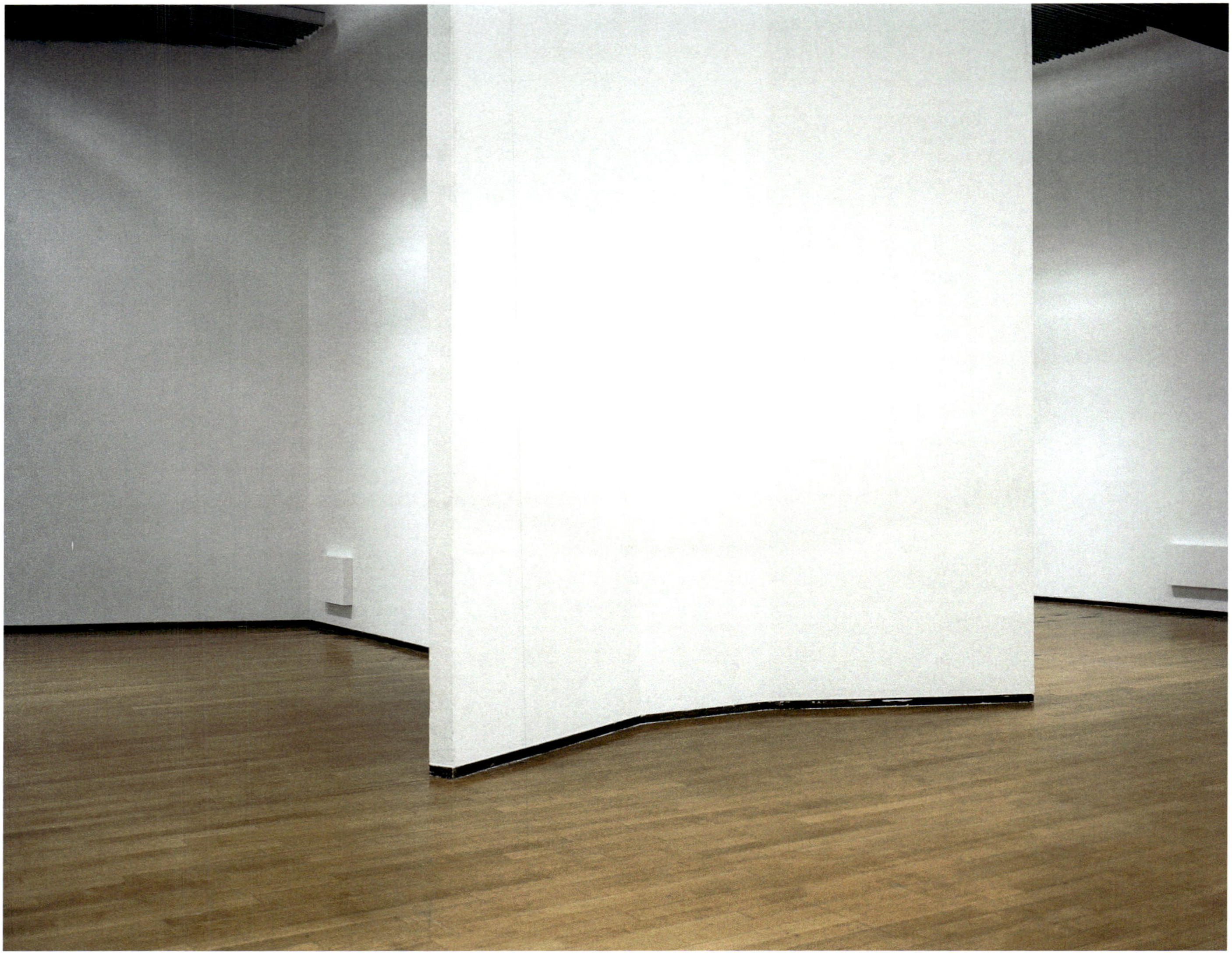

This building, designed by Ignazio Gardella, consists of different types of spaces specifically planned according to the medium exhibited – painting, sculpture, or drawing. After parts of the PAC were destroyed by a bomb attack in 1993, the building was reconstructed in accordance with the original design.

Exhibition space, PAC Padiglione d'Arte Contemporanea, Milan, Italy, 2016

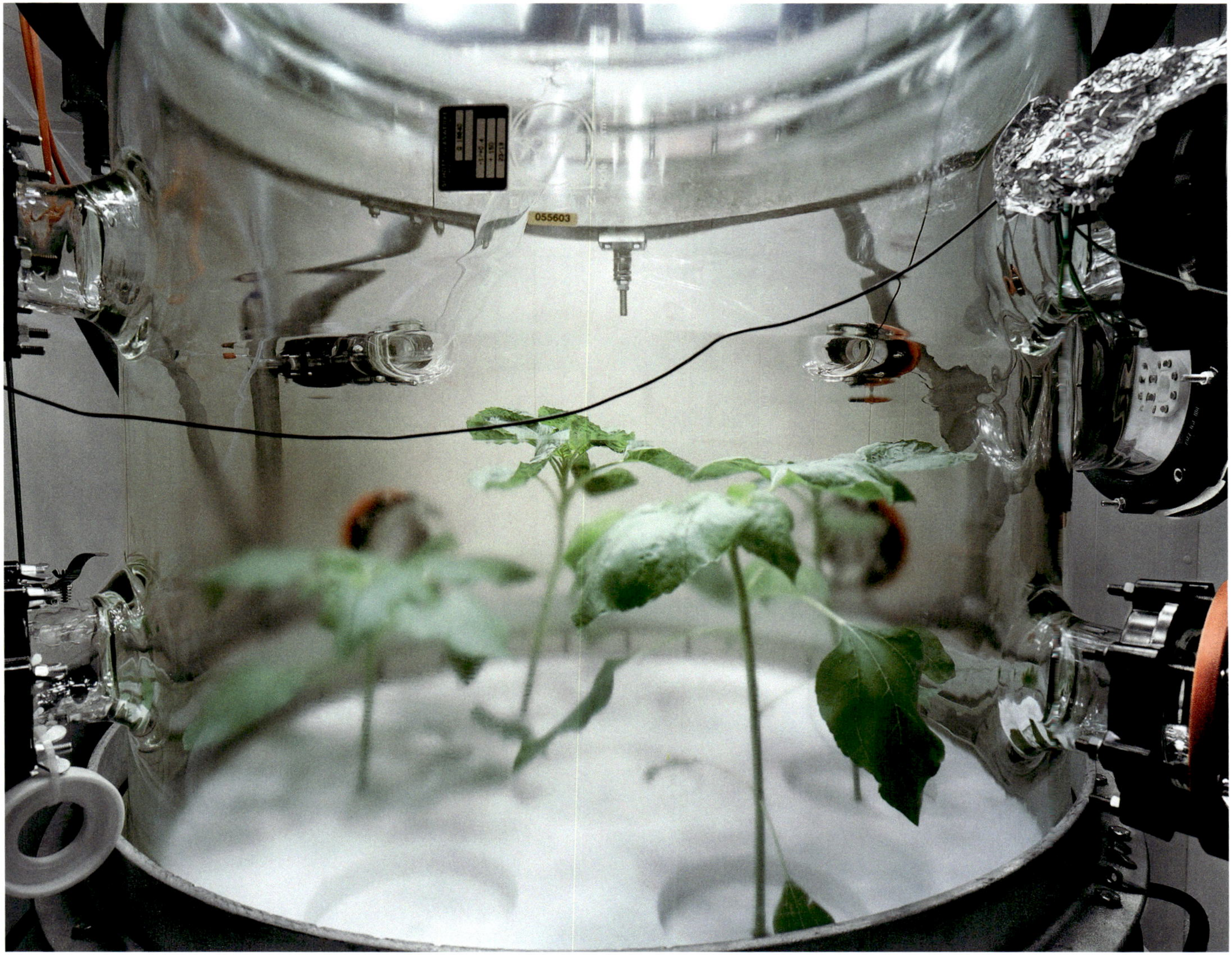

Plants are studied in a compartment with experimentally modified atmospheric conditions. Liquid radioactive tracers are injected to observe the circulation of fluids and the metabolism in the plant during this process.

Forschungszentrum Jülich, plant atmosphere chamber, Jülich (Cologne), Germany, 1999

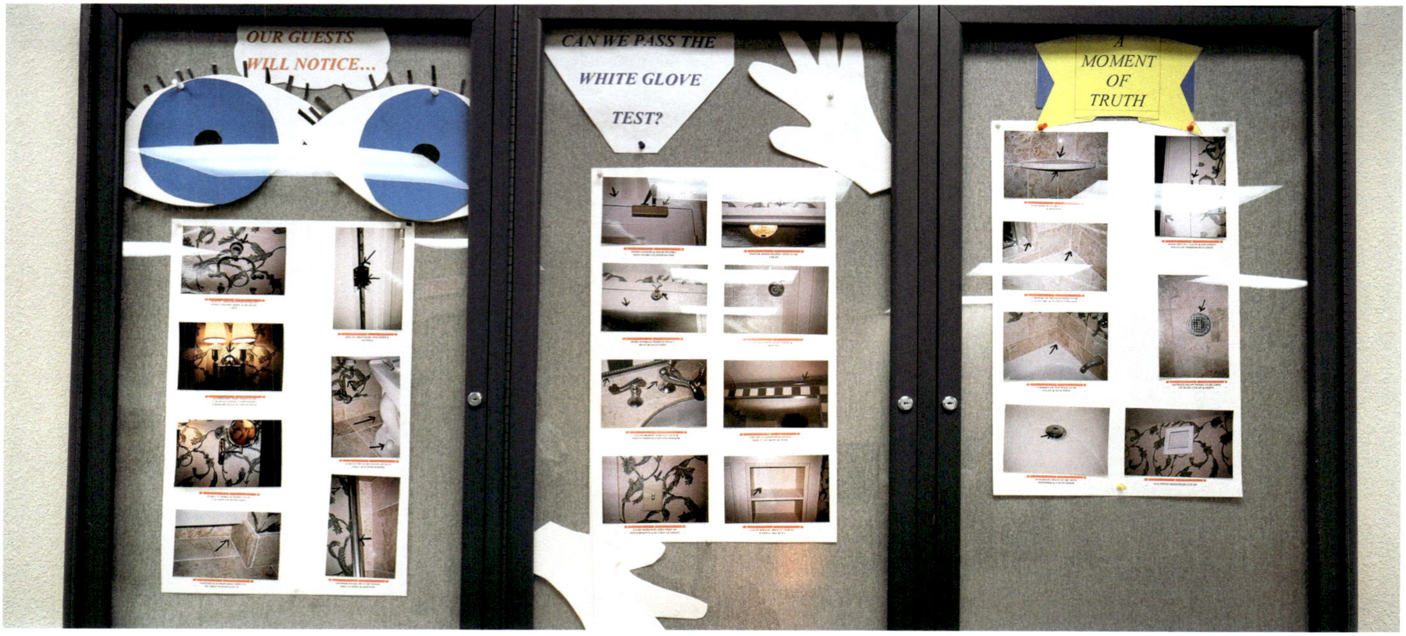

Backstage at the Paris and Aladdin Hotel in Las Vegas, new staff are reminded of cleaning procedures and standards.

Paris and Aladdin Hotel, cleaning instructions, Las Vegas, USA, 1999

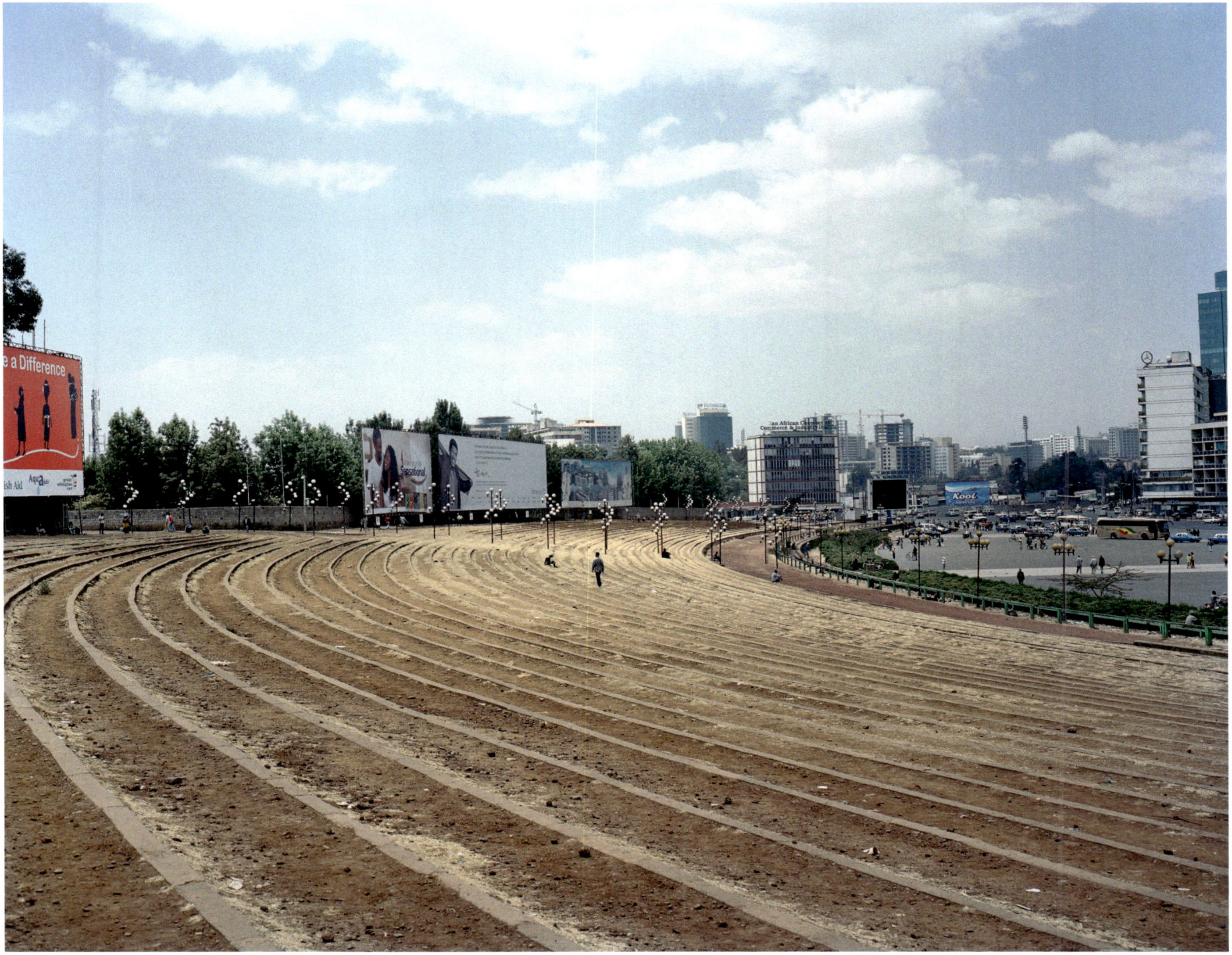

Meskel Square, Addis Ababa, Ethiopia, 2012

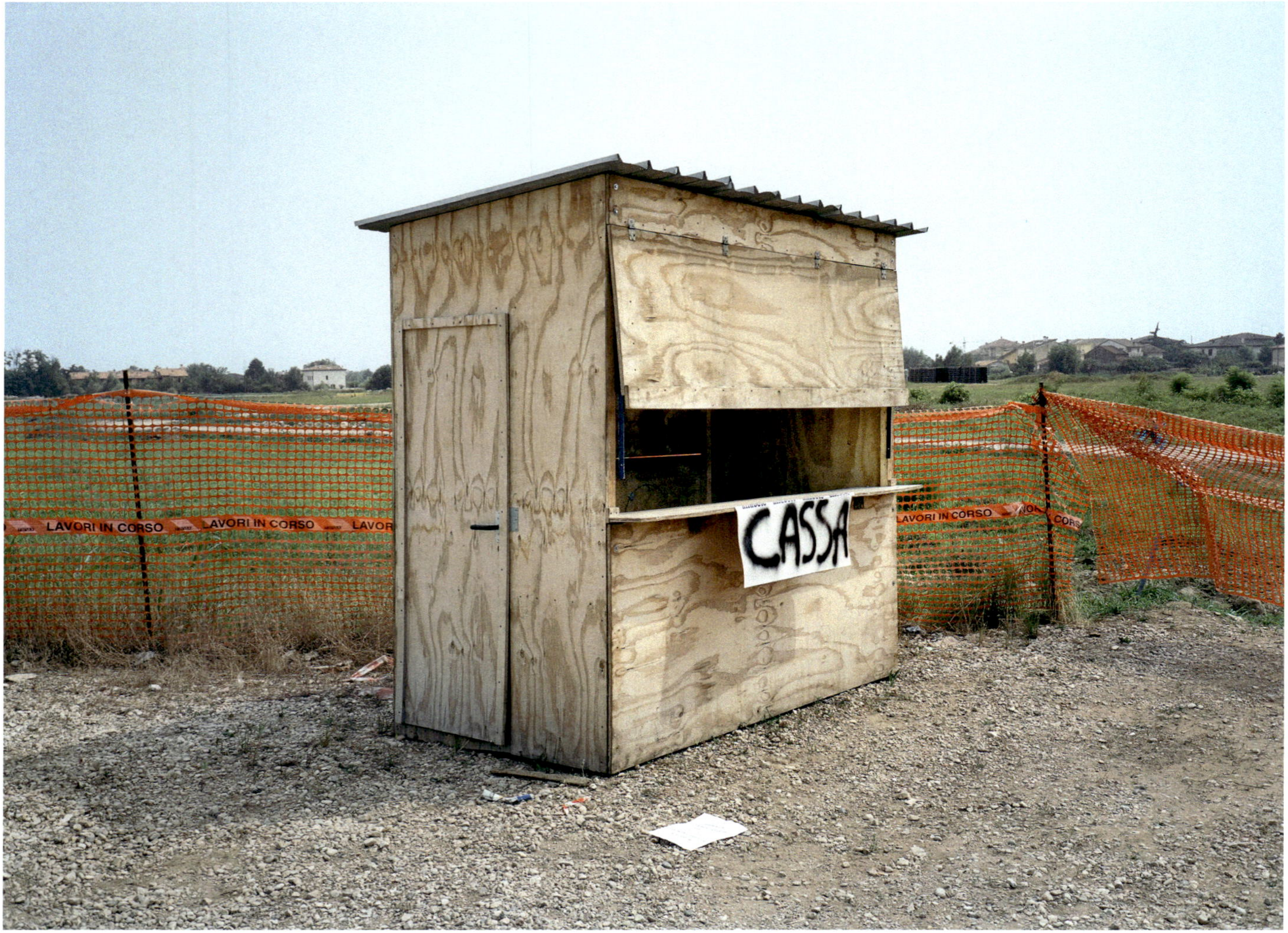

Cashier counter, Caldogno (VI), Italy, 2006

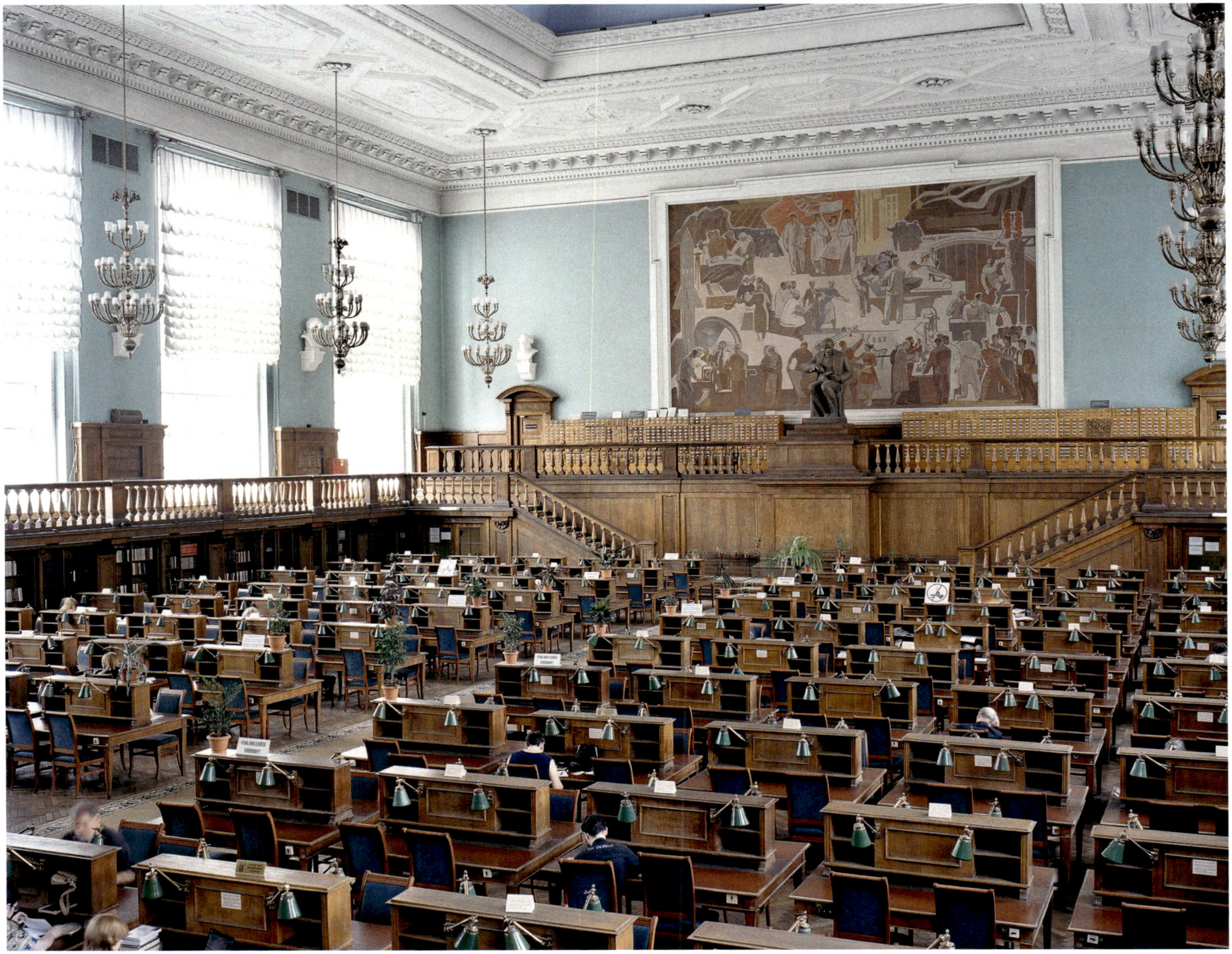

Russian State Library, reading hall, Moscow, Russia, 2011

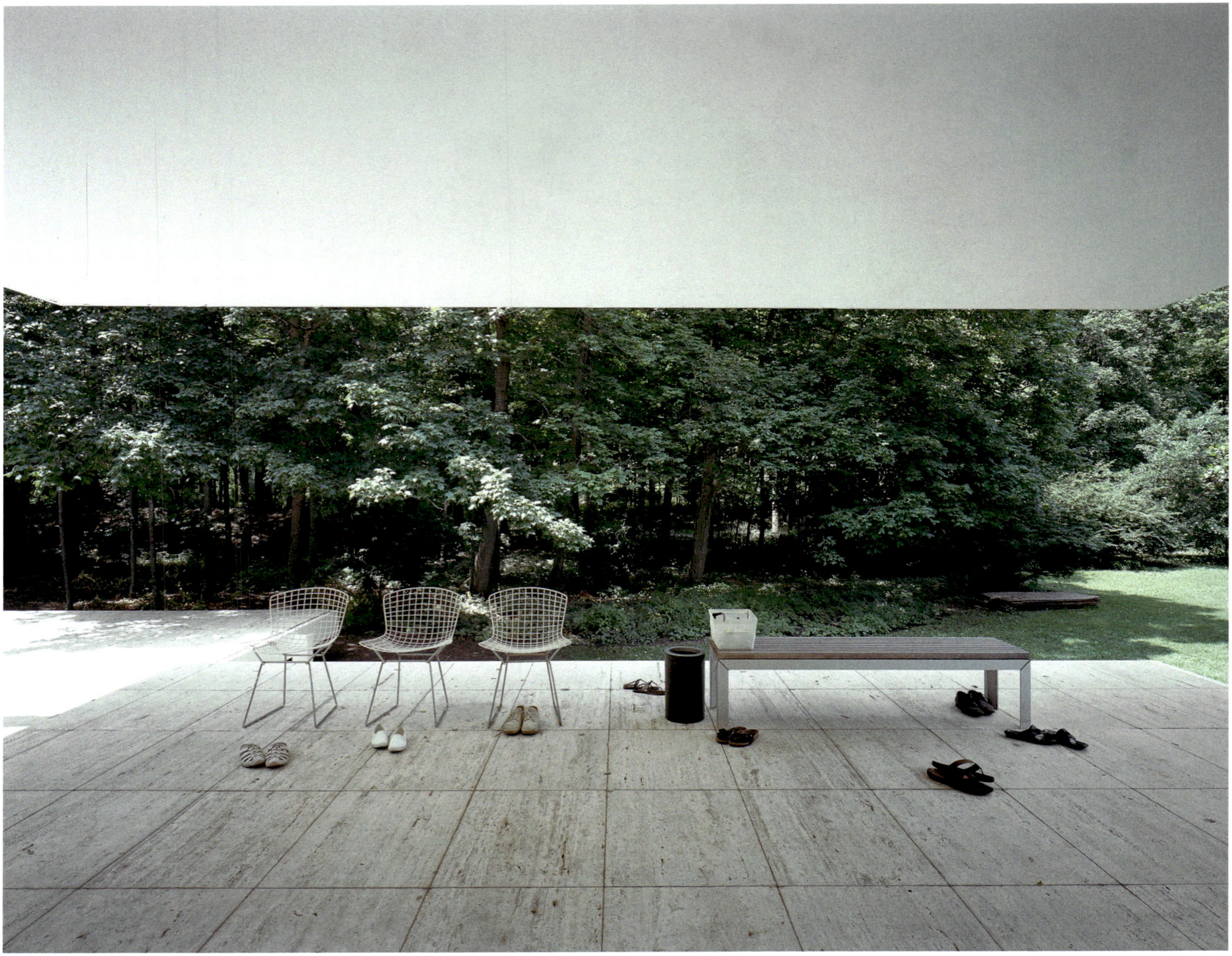

Mies van der Rohe, Farnsworth House, Chicago, USA, 2011

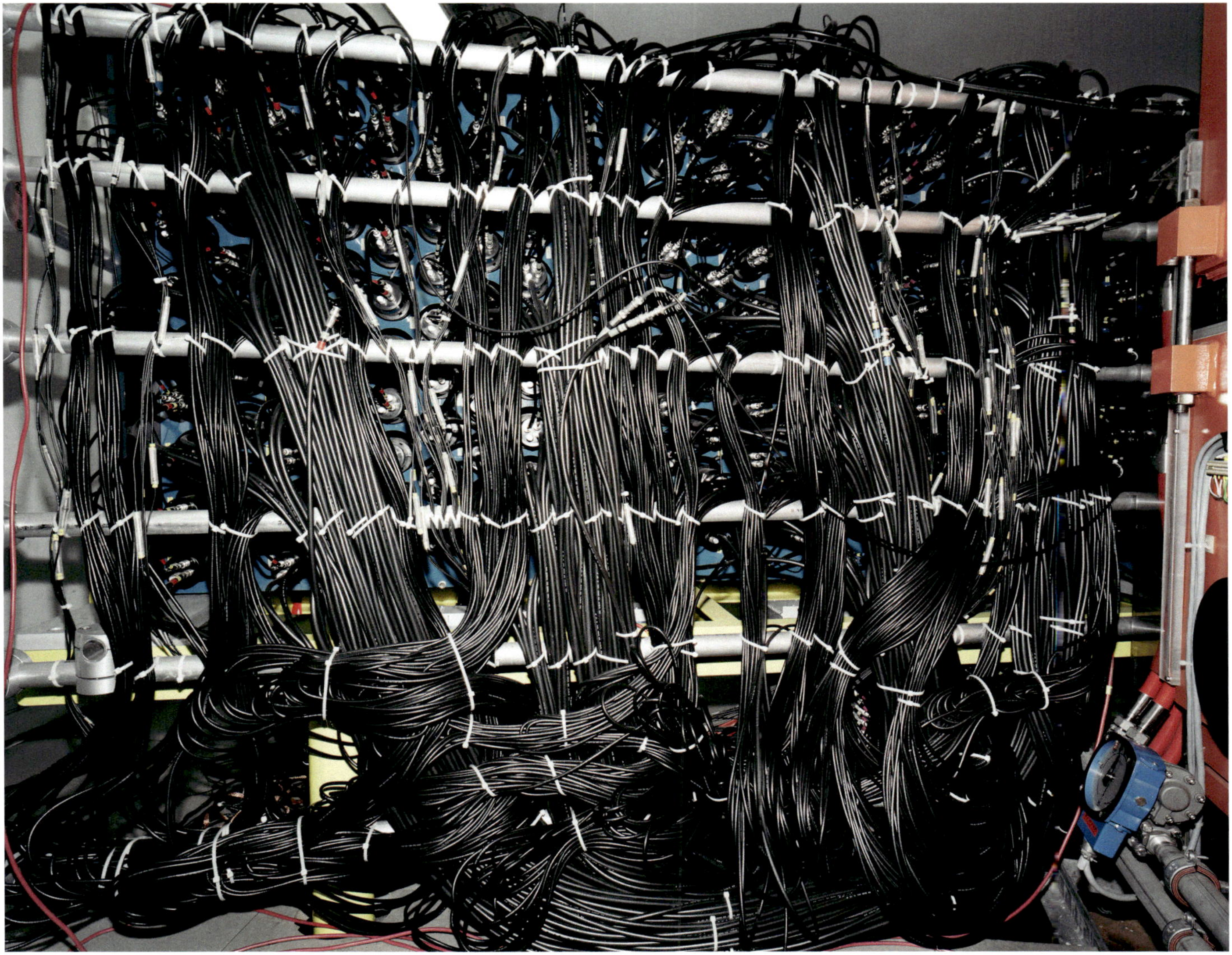

Forschungszentrum Jülich, Jülich (Cologne), Germany, 1999

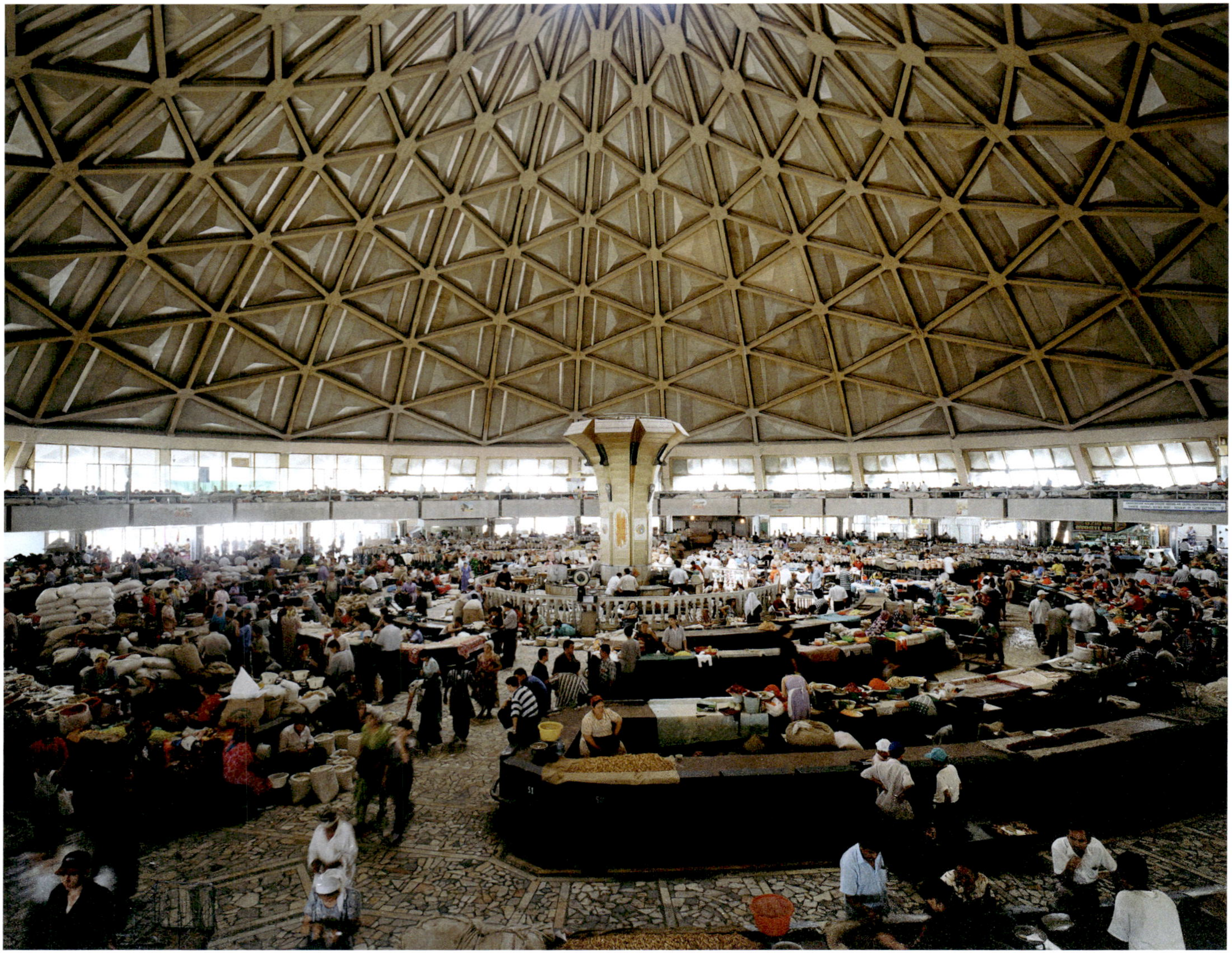

Chorsu Bazaar, Tashkent, Uzbekistan, 2001

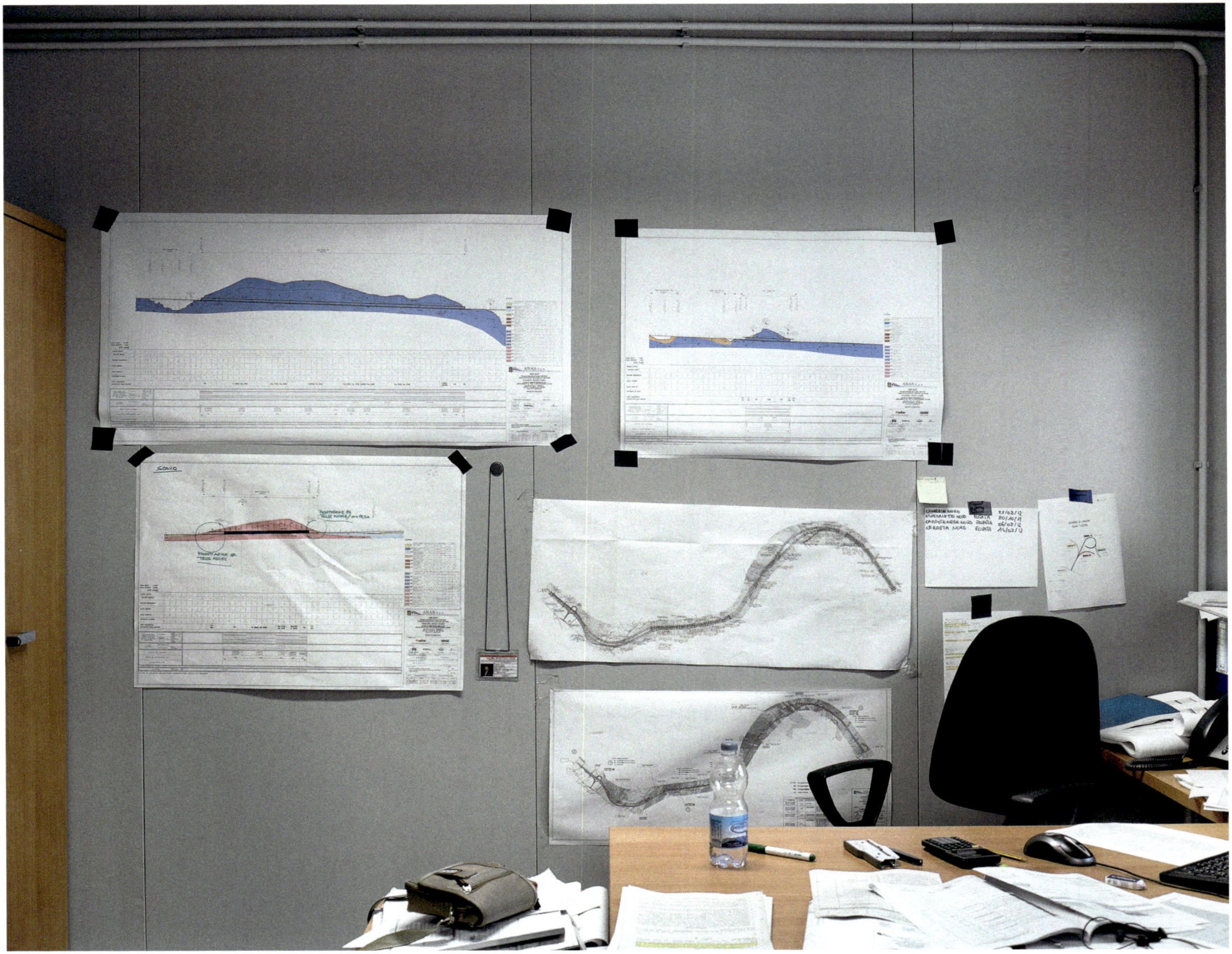

Engineering plans for a tunnel highway in a construction company office

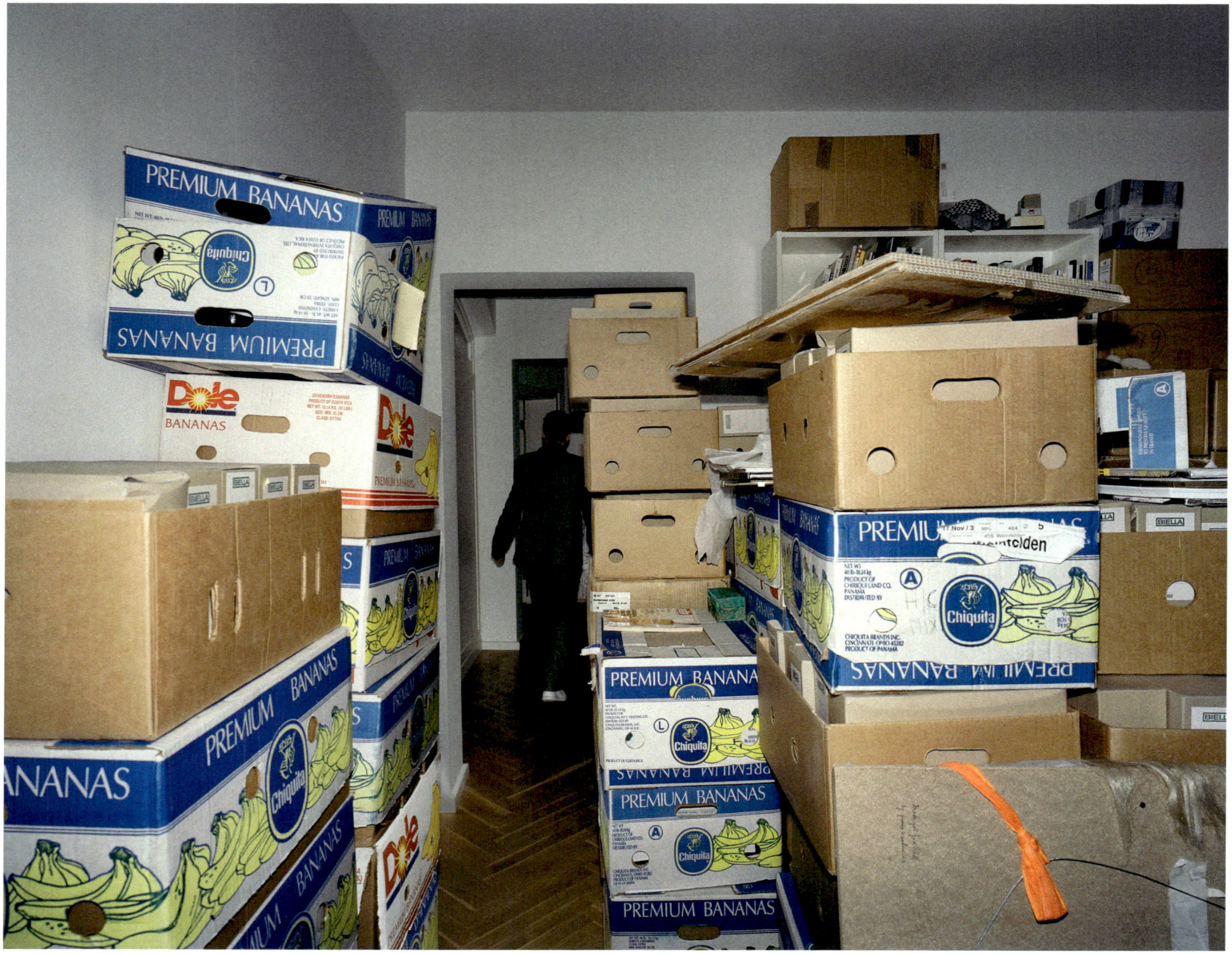

For a period of time, Hans Ulrich Obrist had an apartment in Berlin where he stored banana boxes with books and documents from his research.

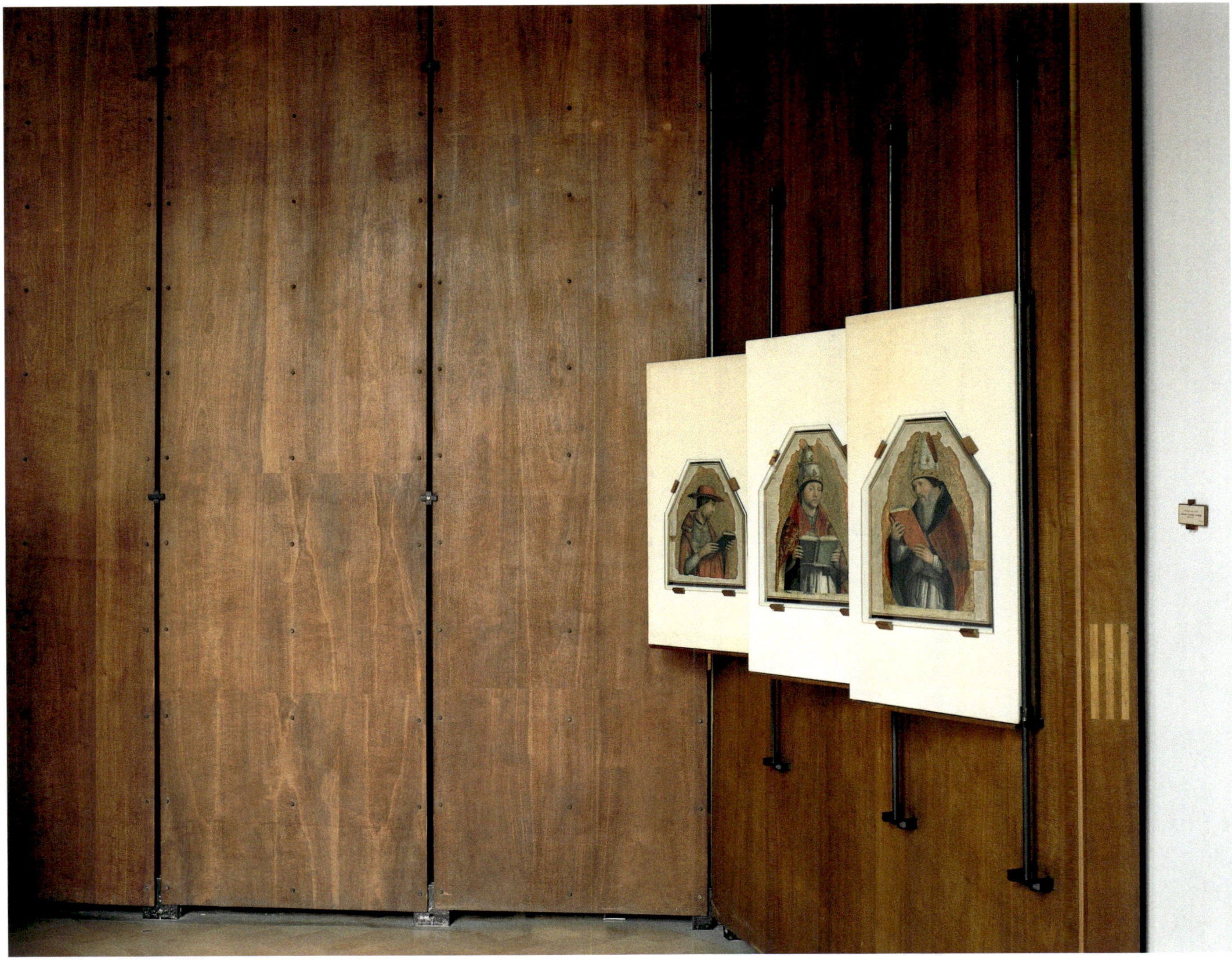

Carlo Scarpa was commissioned to design the displays for the art museum of Palazzo Abatellis in 1953. The three movable panels, showcasing Antonello da Messina's portraits of saints, allow the viewer to move the paintings in order to experience different light conditions and to look at the back of the pictures.

Carlo Scarpa, Palazzo Abatellis, pivoting displays, Palermo, Italy, 2015

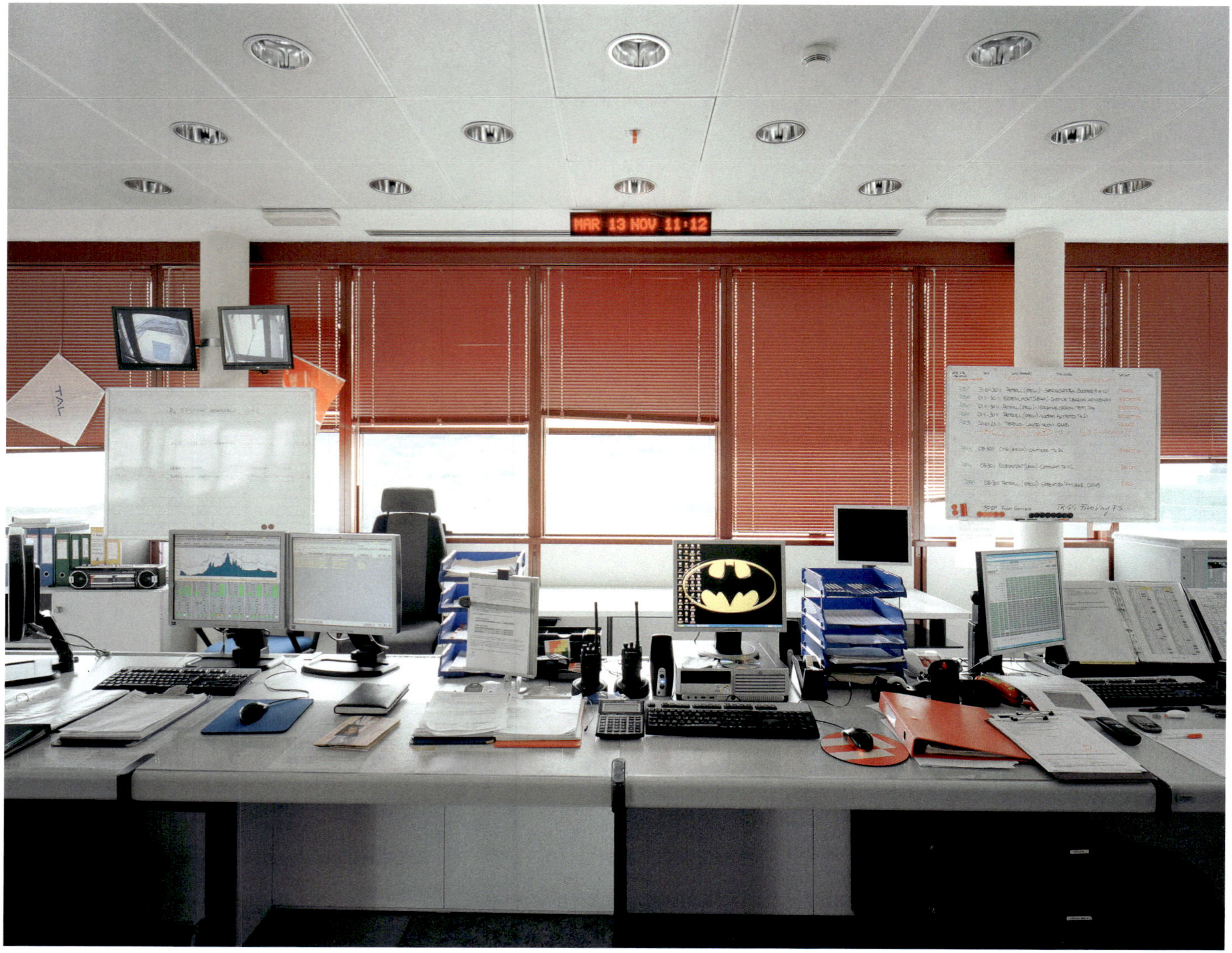

TAL Group Transalpine Pipeline, control room, Trieste, Italy, 2012

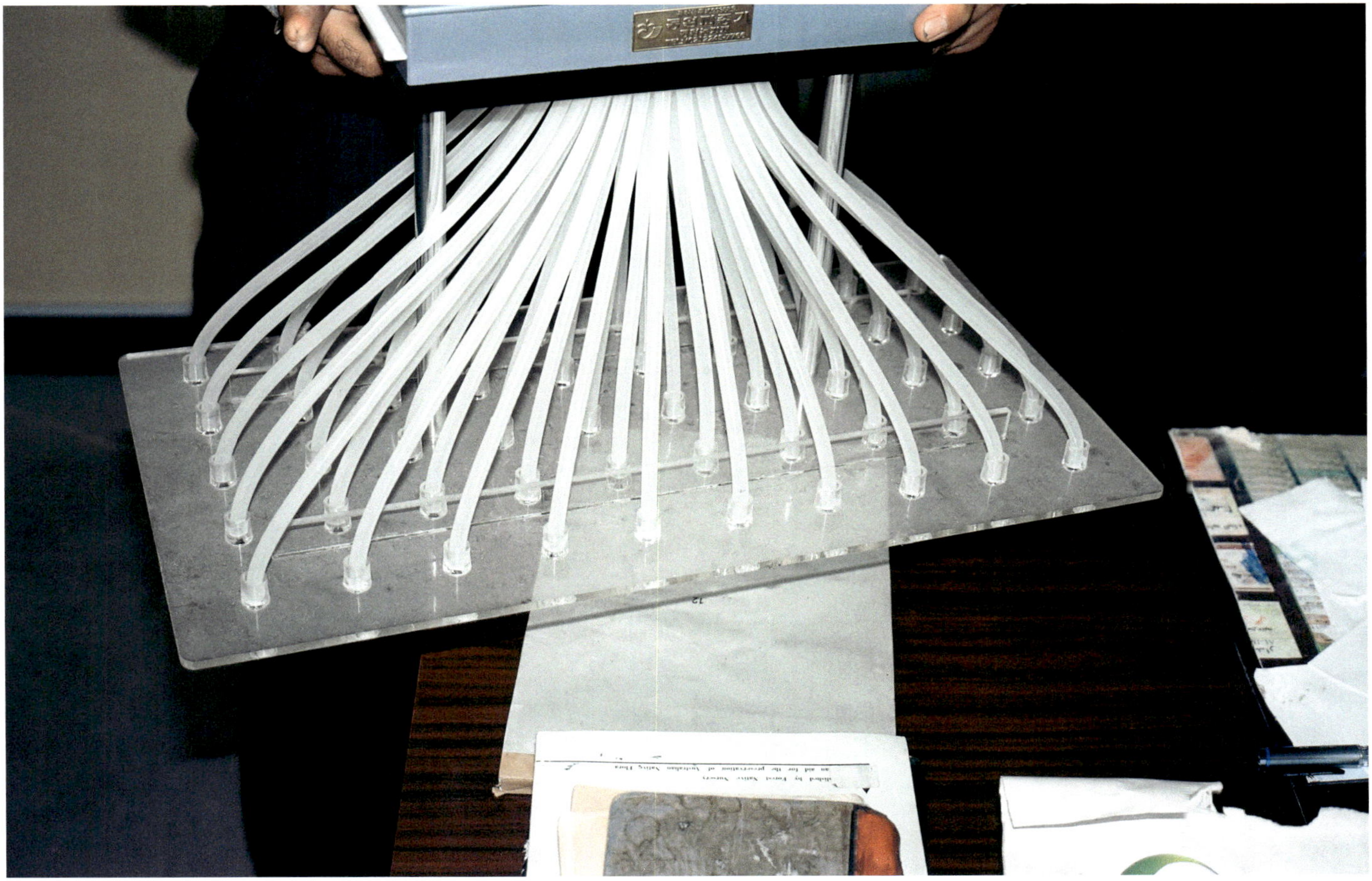

A sowing device for automatically placing seeds into individual containers

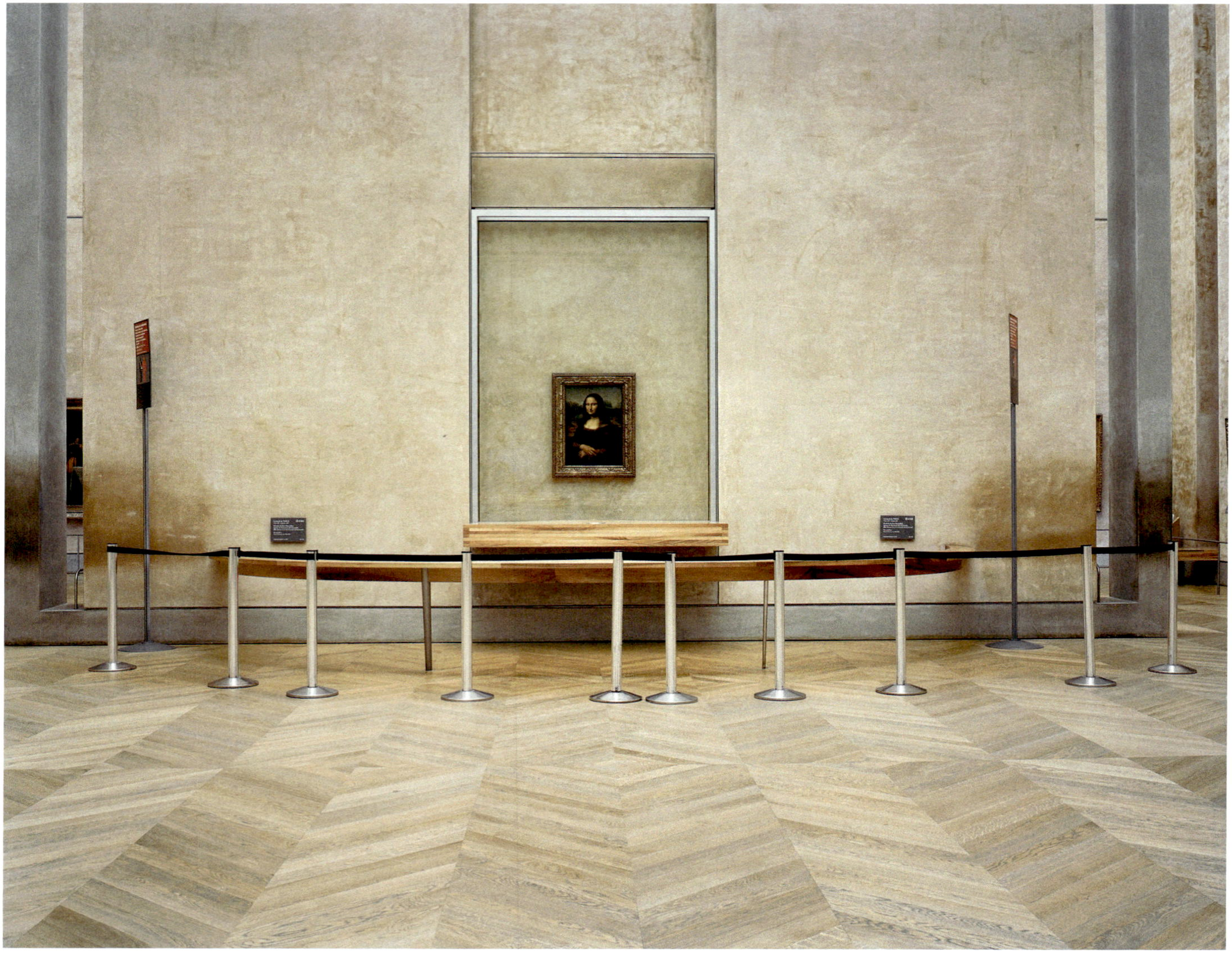

On Tuesdays the Louvre is closed to the public and around 2,000 employees are alone in the museum.

Musée du Louvre, *Mona Lisa* (1503–17) by Leonardo da Vinci, Paris, France, 2013

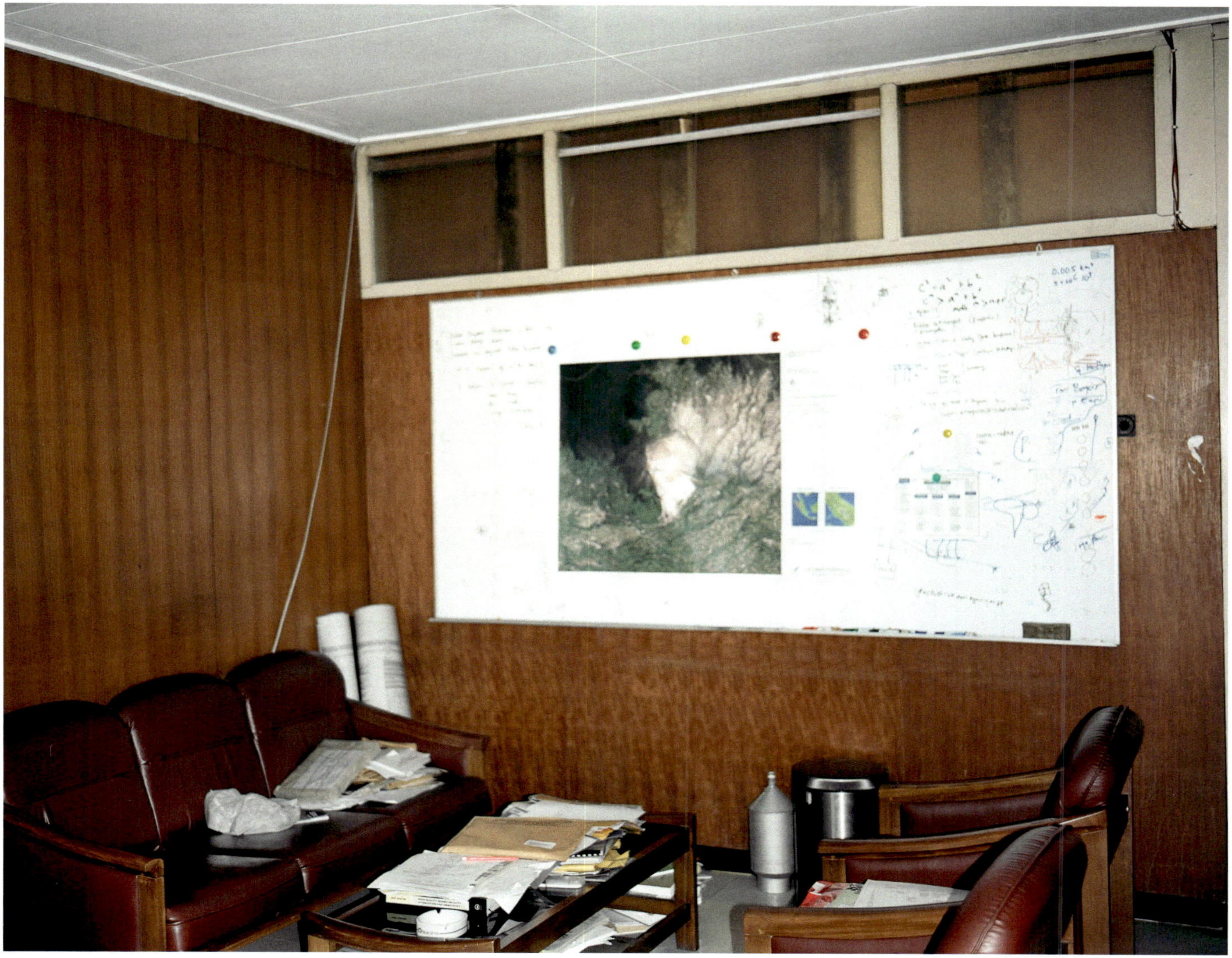

Center for Volcanology and Geological Hazard Mitigation, Bandung, Indonesia, 2016

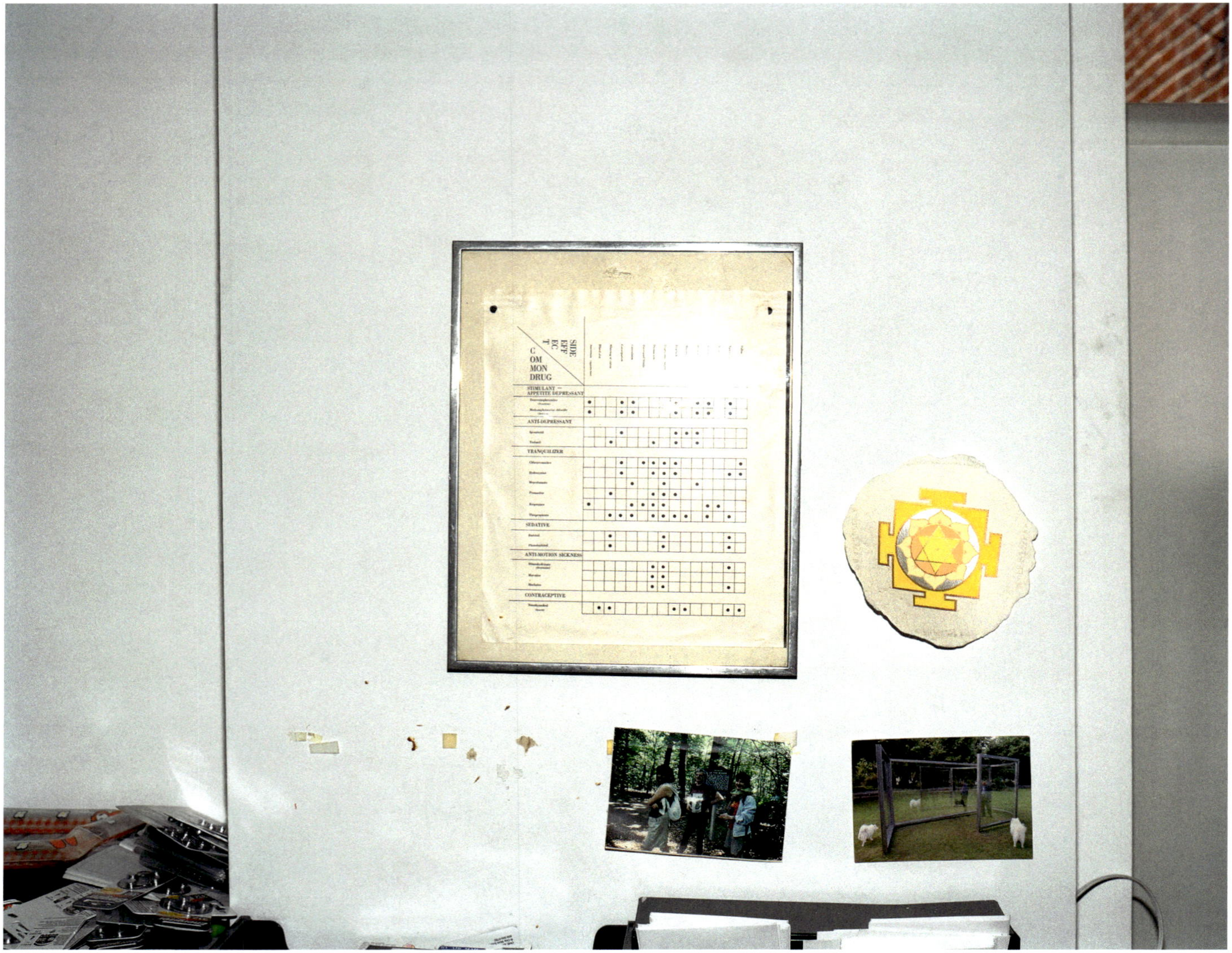

Dan Graham's studio, New York, USA, 2007

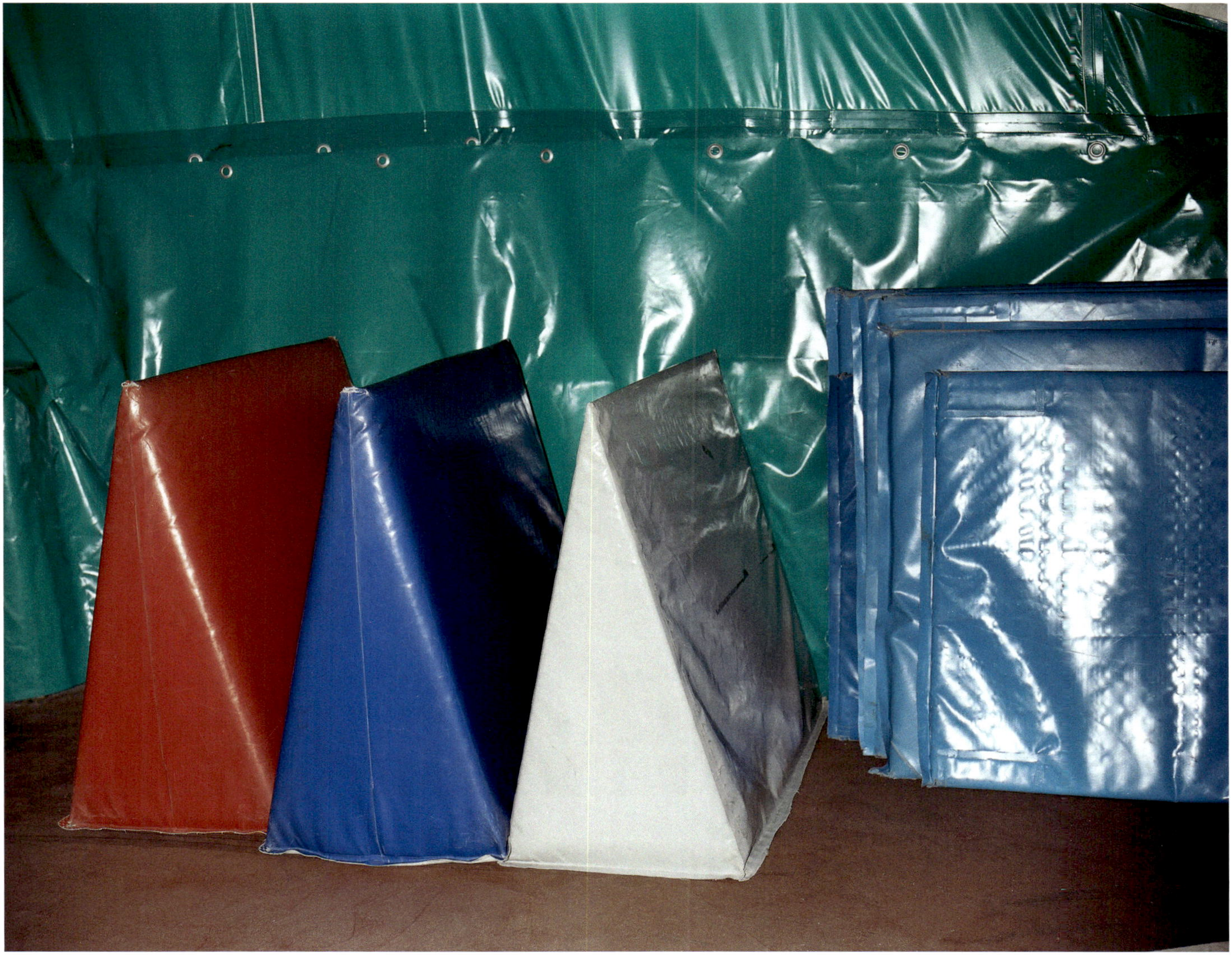

Geometrical shapes filled with foam for gymnastic exercises

Gym, Milan, Italy, 2003

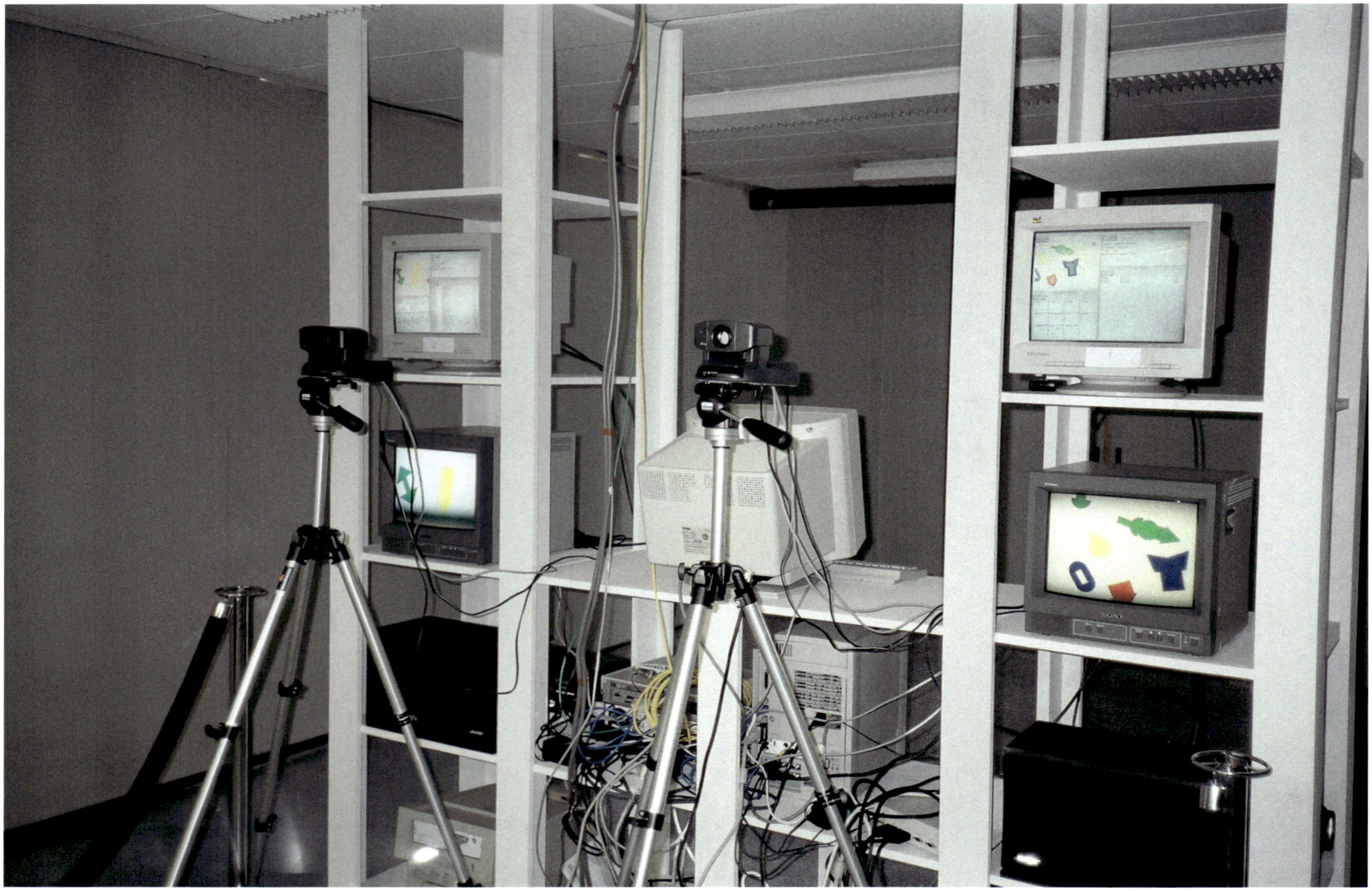

Engaging robots in communication games, Luc Steel's "Talking Heads" experiment investigates the origin of language systems. One unit reads an image using a video camera. After analyzing shapes and colors, it has to suggest a term that best describes this image. The second unit receives and interprets the information. This procedure is used to initiate a dialogue and to construct a shared but more and more complex vocabulary.

Luc Steels, Laboratory for Cognitive Robots and Teleportation, Antwerp, Belgium, 1999

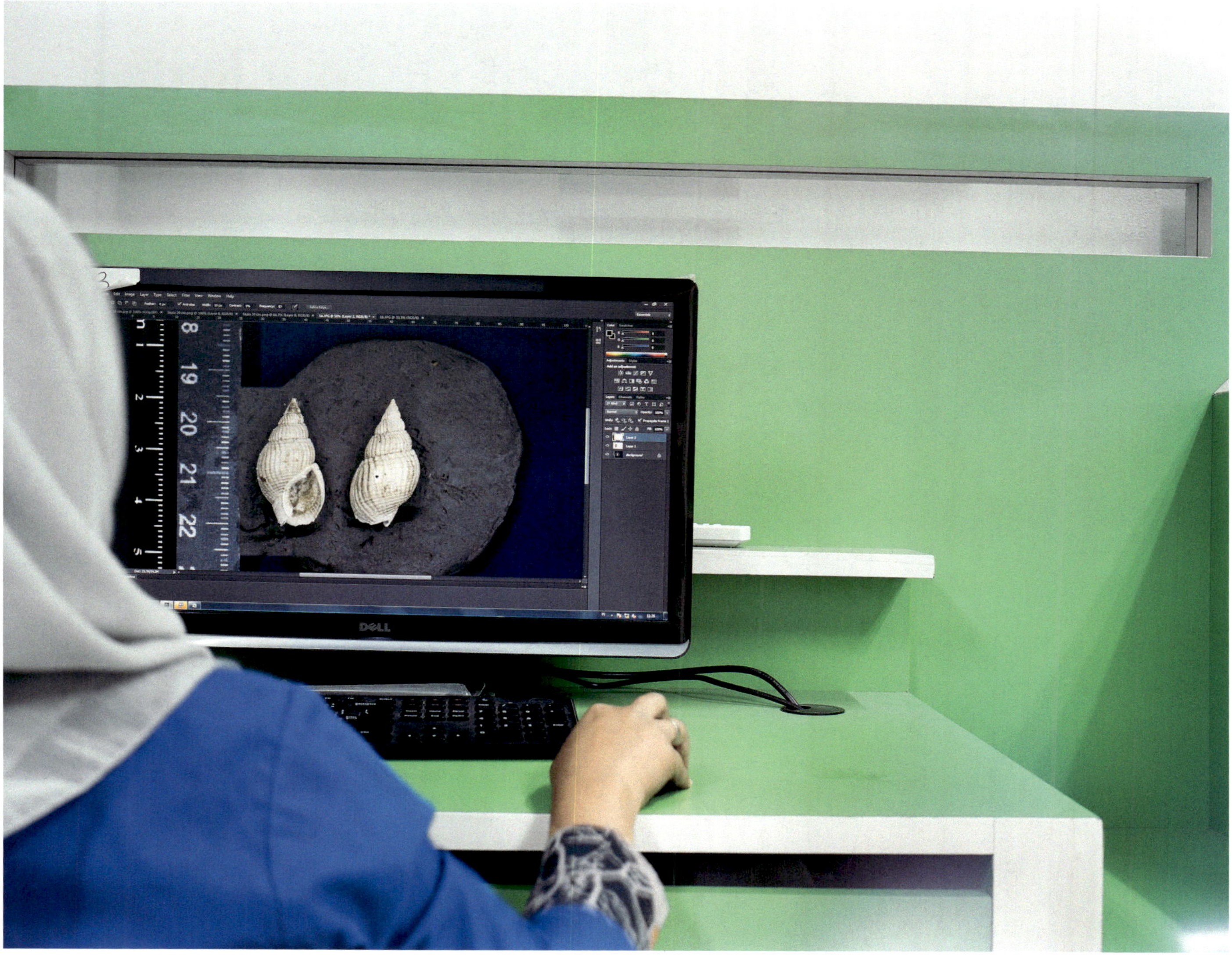

Bandung Geological Museum, Bandung, Indonesia, 2016

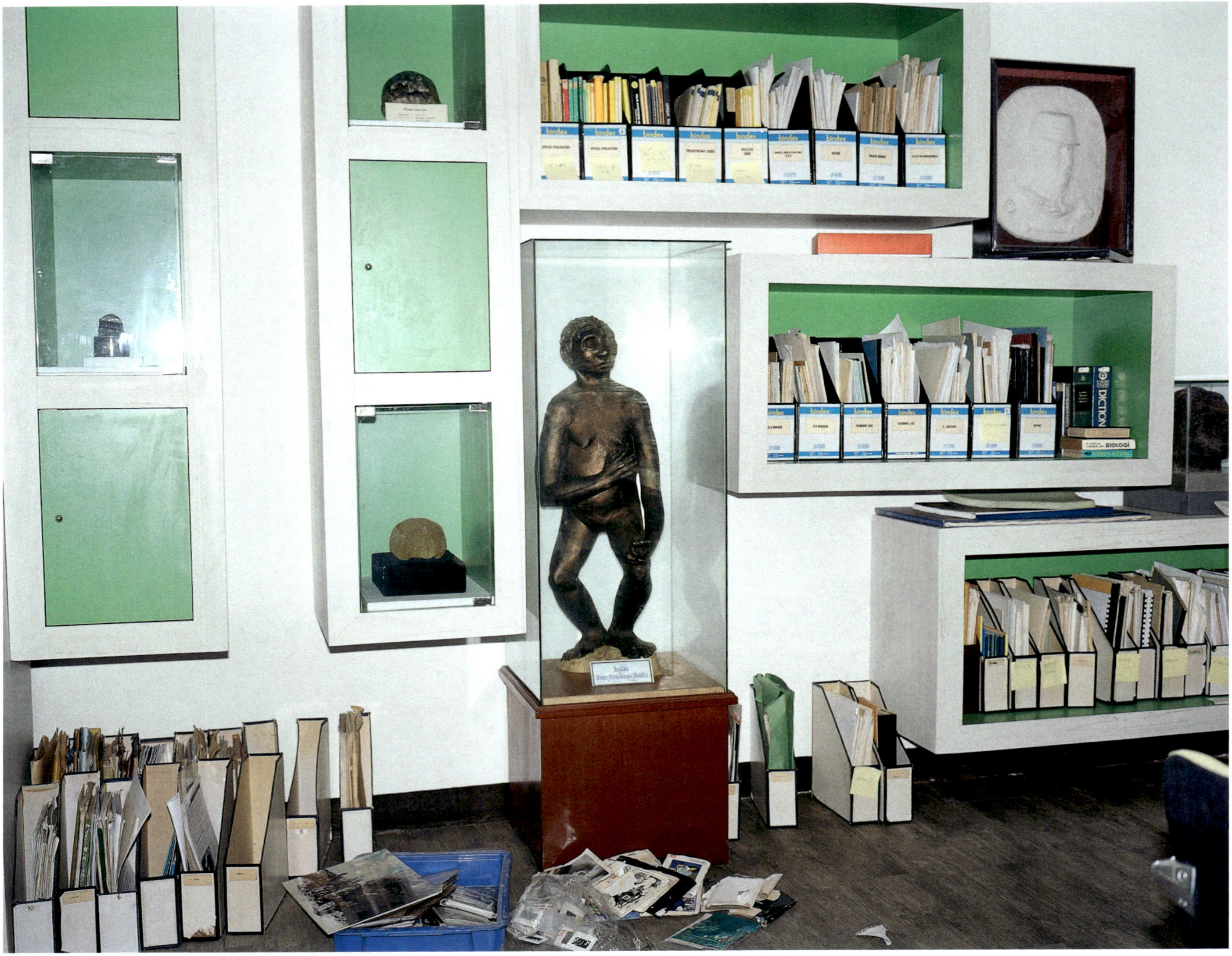

Bandung Geological Museum, office, Bandung, Indonesia, 2016
Photography in collaboration with Giulia Bruno

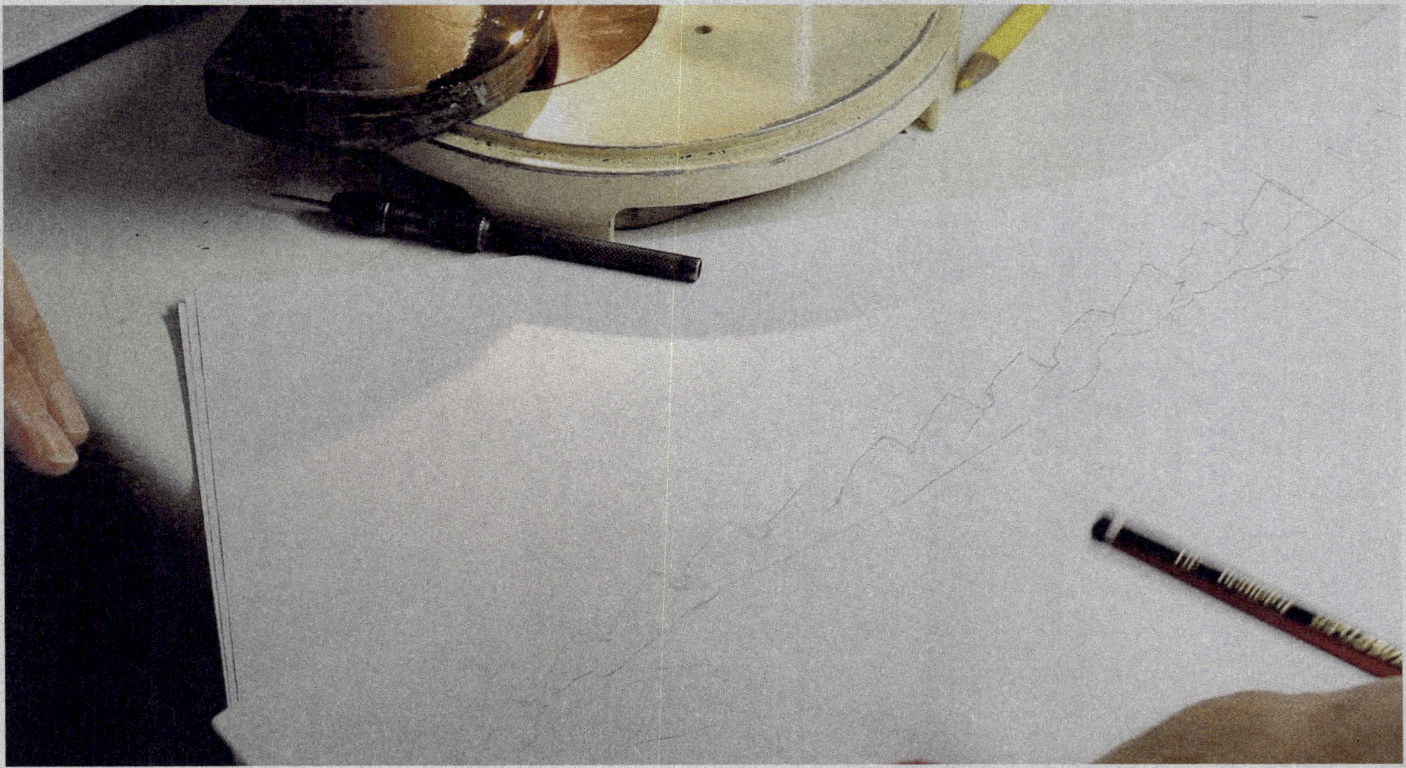

Jan Zalasiewicz

47–86

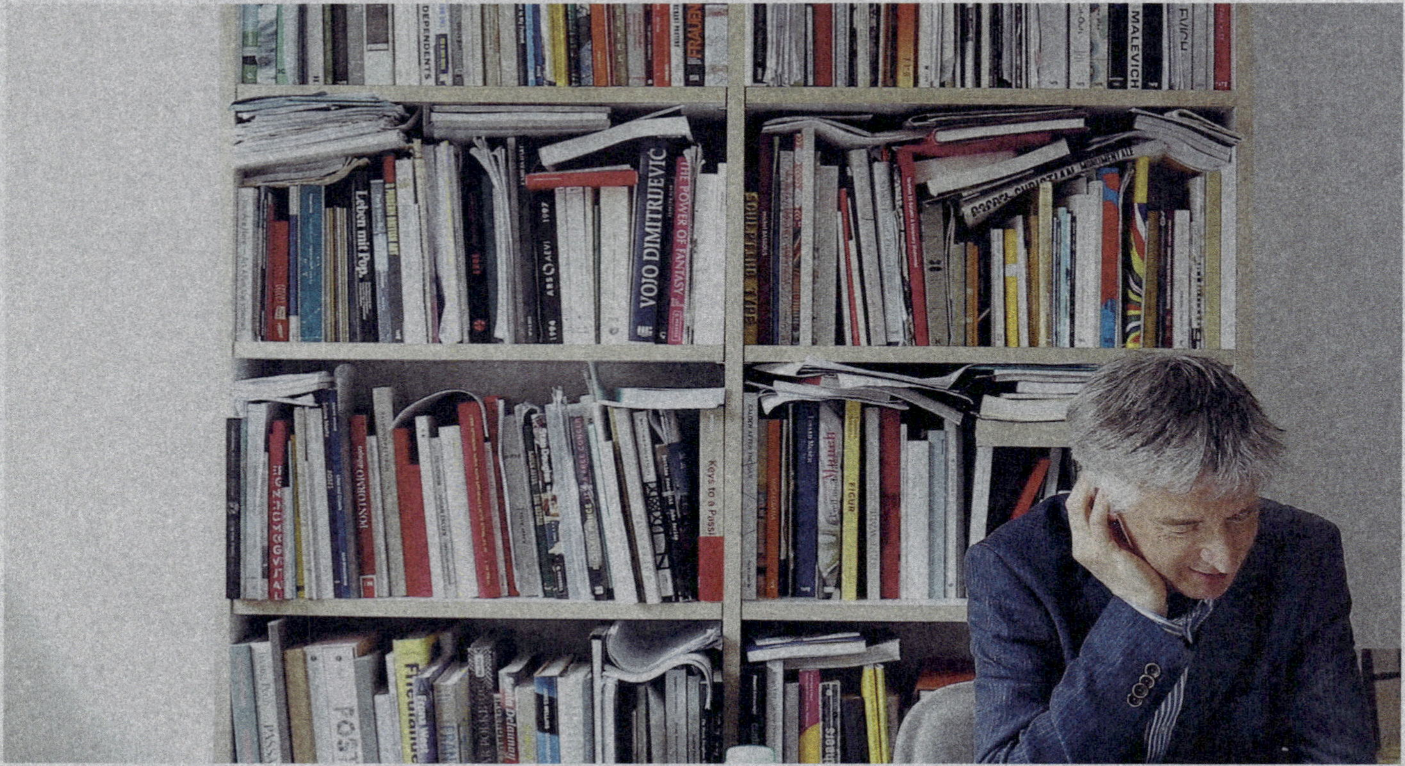

Jan Zalasiewicz and Armin Linke, during a break at *The Anthropocene Project Conference*, Tate Modern, London, June 5, 2015

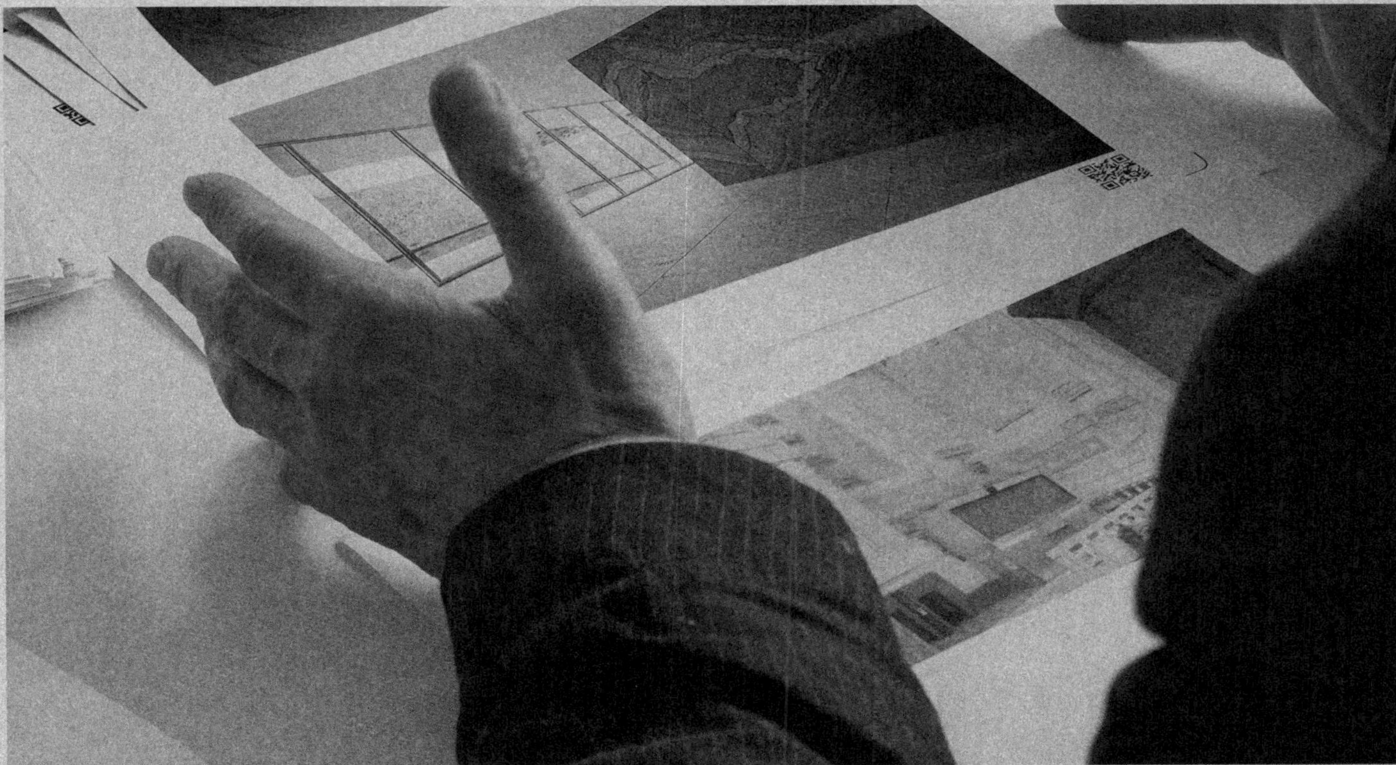

Jan Zalasiewicz and Armin Linke, during a break at *The Anthropocene Project Conference*, Tate Modern, London, June 5, 2015

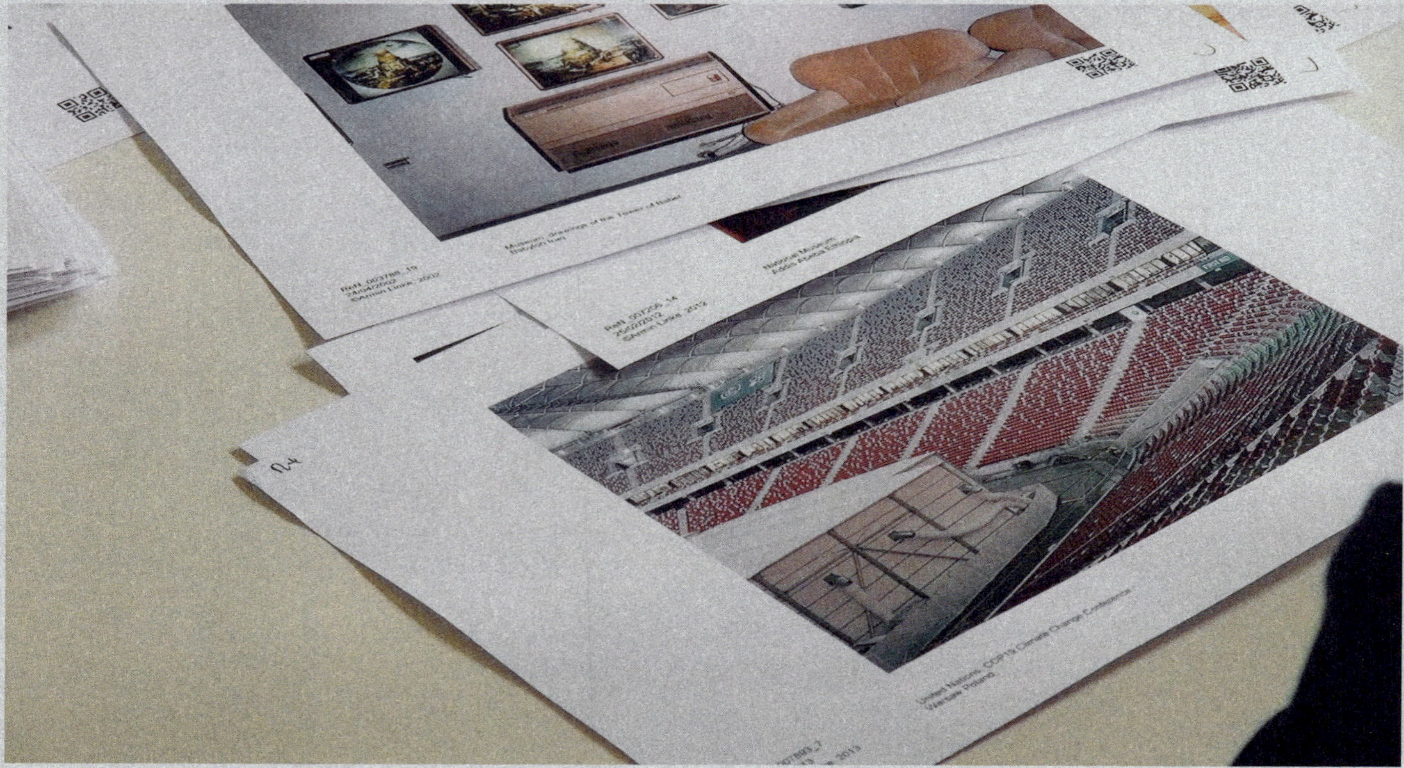

Jan Zalasiewicz and Armin Linke, during a break at *The Anthropocene Project Conference*, Tate Modern, London, June 5, 2015

We are incredibly good at making things, and live in a human world, surrounded by things. One of the results of interpreting it and converting it into geological language is to see just how bizarre, different, and new this multiplicity of things is. Nature has a number of different sorts of mineral types, of rock types and structures, and a great diversity in biology. But the diversity of man-made objects is potentially greater than the diversity of biology, which involves between ten and fifteen million species.

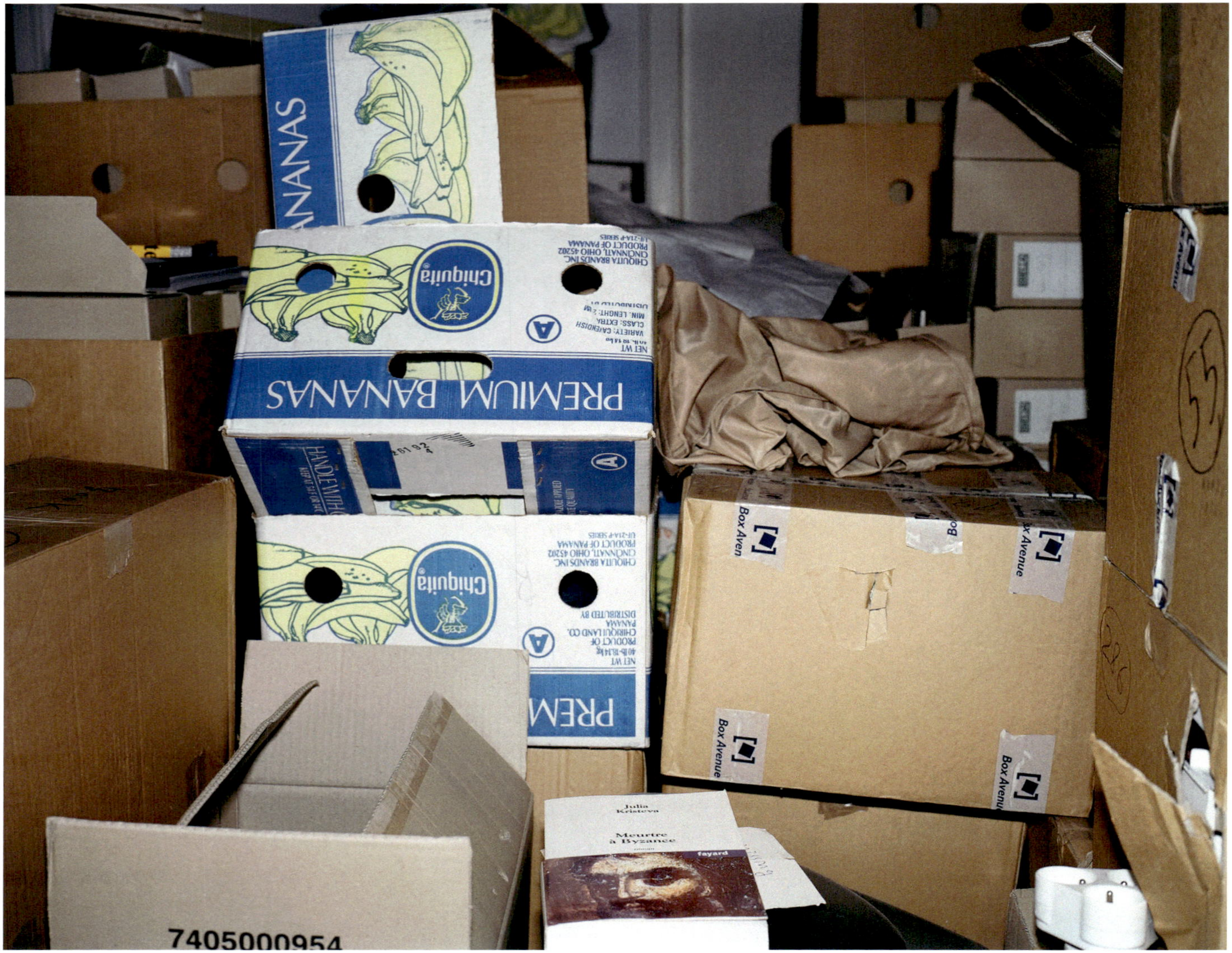

We make many more things, but how would one derive the actual number of things and catalogue them? The only catalogue I have seen is of a tiny part. Someone at Google had been given the job (and somehow survived) of counting the number of different kinds of books that have been published.

Hans Ulrich Obrist, book archive apartment, Berlin, Germany, 2009

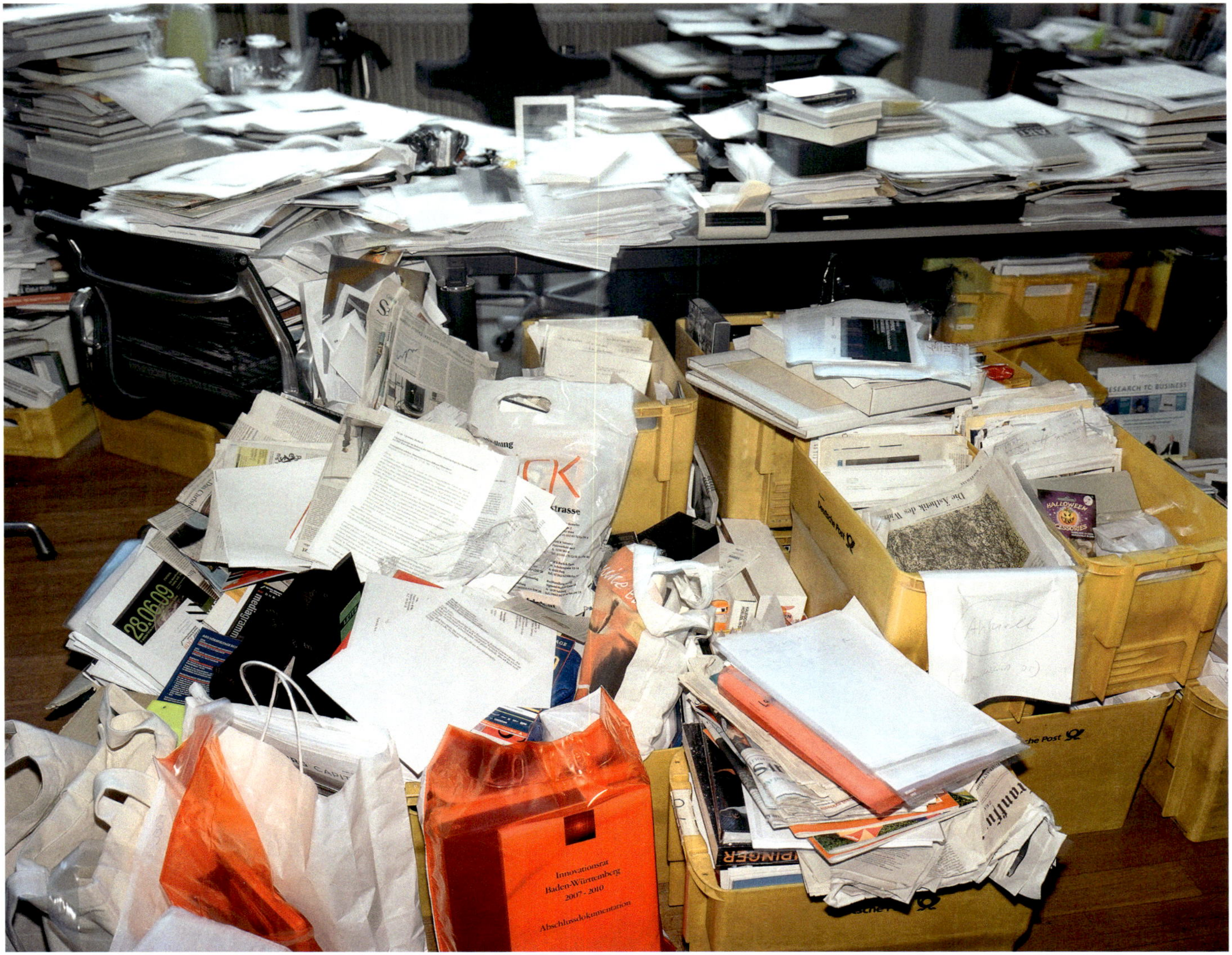

If I remember correctly, the number is about 129 million. Books alone demonstrate more diversity than biology. Translating this into geology is beyond science fiction, a planet you would not think possible if you were designing it from scratch and evolving it.

ZKM | Center for Art and Media Karlsruhe, Peter Weibel's back office, Karlsruhe, Germany, 2011

Pantelleria is a well-known volcanic island, its landscape consisting of vegetation now growing and the plant life that was growing when it was fossilized. Beneath that will be the soil, which some call the critical zone: the interchange between rock, sea, and atmosphere.

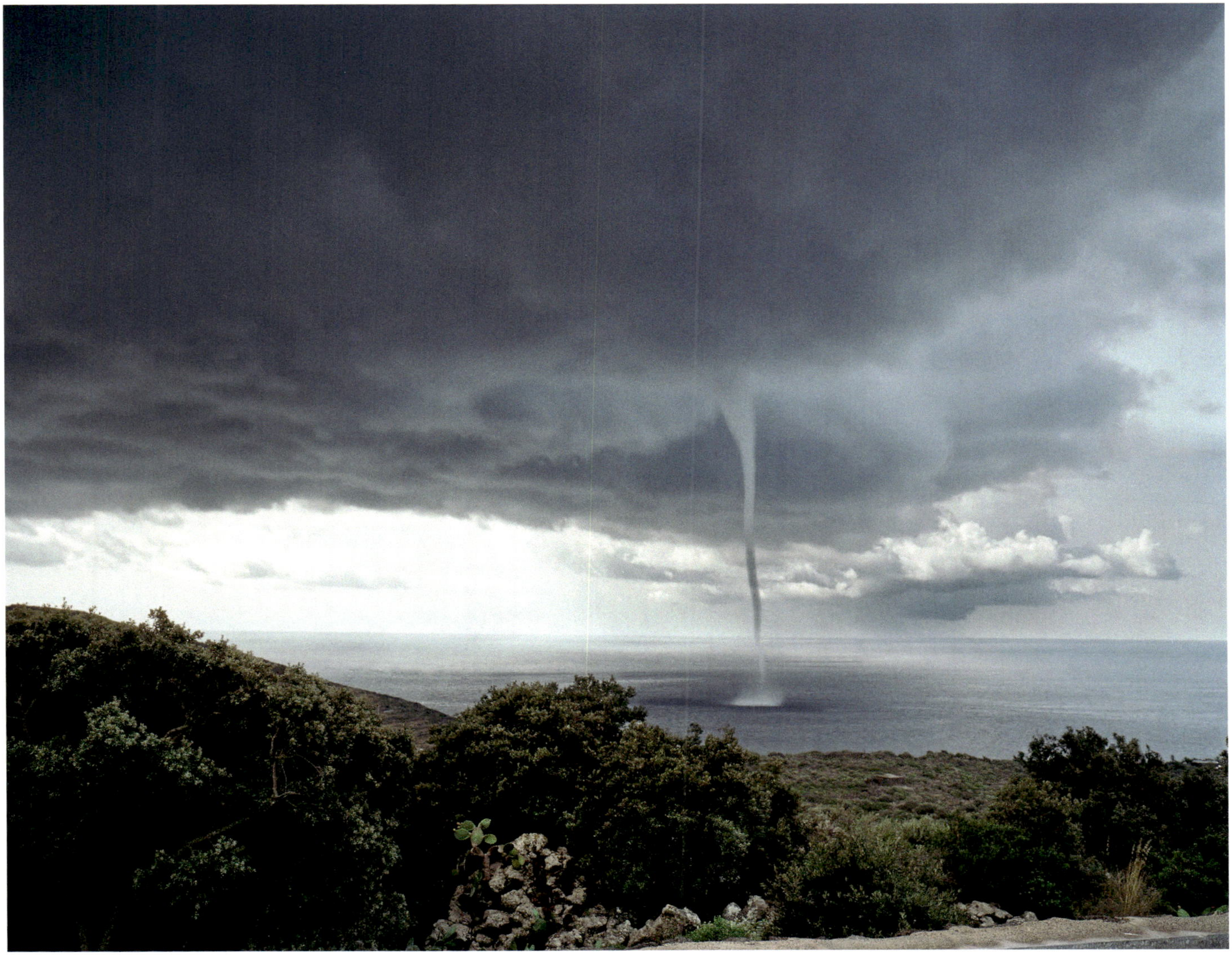

Underneath that there will be rock. And there are clearly two different sorts of rock. You have the steeper hillsides and the gentle hillside, and between them there is a boundary a geologist would call a break of slope, and it clearly separates two kinds of history. So we can read histories into simple things like a seascape.

Whirlwind, Pantelleria (TP), Italy, 2007

The Aral Sea is a classic example of humans changing a piece of nature. Lakes come and go, unlike oceans, which have been constant for at least three billion years. There is a delicate balance between the evaporation of water from the lakes and the input of water into them from rivers.

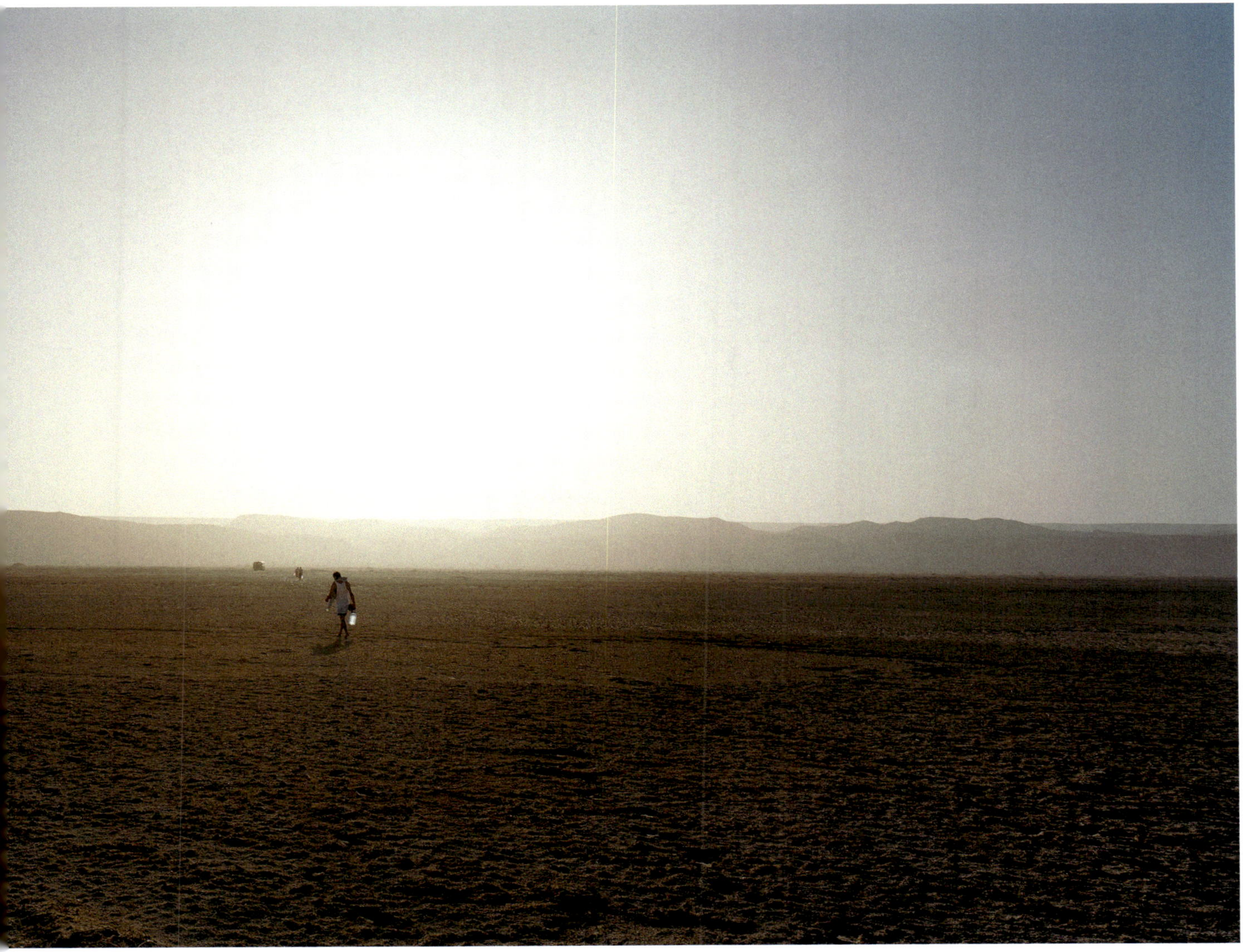

We know this because we find fossil lakes in the rock, which expand and contract, depending on what are usually slight changes in climate or in the shape of the mountains through tectonics, so rivers are cut off or new ones created. Lakes are naturally ephemeral things. This one is particularly ephemeral, because it is large, and the big rivers going into it were diverted, I think, to grow cotton in the old Soviet days.

Aral Lake, Mo'ynoq, Uzbekistan, 2001

A cargo of Lego toys was washed overboard into the sea off the coast of Britain some years ago. People have since then been tracing Lego blocks and figures. Hundreds of thousands, if not millions of Lego blocks were washed up along the coastline. Many effectively became sedimentary particles, parts of present-day layers of sand, gravel, and mud in the sea. As parts of future strata they will mark the age of Lego production: the modern age.

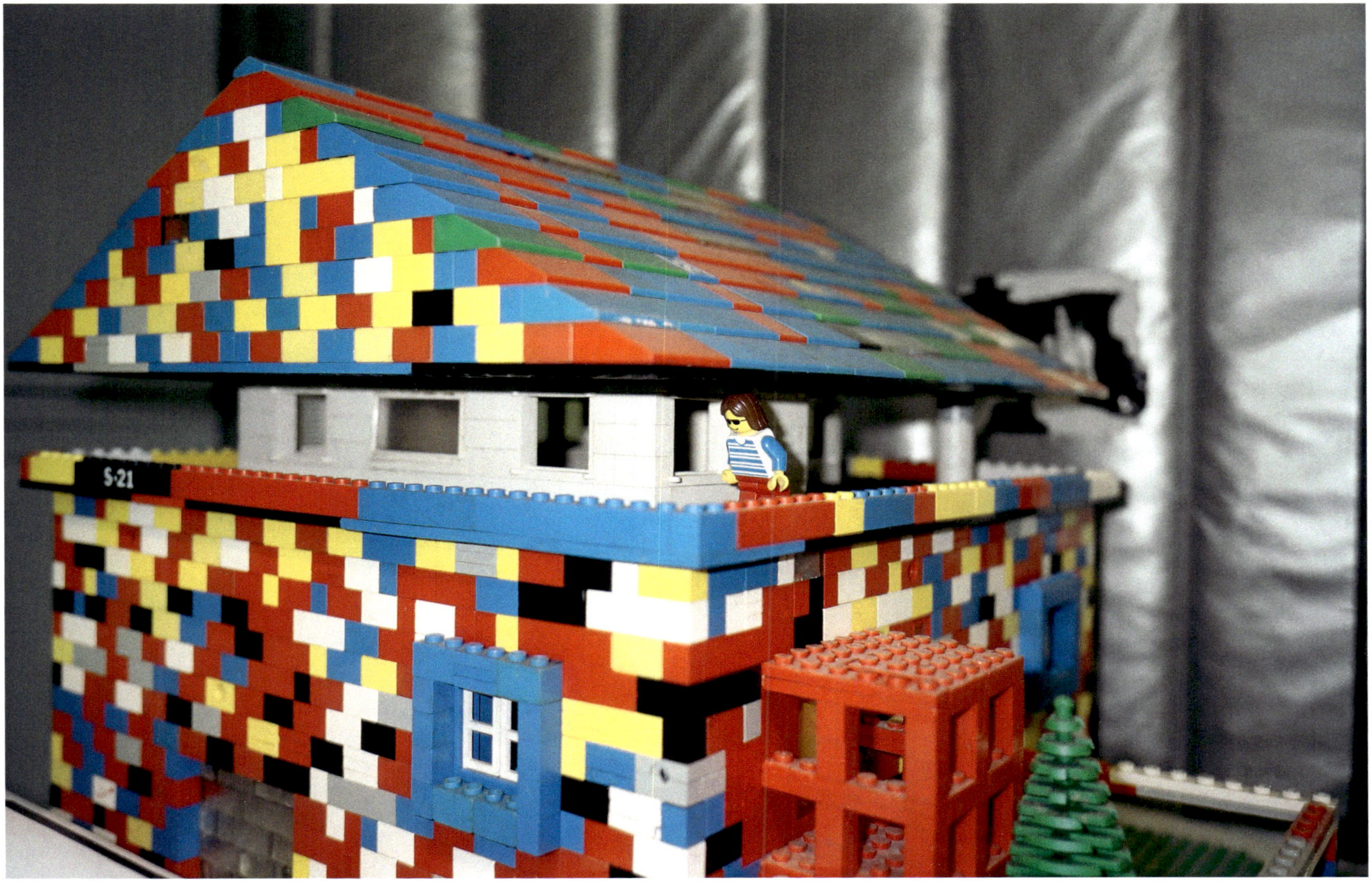

Over 300 million tons of plastic are made every year—hardly any are recycled, some are burned, some buried. A lot of it is now at the bottom of the sea and on beaches around the world. It's another marker for the Anthropocene. And it turns out to be more and more effective as a marker. Tiny bits, plastic microparticles washed off polyester and nylon clothes, go everywhere.

Ettore Sottsass, Lego house model in his studio, Milan, Italy, 1999

It’s a marker because it’s a time-related physical object that is widespread and can therefore get into a variety of different environments, into the sediment of different environments, and those sediments will form strata. An environmental nightmare: it gets into the food chain and causes all kinds of damage—which again leaves a geological trace. Geology as a discipline is fairly dispassionate about life and death.

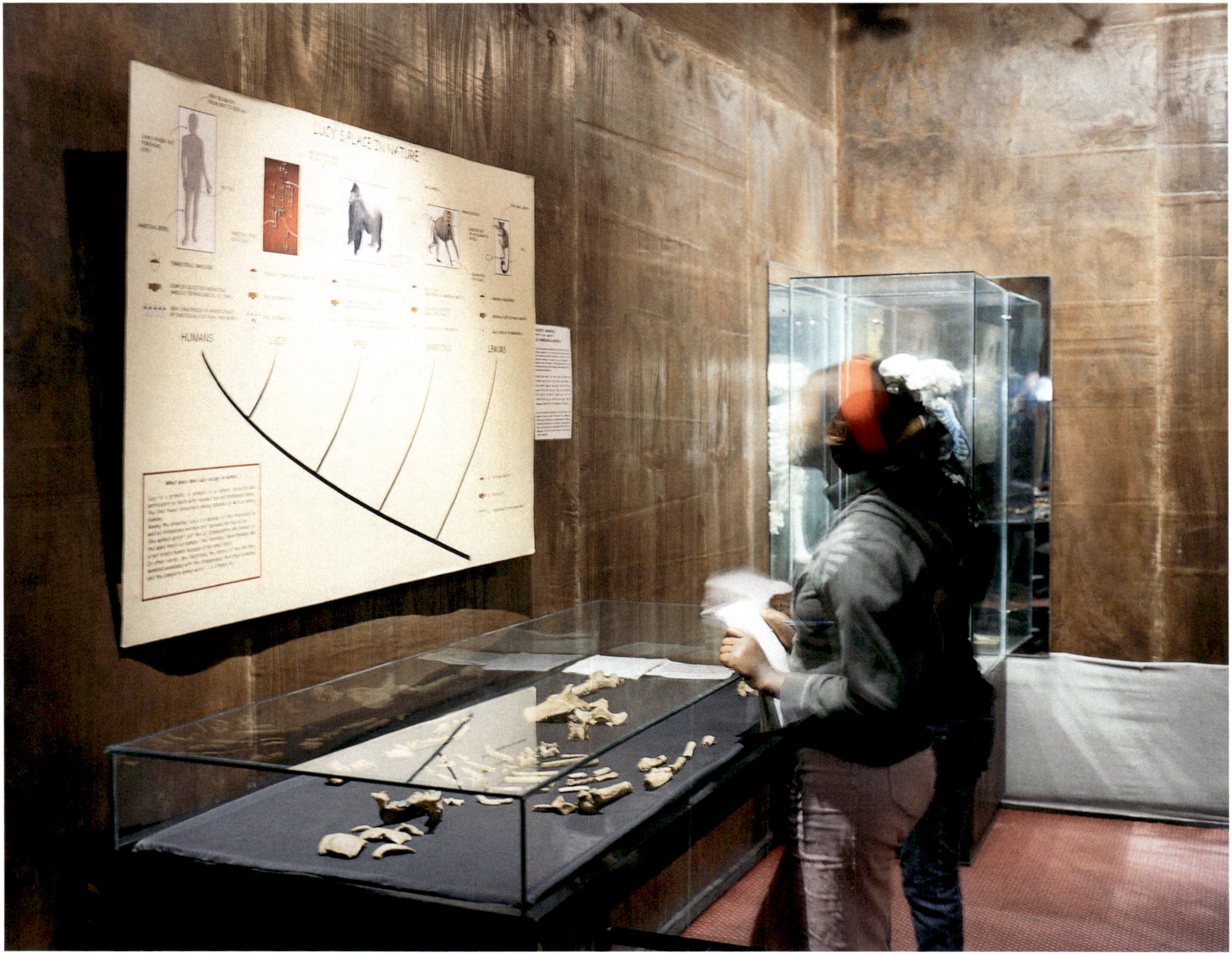

Humans fossilize lots of things. Images of the National Museum in Ethiopia tell us that we are fossilizing fossils, the bones of one of our ancestors, as an early human species and as a model. We fossilize in the sense of preserving the bone that was dug out of some cave, which is then re-fossilized in a museum, where its chances of preservation are better than in the cave. We also fossilize reconstructed shapes.

National Museum, the "Selam" display, Addis Ababa, Ethiopia, 2012

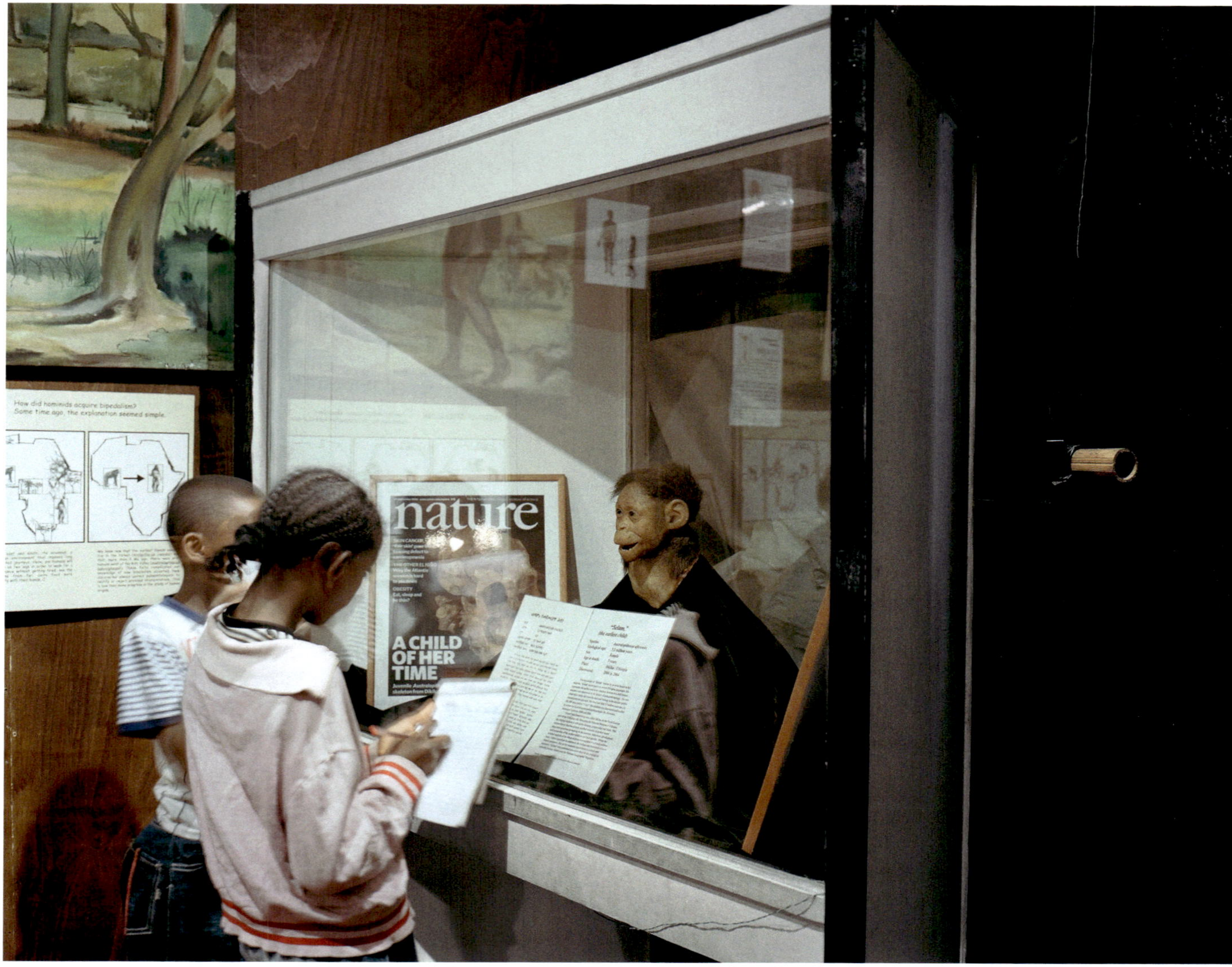

The museum houses the remains of "Lucy," found in 1974 in Ethiopia, belonging to a species classified as *Australopithecus afarensis*. A more recent find (2000–2004) revealed a 3.3 million-year-old partial skeleton of a child, which was reconstructed into a model in order to give an idea of what the first hominid might have looked like. Ethiopian schools visit the museum, as part of their basic curriculum and teaching on cultural heritage.

This is presumably a plastic or rubber model of what these bones represent. One can re-fossilize these bones.

National Museum, replica of "Lucy's" remains, Addis Ababa, Ethiopia, 2012

Let's suppose that in fifty years there is a war and the museum is ruined, as many museums have been in the past. Those bones might then be smashed up; or they might be lucky and simply end up washed out into some sand dune, where the process of fossilization carries on—together with this plastic model, which is less fragile than those bones. It's a reproduction and demonstrates our capacity for preservation.

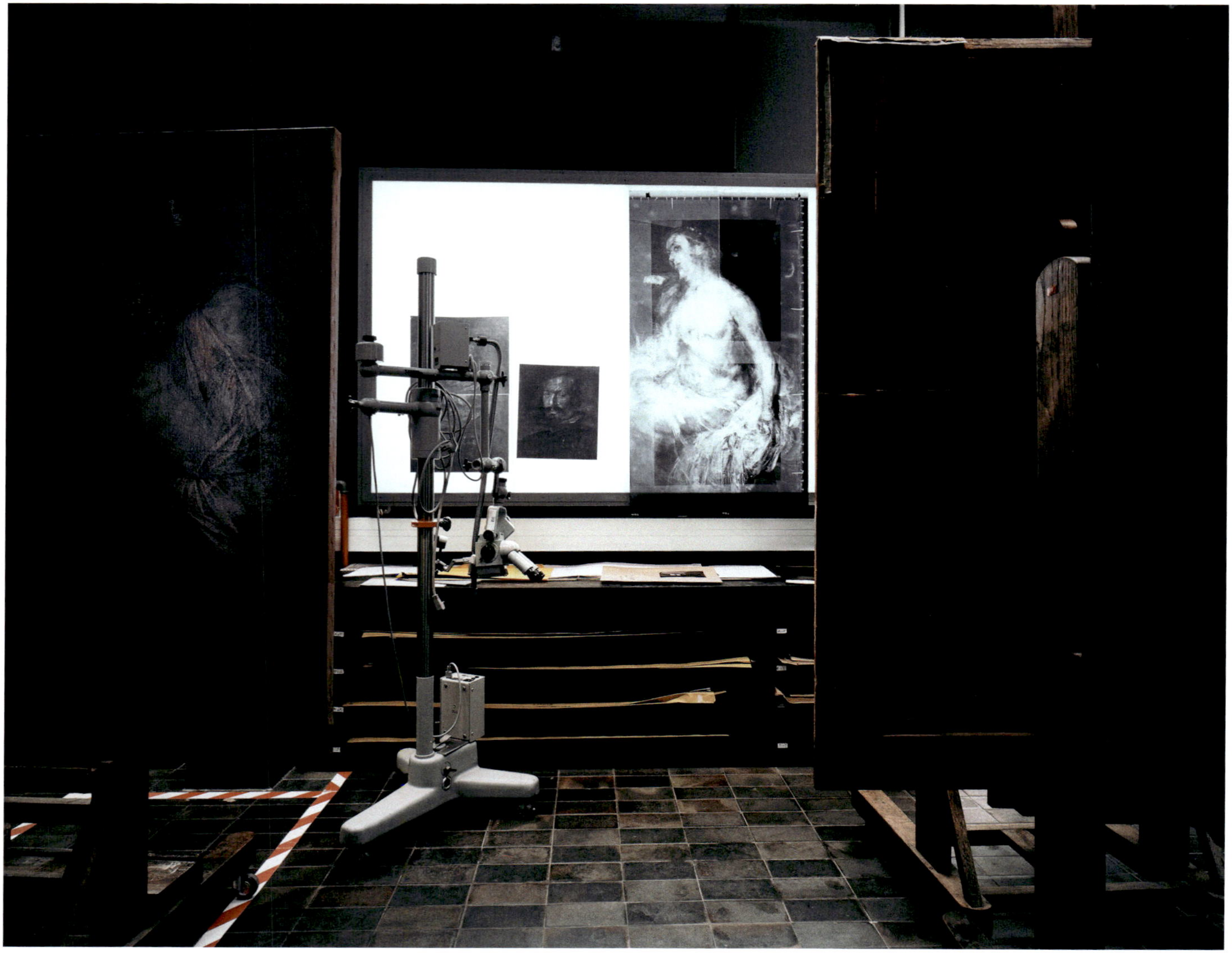

There is a stratigraphy in this Rembrandt painting: he would have painted it layer by layer. These thin strata of paint would have been built up almost geologically. This makes one think about the relationship between people and fossils.

C2RMF, Center for Research and Restoration of the Museums of France, radiographic image of Rembrandt's *Bathsheba at Her Bath* (1654), Paris, France, 2014

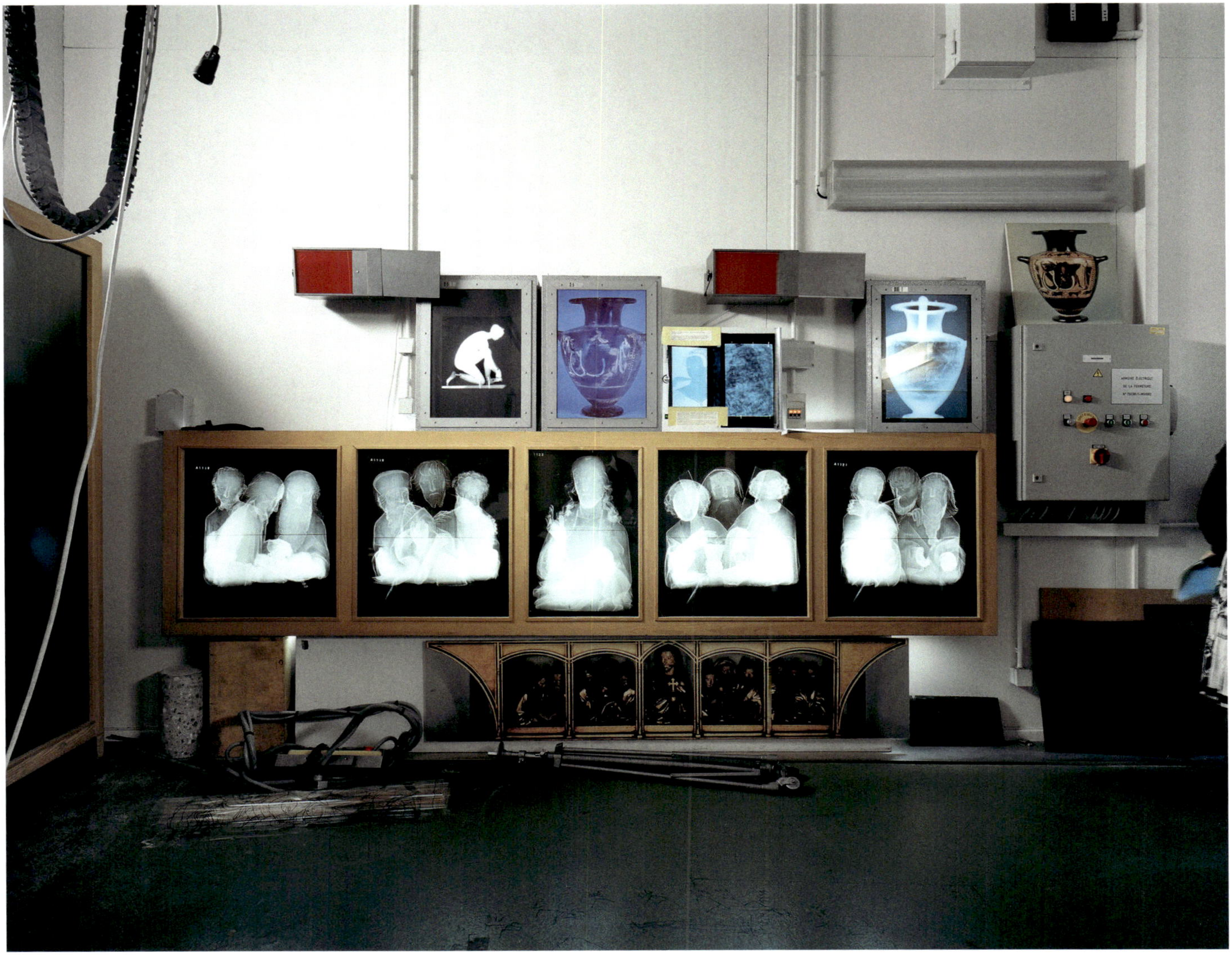

The pictures of these women and the amphorae above are three-dimensional objects, compressed into two dimensions. We do this with paintings and pictures on flat sheets of paper. Nature does it too. In fossilization, it is common to find three-dimensional fossils flattened onto a two-dimensional plane, into a silhouette, an outline.

C2RMF, Center for Research and Restoration of the Museums of France, radiographic laboratory, Paris, France, 2014

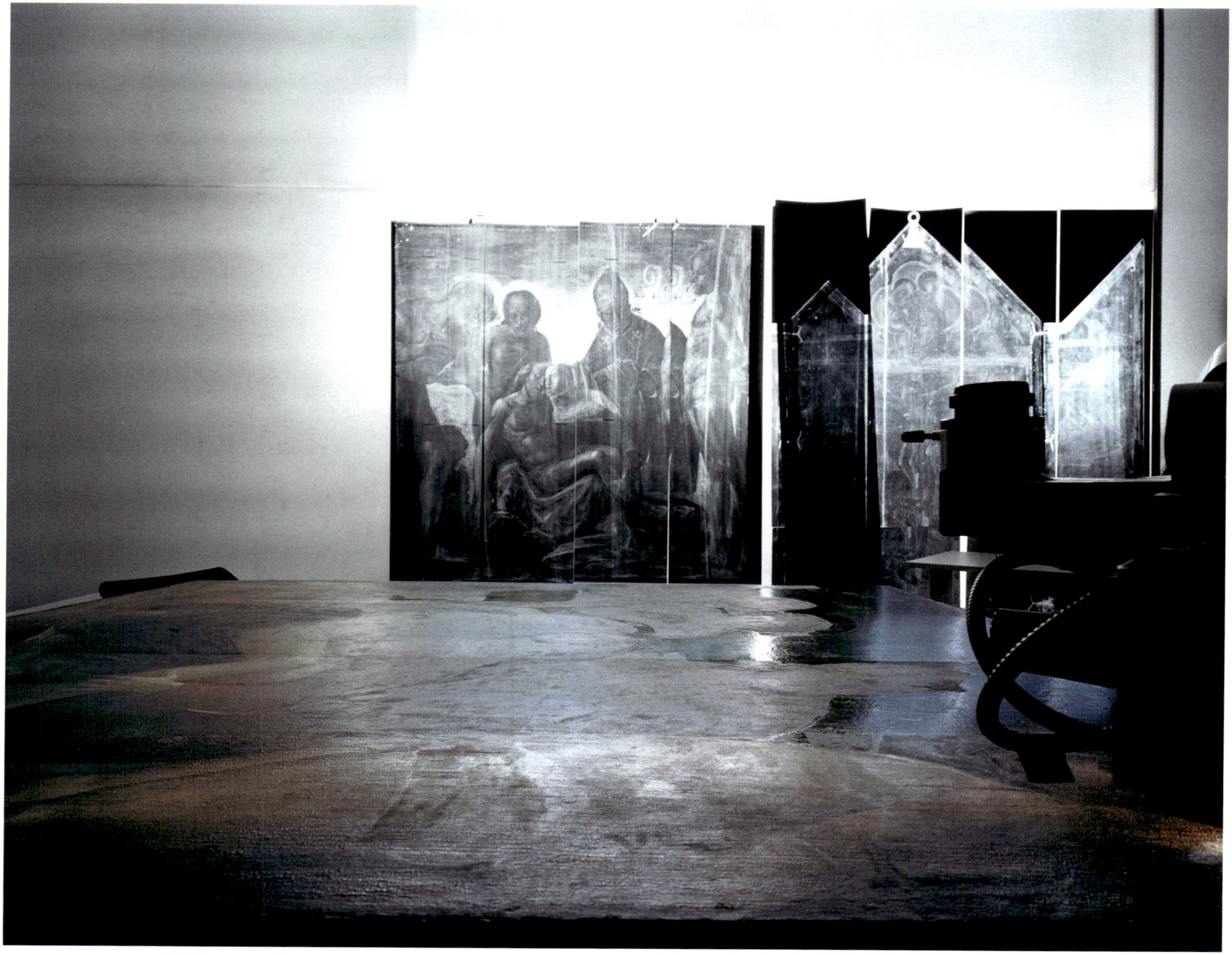

Details emerge within the silhouette, rather like on these X-ray pictures. You can get folds of the animal or openings of tubes; the kind of things one gets from patterns. In this kind of geometry humans imitate geology.

C2RMF, Center for Research and Restoration of the Museums of France, Paris, France, 2014

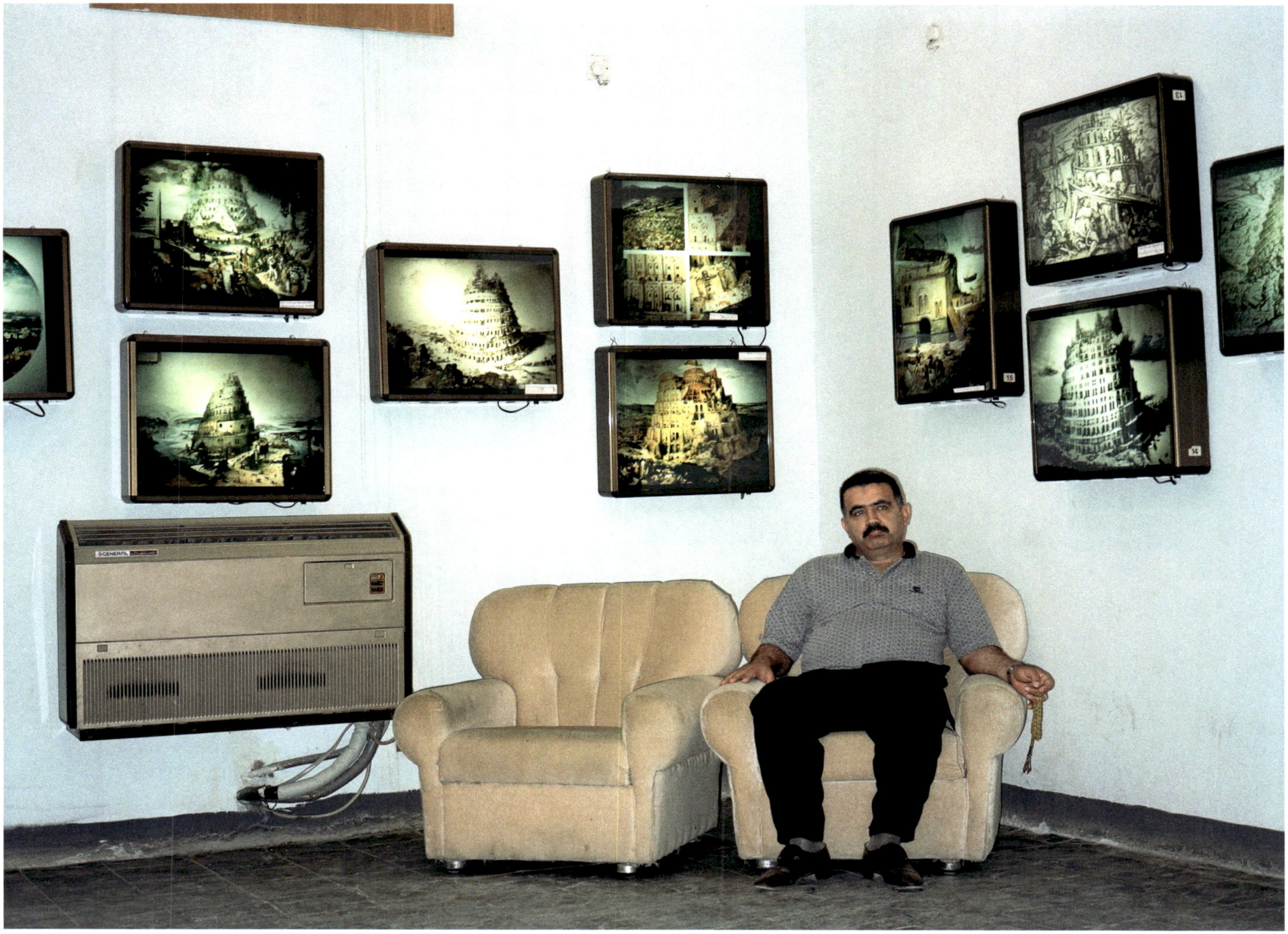

The Tower of Babel was a high, skyscraper-like tower made of weak materials, and it clearly fell down. Human hubris, I think.

Babylon Museum, Babylon, Iraq, 2002

Looking at our skyscrapers, we might wonder what will become of them if the sea level rises by two meters, and ten billion people end up trying to find some space in the world.

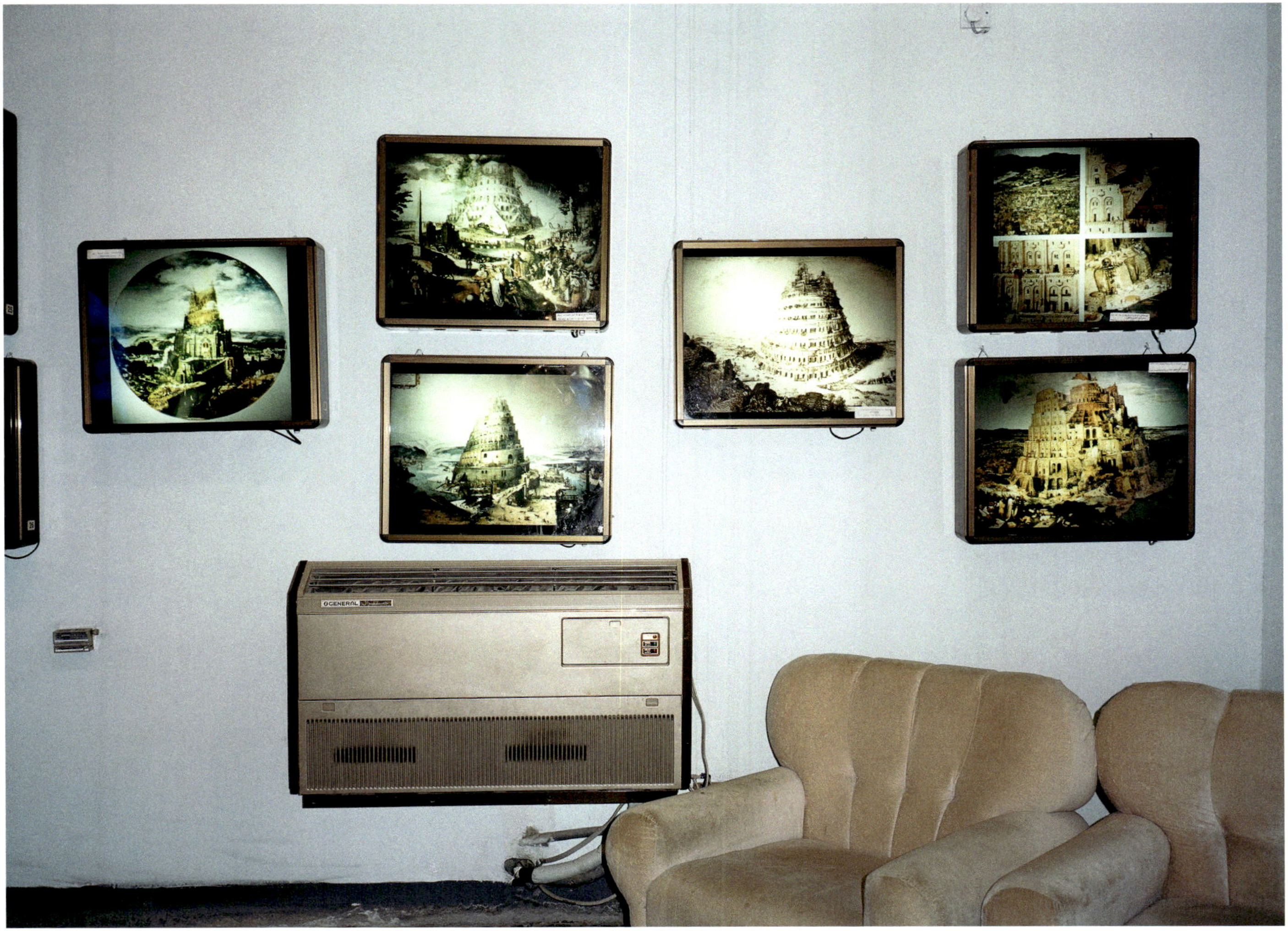

It is part of the technosphere, emblematic of the way in which we humans have developed the facility to make ourselves comfortable in any surroundings, which has made us into an invasive species par excellence. We can go to Antarctica or to the Sahara Desert—technology like this will keep us alive, as long as we can continue making it and running it.

Babylon Museum, Babylon, Iraq, 2002

The decisions arrived at in this place are framed as an air-conditioning unit, cooling down not just a room but the whole planet. This is, for now, a dysfunctional or malfunctioning thermostat; it is operating, but nothing happens. And yet, a planet with the right temperature is a reasonably important thing.

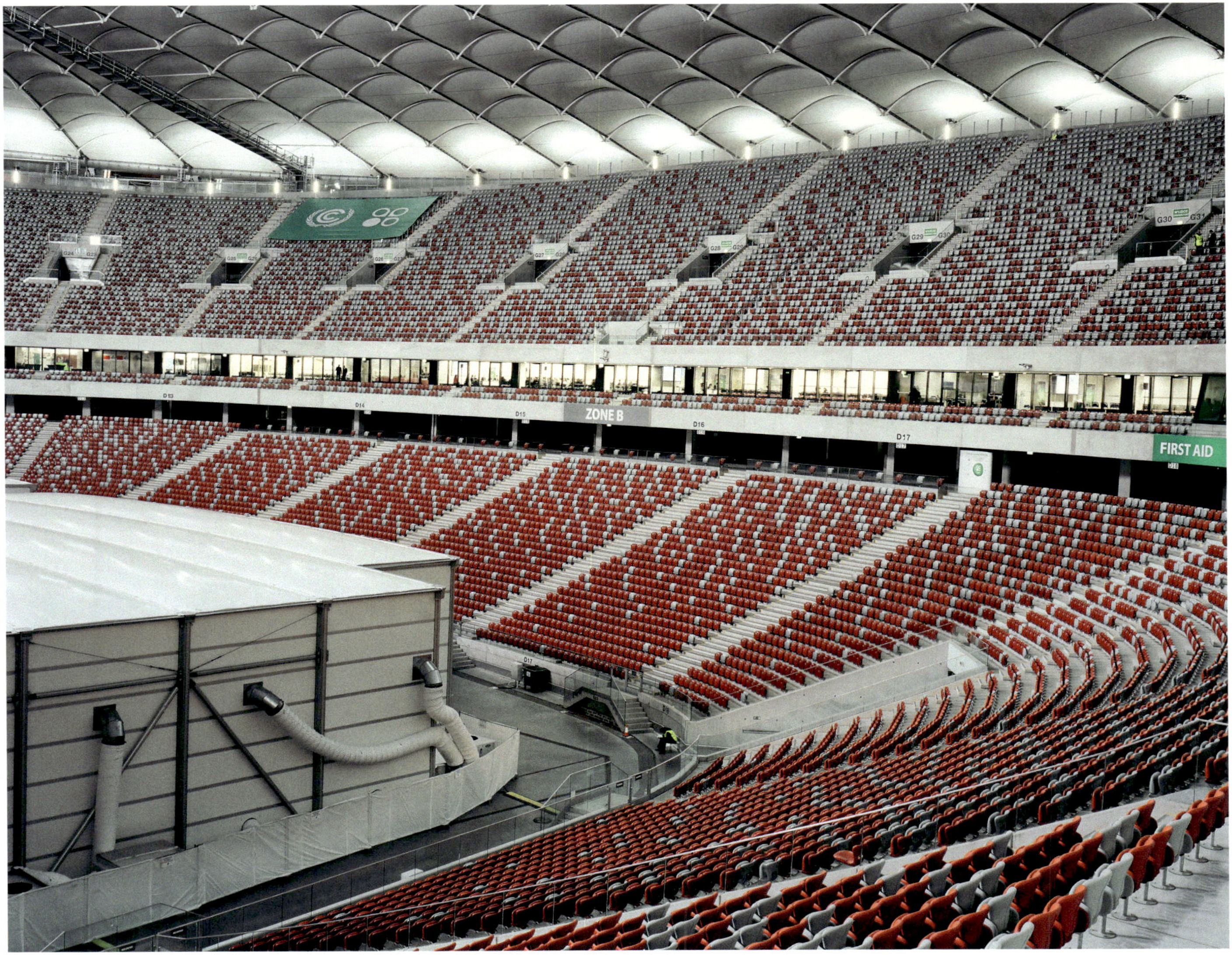

The football stadium is an impressive, well-engineered, expensive part of the technosphere, designed for something none of us needs but a lot of us want, which is to be able to go in large numbers and watch a football match. It is far more important to many people whether, for example, Barcelona or Juventus win the football match tomorrow than whether the Earth's climate will be half a degree warmer or cooler in fifty years time.

UNFCCC, COP19 Climate Change Conference, Warsaw, Poland, 2013
Photography in collaboration with Giulia Bruno

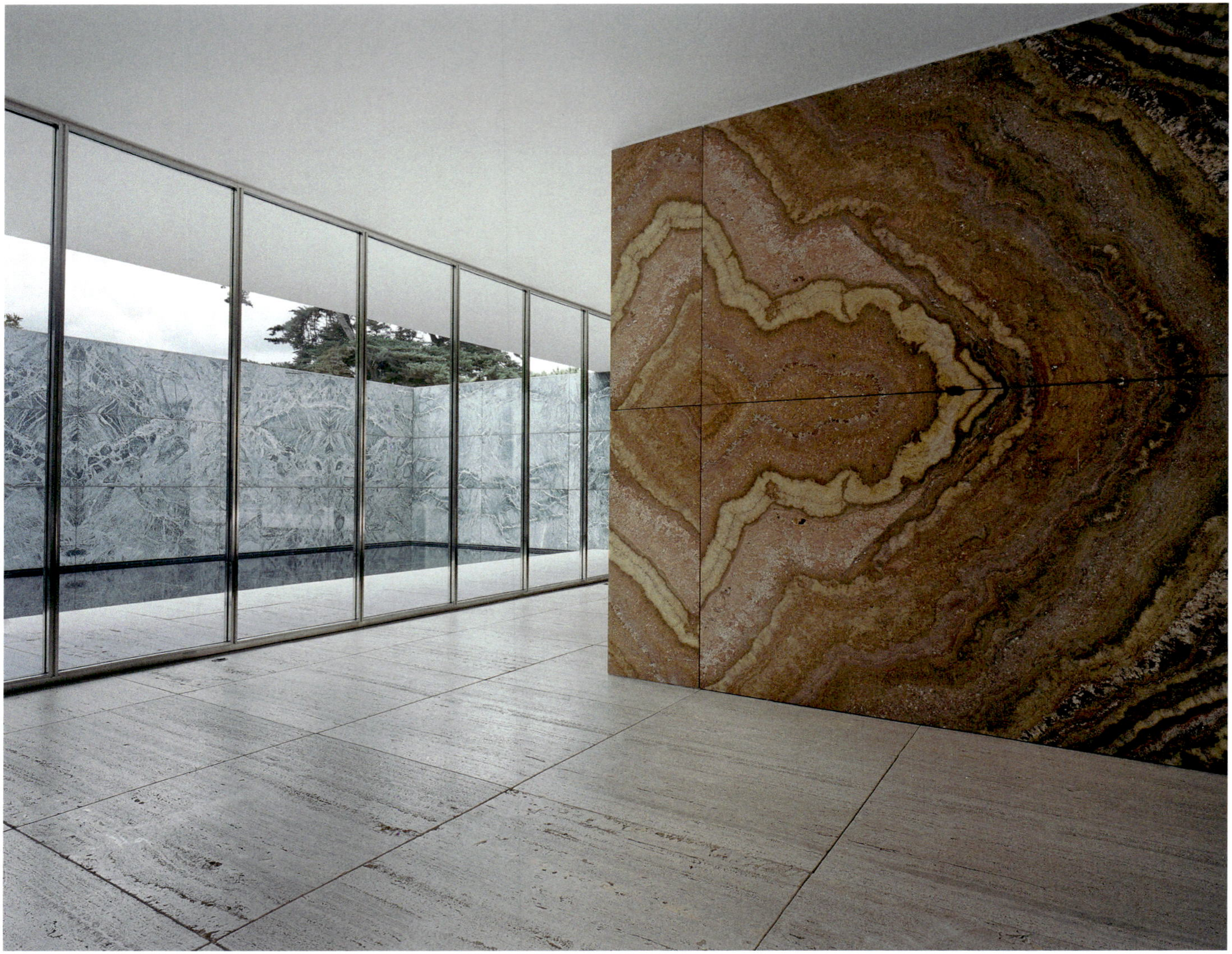

A colleague of mine, an architect, showed me a set of photographs of train stations made in the nineteenth century. The stations, each in a different city, were different, each reflecting local customs. In a later set, from the period a little after Mies van der Rohe, the stations looked almost the same, because of their concrete, steel, and glass constructions and modern, cost-efficient design.

Mies van der Rohe, Barcelona Pavilion, Barcelona, Spain, 2013

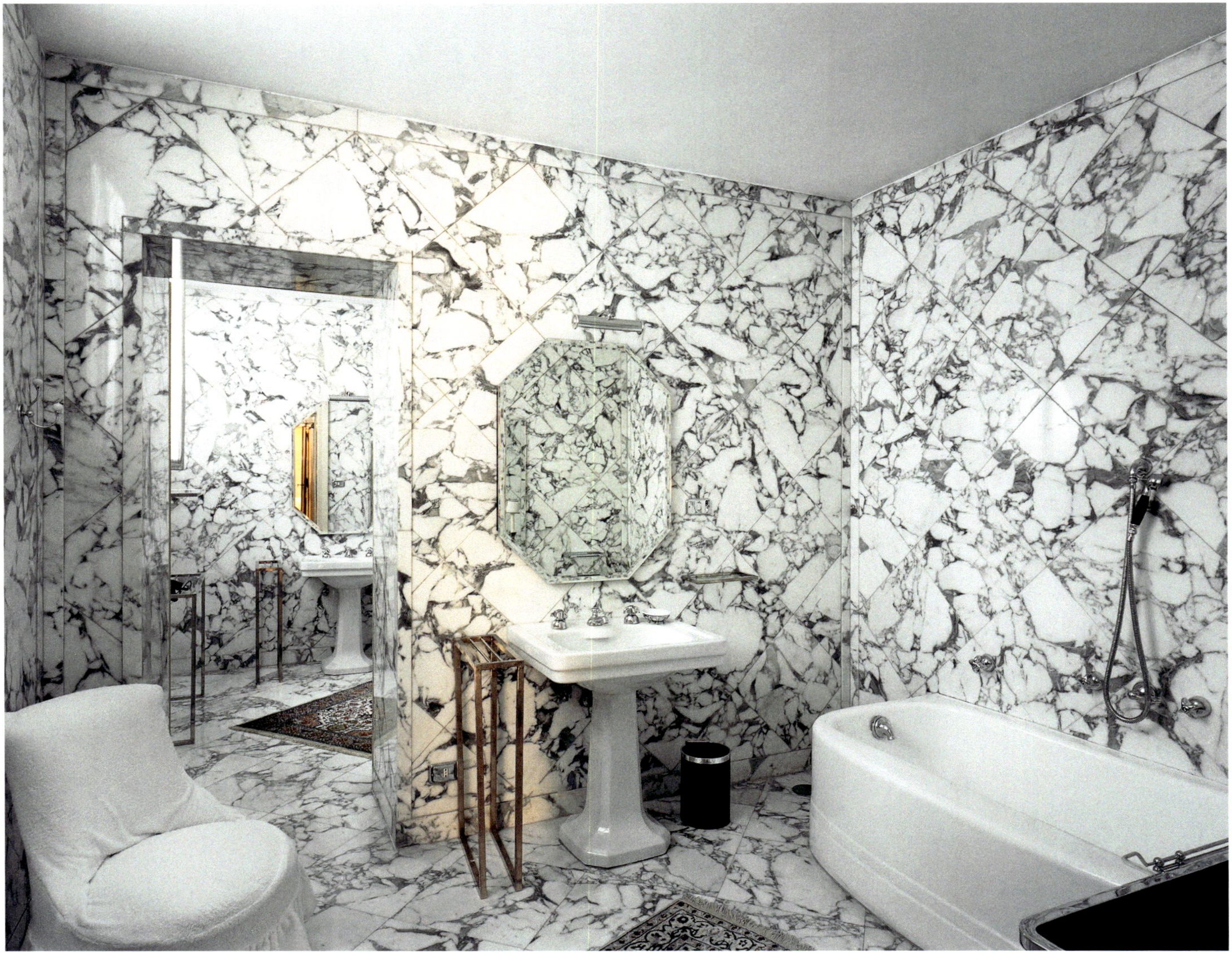

After a phase of diversity in these sorts of constructions, we have returned to a simplified and homogenized design or style. Imagine a science-fiction writer thinking about what an advanced civilization would do as it got richer, more capable, and more powerful: Would it explore greater diversity? Here the opposite has happened—our civilization has become richer, more powerful, and more capable, and it has created uniformity.

Palazzo del Quirinale, official residence of the President of the Italian Republic, bathroom in the guest apartment, Rome, Italy, 2007

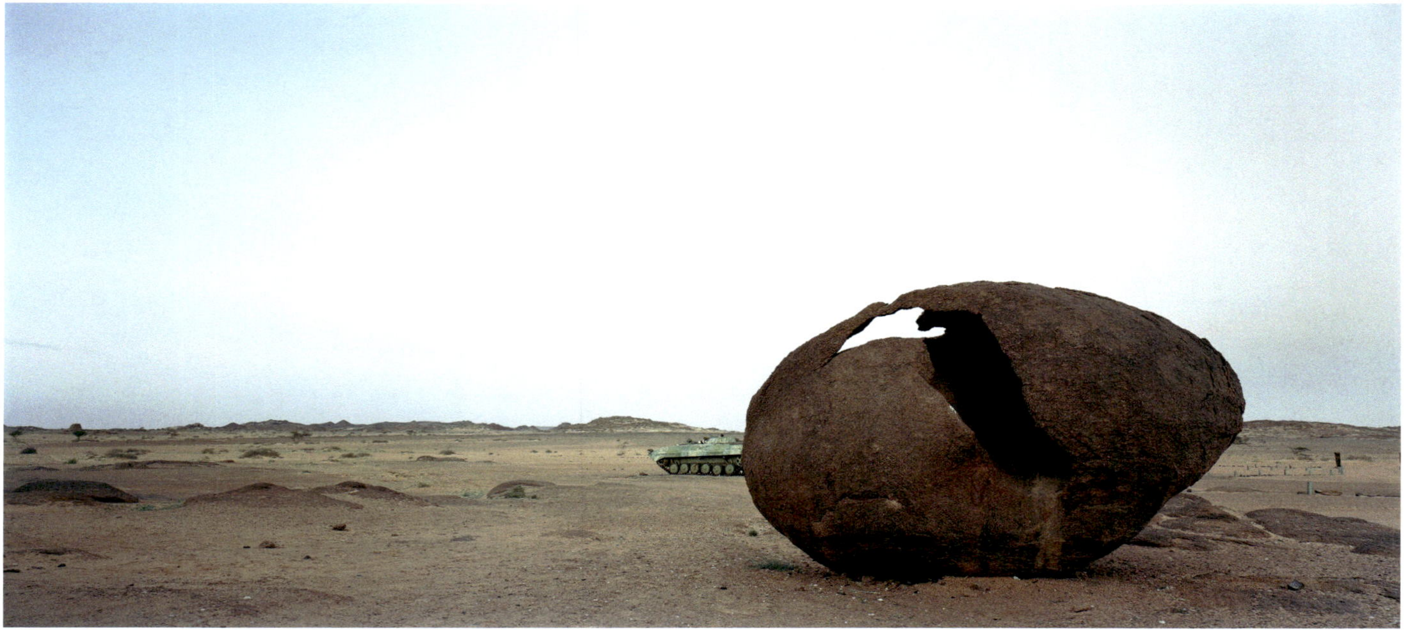

The tank represents an aspect of geology that polite geologists do not mention: war and conflict. When acting territorially, humans direct large parts of their resources into separating off and defending parts of the Earth's surface.

Sahrawi Republic (SADR Territories), Western Sahara, 2004

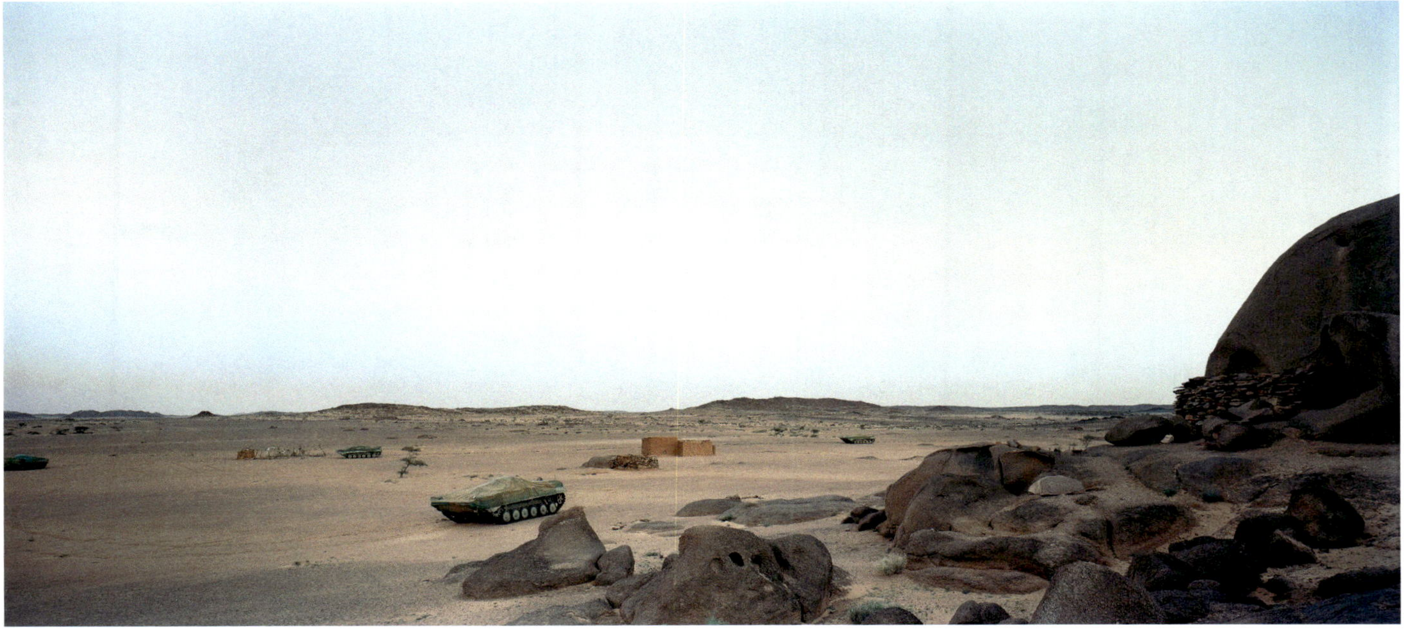

This field is hardly researched at all. In environmental geology we tend to think of all humans as being rather nice creatures acting for the common good, which is clearly not the case in practice. All these things have geological consequences.

Sahrawi Republic (SADR Territories), Western Sahara, 2004

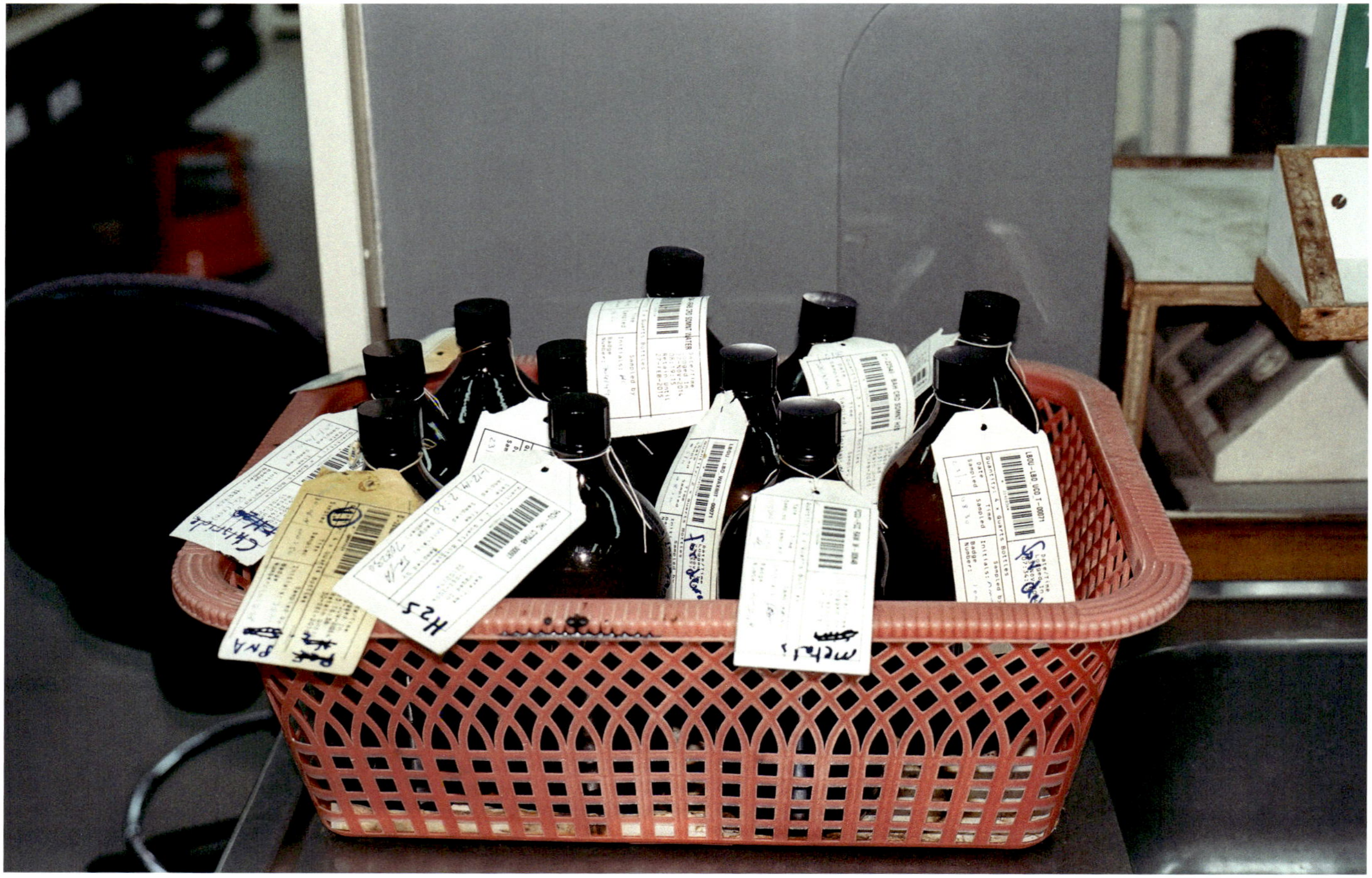

These little bottles of oil are there only because nature is usually very good at recycling, far better than we are. And yet, tiny amounts can escape, drop out of the recycling system, and be buried. This imperfection has led to the storing of old fossil fuels, as a fraction of a percent that escapes the usual carbon cycle. Without the particular conditions for trapping the energy we call oil and gas, what would we as humans have done?

BAPCO Bahrain Petroleum Company, laboratories, Awali,
Kingdom of Bahrain, 2014

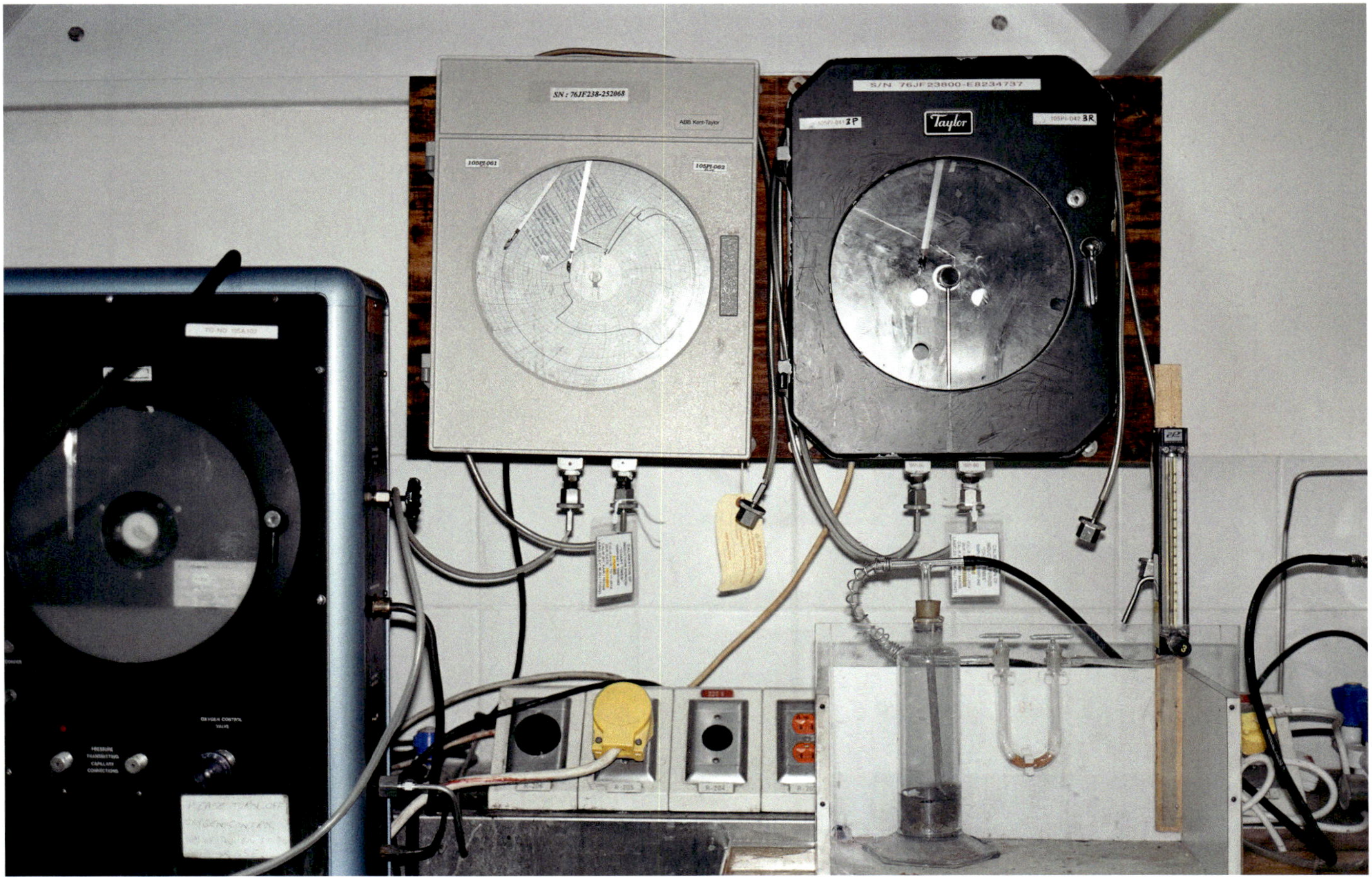

I suspect we would have gotten a lot better at learning how to use energy from plants, from wind, from the sun, from all the other sources that we know are out there and are usable—just not quite as convenient as oil. This is part of the machine that drives the world.

BAPCO Bahrain Petroleum Company, chemical laboratory,
Awali, Bahrain, 2014

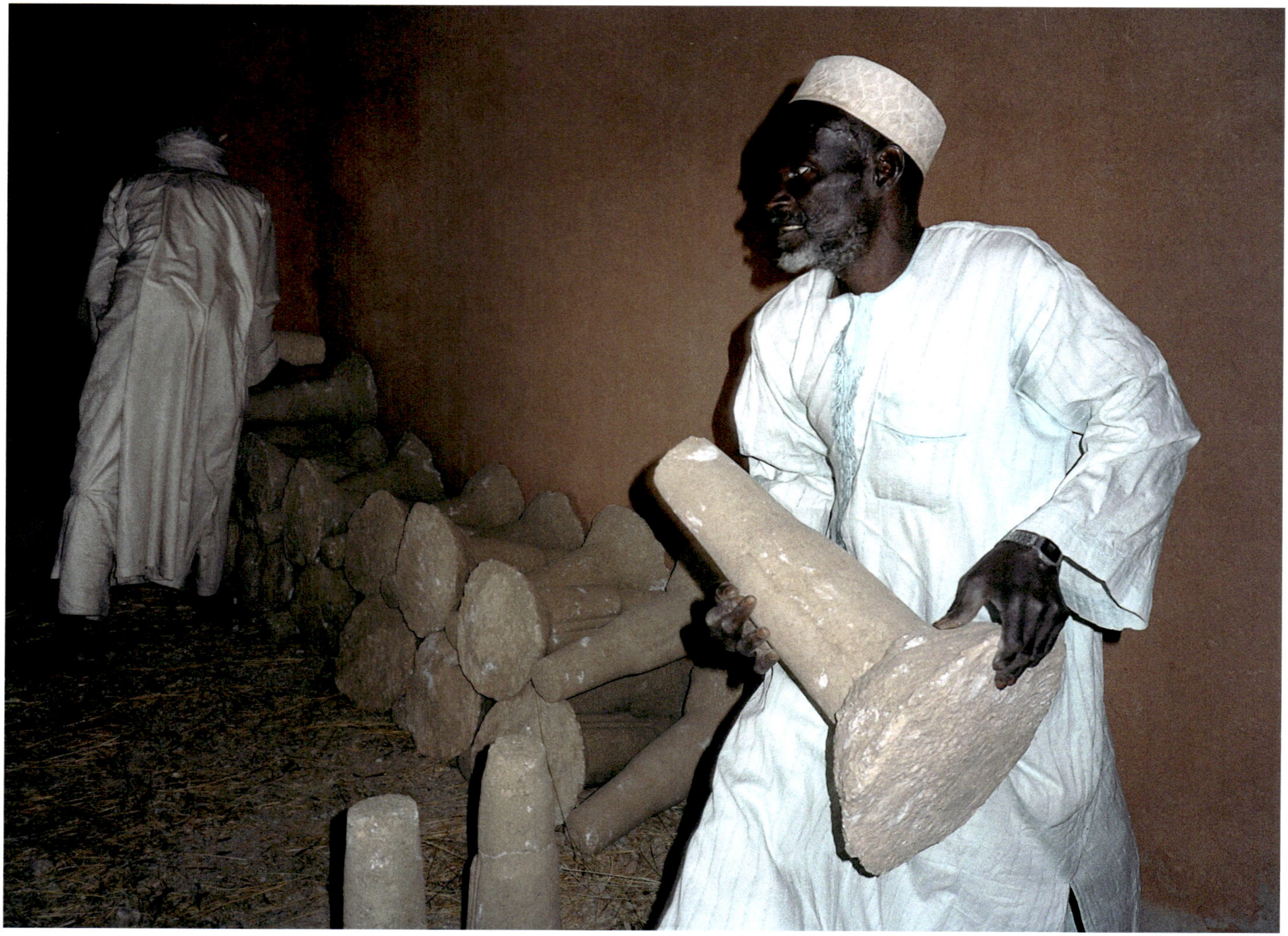

These salt blocks would have been a seafloor millions or hundreds of millions of years ago and were left exposed as the sea dried up. The man is holding a salt rock, as well as an environmental catastrophe. That exposed seafloor would have been far too toxic for any creature to live in, and yet toxic as it was, it has produced matter, stuff that people find useful.

Salt blocks for transportation animals, Agadez, Niger, 2006

Whatever you use salt for—preserving food, the chemical industry—you use past history carved into very particular shapes. We see these little salt columns on pedestals. Whatever they are used for, whether as ornaments or something more practical, a means of carrying salt, they are still part of the mystery. One part of Earth's history is being carried forward and transformed into another part of its history.

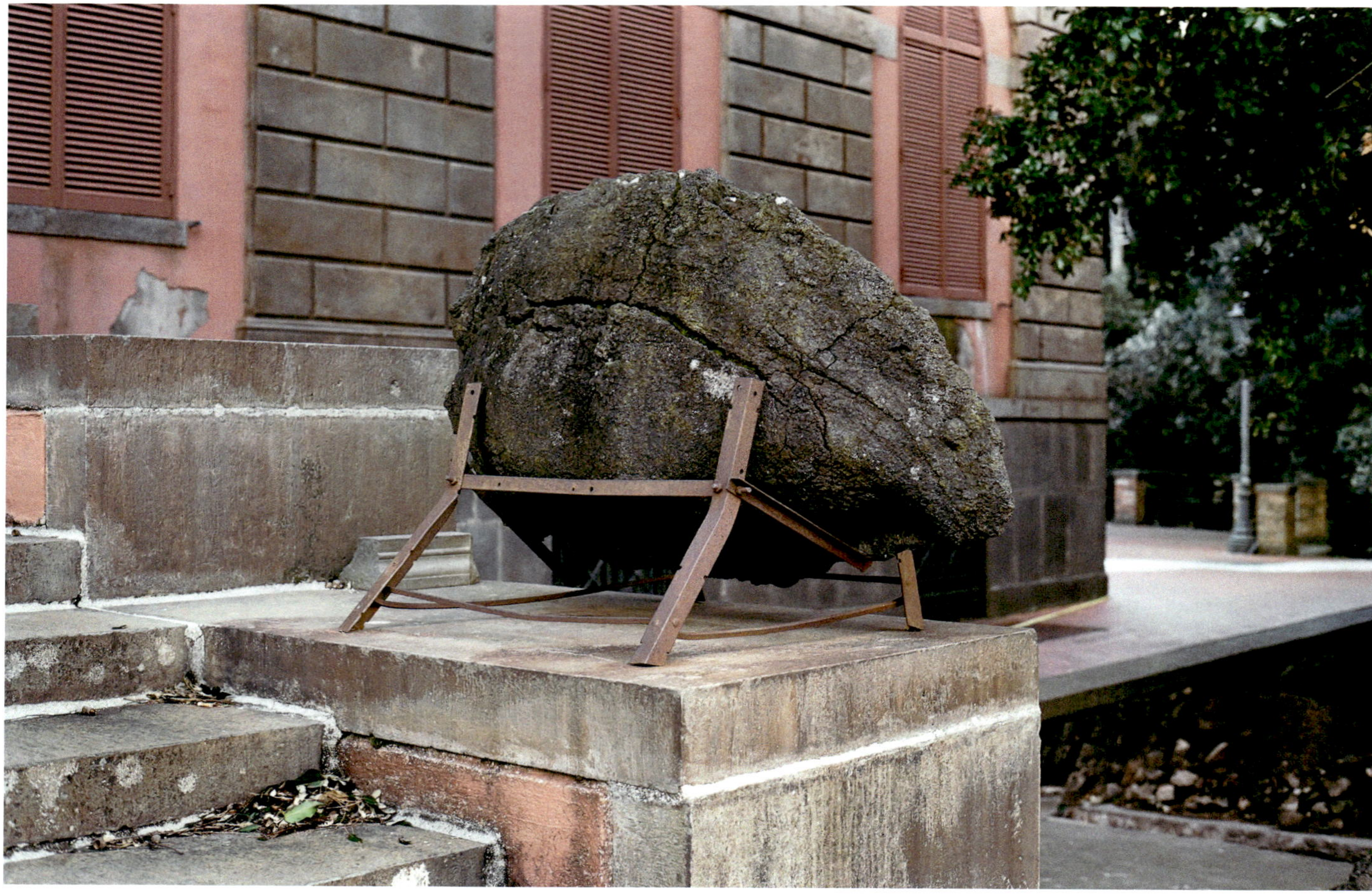

A big volcanic bomb like the one in the photo means a small volcanic eruption, probably more something for tourists to look at than something that can devastate a whole landscape. Nevertheless, this piece of rock was clearly chosen to symbolize the power of volcanism. It is a piece of nature, a relatively gentle part of an otherwise violent nature that has been tamed. It is now clearly within the Anthropocene.

INGV, Vesuvius Observatory, Naples, Italy, 2015

This could be taken as a symbol of the way we control information. Again that is something quite new, the way that we take and store records of objects or happenings or events. I'm not sure what they are, but it's the way we try to bring the whole of the earth within our view—maybe not within our power so much—so that we have this enormous, immense record of it.

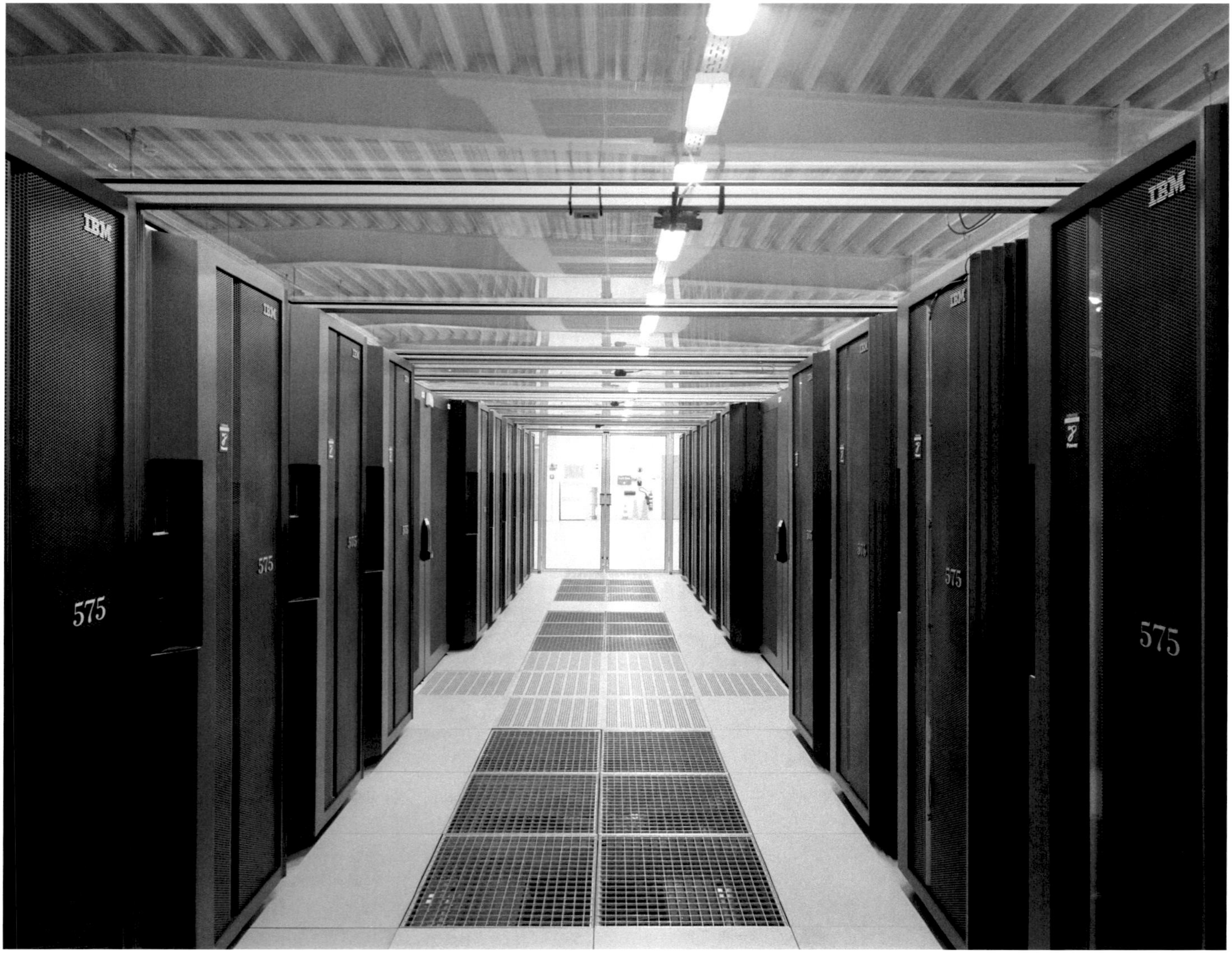

This, I suspect, is very much part of what makes us human. We try to understand things. It is probably what created the Anthropocene. We're trying to look around in the world, make sense of it, and then make use of it.

DKRZ Deutsches Klimarechenzentrum, archives, Hamburg, Germany, 2013

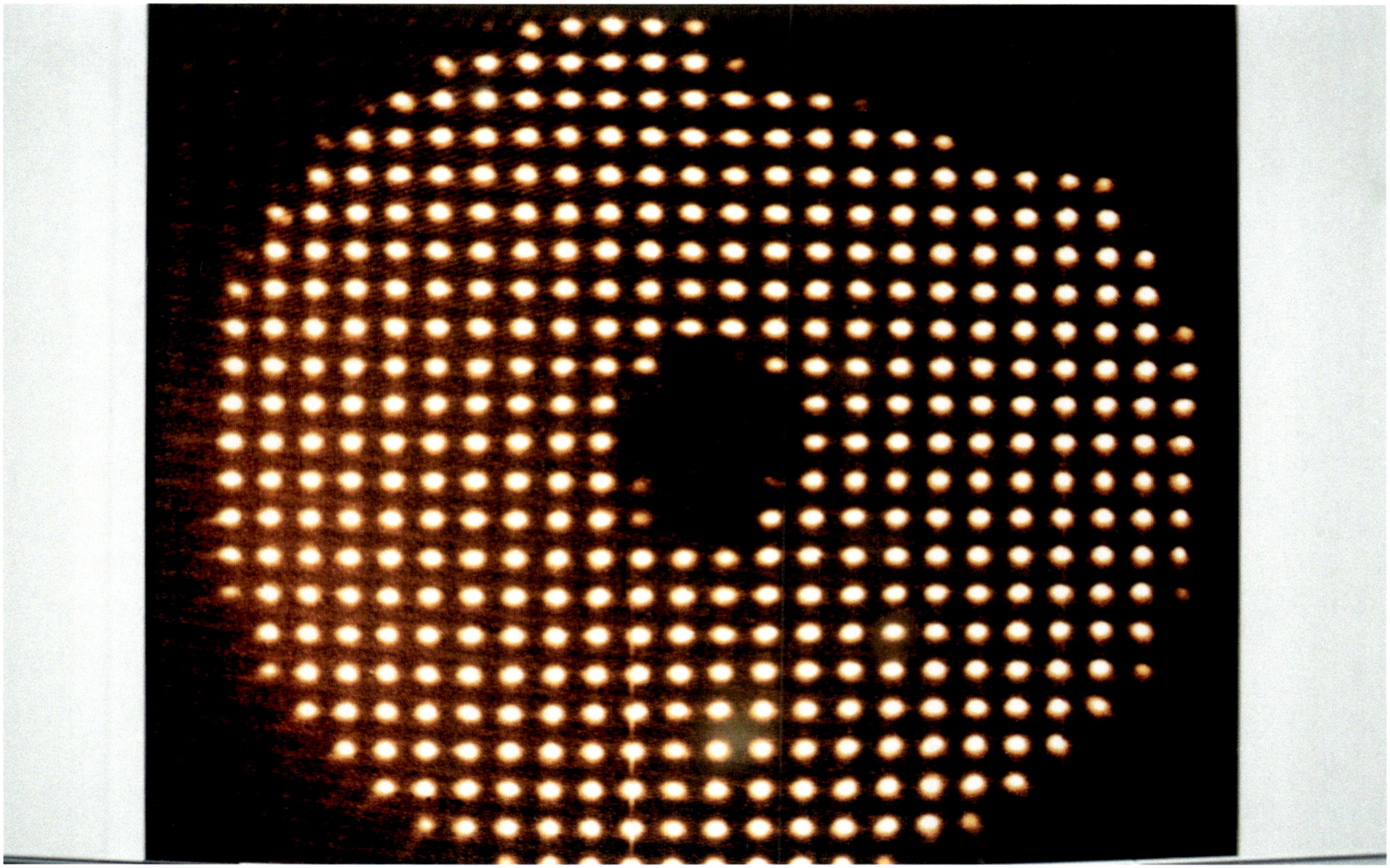

In the circular pattern on this image there are probably a couple of hundred bright dots in parallel lines, going straight up and across. There is also a black hole in the middle, where we do not have any bright dots.

ESO VLT, astronomical observatory, Cerro Paranal, Chile, 1999

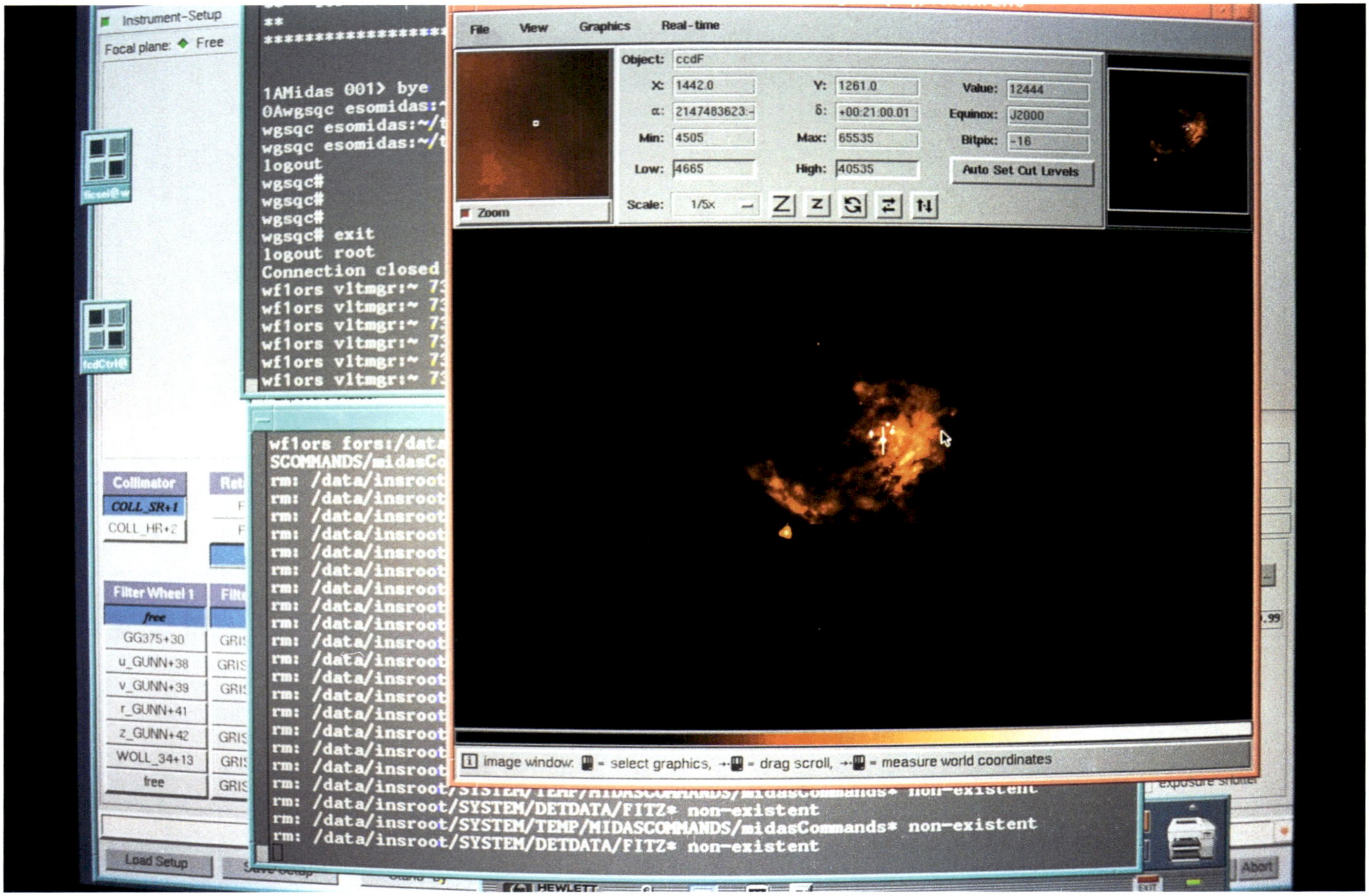

It shows an astronomical observatory, the Magellanic Clouds, and some technical recording of the light of the nebula.

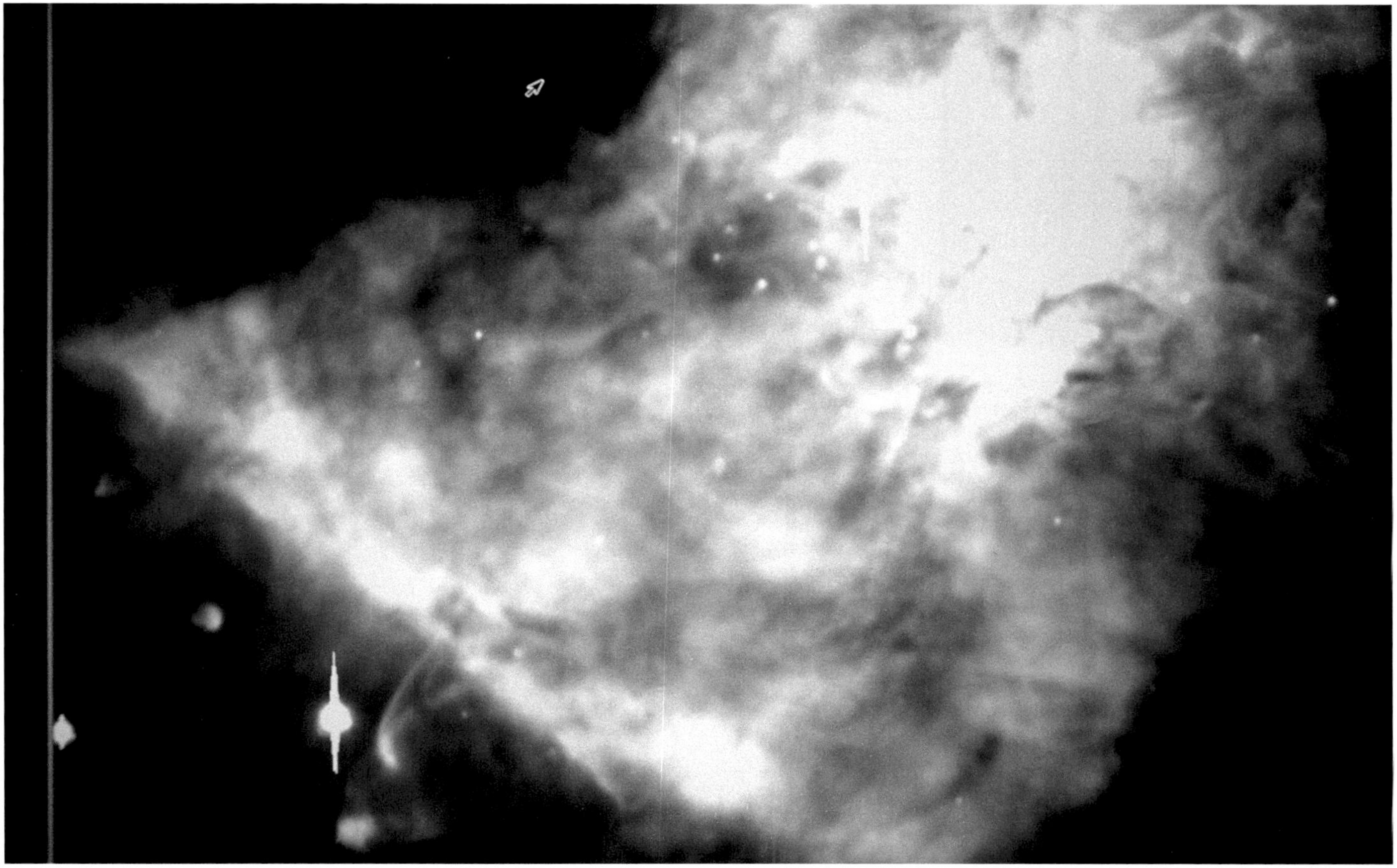

There is so much out there that we often come upon completely new things. We don't know how to begin interpreting them. This sense of being confused, in the dark, is very typical of the life of the scientist, of many of the things we try to understand about the Anthropocene.

ESO VLT, astronomical observatory, Cerro Paranal, Chile, 1999

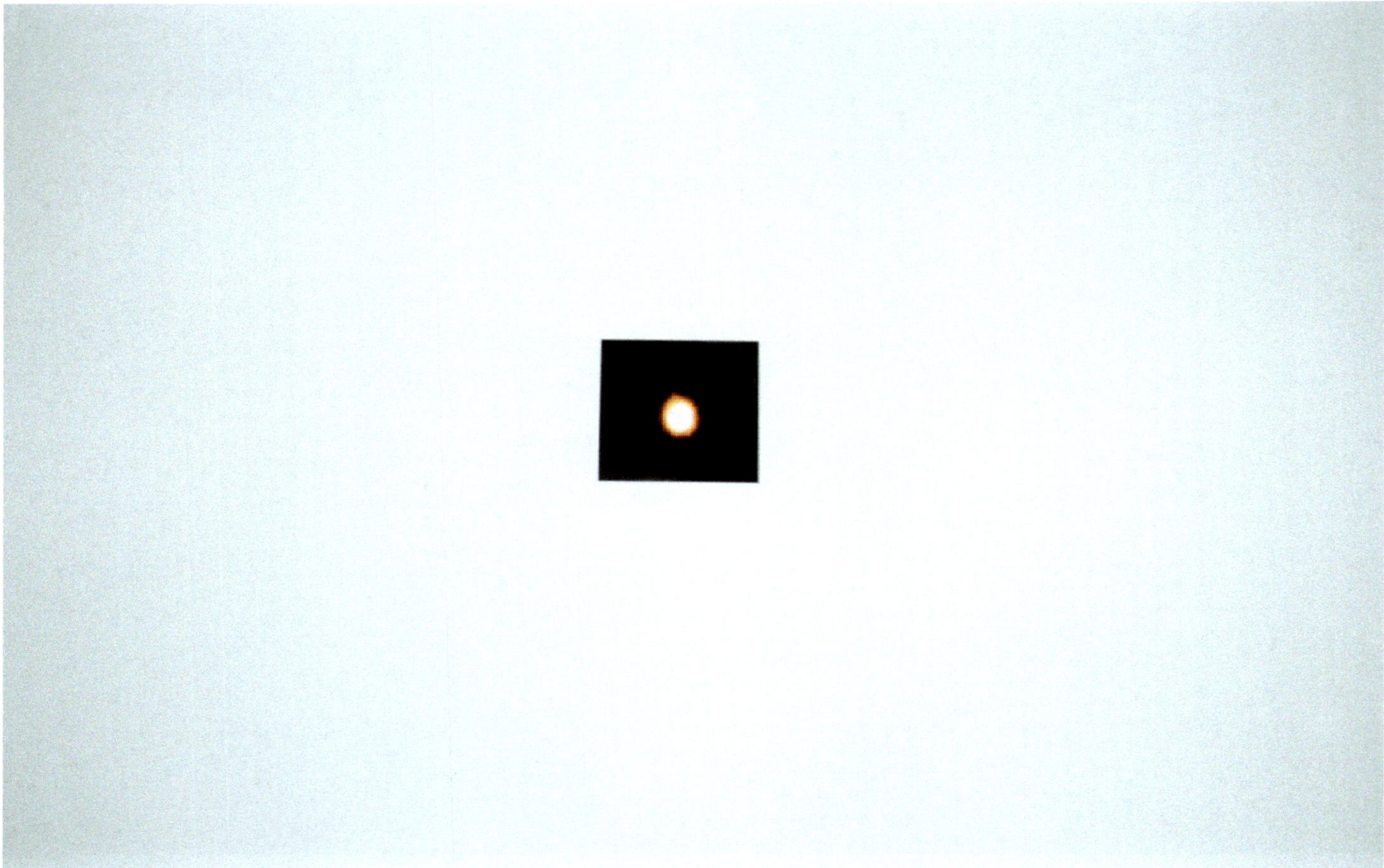

We have incomplete information and new pictures. In order to interpret them, we simply have to start from the very beginning.

ESO VLT, astronomical observatory, Cerro Paranal, Chile, 1999

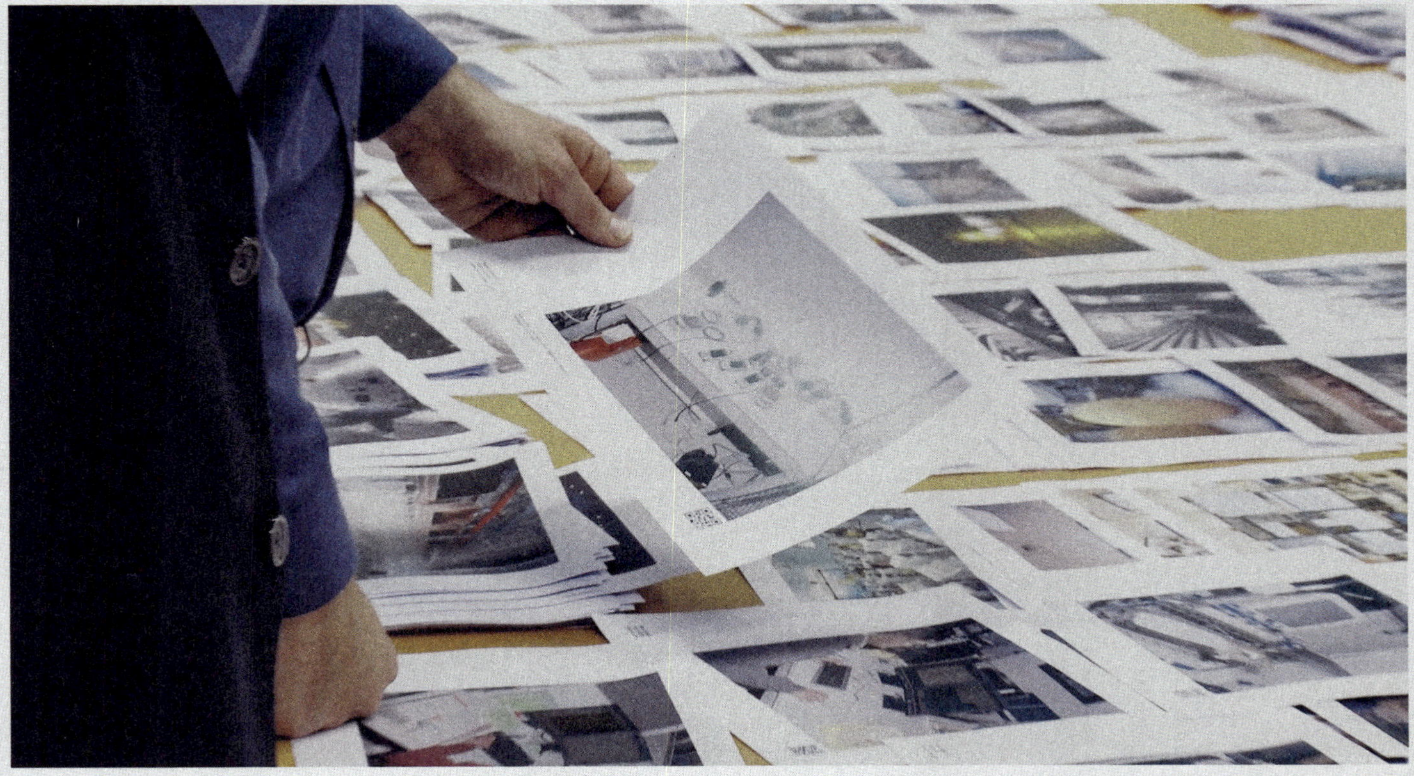

Peter Weibel

87–138

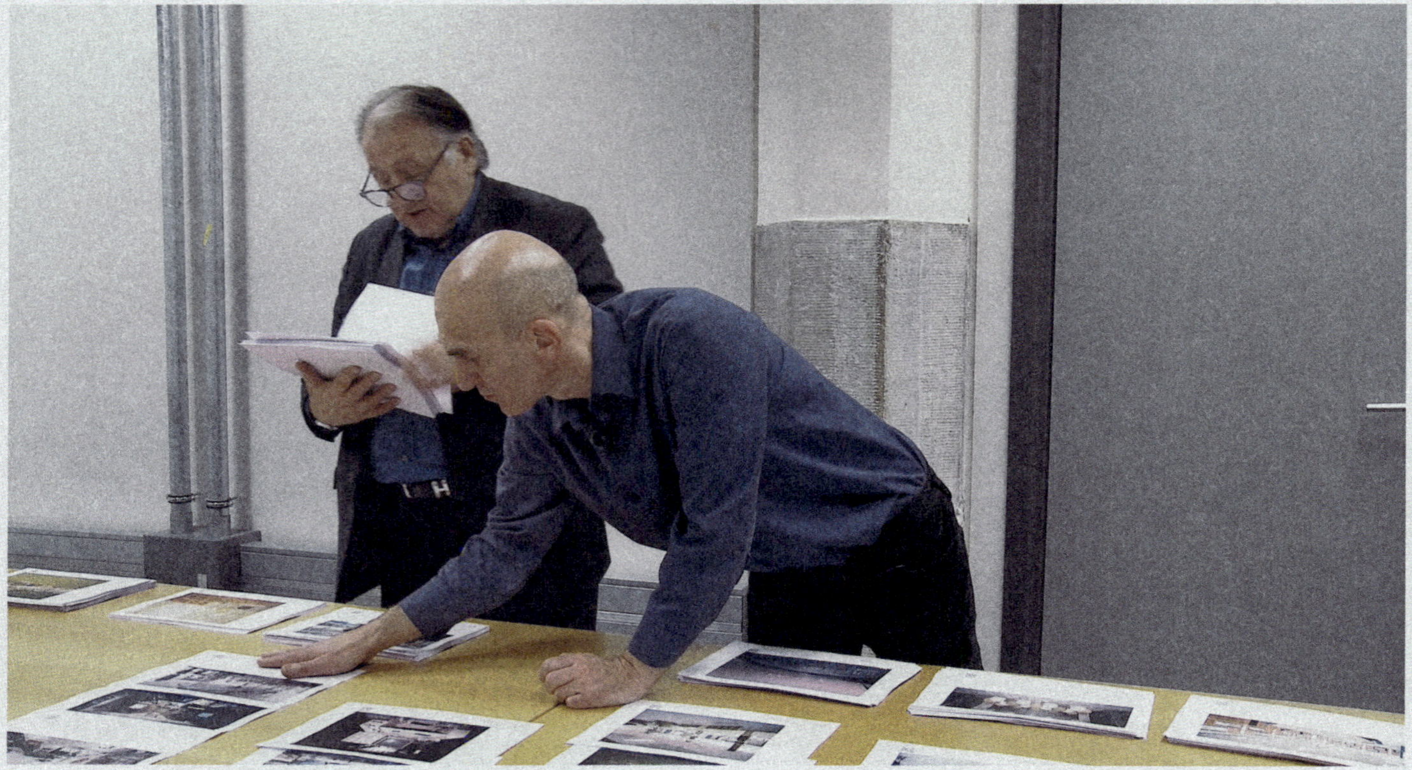

Peter Weibel and Armin Linke, ZKM | Center for Art and Media
Karlsruhe, December 2014

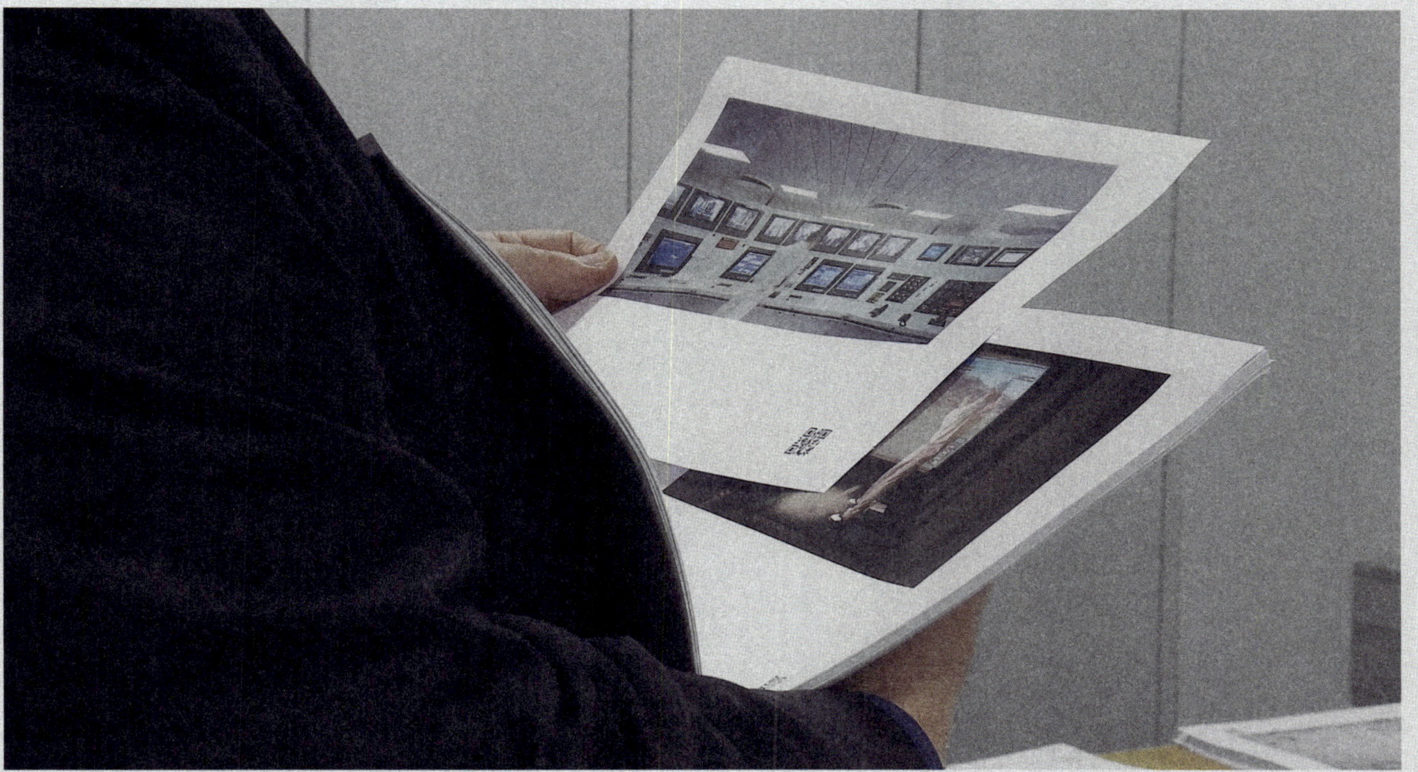

Peter Weibel and Armin Linke, ZKM | Center for Art and Media Karlsruhe, December 2014

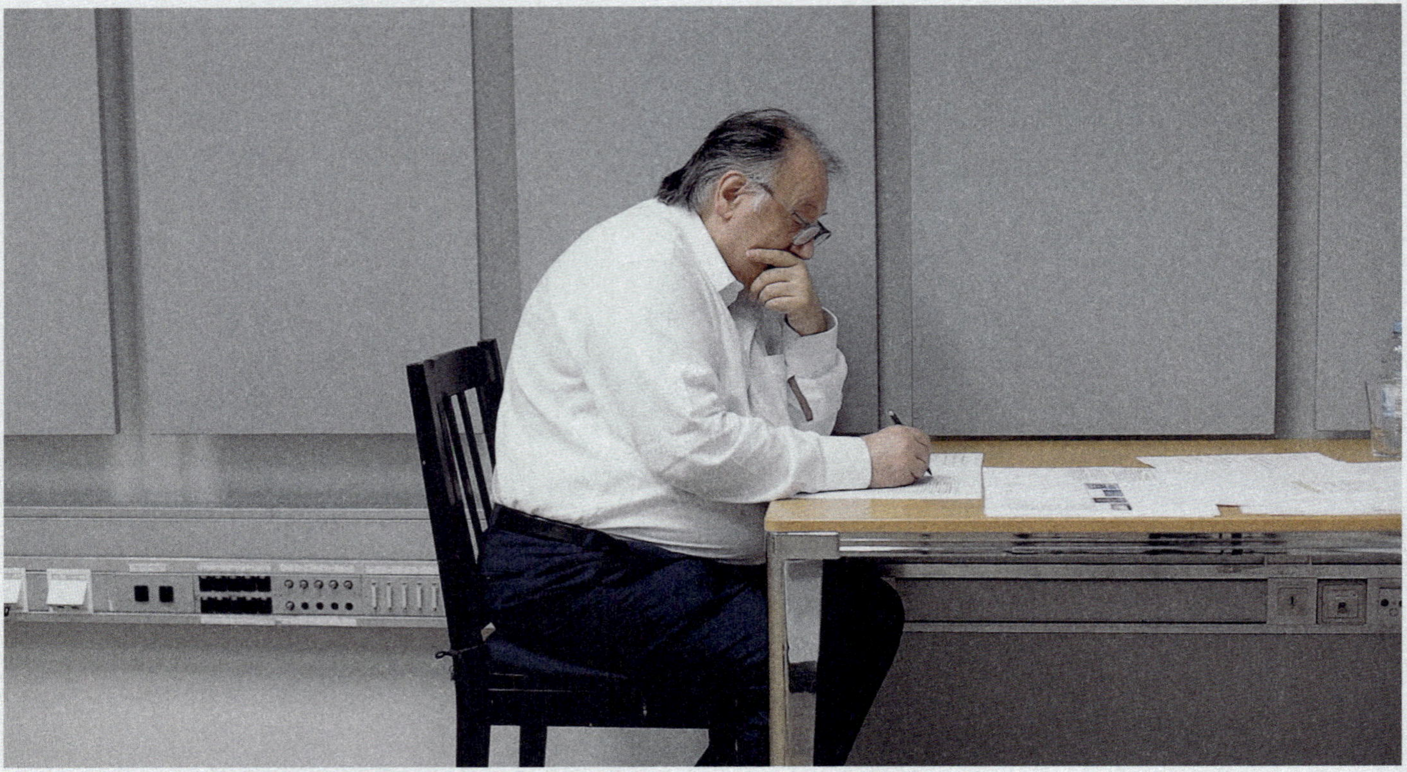

Peter Weibel and Armin Linke, ZKM | Center for Art and Media, sound studio, Karlsruhe, July 2015

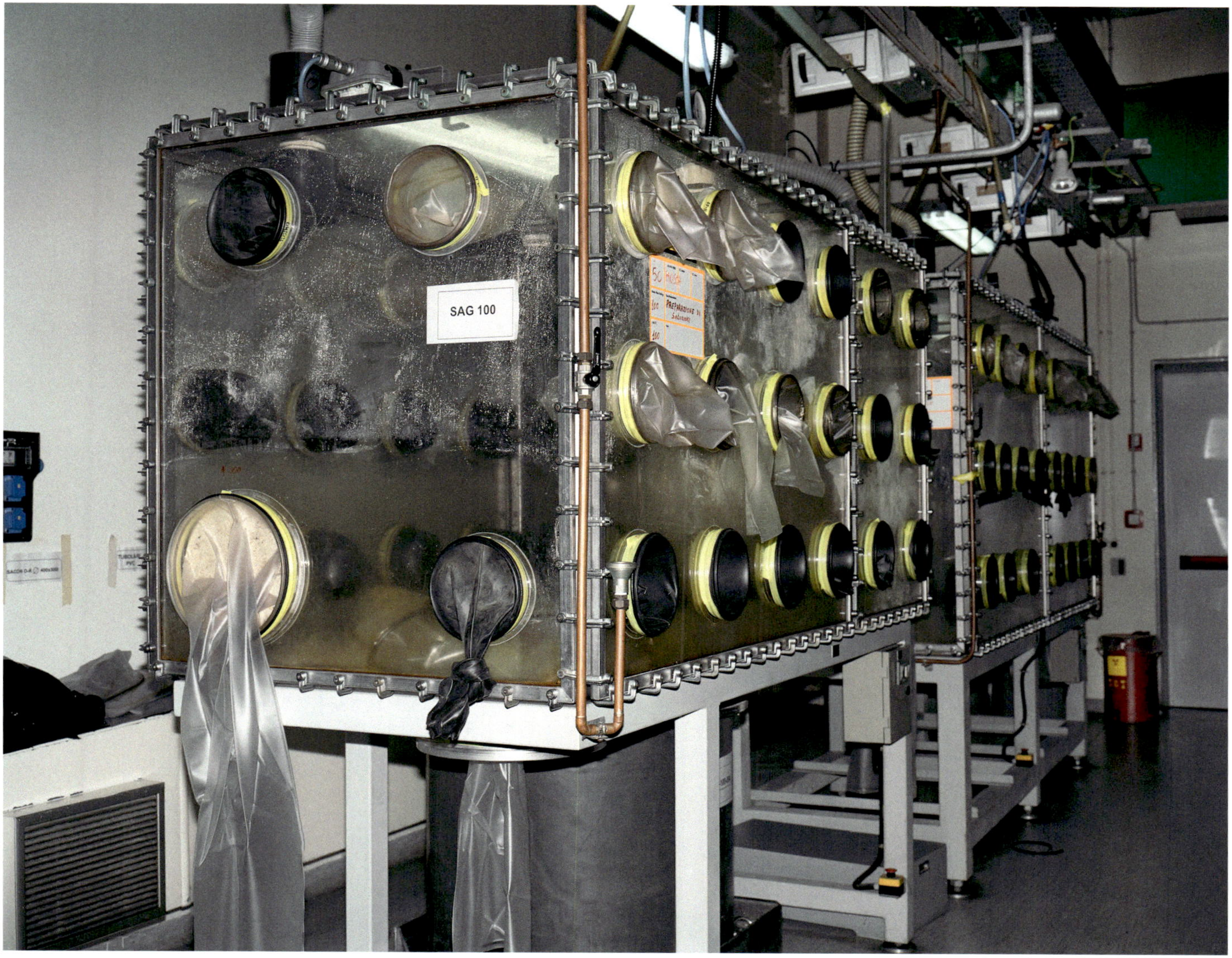

The first and most important tool is the hand. The hand is a human tool, made by nature. But humans have made other tools with their hands, and we therefore speak of *Handwerk* in German. These tools enabled humans to overcome the natural limits of their bodies. The limitations of space and time, as determined by our natural organs, were set to expand.

Sogin, IPU and OPEC plants, plutonium handling device,
Casaccia (RM), Italy, 2007

Humans have increasingly outsourced, exteriorized, or externalized their natural functions and organs in technical tools: we make a hammer as a sort of exteriorization of the hand; a wheel as a kind of exteriorization of the foot; the microscope or telescope as an exteriorization of the eye; the microphone as an exteriorization of the voice.

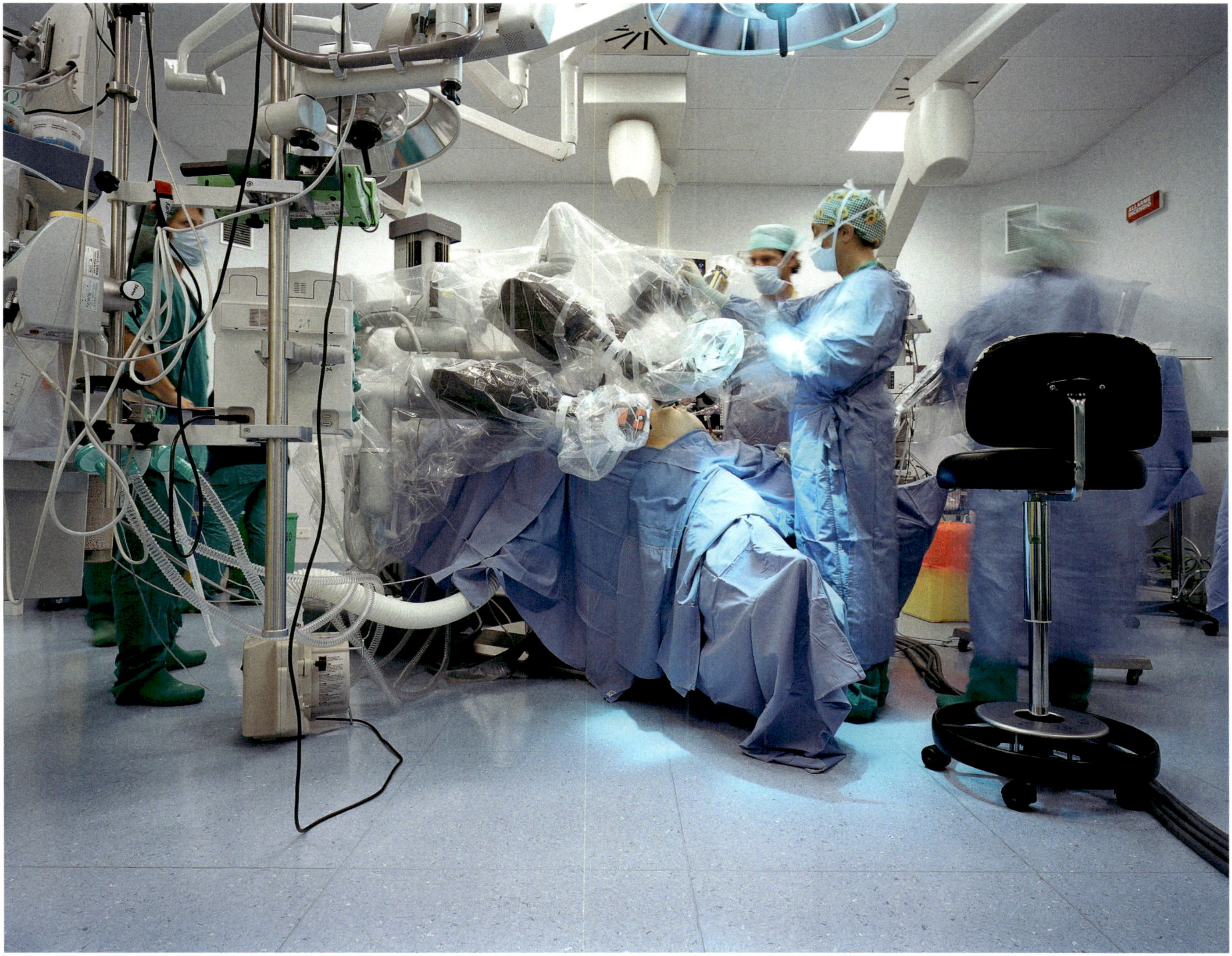

Humans have extended their natural organs through tools. Organs are natural tools, and tools are technical, man-made, artificial organs. With this tool, culture, humankind has stepped out of natural evolution and created an artificial man-made exo-evolution.

Operating theater, remotely controlled surgery, Modena, Italy, 2006

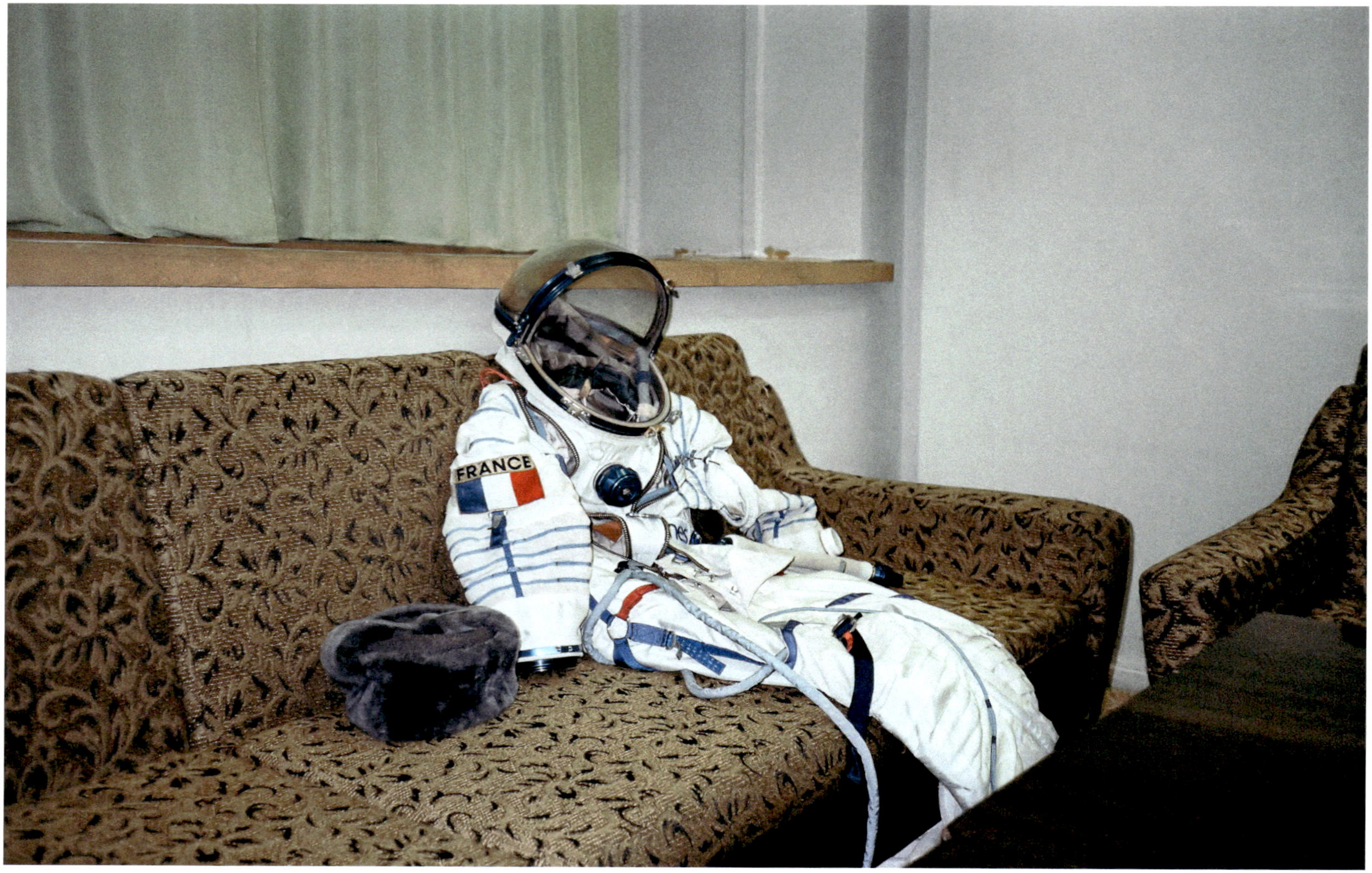

We therefore speak today about exo-planets, exo-suits, exo-biology, etc. Exo-evolution is the result of a noetic turn, a shift from a language- and image-based culture to one that is tool-based.

Star City, Cosmonaut Training Center, Moscow, Russia, 1998

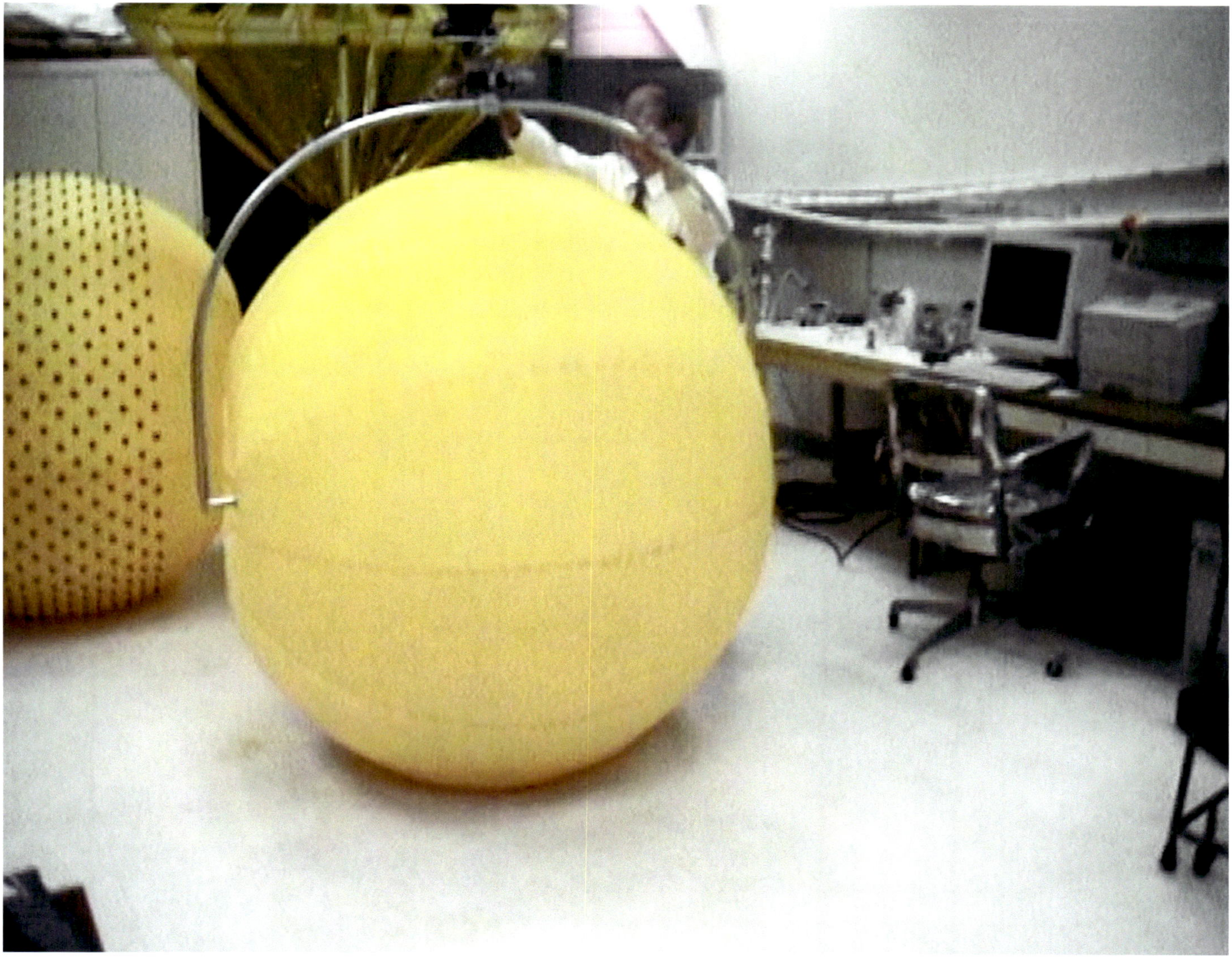

Tools are at the service of survival, and the main tool is the robot. The robot is not merely the externalization or exteriorization of some organs but the exteriorization of the complete human: an artificial double of the human. Initially, it was used to substitute the human in the world of labor. But slowly, the robot became a substitute not only for physical but also for mental activities. Suddenly the robot could calculate and its name was computer.

NASA Jet Propulsion Laboratory, inflatable vehicle for Mars,
Pasadena, USA, 1999

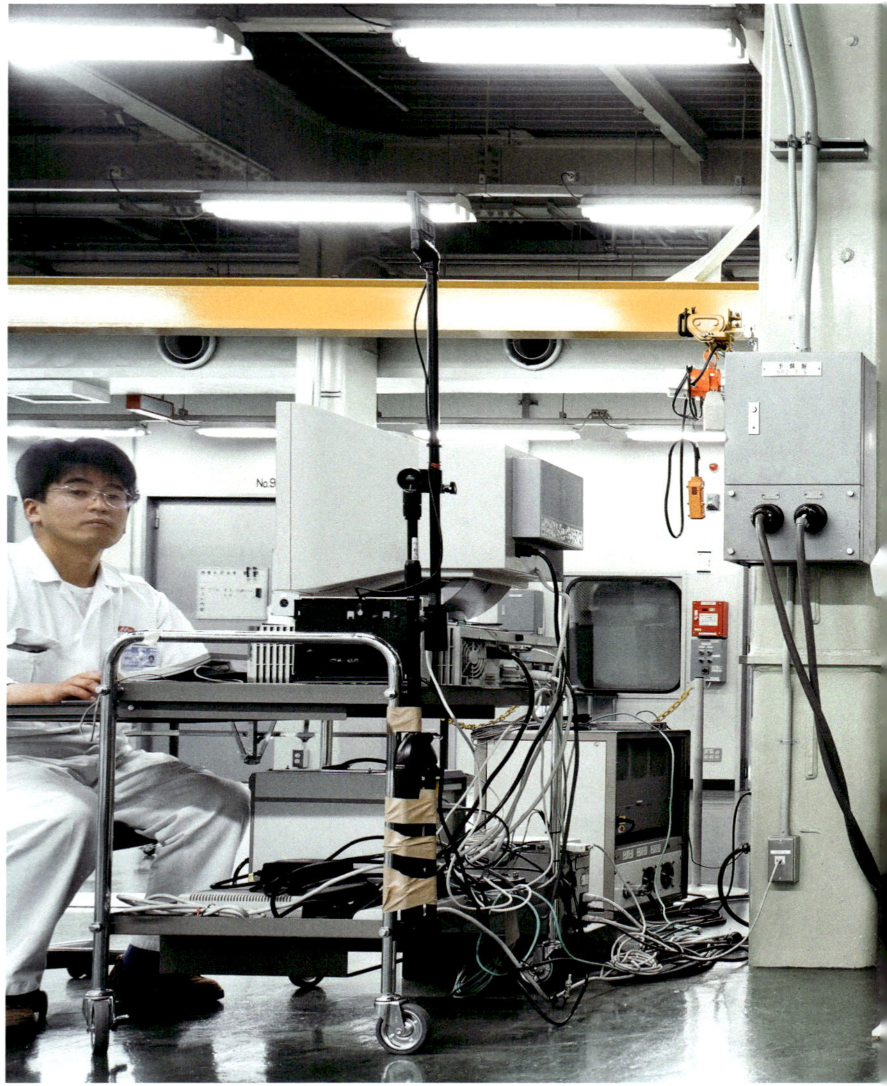

A humanoid robot descending a staircase, protected from falling by a safety harness.

The robot started the idea of artificial intelligence and artificial life. From factory halls to space explorations, from the bank to the airport, robots have become irreplaceable.

Honda Research Center, humanoid robot, Wako, Tokyo, Japan, 1999

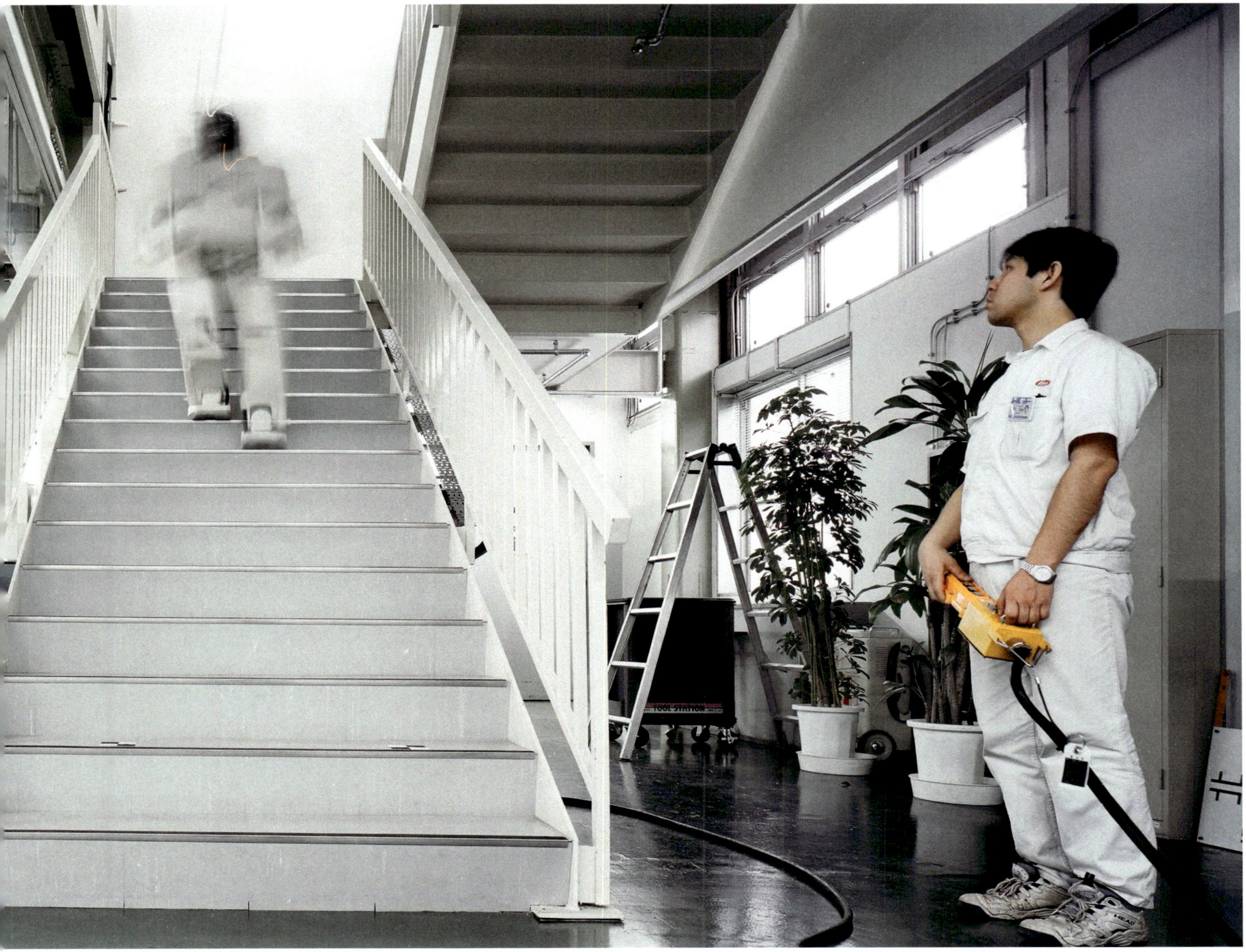

For some people, the robot became a competitor, a rival. But the robot will, in fact, always remain at the service of the human and help him to surpass the limits of his natural organs and functions. But with autonomous driving, with system agents and artificial intelligence, we are now aware that "robots" or "bots" can make autonomous decisions. We must therefore design an ethics for machines.

The architect Frank Lloyd Wright described the analogue world of the past very well in 1930 with his formula “Machinery, Materials, and Men.” In the twenty-first century, we must replace this triad with another: “Media, Data, and Men.”

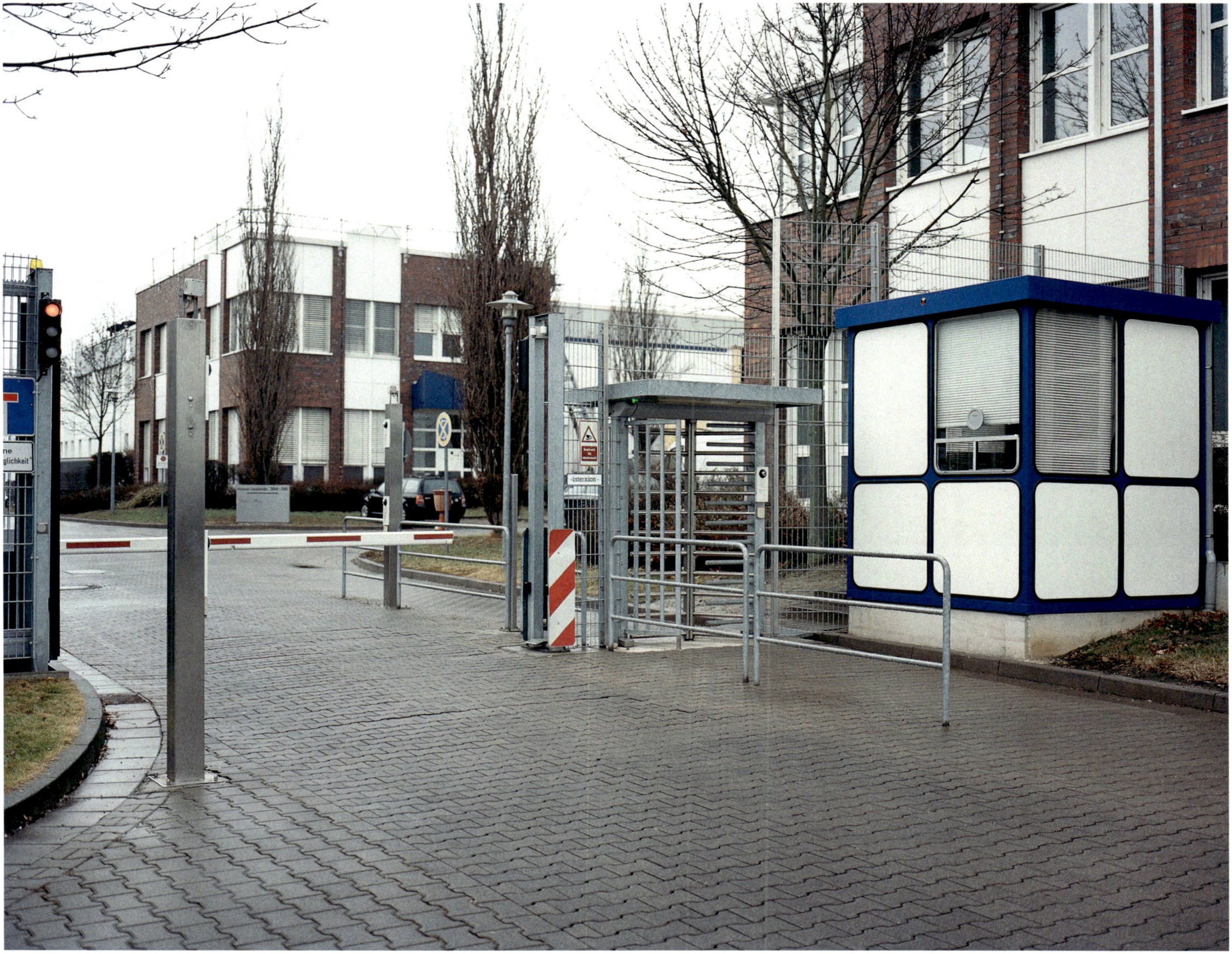

One of the most important submarine communications cables enters Europe in Frankfurt, in the area of Hanauer Landstrasse. Different data centers, such as Colt Technology Service, Interxion, or DE-CIX, provide Internet connections to banks and trading companies that need the shortest possible cable distance for activities such as flash trading.

We need this data world because seven billion people could not live in our world's atmosphere and biosphere without some kind of information sphere.

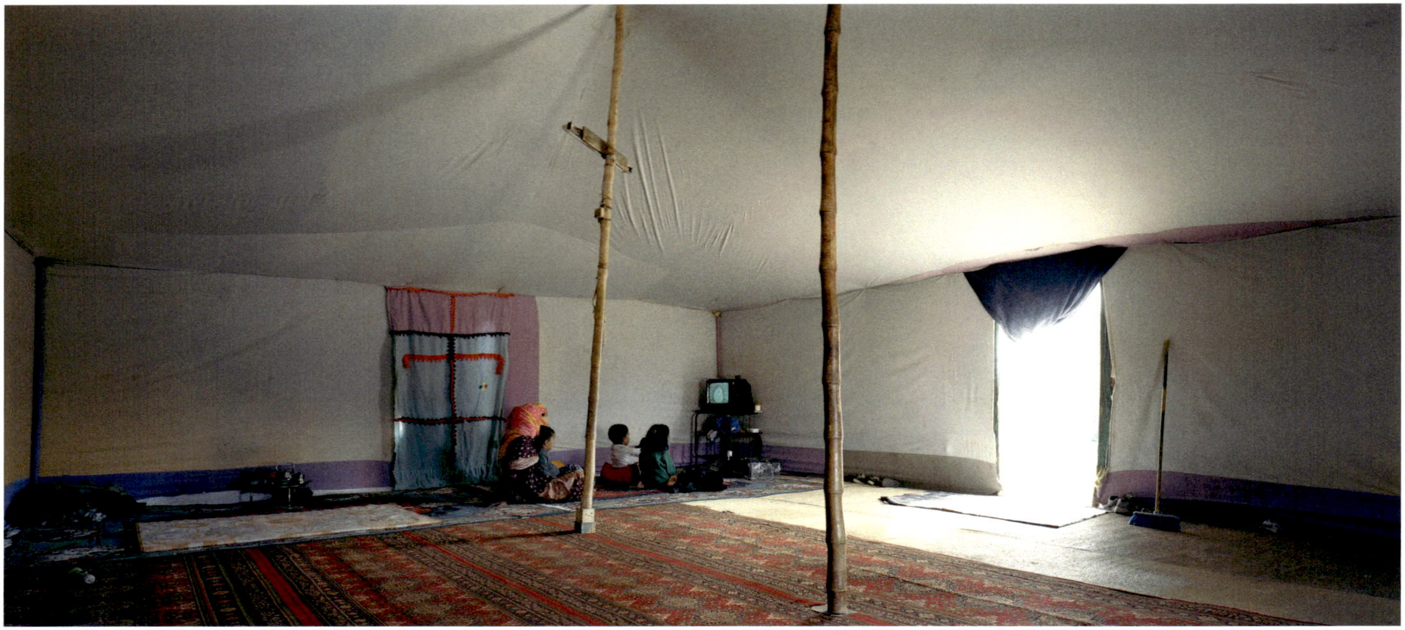

This refugee camp on the Algerian border hosts the Sahrawi families who fled Western Sahara during the conflict with Morocco (1975–91). The UN agencies describe the situation as one of deep ambiguity: with no political solution in sight, the Sahrawis continue to live as a society-in-exile. Their living structures reflect this ambiguity. While it might be possible to construct more definite architecture and infrastructure, many fear that this would endanger their right to return. In the meantime, the 2,700 km long Moroccan Wall separates them from their homes and families.

Smara, Sahrawi refugee camp, tent, Tindouf, Algeria, 2004

I call the electromagnetic waves around our globe the infosphere, which is a part of human exo-evolution.

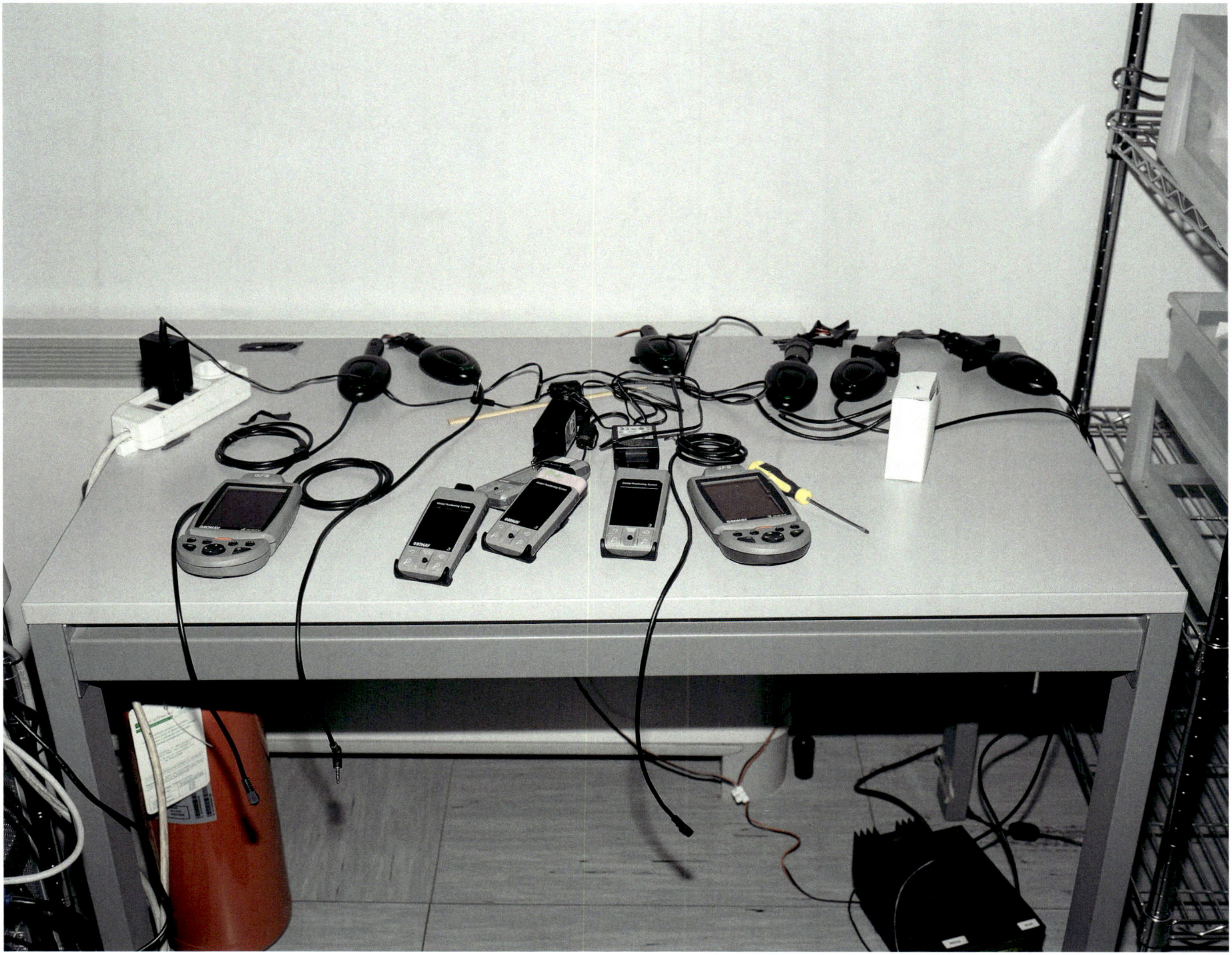

Mankind has made use of this infosphere for the past 150 years via the so-called technology of telematic culture. The prefix "tele-" comes from Greek and means "far." We thus have tele-vision, tele-phone, tele-fax, etc. Signals are transported by the medium of electromagnetic waves, which surround the globe.

Navionics, GPS receivers, testing software, Viareggio (LU), Italy, 2009

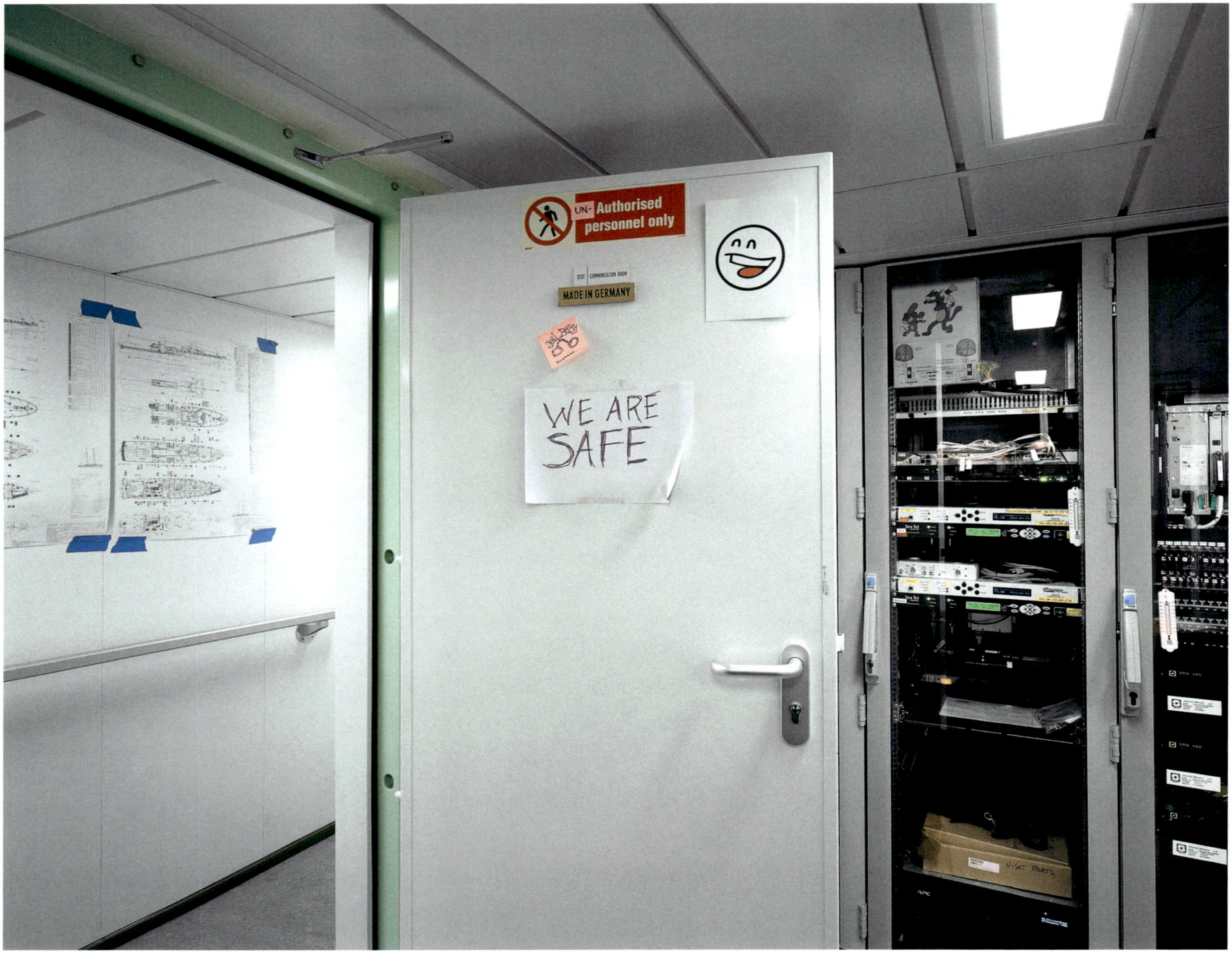

The Greenpeace ship *Rainbow Warrior III* was launched in Bremen in 2012. Its 12 m^2 radio room is fitted with reinforced steel walls and doors, and equipped with high-speed broadband Internet access. It functions as a sort of panic room: it contains all the broadcasting equipment necessary for Greenpeace activists to continue transmitting for twenty minutes even in the event of an attack by military commandos.

Teleportation is an old dream of mankind. In the past, it was called “mind travel.” The author stays at home, but his mind travels to imaginary countries.

Greenpeace, *Rainbow Warrior III*, Bremen, Germany, 2011

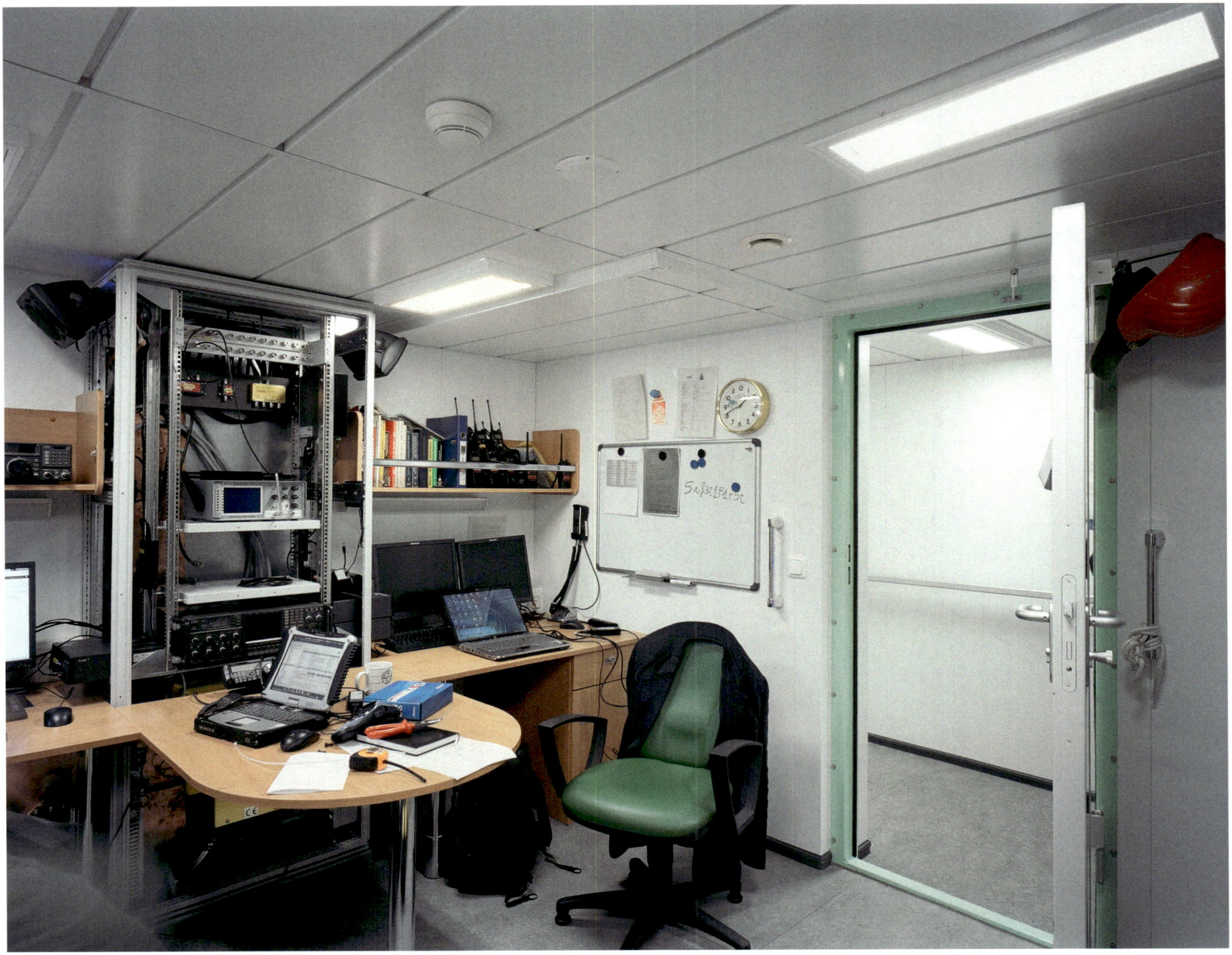

Therein we discover the most important aspect of contemporary teleportation: the separation of the messenger and the message. The messenger stays at home, does not move, but the message, the product of his mind, travels around the globe without any link to the body. This telecommunication, anything from television to telegraphy, is a communication without bodies.

Greenpeace, *Rainbow Warrior III*, Bremen, Germany, 2011

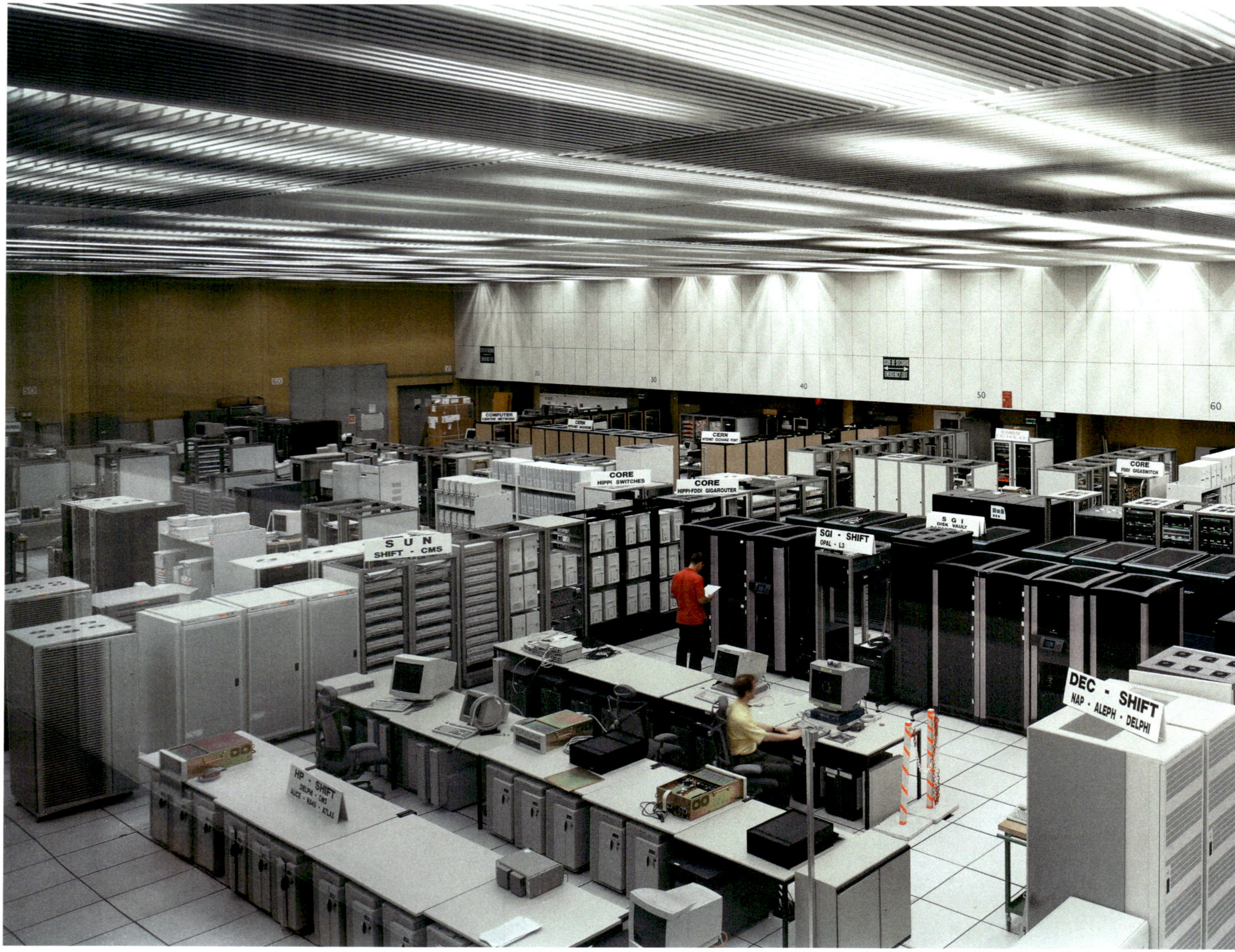

In physics, we speak of quantum entanglement. In 1964, John Stewart Bell showed the simultaneous communication between twin photons. When we change the message in one photon, the information in the other photon at the other end of the universe is changed at the very same time beyond any normal causal explanation.

CERN, European Organization for Nuclear Research, computer room, Geneva, Switzerland, 2000

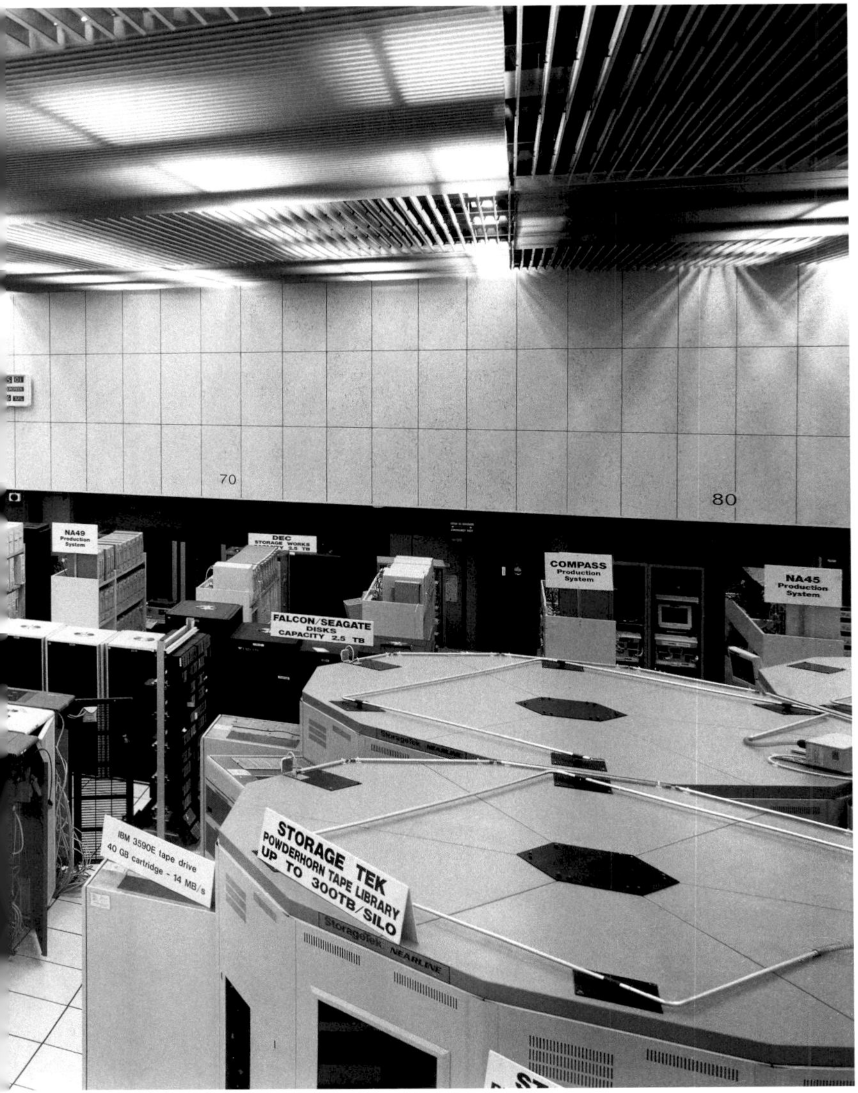

Albert Einstein was against the idea of quantum entanglement, which he called “spooky action at a distance.” People like Alain Aspect and Anton Zeilinger have since proved that it exists. This means that our concept of information needs to be changed.

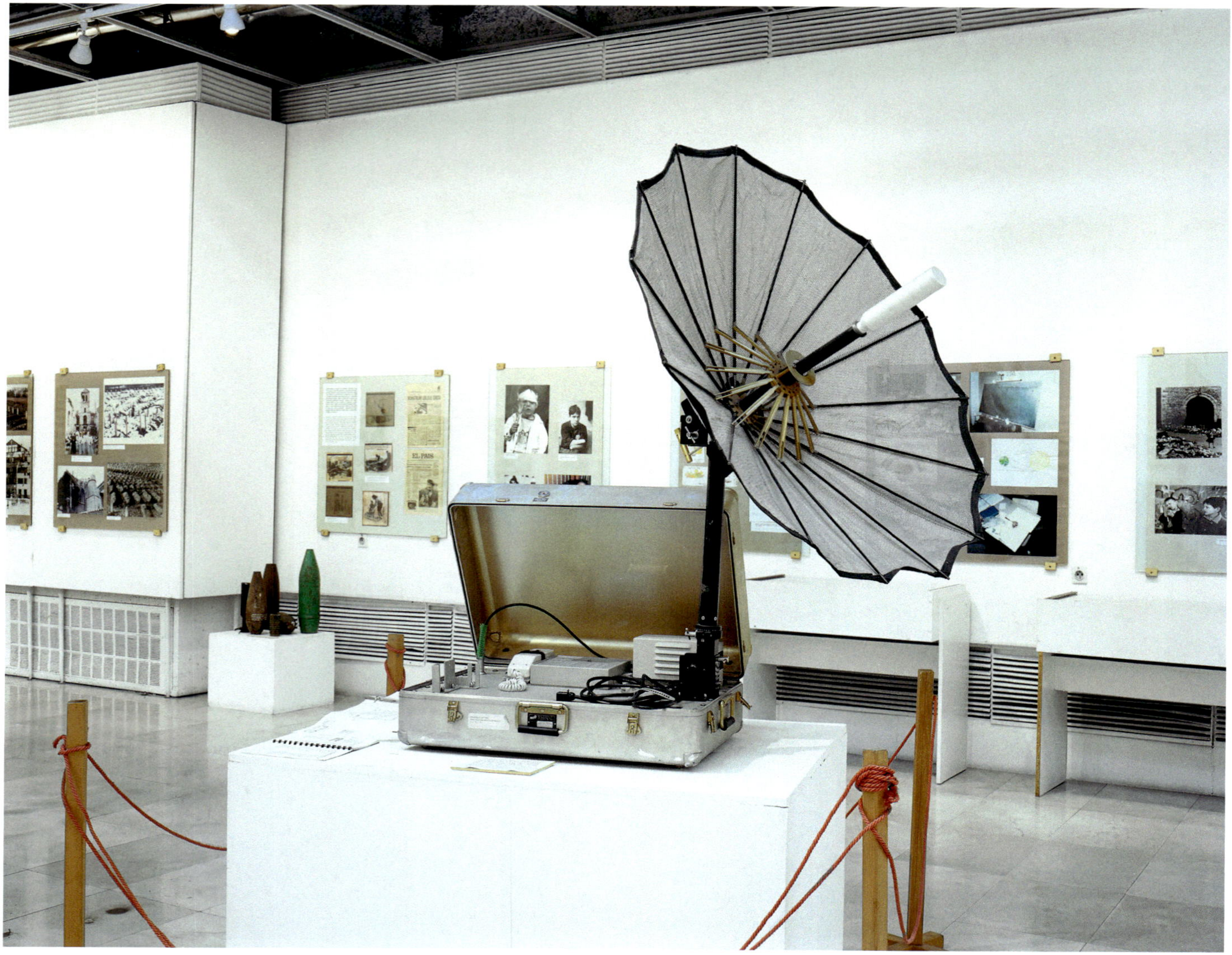

During the 1992–95 war in Bosnia and Herzegovina, this satellite telephone was, for the besieged city of Sarajevo, among the very few means of communication with the outside world. Most of the landline telecommunications infrastructure was damaged and disabled. The phone is exhibited as part of the collection for the proposed Siege of Sarajevo Museum.

Historical Museum of BiH, collection of the planned Siege of Sarajevo Museum, Sarajevo, Bosnia and Herzegovina, 2013

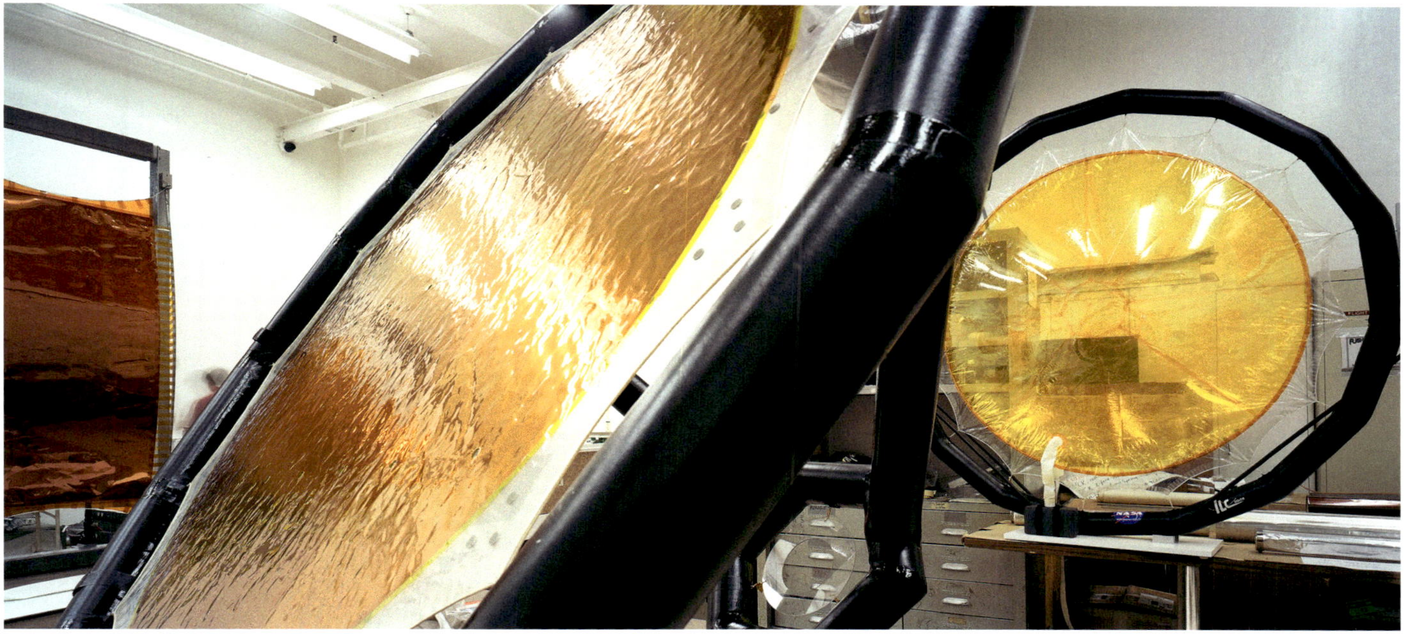

Contemporary social media have made everybody into an emitter and receiver, radically and completely changing our concept of the individual and of mass society. In the 1950s, the crowd was still lonely, as per the title of a book by David Riesman (*The Lonely Crowd*). At that time, the masses were just receivers of messages from the elite and the monopolized mass media. Today, with social media, the crowd consists of individuals with millions of friends.

NASA Jet Propulsion Laboratory, inflatable antennae for Mars, Pasadena, USA, 1999

Through the Internet and smartphones, everyone has become an emitter, a television, or a radio station. We are now surrounded by a new architecture of antennas and satellites, terminals, transmitters, and receivers.

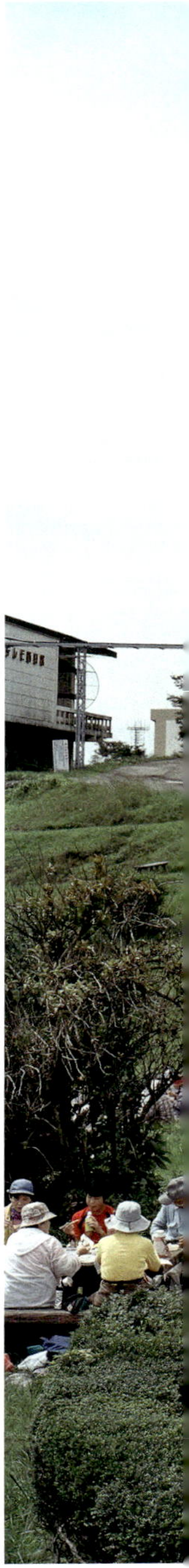

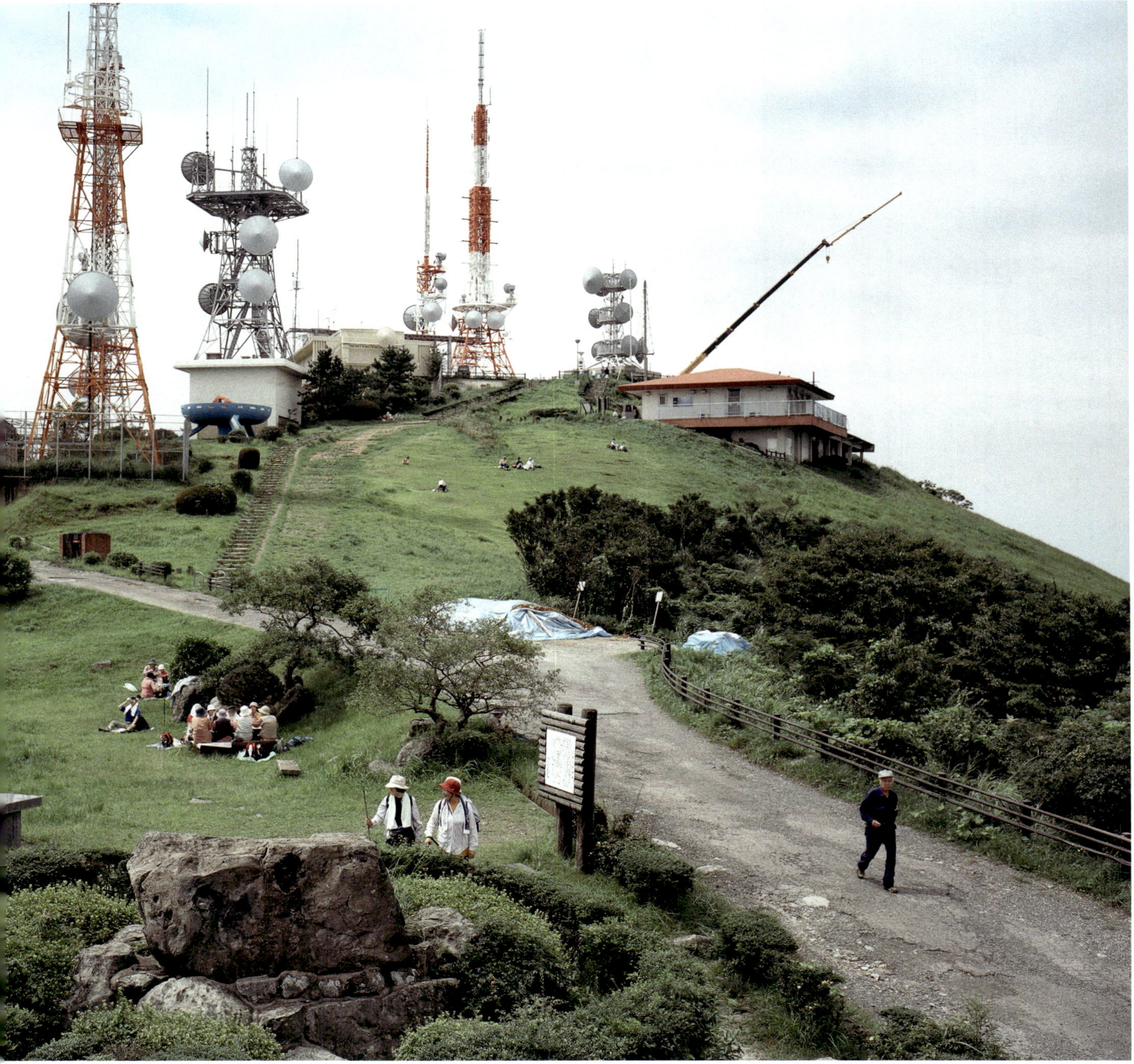

Mountain with antennae, Kitakyushu, Japan, 2006

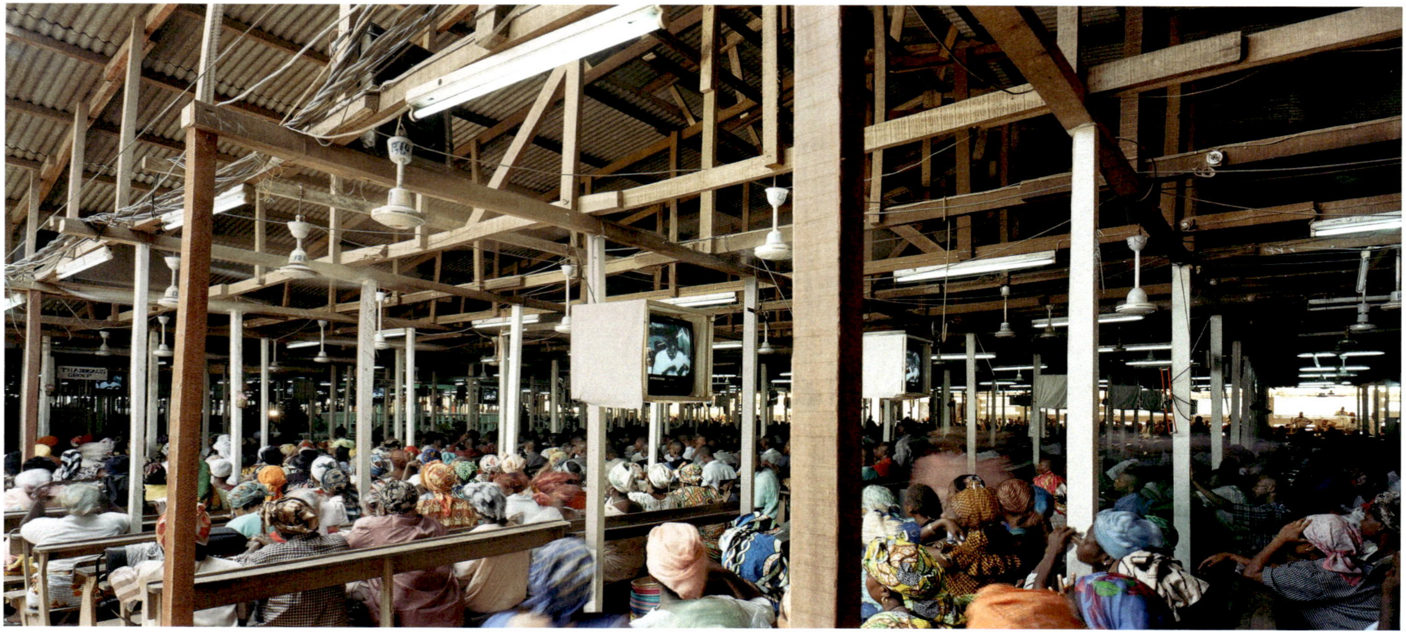

The church functions as a TV studio in which sermons are recorded and transmitted to several West African countries. The hall can accommodate ten thousand people, who experience the ceremony in detail via TV monitors spread around the space.

The Synagogue Church of All Nations, Lagos, Nigeria, 2000

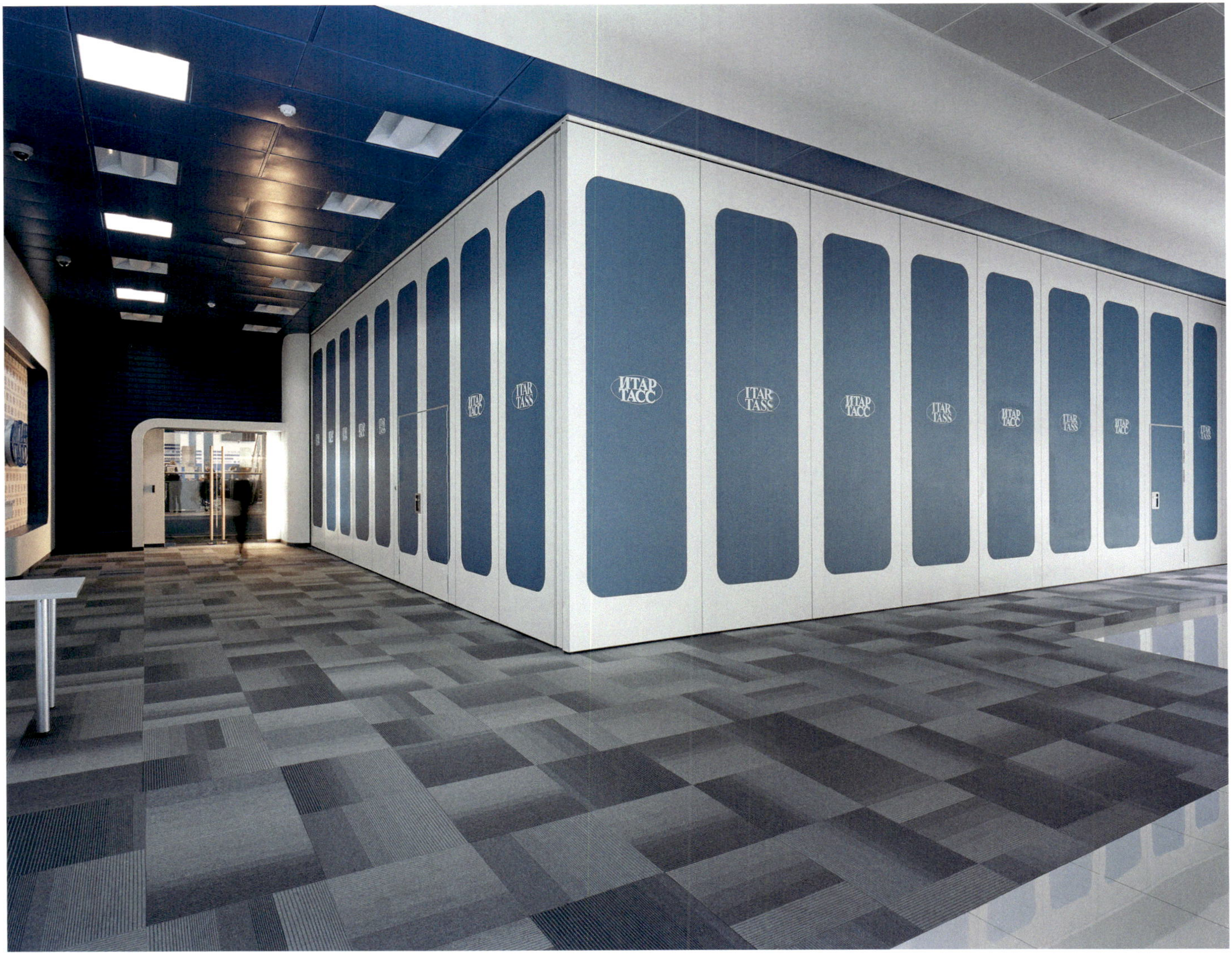

Knowledge was once the privilege of the priests, artists, and philosophers. The mass media, whose hold on the monopoly of being the only transmitter has now been equalized in a democratic way through social media, are being replaced by monopolies of data storage run by the NSA, Google, Facebook, etc.

ITAR-TASS, Information Telegraph Agency of Russia, Moscow, Russia, 2011

This world of transmitters and satellites is usually an invisible zone and thus an ideal area for intelligence agencies such as the National Security Administration (NSA), and the Federal Intelligence Service (BND), etc. A new "Security Securitate," the military occupation of the infosphere is evolving. It is all the more dangerous, since it operates in a discrete, invisible medium.

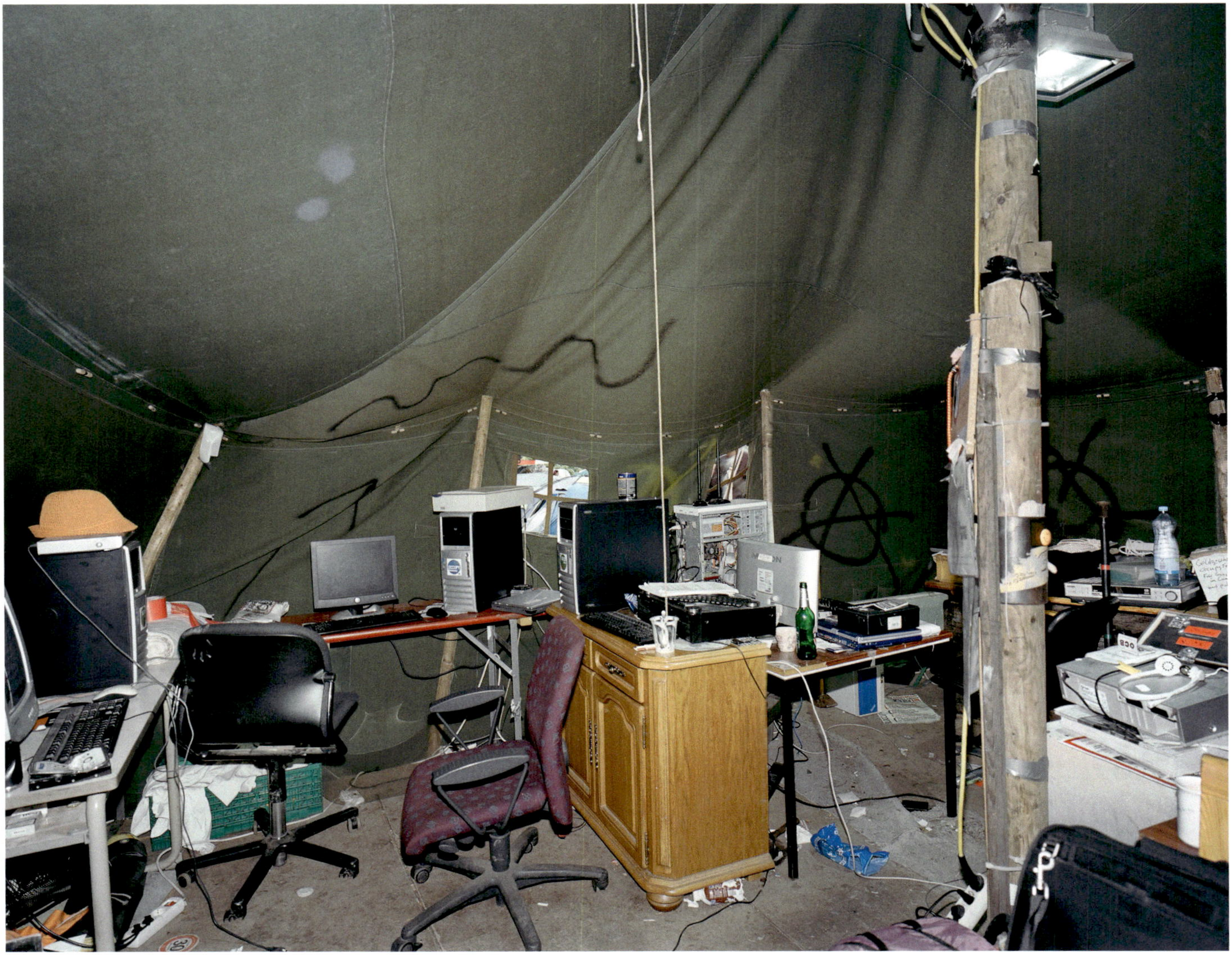

The computer and server room of the Occupy Frankfurt camp just after the raid in which the police seized the camp's hard disks.

Sinv licenses haute couture designer brands in order to produce secondary lines for the wider market. Twice a year, designer teams develop five hundred new prototypes, each reproduced to create fifty to a hundred copies in Eastern Europe, where the production costs are lower. Once back in Italy, the copies travel to distributors around the world for evaluation and orders guided by market predictions. A typical cycle has a six-month time frame, during which a garment in various stages of production and distribution may circumnavigate the world several times.

Sinv, meeting room, Carrè (VI), Italy, 2009

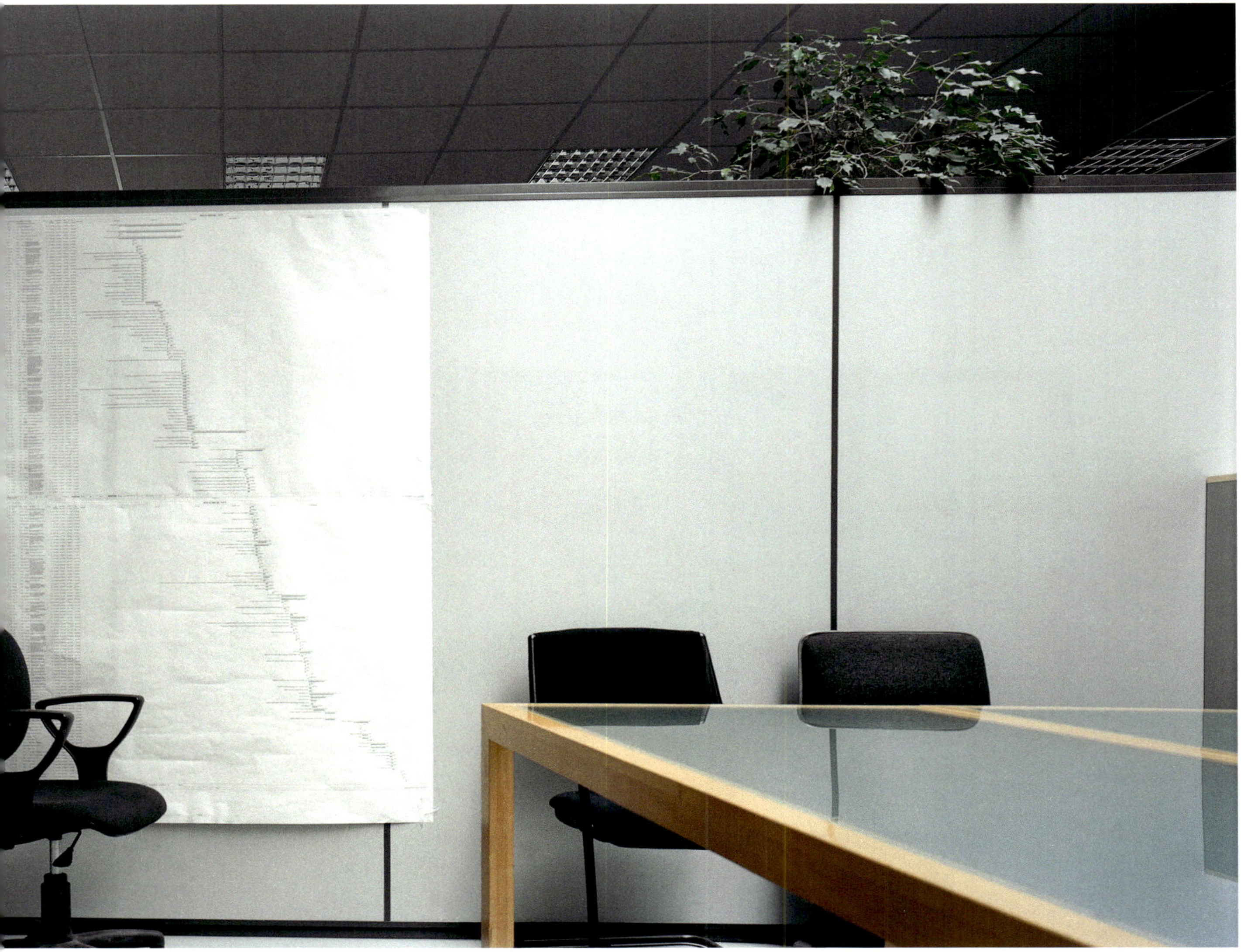

Logistics is the science of the transport, storage, and distribution of goods, data, and people. It is a real science, because today's world of seven billion people has an enormous need to control and govern the transport, storage, and distribution of goods, commodities, people, data, and money. Today, logistics is a superior kind of mathematics, because in order to calculate the mass transport of material, goods, and people, you need enormous support from computers.

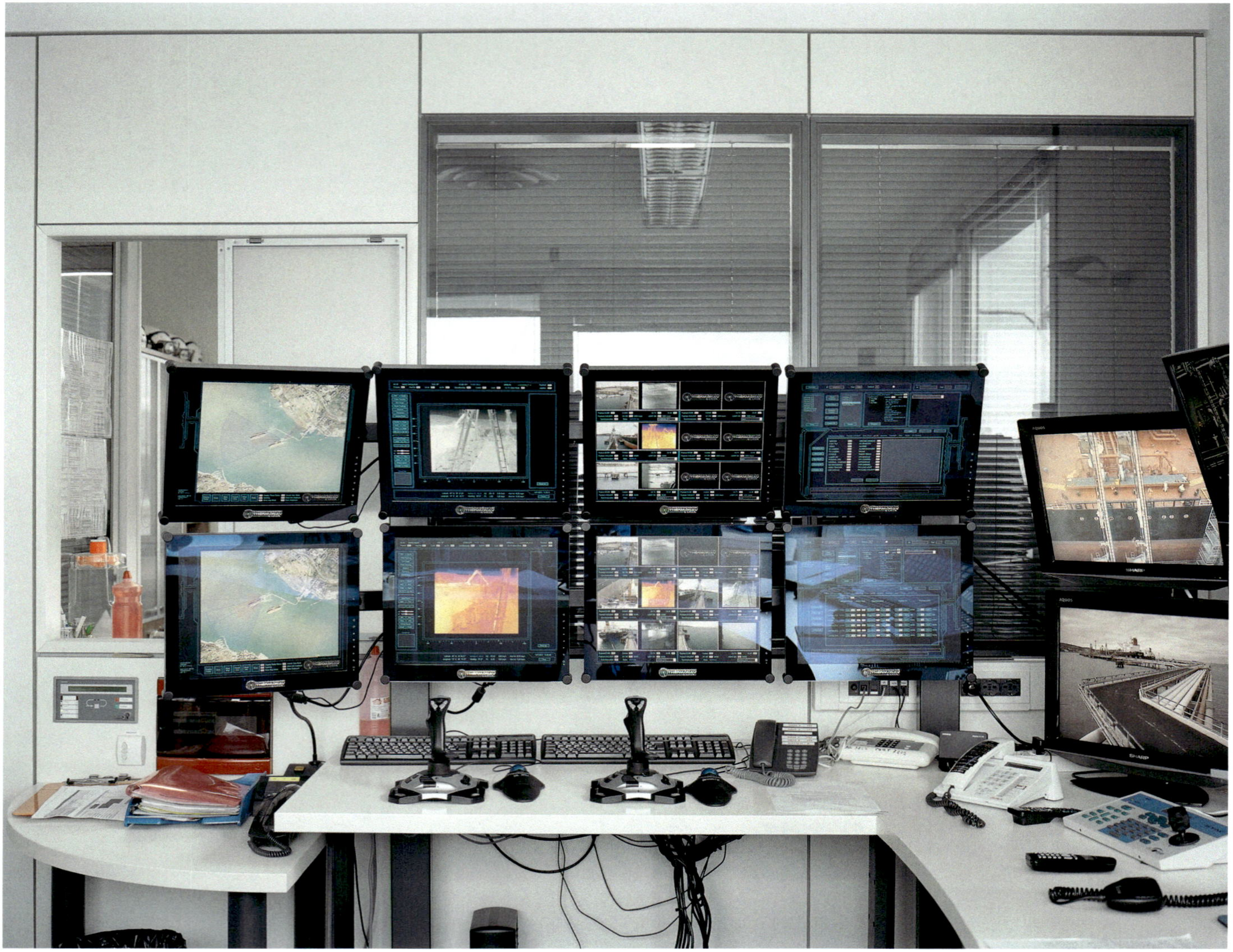

The docking procedure connecting oil tankers to pipelines is controlled with high precision, via multiple sensors, including infrared cameras and satellite imagery, in order to prevent oil spills.

Minimal finger movements on a keyboard can move huge loads.

TAL Group Transalpine Pipeline, oil tanker port, control room, Trieste, Italy, 2012

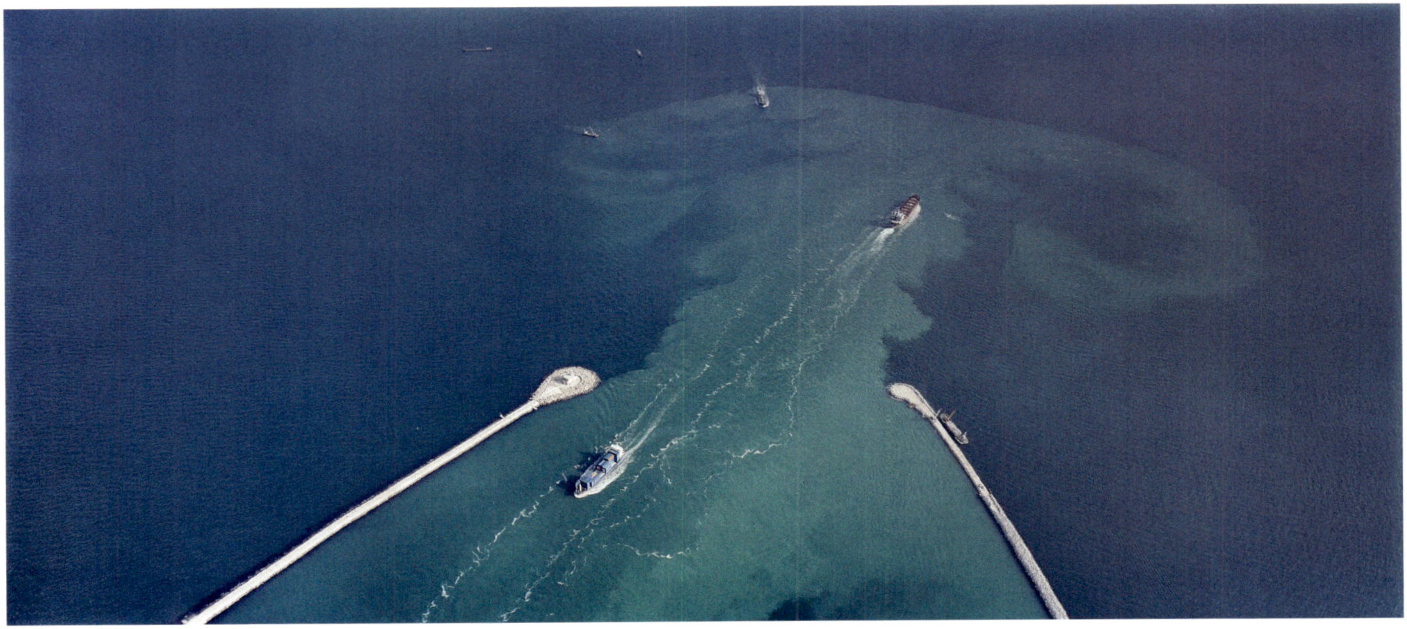

Rows of electromechanical gates extending into the sea make up the MOSE integrated tidal defense system, designed to protect the man-made Venetian lagoon. Venice has a complex port infrastructure, with almost thirty terminals handling cargo and passenger traffic as well as an oil terminal. The MOSE system must accommodate maritime traffic entering the lagoon, such as huge oil tankers and cruise ships, and offer crucial protection for the sensitive and complicated docking logistics within the port of Venice.

At the same time, the real goods of the analogue world are transformed into digital data on the screen.

MOSE Project, tidal defense system, Venice, Italy, 2005

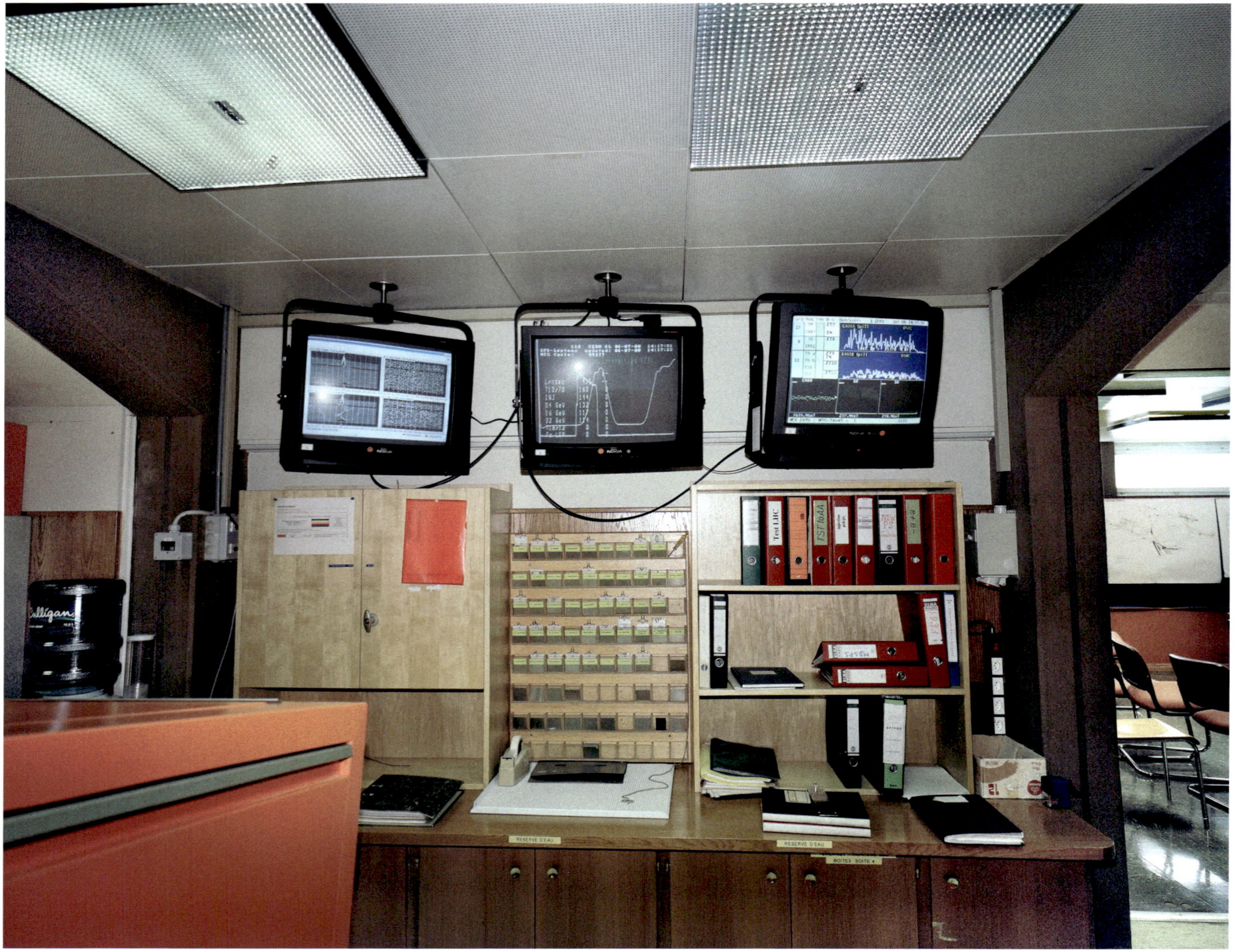

If you cannot calculate data and the transport of data on a screen, you cannot control the real transportation of commodities and goods. The whole freight transport and cargo industry could not function without computers.

CERN, European Organization for Nuclear Research, control room, Geneva, Switzerland, 2000

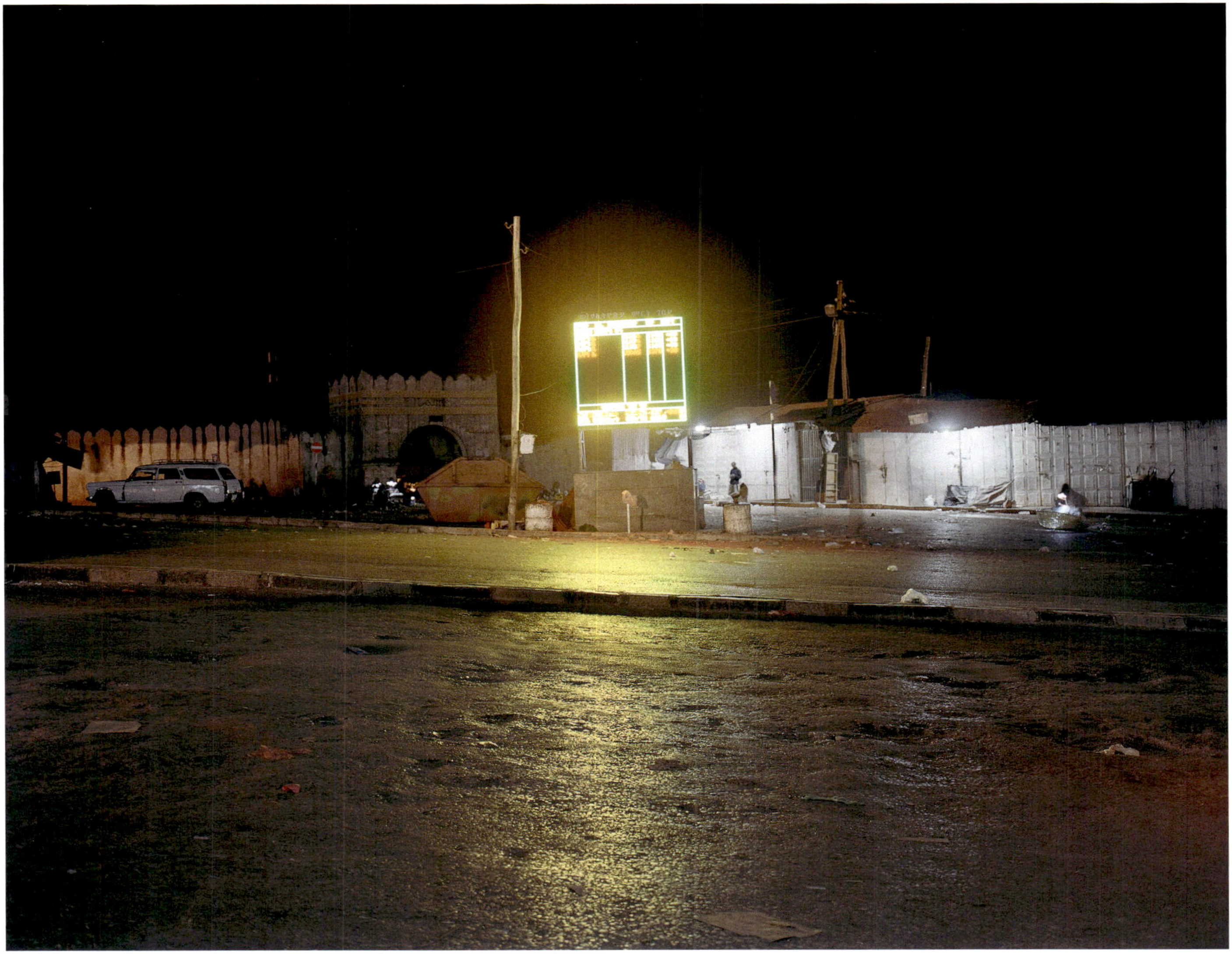

Near the Harar central market in the Ethiopian Highlands, coffee stock prices are displayed digitally in real time, connecting local production with global market information.

Digital stock market ticker for coffee, Harar, Ethiopia, 2012

In economics, the effects of globalization and digitization become most evident. If you look at the economy today, all you see in the headquarters of banks or on trading floors are screens, because today money is not about labor but about figures, numbers, and data.

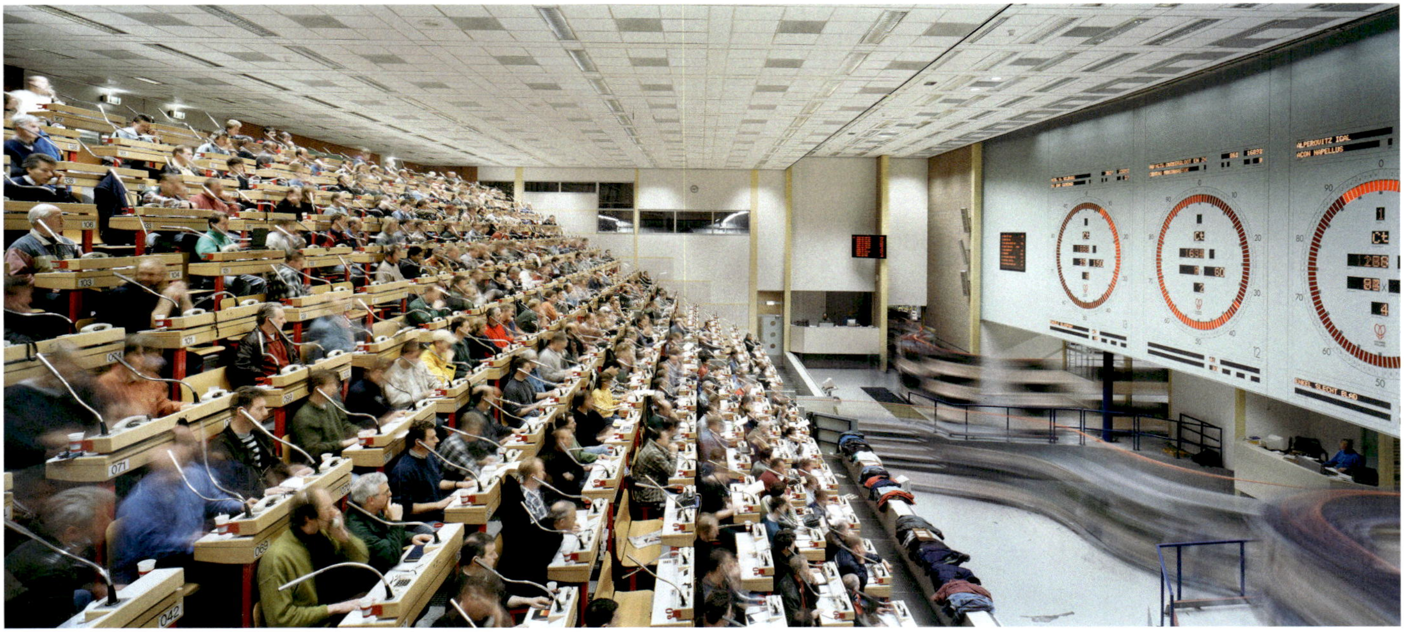

This auction complex is one of the largest industrial buildings in the world, located near Amsterdam's Schiphol airport. The auction hall screen displays basic information about flowers on sale, as well as quality remarks, country of origin, and the names and exact contents of the batches. Buyers bid electronically, and, once sold, the flowers are immediately transported to the buyer's logistics chain. The link between flowers and the economy in Holland can be dated back to one of the earliest recorded economic crises: the Tulip Mania of 1636.

As a result, there has been this recent tendency toward abolishing paper money. You cannot pay with real money anymore. This means that money has become the most abstract interface in the world.

Bloemenveiling Aalsmeer, flower auction, Aalsmeer, Netherlands, 1998

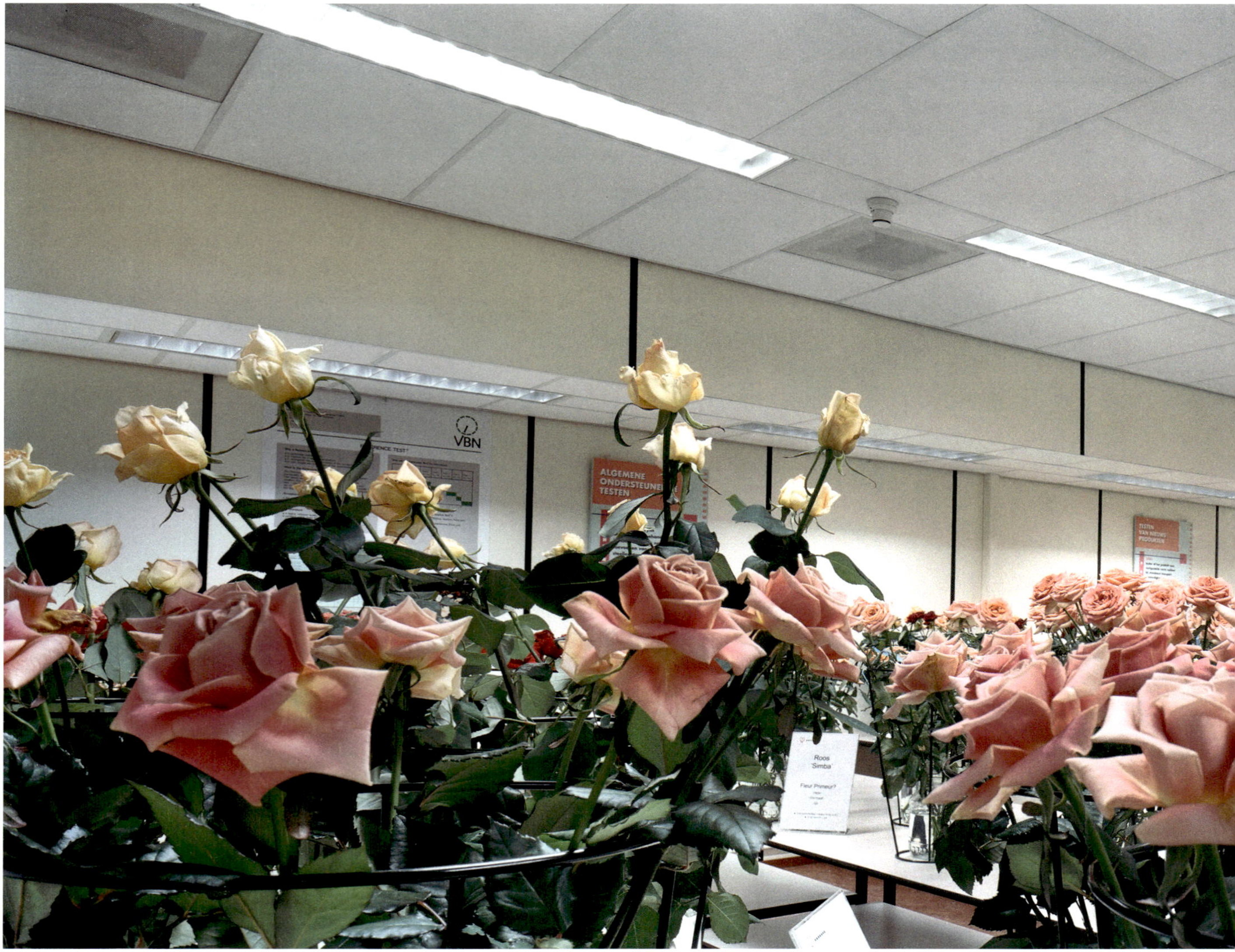

Laboratory tests performed under specific atmospheric conditions ensure the quality of flowers before the auction.

The old economy was based on labor and how labor changes into value and value into money.

Bloemenveiling Aalsmeer, flower auction, test room, Aalsmeer, Netherlands, 1998

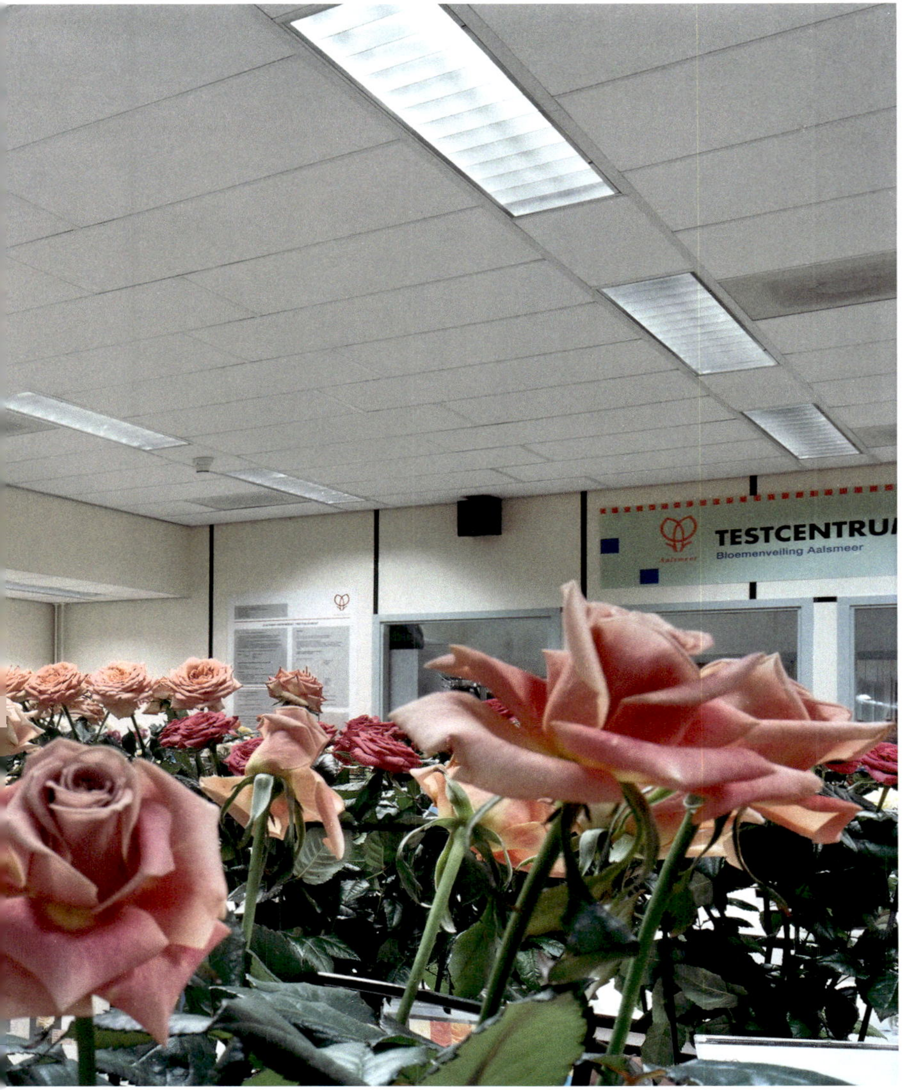

What we see today in the financial industry is that capital is not the heart of the economy. The heart of the economy is credit; credit is a business within which you sell your present to the future and make exchanges in the name of the future. You calculate profit in the future. This is the basis of credit, because this future value defines your current value.

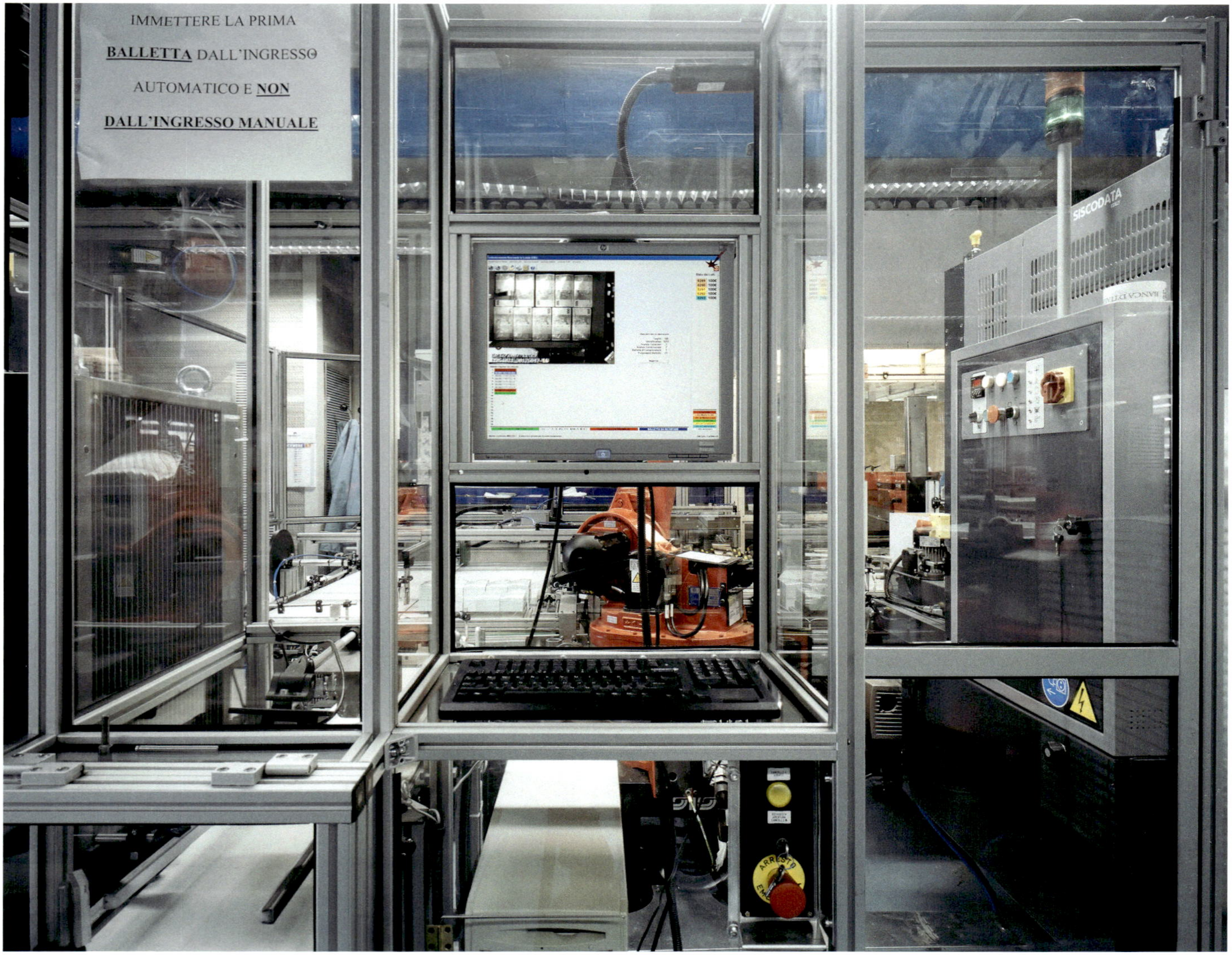

In the final production phase, euro banknotes are printed and cut. Optical control systems check both the visible and the invisible print layers. A robotic arm with an inbuilt camera packs the banknotes and photographs into containers, each holding about one million euros. This image functions as a digital signature with legal weight, confirming that each million euros photographed does indeed exist.

Economics has become a very difficult mathematics, dealing with data instead of money.

Bank of Italy, Department Cut2000, Rome, Italy, 2007

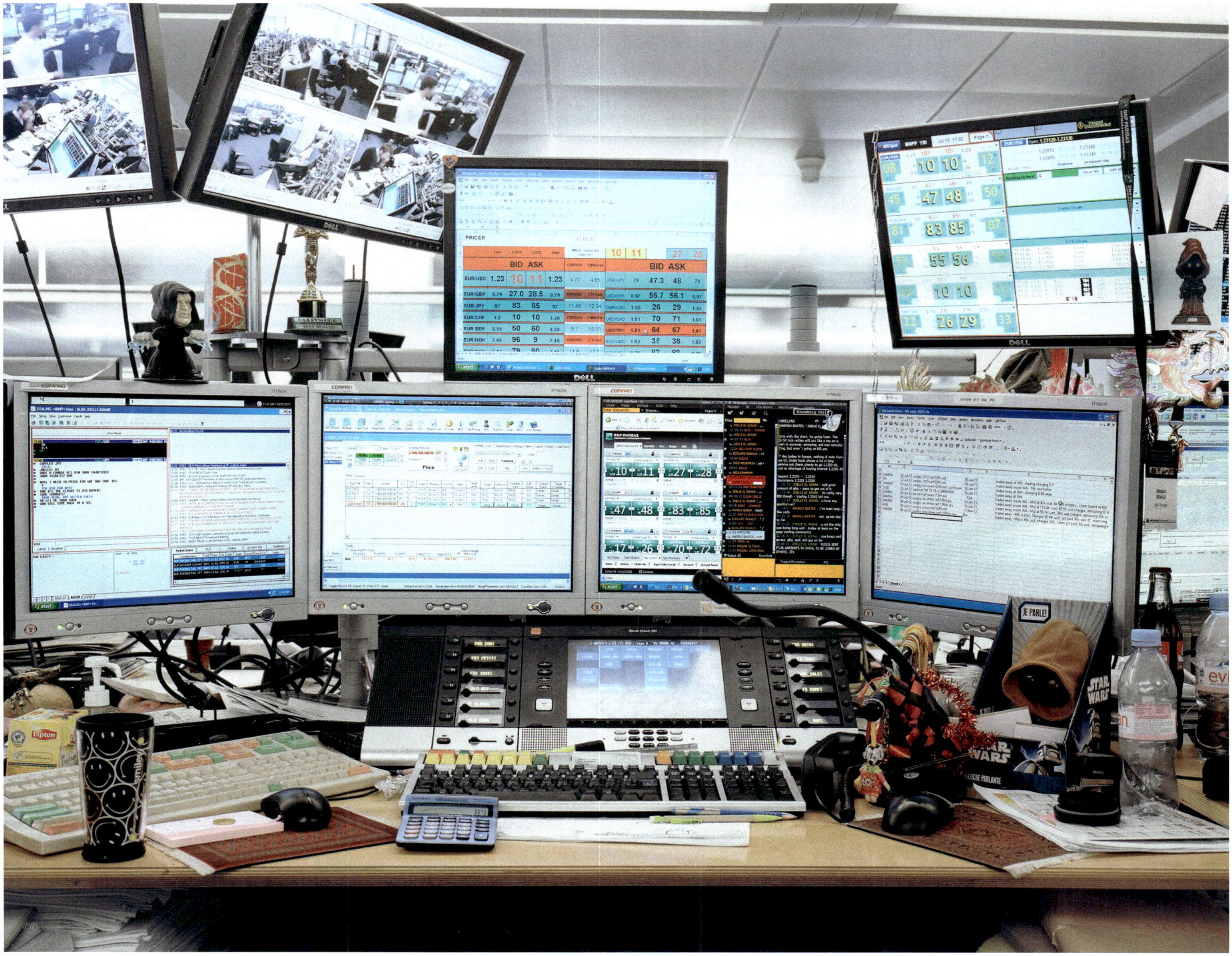

Foreign exchange and investment desk in the BNP Paribas Trading Room. The operator is in permanent communication with desks in Tokyo, London, New York, and Frankfurt. All information is conveyed in real time in order to prompt immediate decisions.

The financial industry has separated from so-called real industry. Money has dematerialized into data and we have therefore lost control. The economic crisis is just a crisis of abstraction.

BNP Paribas, headquarters, trading floor, Paris, France, 2012

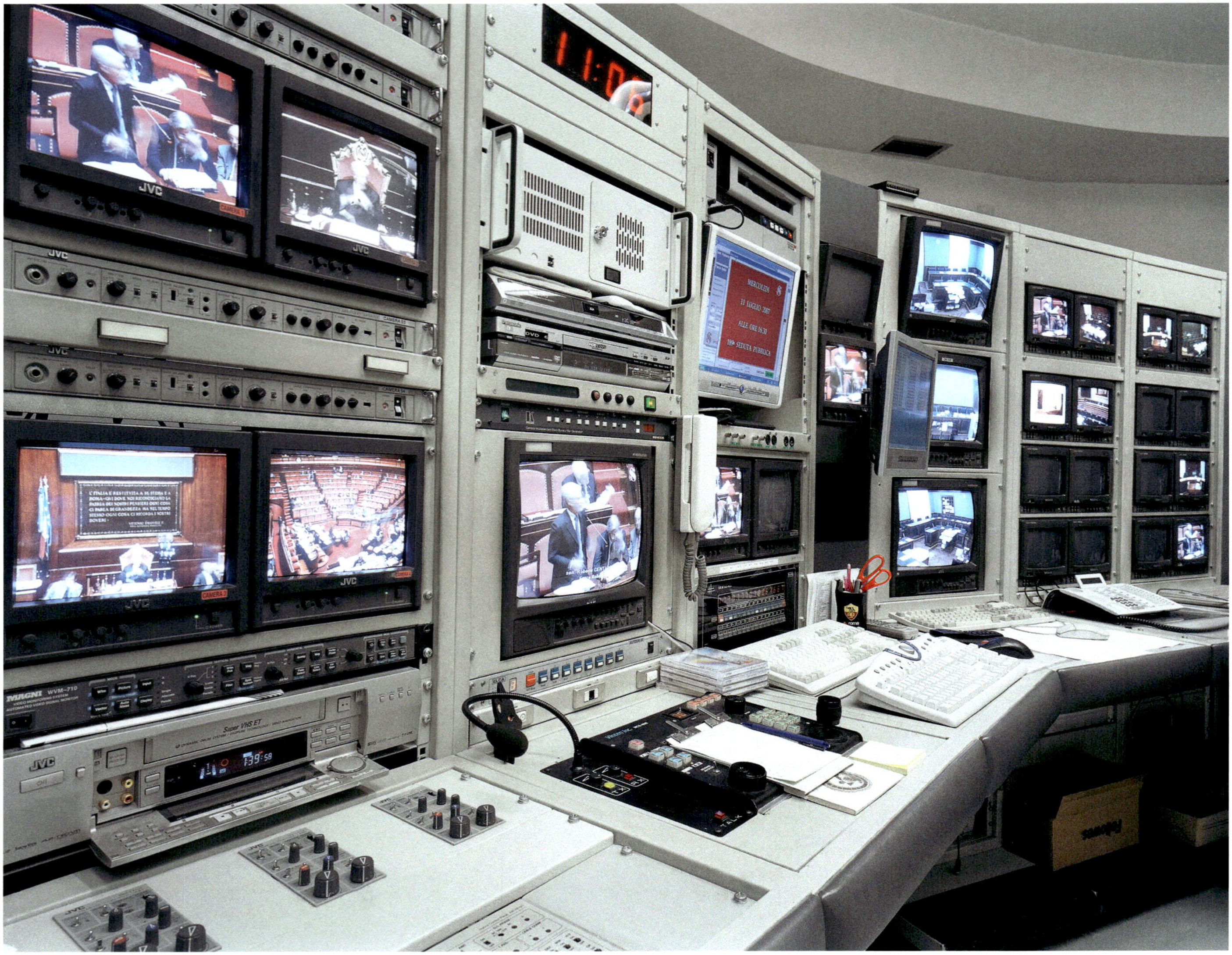

The Senate of the Italian Republic runs a YouTube and satellite TV channel transmitting live or recorded sessions. Transmissions are coordinated from this control room.

We need control as biological organisms, because our bodies would collapse without organs to control them.

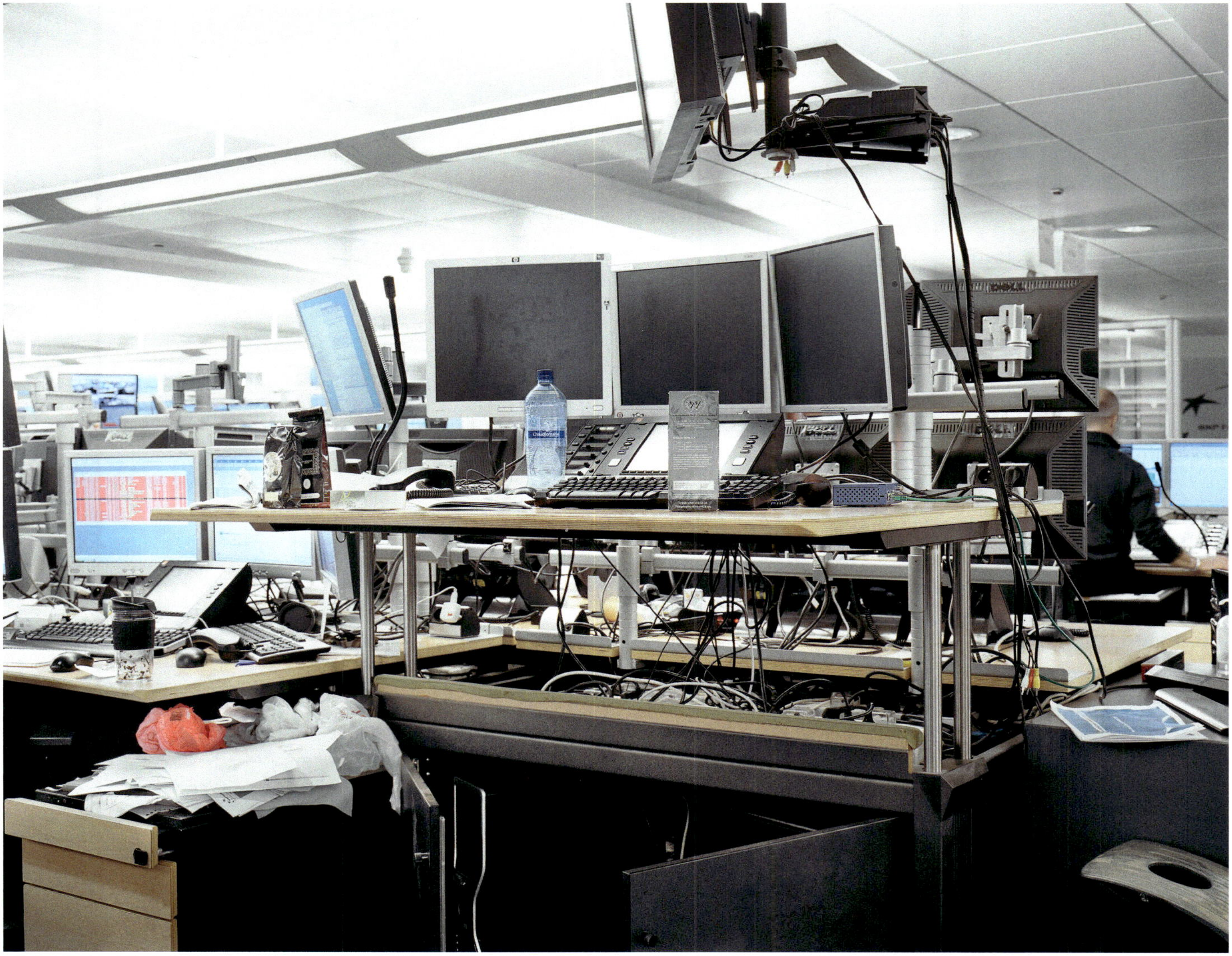

The fact that we can move upright has to do with having a sensory organ in our brain that controls our equilibrium.

BNP Paribas, headquarters, trading floor, Paris, France, 2012

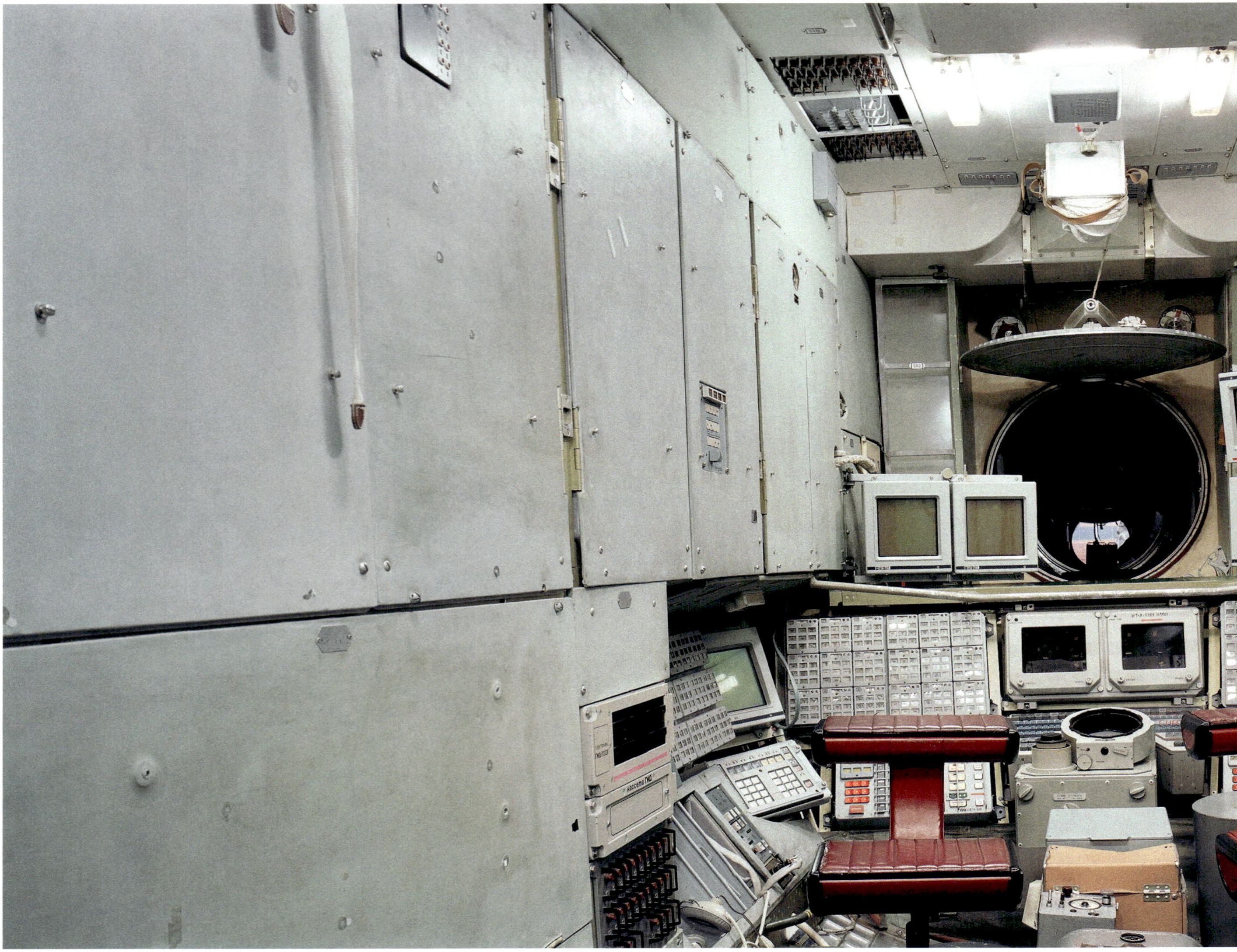

This facsimile of the Soviet Space Station Mir enabled simulations of procedures that would be followed in case of an emergency on the "original" orbiting the Earth.

So when we fly in a plane, we not only need a pilot but also the help of ground control.

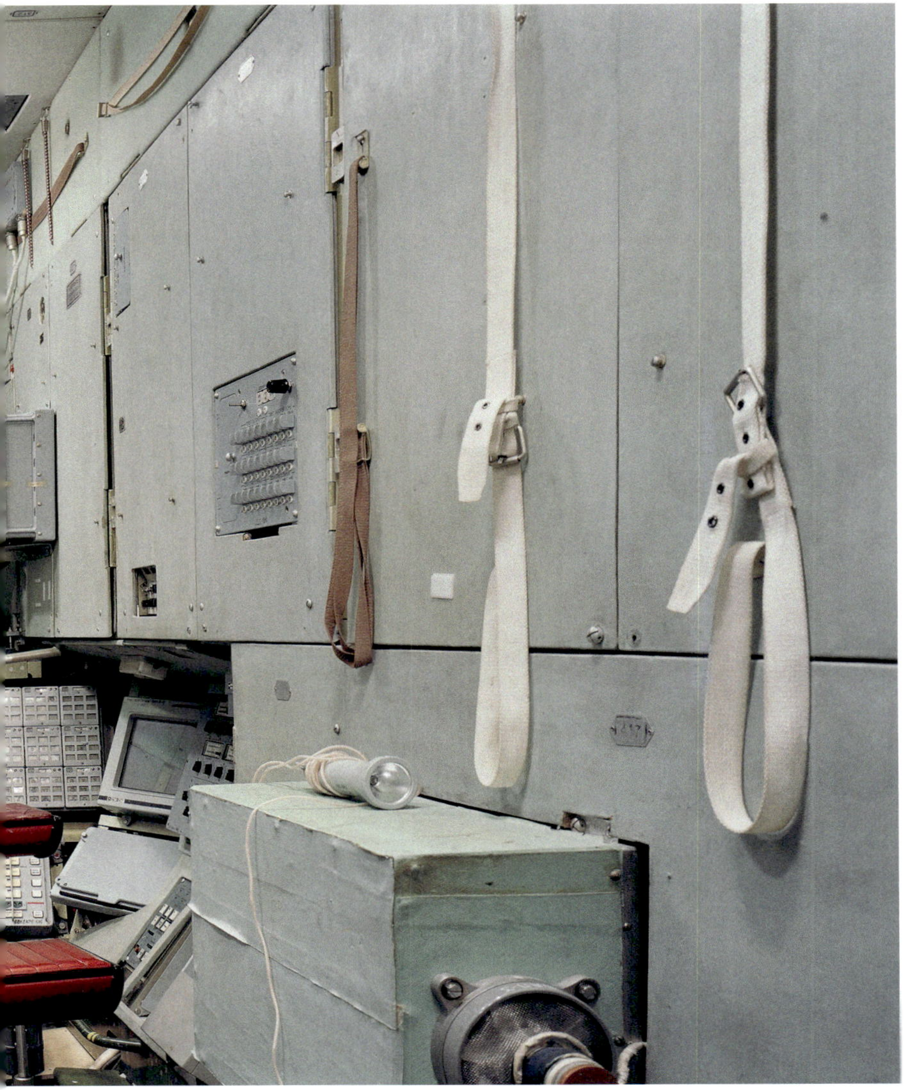

This is a kind of feedback that we owe to the science of cybernetics: we learn about control as being nothing but the organism's measurement and governance of itself. Feedback is the true name for control. Without this coordination, controlling, and governing of our organs, our organism would not function. And the same happens with societal systems: the movements of masses, of trains and ships, the movements of data and media would collapse without control, without a system of feedback.

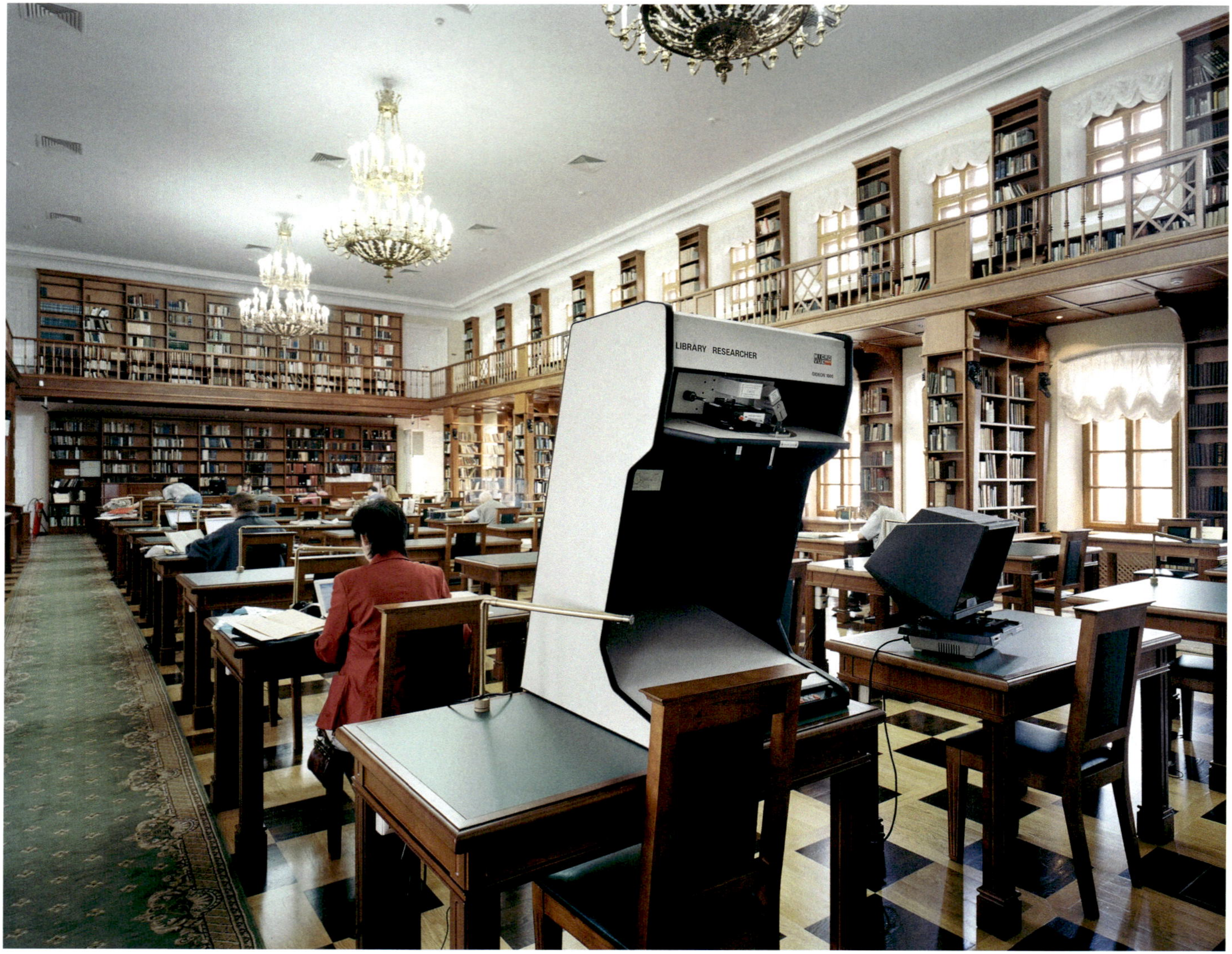

Storage means to keep, temporarily save, and collect for future use. Material goods, natural products, energy, and, above all, information and digital data are stored. In order to store, you need storage space, as in agriculture, in which information is kept for later use.

Russian State Library, reading hall, Moscow, Russia, 2011

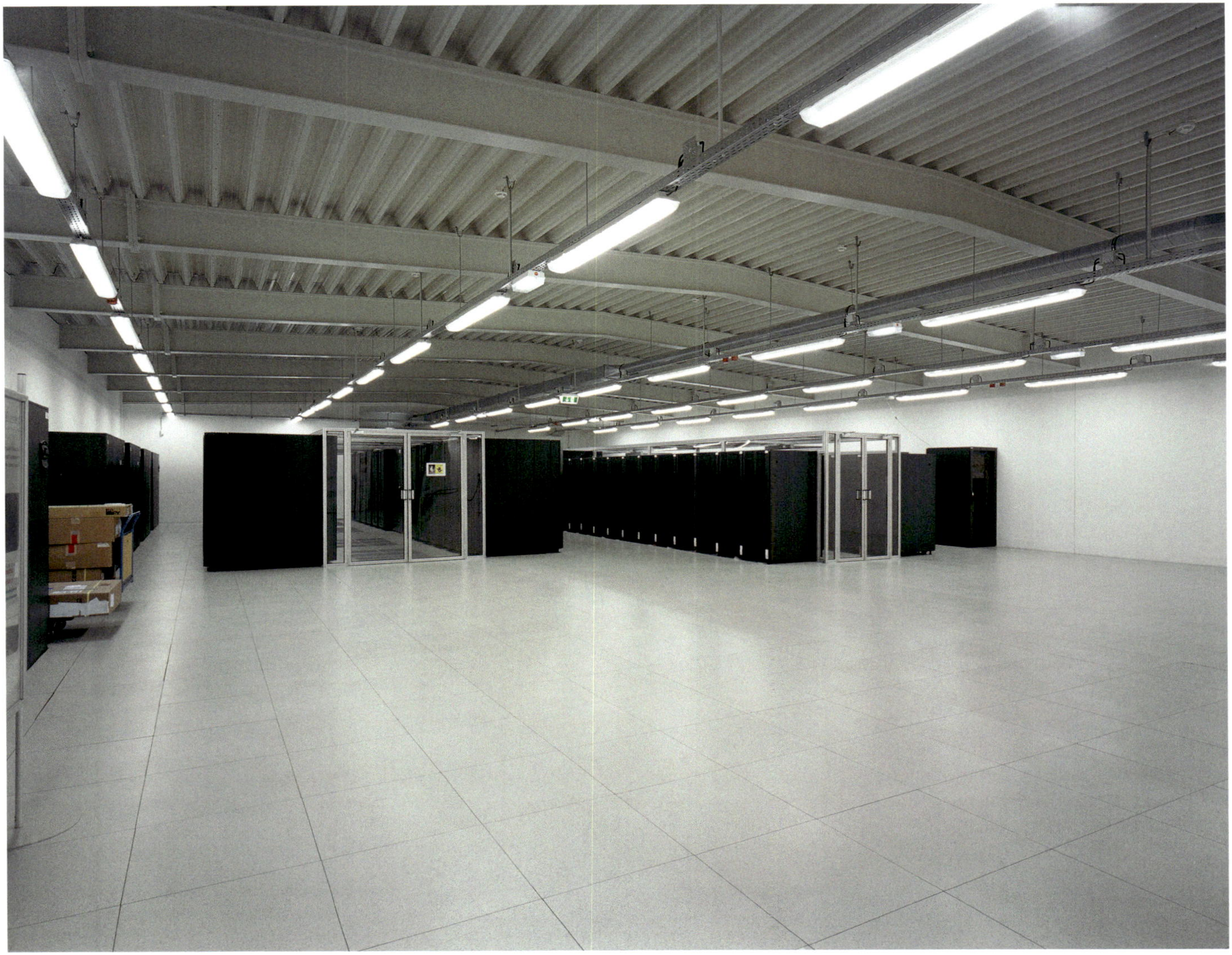

A large building constructed around the computer room cools the machines. Every six years, computers are upgraded to more energy-efficient models. The annual electricity bill for the German Climate Computing Center runs to about two million euros.

So it is not just about storage space but also about storage time. Storage spaces are cooled rooms—be they film archives, meat halls, or computer centers.

DKRZ, German Climate Computing Center, archives, Hamburg, Germany, 2013

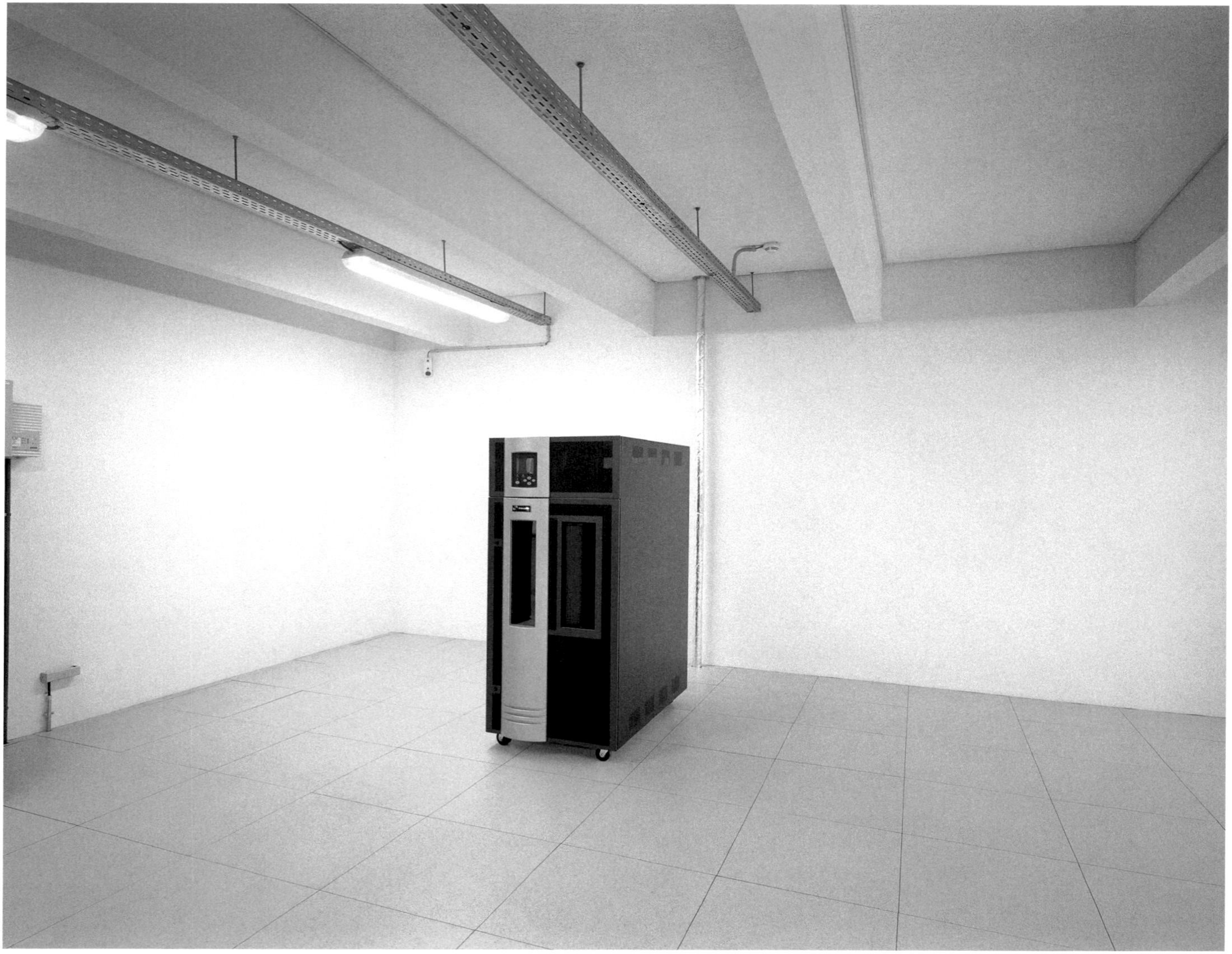

The German Climate Computing Center conducts high performance computing for research into climate and Earth systems.

The cooling tries to solve the problem of storage time. We encounter a strange paradox in our contemporary data world.

DKRZ, German Climate Computing Center, archives, Hamburg, Germany, 2013

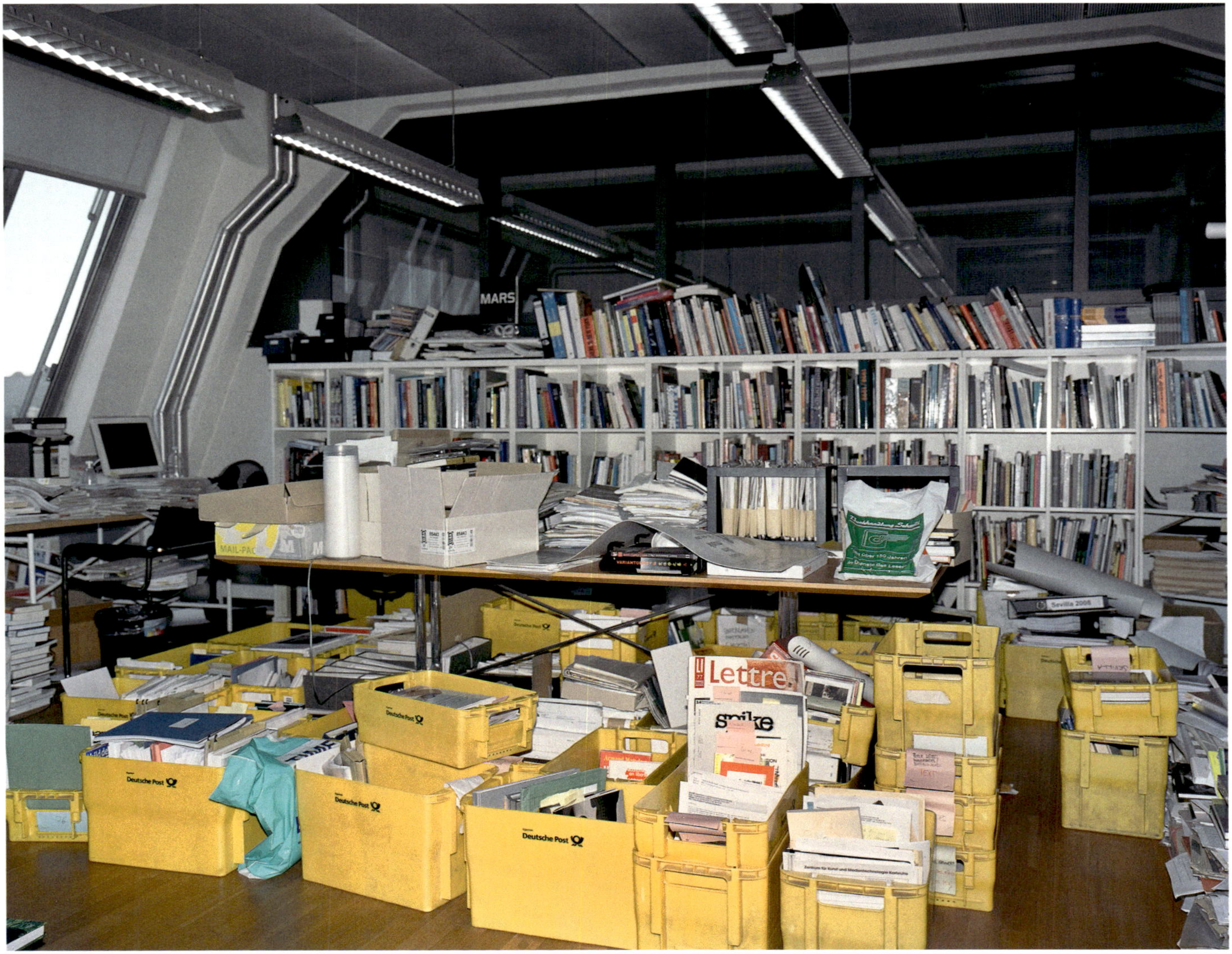

A book can be a storage medium for two thousand years, but a DVD is a storage medium for only a decade. Because the storage media have to be renewed every few years, storage time is getting ever shorter, tending toward zero, while storage space is getting ever larger, tending toward infinity. Civilizations are basically nothing but the proliferation of storage spaces and the decline of storage time.

ZKM | Center for Art and Media Karlsruhe, Peter Weibel's back office, Karlsruhe, Germany, 2011

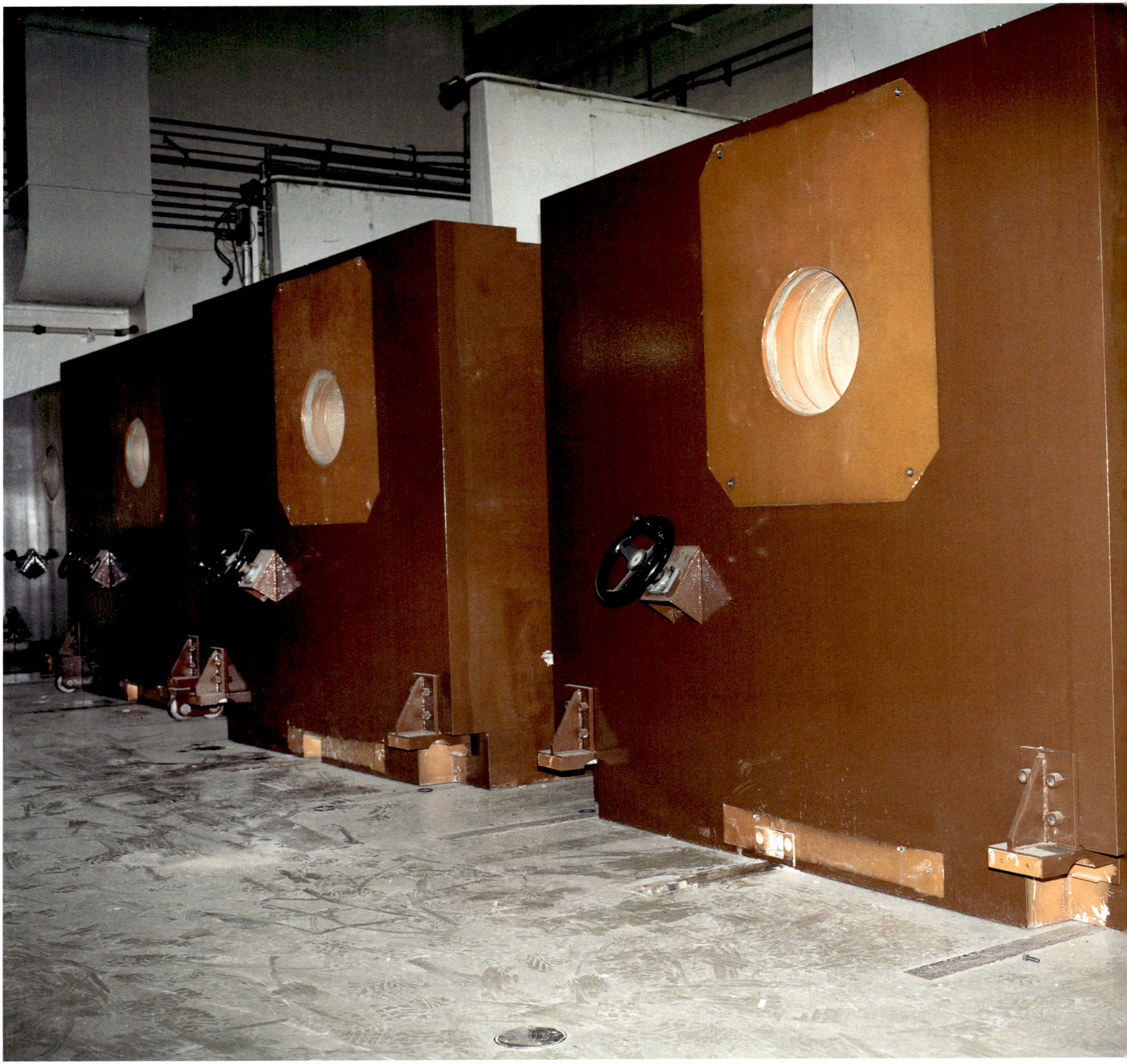

Sogin, IPU and OPEC plants, plutonium handling device,
Casaccia (RM), Italy, 2007

In 1968 Buckminster Fuller (*Operating Manual for Spaceship Earth*, 1968) observed that our planet is just a spaceship with limited energy and limited resources. Energy has since become one of the key concepts of the twenty-first century.

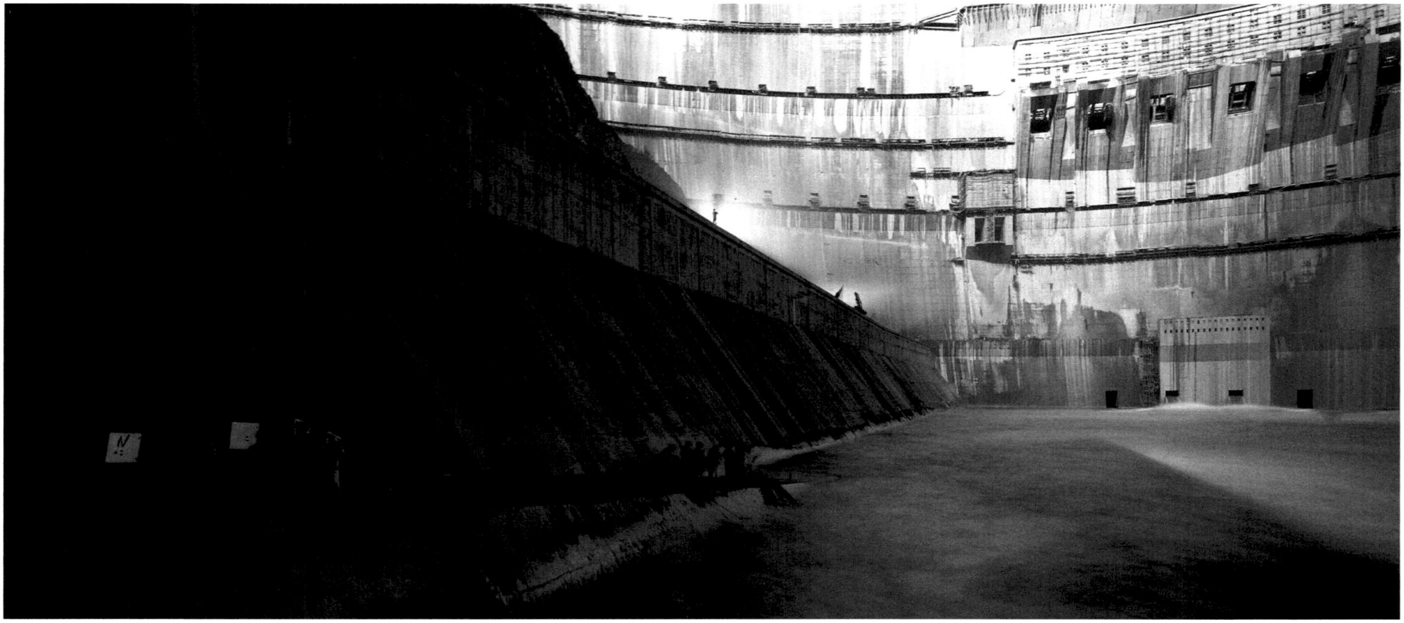

Ertan Dam, seen from downstream where the outtake jet releases water from the turbines. A group of villagers rely on the strong current to bring fish into their nets.

Ertan Dam, downstream side, Panzhihua, Sichuan, China, 1998

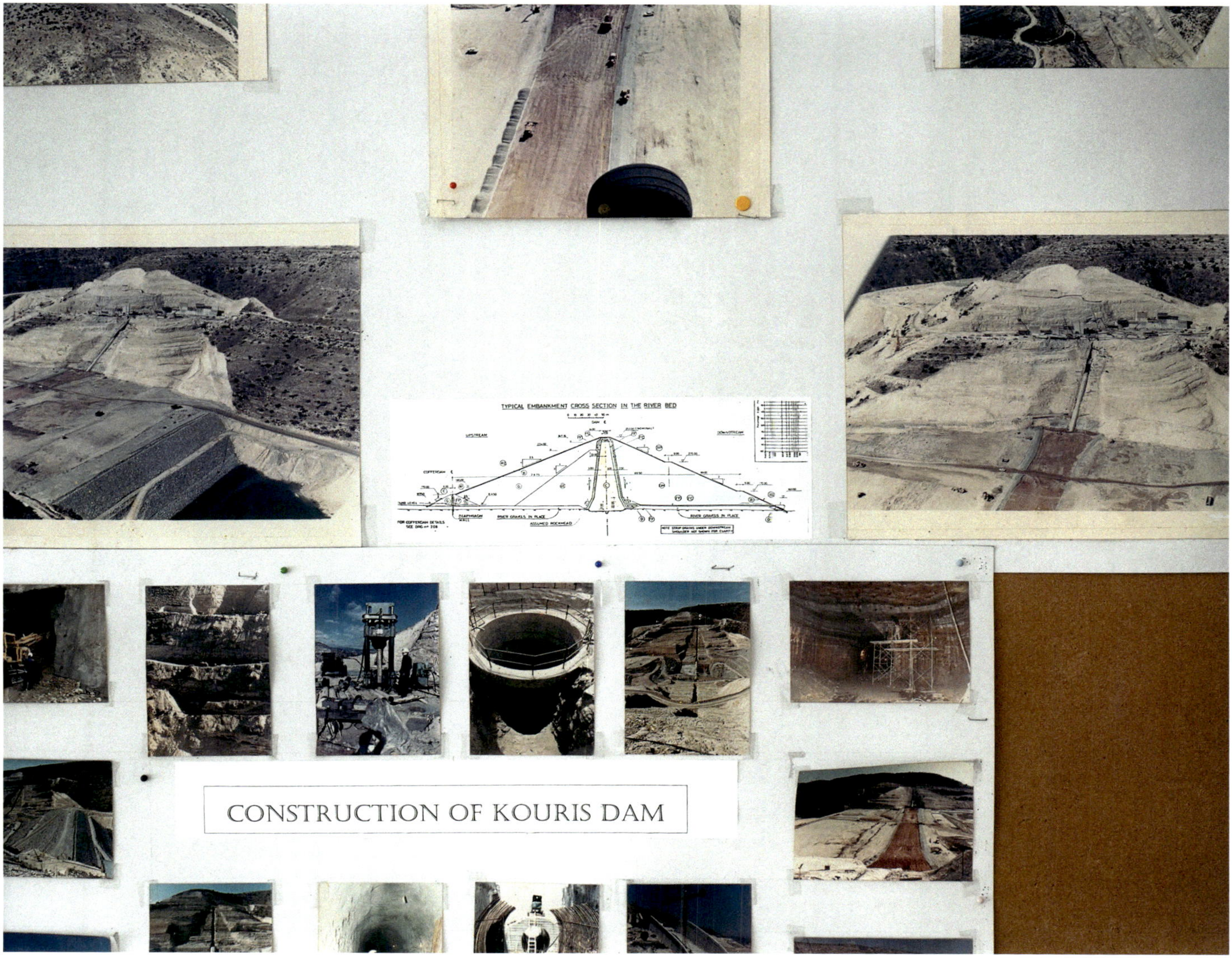

We have become embroiled in an energetic furor. For billions of years, humans were satisfied with the natural energy source that is the sun, which to us is nothing other than an eternal nuclear bomb, an infinite nuclear fission. The era of fossil fuels and planetary oil and gas reserves is coming to an end today. At the same time, we are discovering the energetic costs of the information society.

Kouris Dam, offices, Limasol, Cyprus, 2008

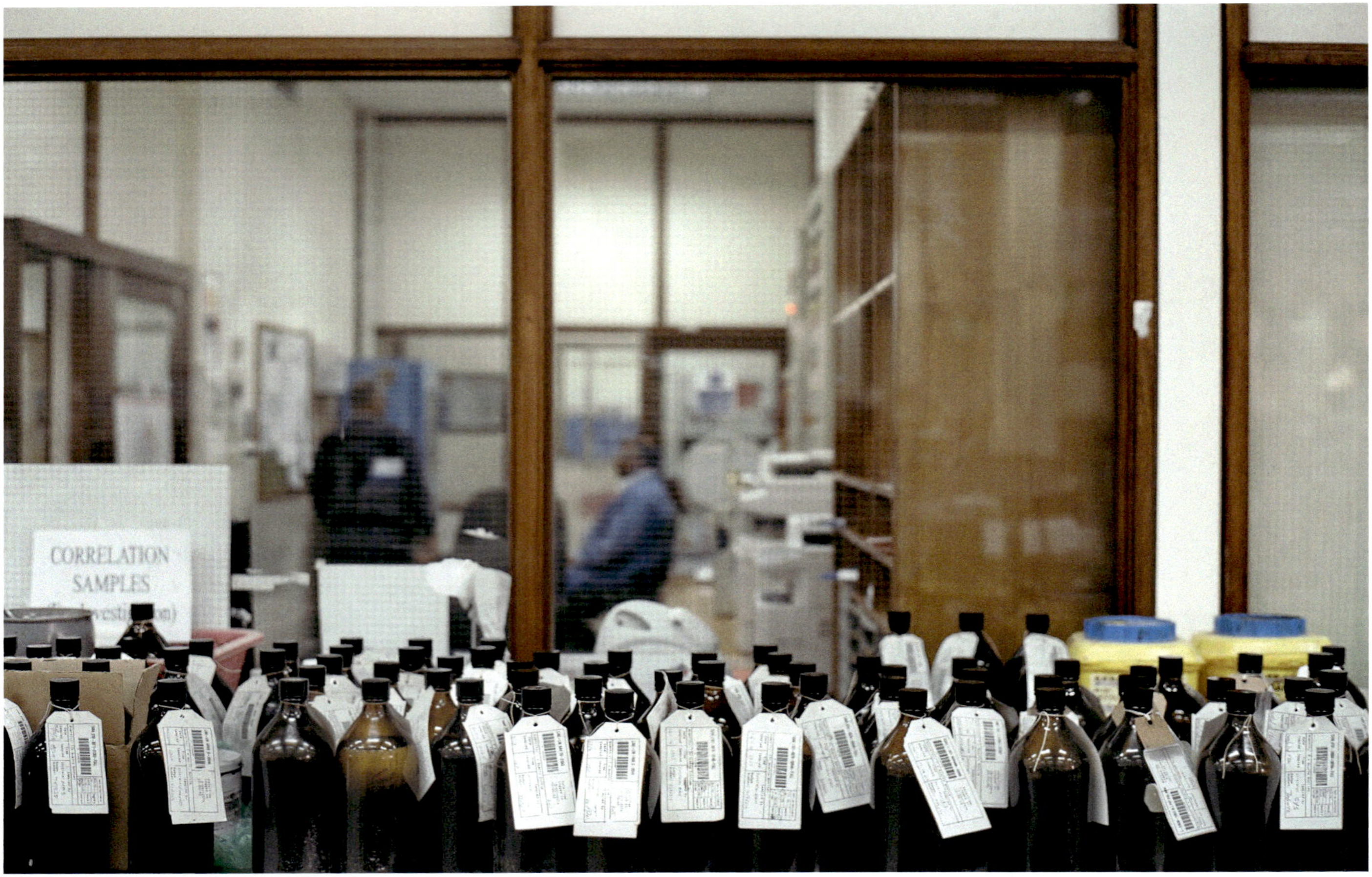

We should therefore follow the "energetic imperative" pronounced by Nobel Prize winner Wilhelm Ostwald in 1912: "Do not squander energy—utilize it!"

BAPCO Bahrain Petroleum Company, chemical laboratory, Awali, Bahrain, 2014

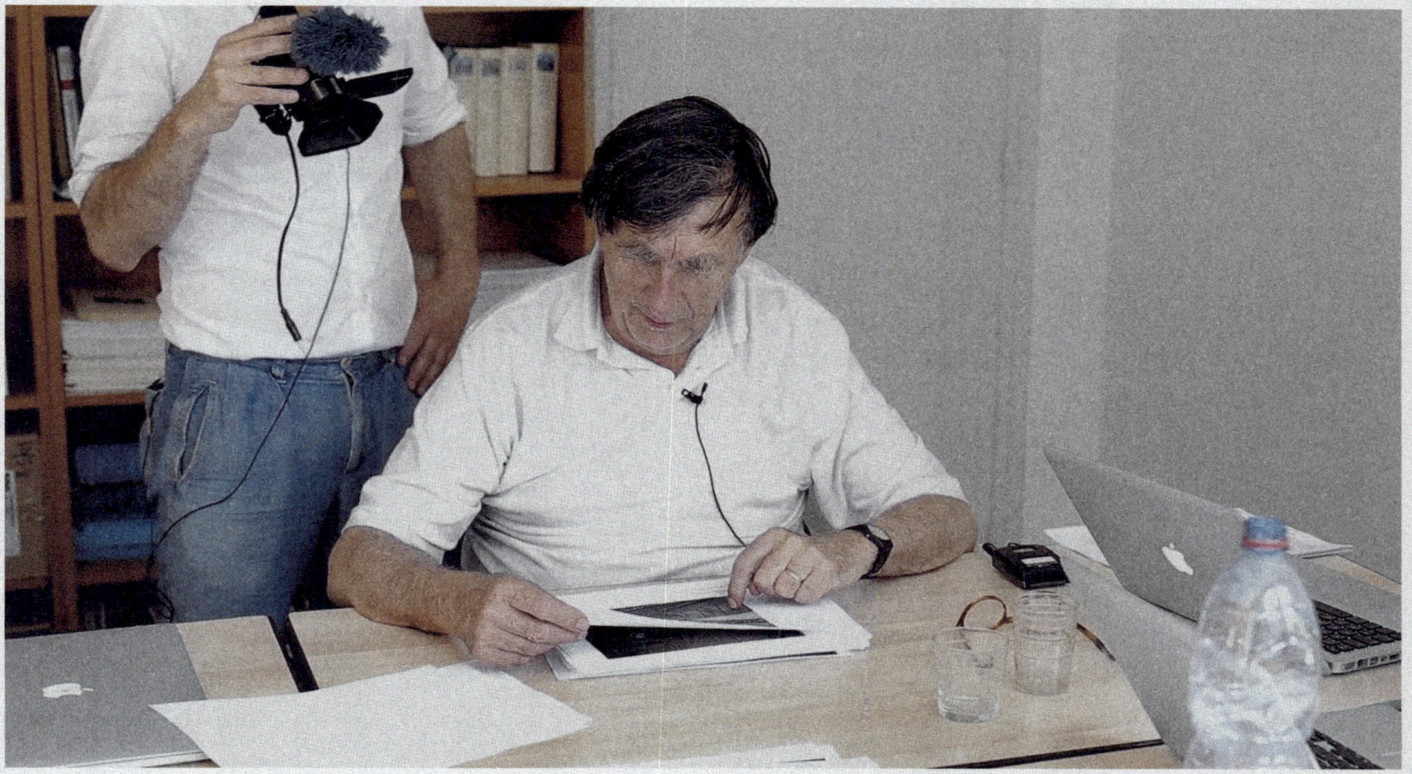

Bruno Latour

139–190

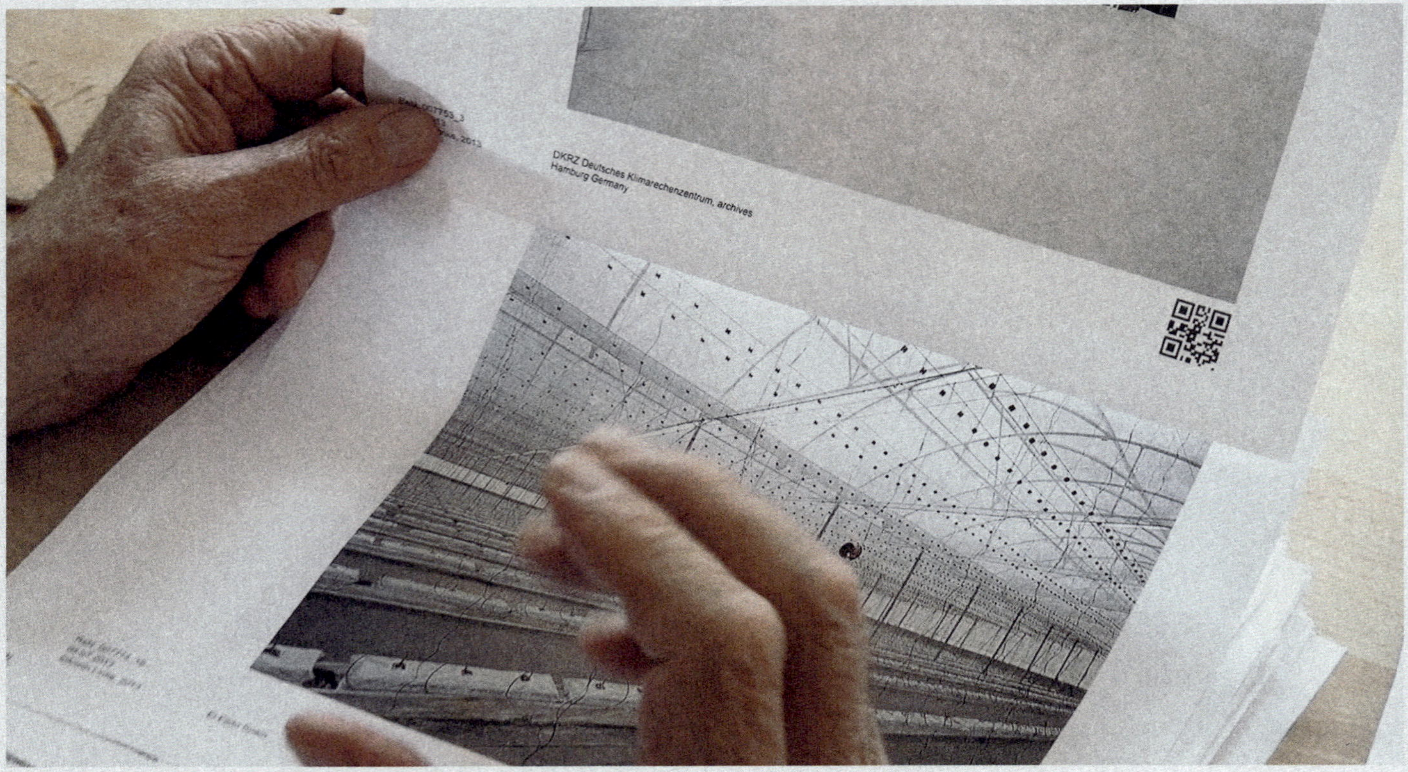

Bruno Latour and Armin Linke, Sciences Po campus in Paris,
January and July 2015

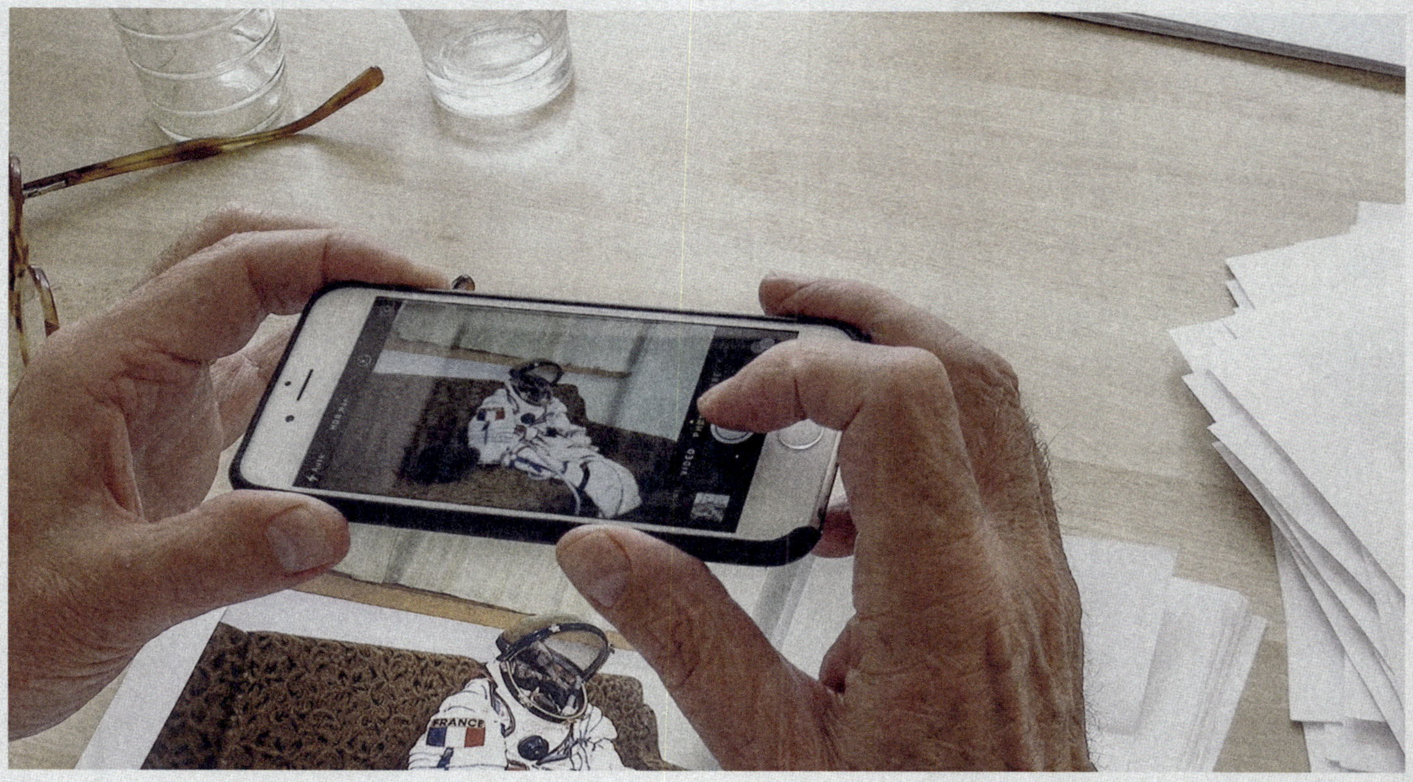

Bruno Latour and Armin Linke, Sciences Po campus in Paris, January and July 2015

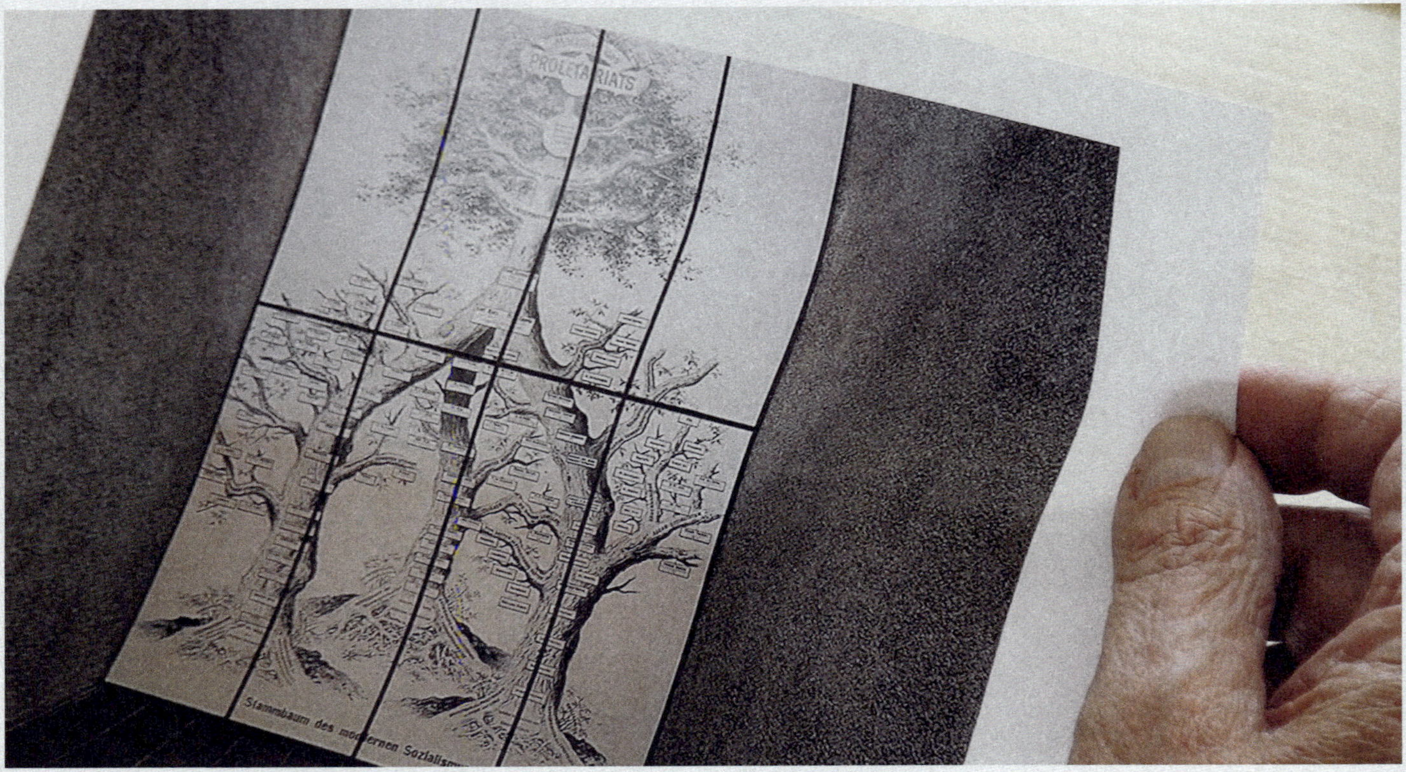

Bruno Latour and Armin Linke, Sciences Po campus in Paris,
January and July 2015

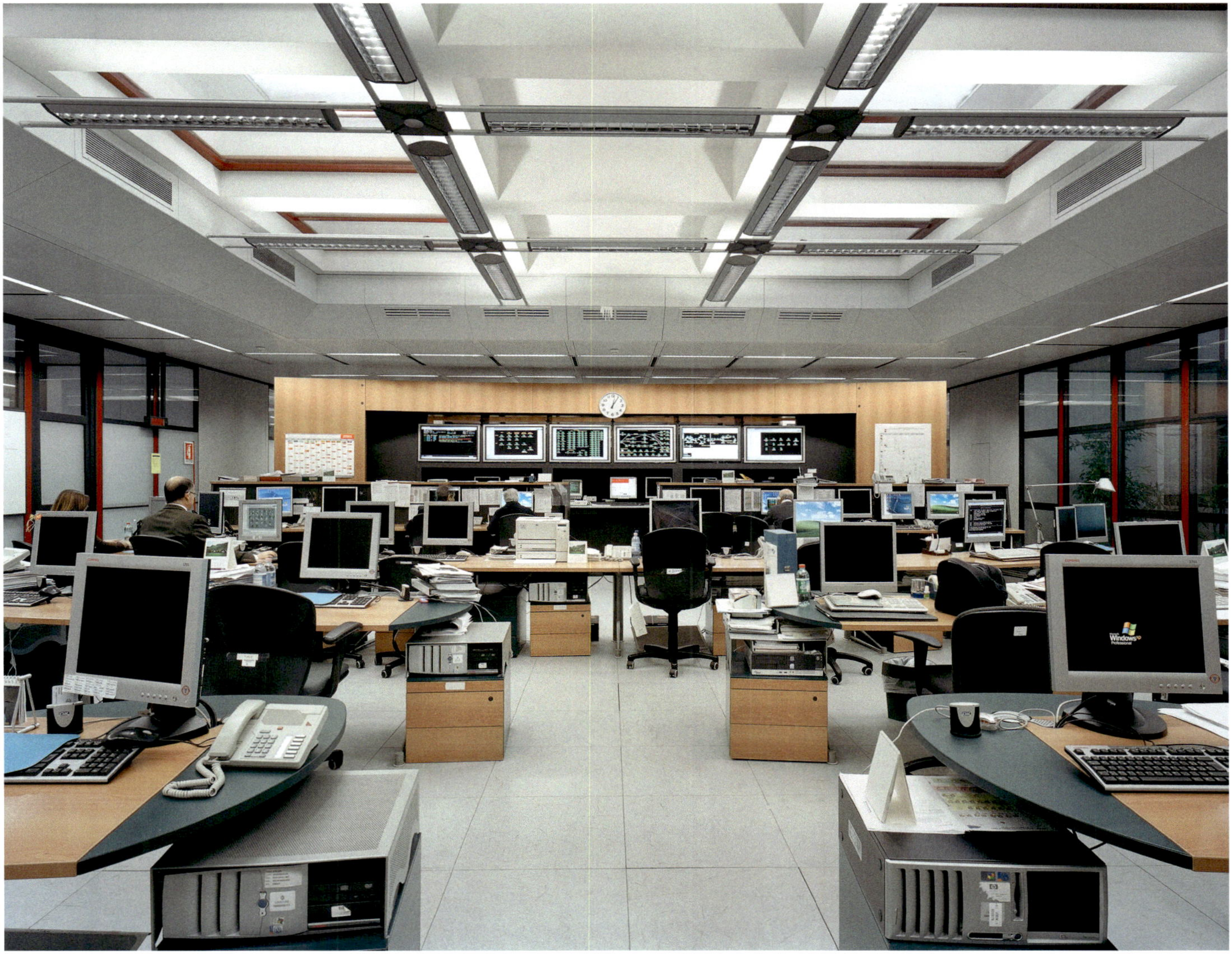

TARGET2, is the European inter-banking system regulating payments between banks. A back-up replica or twin room is based in Frankfurt at the European Central Bank to take over in case of emergency.

The economy is a great mystery.

Bank of Italy, Donato Menichella Center, the TARGET2 European inter-banking system room, Frascati (RM), Italy, 2007

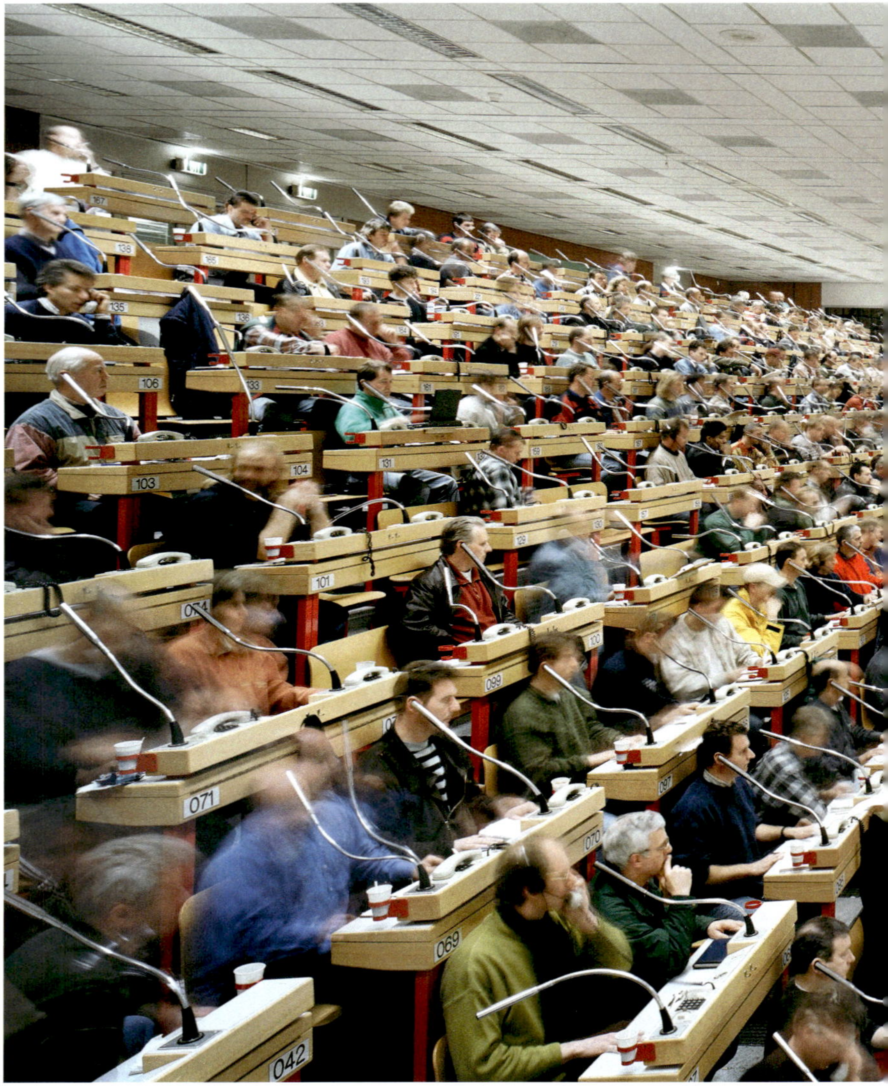

This auction complex is one of the largest industrial buildings in the world, located near Amsterdam's Schiphol airport. The auction hall screen displays basic information about flowers on sale, as well as quality remarks, country of origin, and the names and exact contents of the batches. Buyers bid electronically, and, once sold, the flowers are immediately transported to the buyer's logistics chain. The link between flowers and the economy in Holland can be dated back to one of the earliest recorded economic crises: the Tulip Mania of 1636.

Bloemenveiling Aalsmeer, flower auction, Aalsmeer, Netherlands, 1998

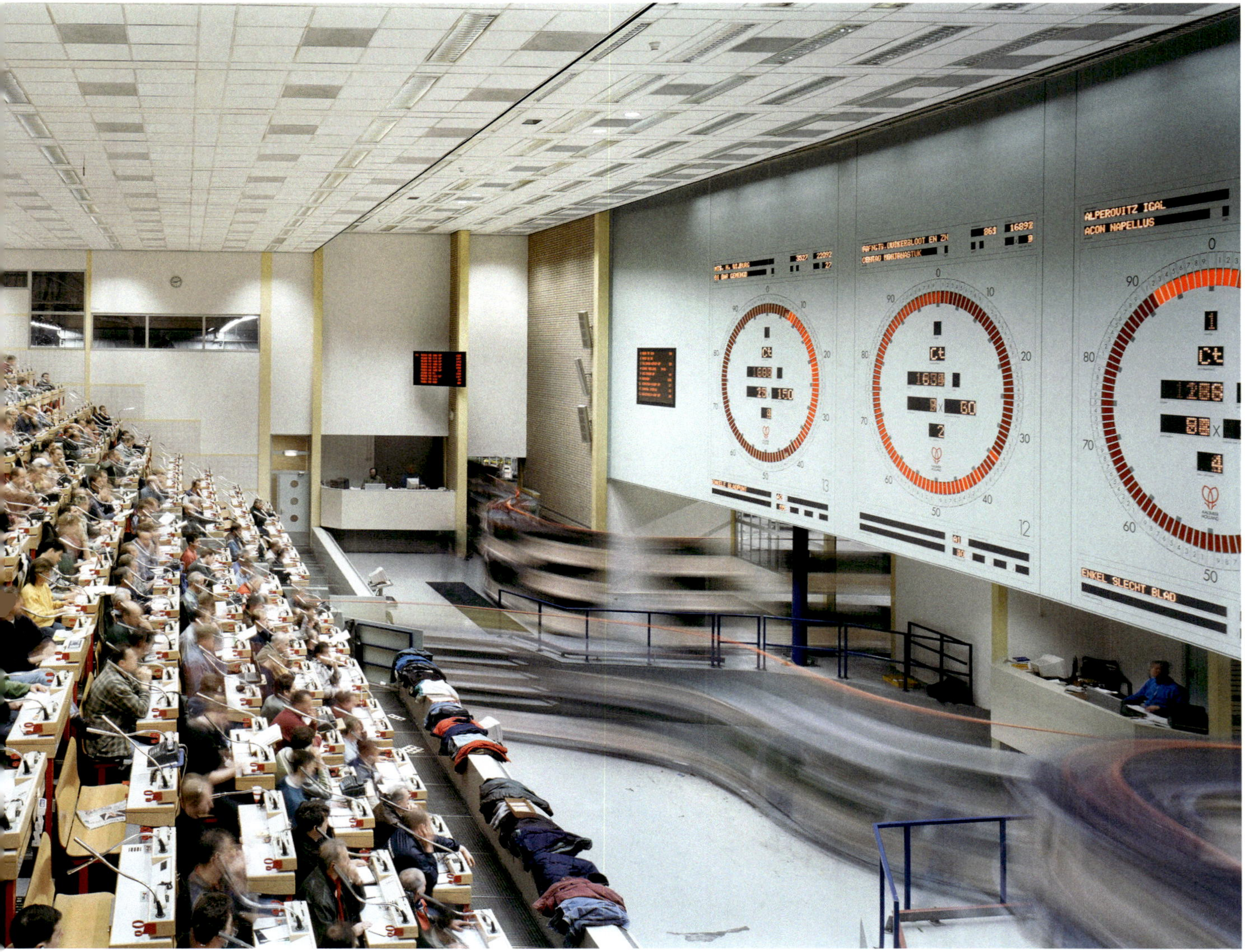

We are supposed to live in it, to be *homo oeconomicus*, a new species of people capable of calculating.

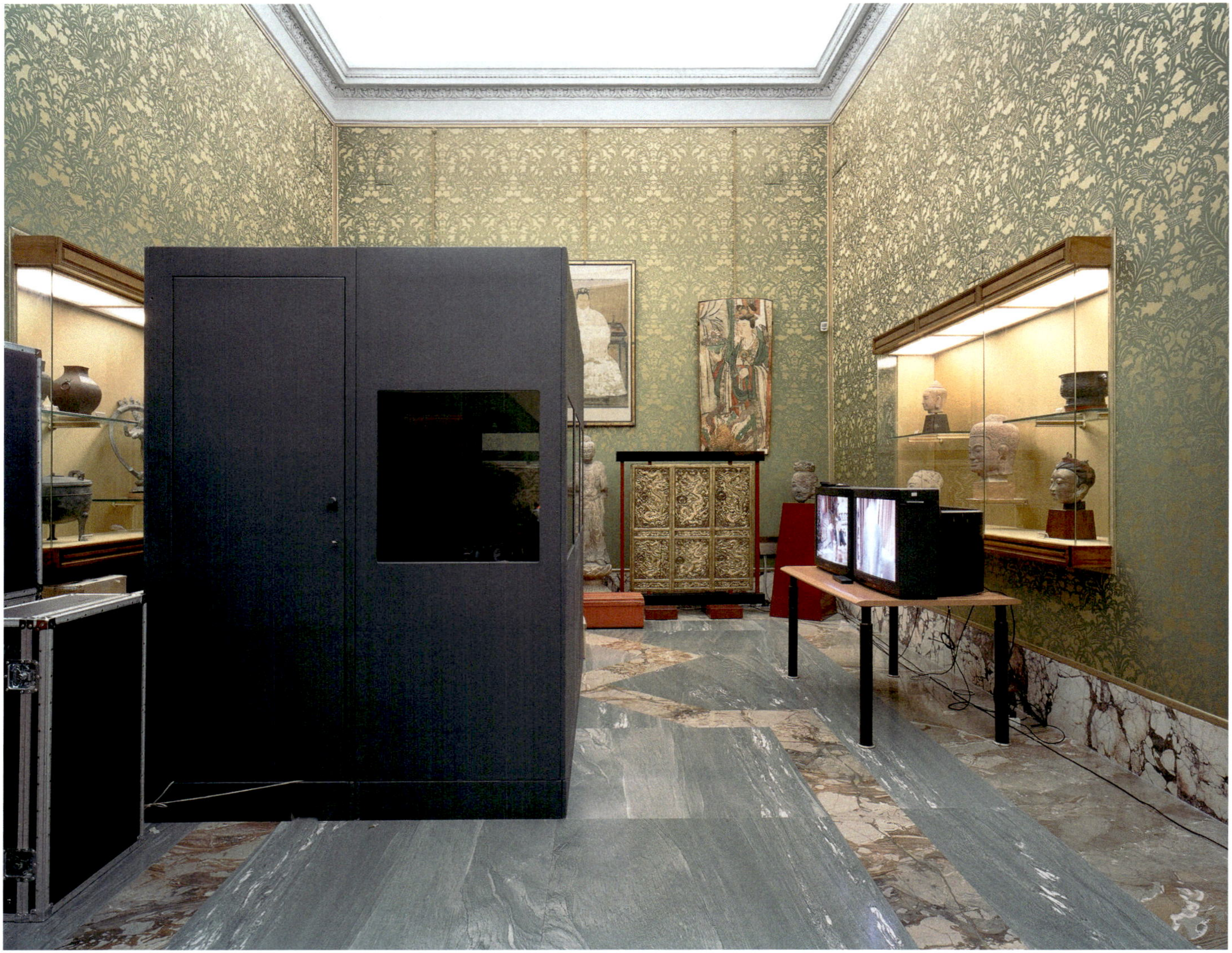

In fact, we have absolutely no idea how this is done, how we are formatted to make calculations or evaluations, or how the instruments that allow us to limit the calculations to, say, our bank account or the nation's bank accounts in the form of a currency, are produced.

Bank of Italy, Palazzo Koch, Chinese Room (Oriental Room), temporary simultaneous interpretation booth, Rome, Italy, 2007

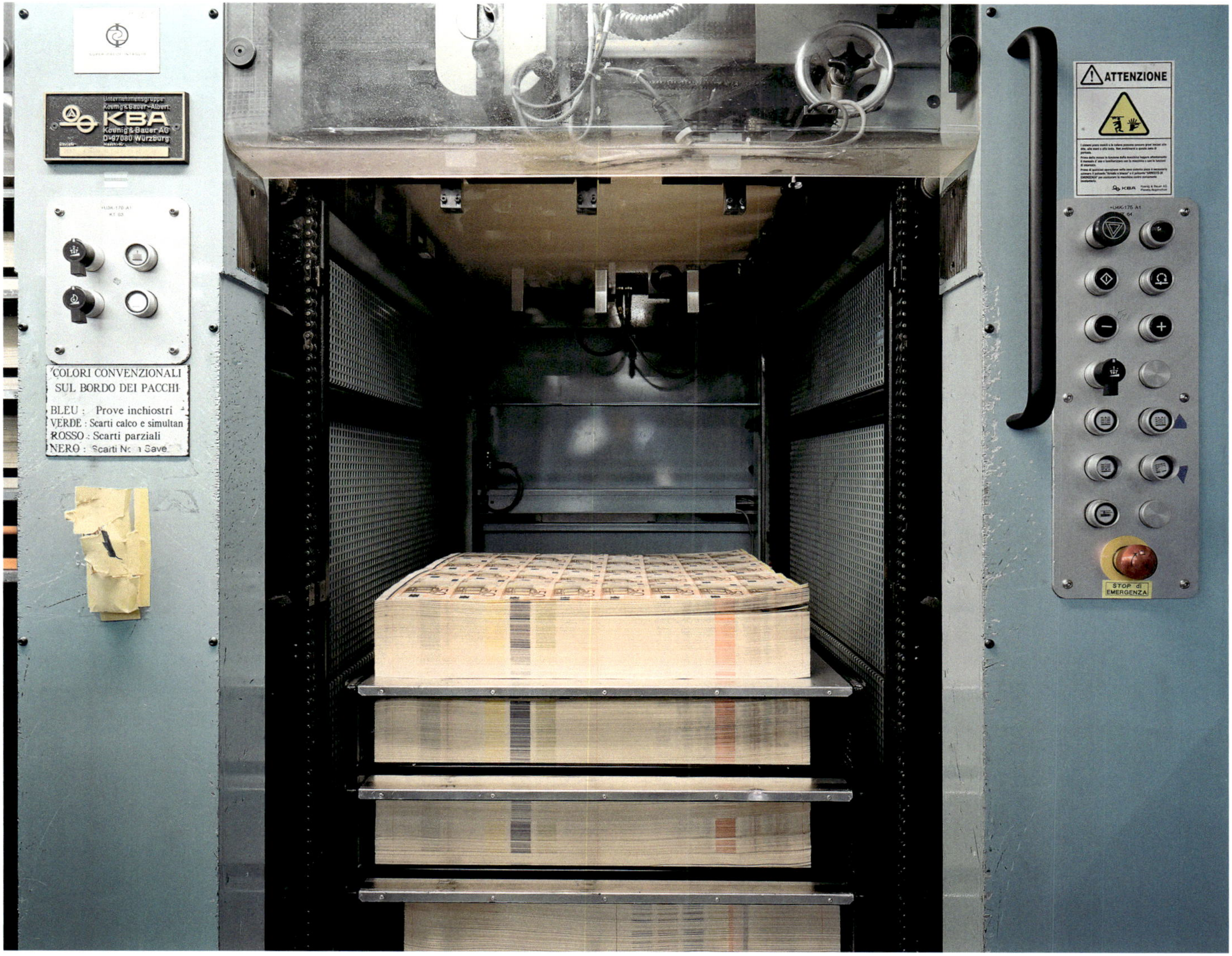

Bank of Italy, printing work, Rome, Italy, 2007

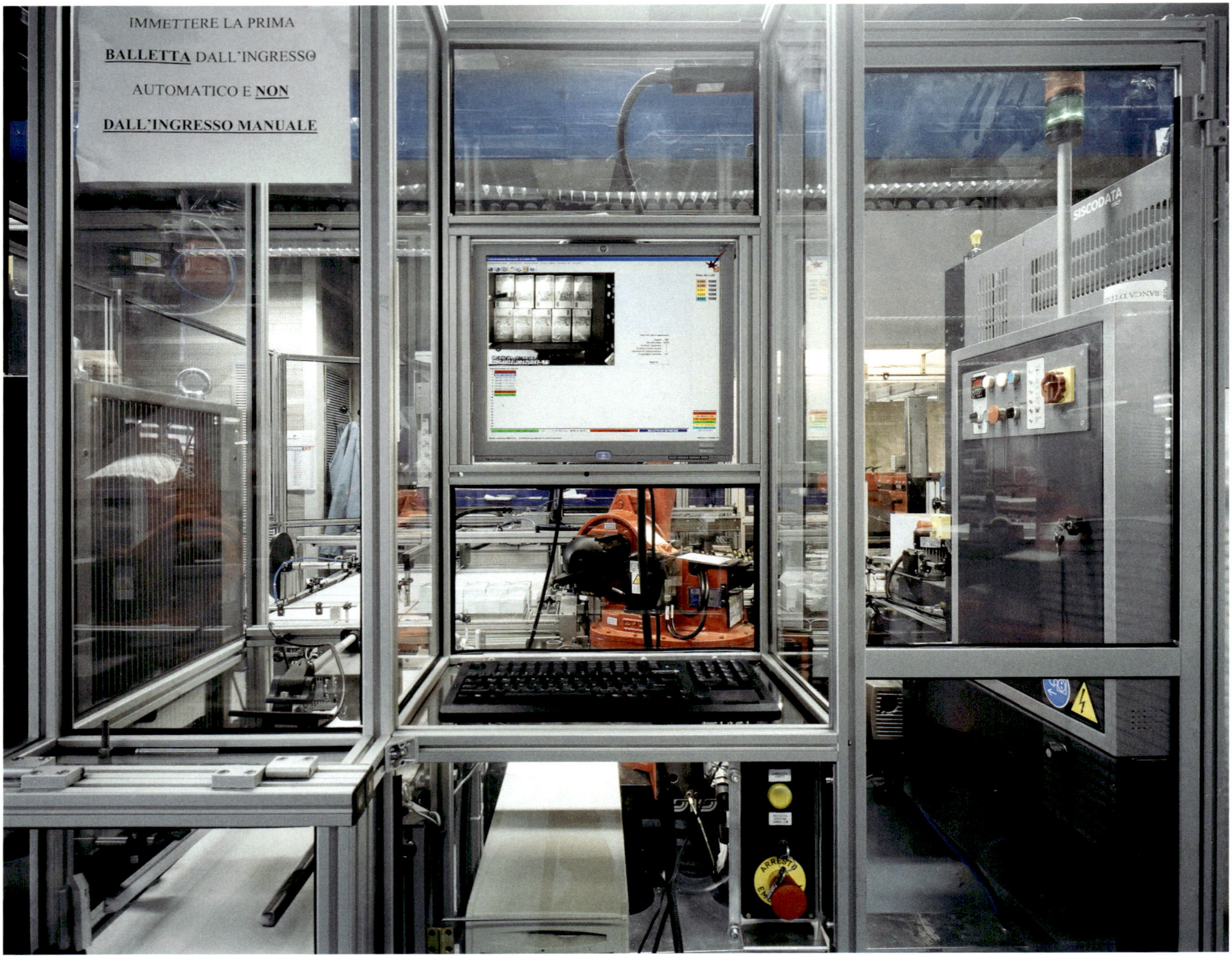

In the final production phase, euro banknotes are printed and cut. Optical control systems check both the visible and the invisible print layers. A robotic arm with an inbuilt camera packs the banknotes and photographs into containers, each holding about one million euros. This image functions as a digital signature with legal weight, confirming that each million euros photographed does indeed exist.

All of that is completely invisible to common sense. The most important elements of the way we organize our lives are unseen.

Bank of Italy, Department Cut2000, Rome, Italy, 2007

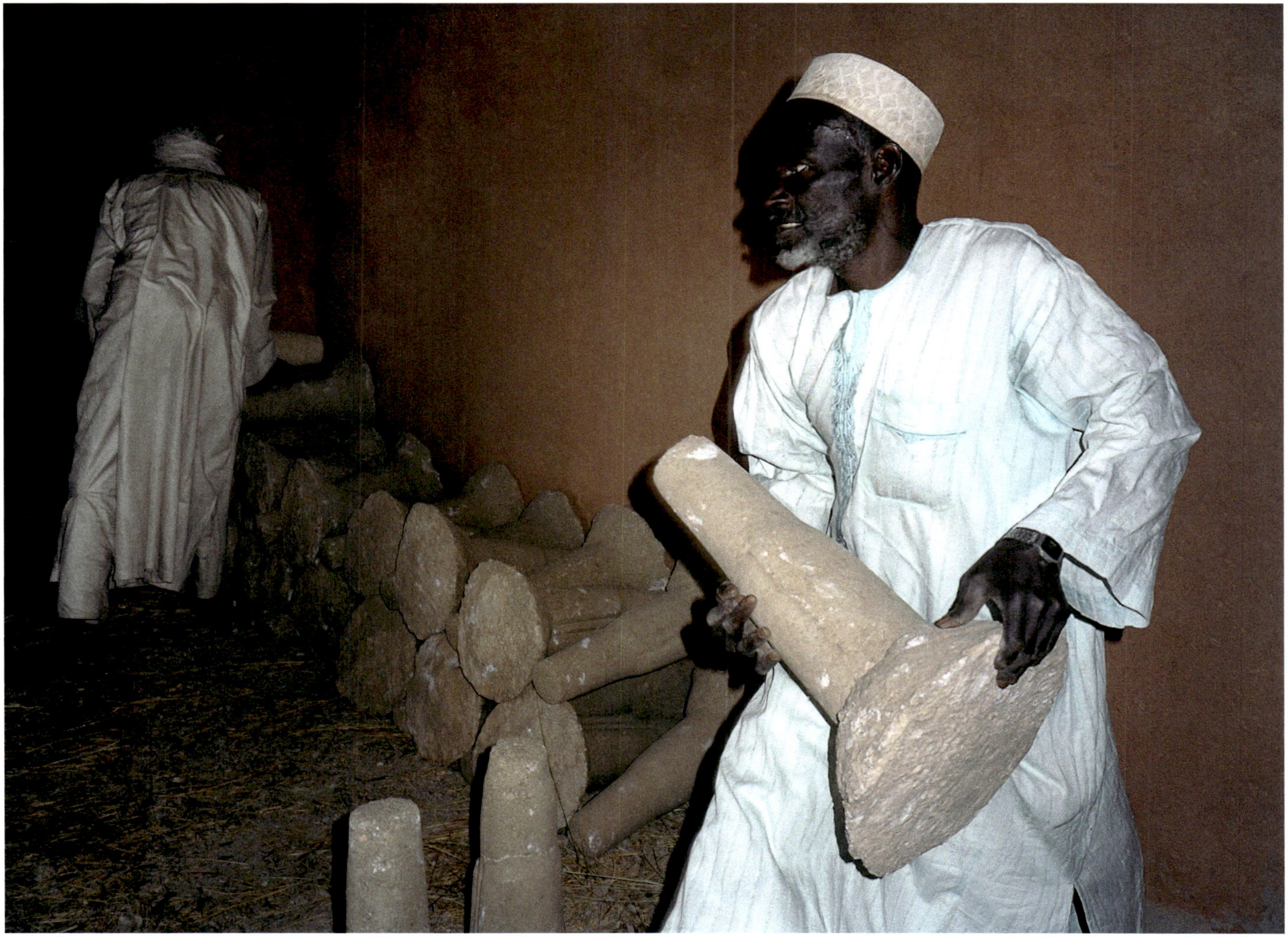

The visibility—which the anthropologists of the economy knew about in the old days—evident in this image of salt blocks for transportation animalsrelates to the question of value and all sorts of exchanges. Salt blocks are a very important currency in Africa.

Salt blocks for transportation animals, Agadez, Niger, 2006

Contrary to many other images, we feel that politics can be seen. Politics is never done in a vacuum. Not only because it is always connected to specific issues and matters of concern but also because it always requires a specific setting, place, architecture, and ambiance.

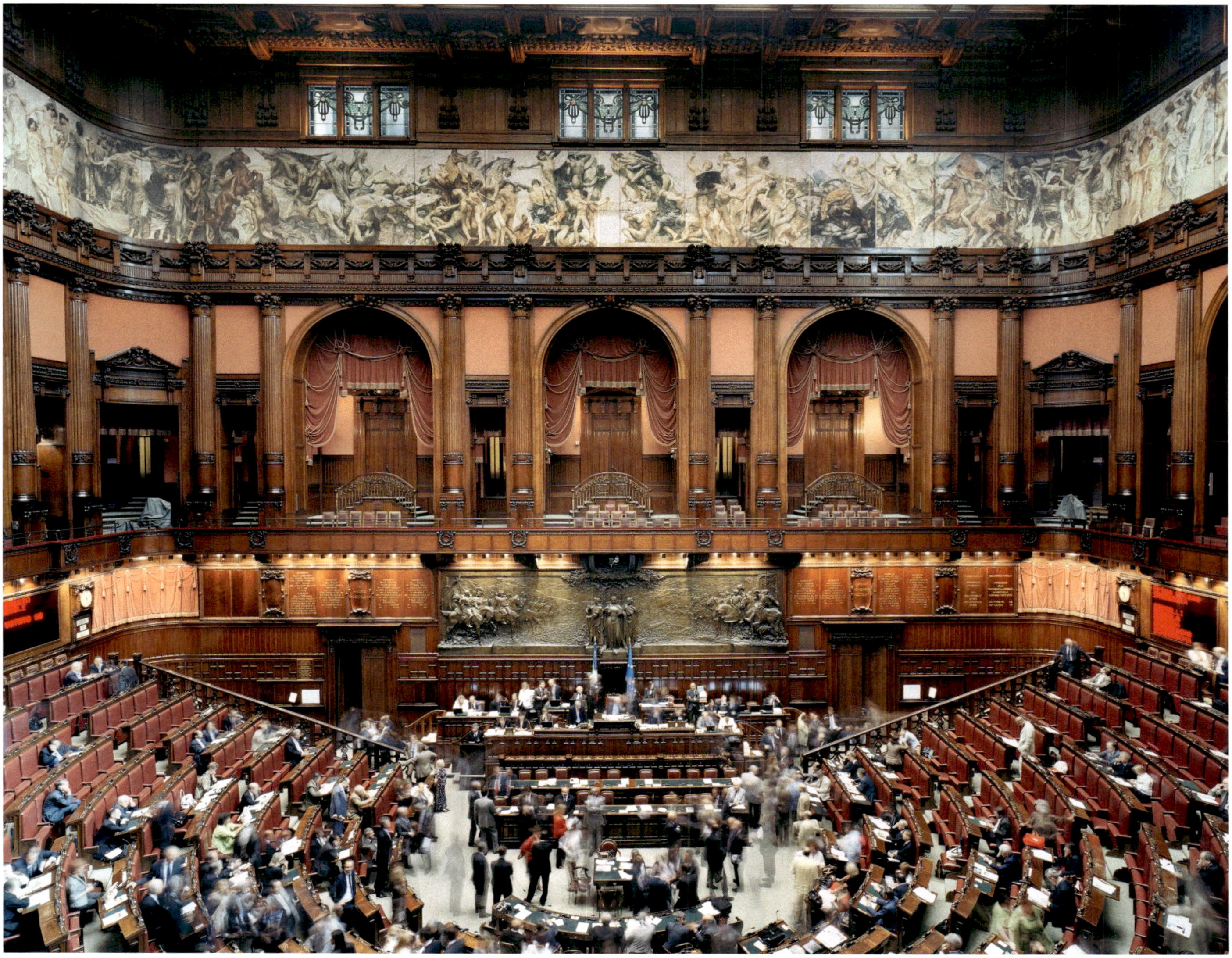

The symbolist encaustic frieze by Giulio Aristide Sartorio (1912) encircling the walls of the Chamber of Deputies, depicts the formation of the Italian nation, with young Italy in the center, personified as a maiden.

We enter those palazzi or huge dome-like structures, such as the Chamber of Deputies in Rome, and know from the outset that we are in politics, because of the way the space is organized, the way people are seated.

Chamber of Deputies, Palazzo Montecitorio, Rome, Italy, 2007

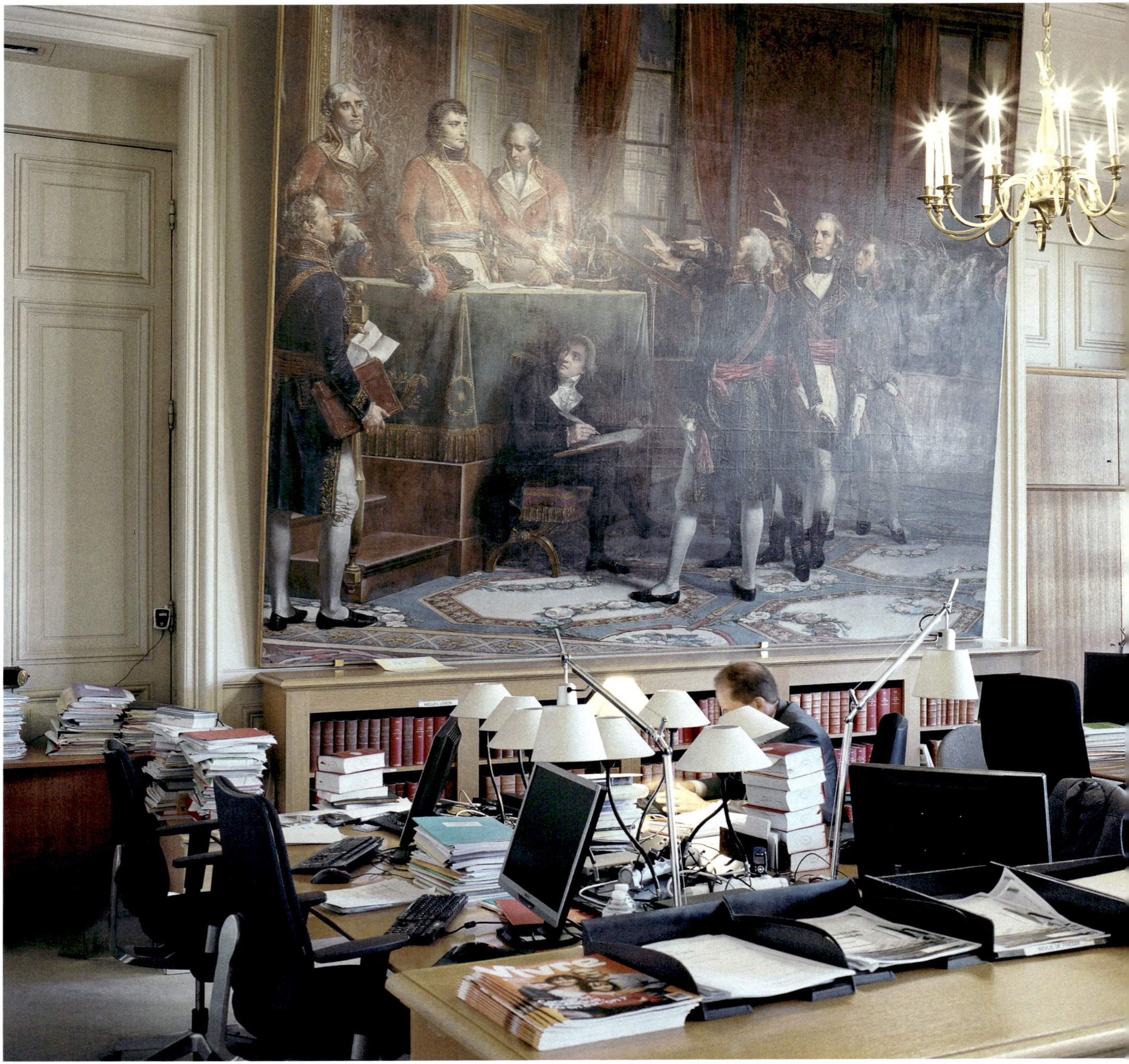

Council of State, small library, Paris, France, 2013

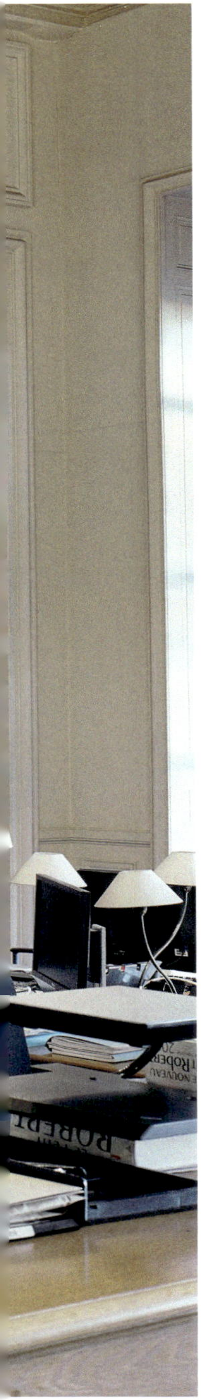

There is a huge literature on what could be called the architecture of political rhetoric or the rhetoric of political architecture.

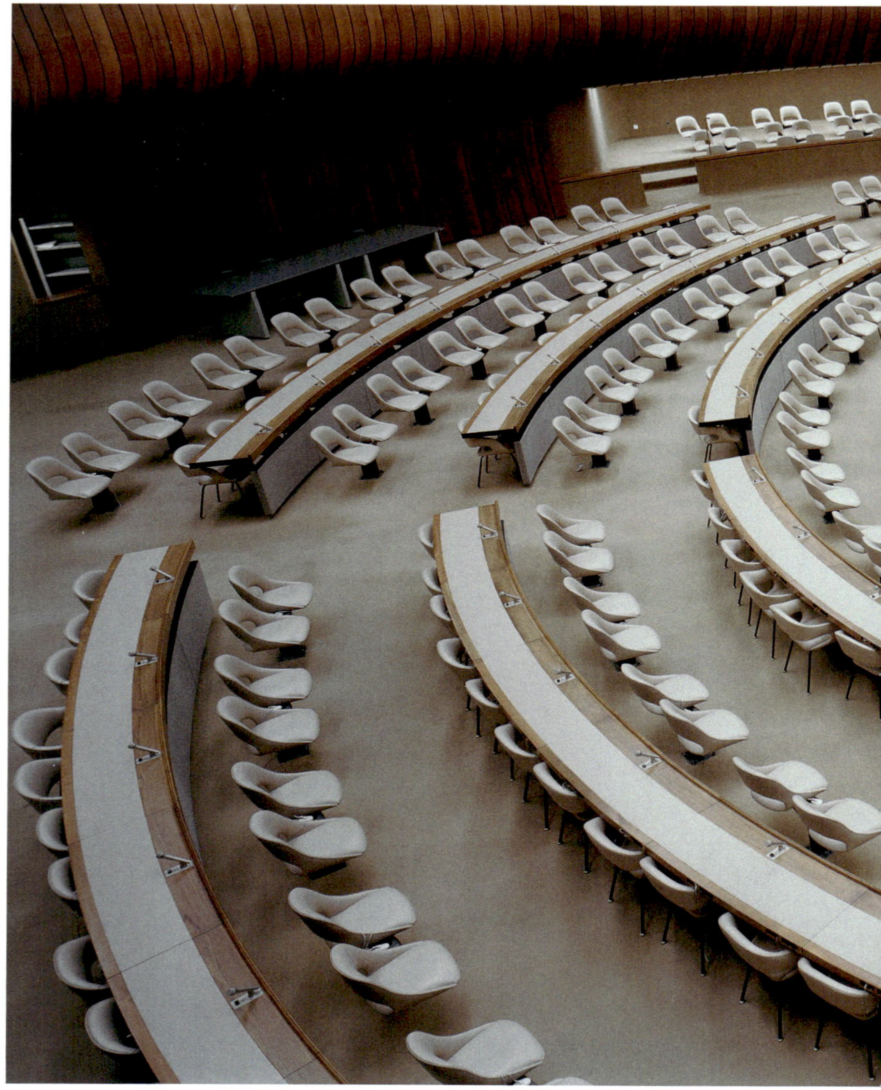

That is, how to practically solve the question of how many people can be seated—which means that the representativity question has to be solved, then who speaks from where, and how parties, factions, and votes are to be rendered visible—the famous Left / Right segmentation.

United Nations Organization, conference room, Geneva, Switzerland, 2001

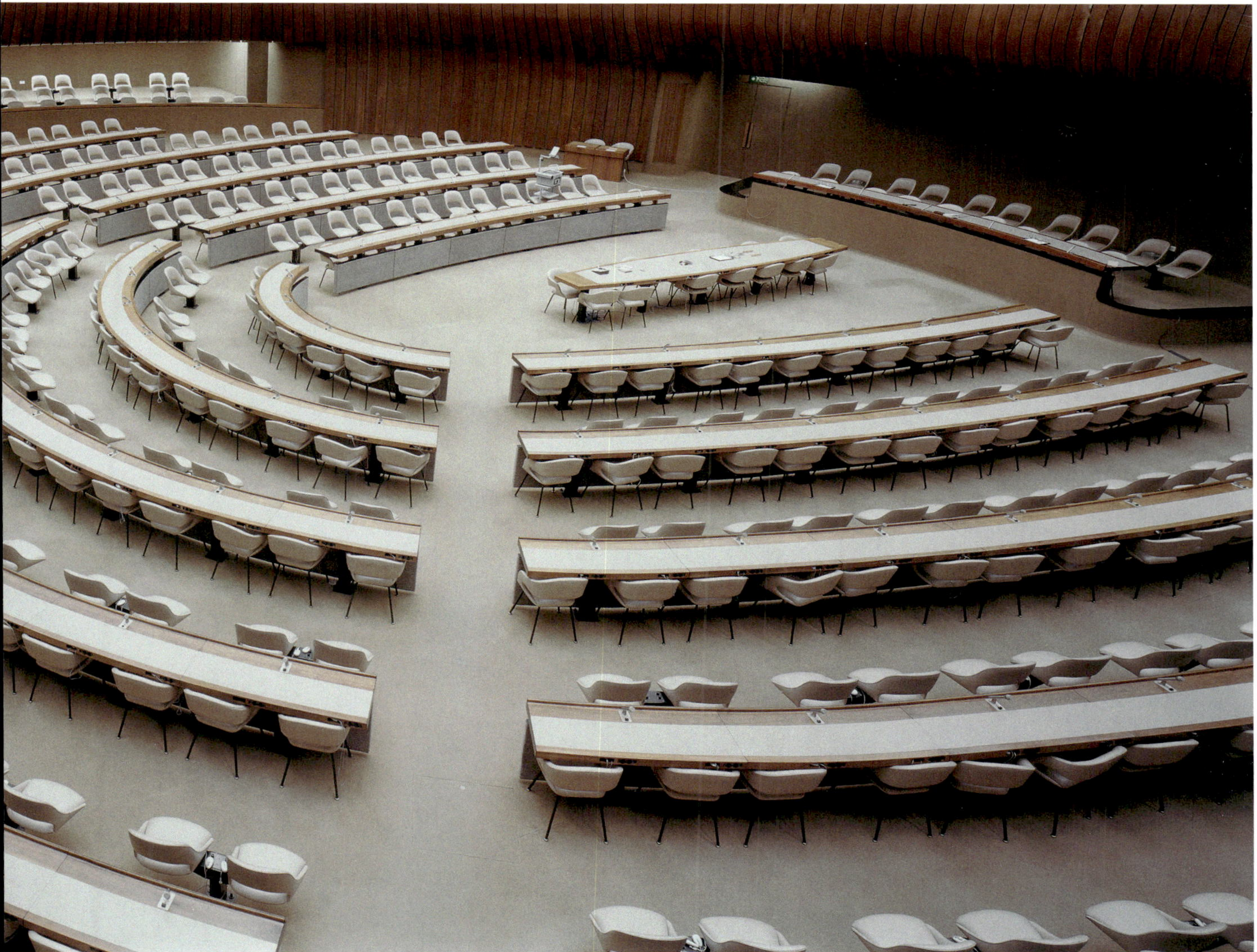

As is well known, many of those architectural decisions came from the reinvention the internal organization of churches during the Reformation. Here we have the sort of abstract ideal type of what it is to be seated in a hemisphere as proposed by Sieyes during the French Revolution and since extended to many settings.

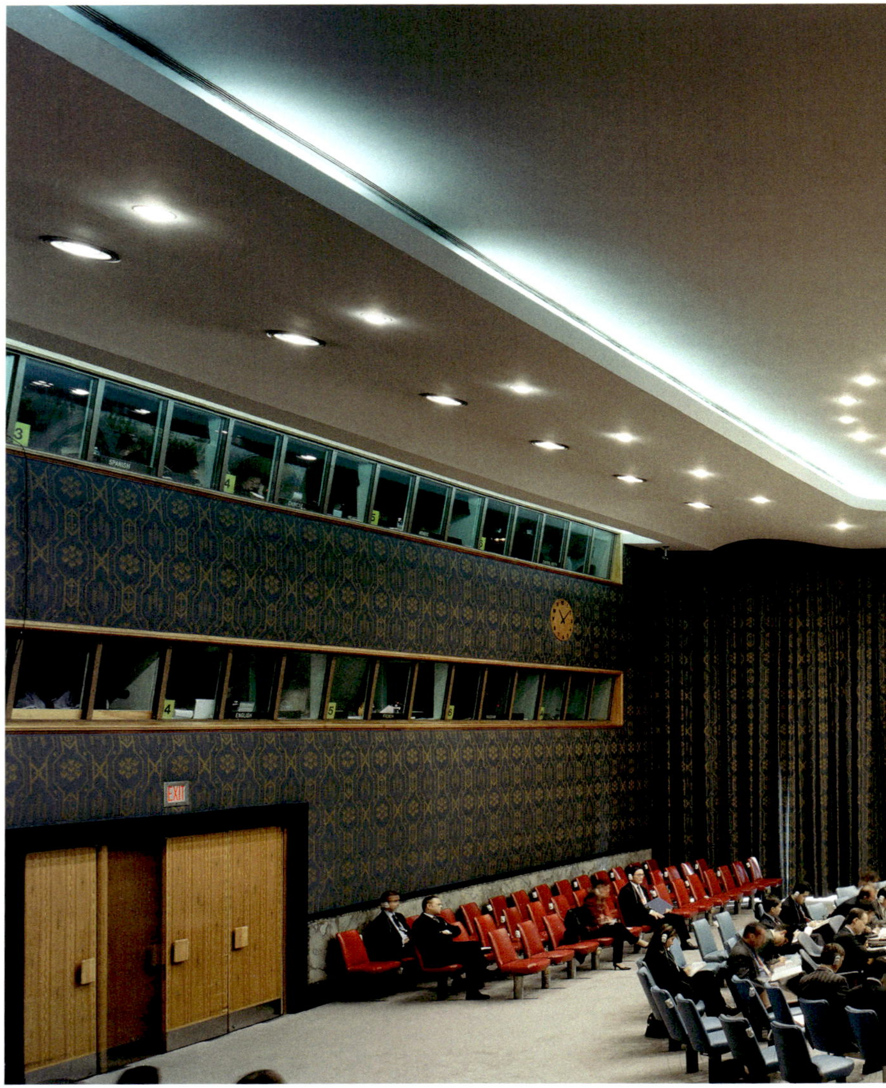

This image associated with the architectural rhetoric of space, doesn't show the parliament (i.e., the legislative branch) but the "centers of powers" (i.e., the executive branch—or what we imagine to be the executive branch). Here is the room of the UN security council.

United Nations Organization, Security Council Chamber,
New York, USA, 2001

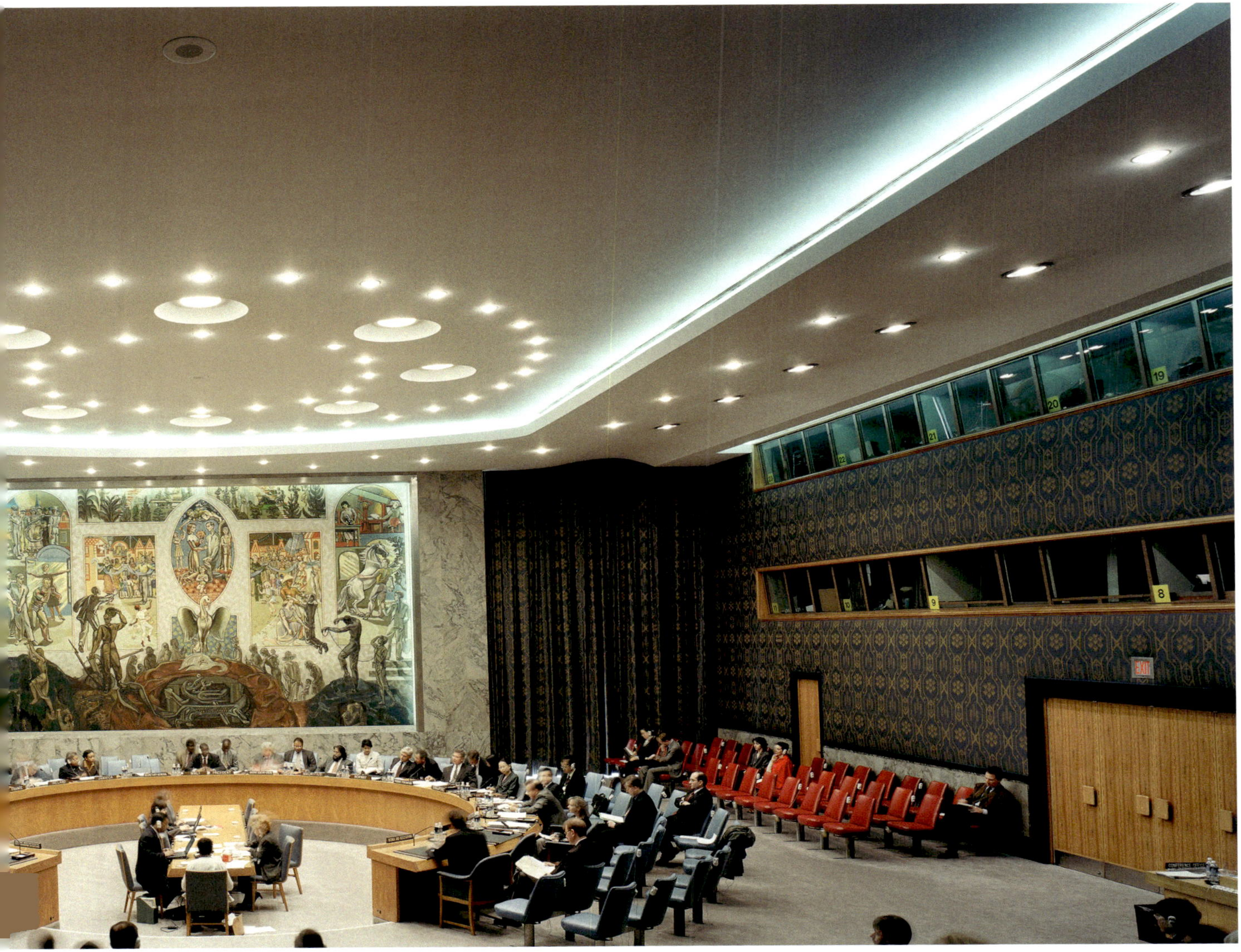

The United Nations COP19 meeting is held in an empty stadium. The stadium itself is not the assembly. You might think, at a glance, that it is filled with an applauding crowd, participating in climate negotiations.

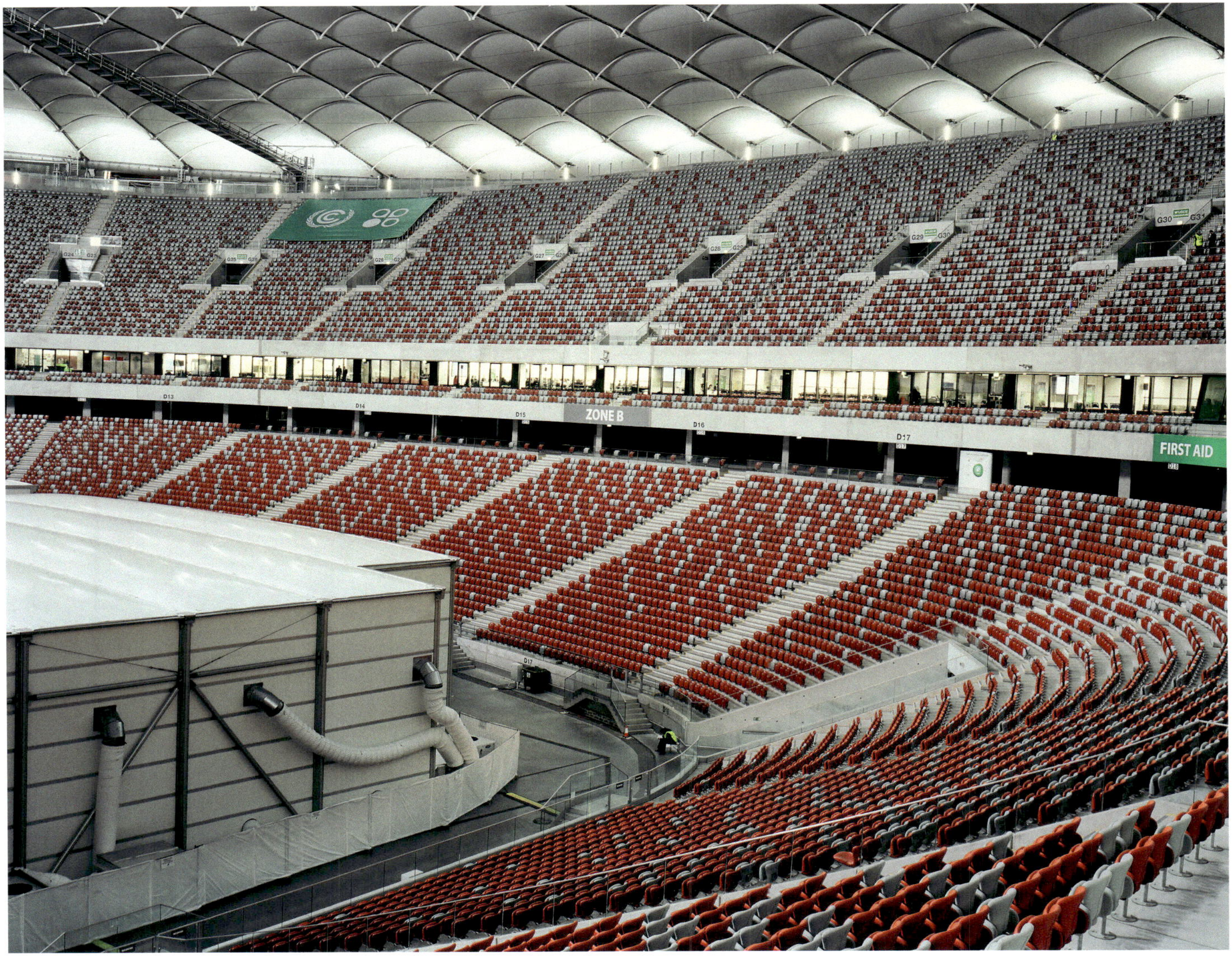

It is completely empty, though, and the people actually negotiating are in this artificial, air-conditioned building inside the stadium. There is a great irony in this image.

UNFCCC, COP19 Climate Change Conference, Warsaw, Poland, 2013
Photography in collaboration with Giulia Bruno

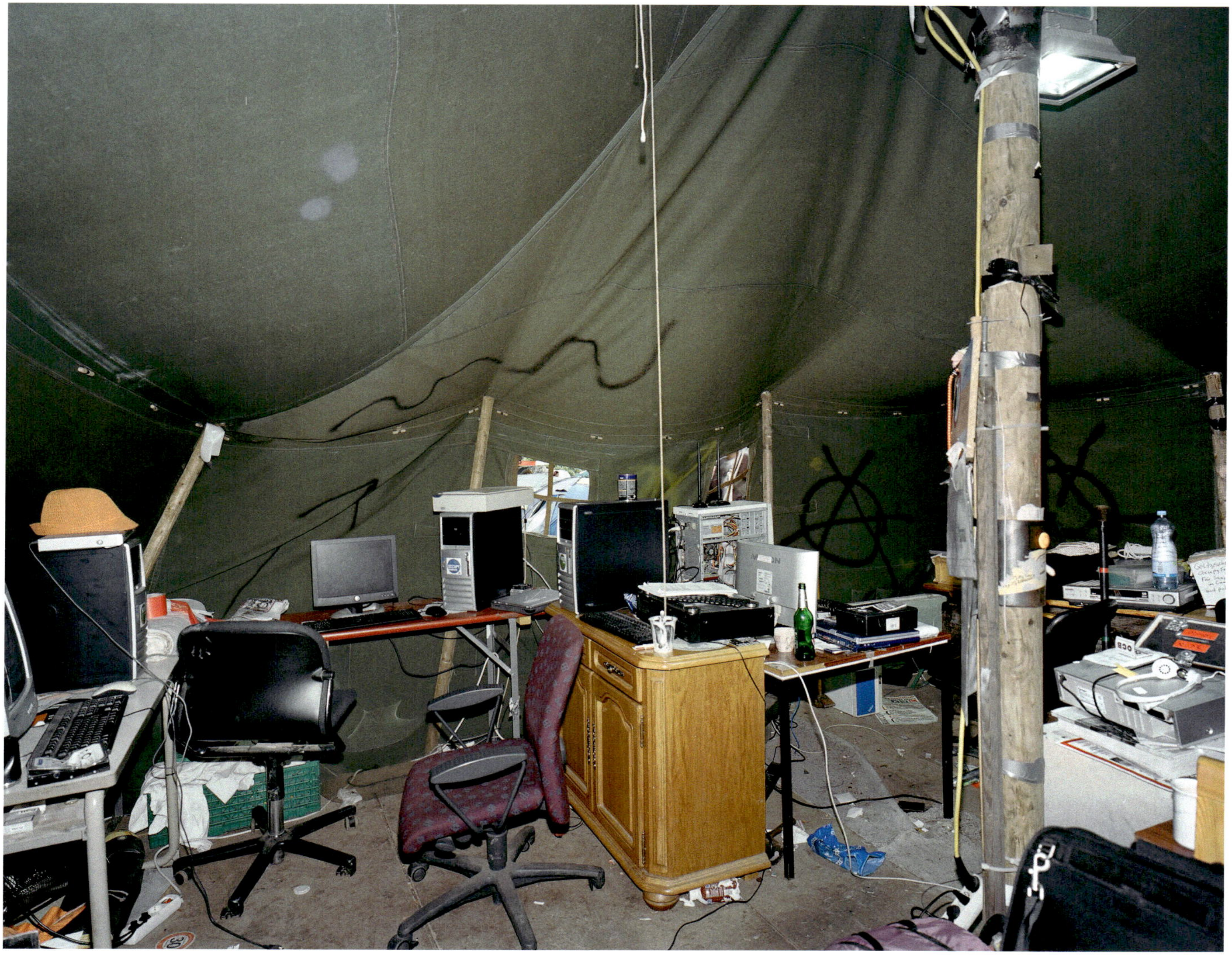

The computer and server room of the Occupy Frankfurt camp just after the raid in which the police seized the camp's hard disks.

Here, you see Occupy Frankfurt in 2012, where the same techniques are used—you need screens and paper, you need to provide chairs, and even beds for people to sleep in.

Except, of course, that the institutional support is absent and has to be invented. Interestingly, in the architectural setting that the movement had to create, people were not permitted to fix their tents with pegs stuck in the ground. So there is indeed a whole political architecture to be invented, but it is not allowed to be grounded or durably instituted.

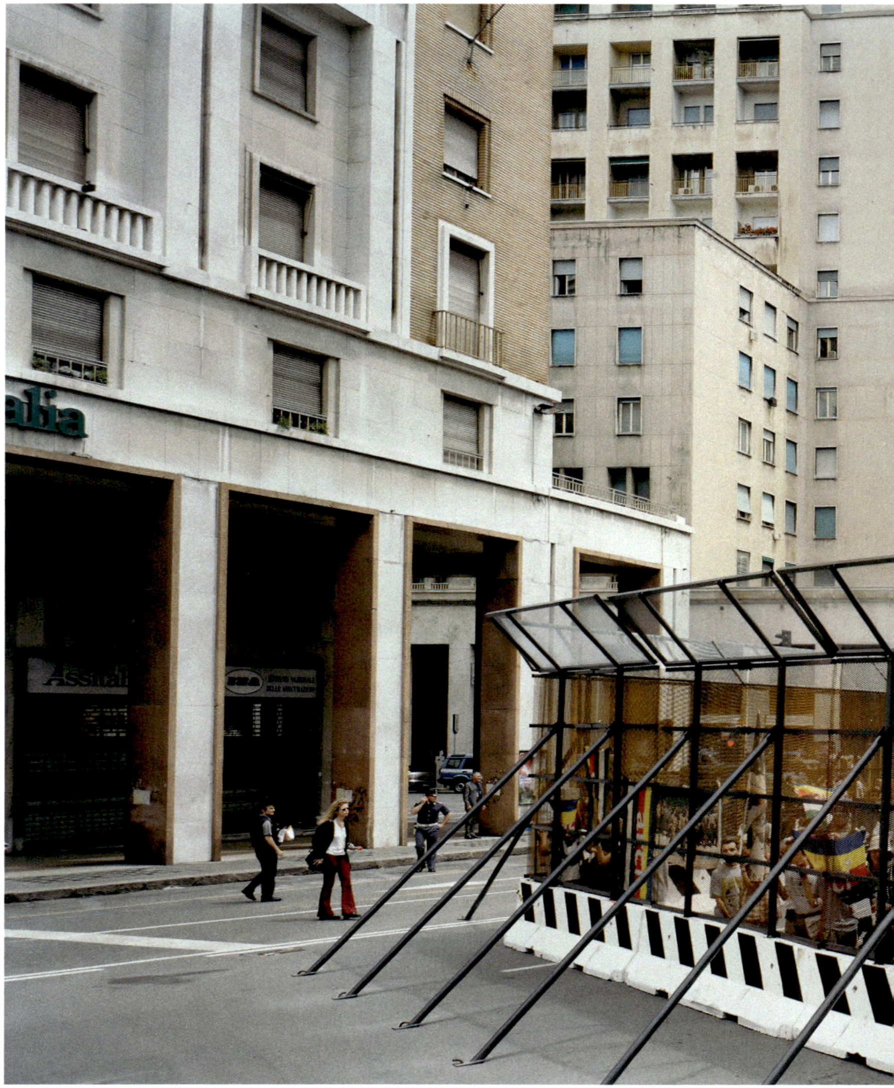

A completely different definition of the link between private and public sphere is when the security question gets in the way of peoples' freedom to move in a city because of the perceived need to protect the "peace" and "autonomy" of discussions.

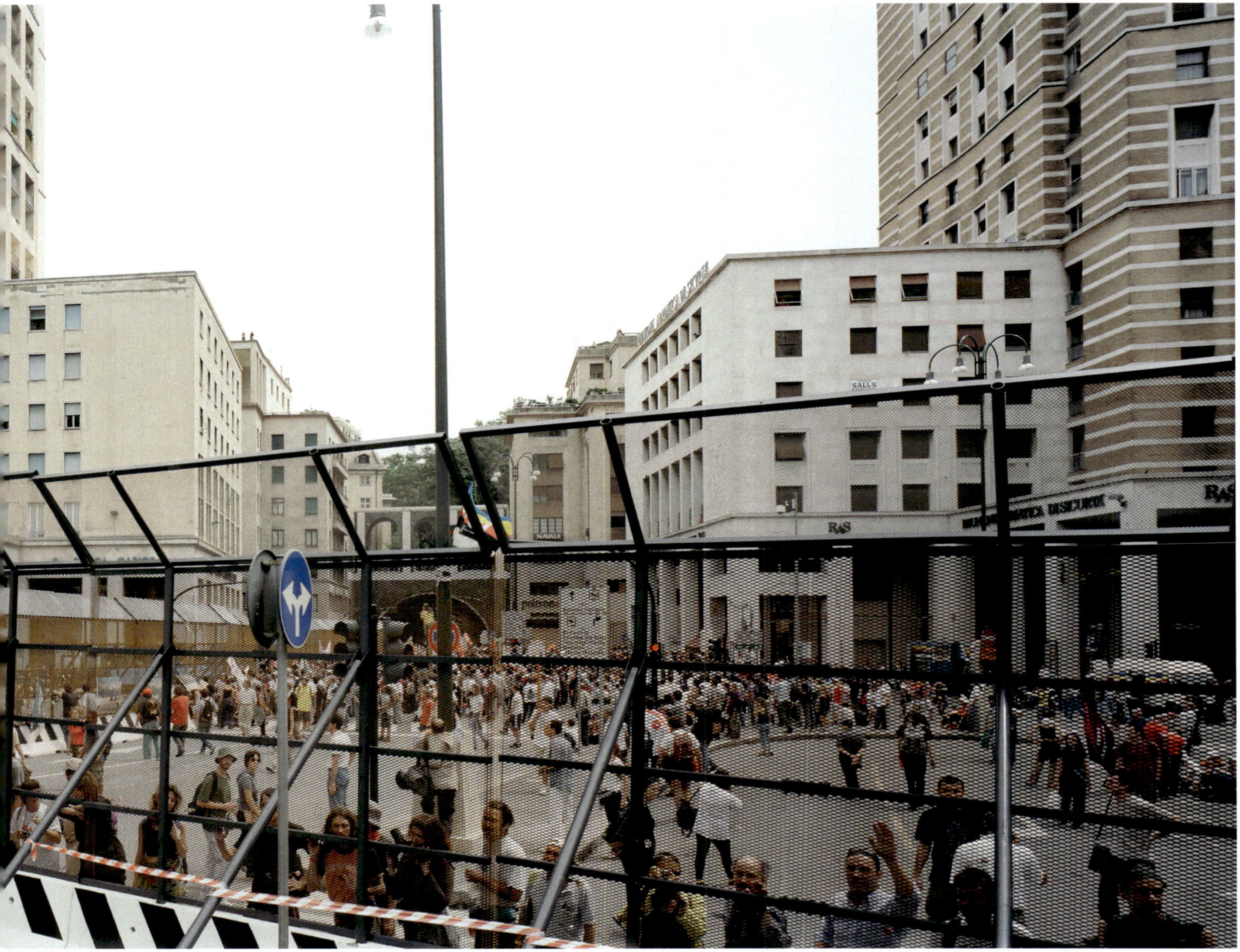

It took only a week for forty steel construction and locksmith companies to erect around 450 fences, closing off the historical center of Genoa and its intricate urban labyrinth of *caruggi* alleys, as part of security measures for the 2001 G8 Summit. People living within the fenced-off area had to pass through metal detectors and X-ray stations upon leaving and entering.

Here, all the clever inventions of the architecture of rhetoric are forgotten and what we get is just a solid gate imposing a distinction between inside and outside.

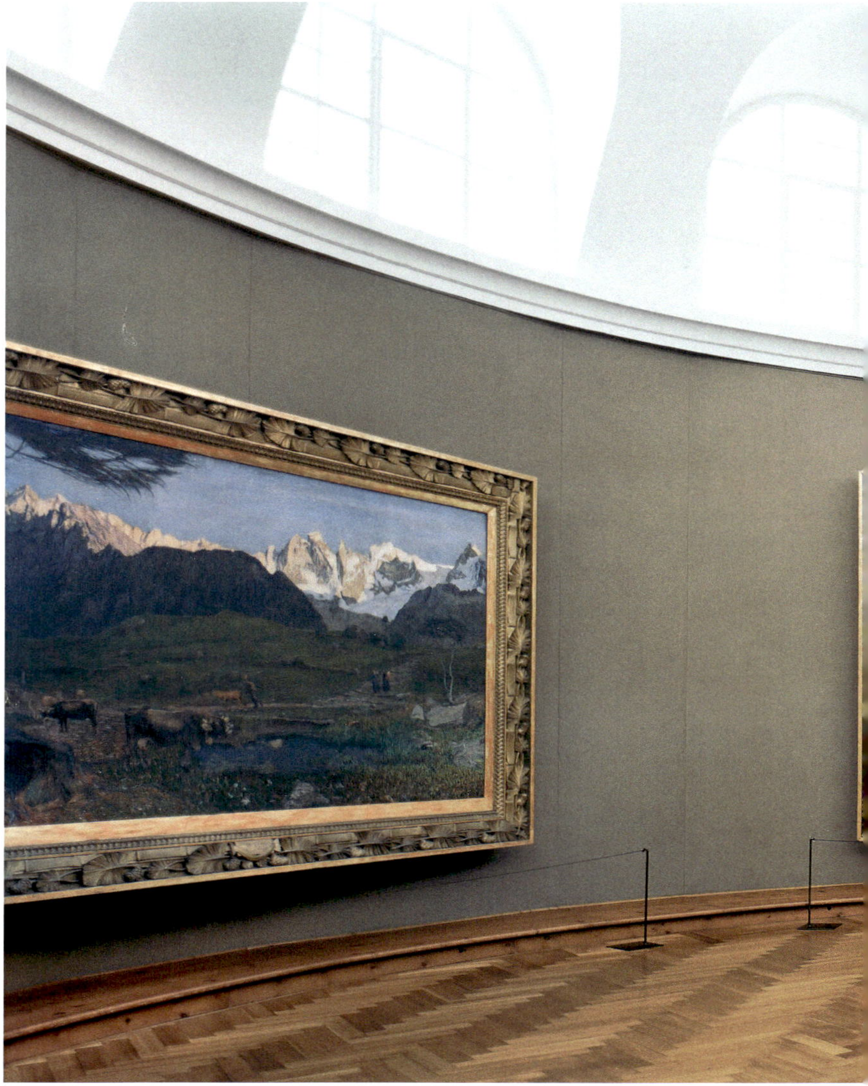

These paintings were made for an immersive installation Giovanni Segantini planned for the 1900 Paris World Exposition and which was to be financed by all the hoteliers of Engadin. A panoramic painting was to be installed in a pavilion with plants and livestock supplying the sounds, smells, and other sensory experiences of Alpine life.

One of the most interesting aspects of what it means to show the unseen is to work out the boundary between the inside and the outside. We are always inside a place, inside this exhibition, for example.

Segantini Museum, St. Moritz, Switzerland, 2004

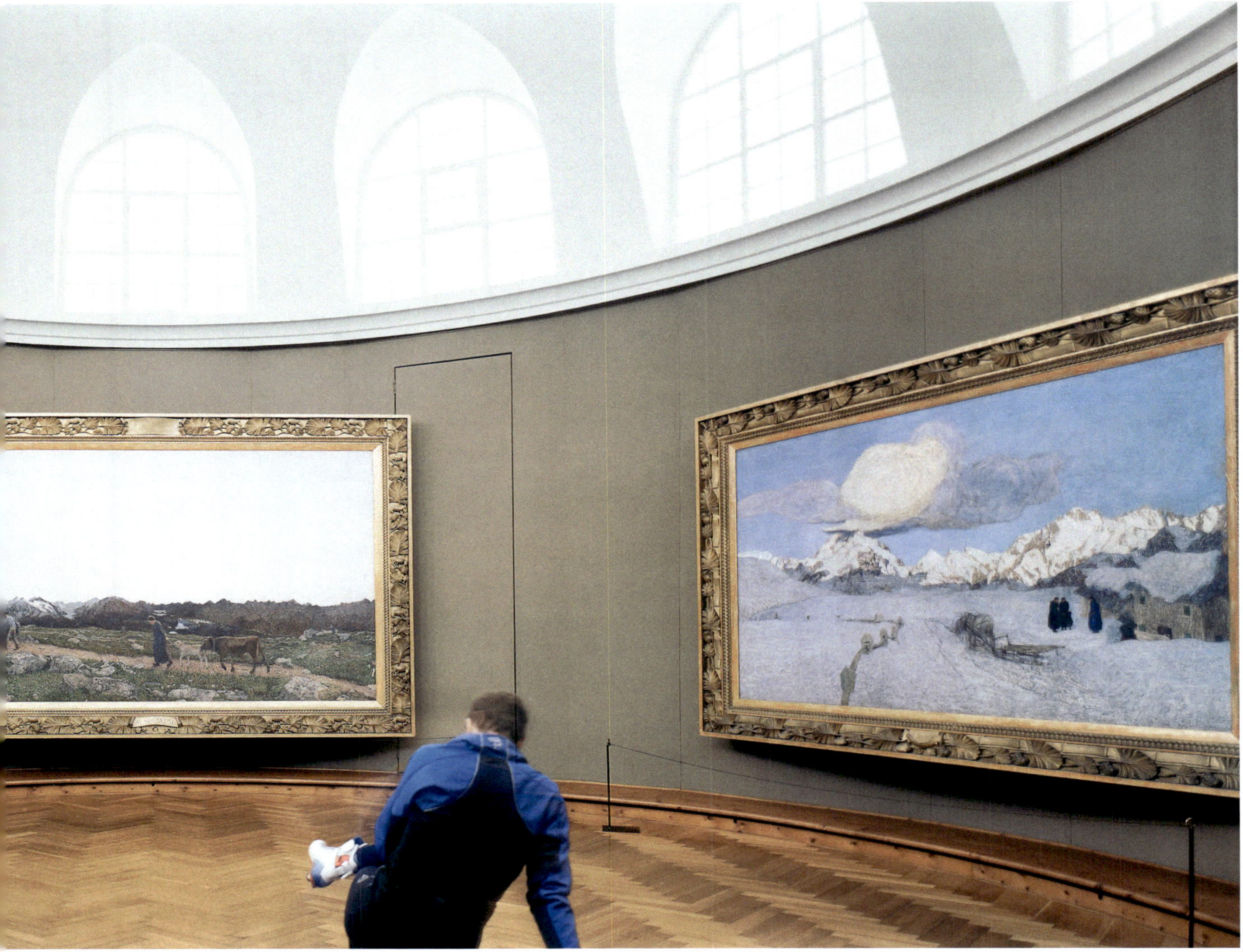

The outside is always an artifact we construct, the architecture in a zoo or in a theater, or inside a house in the middle of the Alps. So you look at the Alps by looking at a cliché, a painting or a scale model of the Alps. It is very difficult, however, to photograph the way in which clichés themselves are produced. What is the screen? What is the boundary between the inside and the outside?

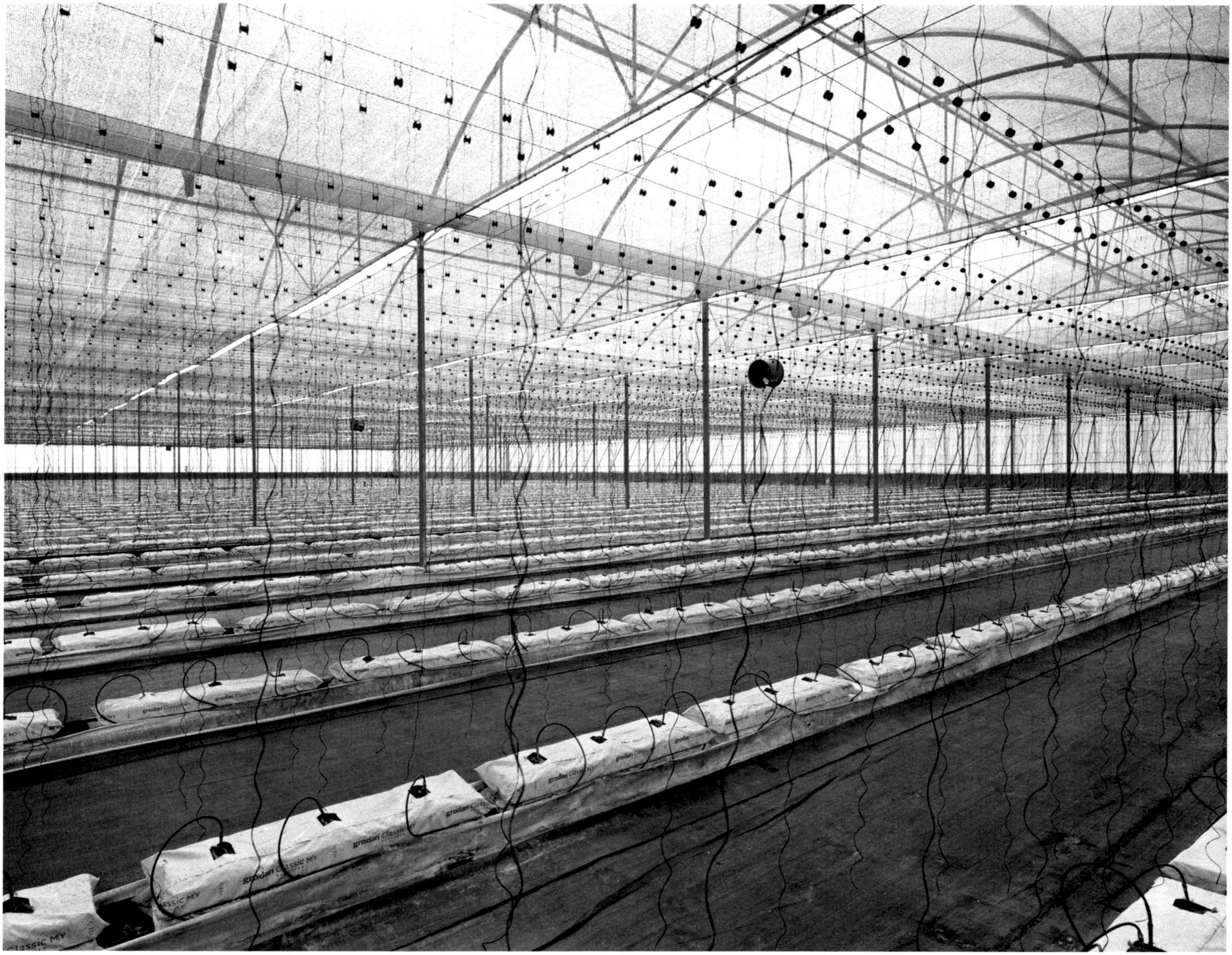

Intensive agriculture in the El Ejido area produces vegetables for most of Europe, throughout the year. This greenhouse covers a ground space of about 0.5 km^2. An English supermarket company rents the greenhouse and ships young tomato plants from Britain to Spain, where they are grown and harvested, and then shipped back to the British chain.

These are two interesting cases of an artificial inversion of the inside/outside. These tomatoes on hydroponic soil—meaning soil without soil—are inside a completely artificial glasshouse. This is one way of envisioning the future of soil.

Greenhouse, El Ejido, Spain, 2013

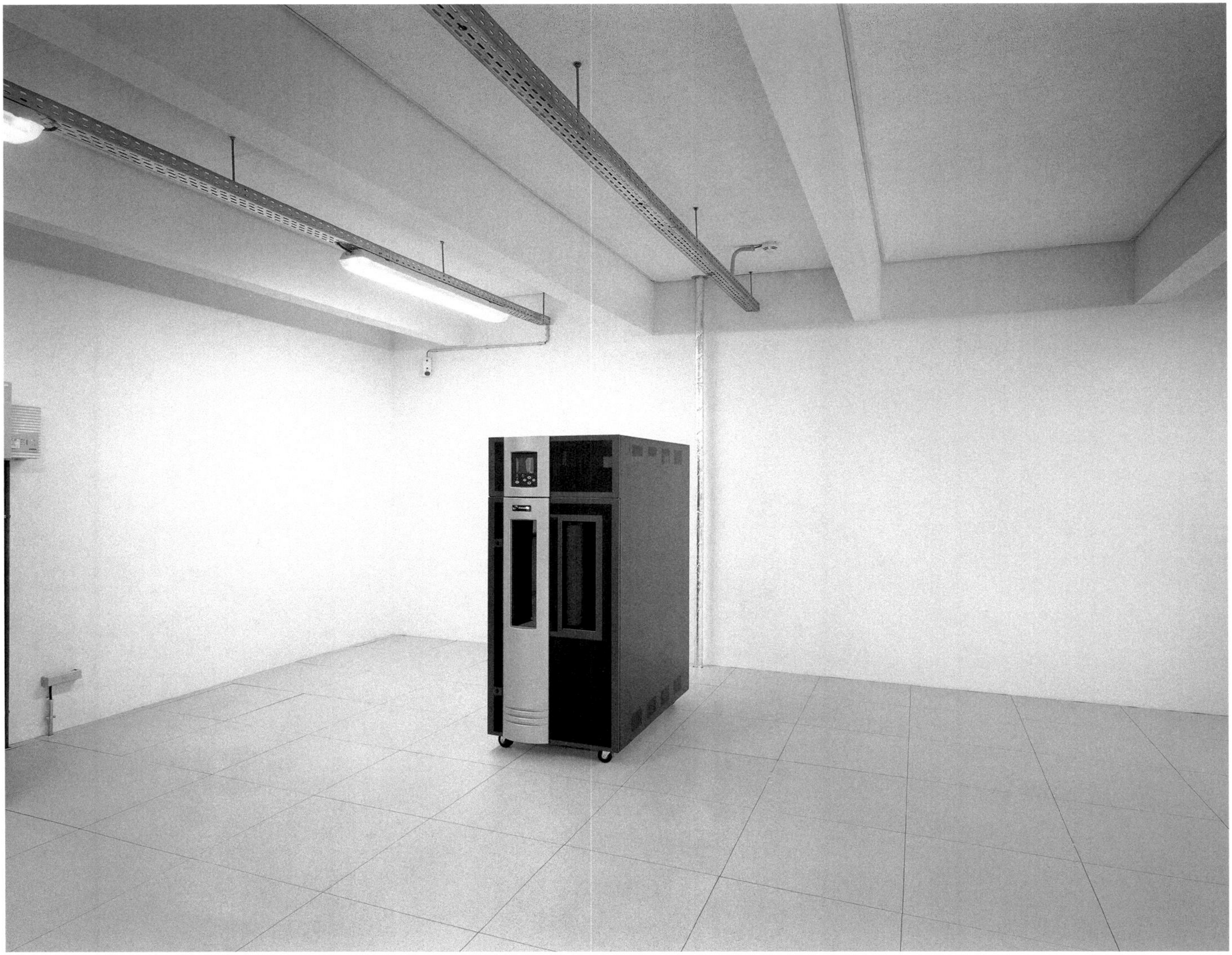

The case of the center for climate modeling in Hamburg is mediated by a more important, harder science. This place is doubly paradoxical because the climate of the whole Earth is calculated in this room. This would be the first inversion of inside out.

DKRZ, German Climate Computing Center, archives, Hamburg, Germany, 2013

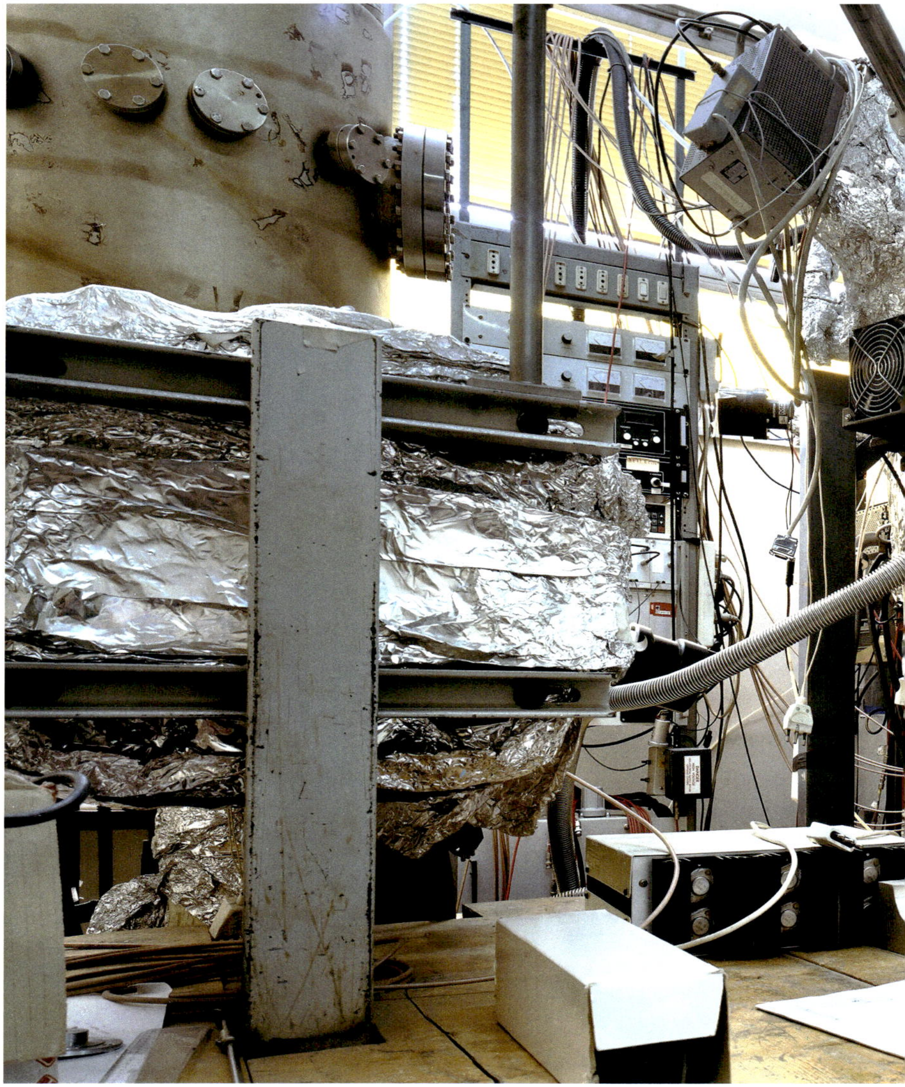

Italian Climate Observatory Ottavio Vittori, lab, Monte Cimone,
Italy, 2006

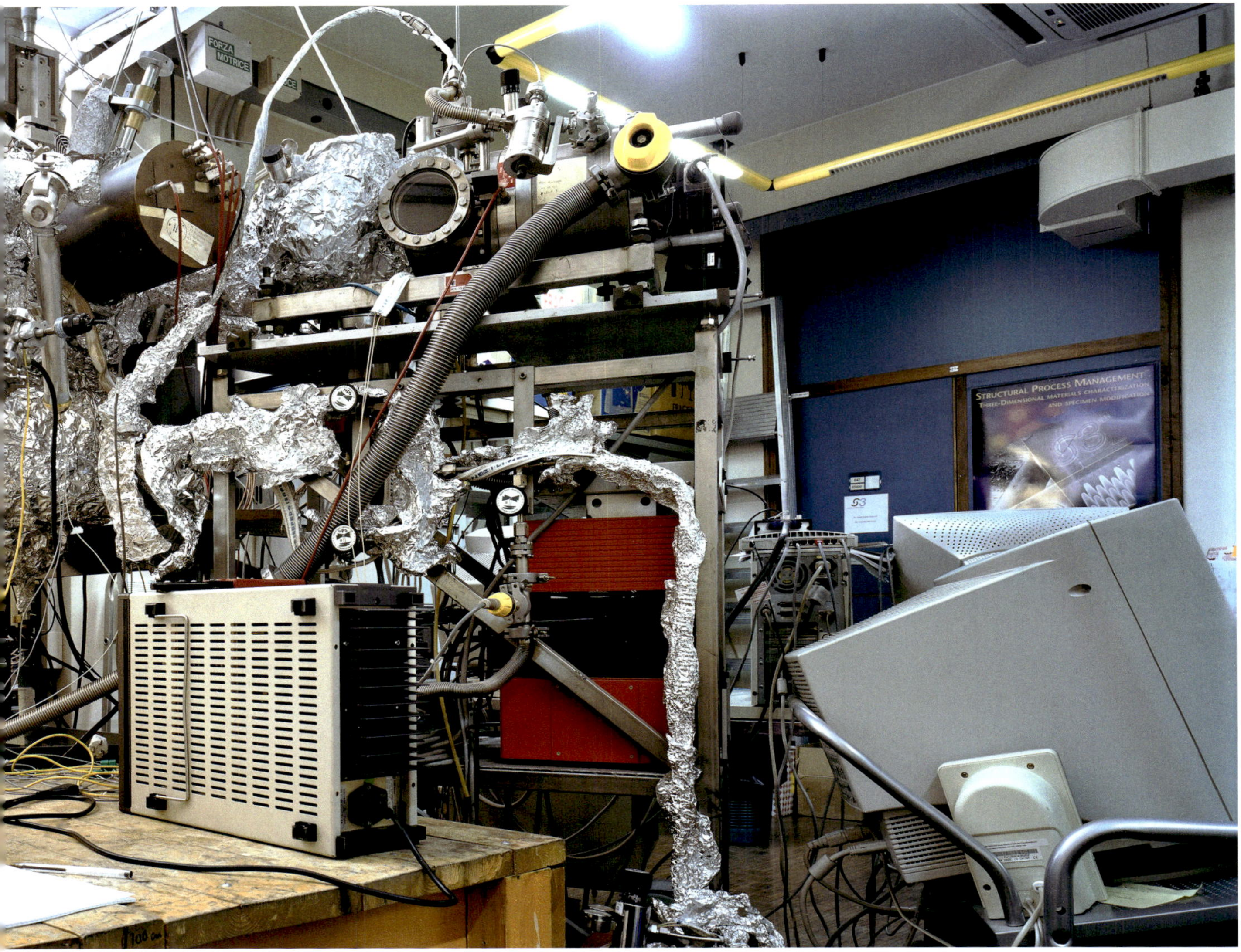

It is another way of explaining the extent to which we live in an artificial space. This is not necessarily bad. It only means that it is difficult to detect all the different ways we cover up the boundaries between the inside and the outside.

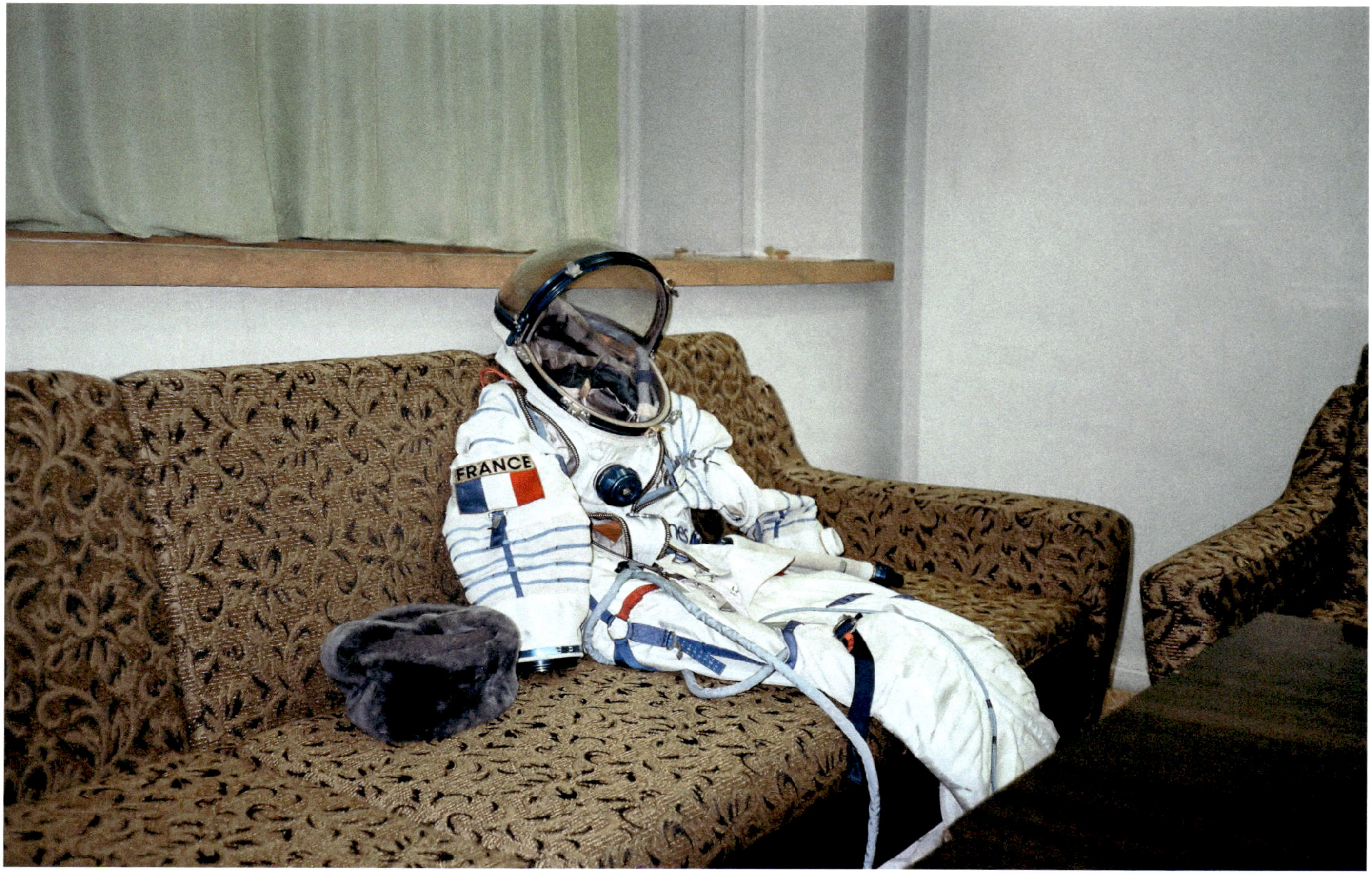

We are never really outside. If we were to really be outside, we would be lost entirely, like someone out in space without a spacesuit. It is very difficult to document how we move from an inside to an outside.

Star City, Cosmonaut Training Center, Moscow, Russia, 1998

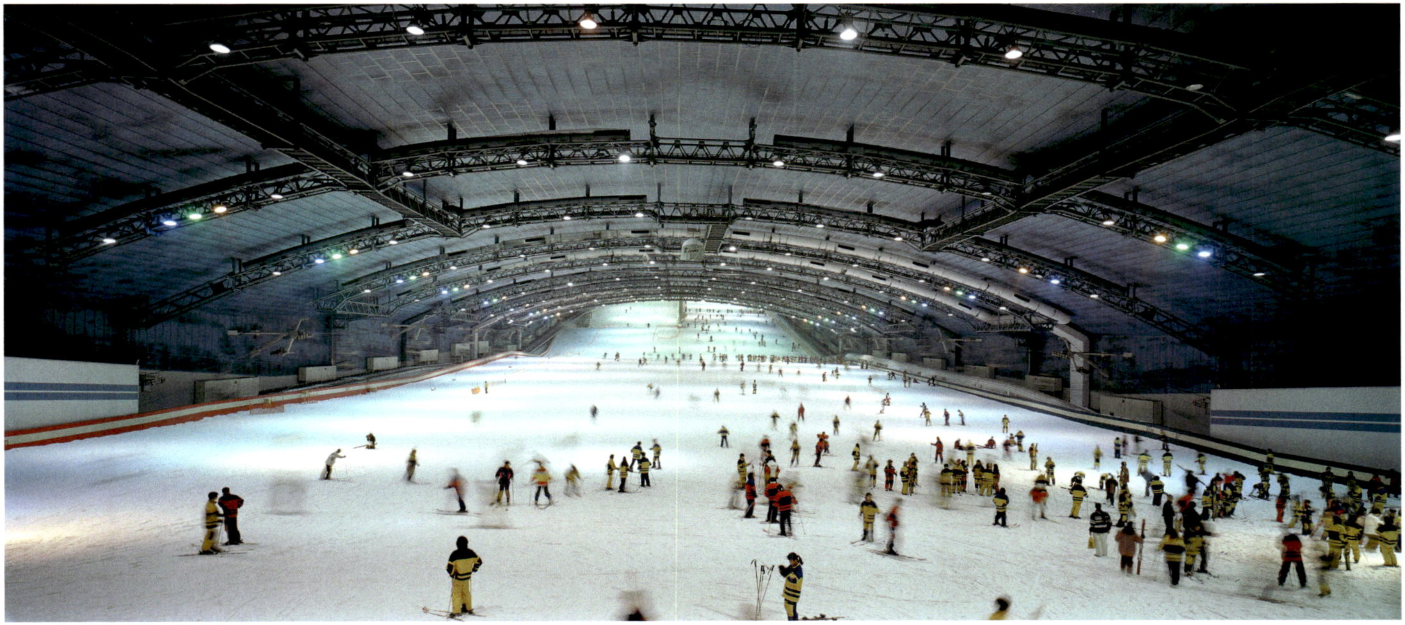

The SSAWS (Spring, Summer, Autumn, Winter Skiing) Dome was the world's biggest indoor downhill-ski arena. It was demolished in 2002 to make space for the first IKEA in Japan.

In order to let you sense how a cliché itself is produced, the photographer must place the aesthetic of the camera at the boundary between the inside and the outside.

Ski Dome, Tokyo, Japan, 1998

The essential difference between the different types of value meters is not easy to detect because what could be more similar than a desk with a computer screen than another desk with another computer screen? These sites are simultaneously banal, ubiquitous, and rarely documented.

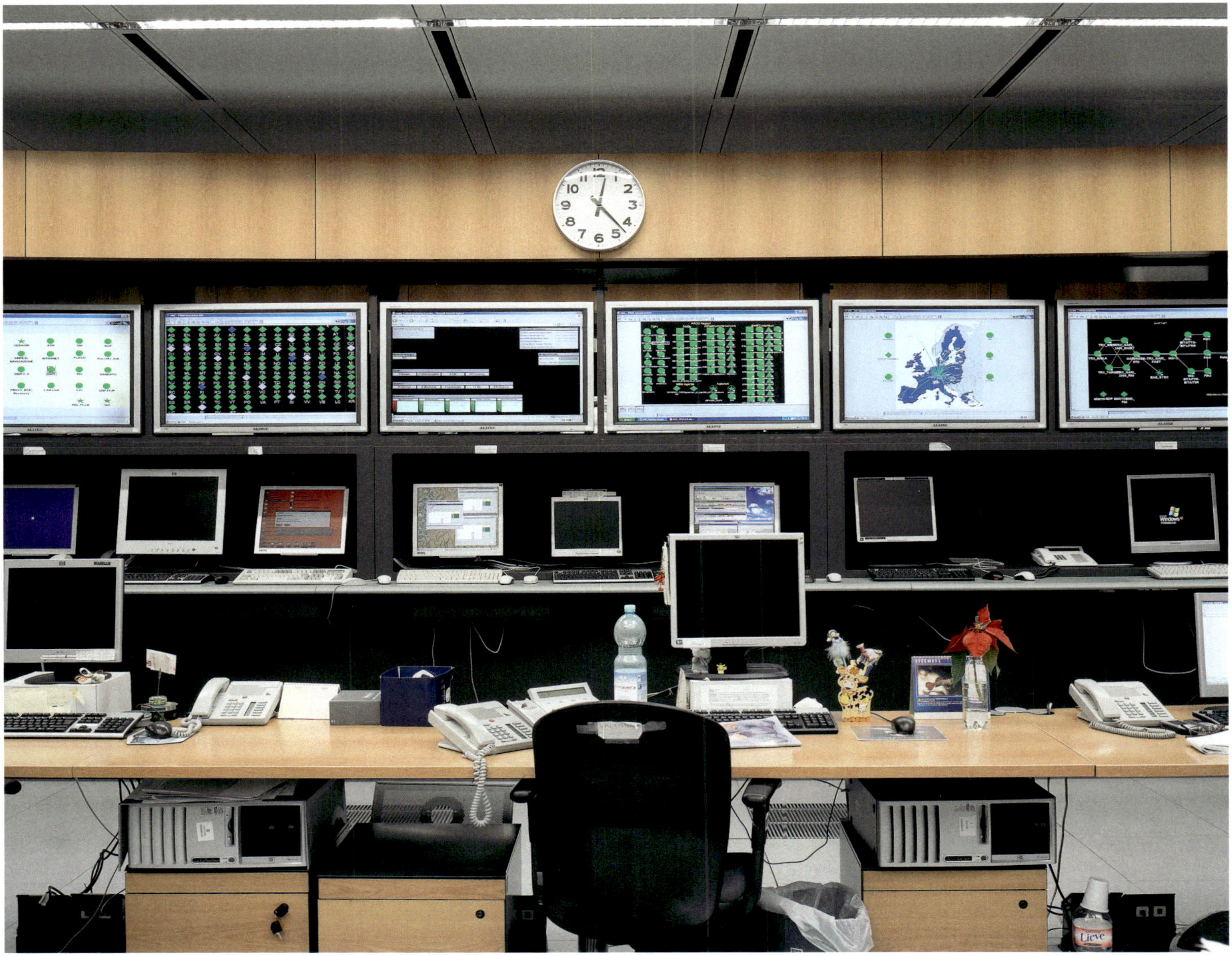

Bank of Italy, Donato Menichella Center, the TARGET2 European inter-banking system room, Frascati (RM), Italy, 2007

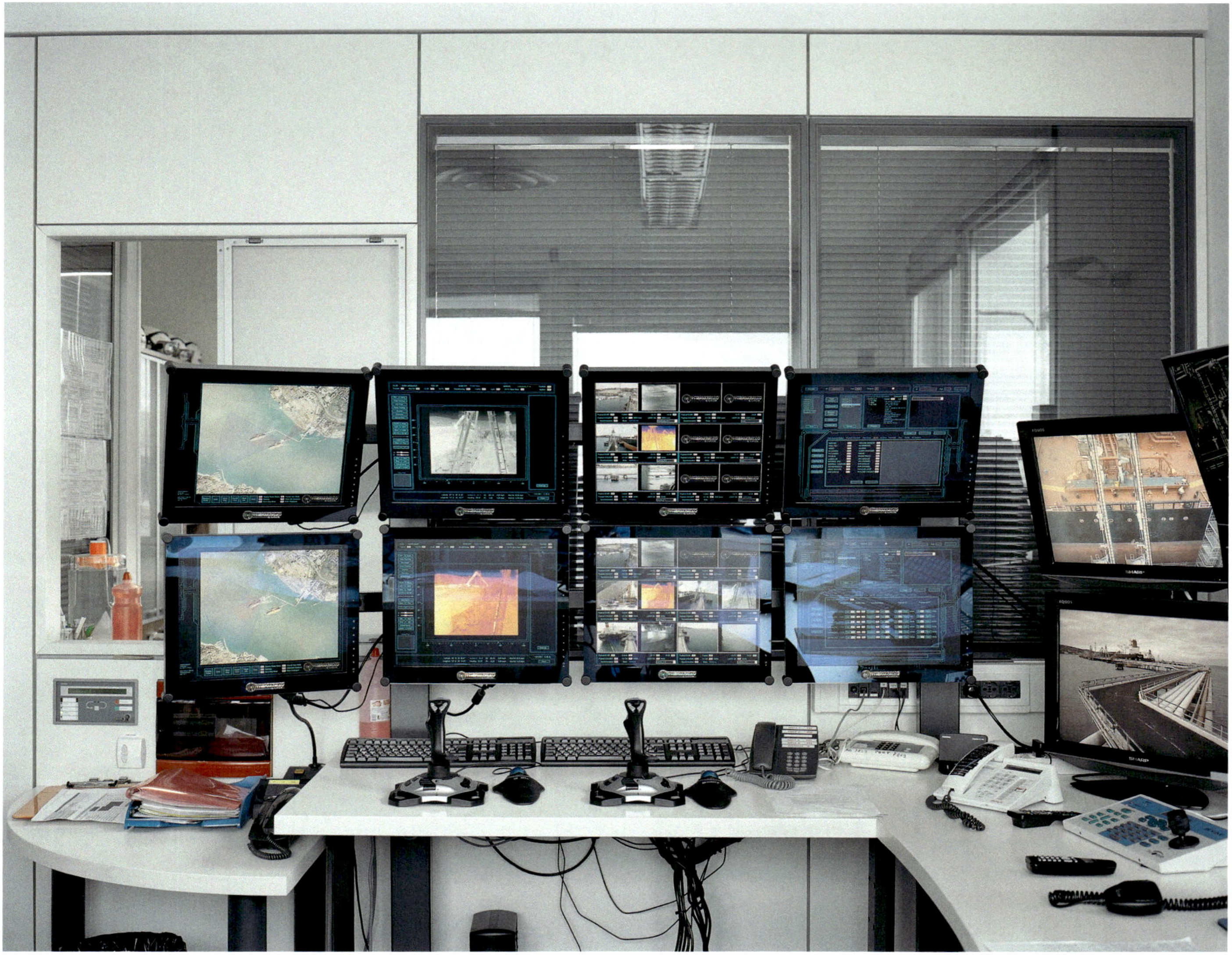

What they all have in common is that they are inside closed rooms and arranged so as to make it possible to see something that is outside of them to which they are linked by two-way connections, with the omnipresent screens making these connections visible.

TAL Group Transalpine Pipeline, oil tanker port, control room,
Trieste, Italy, 2012

“Oligoptica” is a way of capturing this mixture of blindness (isolated operators in closed rooms who see nothing) and vision (through the connections they see a tiny spectrum of data very clearly). Some of these rooms are two-way rooms: that is, not only do they receive information through sensors, they may also act in return by pushing buttons (actuators) or by sending alarms or signals of some sort.

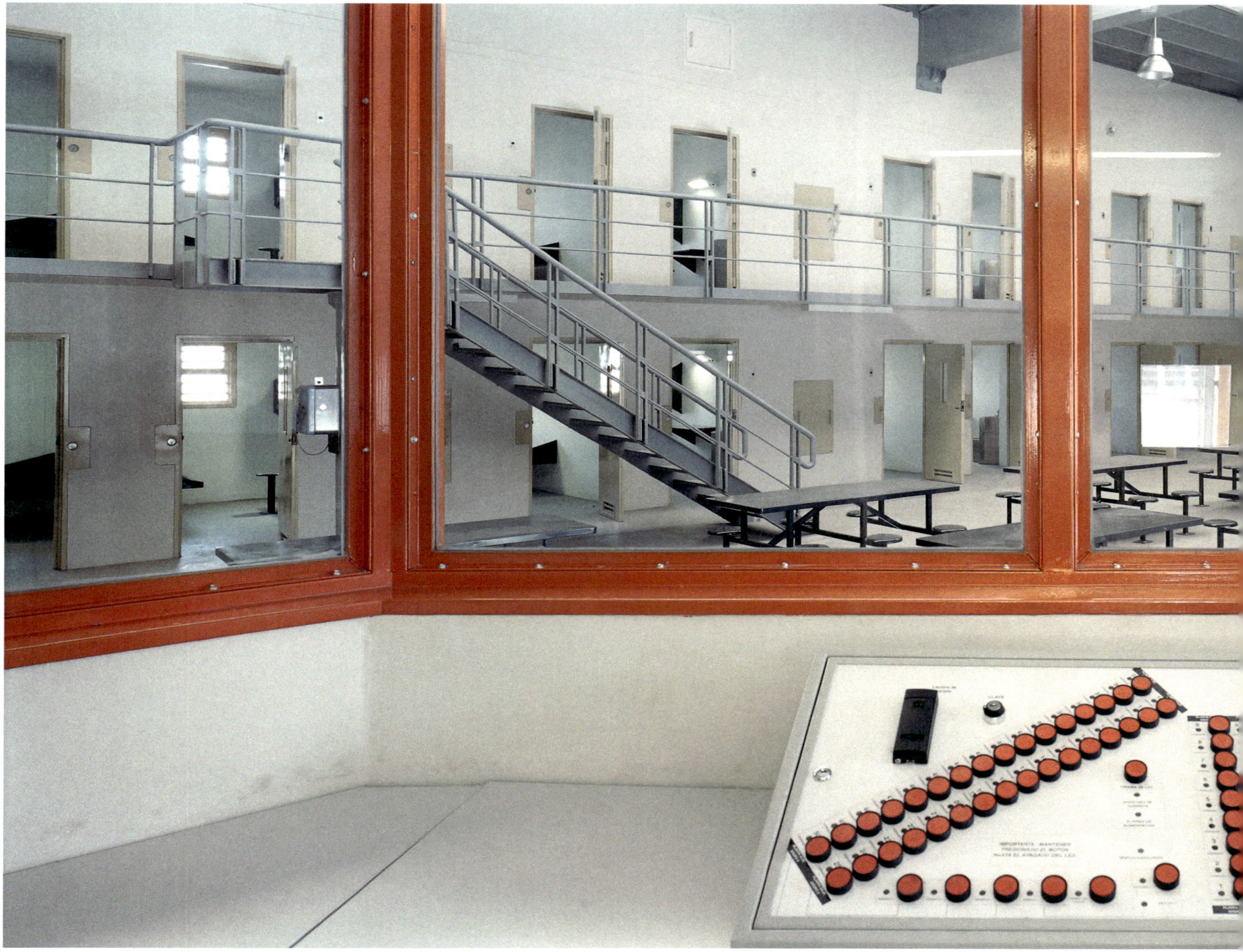

This electromechanical interface controls access to the common area of one of the Ezeiza Penitentiary buildings. Enclosed in the secure booth, the guard has no contact with the inmates. The triangular button layout on the interface echoes the architecture of the prison complex: triangular buildings are positioned around the triangular outdoor area. An industrial group specializing in major infrastructure construction designed, built, and equipped the prison complex, and is now leasing it to the Argentinian government.

Here, we are clearly in what Michel Foucault would have called a panopticon, that is, a visual device invented for prisons in the eighteenth century and almost exactly replicated here in the design of the control room.

Ezeiza Penitentiary, Buenos Aires, Argentina, 1999

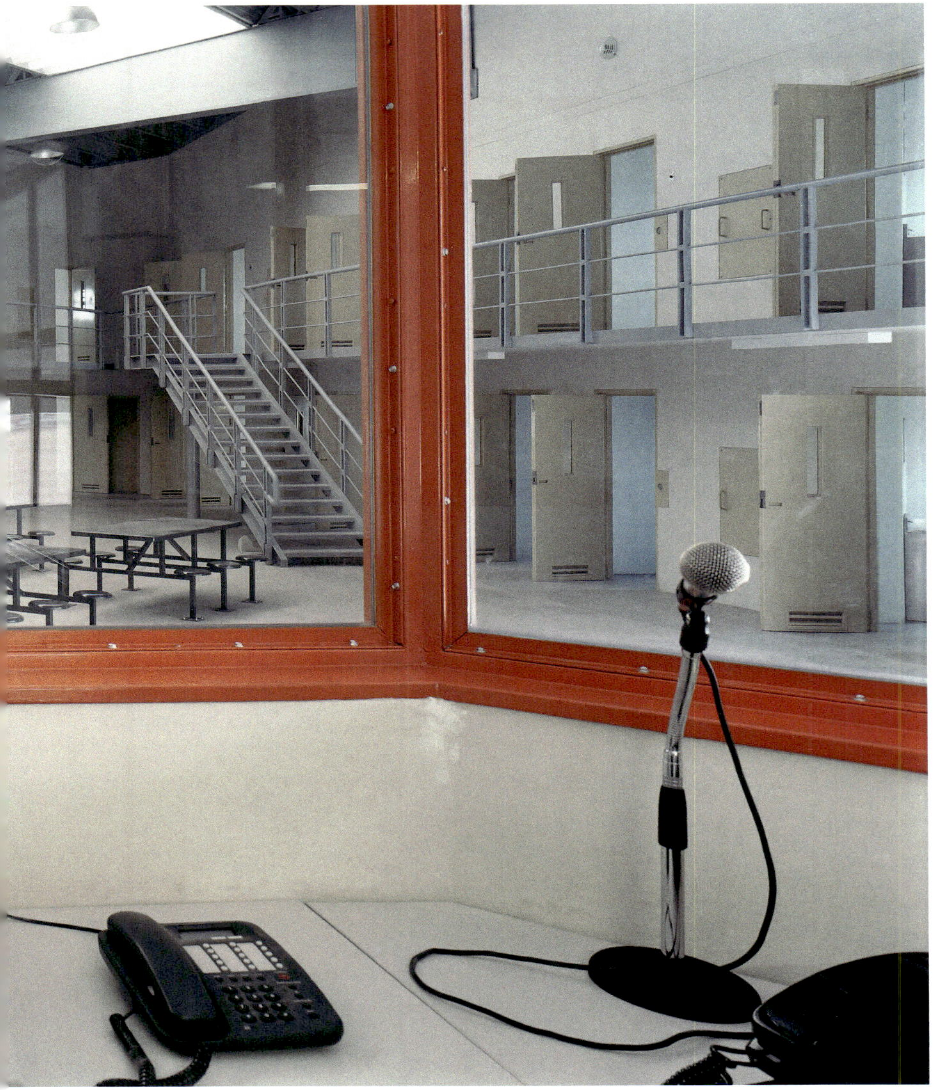

A single guard, protected by a glass wall, oversees the opening and closing of cells. Surveillance gives a commensurable element to the lives of prisoners in this high-tech and probably very depressing prison.

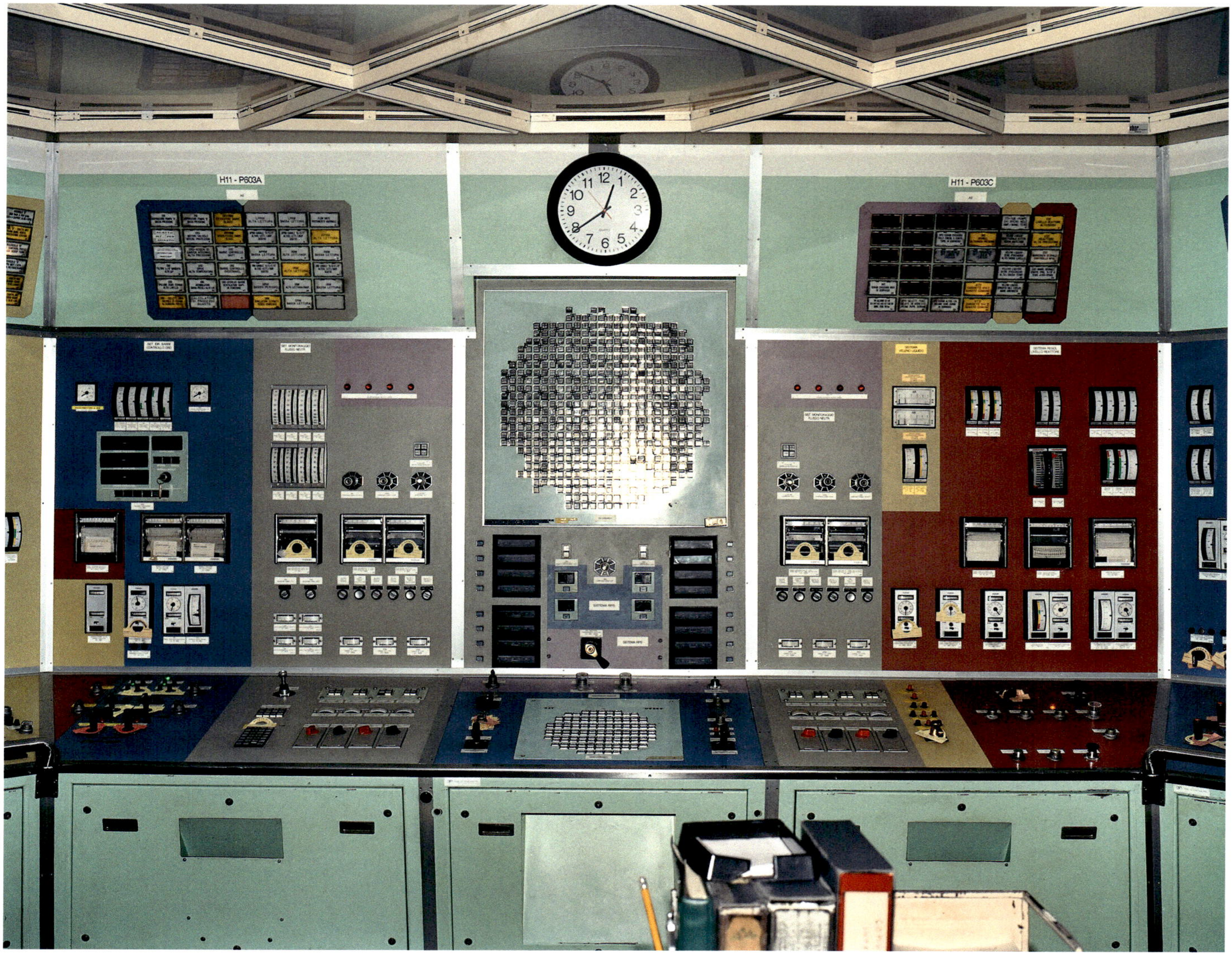

After the Chernobyl disaster in 1986, Italy decided in a public referendum to stop using nuclear power. Opened in 1982, the power plant depicted in this image is the same model as the US Three Mile Island power plant, the setting of a serious meltdown in 1979. This prompted the introduction of a color scheme for control interfaces.

Control rooms of nuclear plants are the most advanced type of ergonomical device. This time, control is not exerted on humans but on non-human agencies.

The disused Caorso Nuclear Power Plant, control panel, Caorso (PC), Italy, 2007

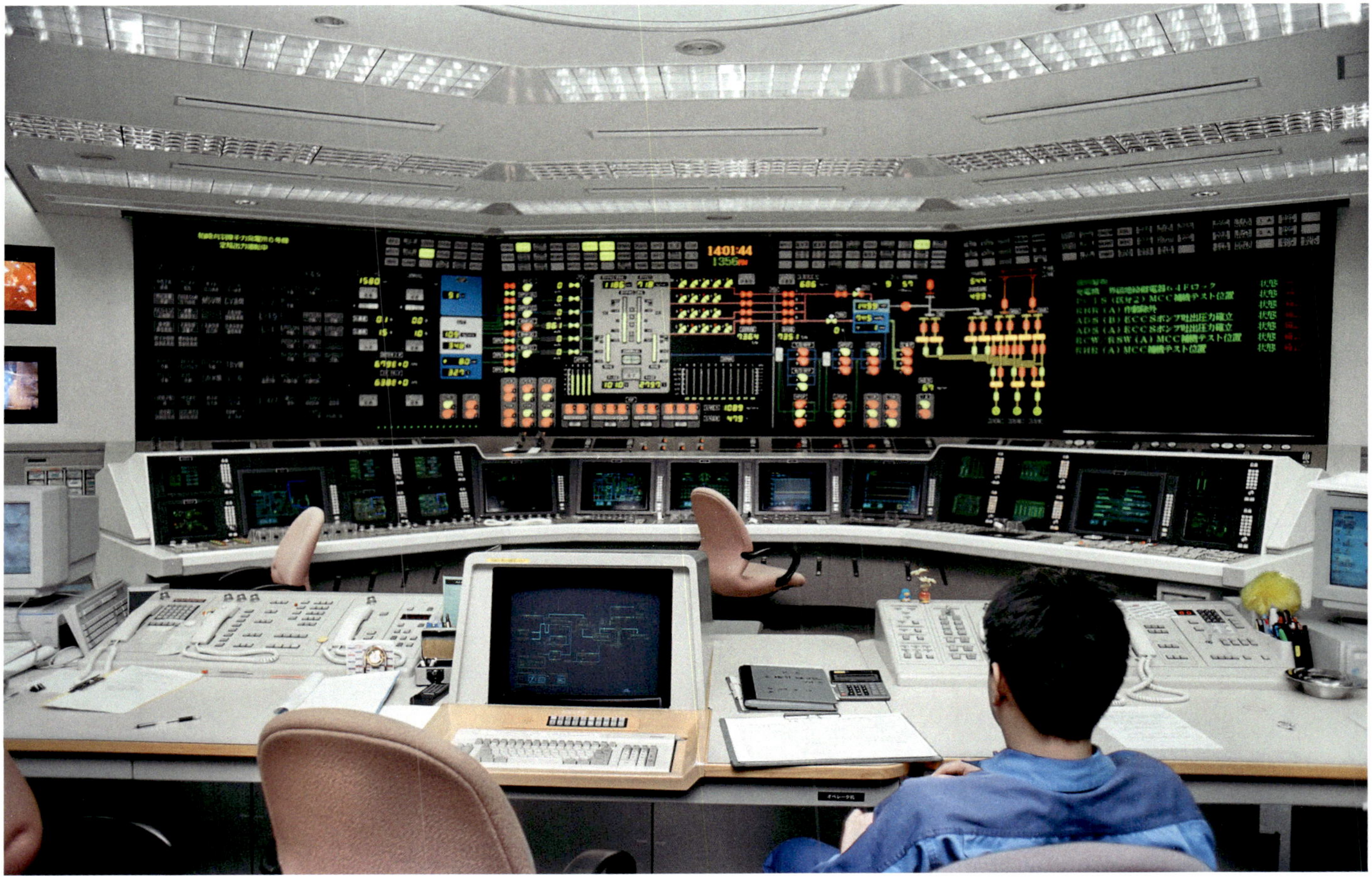

It is in such rooms that all of the feedback loops of the complex plants end up and have to be assessed by a human brain, a highly skilled operator who has had to learn the routine reactions through continuous drills. The whole process is built up so that there is as little new information as possible injected into it. And yet the operator should remain alert, but alert to a totally routine set of formats. A cognitive puzzle for ergonomists.

Kashiwazaki-Kariwa Nuclear Power Station, control room, Kashiwazaki, Japan, 1998

At Mount Etna, the physical phenomena to be monitored are not man-made and are not susceptible to corrective actions through any sort of actuator (for instance, shutting down or increasing the level of volcanic activity). It is a control room with half of the feedback loop: sensors sending information to one single *oligopticon*. The real difference compared to the other images is that this “monitoring station” is established so as to detect the abnormal.

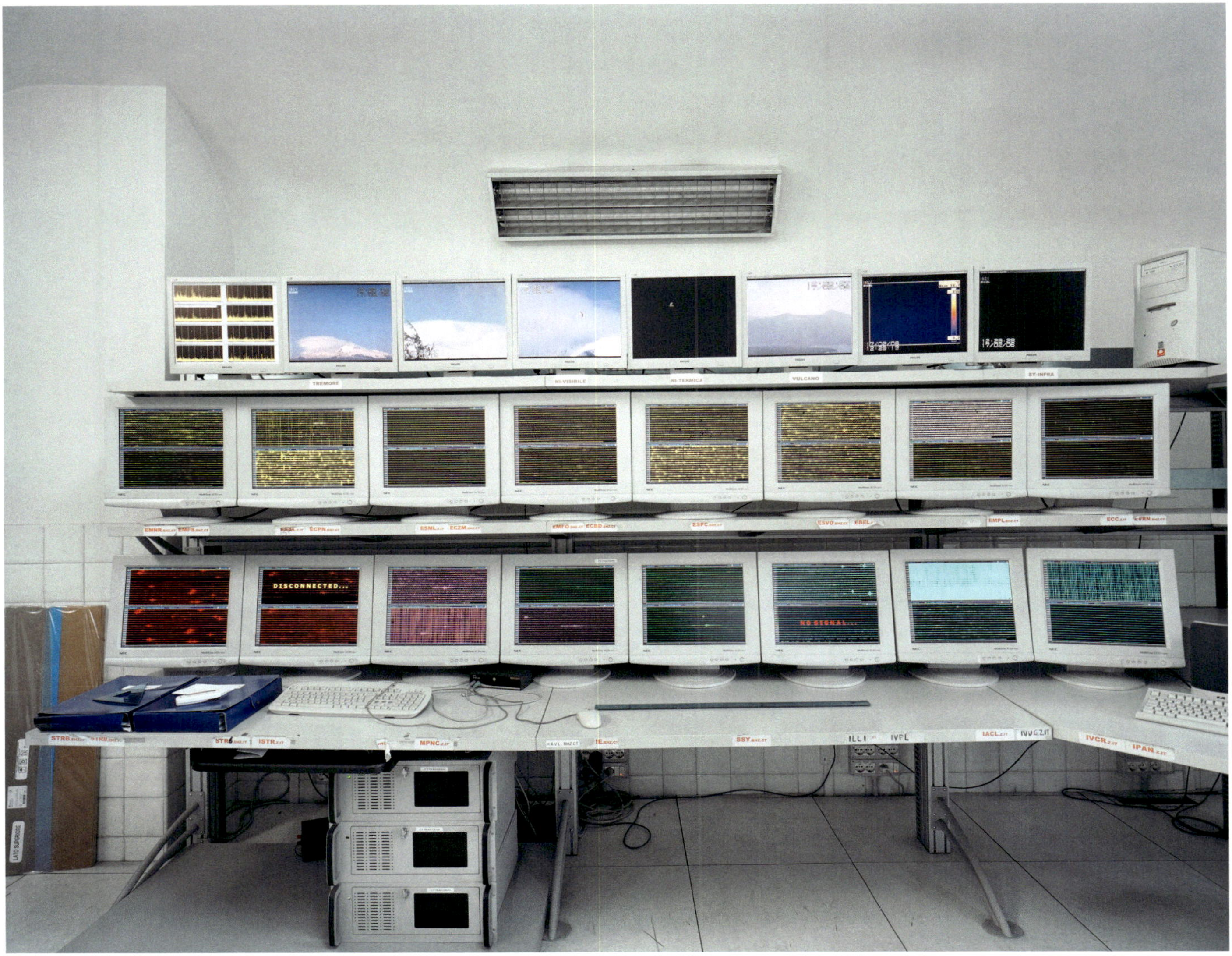

Several sets of video cameras, GPS and seismic detectors, UV scanners, gas correlation spectrometers, and other data collectors installed in different areas of the Etna crater region allow seismologists to remotely monitor volcanic activity.

Etna Observatory, National Institute of Geophysics and Volcanology, monitoring room, Catania, Italy, 2006

The reaction of the operator, meanwhile, is totally unformatted. It is these sources of uncertainty about what is to be detected and what we should do that make this monitoring station closer to an instrument.

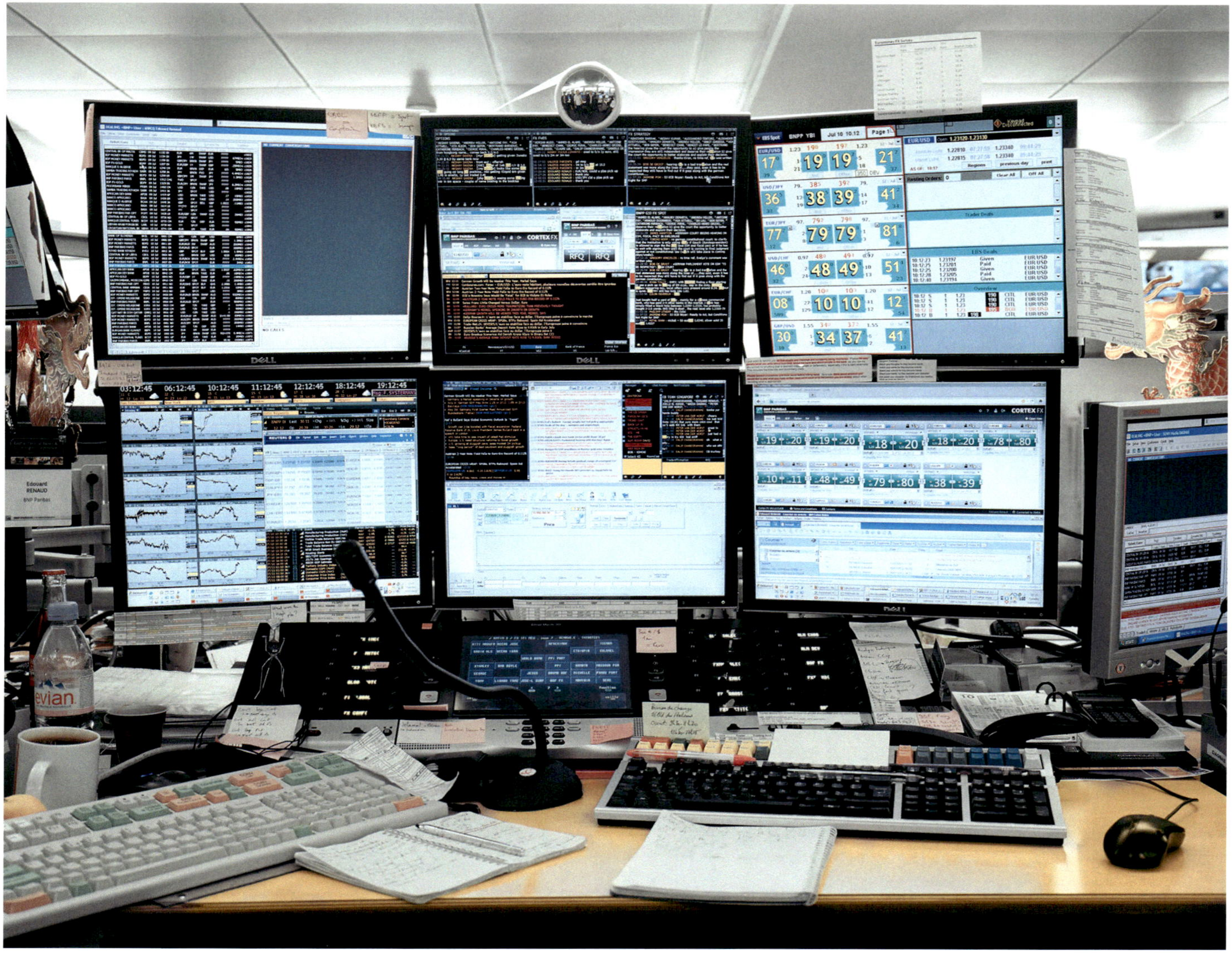

Up to 150 people operate from the foreign exchange and investment desk in the BNP Paribas Trading Room. Each operator multitasks by participating in four different data transmission layers: information from external agencies, information from the internal system, information exchanged with colleagues in other desks around the world, and information exchanged with colleagues in the same room. Different sound signals and alarms orientate operators through the screens, highlighting and directing specific procedures.

Traders work with this amazing mass of instruments, measuring something that is not quite objective: values. In an entirely quantified world, quantification is the product of these instruments.

The set of entities that are to be surveyed is not fixed and requires very fast actions from the operator. The bulk of the screens give instant information about other agents around the world who are equipped in exactly the same way as this one. So every time they act, it shows up on the screen and vice versa. This is where the difference lies between "performativity," as it is understood in the social studies of finance and economics, and the formatting that goes on in all scientific apparatuses.

We do not live in a society but in a collective. If we are in a collective, it is because we collect things. A major aspect of the history of our so-called modern world, especially the scientific modern world, is our invention of collections. Why?

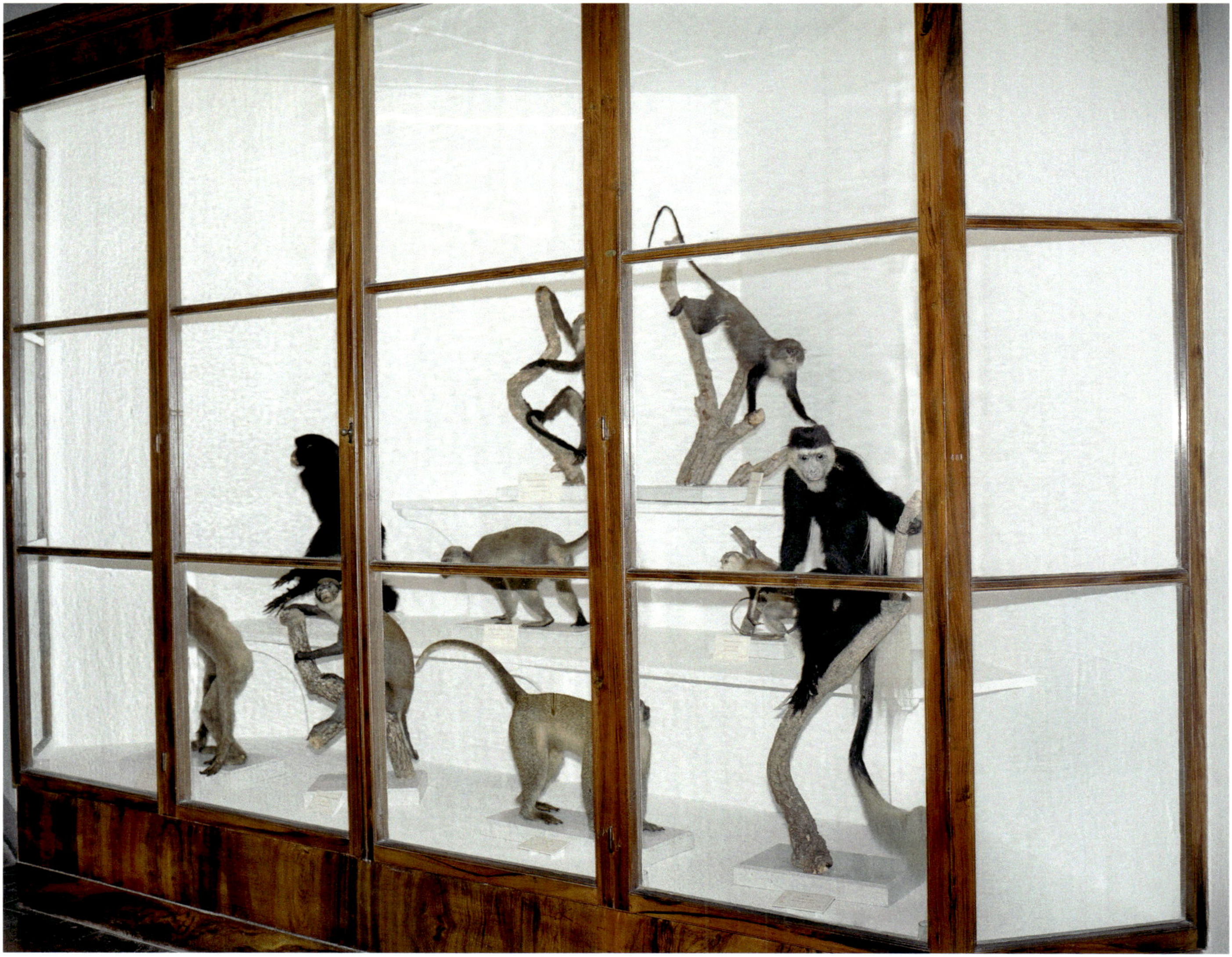

When you build up a collection, you survey a lot of elements simultaneously, and you can make a lot of comparisons. Analogism is defined as the relation between the parts and the whole so that any relation in one part is seen as one example of another relation in another part. It is a powerful way of ordering the world.

La Specola Museum of Zoology and Natural History, Florence, Italy, 2008

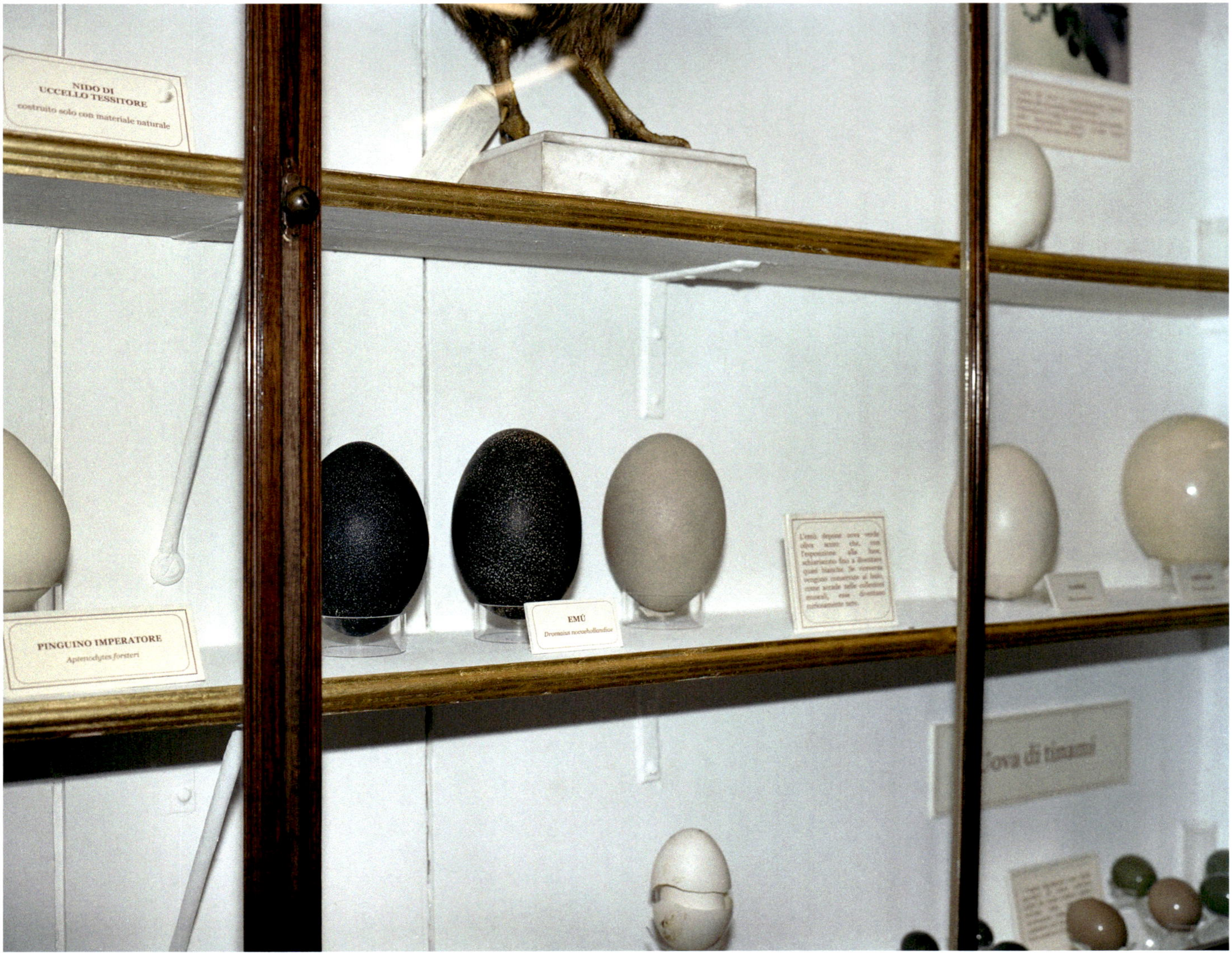

The Museum of Zoology and Natural History in Florence is an intermediary between a baroque definition of a collection and what is considered the modern, systematic way of separating the different genres such as nature, art, artifact—the Museum of History separated from the Museum of Science, technology separated from natural phenomena, and so on.

La Specola Museum of Zoology and Natural History, Florence, Italy, 2008

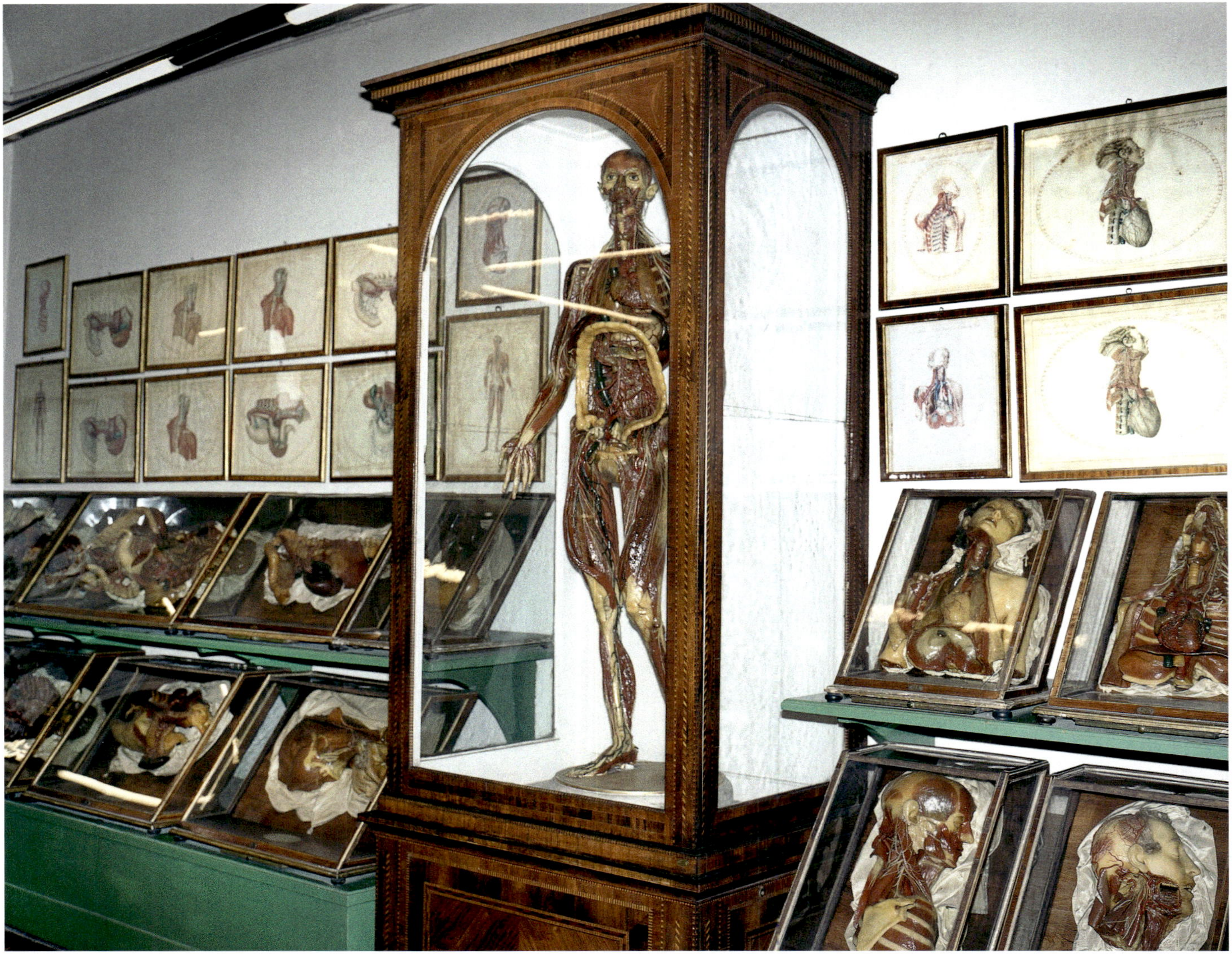

The museum's displays have barely changed since it opened to the public in 1775. It is renowned for its collection of anatomic waxes, produced in Florence between the seventeenth and nineteenth century, for medical and educational purposes. Under the pretext of science, it became possible to depict parts of the human body that could not have been shown publicly in the past.

La Specola Museum of Zoology and Natural History, Florence, Italy, 2008

There is a rich way of documenting how these different domains are simultaneously collected and made synoptically visible, first to the eye of the scientist or, in the old days, of the collector, and now of the visitor.

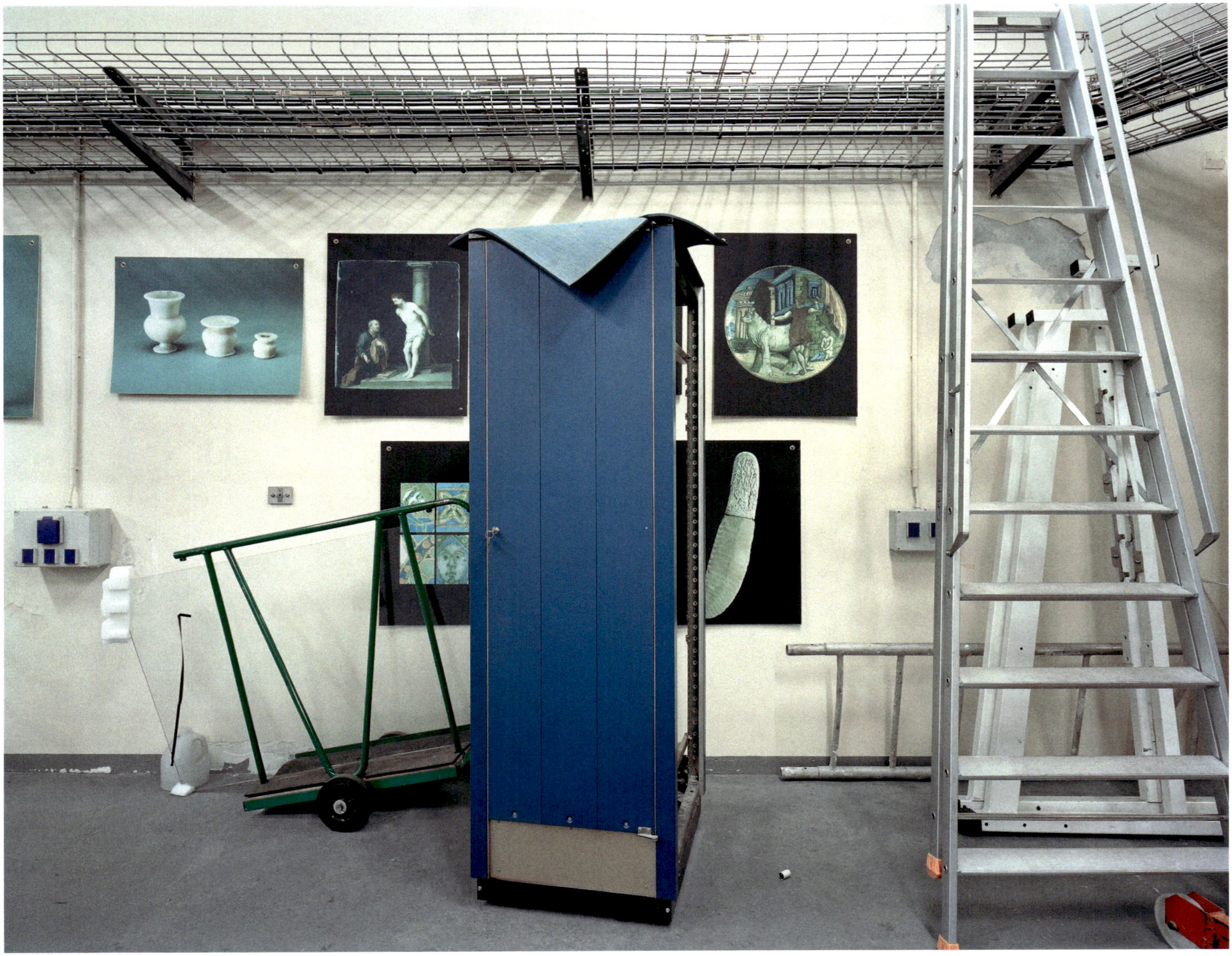

C2RMF, Center for Research and Restoration of the Museums of France, Paris, France, 2014

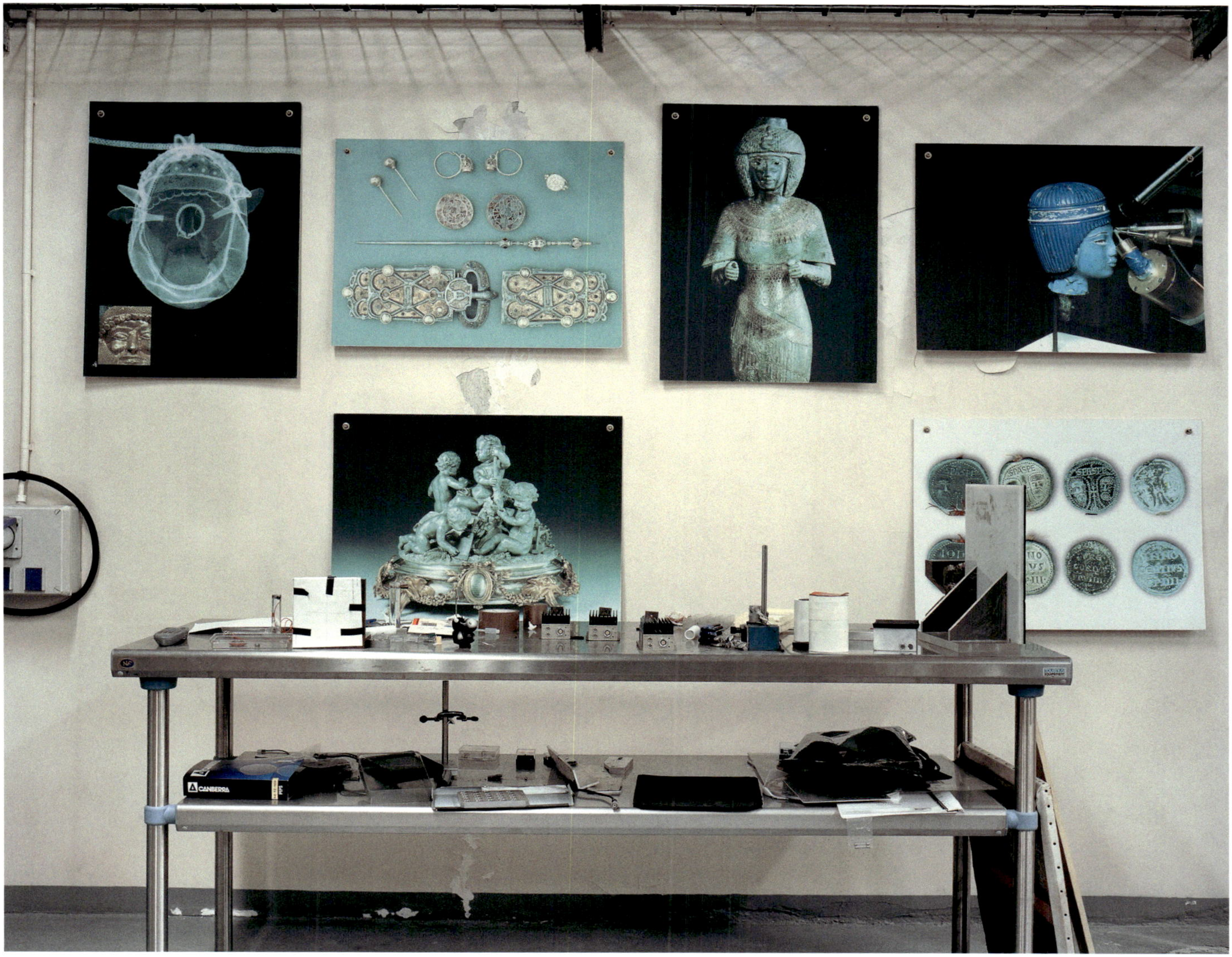

The image of Factum Arte in Madrid, however, shows a return to a baroque confusion of many different genres: an element of artifact, an element of nature, an element of art history, and an element of the new politics of art—all collected in the same place.

C2RMF, Center for Research and Restoration of the Museums of France, AGLAE particle accelerator laboratory, Paris, France, 2014

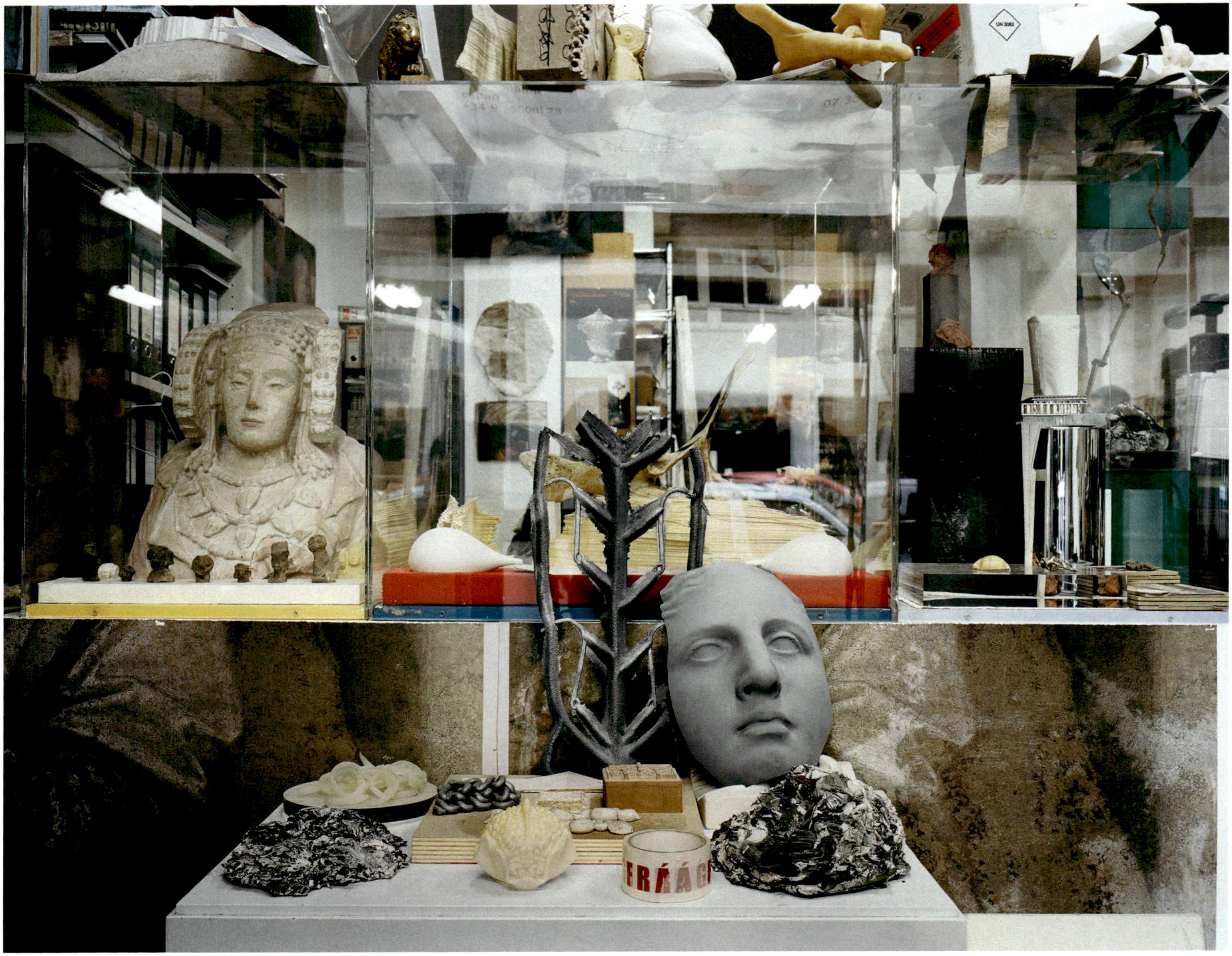

So there is a great interest in following how collections collect, how they disseminate, how they organize, how they actually remix things that were separate before. The fact of having all the projects in the same space allows many connections to be made. This is what collection really allows: by collecting elements, it allows people to "collect their thoughts."

Factum Arte workshops, Madrid, Spain, 2011

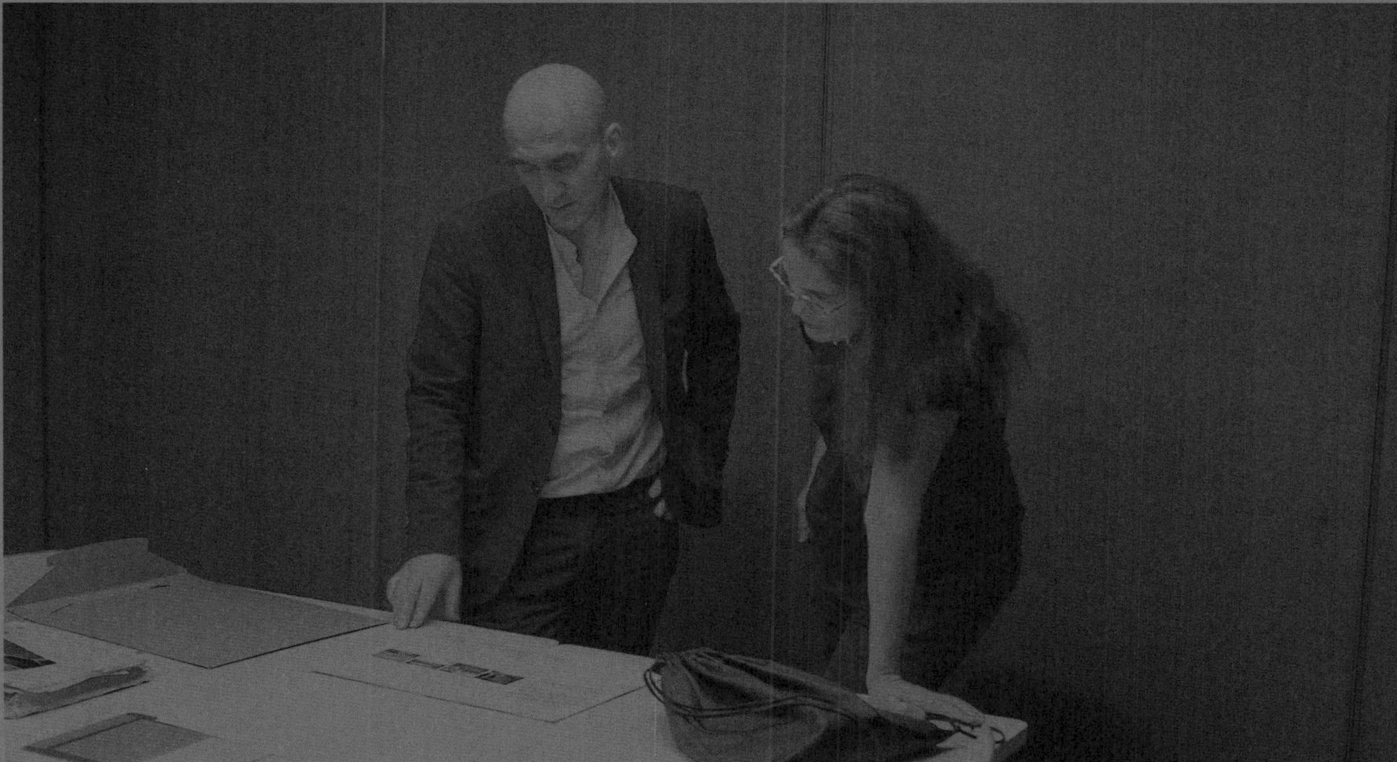

Ariella Azoulay

191–242

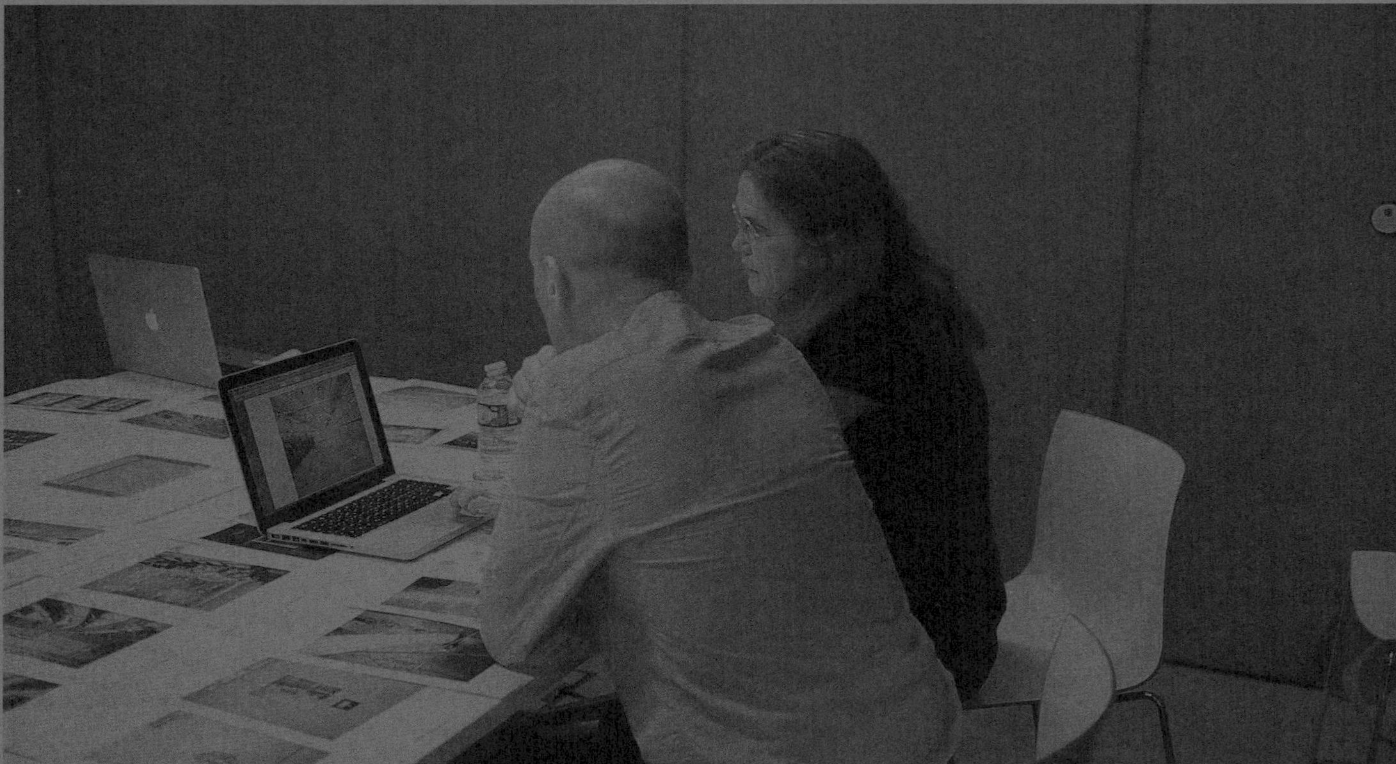

Ariella Azoulay and Armin Linke, Sciences Po library room,
Paris, June 2015

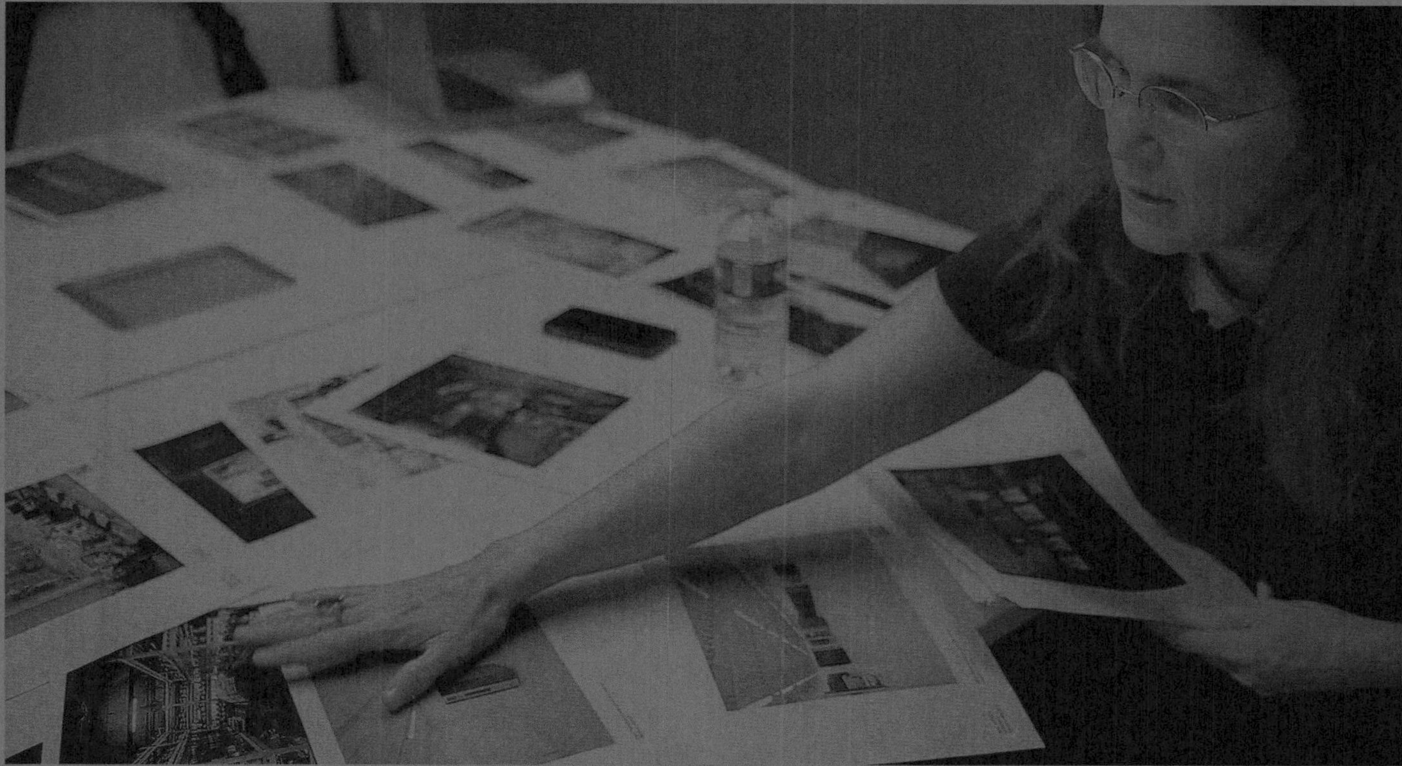

Ariella Azoulay and Armin Linke, Sciences Po library room,
Paris, June 2015

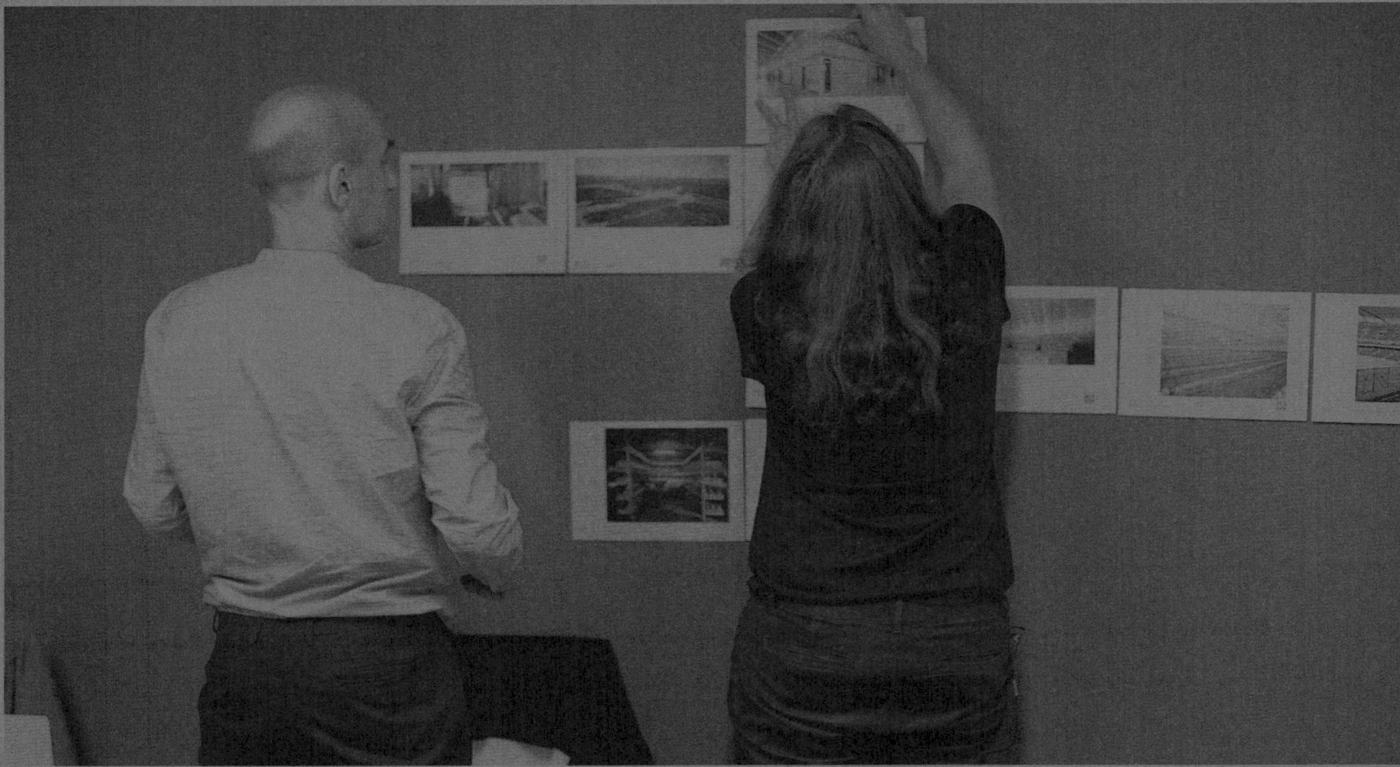

Ariella Azoulay and Armin Linke, Sciences Po library room,
Paris, June 2015

The imperial condition is encapsulated in these red, juicy, vertically growing tomatoes. Cost and benefit, efficiency, and fantasies of reducing risk through the creation of secure zones appear as common reasons for preferring walls of tomatoes to traditional horizontal farming. These arguments, however serious and accurate, are as groundless as the tomatoes—both grow on imperial soil. Their proximity intrigues me.

Our thinking and farming continue to be bounded by this imperial conception of progress and the belief that the outcome of our deeds is totally masterable and predictable. To that end, people should be eliminated. Hence, people are not absent from this photo because it is low season, but rather because they endanger the desired outcome. Besides their labor power, they have been made superfluous.

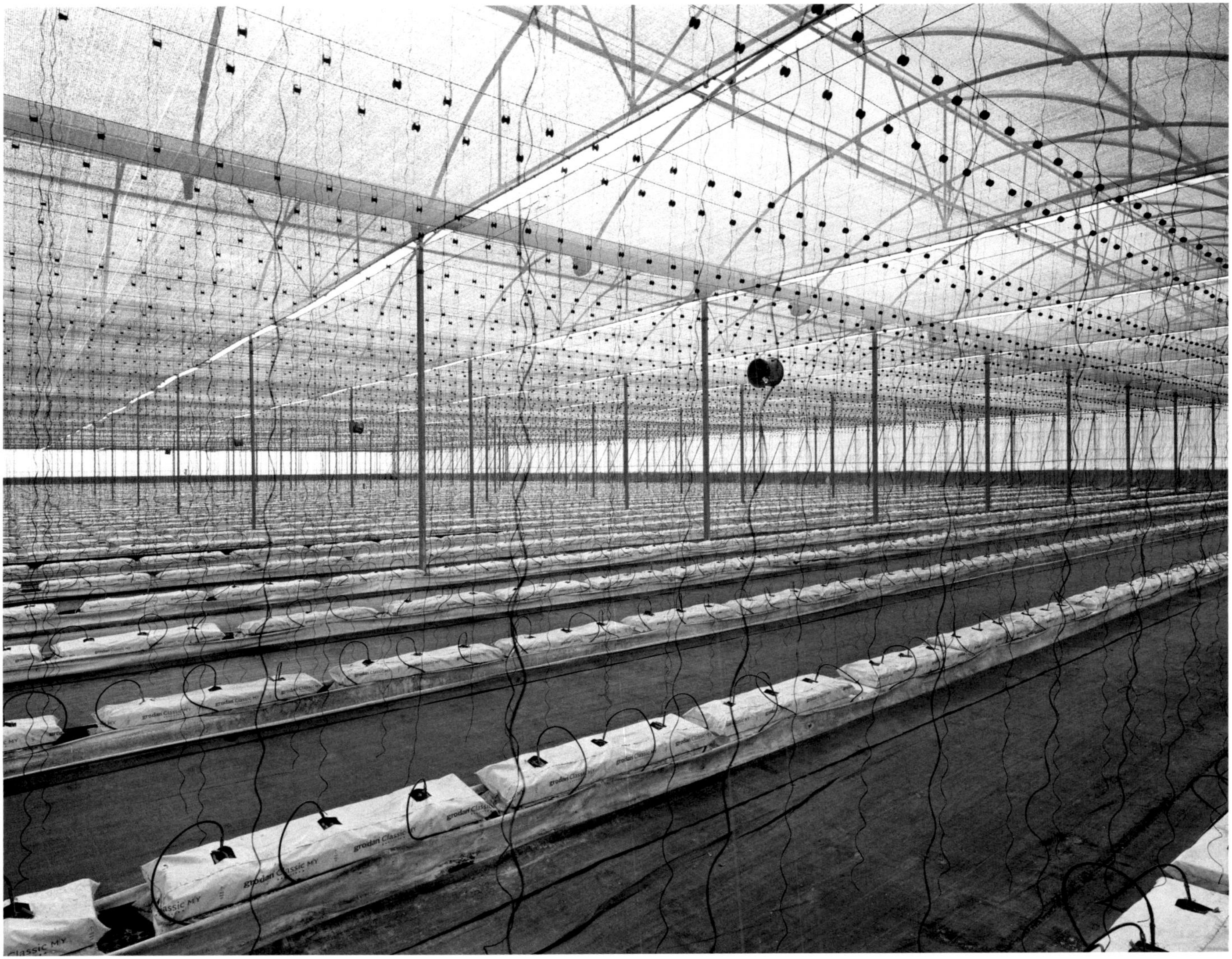

Intensive agriculture in the El Ejido area produces vegetables for most of Europe, throughout the year. This greenhouse covers a ground space of about 0.5 km^2. An English supermarket company rents the greenhouse and ships young tomato plants from Britain to Spain, where they are grown and harvested, and then shipped back to the British chain.

Originally, tomatoes grew in South America. With the Spanish occupation, they spread all over the world and quickly became as cherished on people's plates as sugar, cocoa, and coffee were in their cups.

Greenhouse, El Ejido, Spain, 2013

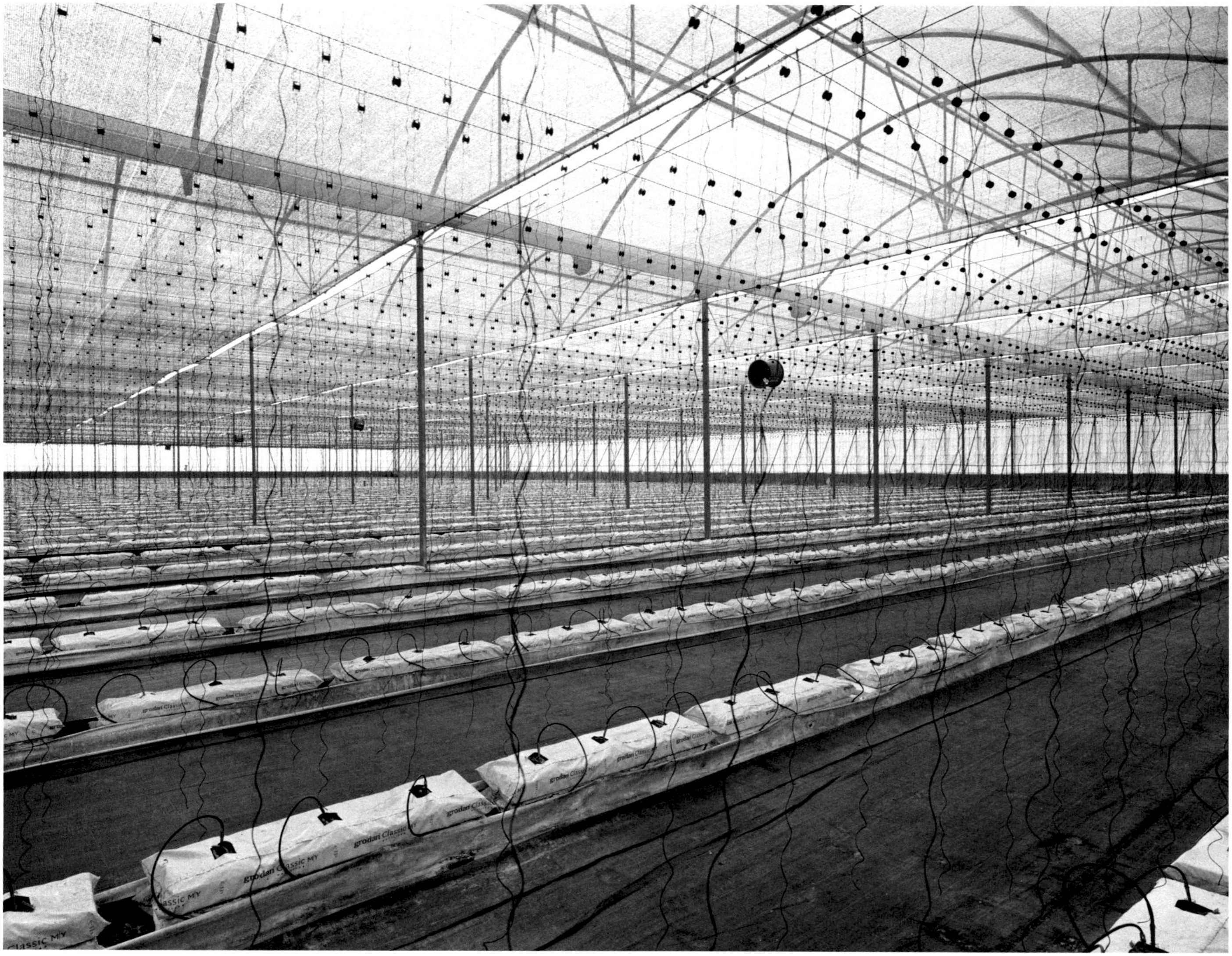

The best tomatoes my Jewish Israeli mouth had ever tasted came from occupied Gaza, in Palestine. One day these tomatoes disappeared from the market and were replaced by another species, better engineered. Today, the relatively decent wage they provided Gazans with is no more. Their glory may return one day with “peace,” perhaps in the form of walls of groundless tomatoes.

Greenhouse, El Ejido, Spain, 2013

In which imperial soil was this photo taken? Morocco? Southern Morocco? On the border? El Ejido, Spain, as the photograph was tagged? Was it in Western Sub-Saharan Africa, a place whose name is often accompanied by the title "the last colony in Africa," as if other places in the world are free of the imperial imprint. Thus the "economic miracle" El Ejido stands for was made possible through the labor of transparent immigrant workers without rights.

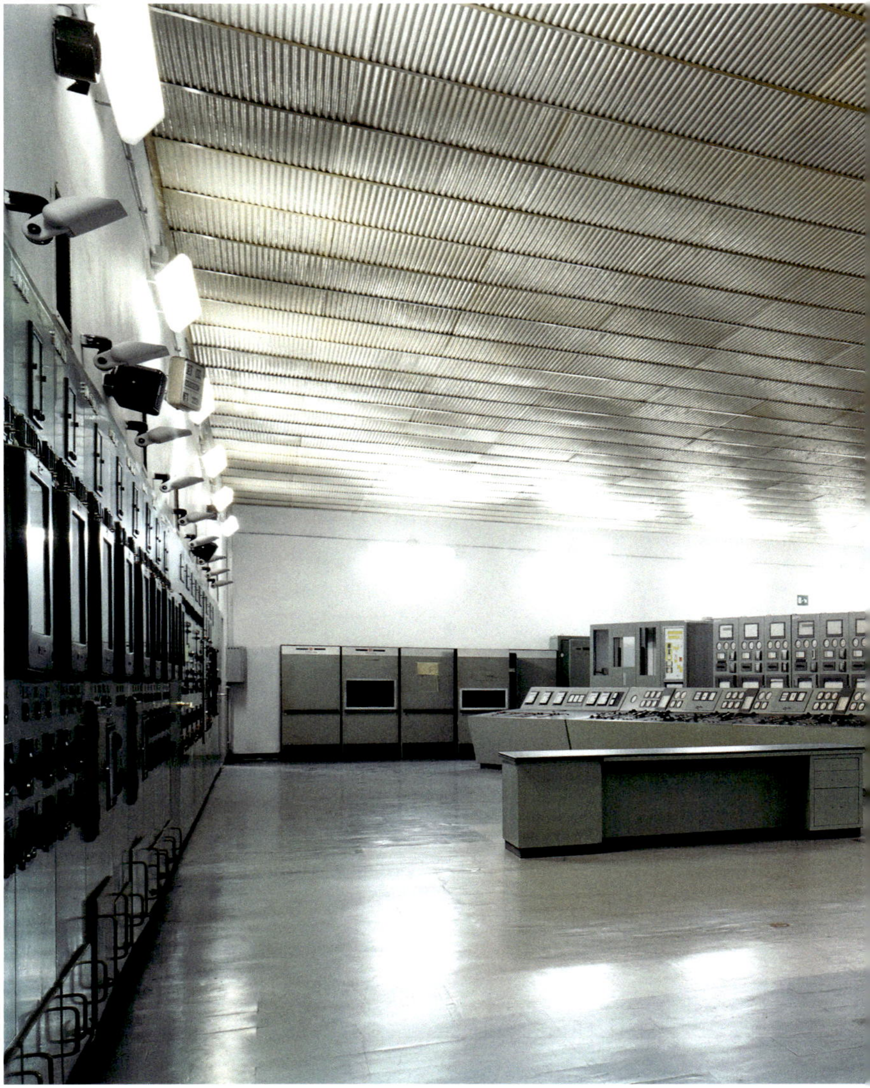

With the creation of the "New World" came the evacuation of people, for the *bien-être* of the unstoppable force of imperial progress.

Disused nuclear power station, computer room, Latina, Italy, 2007

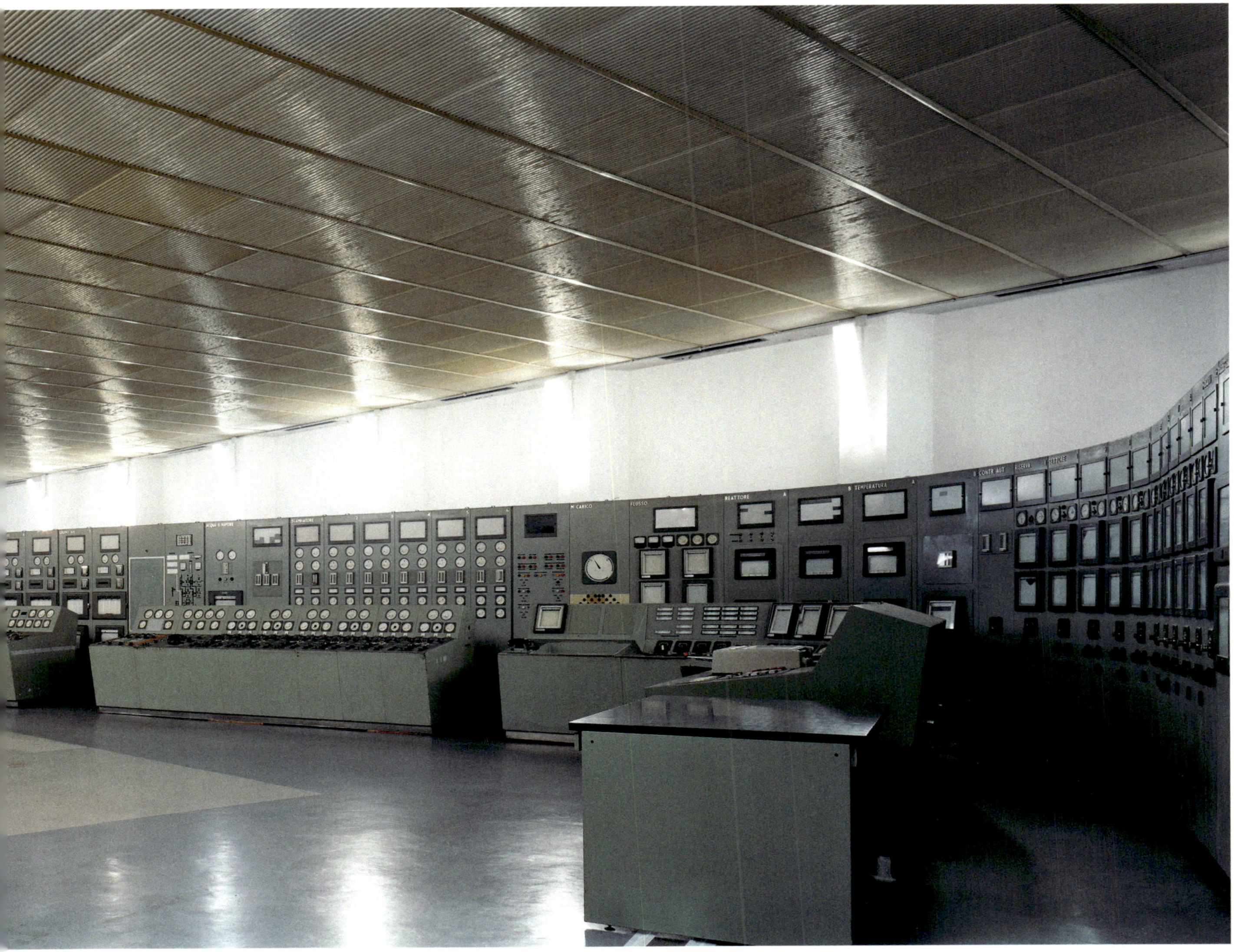

Our absence—whoever we are, consumers, citizens, neighbors—guarantees that those who are there, toiling for the workless enterprise, remain transparent. This is our role in maintaining the groundless arguments of progress. A photograph is sometimes an opportunity to account for the perpetual motion of imperialism rather than for ecological progress. Tomatoes and nuclear energy seem unrelated, unless we assume that processes are never predictable, even if initiated under controlled laboratory conditions.

As regards nuclear facilities, their explosive unpredictability is not related solely to initiatives designed to start processes but to the possibility of ending them, deliberately. The use of the verb "decommissioning"—as if a commission can simply be reversed—in protocols for dismantling nuclear facilities is symptomatic of this denial.

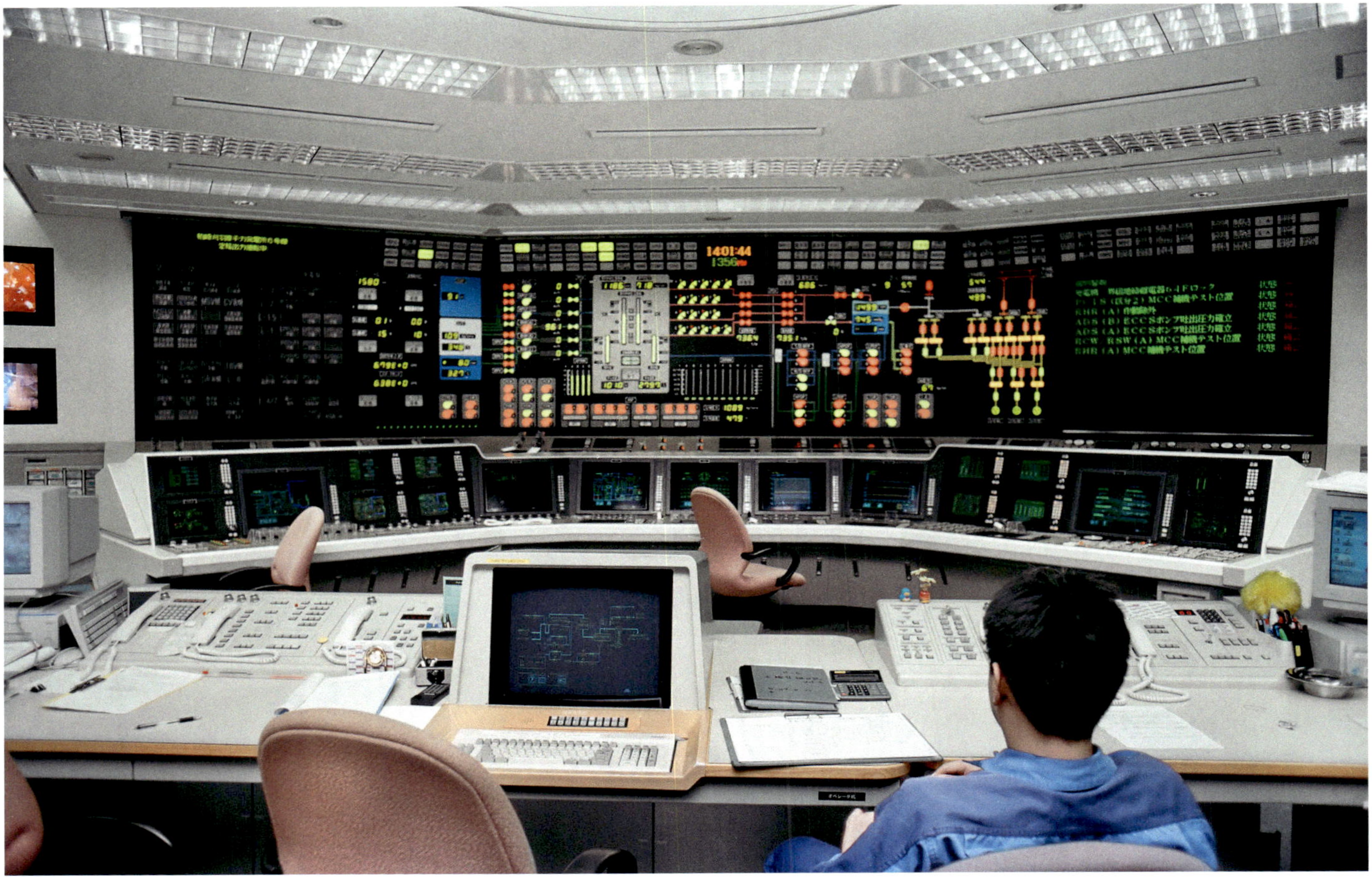

The catastrophic arrogance of imperial modernity lies in the belief that everything is predictable and therefore masterable, and that whatever was started, regardless of the violence it required, can be brought to a decent end.

Kashiwazaki-Kariwa Nuclear Power Station, control room, Kashiwazaki, Japan, 1998

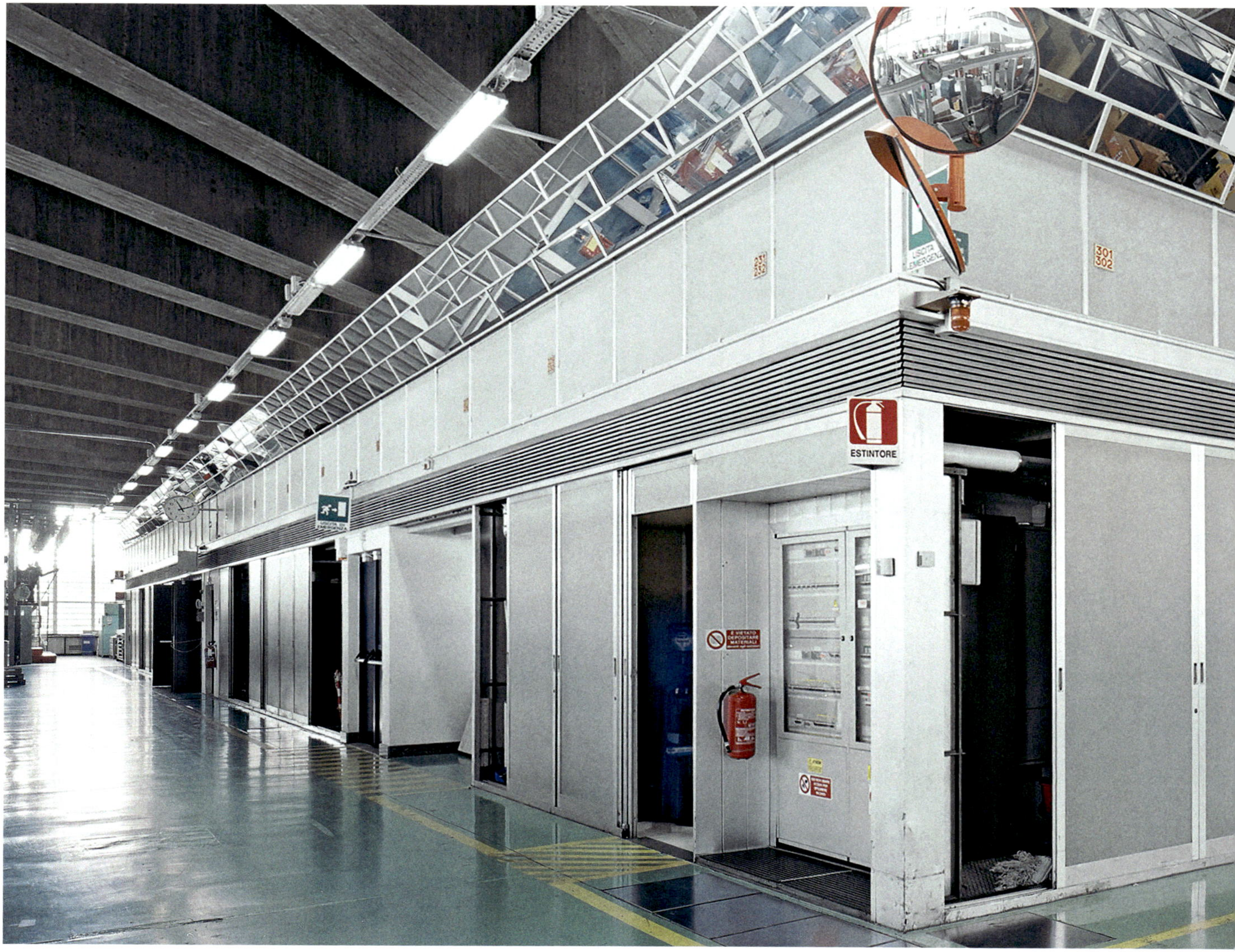

The banknote printing works and storage building was designed by the engineer Pier Luigi Nervi in 1968. Structural concrete beams in the center form a shaft housing the banknote storage bunker. The workers are monitored by means of two-way mirrors placed on the ceiling.

Here is another reason for evacuating people from places where they are still needed. But just as the process of producing banknotes cannot be exposed to people who may mess everything up, it is impossible to completely remove people from it.

Bank of Italy, banknote storage, Rome, Italy, 2007

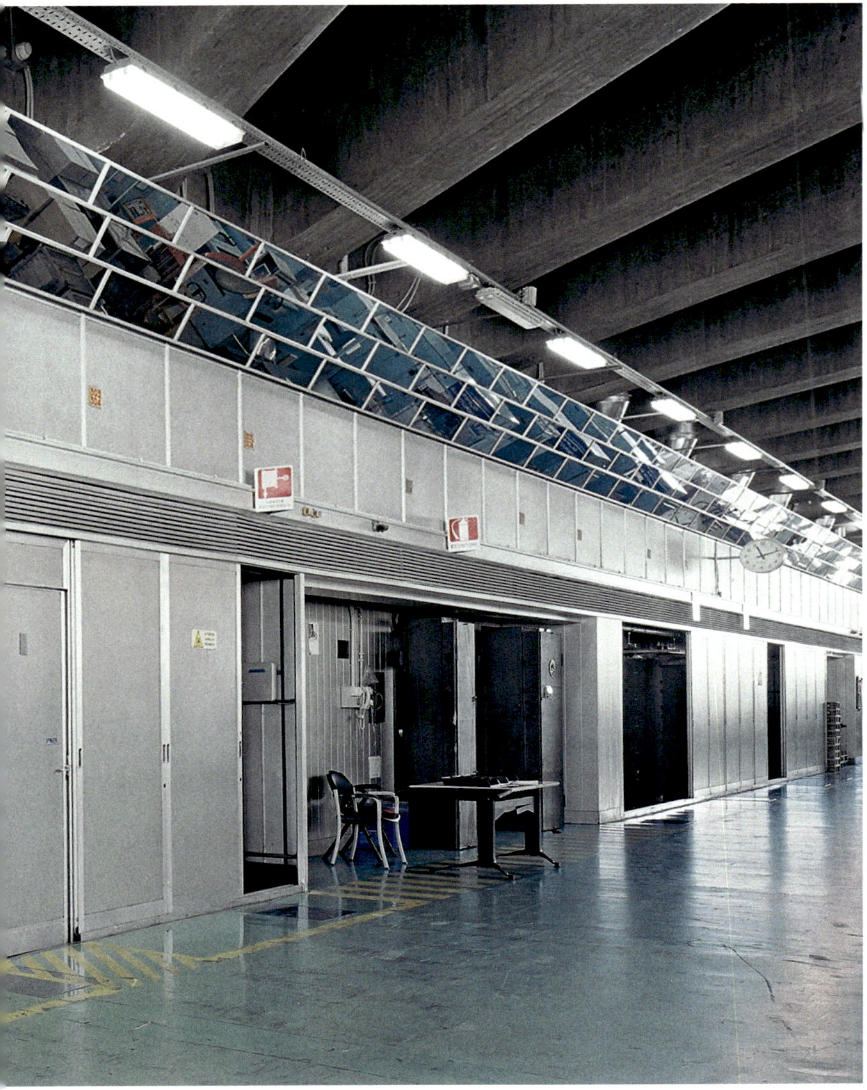

The absence of people in this image is not solely about money but also about architecture and photography, whose function in this installation is reduced to registering the fantasy of a people-free mode of operation. We see in the photo something like an inverted panopticon, called upon, with the programmed camera, to guarantee that the minimal human presence will not interfere in the perfect global crime of producing the groundless currency—money.

The final photograph produced in this chamber is expected to act as a proof of success in preventing a crime: the money is shown as safely encased and ready to go. Why, however, were these photos of a highly secured space authorized, perhaps even desired? Why are we as spectators of this image made complicit in an anticipated crime whose blueprint is scripted as an option in this enclosed space where the photographed camera is located?

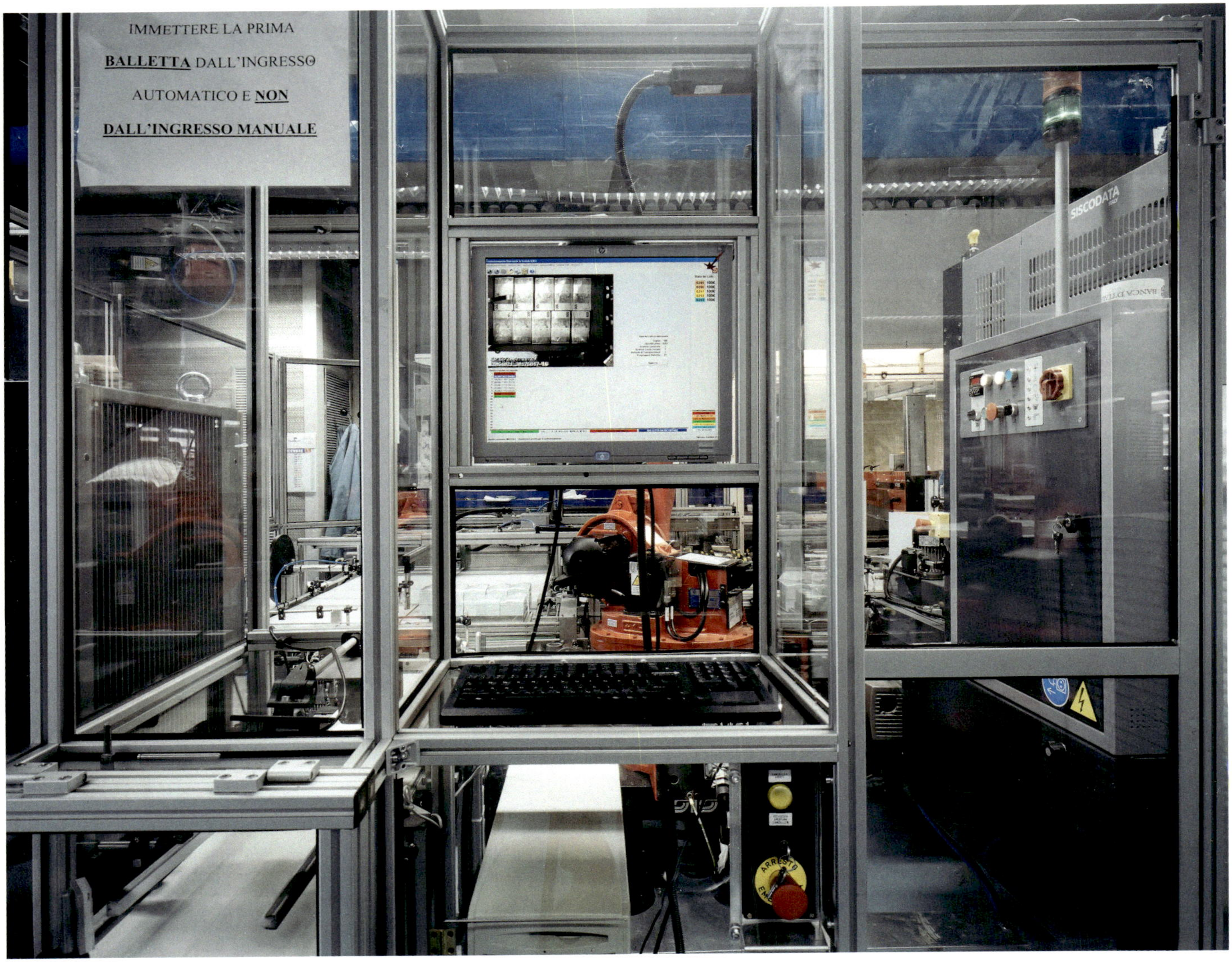

In the final production phase, euro banknotes are printed and cut. Optical control systems check both the visible and the invisible print layers. A robotic arm with an inbuilt camera packs the banknotes and photographs into containers, each holding about one million euros. This image functions as a digital signature with legal weight, confirming that each million euros photographed does indeed exist.

We were given permission to view/acknowledge that in the process of money production there is only one type of crime—its theft by ordinary people—and that it is under control.

Bank of Italy, Department Cut2000, Rome, Italy, 2007

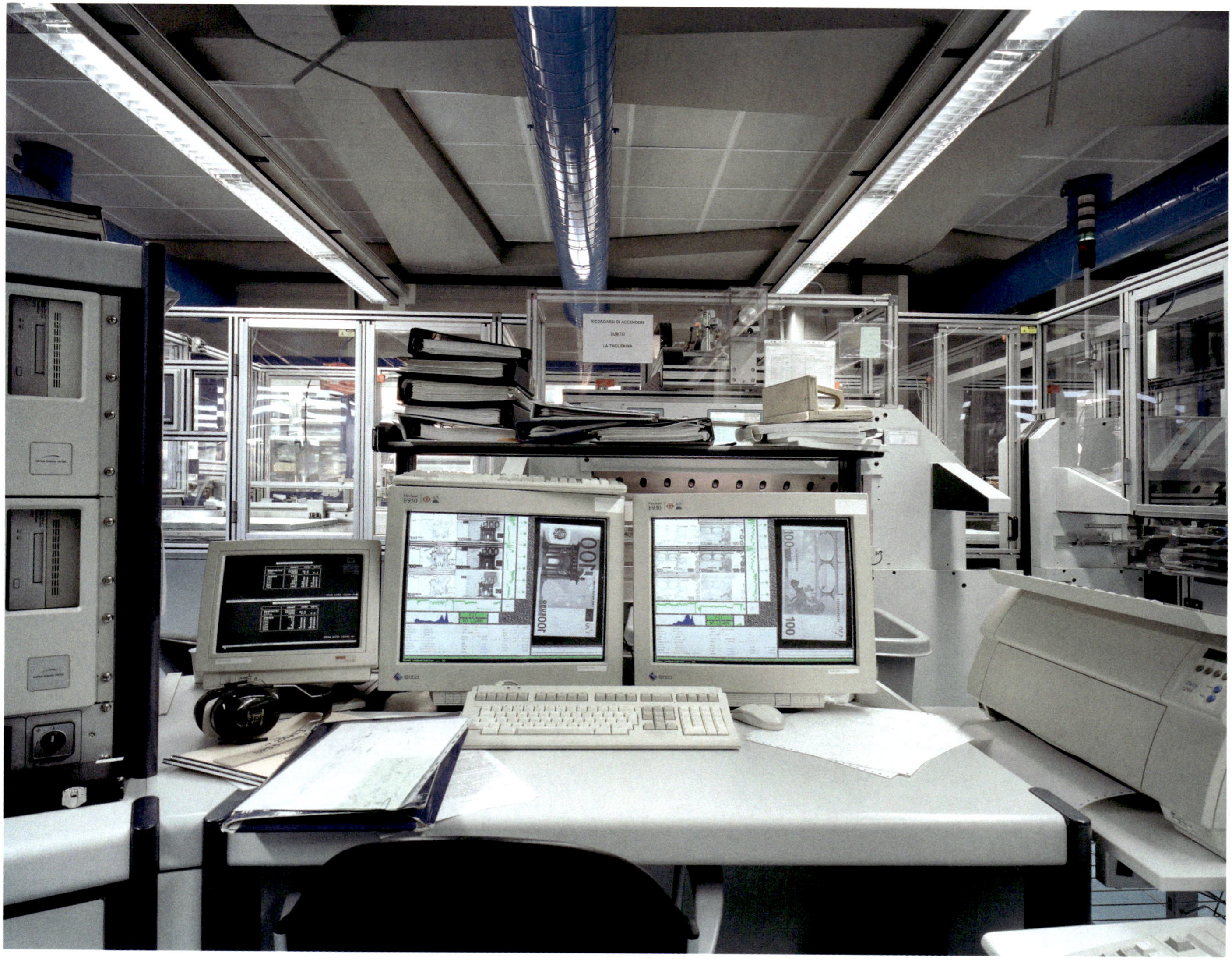

Surprisingly, no draconian contract was signed between those responsible for this installation and the photographer concerning the conditions of public display once the official exhibition for which the pictures were commissioned is over, which leaves some doubt as to what would constitute an infringement of such a contract—sharing with others that bypassing the programmed camera will enable them to commit the perfect crime.

Bank of Italy, Department Cut2000, infrared and ultraviolet checking system, Rome, Italy, 2007

Or that the perfect crime is in making us believe that this is the perfect crime, rather than the continuous and orchestrated dispossession of people through the way they are enslaved to money and forced to give their consent to being exploited to death?

When we think about the archive and seek to conceptualize it, we tend to forget one of its intriguing features: it consists of an overwhelming quantity of material. The more transparent its principles of collecting items are and the less affected by filters, the more opaque it becomes for its users.

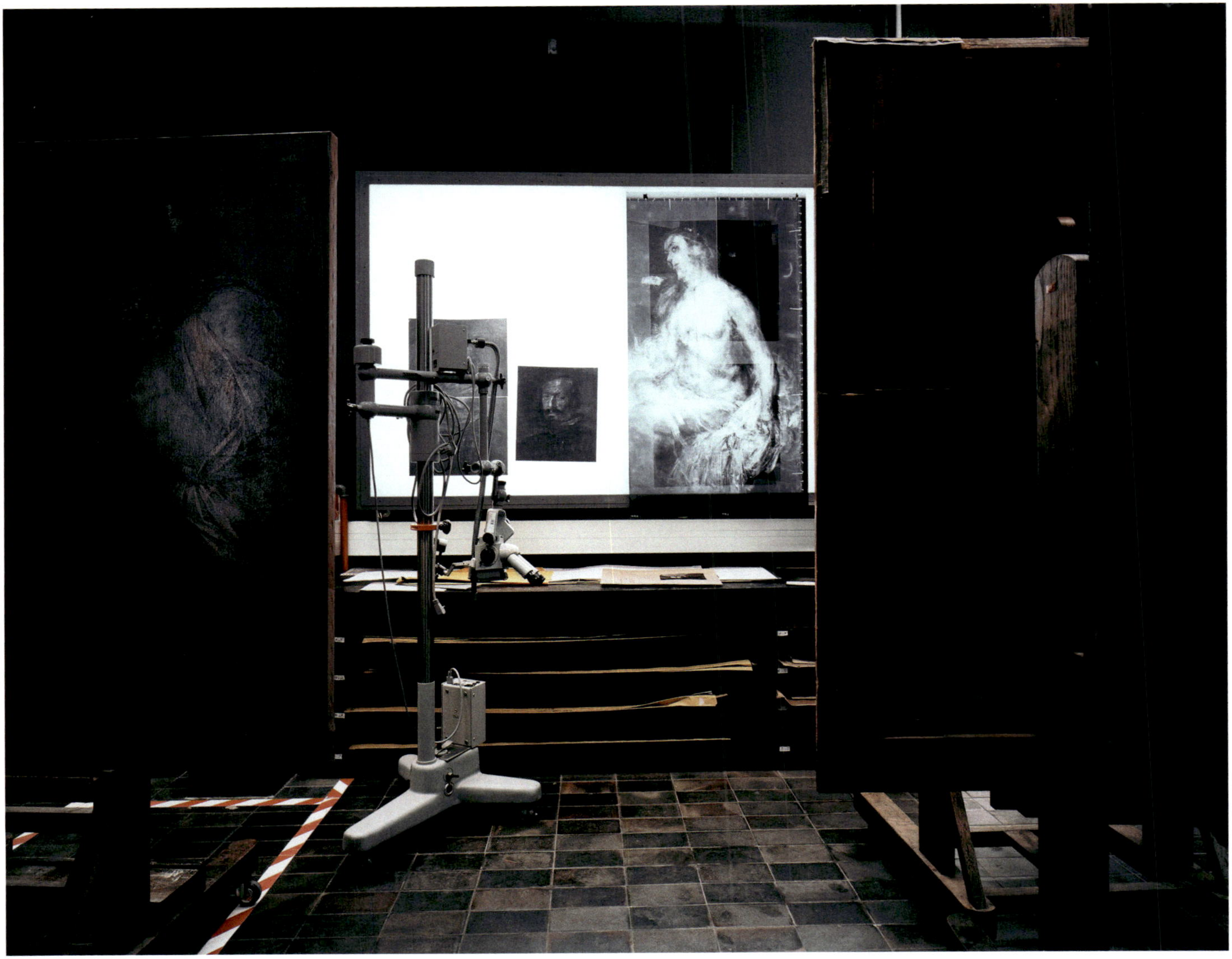

The site of preservation is usually isolated and inaccessible in its material form of organization, as archives are often accessible only through indexes.

C2RMF, Center for Research and Restoration of the Museums of France, radiographic image of Rembrandt's *Bathsheba at Her Bath* (1654), Paris, France, 2014

These jars storing five thousand types of rice on a farm in Bangladesh function as drawers in an archive rather than as showcases in a museum. In terms of physical proximity to what they contain, these jars are on one end of the scale of archival types.

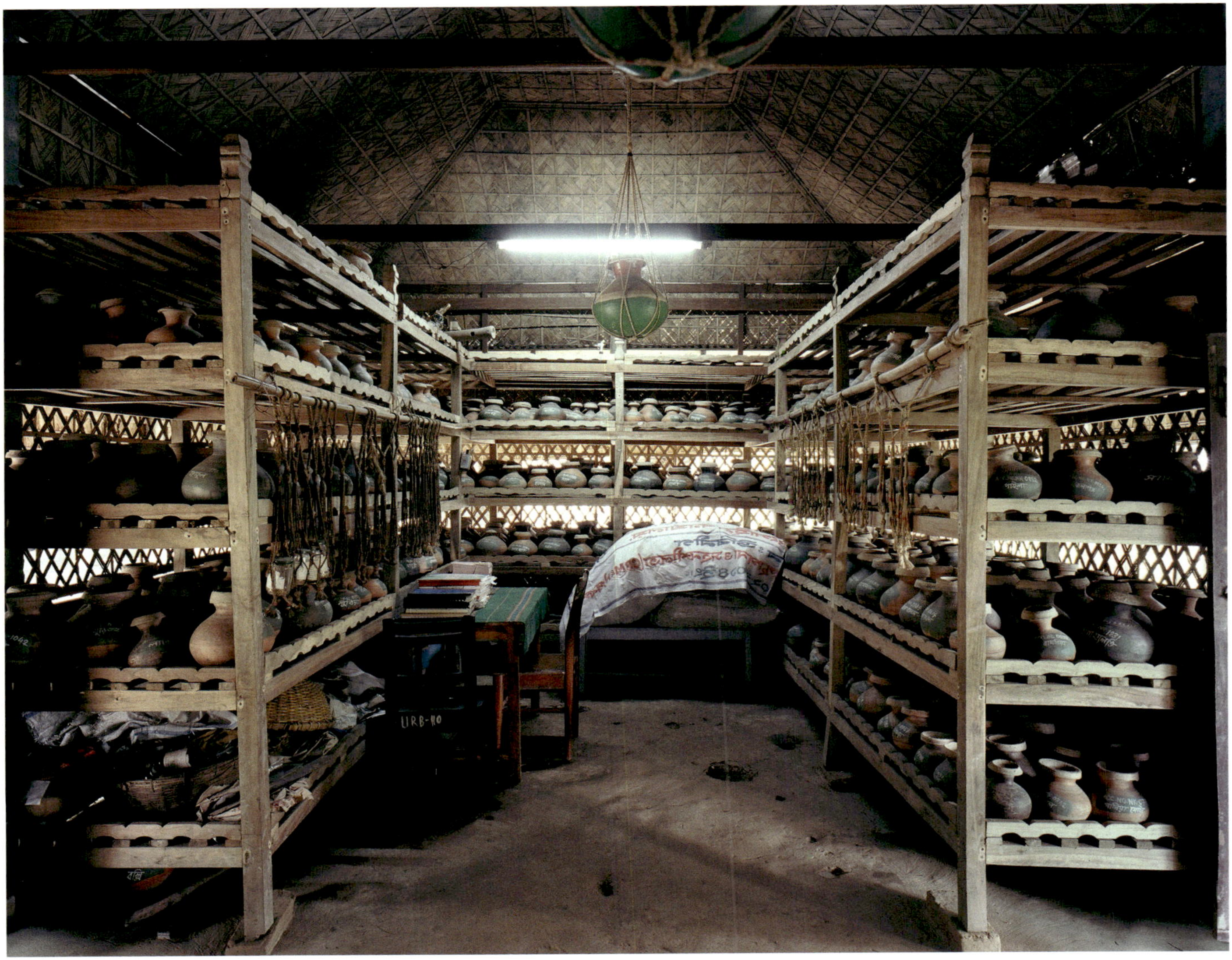

This local farmers' association archives about five thousand of the ten thousand traditional Bangladeshi rice-seed types. Recently introduced industrial farming practices make use of only about ten varieties of rice. The farmers can have rice seeds for free, provided they bring twice the amount taken, after their harvest.

Nayakrishi Andalon, ecological farm rice-seed vault, Tangail, Bangladesh, 2014

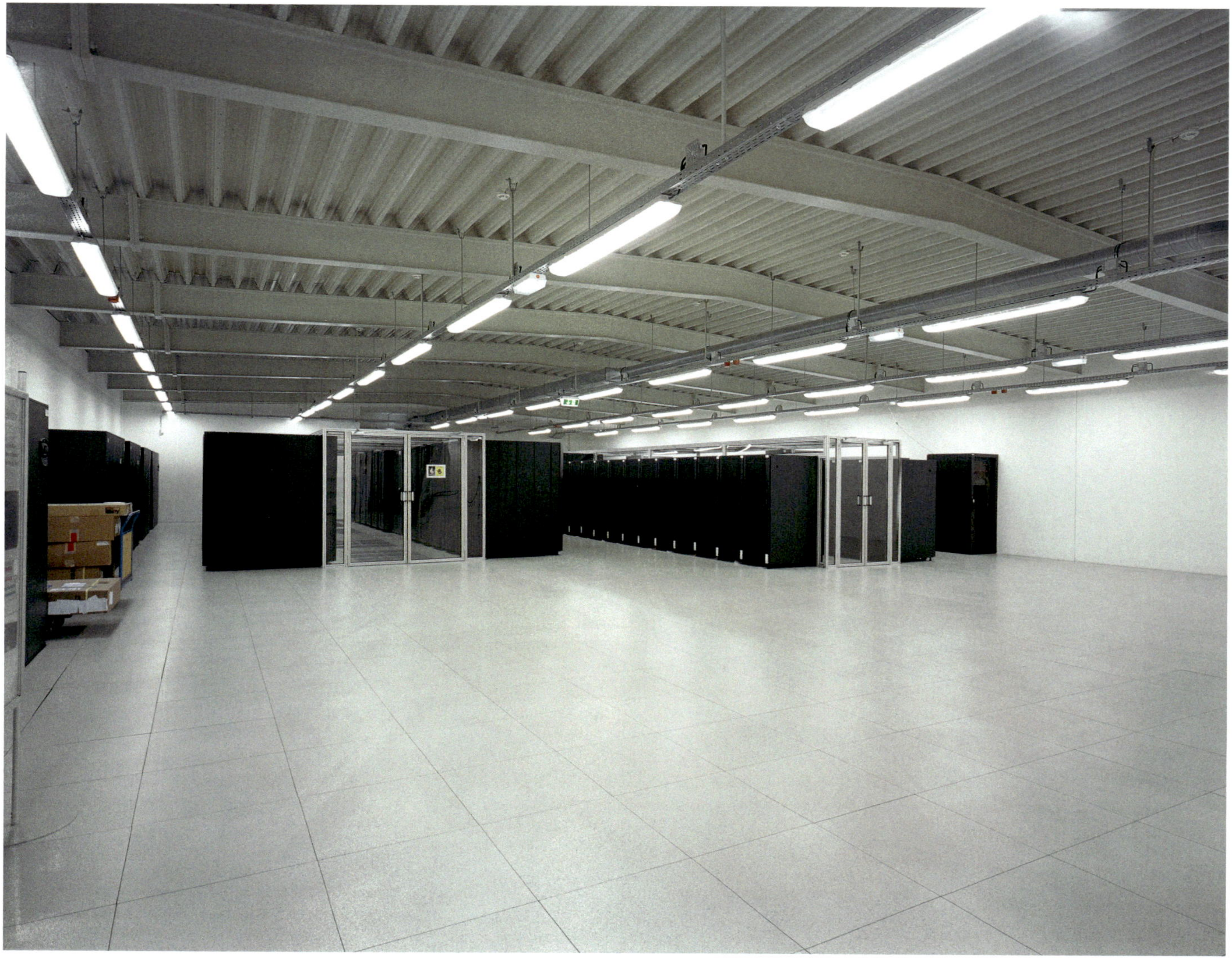

A large building constructed around the computer room cools the machines. Every six years, the high performance computers are upgraded to more energy-efficient models. The annual electricity bill for the German Climate Computing Center runs to about two million euros.

The archive of climate-change data at DKRZ can be used to illustrate the other end of this scale.

DKRZ, German Climate Computing Center, archives, Hamburg, Germany, 2013

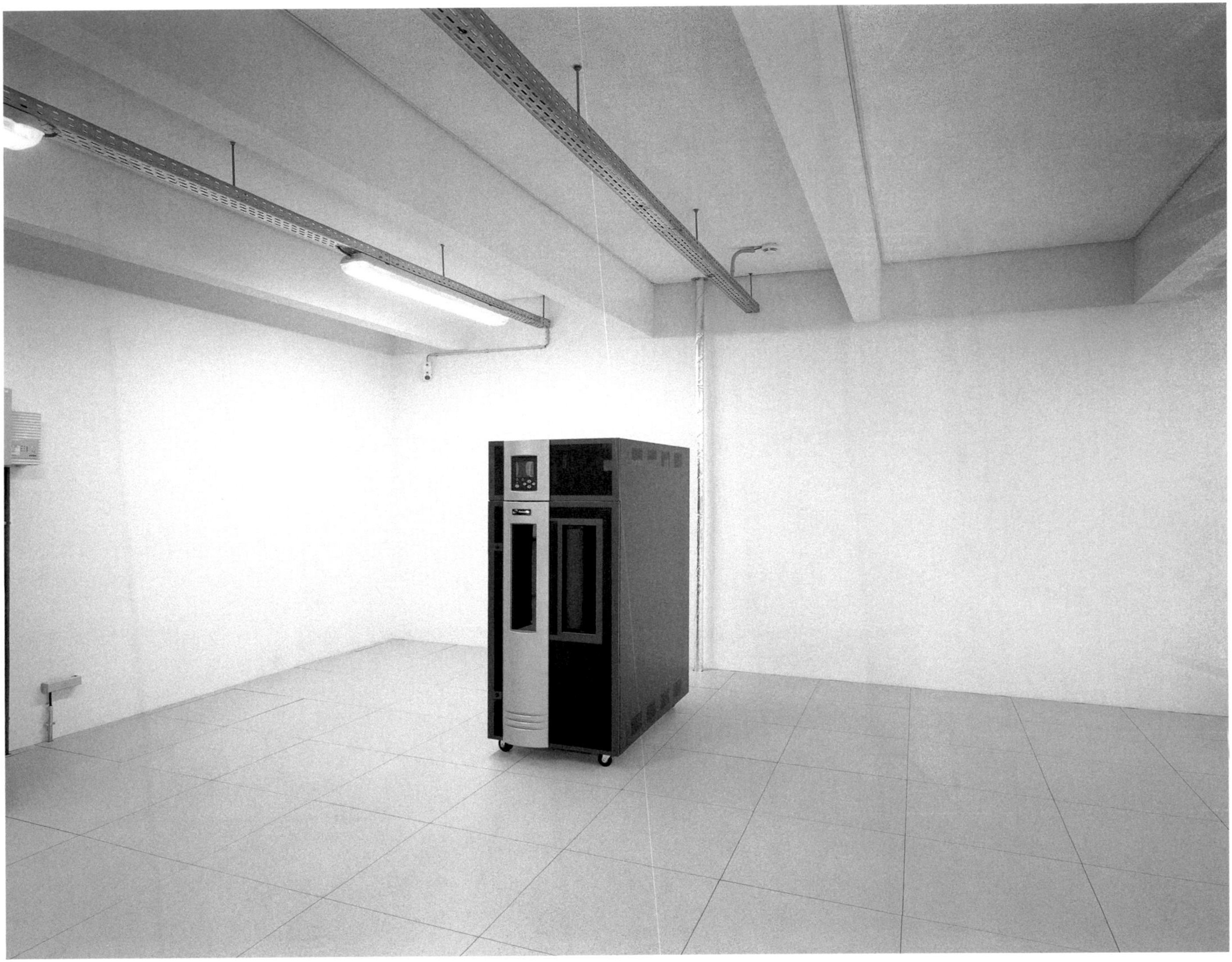

Here we see a single object, a server with the capacity to contain information far greater than those thousands of jars, whose optimal functioning depends on physical isolation in a big, cooled, sealed-off room. Designating this server as an archive and distinguishing it from other servers continuously processing climate-change data are part of the standardized archival operation of differentiating between tenses—past, present, and future—and articulating them in a unilinear sequence.

DKRZ, German Climate Computing Center, archives, Hamburg, Germany, 2013

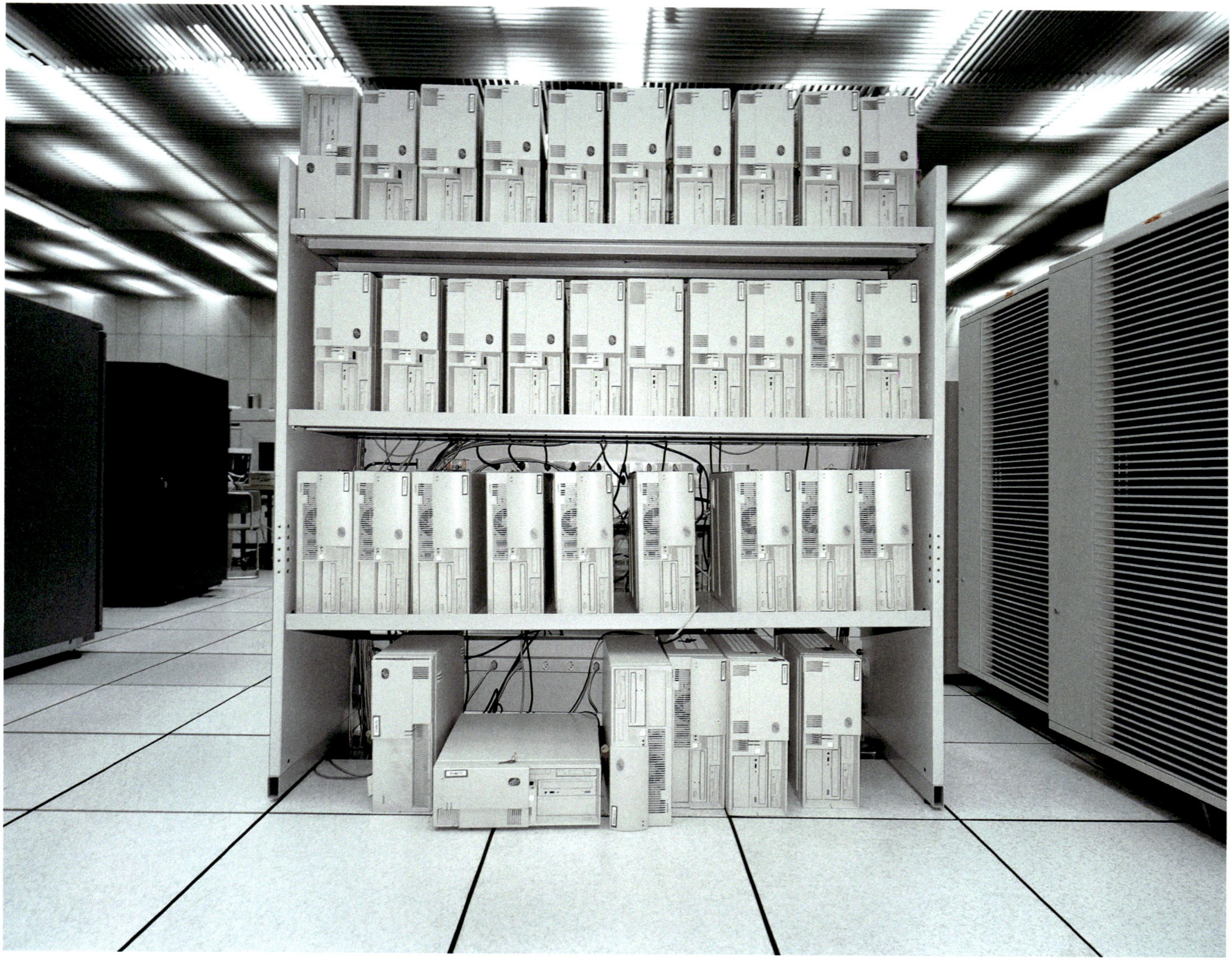

The archive trains us to believe that what we are doing now will be over in a minute and should make room for another thing that will replace it. All these operations, from sealing off data in jars to indexing procedures, partake in the modern archival enterprise of keeping us outside and giving us modest, individual licenses to intervene in the production of the past as "over." They limit us to the position of knowledgeable external scholars in, and spectators of, the catastrophes unfolding before our eyes.

CERN, European Organization for Nuclear Research, control rooms,
Geneva, Switzerland, 2000

We are viewing a spot that is supposed to stay out of sight. There is something frightening about the sudden desire to show it expressed by those whose role is to keep it hidden from the public gaze. I'm intrigued by the burden of holding for oneself what is declared secret, prohibited, classified, but also by the semi-burden of the photographer once he was interpellated into revealing and exposing this secret material (though never fully), as well as the burden of being entrusted with confidentiality against, or as distinct from, others.

The critical task and position of "exposing" and "revealing" often divert us from recognizing the most basic given of being ruled under the imperial principles that made us complicit in the systems conducted through us.

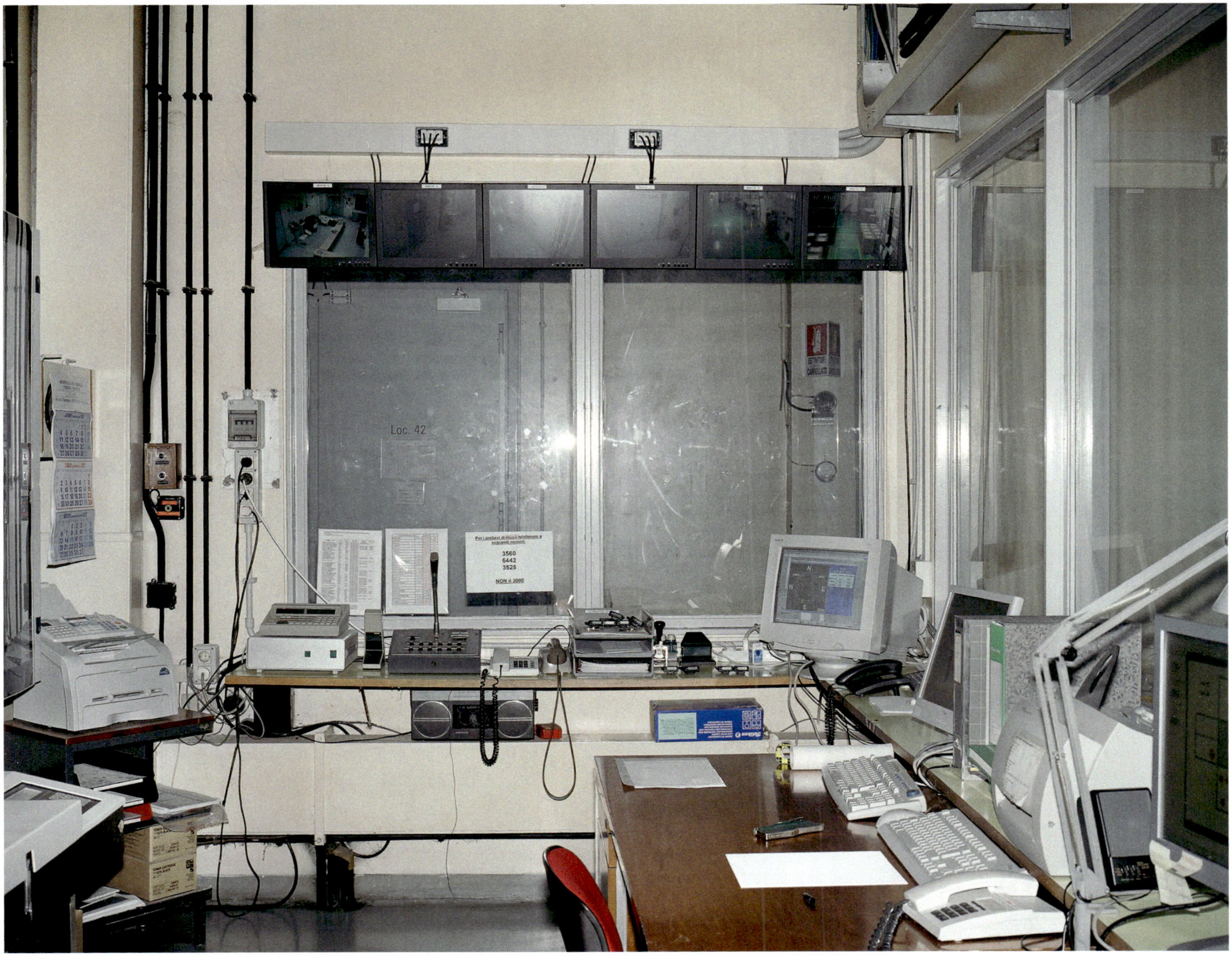

The failure of the critical project is thus constitutive, as both the project and its failure are based on the isolation of (mostly heroic) actions by individuals, often acting separately from others.

Sogin, IPU and OPEC plants, Casaccia (RM), Italy, 2007

A photo opportunity is usually associated with an event that will not recur. But when the idea of security is the major governing principle, a photo opportunity has different manifestations. The production of certain static spots as highly secure, unreachable, and classified—access to which means waiting for hard-to-obtain permission—interpellates citizens, through the mediation of the photographer, into being complicit in the production of a certain spot, moment, or event seen as decisive in bringing about a catastrophe.

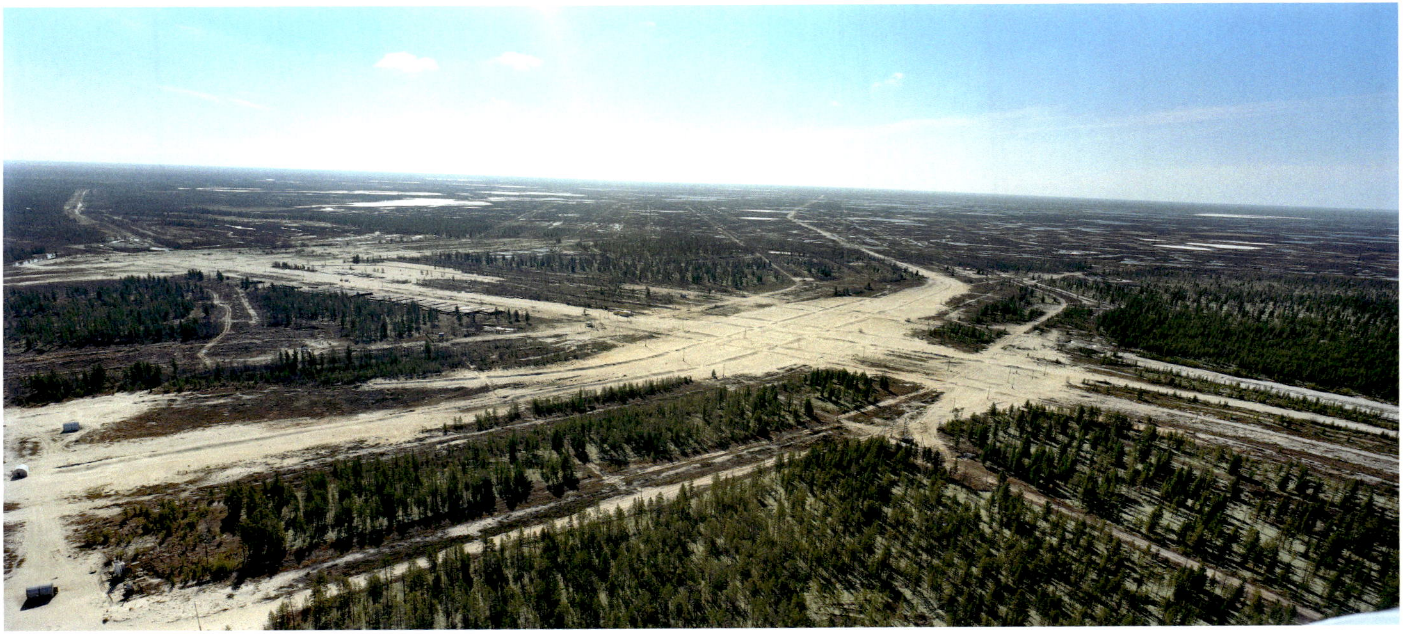

According to a 2009 CIA document released in 2010 by WikiLeaks, the Nadym Gas Pipeline Junction is considered to be one of the most critical gas infrastructures in the world.

The Nadym pipeline junction is on the list of three hundred installations in over fifty countries known as the Critical Foreign Dependencies Initiative (CFDI), which "if attacked or destroyed would critically impact the United States."

Gas pipeline junction, Nadym, Russia, 2011

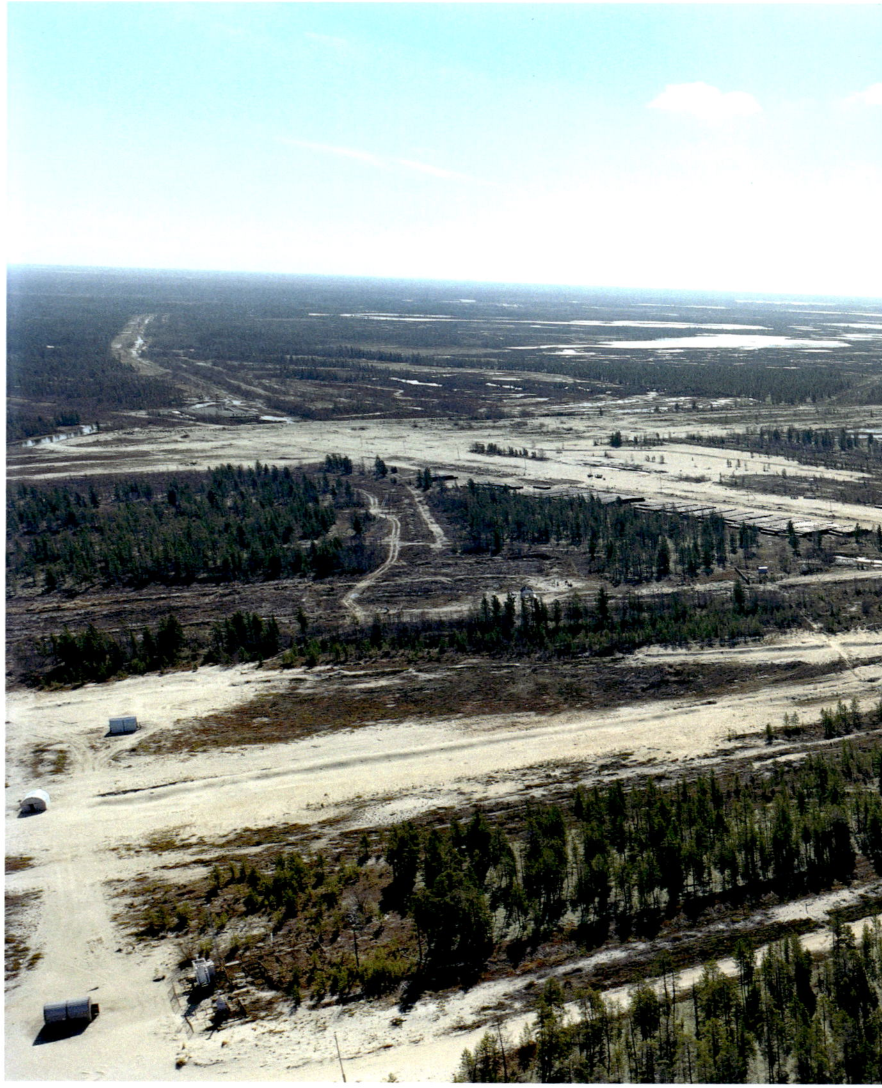

The exposure of these classified spots does little to increase their vulnerability; rather, it increases our vulnerability, as citizens, to ever-greater compliance with information provided by official, authorized institutions. This endangers our citizenship, as the catastrophe that we are being warned of may come if x, y, or z has already unfolded in the fabric of our life, in the form of regime-made disaster, in which millions live outside the protective shell promised to privileged citizens by those institutions.

Gas pipeline junction, Nadym, Russia, 2011

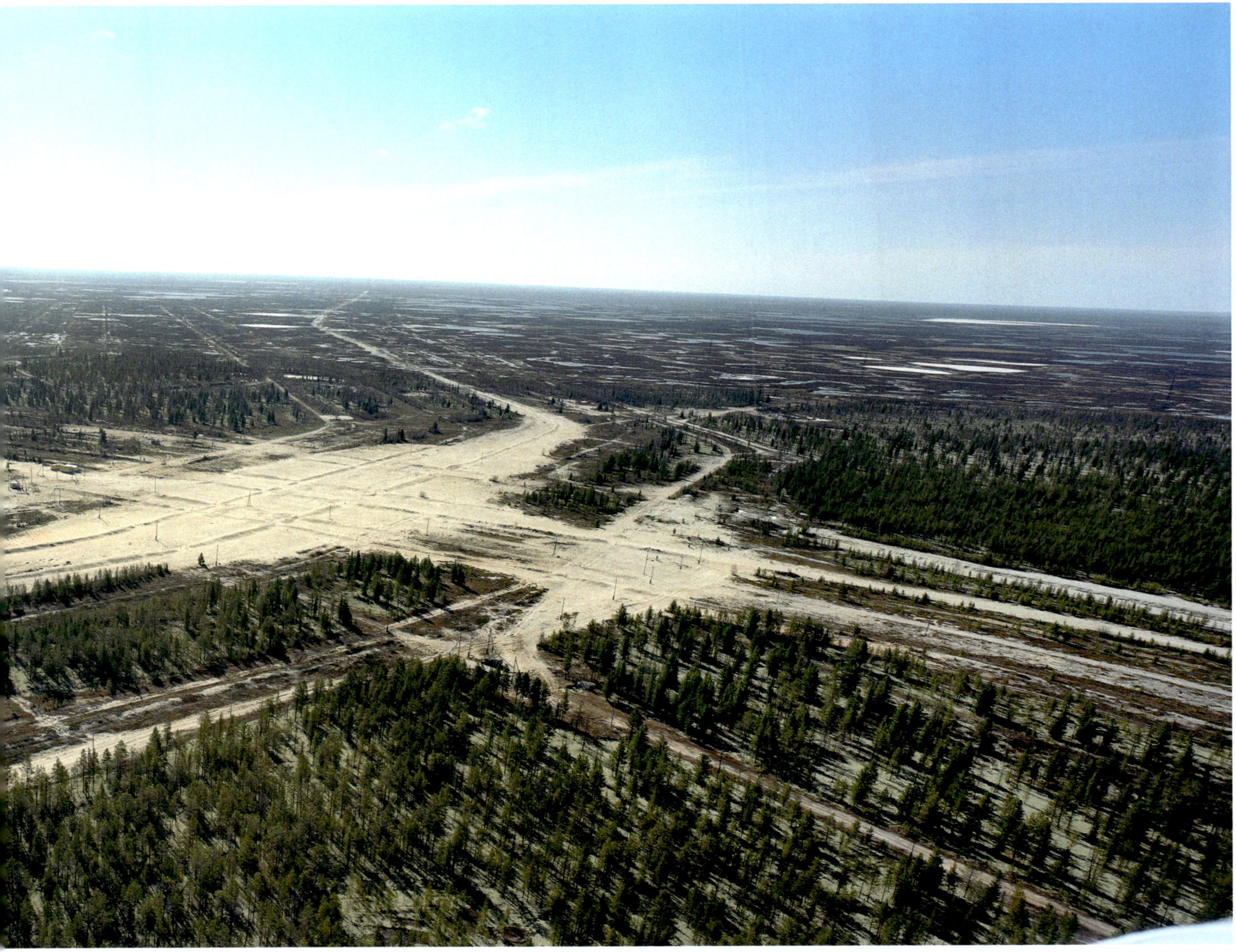

And the camera? Can it act differently in these theaters of display that fetishize the weakest points in networked systems?

The spectators' benches in the Warsaw National Stadium are empty while the United Nations (UN) Climate Change Conference COP19 takes place. Based on past experience, were these benches to have been occupied, it would not have been by people. Since its founding in 1945, the UN has been promoting the "new world order" to end war. This has been a violent process, perpetuating violence in other forms.

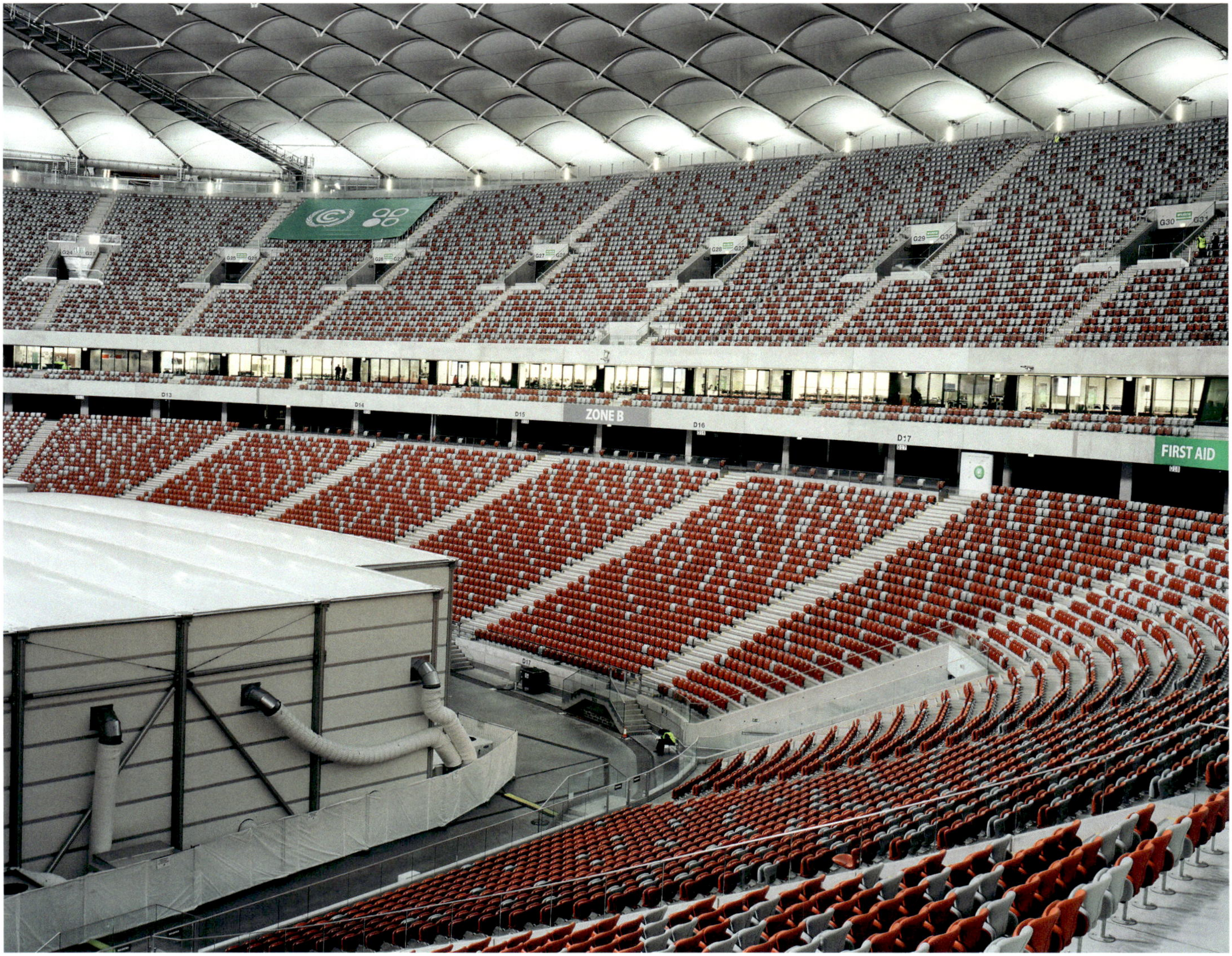

For as long as the UN is actually run by and serves the interests of different sovereign nation-states, its association with the role of an international arbiter is misleading. Nation-states are imperial products and serve imperial interests rather than civil ones. Behind closed doors, the representatives of the "developed" and "developing" states negotiate the future of the planet. They come up with agreements they consider beneficial to poor countries.

UNFCCC, COP19 Climate Change Conference, Warsaw, Poland, 2013
Photography in collaboration with Giulia Bruno

Grassroots organizations cannot be heard within these summits. The protesters encircling the stadium during the COP19 conference were well isolated in order to provide secure space for the growth of groundless arguments, to be delivered to the public as desired policies to be adopted. This isolation of the many is not merely about participation in the actual event but about refusing to admit civil knowledge as a competitor to expert knowledge.

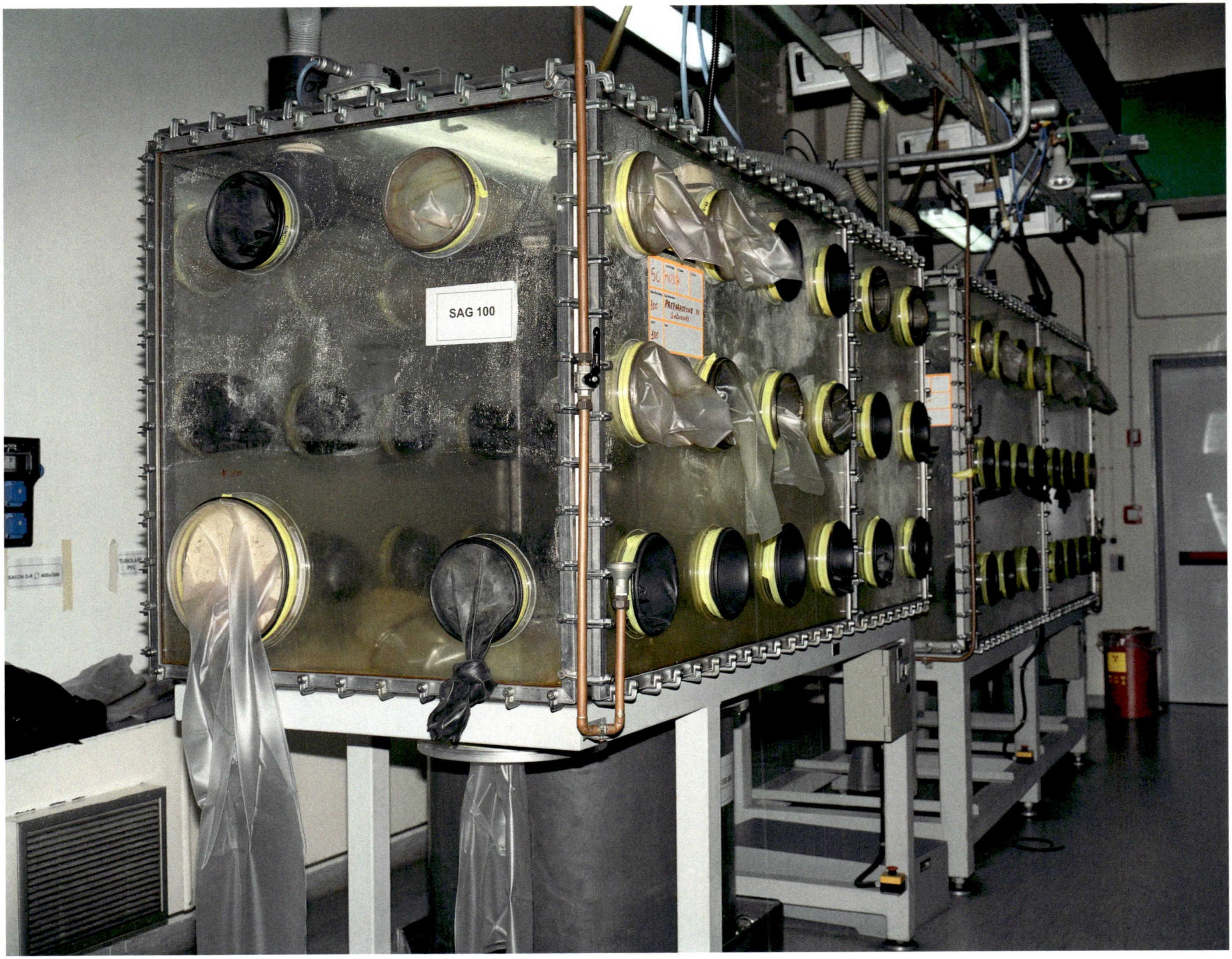

The replacement of the "human condition," as the condition sine qua non of sustainable life, with the imperial condition is visually emblematized in this image of the bunkerization of what should have been an open space.

Sogin, IPU and OPEC plants, plutonium handling device,
Casaccia (RM), Italy, 2007

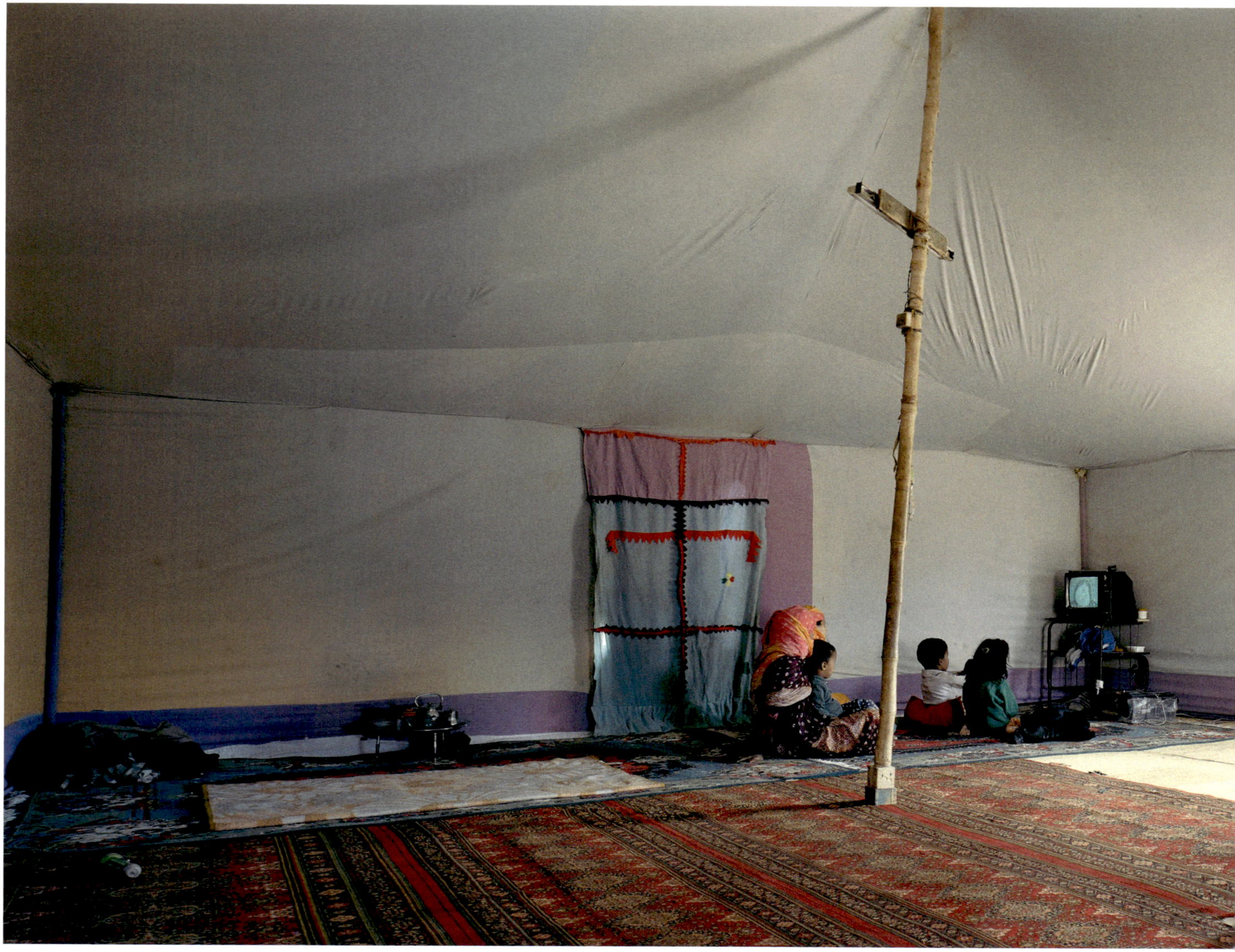

This refugee camp on the borders of Algeria hosts the Sahrawi families who fled Western Sahara during the conflict with Morocco (1975–91). The UN agencies describe the situation as one of deep ambiguity: with no political solution in sight, the Sahrawis continue to live as a society-in-exile. Their living structures reflect this ambiguity. While it might be possible to construct more definite architecture and infrastructure, many fear that this would endanger their right to return. In the meantime, the 2,700 km long Moroccan Wall separates them from their homes and families.

A tent is a temporary shelter often identified with refugees, people uprooted from their homes and homelands or impounded in settlements wherever they are.

Smara, Sahrawi refugee camp, tent, Tindouf, Algeria, 2004

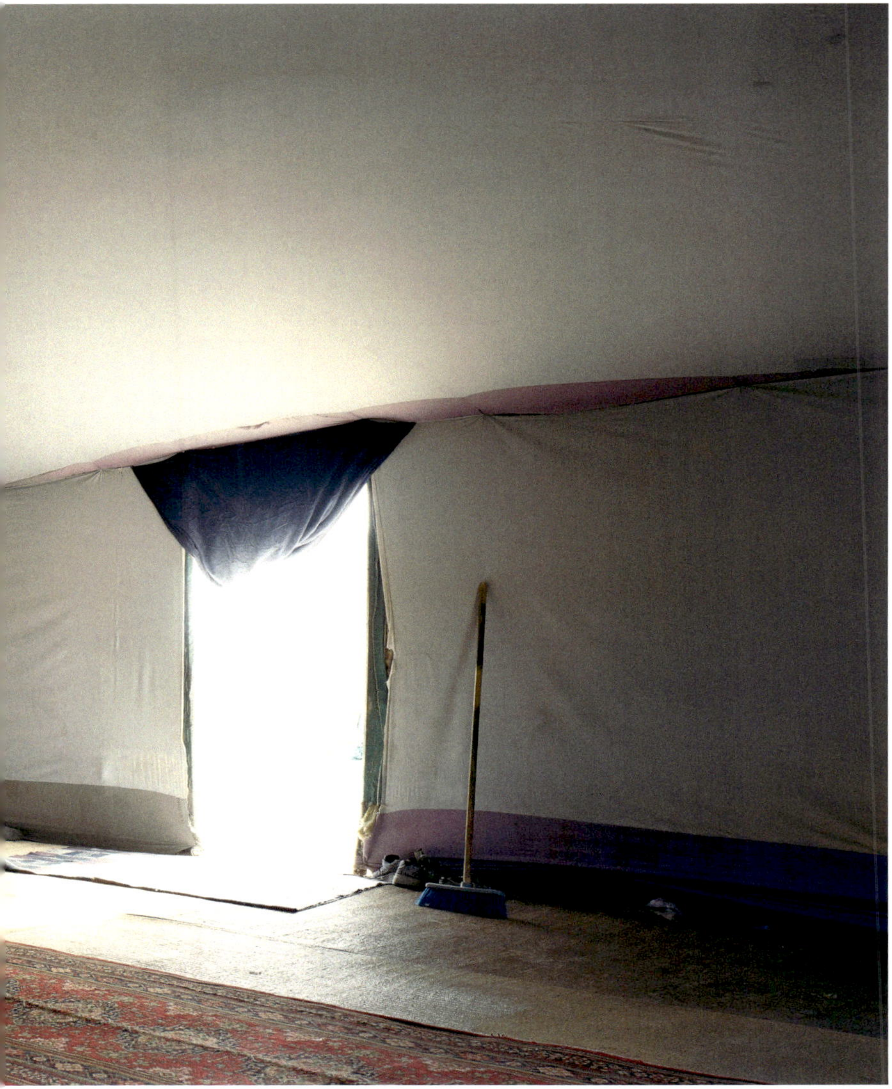

The use of tents in the protests of the last decade has created a fascinating collusion with sovereign imperial gestures. With these temporary cloth shelters, protesters have exercised their right to negotiate imperial temporality and question the source of authority to transform the temporary into the permanent.

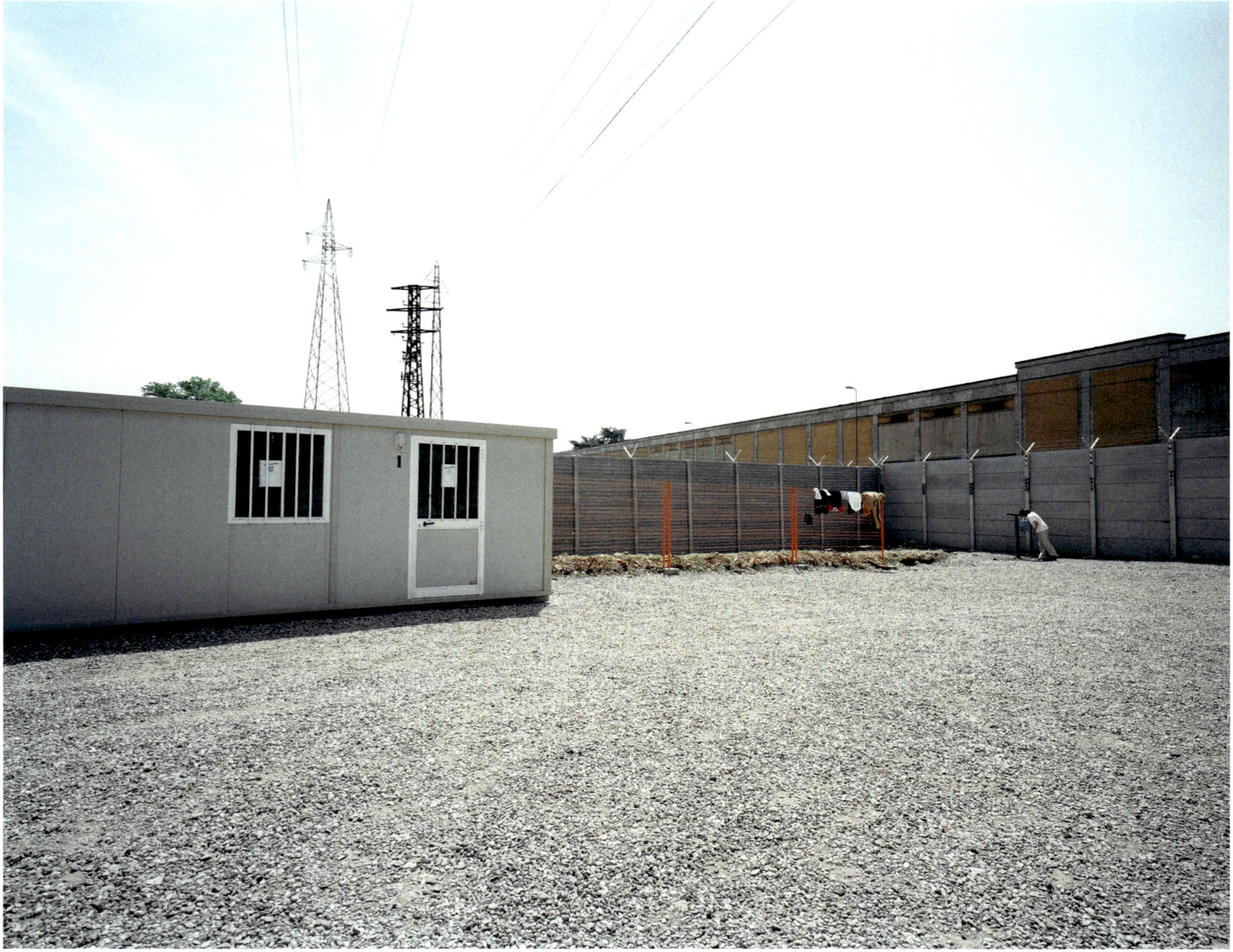

Looking at this authorized Roma camp, one cannot help asking about the origin of the sovereign states' right to steal people's time. These questions could not be abstractly formulated in parliaments; corporeally, they were brought to the fore in urban spaces through these encampments.

Via Barzaghi, Roma camp set up by the city authorities, Milan, Italy, 2004

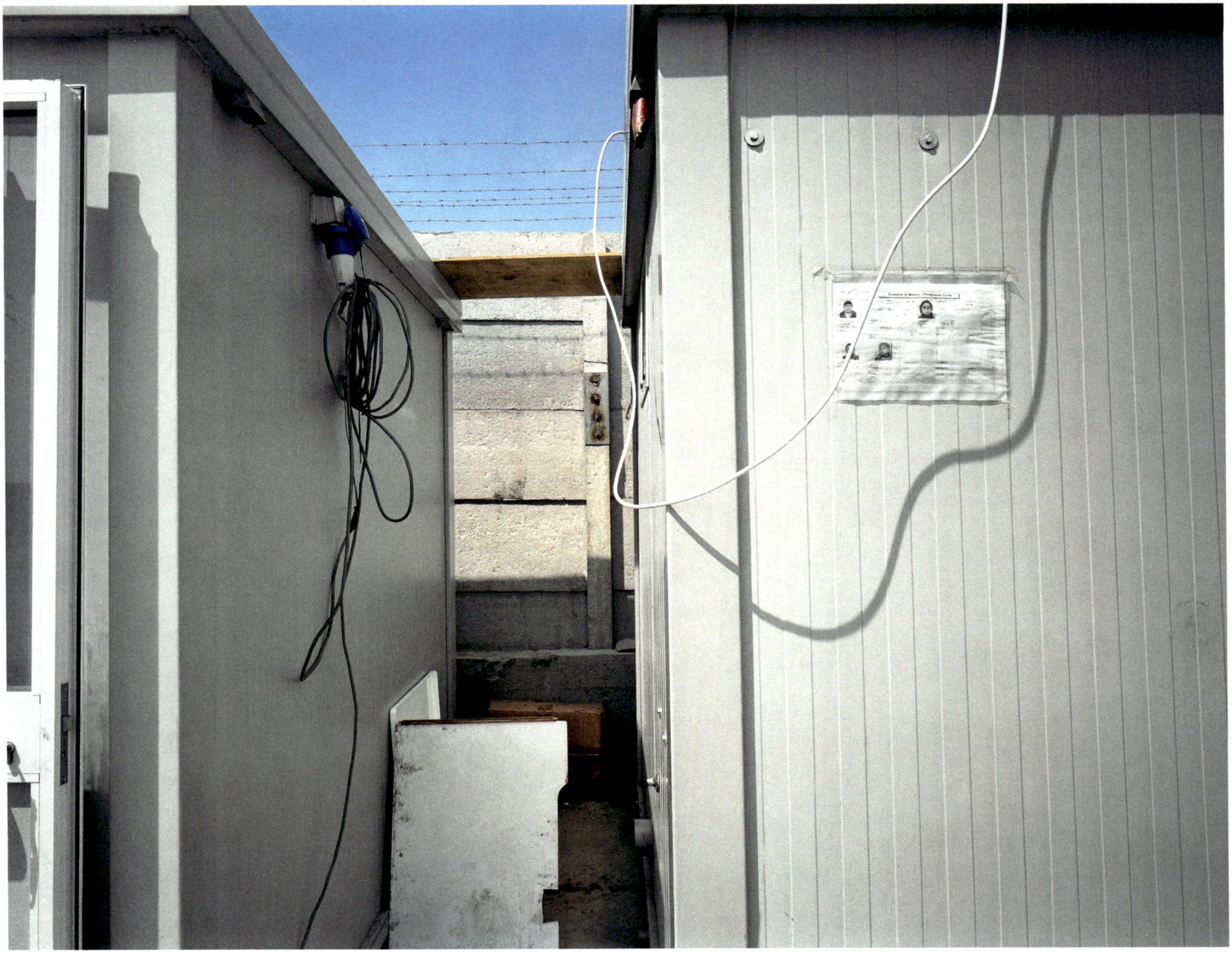

The first political act of the newly elected Lega Nord administration of the city of Milan was to displace the informal self-organized Roma living structures from the center to the outskirts of the city where they would be less visible. Municipal camps were constructed in order to enforce police control via formal infrastructure.

They publicly imposed an ur-form of our political regimes, and it seems that we are only at the beginning of this conversation.

Via Barzaghi, Roma camp set up by the city authorities, Milan, Italy, 2004

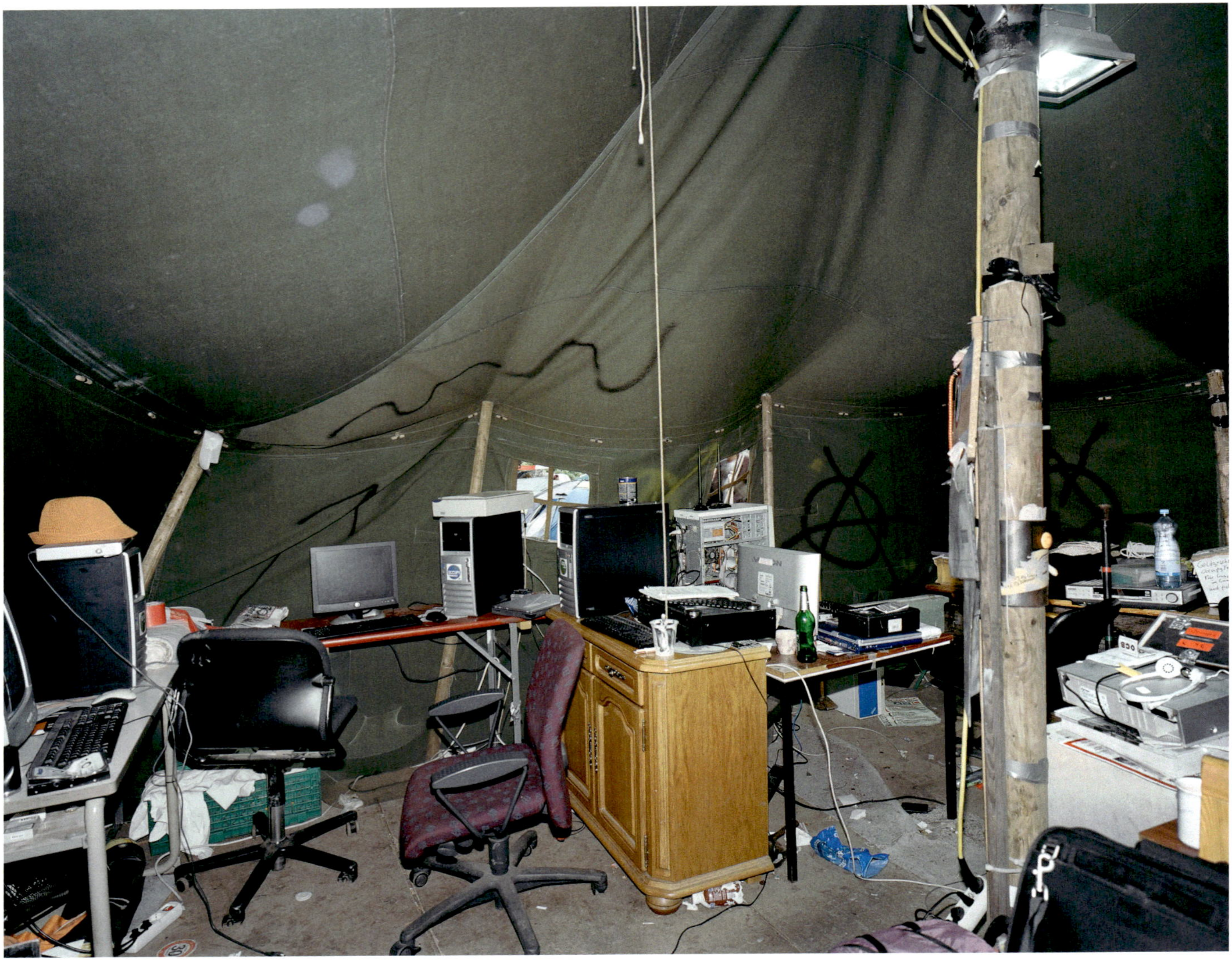

The protestors of Occupy Frankfurt are free to go in and out of the camp. Technological devices are used in protest camps to amplify civil activity and are an indication of temporariness, while the TV in the Sahrawi refugee camp indicates that people there are inmates, deprived of the right to bring to an end their temporary situation.

Occupy Frankfurt, camp in front of the ECB, Frankfurt, Germany, 2012

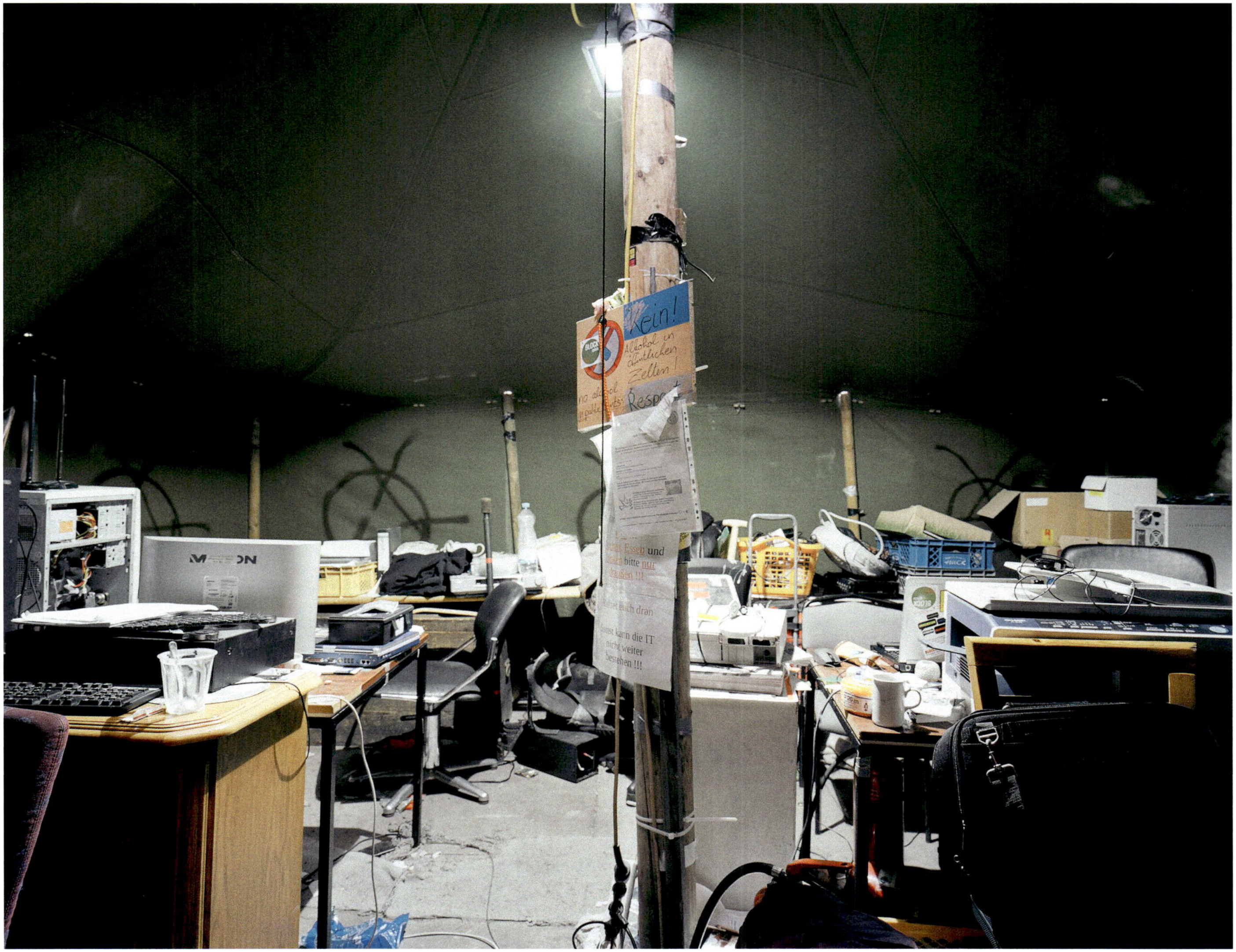

How long are we, as citizens, going to continue reiterating the political idioms of temporariness provided by sovereign political regimes and the international law in relation to people incarcerated in camps and disallowed from sharing one continuous space with us?

Occupy Frankfurt, camp in front of the ECB, Frankfurt, Germany, 2012

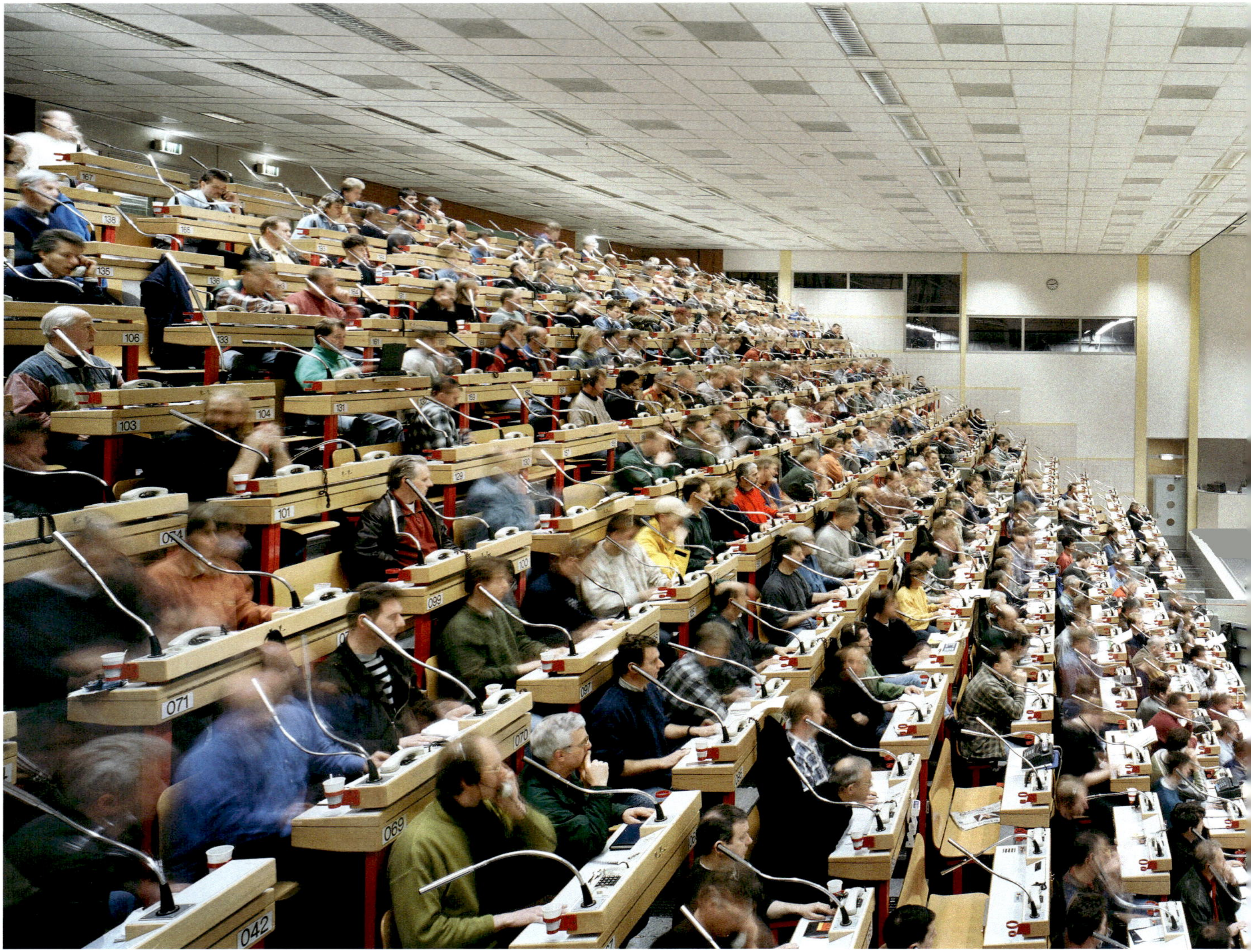

This auction complex is one of the largest industrial buildings in the world, located near Amsterdam's Schiphol airport. The auction hall screen displays basic information about flowers on sale, as well as quality remarks, country of origin, and the names and exact contents of the batches. Buyers bid electronically, and, once sold, the flowers are immediately transported to the buyer's logistics chain. The link between flowers and the economy in Holland can be dated back to one of the earliest recorded economic crises: the Tulip Mania of 1636.

Bloemenveiling Aalsmeer, flower auction, Aalsmeer, Netherlands, 1998

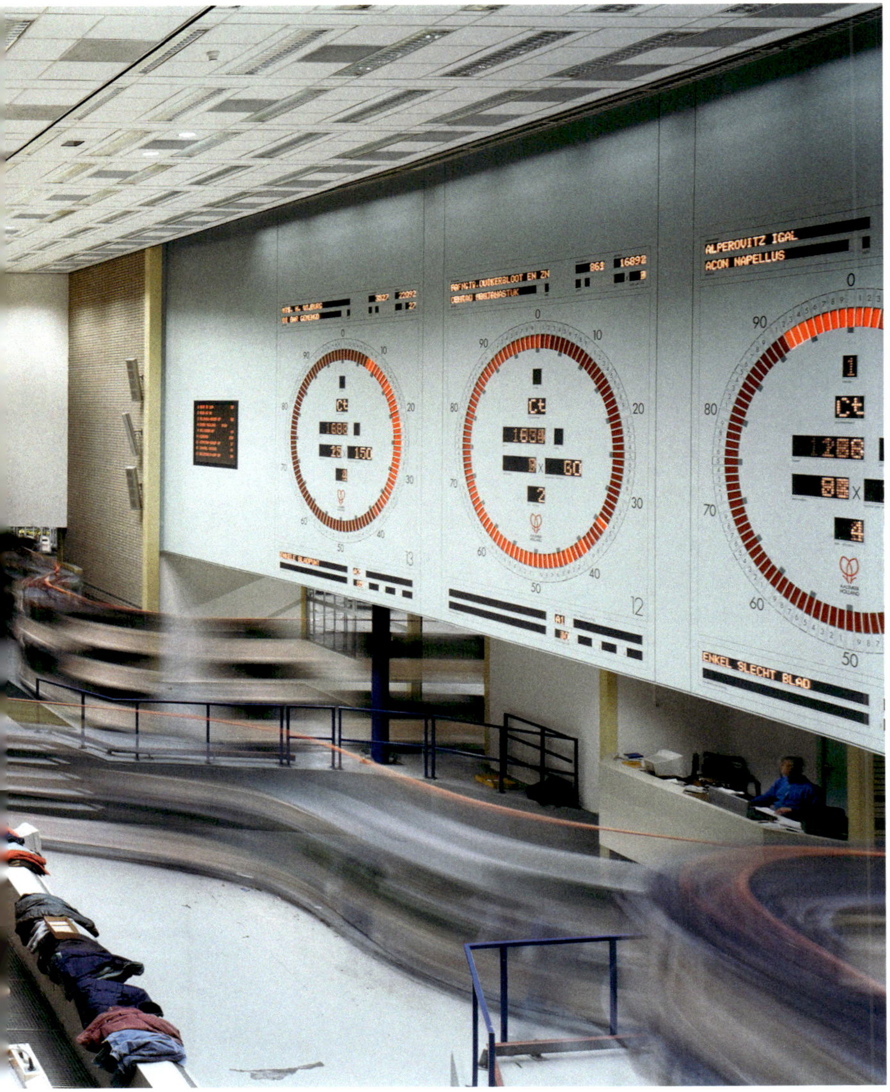

This part of the Aalsmeer Flower Auction is something between a stock market and a museum. Each day, twenty million flowers are sold via screens. In comparison, tiny crowds convene in show rooms to smell the real thing, flowers from Uganda, Spain, France, Colombia, India, Kenya, and other countries linked in an imperial circuit.

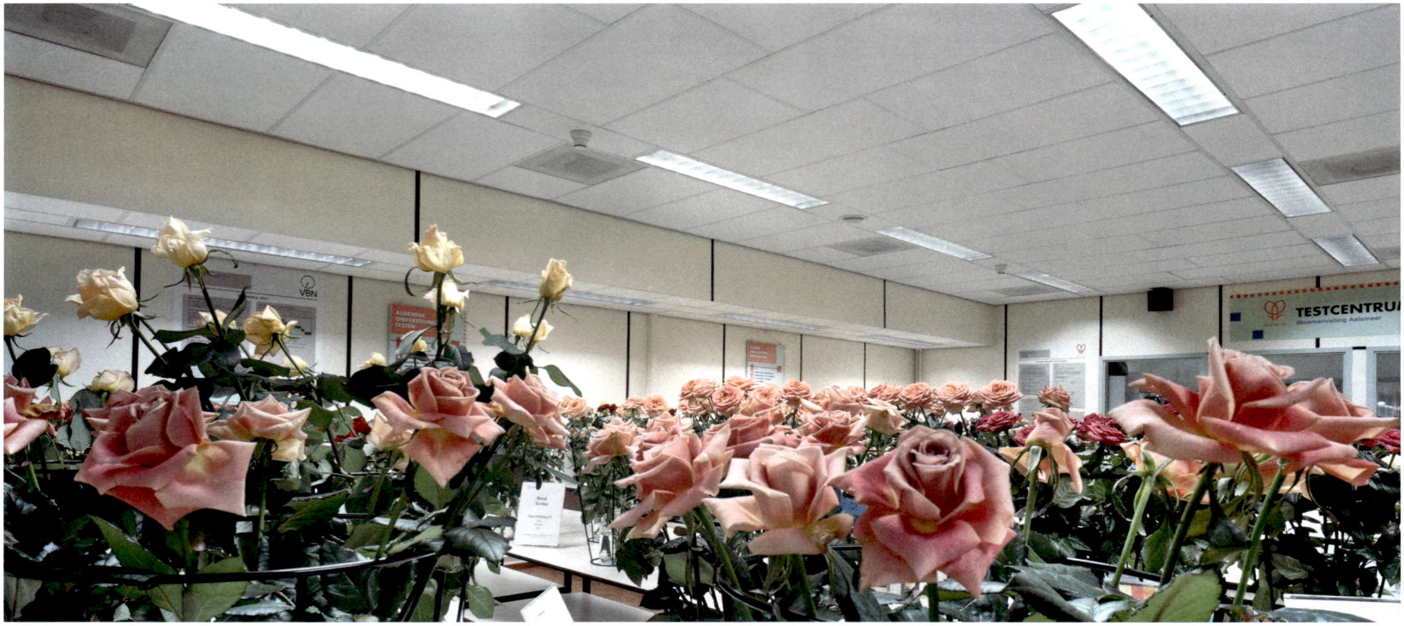

Specially prepared so as to survive long global transportation until they are put into vases in homes on other continents, the flowers are enriched with preservatives so as to appear freshly cut. The camera's symbolic feature of "capturing" operates literally: the weariness of the journey is revealed by the effort to display perfection. A colorful reminder of our own exhaustion and finitude, which the flowers we are ready to admire share with us.

Bloemenveiling Aalsmeer, flower auction, test room, Aalsmeer, Netherlands, 1998

Much of the reporting on the Arab Spring shed special light on technology and its progress, as if people resisting the imprint of long-experienced imperialism are secondary to the celebration of technological advances. Many referred to the Arab Spring as “the first Twitter Revolution” or “the first Facebook Revolution.” People’s resistance to oppression and abuse is often spatially and temporally delineated and associated with symbolic objects, preferably technological.

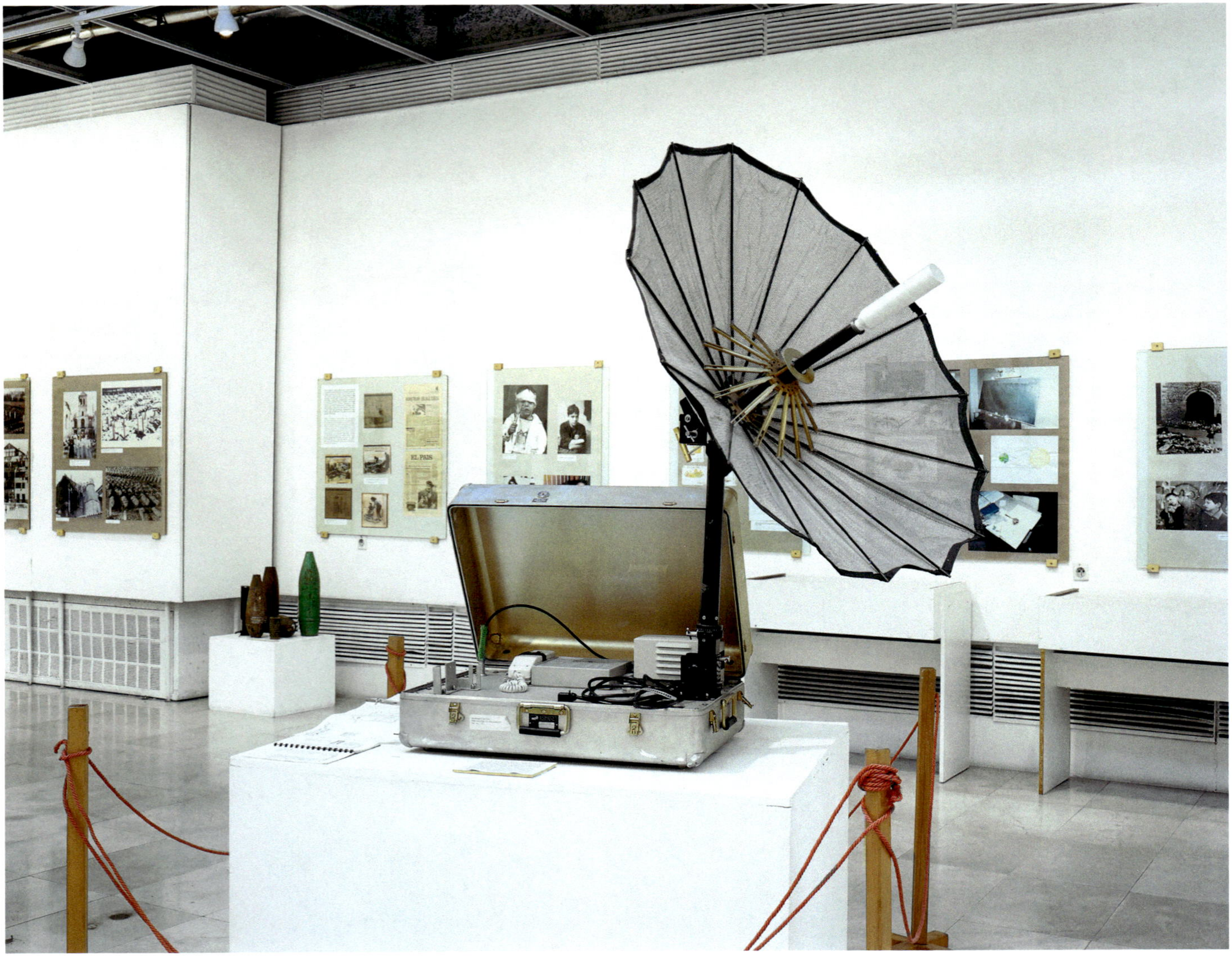

During the 1992–95 war in Bosnia and Herzegovina, this satellite telephone was, for the besieged city of Sarajevo, among the very few means of communication with the outside world. Most of the landline telecommunications infrastructure was damaged and disabled. The phone is exhibited as part of the collection for the proposed Siege of Sarajevo Museum.

Historical Museum of BiH, collection of the planned Siege of Sarajevo Museum, Sarajevo, Bosnia and Herzegovina, 2013

This is how the dispersal of people who gather in public is accelerated and anticipated, expected in advance. Similarly, museum objects are fascinating not solely for what they are, or what those in charge of speaking through them wish them to be, but also for what they are not meant to be, what they are meant to escape from, avoid, or distort. This satellite phone, even without anyone having told its story, already looks like a storytelling kit made up of a suitcase, some black boxes, and an umbrella.

In a museum focused on the siege of a city in yet another war in which people were interpellated and forced to partake, the fetishization of this object as the "only contact to the outside world" is intriguing. The object onto which this fantasy burden is projected is in itself a relic of the loss of contact with the world, not merely the outer one but also, or primarily, the internal one.

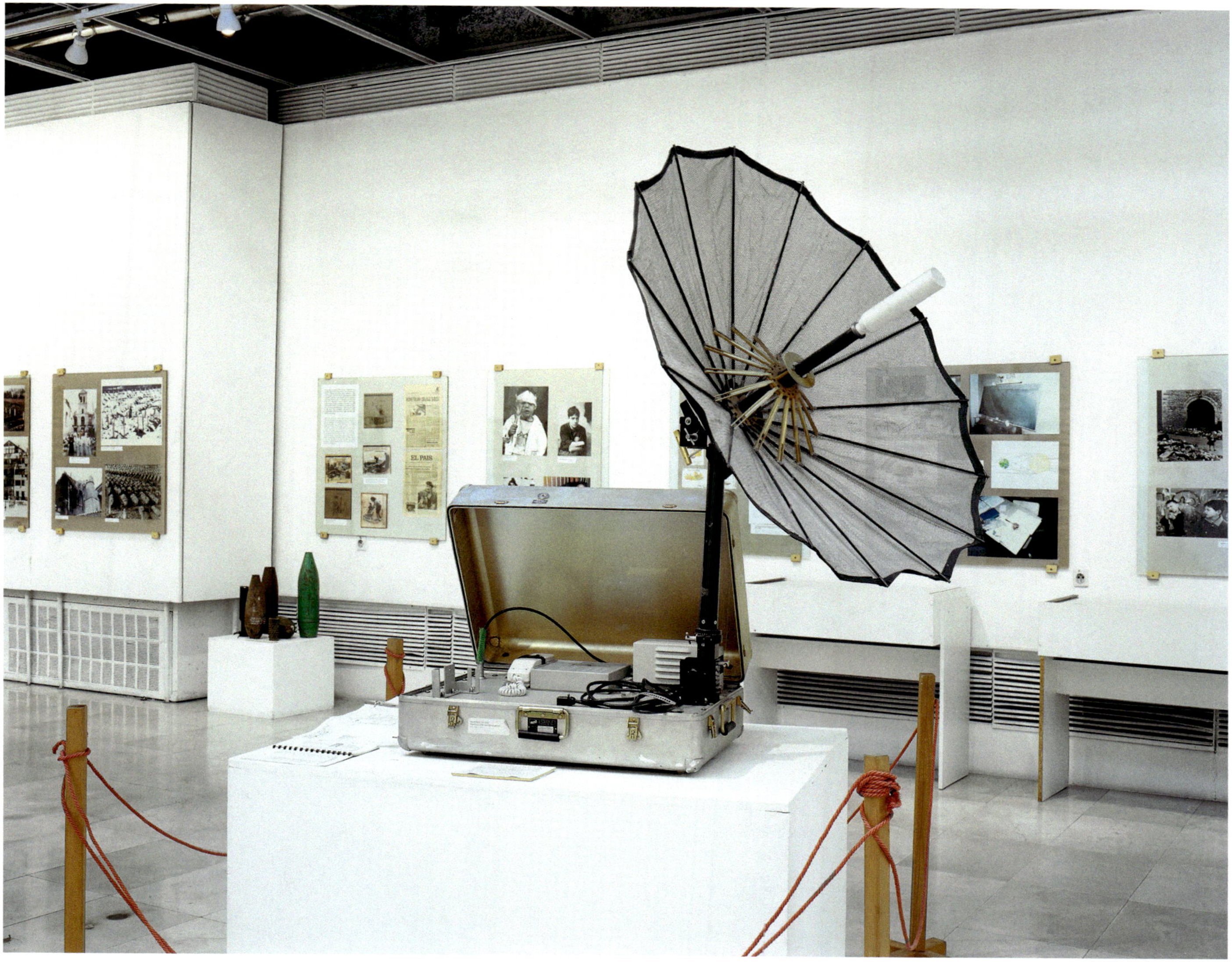

Left behind by one of the international peace troops, this satellite phone could also be read as emblematizing the disastrous role of the national/international system of sovereignties in igniting lethal violence. Our civil imagination, like the photographer's, is attracted to and affected by the presence of a seemingly not-very-advanced technology, in which the commands to pursue the new and worship the old coincide.

Historical Museum of BiH, collection of the planned Siege of Sarajevo Museum, Sarajevo, Bosnia and Herzegovina, 2013

In endowing a single object with the power to enable "sole contact with the world," we are interpellated into forgetting and setting aside other forms of contact, without which our civil imagination is conditioned by sovereign fantasies.

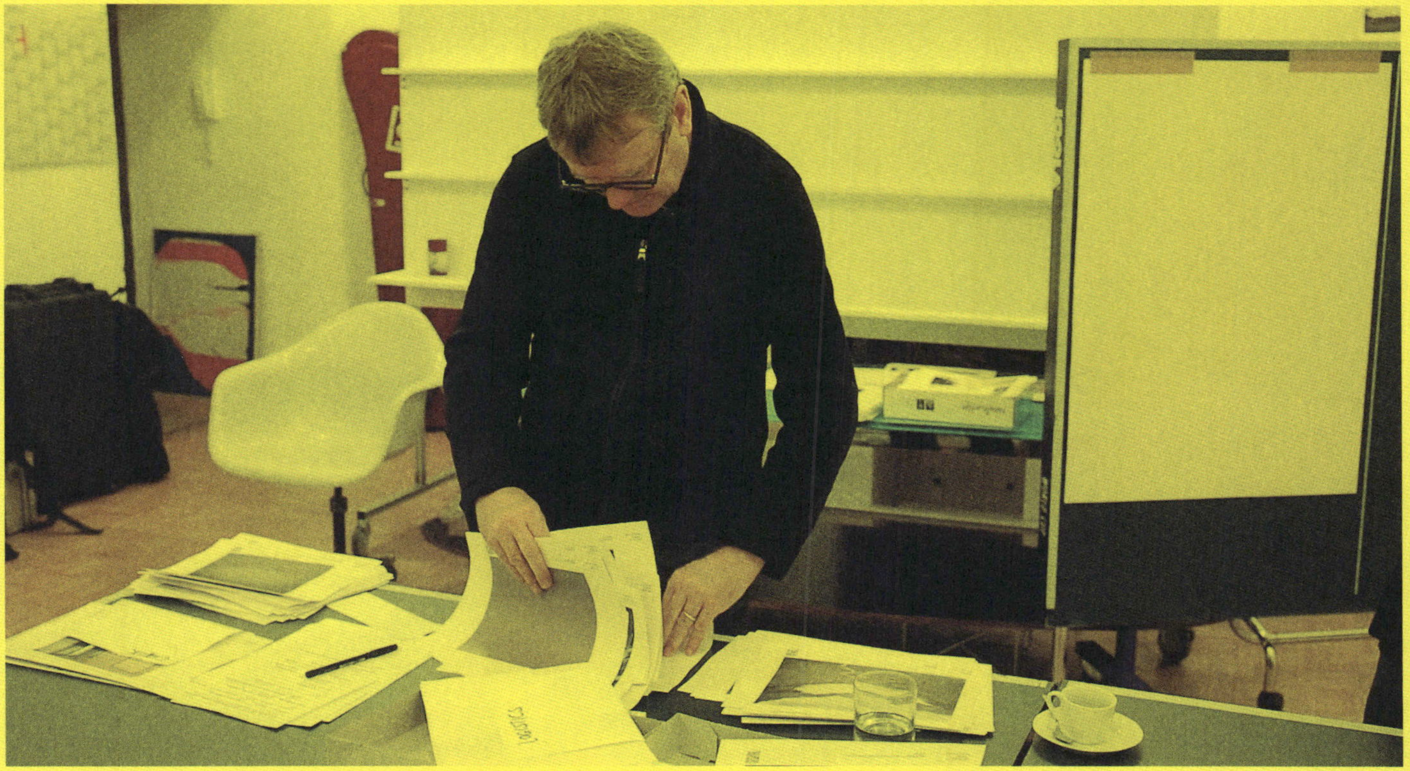

Mark Wigley

243–294

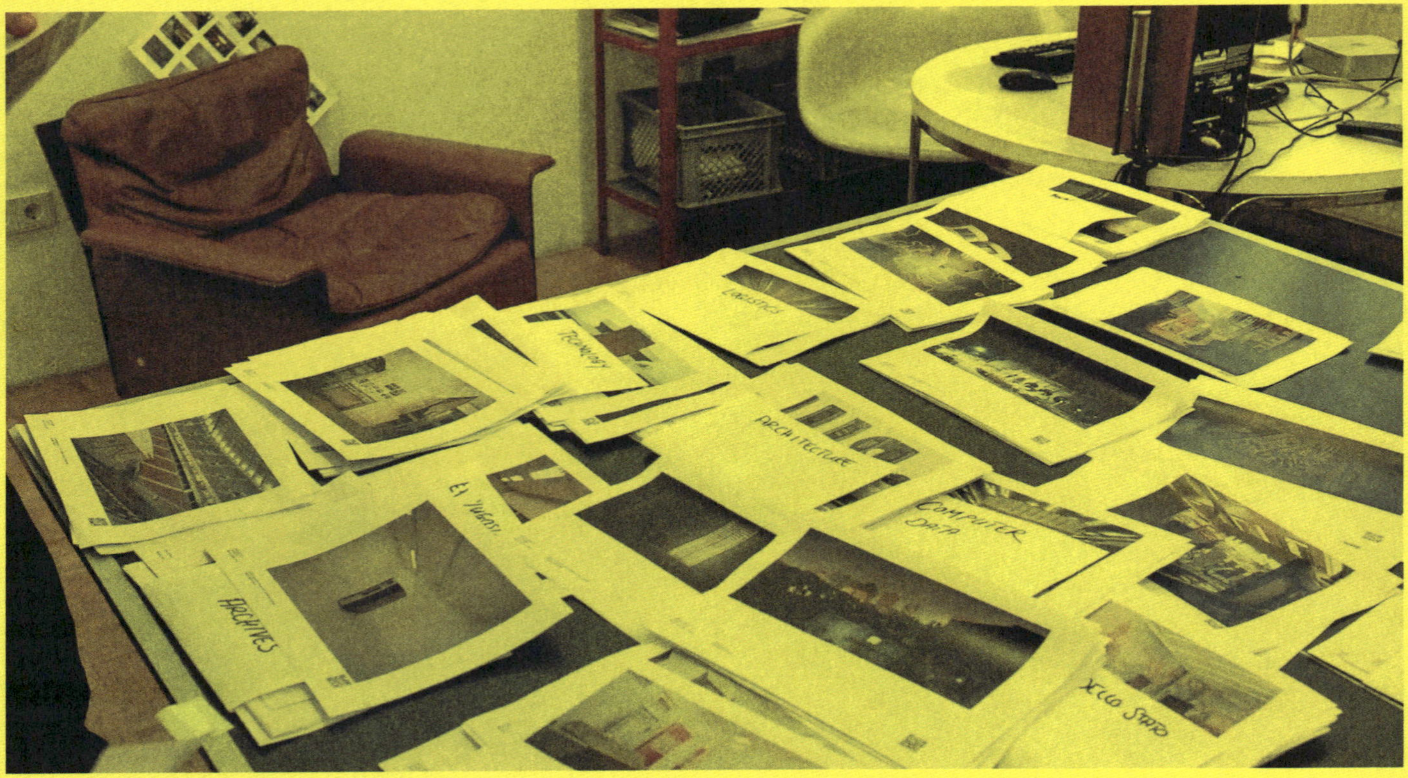

Mark Wigley and Armin Linke, Armin Linke's studio, Berlin,
November 2014

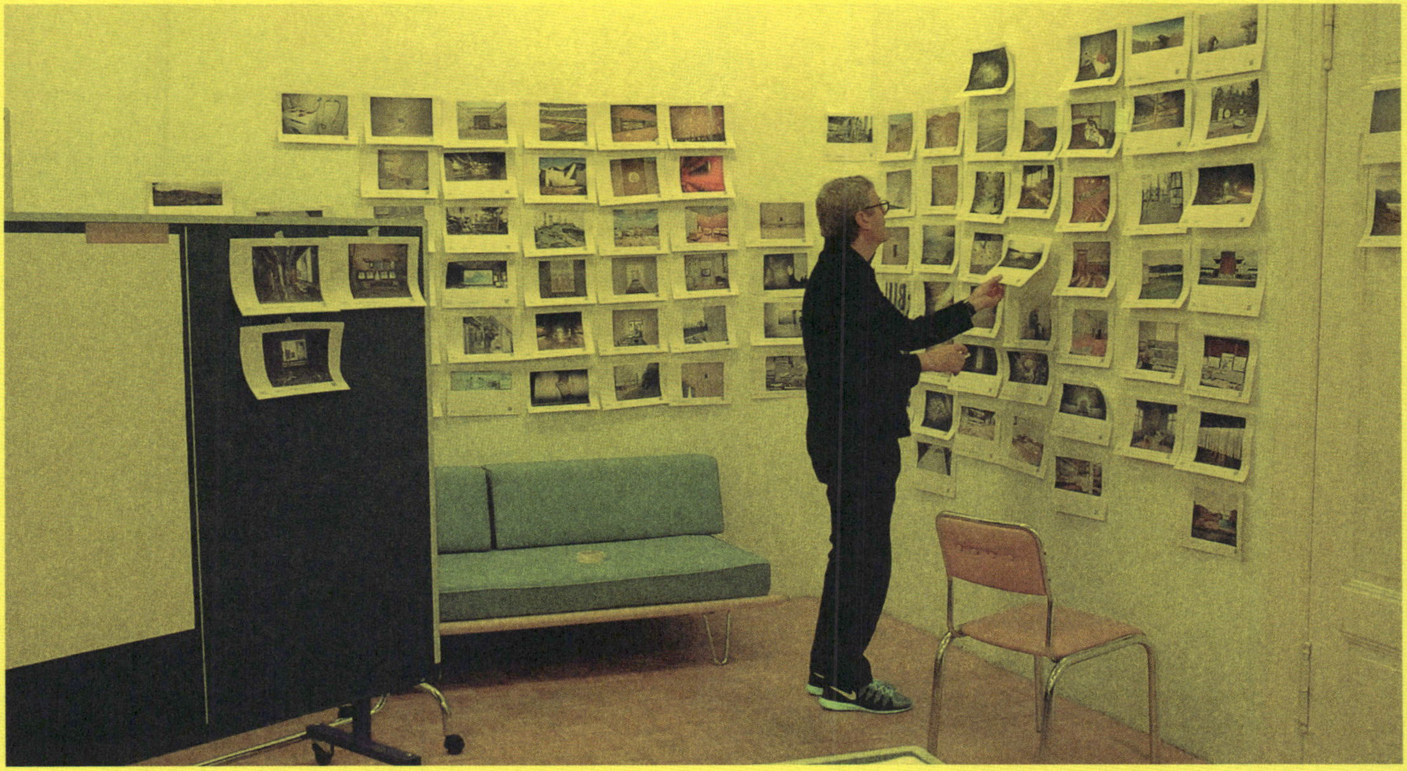

Mark Wigley and Armin Linke, Armin Linke's studio, Berlin,
November 2014

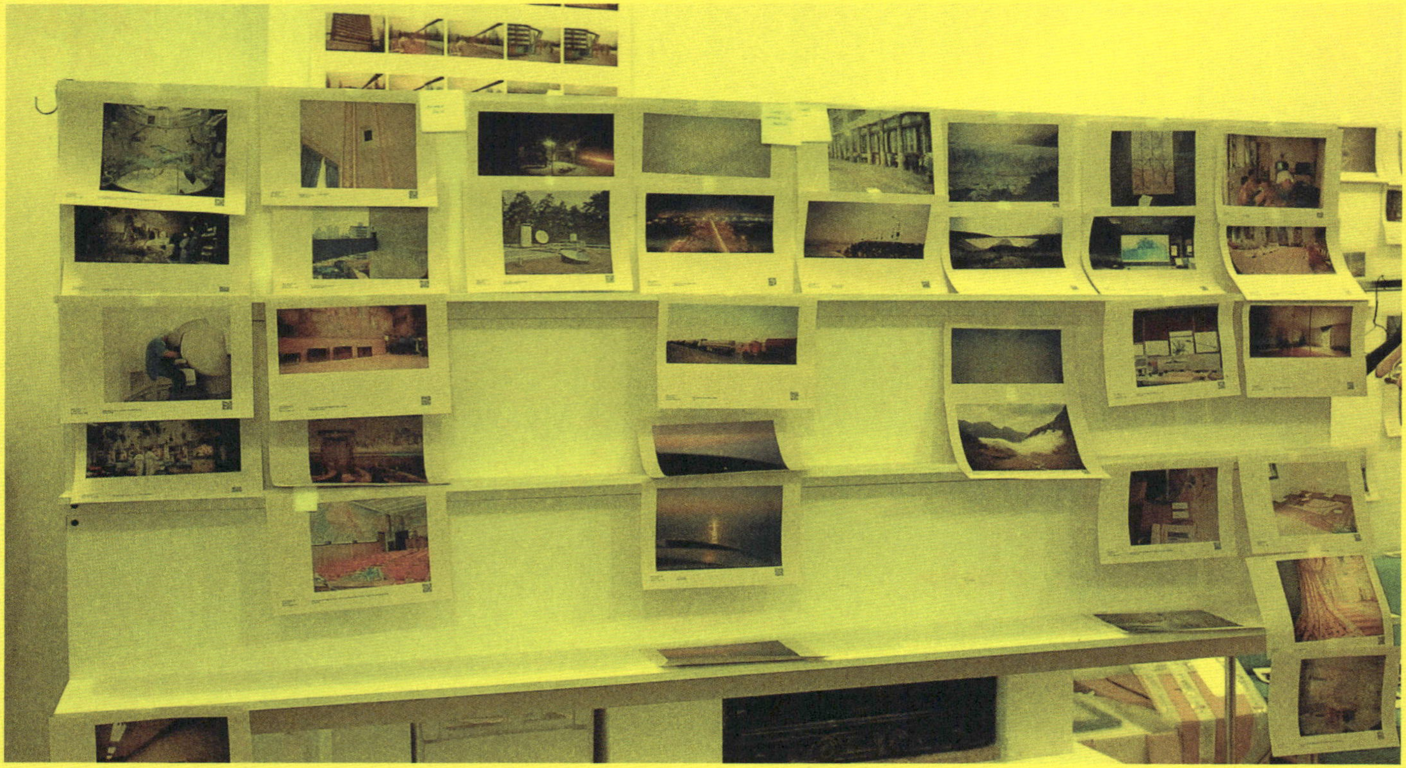

Mark Wigley and Armin Linke, Armin Linke's studio, Berlin,
November 2014

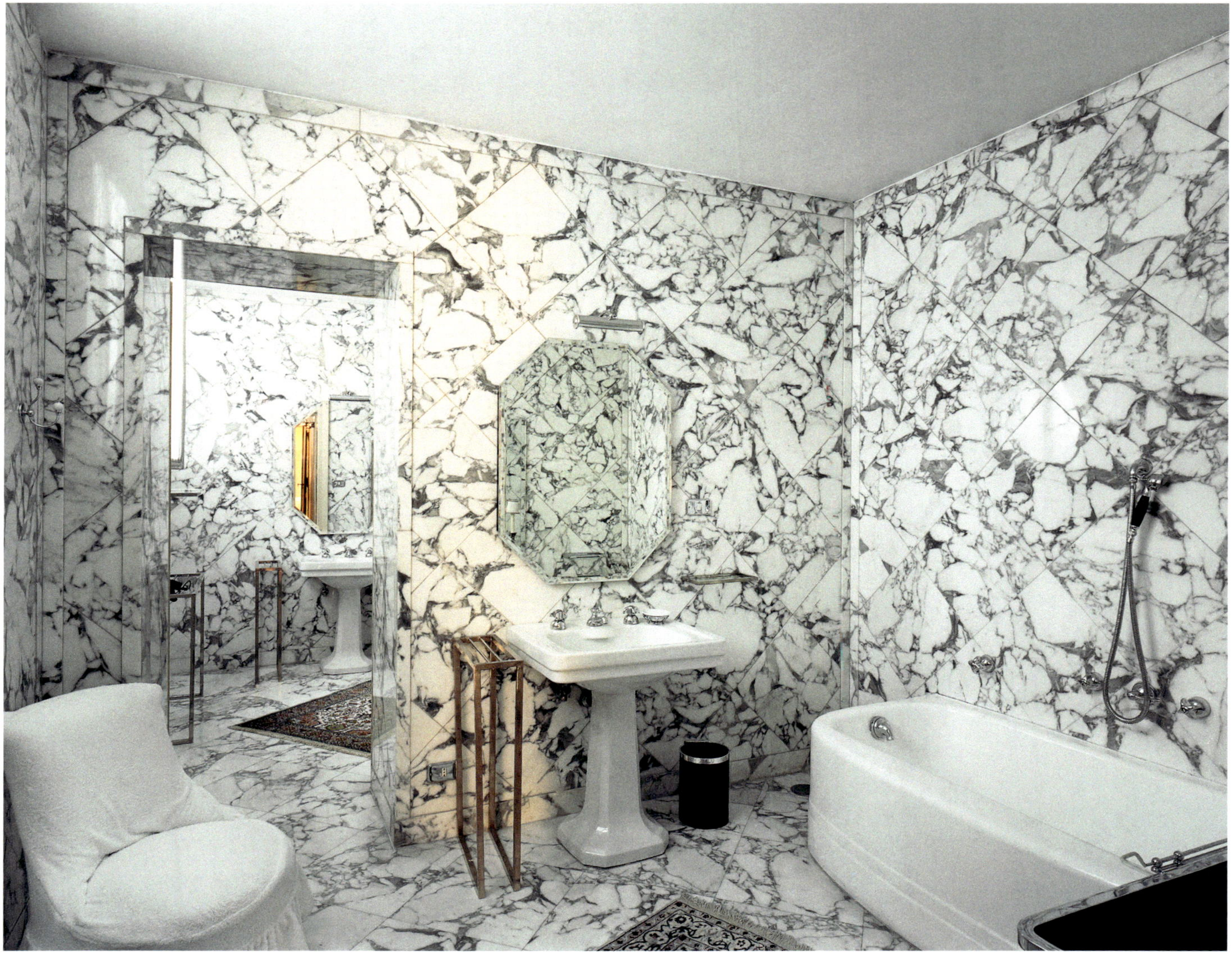

The theory would be that the main concern of architecture appears when the plumbing meets the fabric; in each of these moments the fabric is in some way violated by the plumbing.

Palazzo del Quirinale, official residence of the President of the Italian Republic, bathroom in the guest apartment, Rome, Italy, 2007

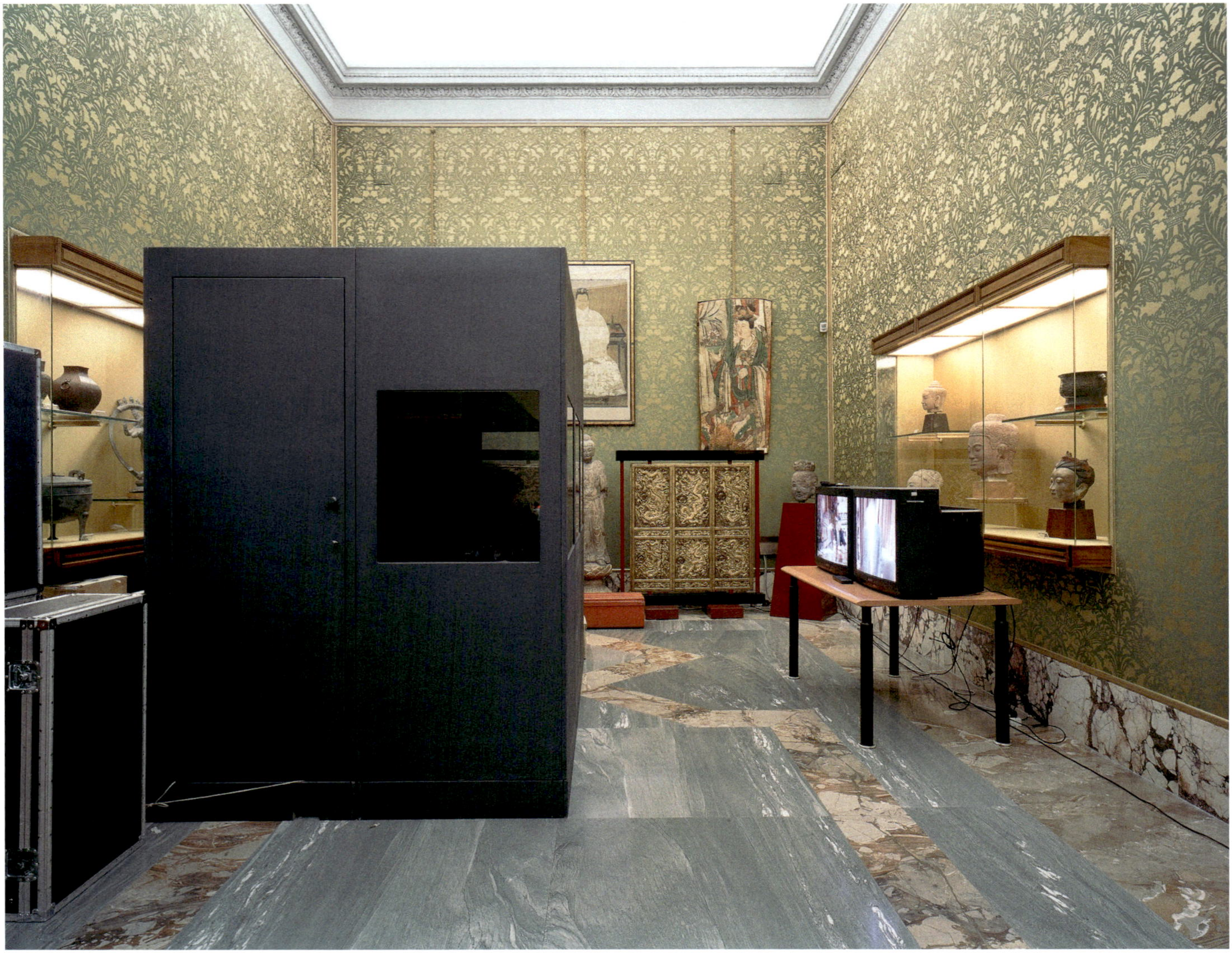

Bank of Italy, Palazzo Koch, Chinese Room (Oriental Room),
temporary simultaneous interpretation booth, Rome, Italy, 2007

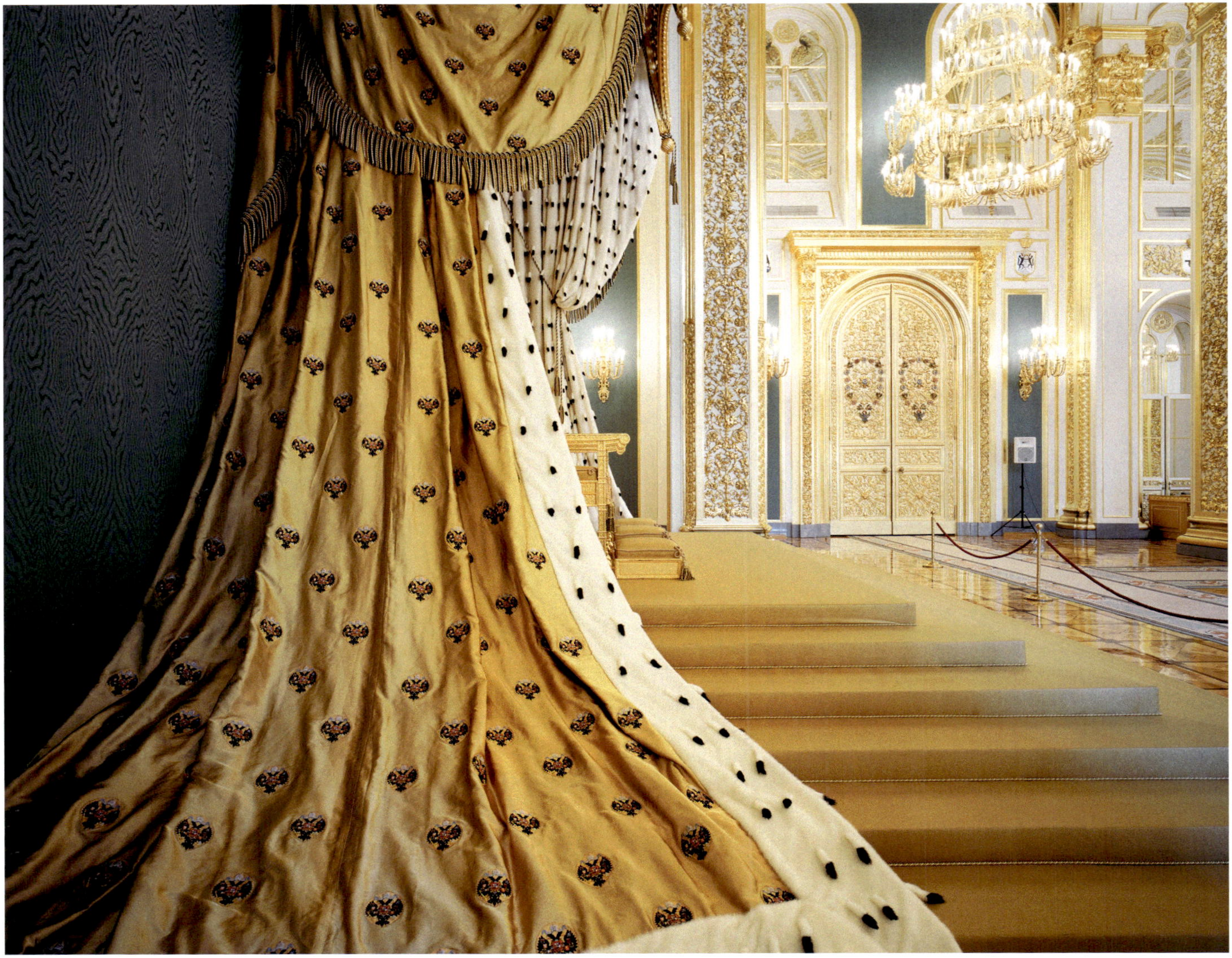

These are also the sites of exchange, negotiation, and sexual economic drama. Architecture mostly hides this, represses it. The trick is, of course, that the fabric hides the plumbing. The fabric of the human skin is, for example, very efficient at hiding the plumbing. Our plumbing is a very complex system: we breathe through billions of holes in the skin. Our skin is a fabric, and an organ.

Grand Kremlin Palace, the throne in St. Andrew's Hall, Moscow, Russia, 2011

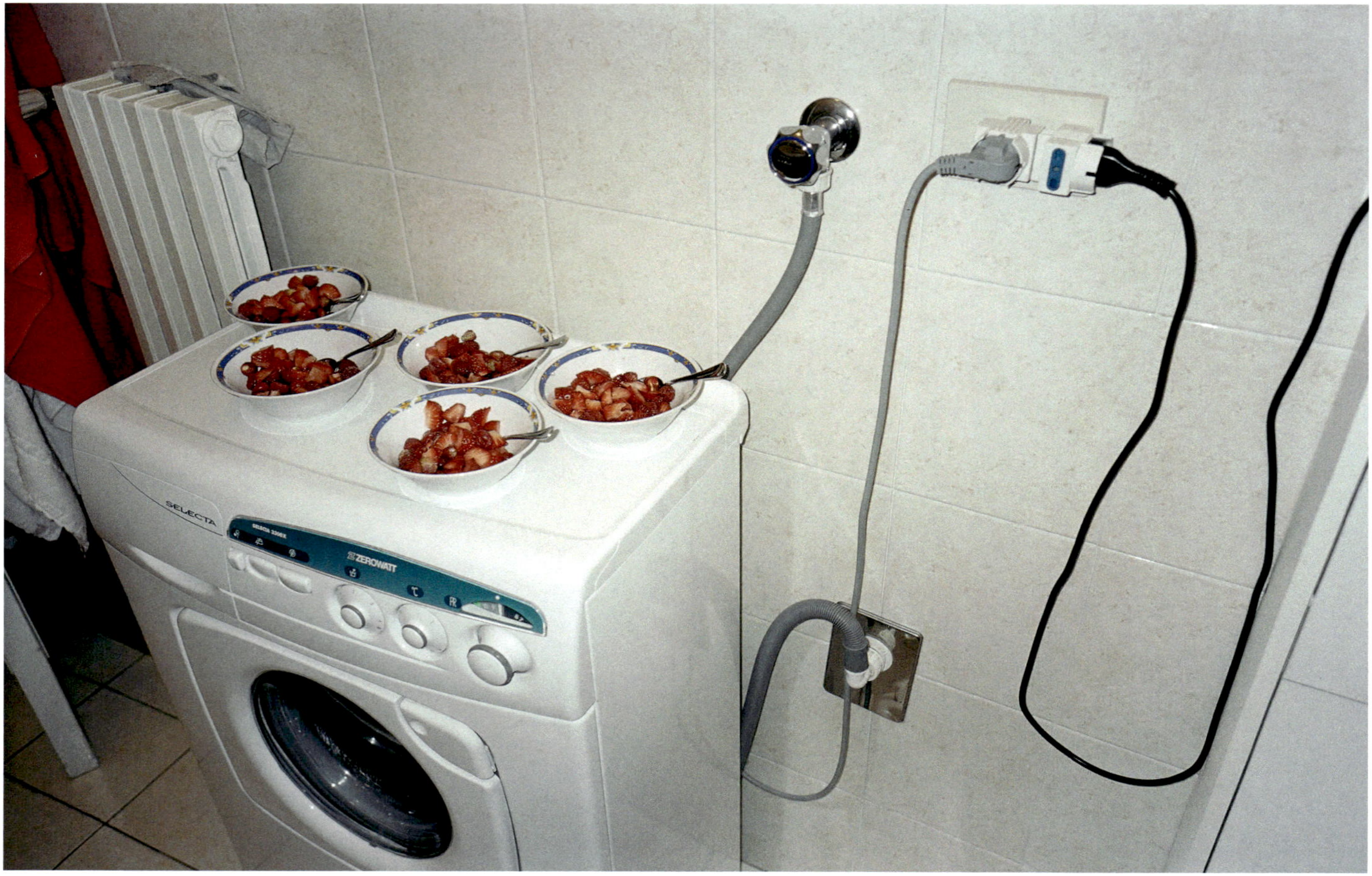

Each type of fabric is made of plumbing, on a different scale. Depending on where your gaze turns, you either see fabric or plumbing. Plumbing is like a snake. Plumbing does not obey the law. That is the great thing about it: it violates the laws it supports.

Strawberries, Milan, Italy, 2000

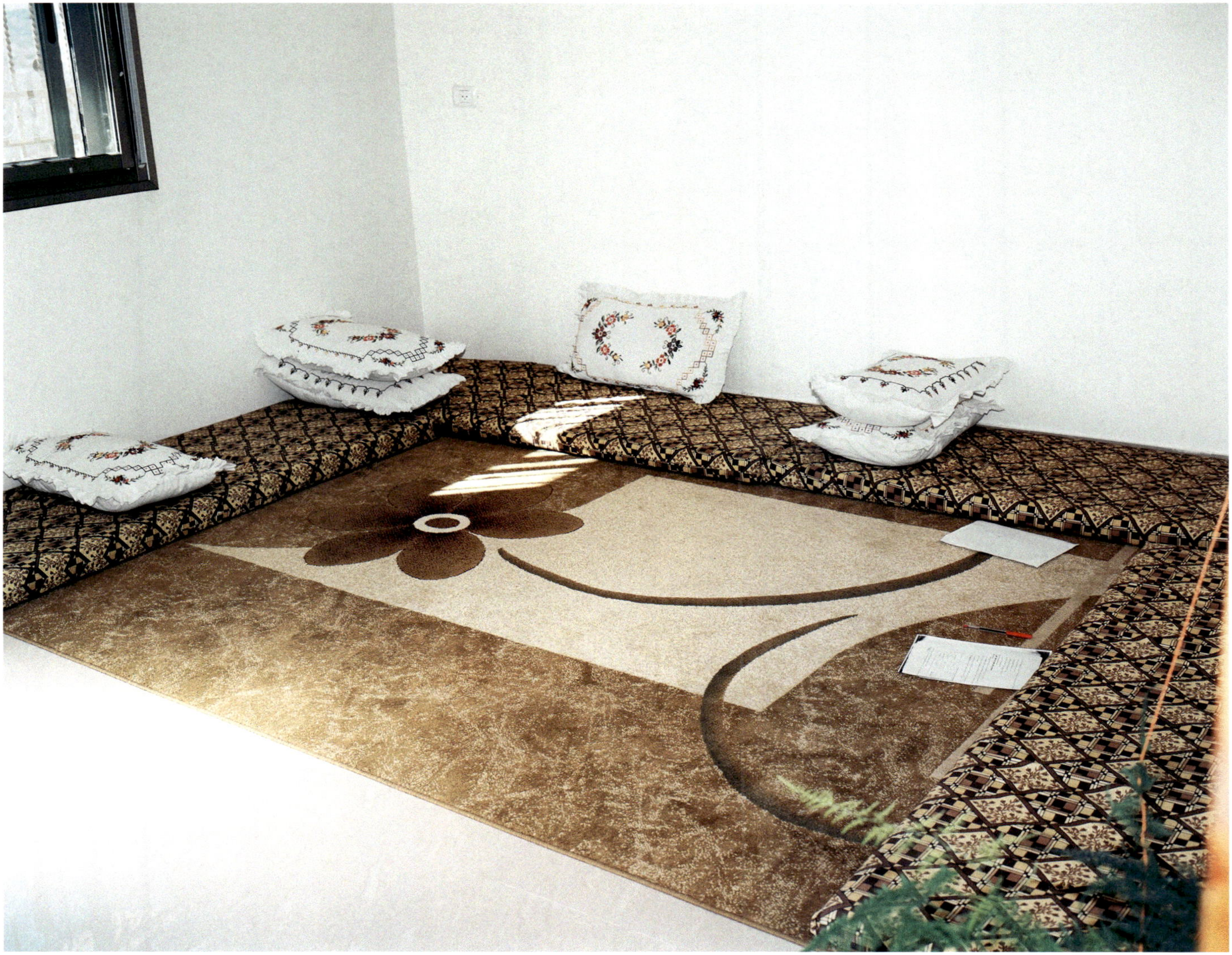

The law of this room, for example, is a square, more or less, very continuous. They have detailed the room so you have the sense of being in a bubble. The bubble is, of course, filled with plumbing of different types, which you do not see.

Refugee camp, Hebron, West Bank, 2007

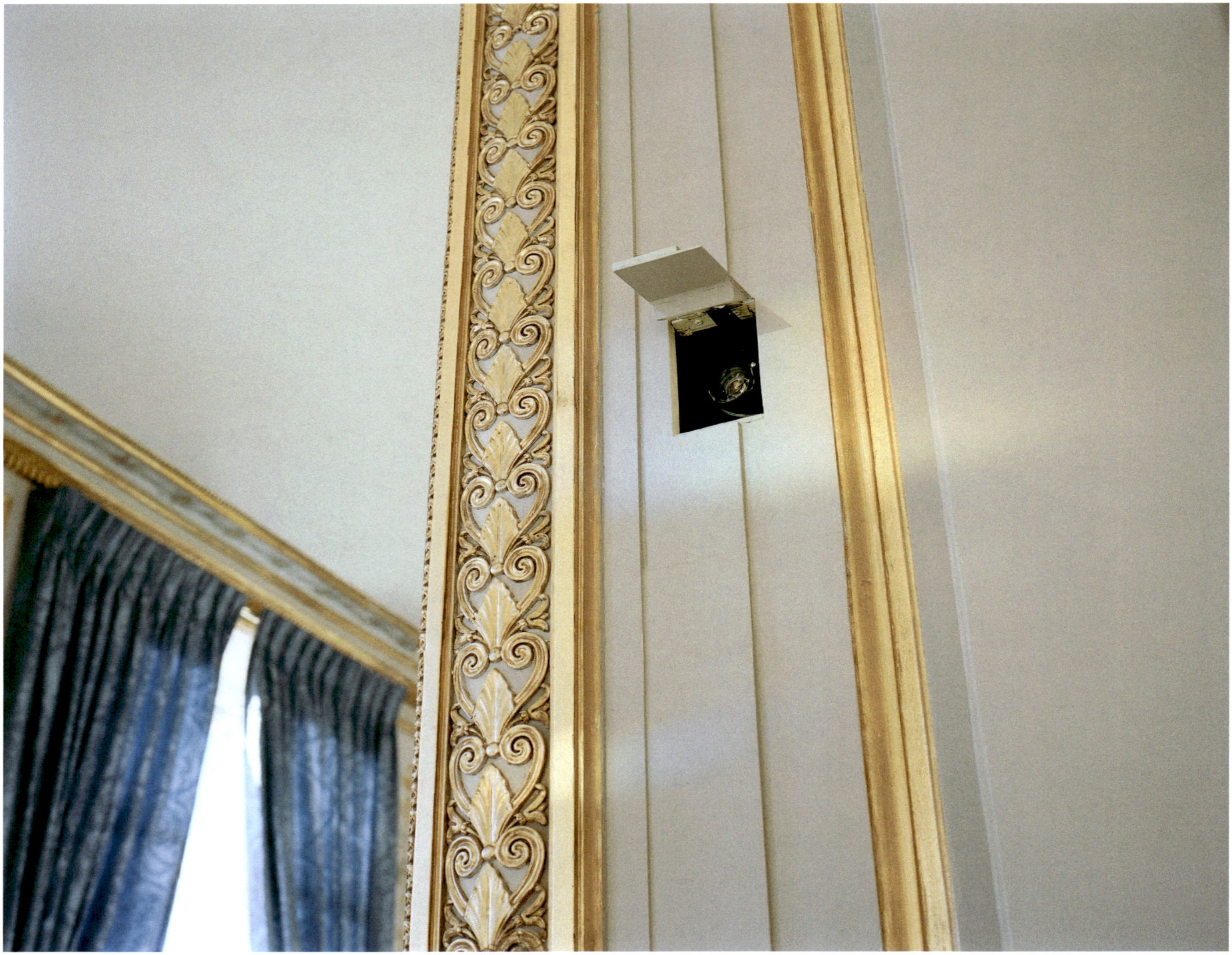

Fabric creates a sense of continuity. In order to sustain this image of a single sealed room, however, the plumbing has to violate the room.

Constitutional Council, board room, Paris, France, 2013

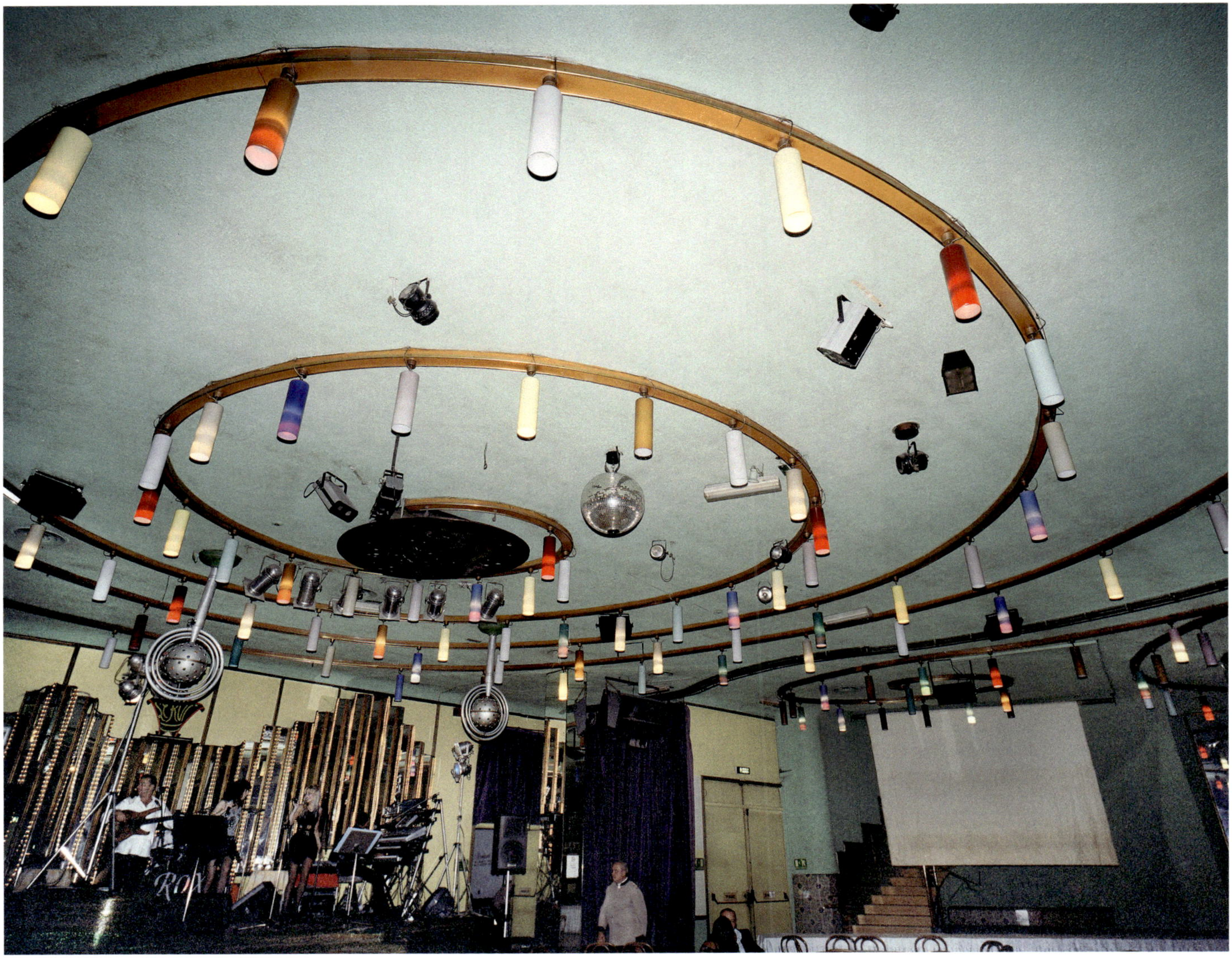

The light bulb works because there is a wire that we do not see: it disappears into the next room, then the next and the next room again. In order to be on, the light in this room must connect to a transformer in the street connected to a big wire that is in turn connected to a power station, probably somewhere in the countryside.

Carlo Mollino, Lutrario dance hall, Turin, Italy, 2006

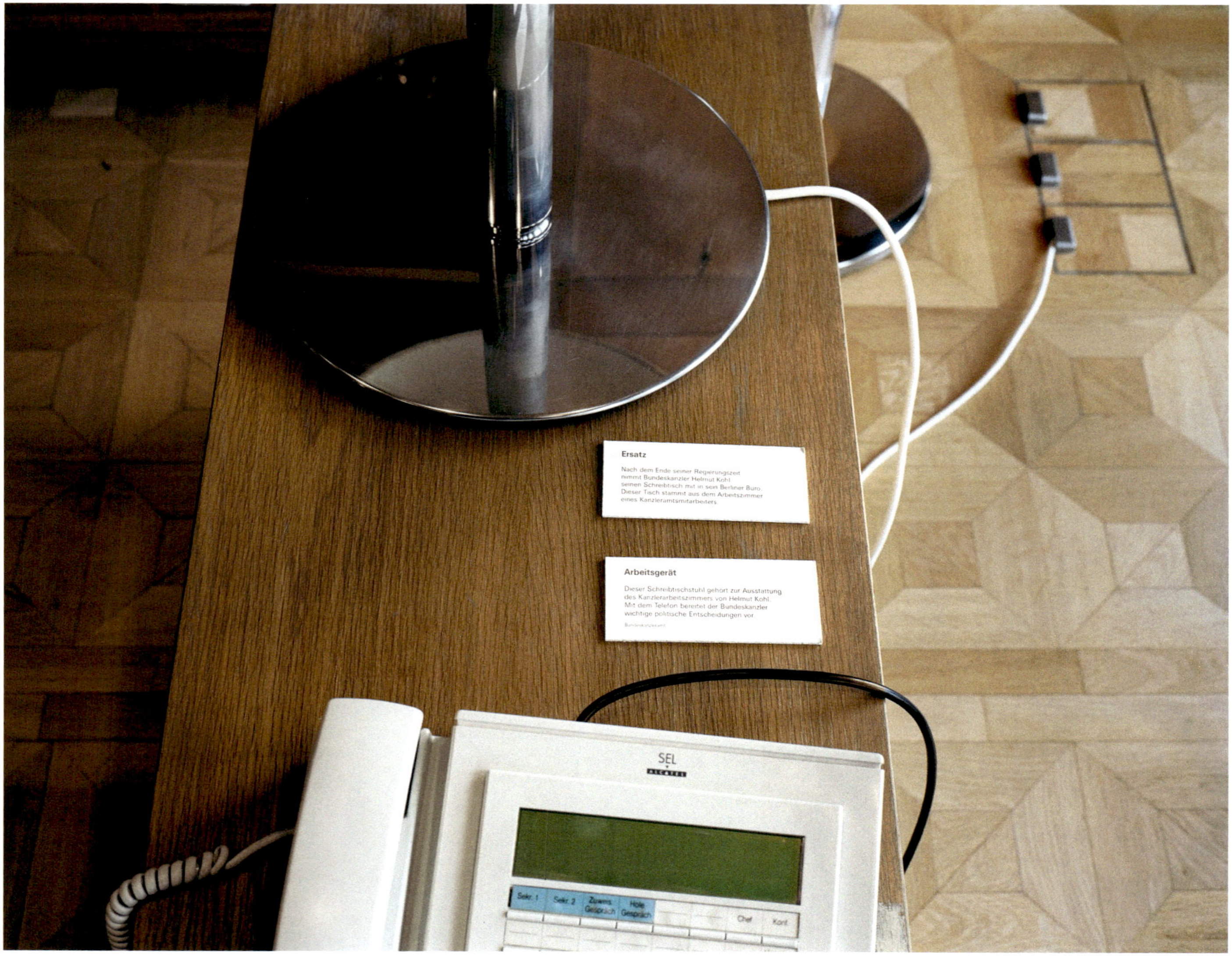

We have the telephone cable and the electric wire. You see them disappear. The place through which they disappear has to pretend to be part of the floor. So we are being told: "Don't worry, the floor is continuous. We're safe."

Federal Ministry for Economic Affairs and Energy, formerly the German Chancellor's office, Bonn, Germany, 2014

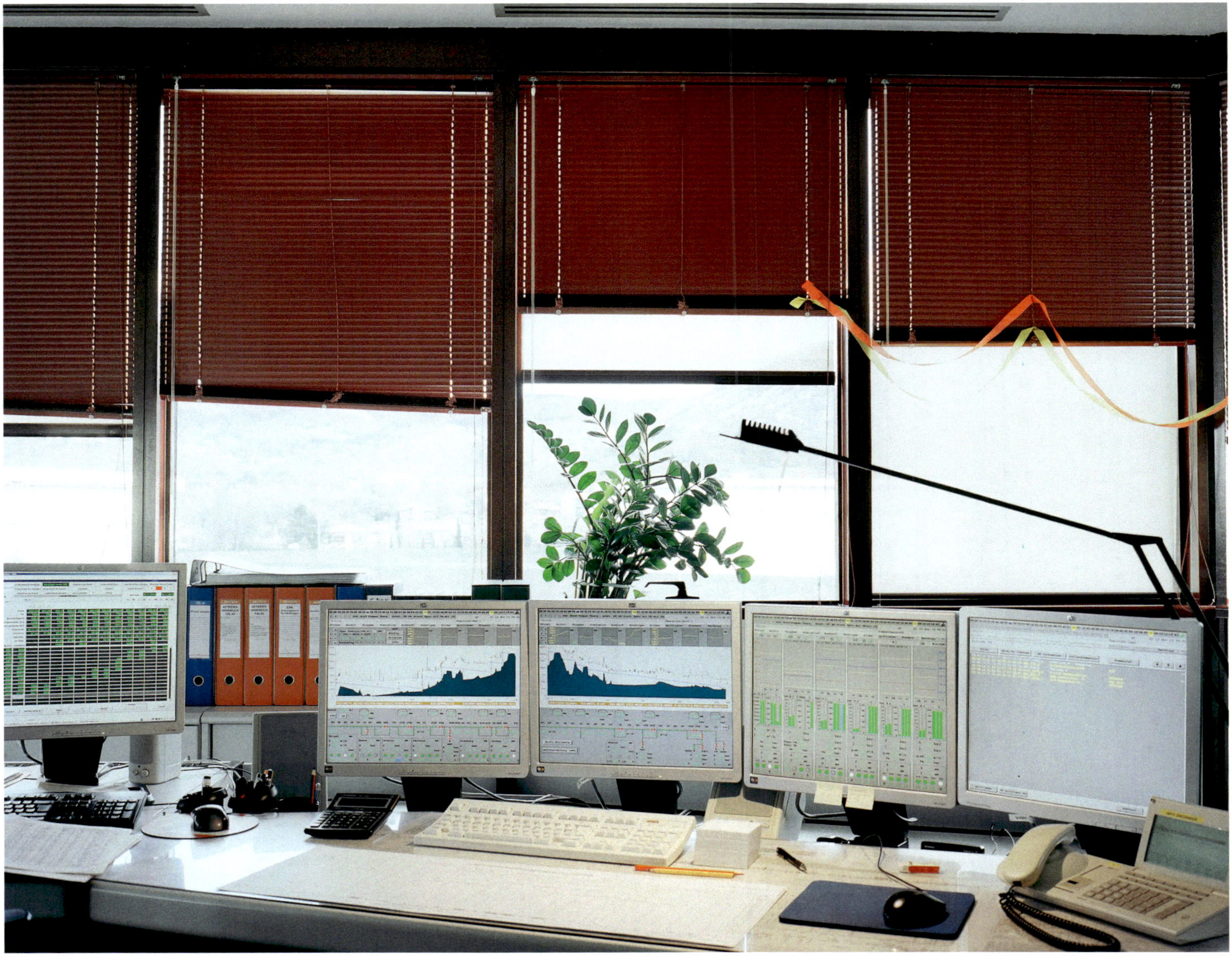

The variety of windows—in the room and on the screens—is what's really interesting in this photograph. The setup, with screens in front of the windows, points to the fact that for people working there, the real window is the one on the screen; that is where the real information is. The other one is optional.

TAL Group Transalpine Pipeline, control room, Trieste, Italy, 2012

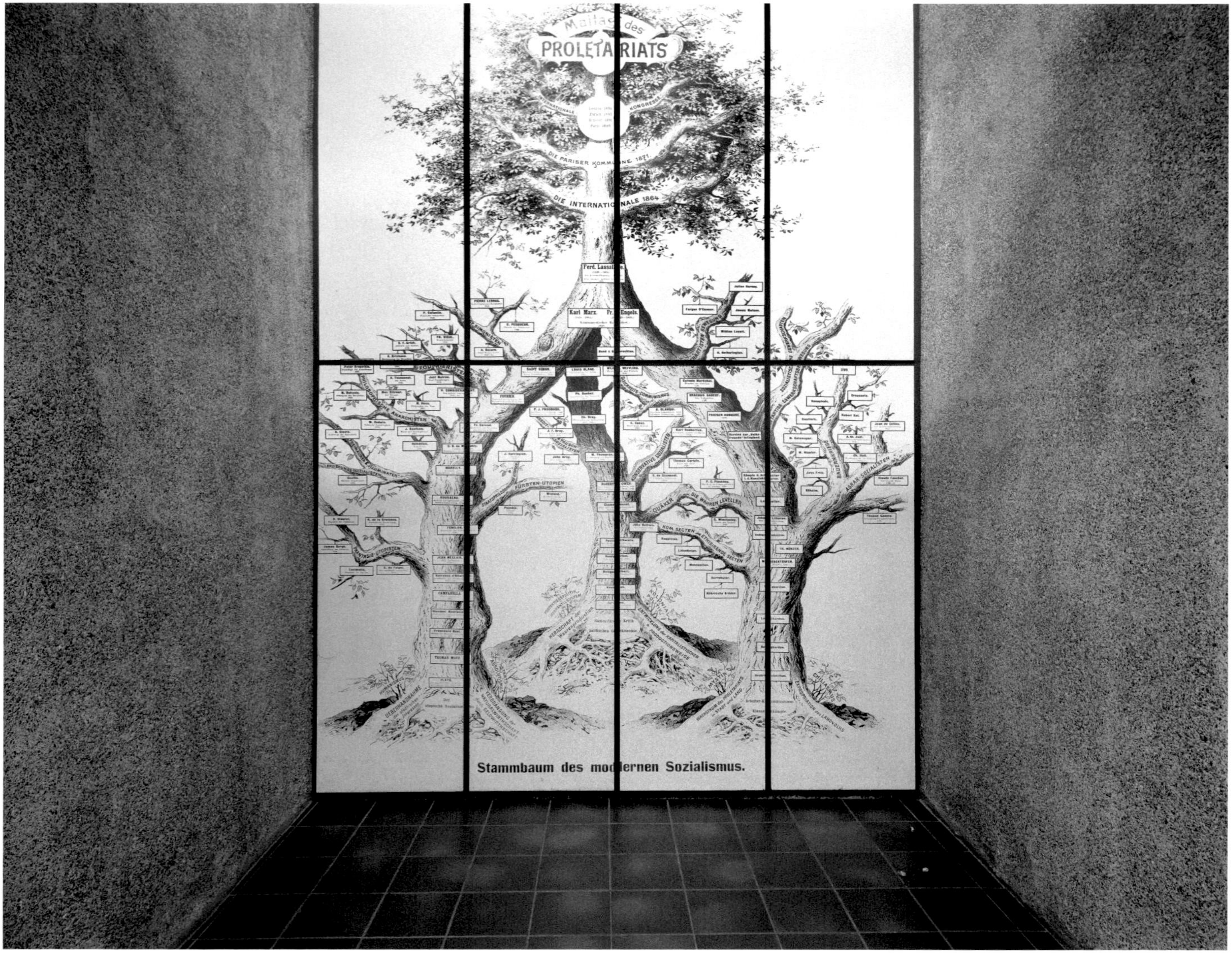

And then there are many different kinds of windows: a normal window through which you can see a tree, or a screen window with a painting of a tree or a diagram. The law of the room is that you are in this space with one, two, or three doors that you can apparently control. You think that you enter the room by stepping through a door.

Erich-Ollenhauer Haus, former SPD headquarters, Bonn, Germany, 2014

But in order to feel that you are now inside, you have to be directly connected to the outside. Not merely through a window, as in, "Ah, I see the outside." The real outside appears through the plumbing.

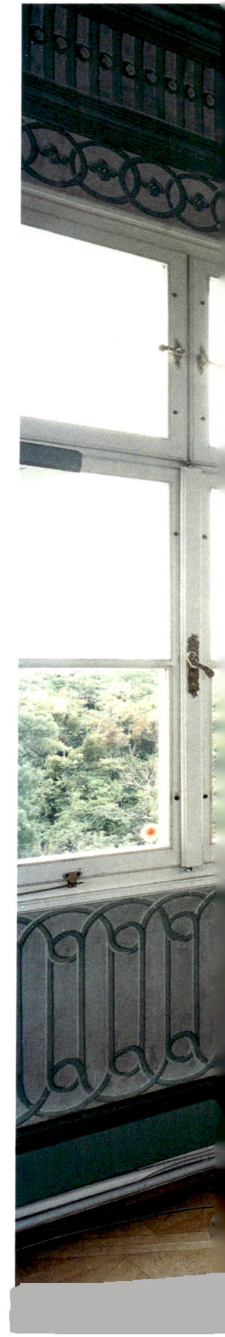

As a non-governmental research organization, founded in 1972, IIASA conducts research into critical issues—relating to the global environment, economics, technology, social change, etc.—that are too large or too complex to be solved by a single country or academic discipline.

International Institute for Applied Systems Analysis (IIASA), office, Vienna, Austria, 2013

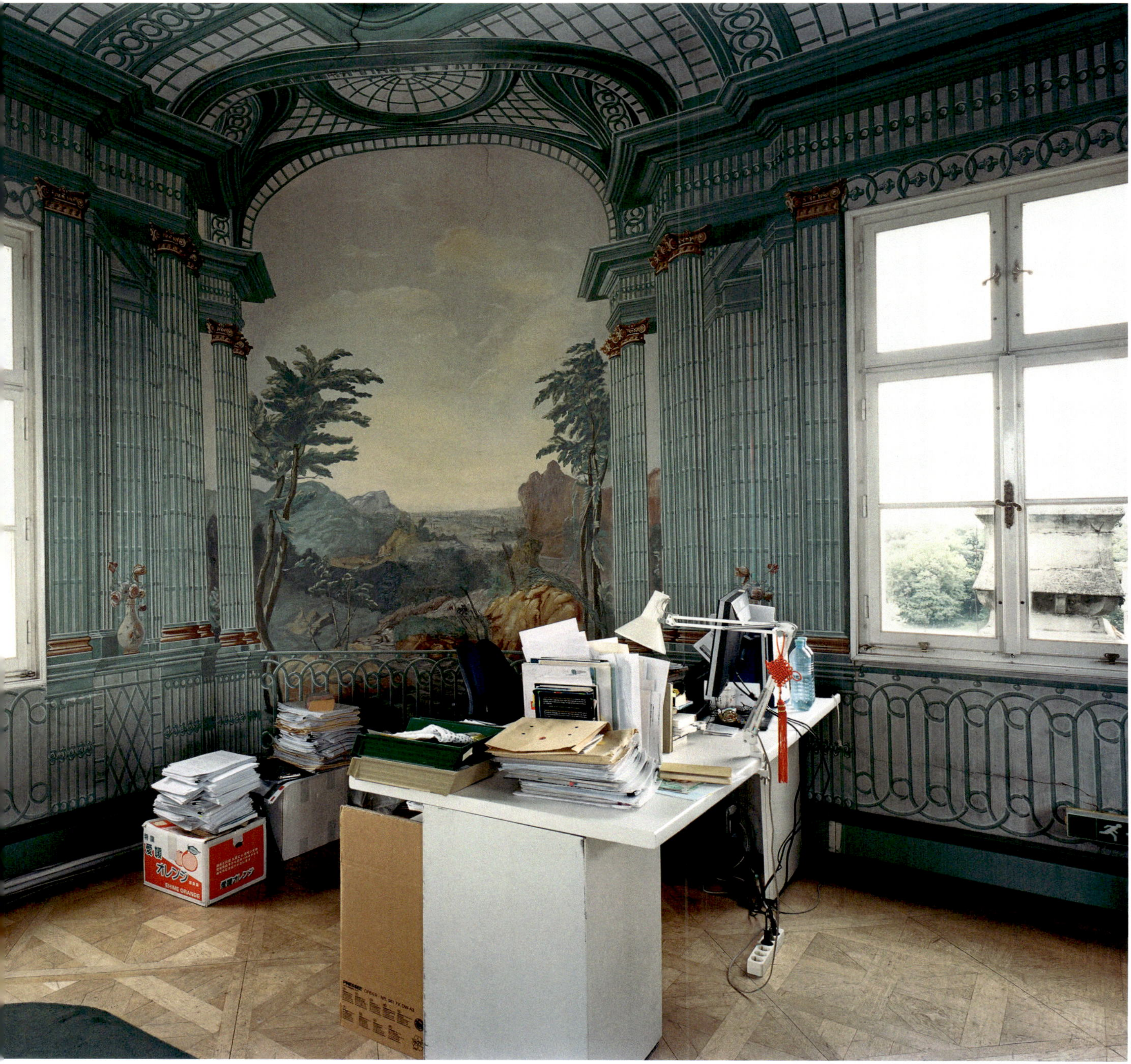

We only have one concept here, a love story between the fabric and the plumbing. We learn that the fabric is not quite what we thought it was, that the plumbing is not what we thought either.

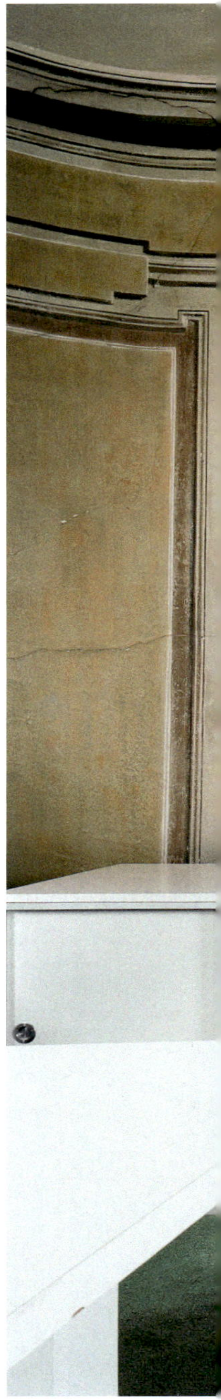

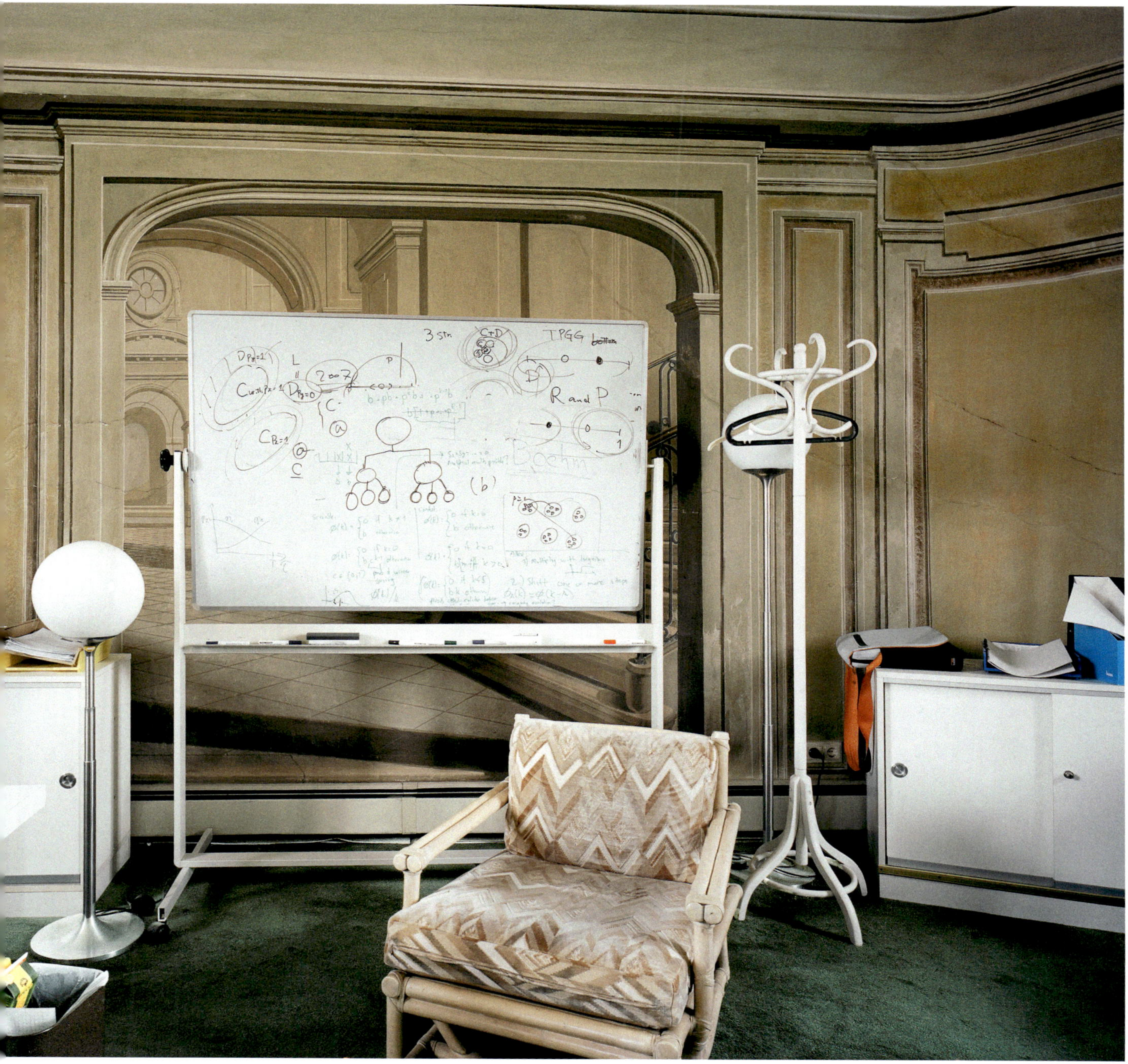

Ilasa International Institute for Applied Systems Analysis, Vienna, Austria, 2013

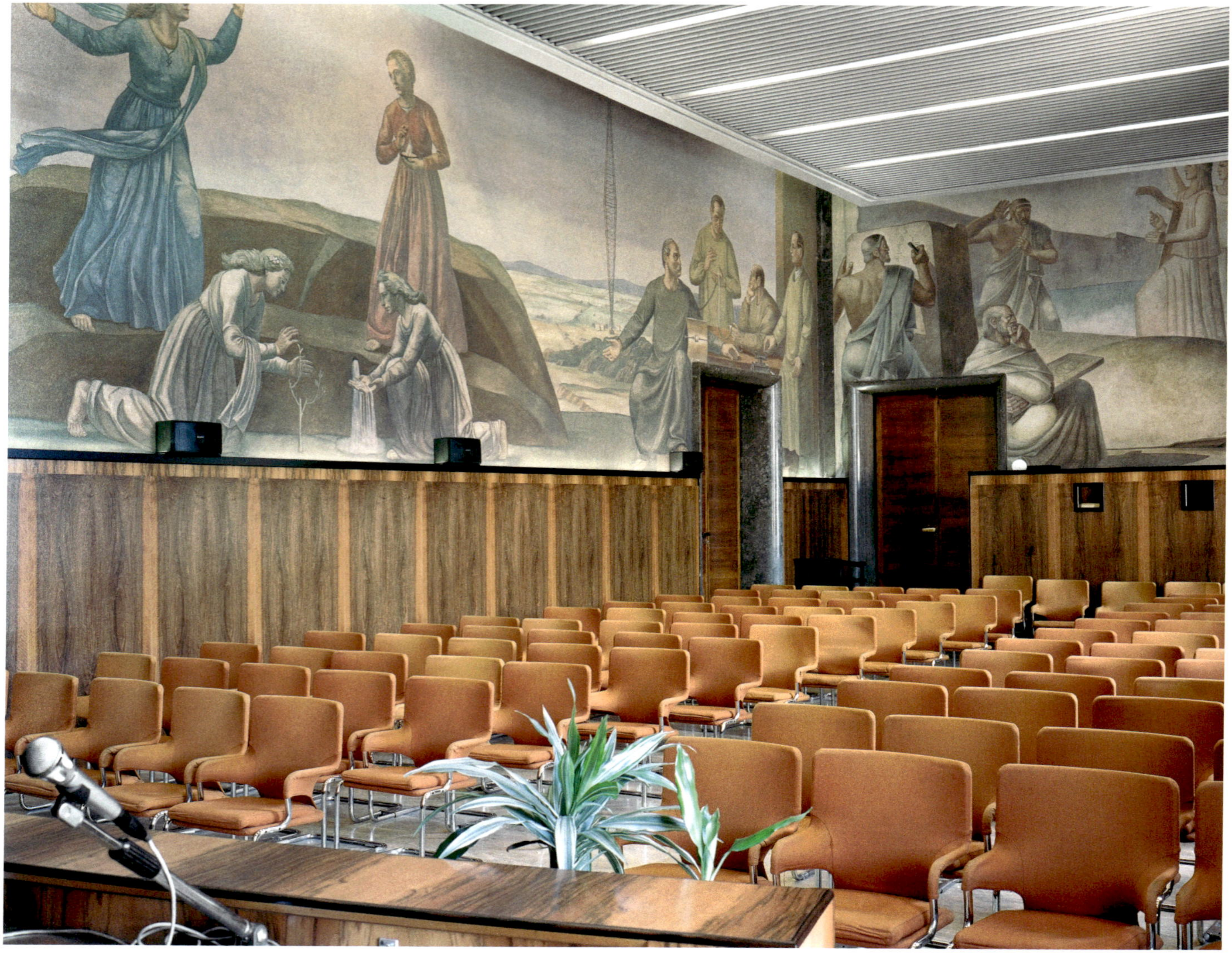

The Fascist-era frescos by Antonio Achilli celebrate Italian scientific achievements through history, from Archimedes to Lucrezio Caro, Galileo Galilei to Christopher Colombus.

We then see them dance and we see the architecture somehow emerging in the moment of plumbing becoming fabric and fabric becoming plumbing.

CNR, National Science Research Council, Marconi conference hall, Rome, Italy, 2007

In that very moment architecture enters as a fabric to disavow this slippage between fabric and plumbing. It gives you a beautifully designed faucet and says, "Don't worry, this is architecture, this is design. You don't have to think about the mountains, your neighbors, the economy, the ecology, or the rivers." Looking at these images, my double question is always, What is the fabric? Do we see the appearance of the plumbing?

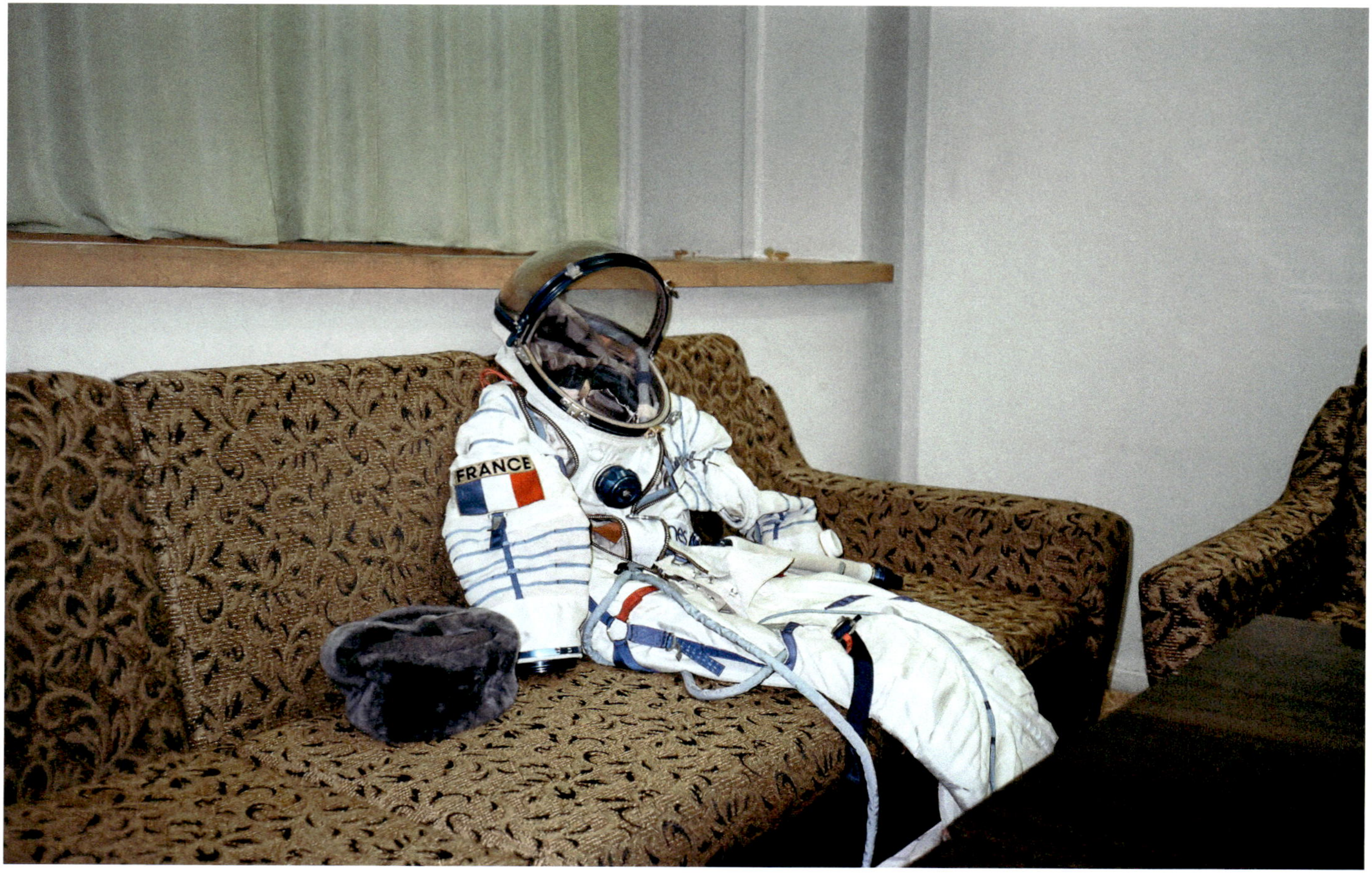

The brilliant thing about the spacesuit is that it does not really need the astronaut. It is perfectly operational. I love this image because the suit sits, resting on a couch, in an utterly domestic situation. The room becomes a spaceship. Plumbing doesn't simply support human life. It has a human life.

Star City, Cosmonaut Training Center, Moscow, Russia, 1998

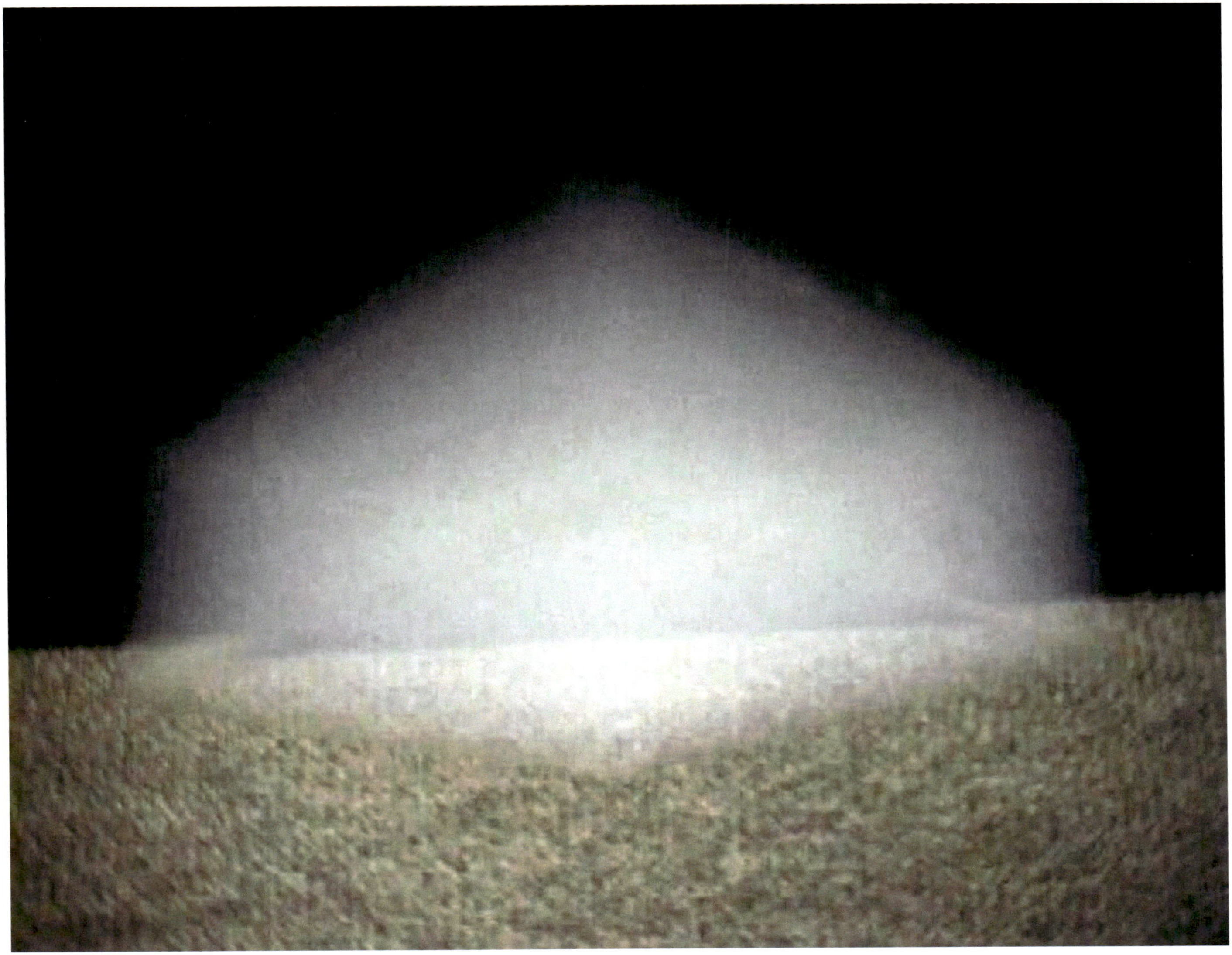

Aerogel is an ultralight nanoporous material: a gel in which the liquid element is replaced with gas. This translucent, extremely low-density substance has the lowest-known heat conductivity in a solid and is used as insulation in space exploration.

NASA Jet Propulsion Laboratory, Pasadena, USA, 1999

The walls of the seminar hall in this theoretical physics center are lined with portraits of famous physicists. So the idea is that you could be just a head. Stephen Hawking is the perfect image, telling us, basically, that you just need a brain and whatever technology necessary to keep it operating. There is this idea that the brain of a physicist can make the invisible world of the universe visible: the brain, not the feet or the hands. So, you just need the heads, sort of decapitated.

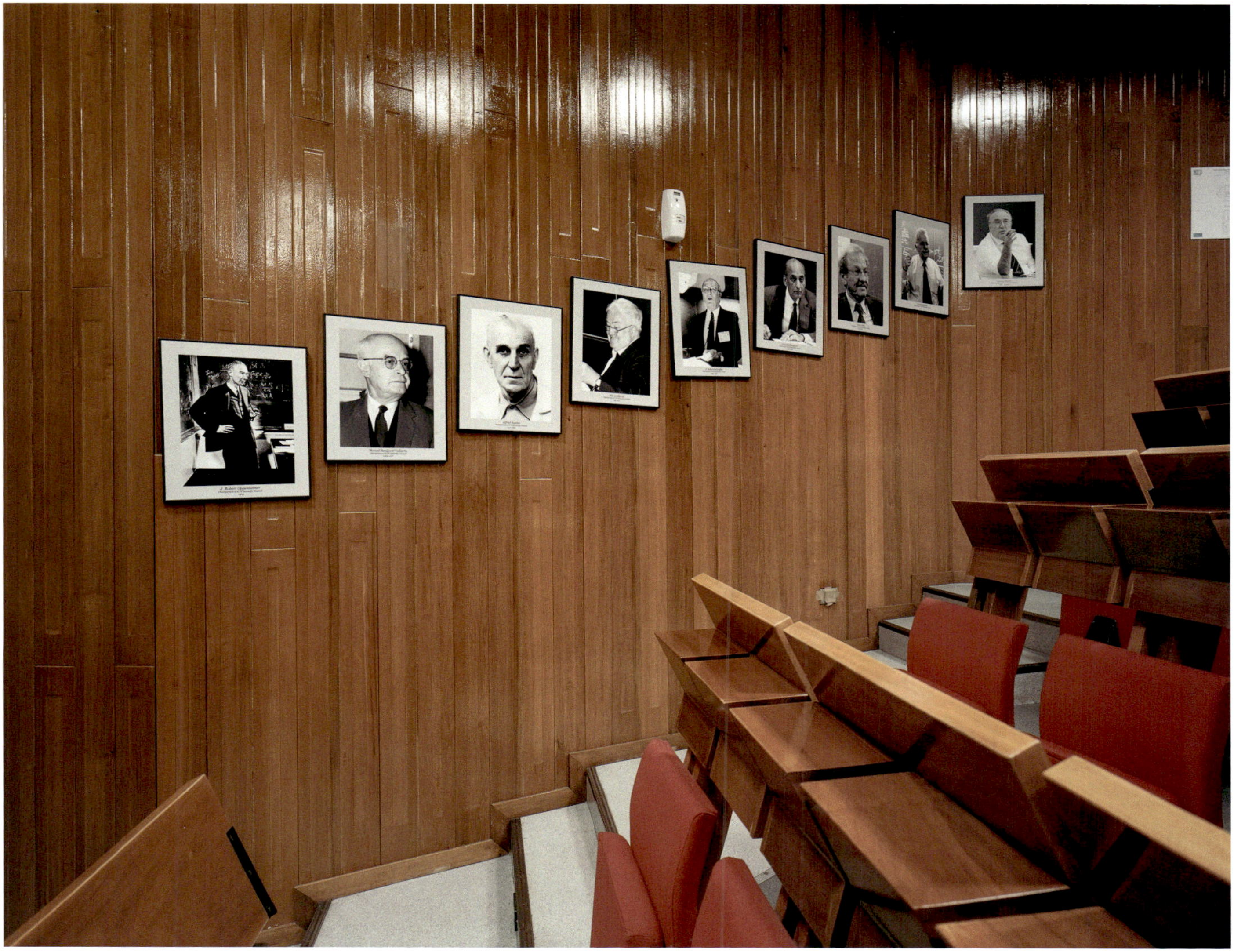

You could imagine a body under each head, or perhaps the classroom has become the body. When this hall, this classroom is full, a hundred heads of young scientists will be accompanied by these floating heads, portraits of physicists lined up on the wall. They are all looking at images, models, words, and formulas. In that way, a lecture room is the meeting of fabric and hidden world.

The Abdus Salam International Centre for Theoretical Physics, Trieste, Italy, 2012

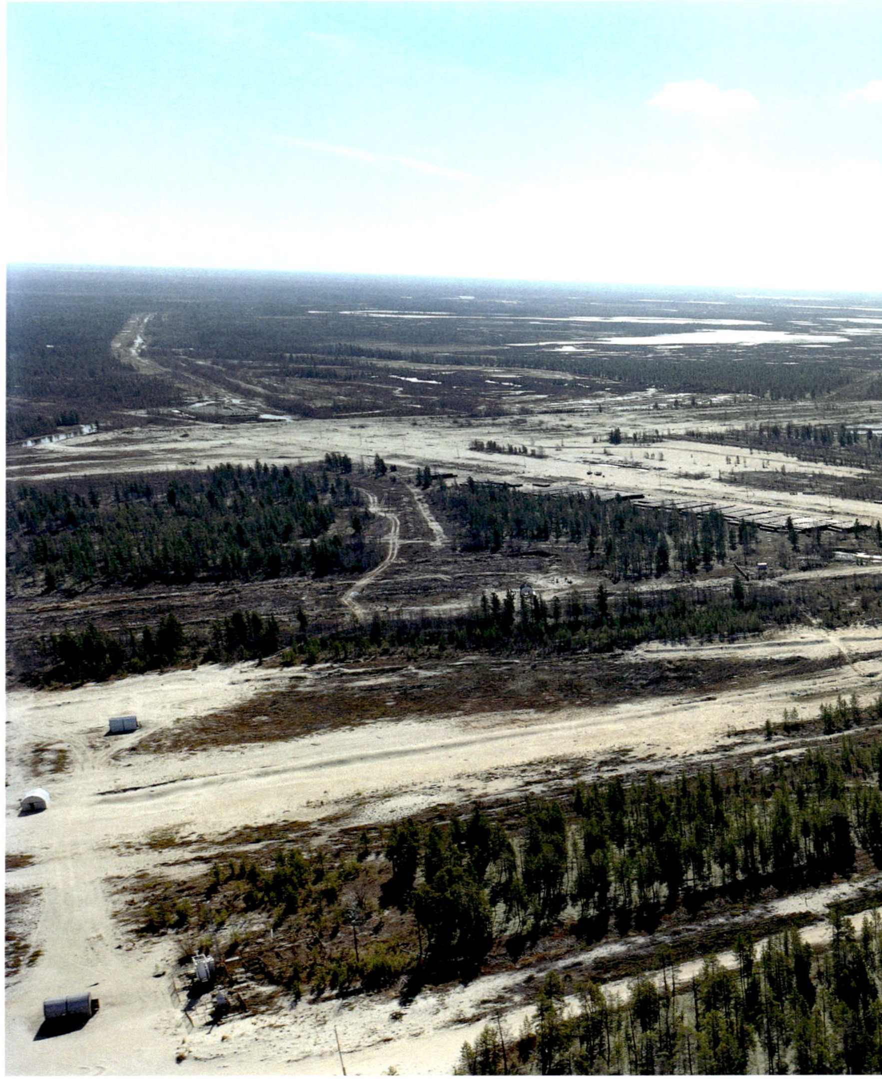

According to a 2009 CIA document released in 2010 by WikiLeaks, the Nadym Gas Pipeline Junction is considered to be one of the most critical gas infrastructures in the world.

Gas pipeline junction, Nadym, Russia, 2011

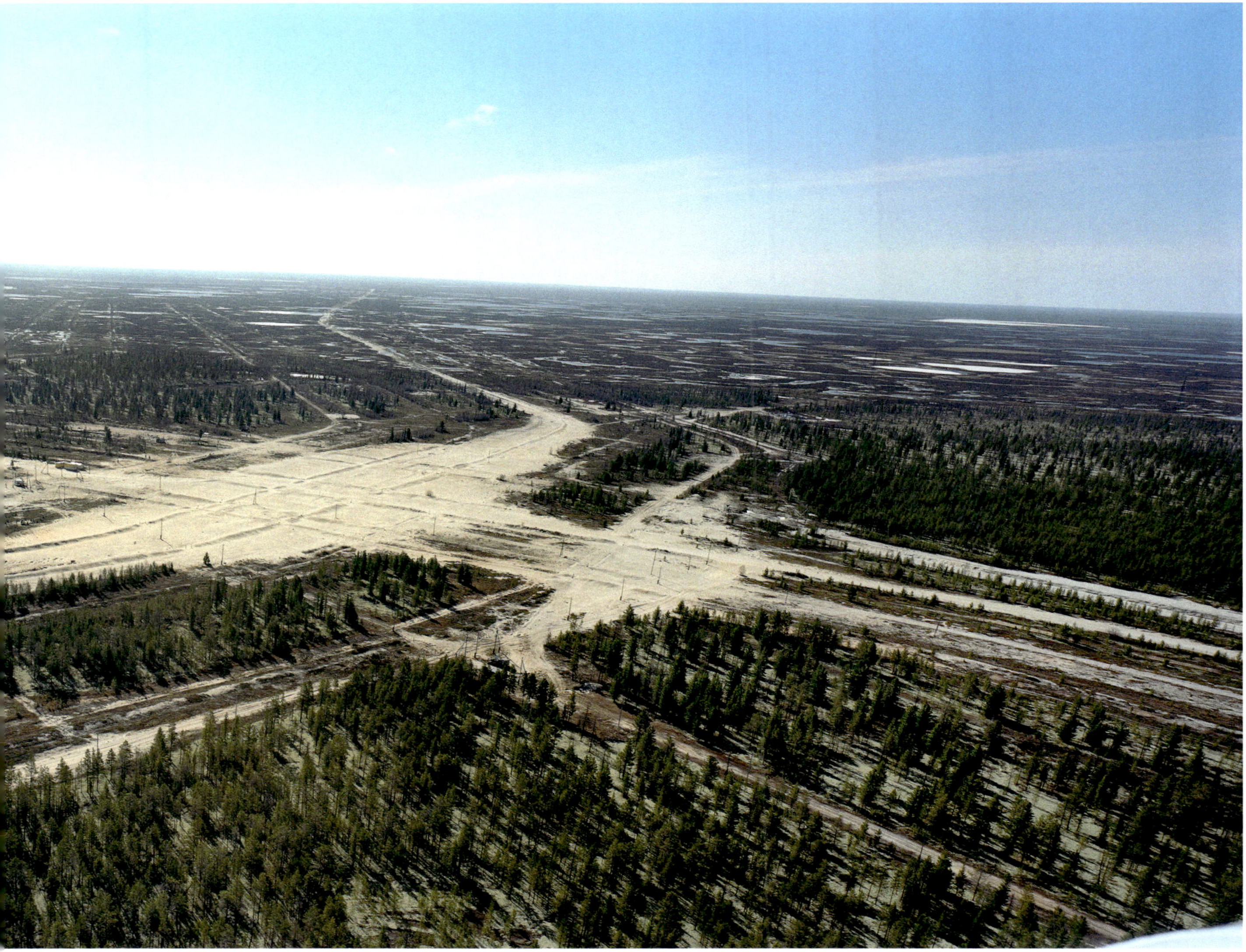

The image of the Nadym gas pipeline junction gives you a sense of mega-scale. This is fantastic, this bird's-eye view of such expansive gas infrastructure. In this case, fabric acts as a visual cover for a world that is impossible to visualize. This system is completely different from the system you can see. The world it enters is not merely a world you cannot see but a world beyond vision.

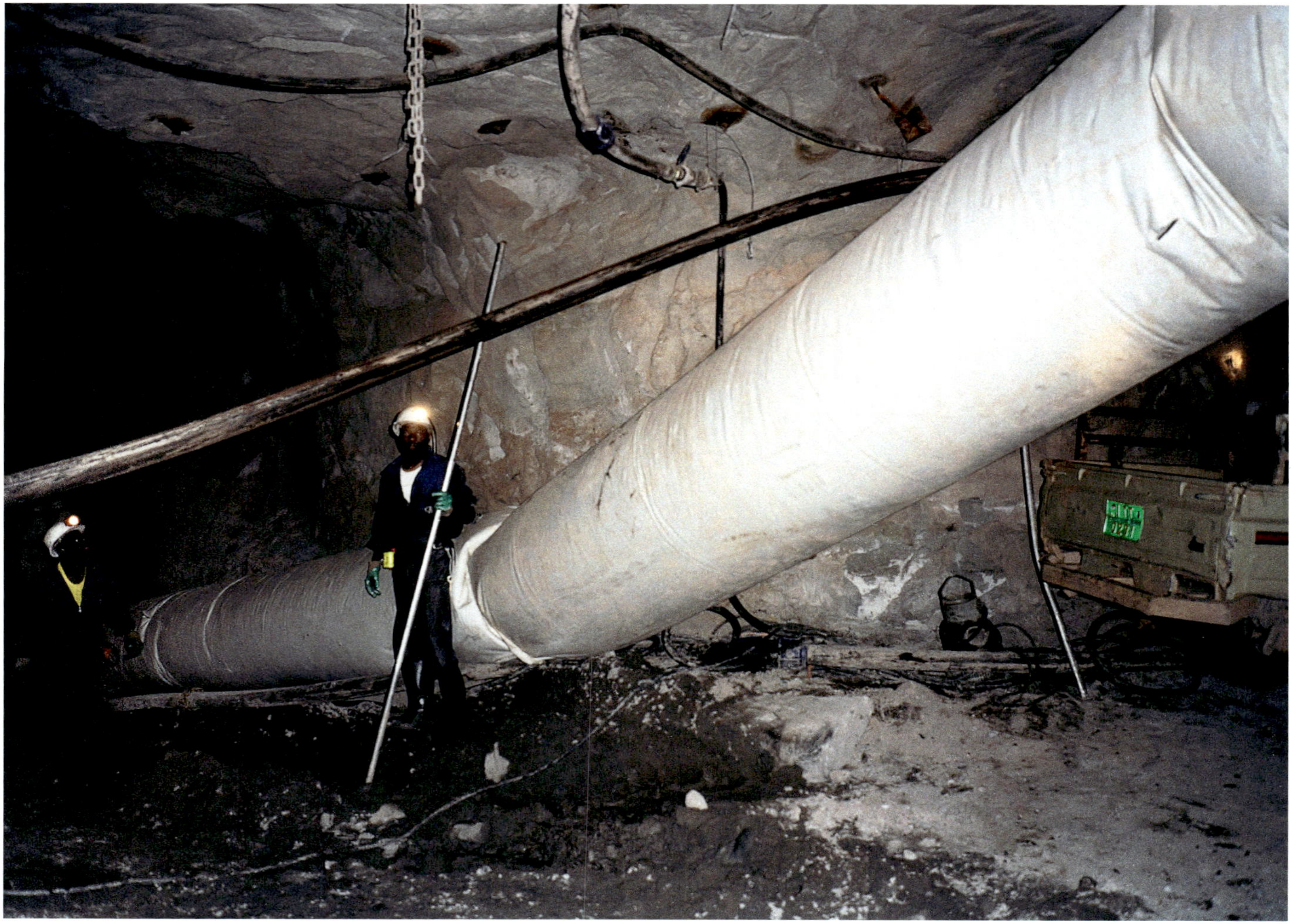

The Saharan city of Arlit began developing advanced infrastructures in 1969 with the opening of the Arlit uranium mine, through French government investments. Although the end of the Cold War and the Chernobyl meltdown caused a slump in demand, the industry has recovered since. The Arlit mine was at the center of the “Yellowcake” controversy at the onset of the Iraq War, in 2003, as false information spread that Saddam Hussein was looking to purchase uranium.

A piece of plumbing in a house, for a kitchen sink, for example, is always designed to look as if it belongs to the room and not to the pipe. A pipe covered with chrome is not a pipe but a piece of design.

Uranium miner, Arlit, Niger, 2006

But if I touch the inside of the pipe with my finger, I can feel that it is cold and wet. The surface I am touching must connect to all the other inside surfaces of all the other pipes in the house. They all run from the same water input, and are connected to all the water inputs in all the other houses on the same street.

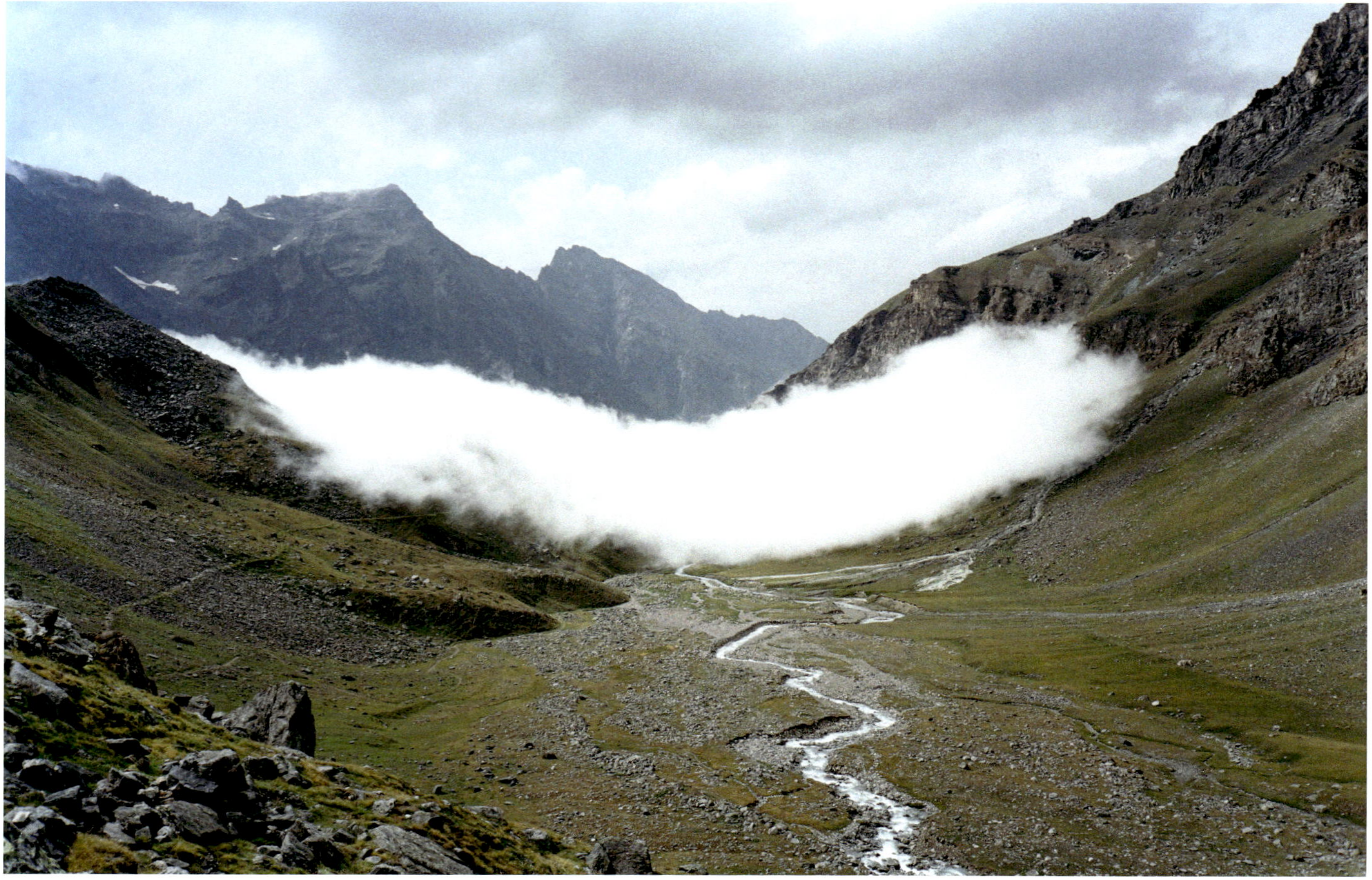

The inside of the pipe is a surface, completely continuous: all the way to the mountains the water comes from. This is only the pipe that brings the water in. Underneath the tap, under the sink, there is another pipe, which I can also touch the inside of. For that pipe to work, its inside surface must be connected to all the other pipes going out of your house—as well as all the other pipes out of all the other houses—to the ocean or perhaps to a river in Berlin and then the ocean.

Moving cloud, Aosta, Italy, 2000

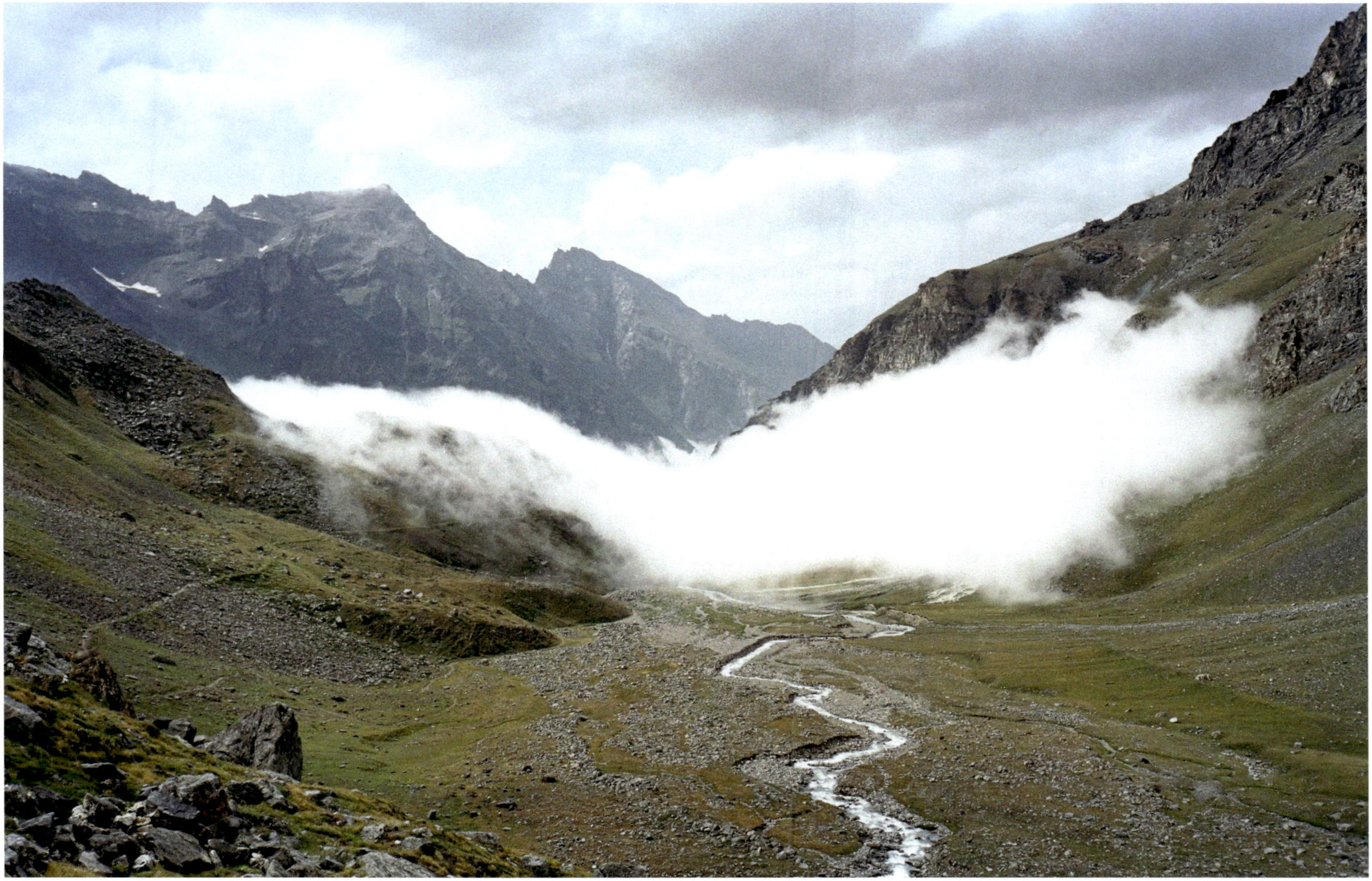

It is completely obscene, unthinkable, unimaginable, and horrific that when I want a glass of water, I put my body inside a pipe that offers an opening between the tap and the sink, and that in that moment I am connected to every other pipe in my city and other cities, connected both to the mountains and to the ocean. The plumbing system is, moreover, one interior, a single interior space.

Moving cloud, Aosta, Italy, 2000

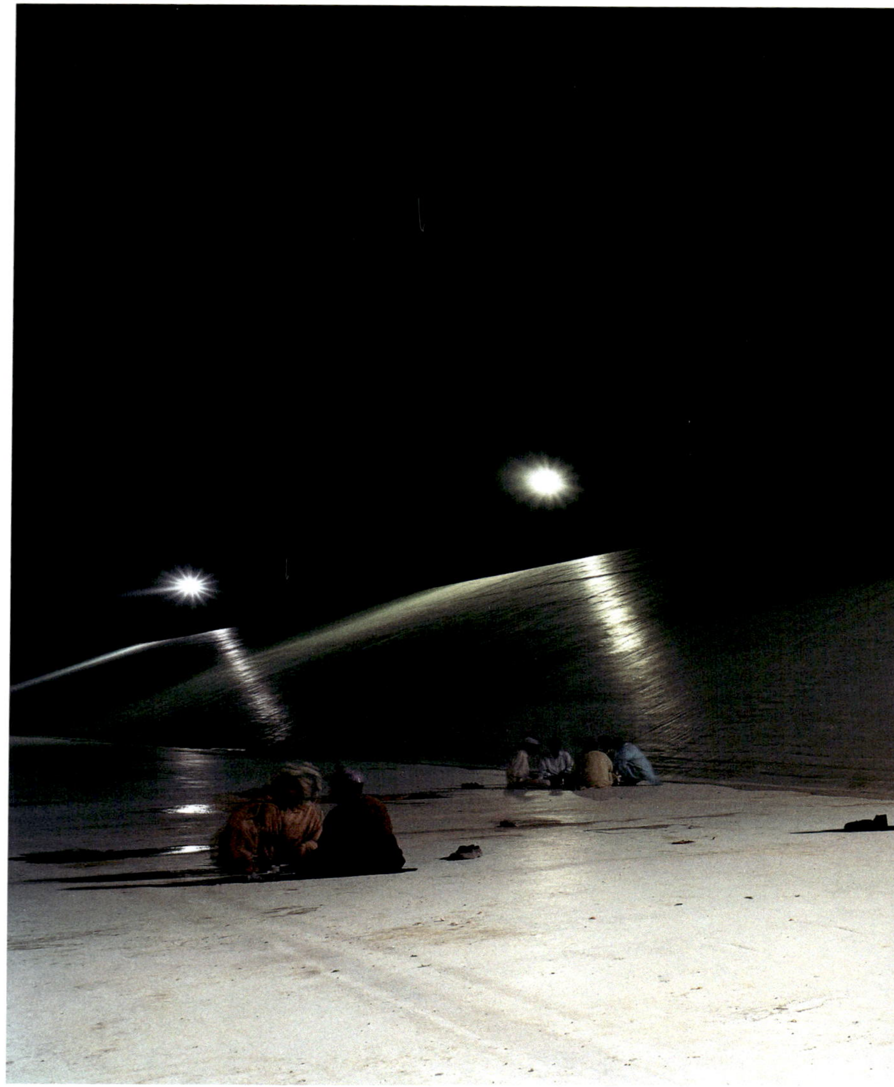

Workers praying during the construction of the Ghazi Barotha hydroelectric project. Excess sedimentation rendered the original Tarbela dam (1976) inefficient. The Ghazi Barotha project diverts its barrage water through a 52 km long channel to a powerhouse near Barotha. Funded by the World Bank, the project was implemented by an international consortium of engineering companies.

Just like on the inside of the lungs, there are millions and millions of little pathways forming one incredibly elaborate interior.

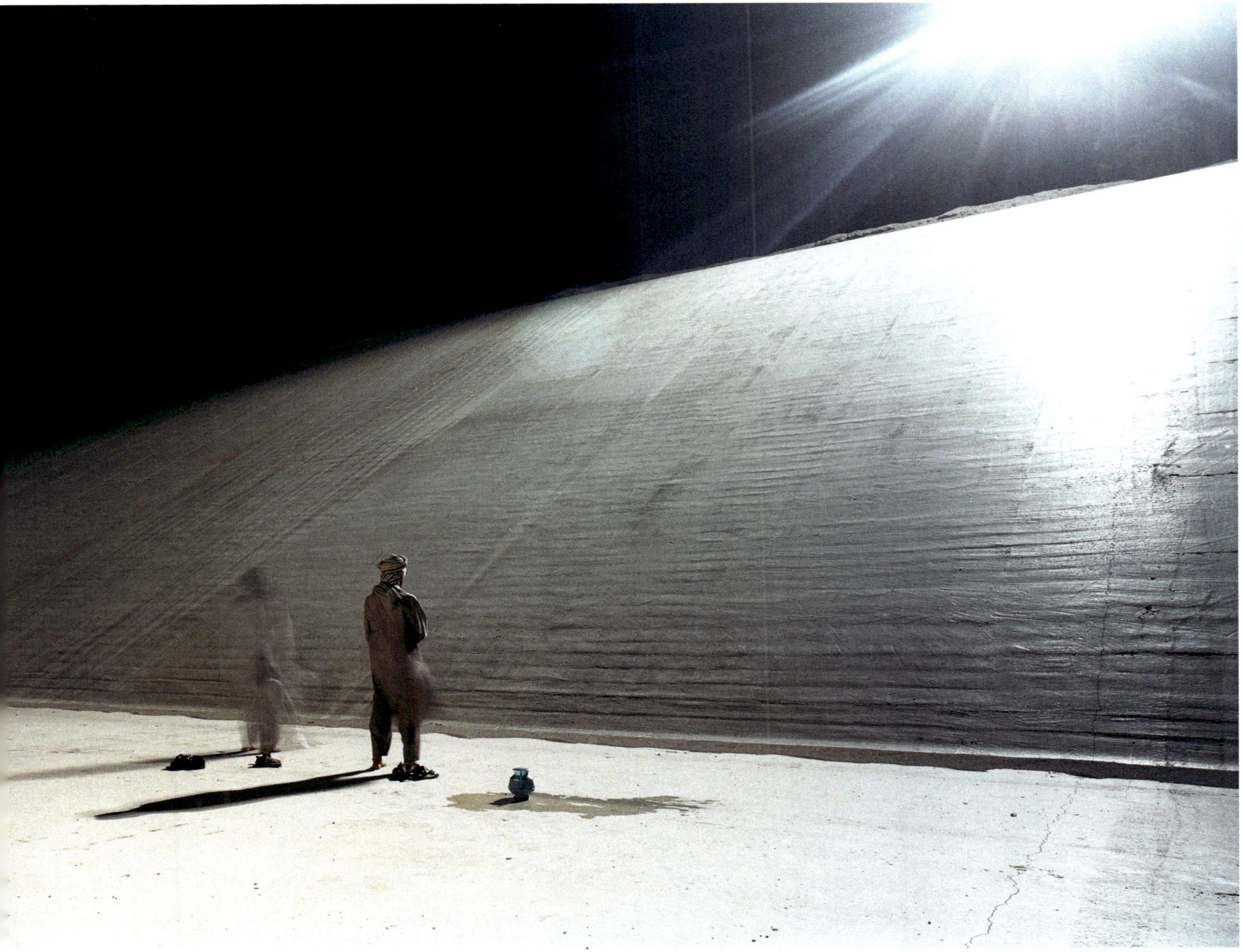

Ecological thinking is an attempt to make you look at this impossible-to-see world; to see the interconnections, to see that you are sharing water with your next-door neighbor. Every time you pour a glass of water, you perform a highly political act activating the full force of the economy—political, sexual, psychological, and architectural. This enormously charged gesture is the perfect example of a very small domestic gesture.

Every small domestic gesture is only domestic because there is some kind of fabric allowing you to feel isolated, suspended from this expanded, networked world—which is also a world of responsibility. While you drink the water you share with your city, as part of the efficiency of living together, you dream of private water.

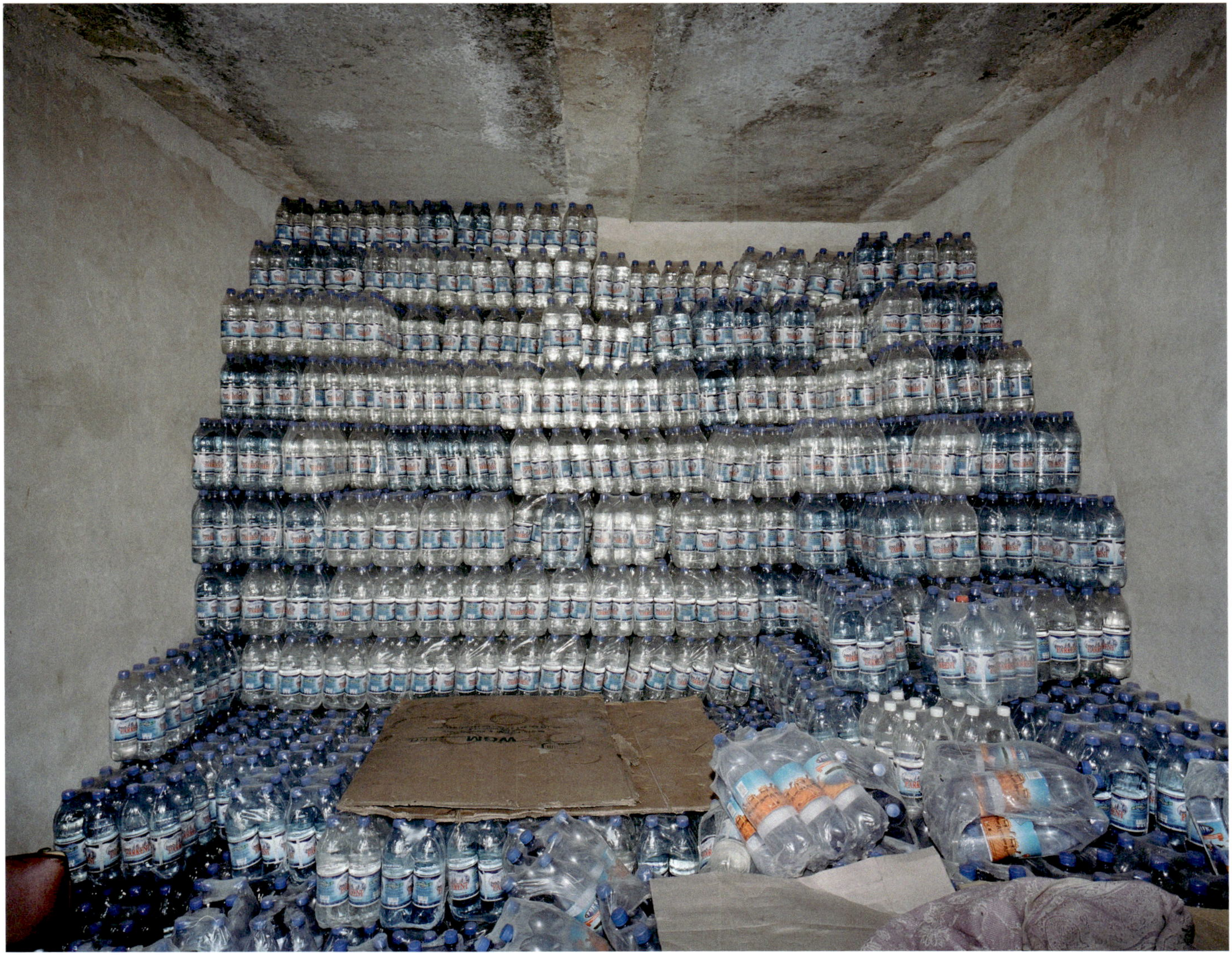

People who filter water in their homes add another layer of disconnection from their neighbors. The super-European and now super-American tradition of bottled mineral water is, in this sense, a desire to not be in the world of pipes, of plumbing and interconnection: to not be in a shared world.

Water shop, Nukus (Aral Lake), Uzbekistan, 2001

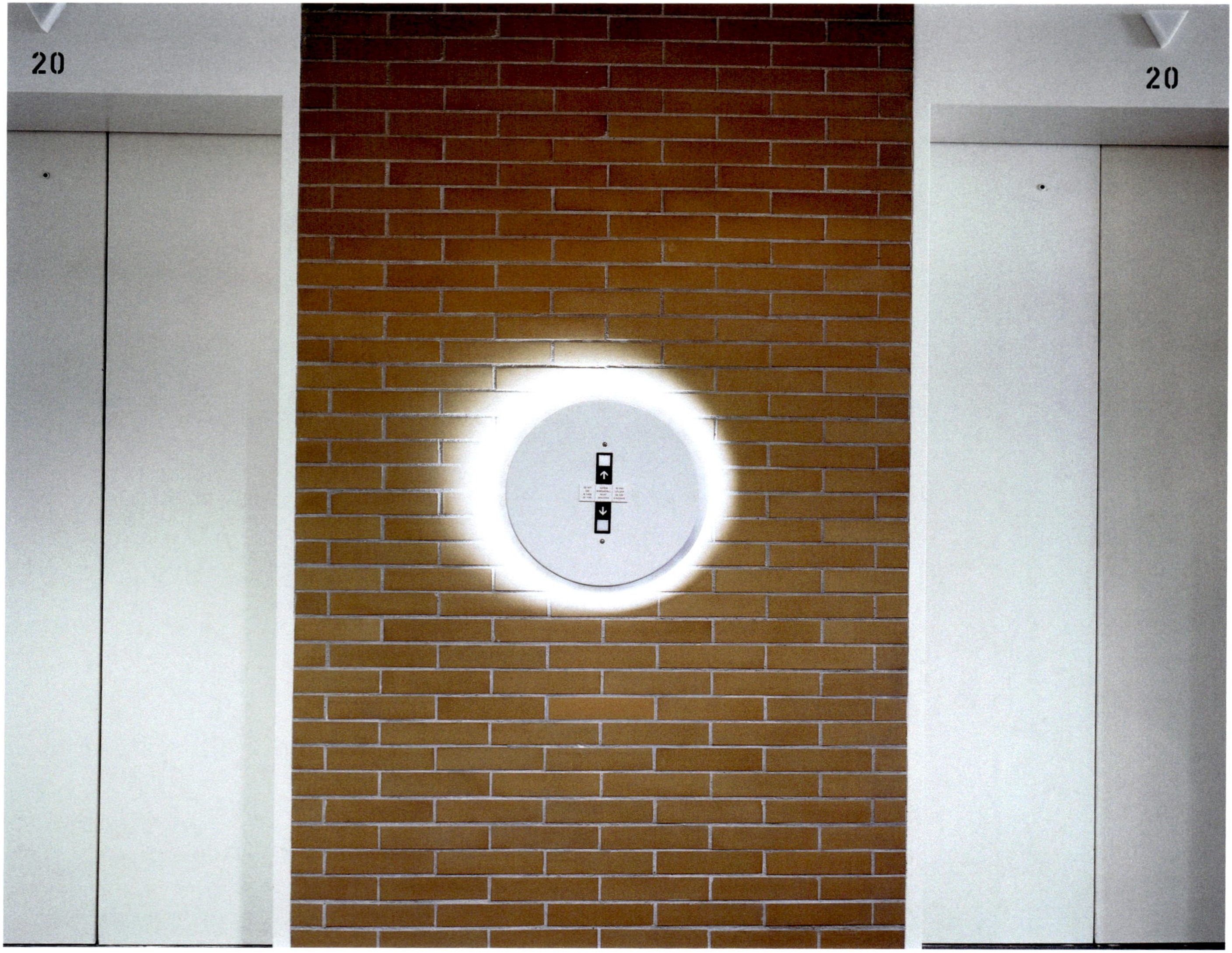

The idea of an elevator, I suppose, is that you enter into the plumbing, into a tube that takes you up within the building. This small piece of architecture enables you to forget you are in a tube. When you push a button in an elevator, there is this micro-delay, less than half a second, before the door opens. People experience high levels of stress within this delay, many already moving into the fight-or-flight mode. It is a complicated negotiation.

Egon Eiermann, “Langer Eugen” building, lift, Bonn, Germany, 2014

Elevator

music was there to make you feel all right. Now they might have a woman's voice saying, "One, two, three," or a TV screen—all sorts of anesthetics. The fabric/plumbing argument here is that architecture is a form of anesthetic, covering the moment of trauma with a kind of fabric.

Sometimes the plumbing, the tube, is constructed out of information, like the inside of a plane on approach to landing. In order to land, the aircraft has to occupy a virtual piece of plumbing, a corridor. If the inside of the plumbing is made out of fabric, this fabric could be information or light or economic pathways.

Runway lights, Bergamo, Italy, 1998

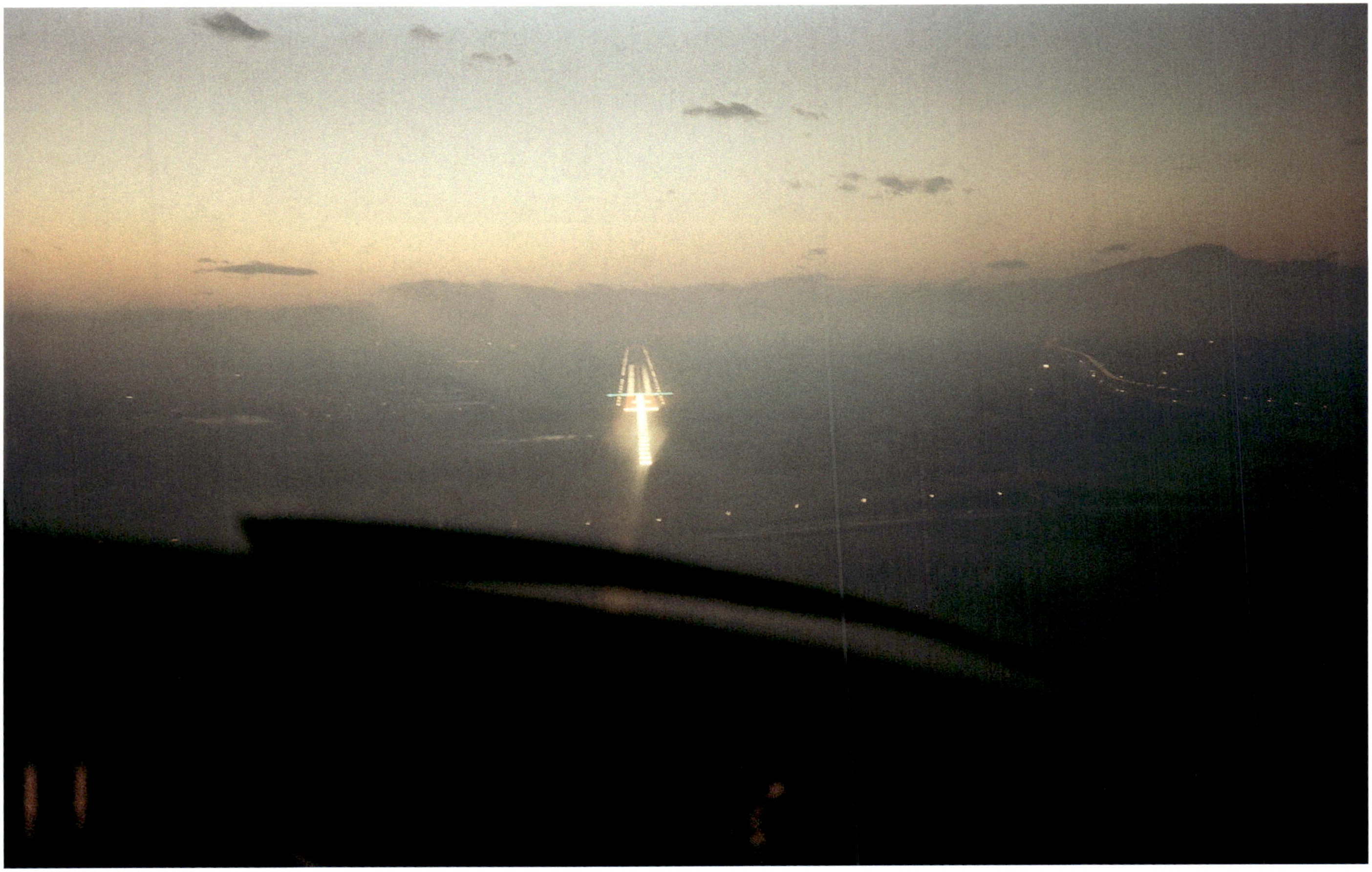

This fabric is so fine that you do not see it well. But when you hit the interface, you have all these kinds of virtual plumbing. When you are inside the plumbing, the fabric is a form of friction. When you are really deep in the system—it is the same with the aircraft coming in—when you are completely inside the plumbing, the experience is very different.

Runway lights, Bergamo, Italy, 1998

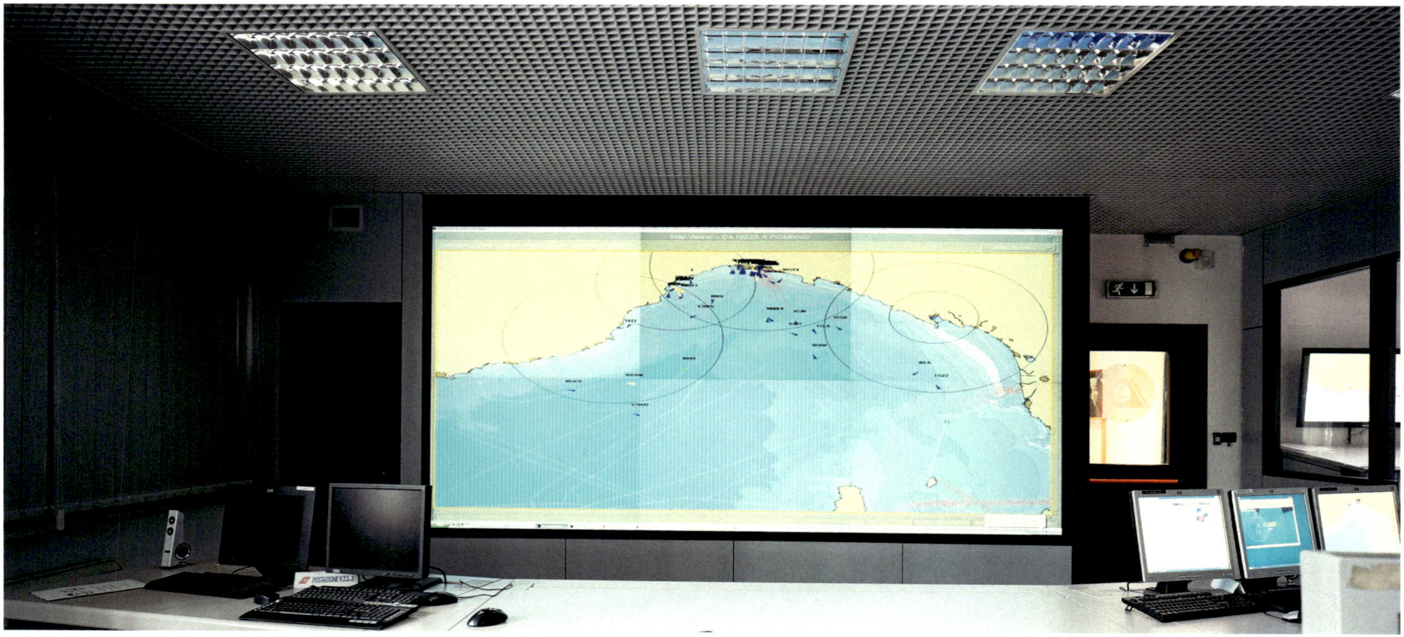

From this control room, the General Command of the Port Authority Corp for the Italian Coast Guard monitor the movements of cargo, fishing, and other vessels in the Mediterranean, and coordinate maritime rescue operations by the coast guard, the navy, and merchant vessels of all flags responding to SOS calls, including those giving alerts of migrants in danger.

Italian Coast Guard, General Command of the Port Authority Corp, Rome, Italy, 2009

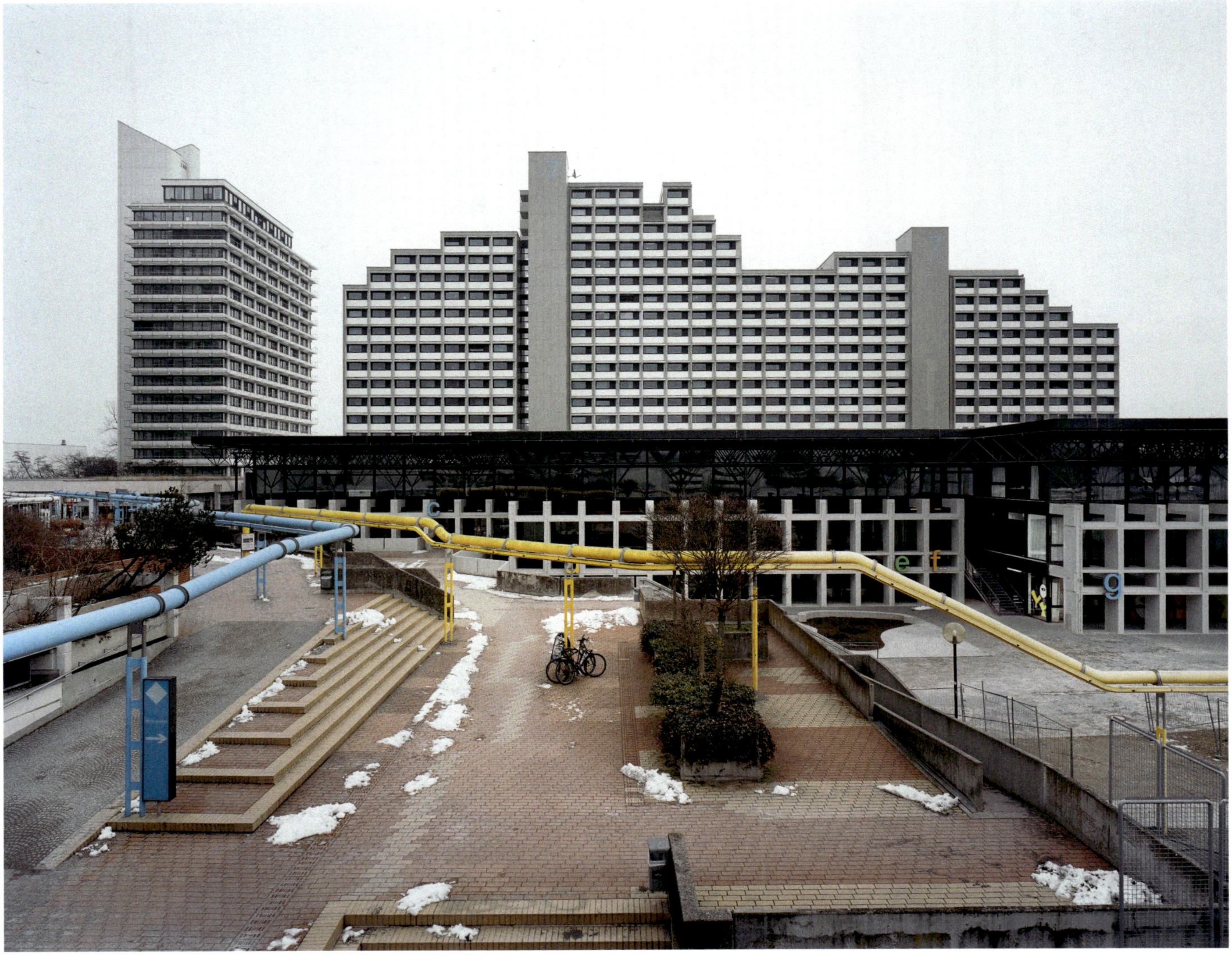

You can make a tube with tracks, cars, or in nature. Sometimes there are secrets. You can make a tube with people. Sometimes the tube is the size of the landscape.

Hans Hollein, "Media Linien," Olympic Village (1971–72), Munich, Germany, 2014

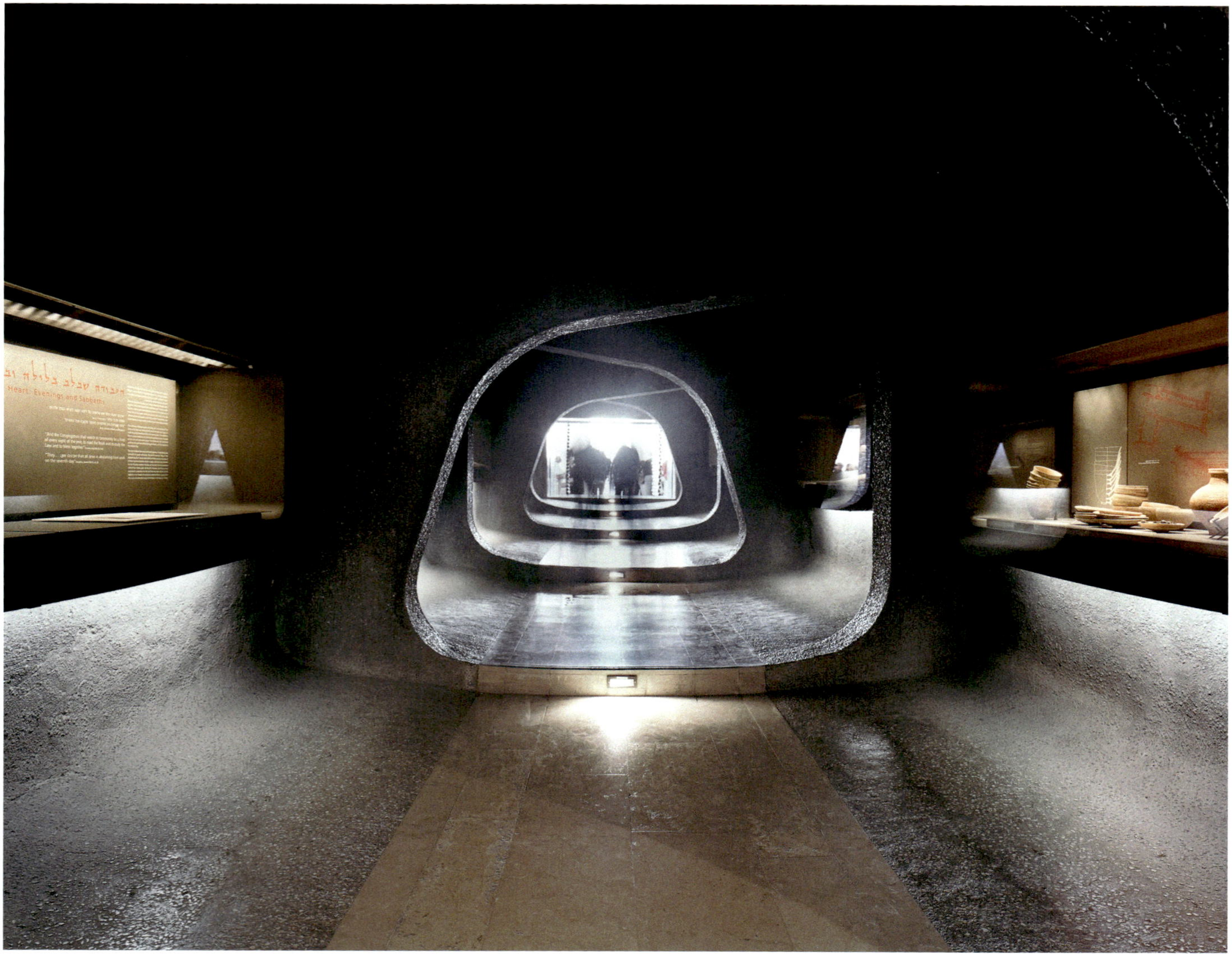

Richard Buckminster Fuller writes about the highway as a tube, a pipe that does not have the upper half. You are in a channel. He hates channels, however, because they take choice and freedom away. He believes in omnidirectional, not unidirectional movement. He does not like going from A to B.

Friedrich Kiesler, Armand Bartos, Shrine of the Book, The Israel Museum, Jerusalem, Israel, 2008

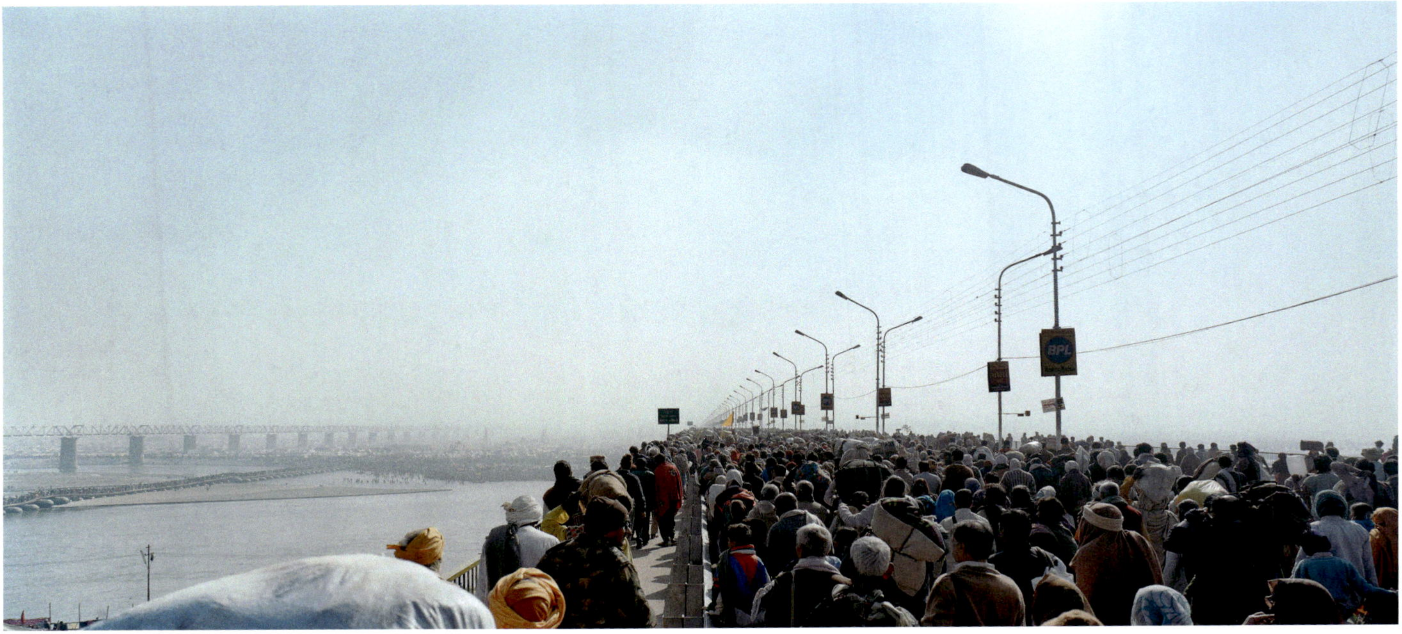

Twenty to forty million people gathered in the city of Allahabad to bathe in the Ganges River for the Maha Kumbh Mela religious festival. Supplemented merely by temporary pontoon bridges, the infrastructure of Allahabad, a city of around six hundred thousand inhabitants, coped with vast crowds.

Maha Kumbh Mela, Allahabad, India, 2001

What interests me is, when does carpet turn into fabric, and when does fabric turn into carpet? Usually, multiple things happen.

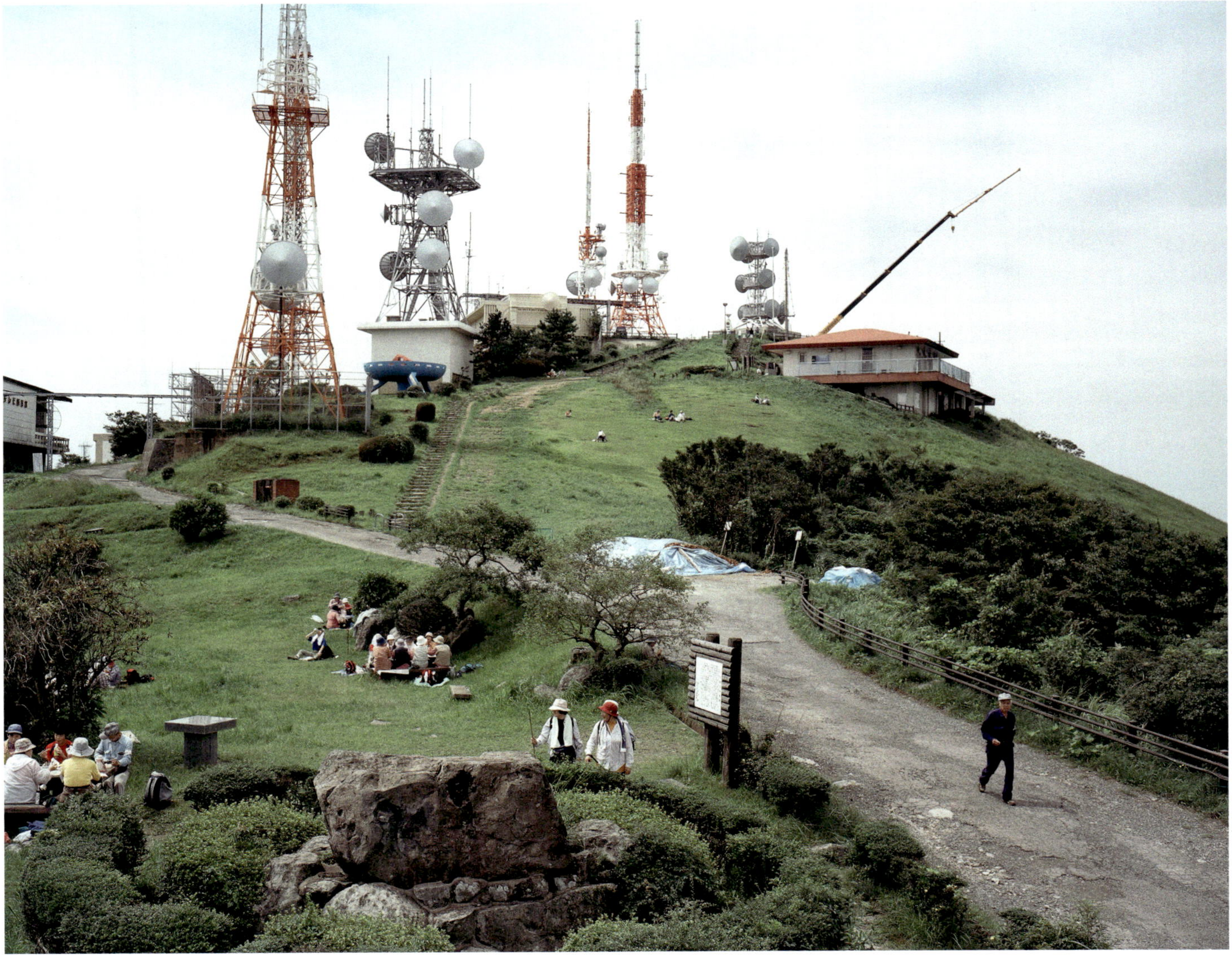

Radio is plumbing, for example, and so is the big cell-phone mast we see in the image. It is woven like a carpet in the sky. If you look into a carpet, it is made of plumbing, in a way. And the Internet is also a carpet. And so on. This fits with the idea of being inside the plumbing, because you first install the plumbing, and then everybody gathers around.

Mountain with antennae, Kitakyushu, Japan, 2006

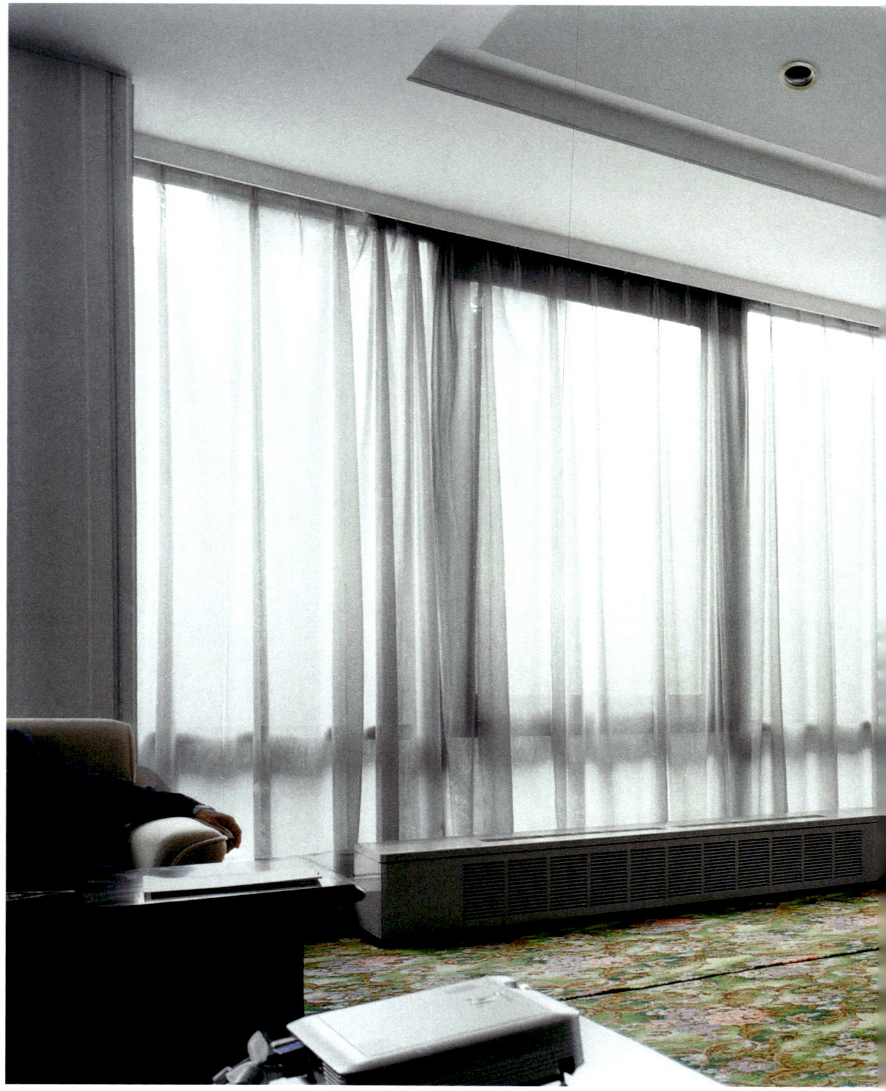

Mount Paekdu Architecture Academy, Ryugyong Hotel engineer,
Pyongyang, North Korea, 2005

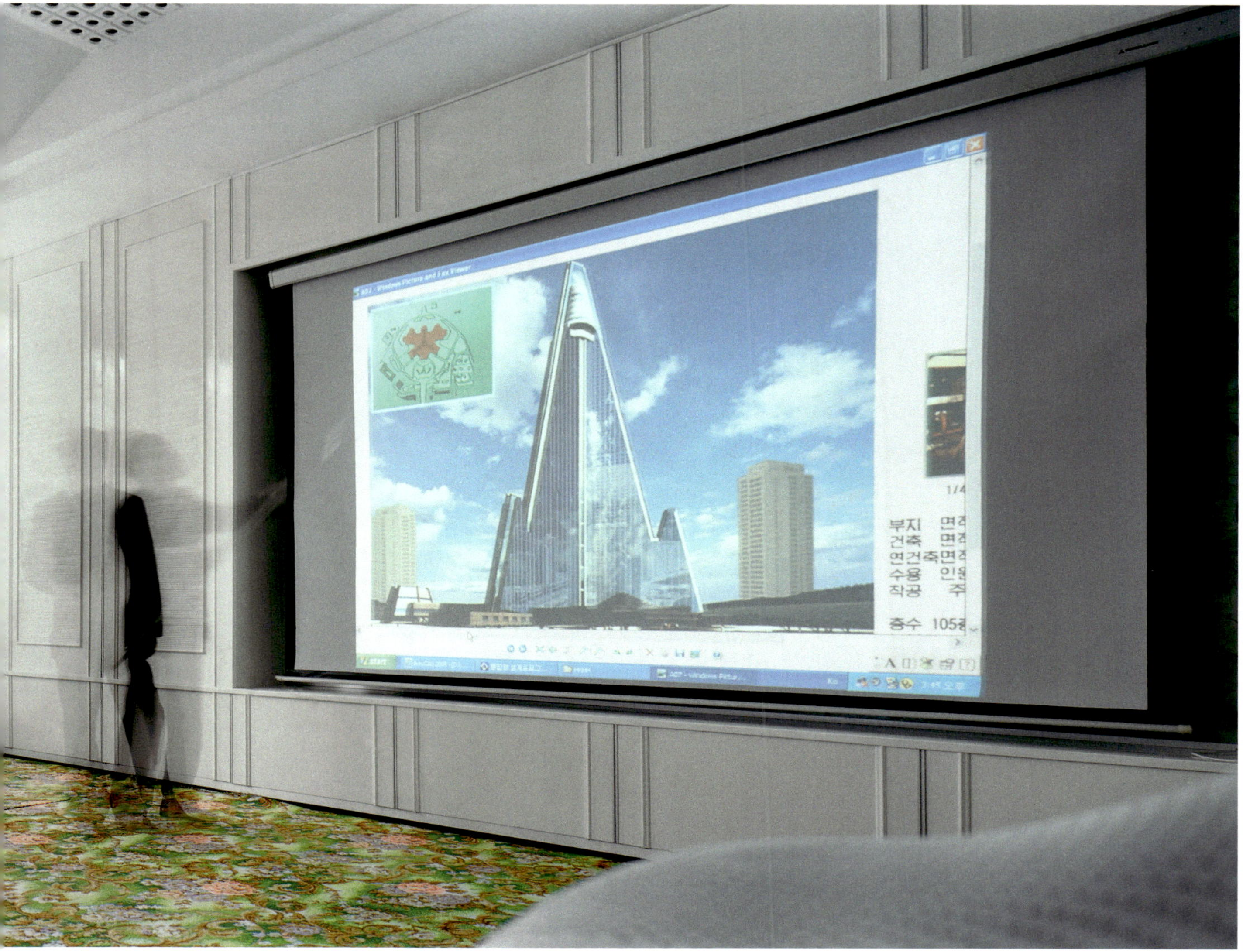
1/4
부지
건축
연건축
수용
층수 105

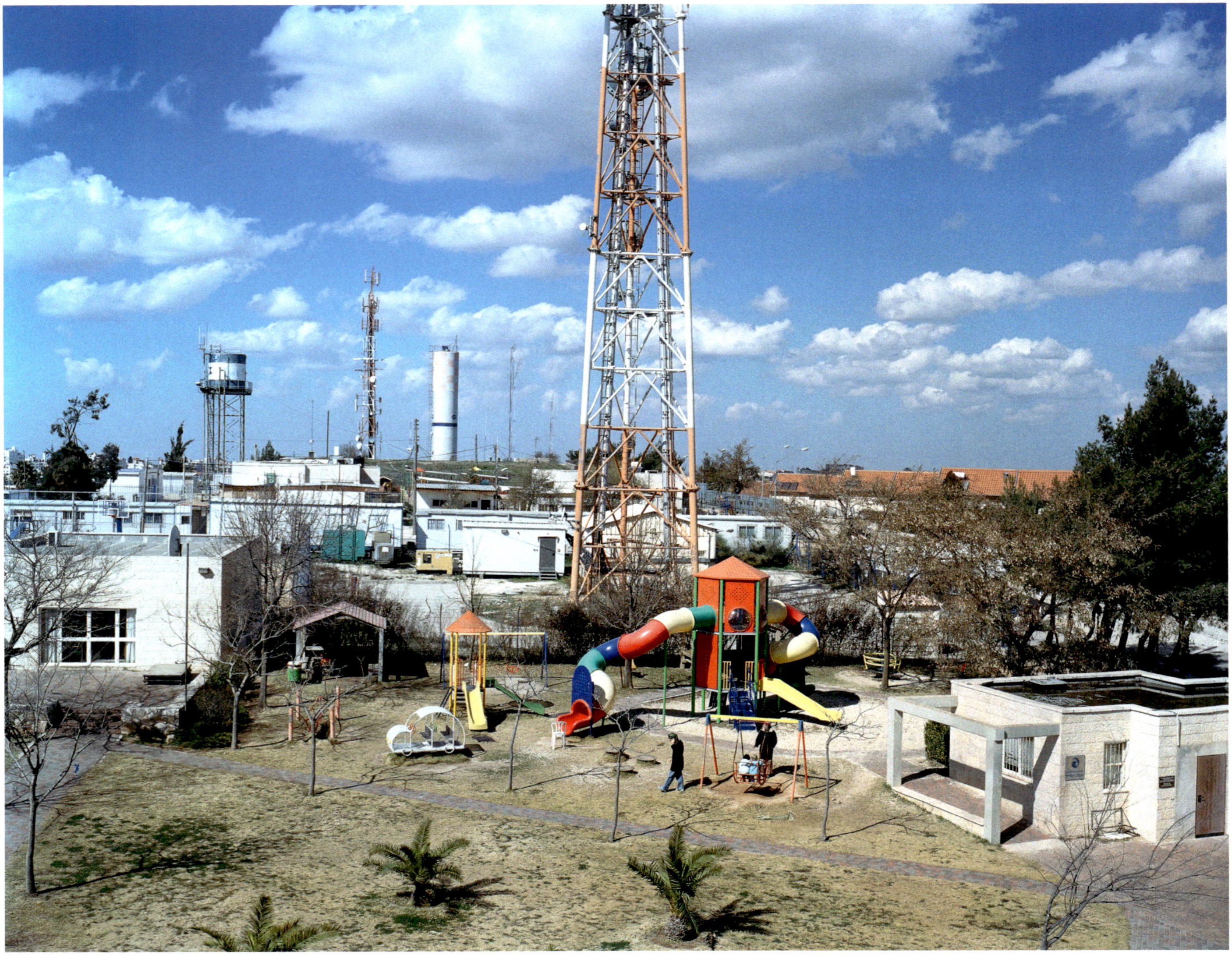

During a visit to the Psagot Settlement overlooking the city of Ramallah, Eyal Weizmann and Alessandro Petti from the Decolonizing Architecture project explained that the moment of occupation often starts with the installation of mobile telephony infrastructure, the cell-phone masts, around which the colonizers then build their settlement.

The Psagot Settlement, West Bank, 2008

In the image with the playground and the cell masts, however, the children get to be in the plumbing, they play in these tube slides. They are their little tower. And then there is another radio mast. And in the distance you see many communications masts. In Israel, military is, of course, domestic and domestic is military.

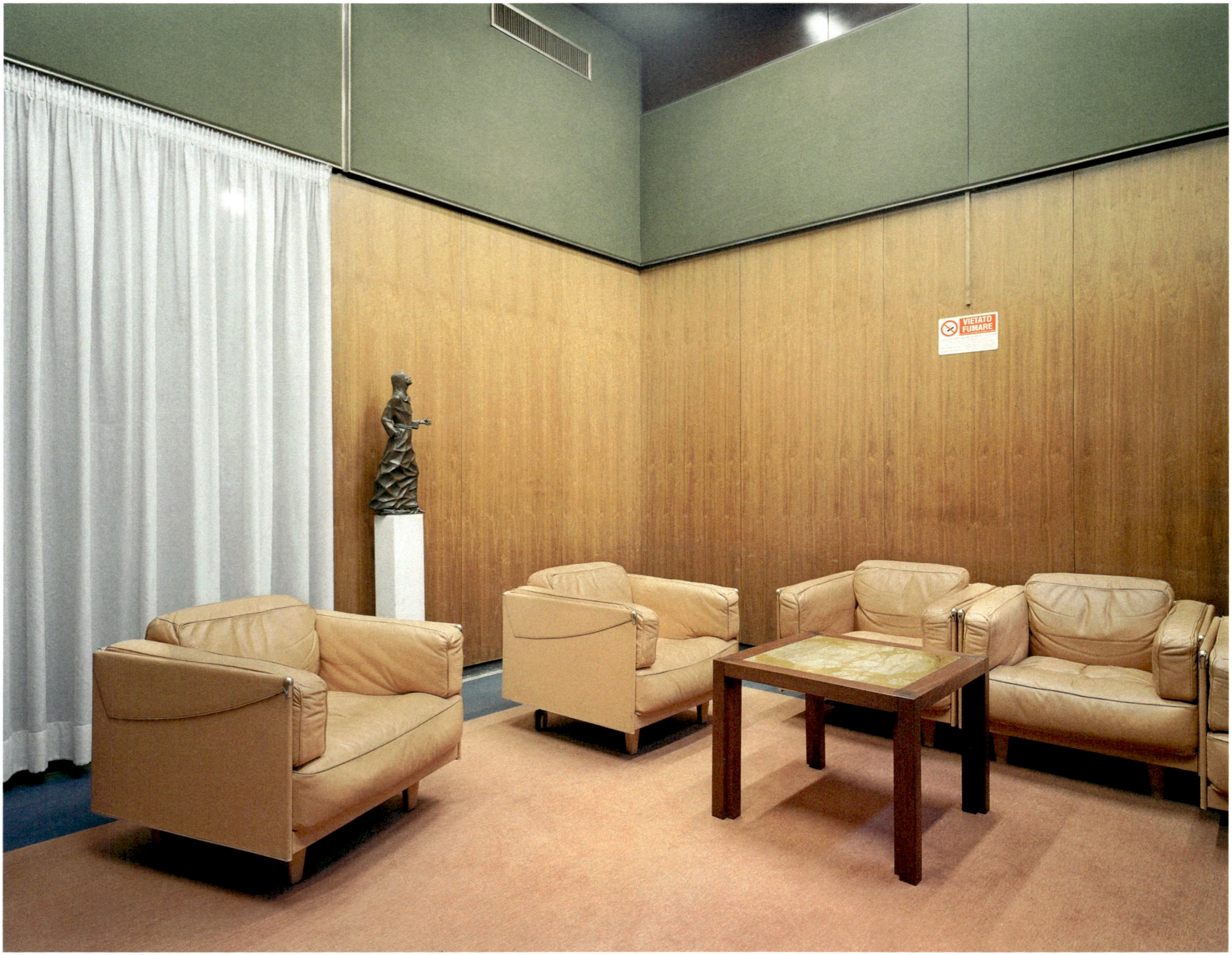

A sculpture of Saint Clare of Assisi, who was canonized in 1255 for her work with Saint Francis of Assisi, graces a RAI building interior. In 1958, Pope Pius XII declared Saint Clare of Assisi the patron saint of television and telecommunications.

RAI, Italian Broadcasting Corporation, Rome, Italy, 2008

Many years ago, Beatriz and I visited this Alvar Aalto house. Maire Gullichsen, the original client, was still alive. The owner wished to talk about putting a satellite dish on the roof and wondered if Aalto would have wanted to do this.

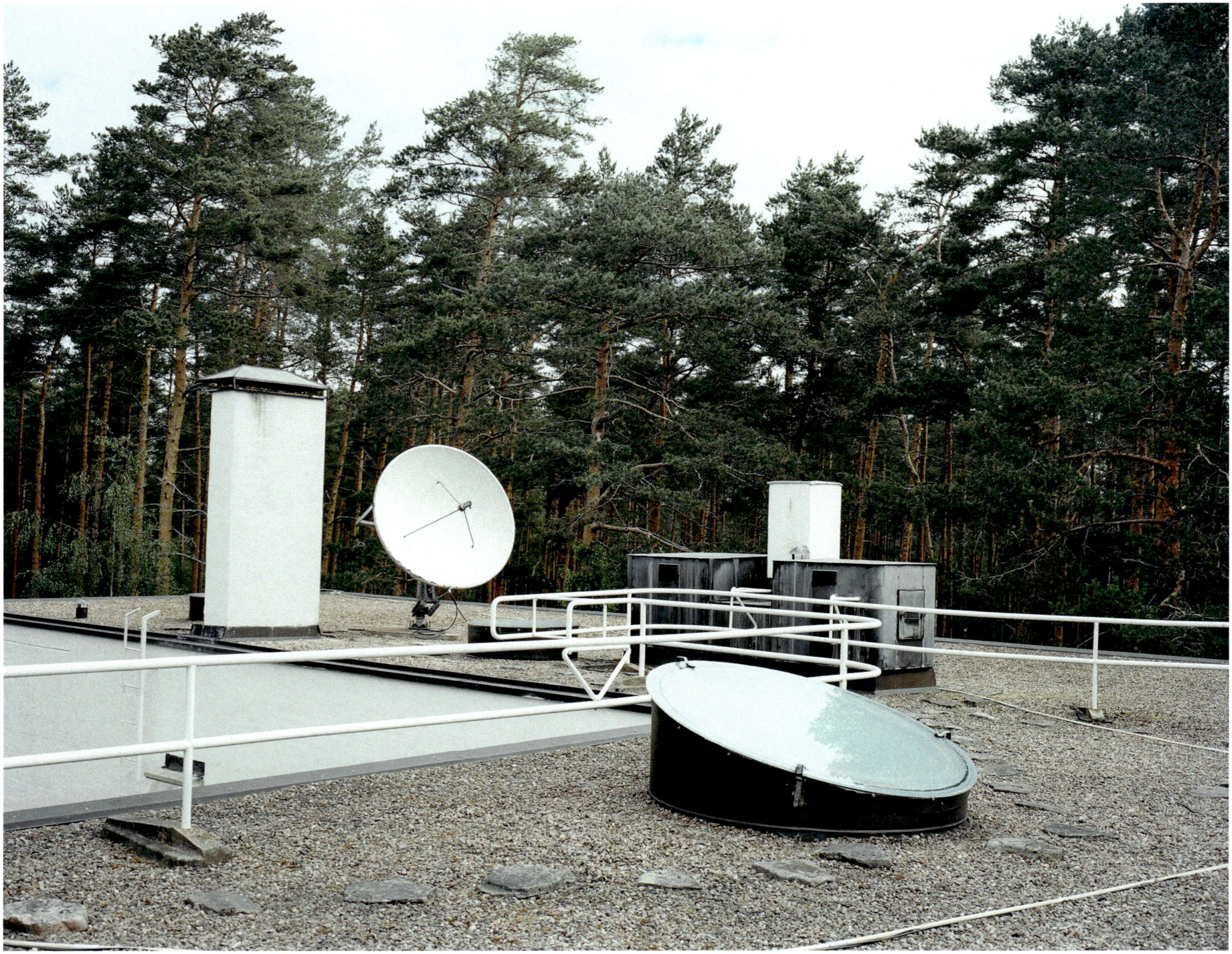

Being addicted to television, I said, “Of course!” And Gullichsen, she would have wanted it, too. We were with Juhani Pallasmaa, and he was a bit more nervous about this. In the end we said, “Anyhow, it would look good.”

Alvar Aalto, Villa Mairea (1939), Noormarkku, Finland, 2014

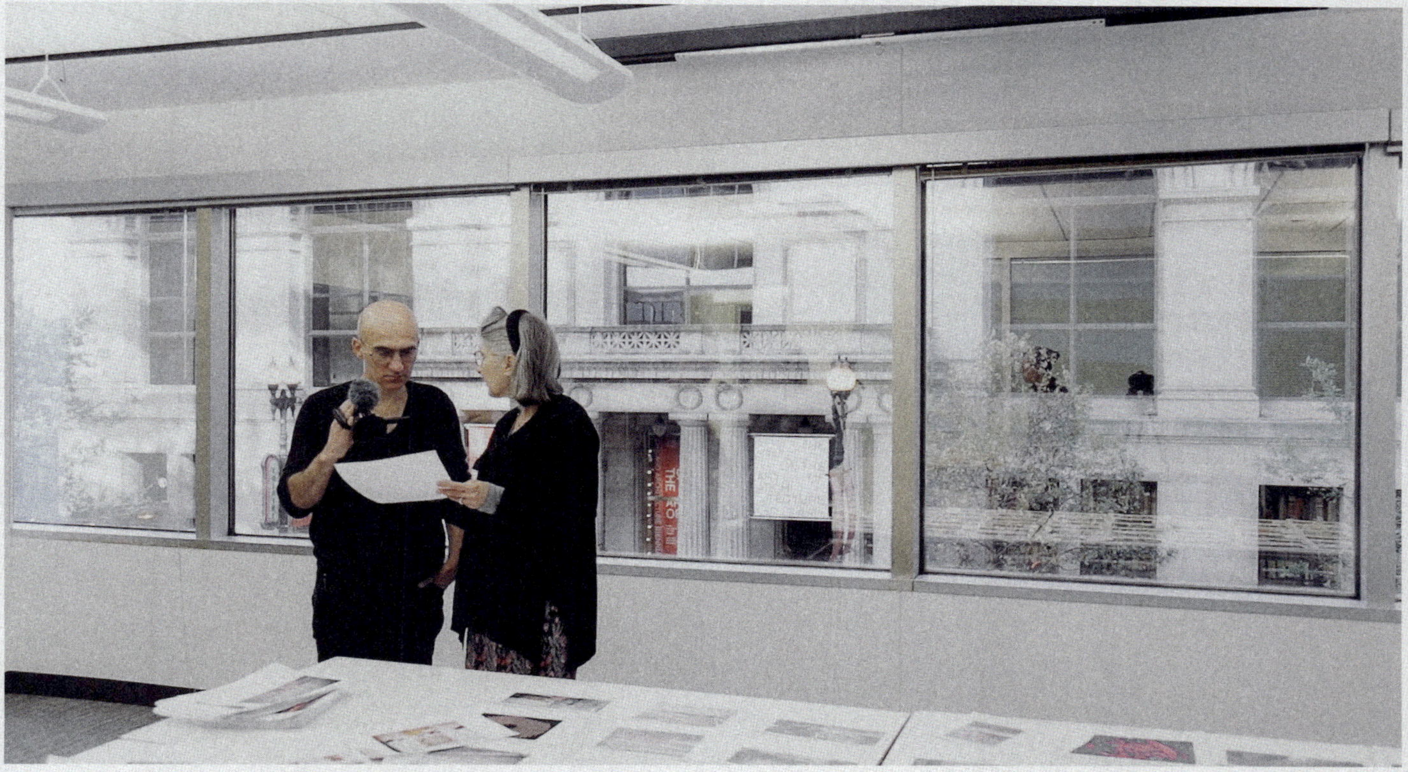

Lorraine Daston

295–334

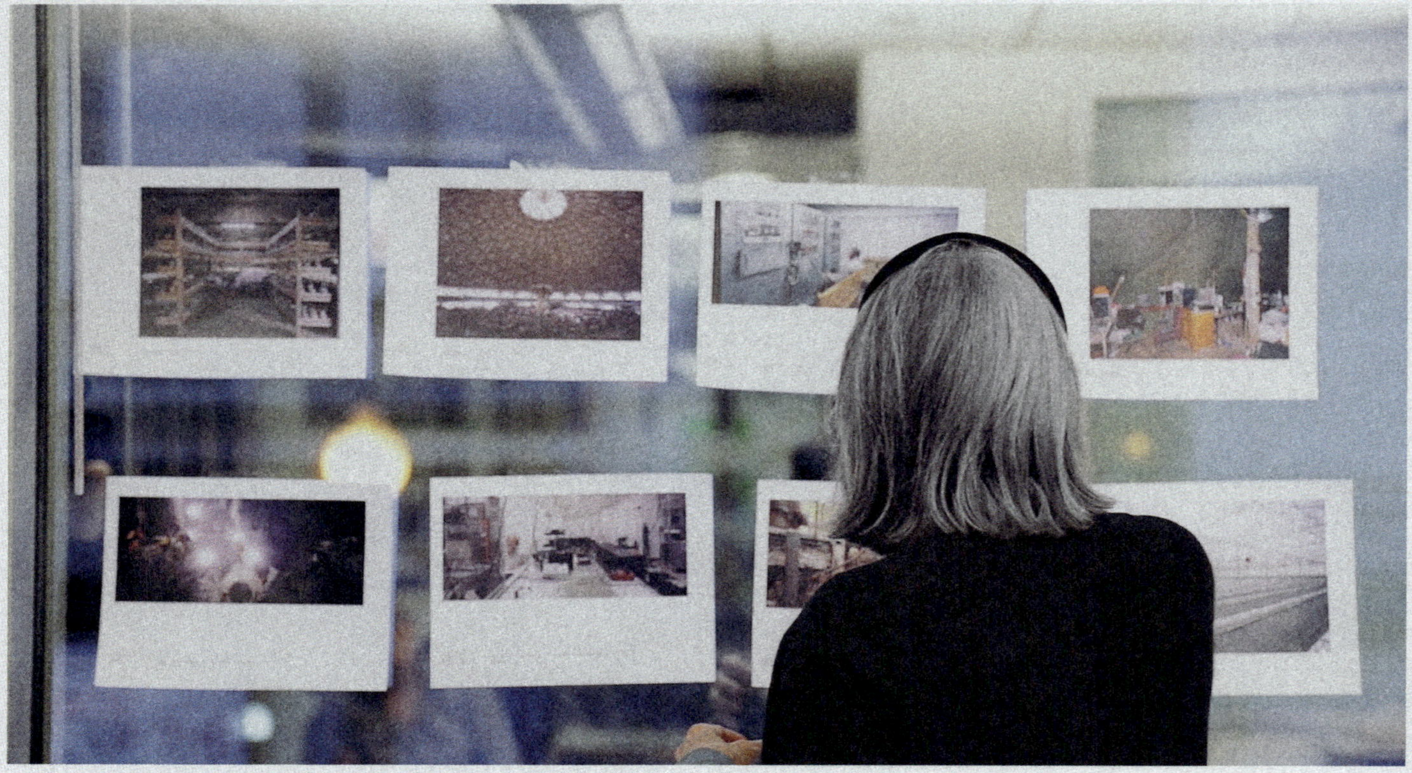

Lorraine Daston and Armin Linke, Goethe Institute, Chicago, October 2015

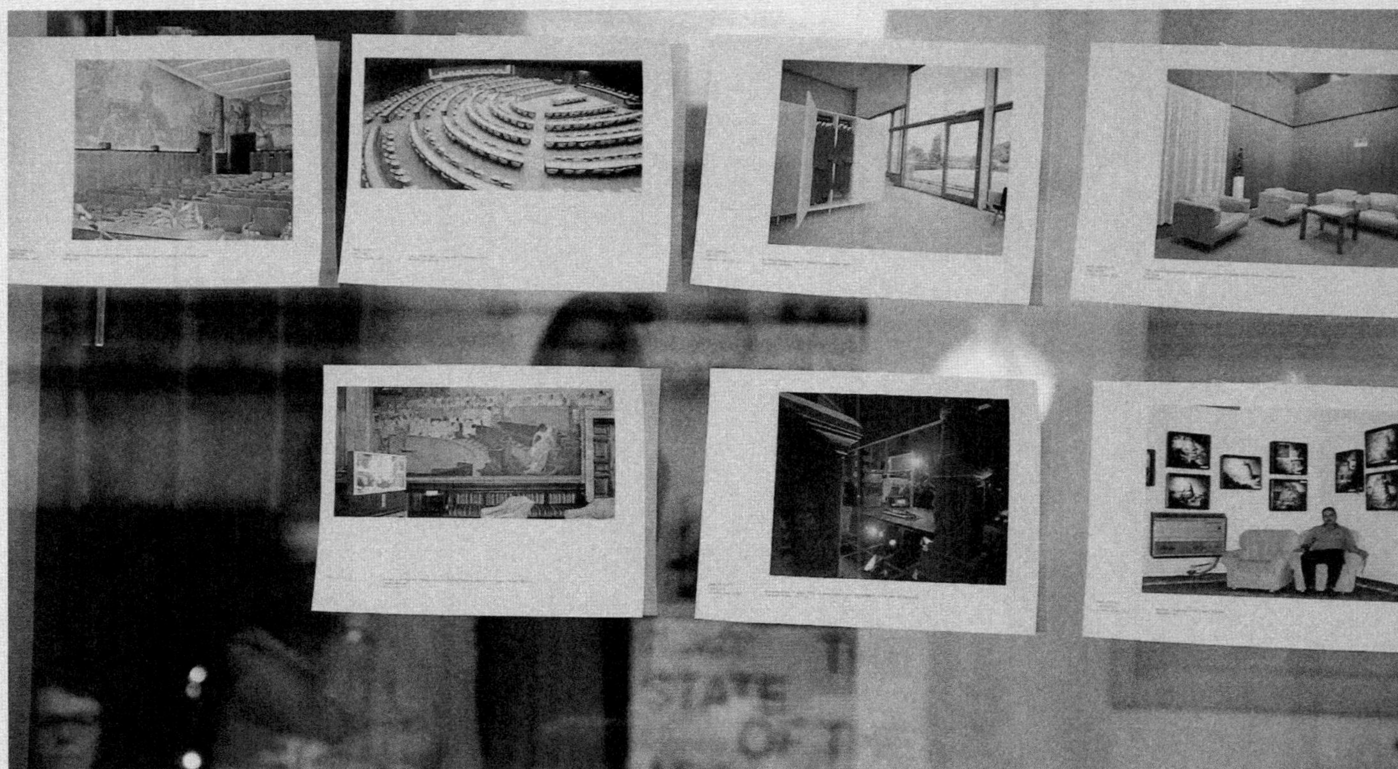

Lorraine Daston and Armin Linke, Goethe Institute, Chicago, October 2015

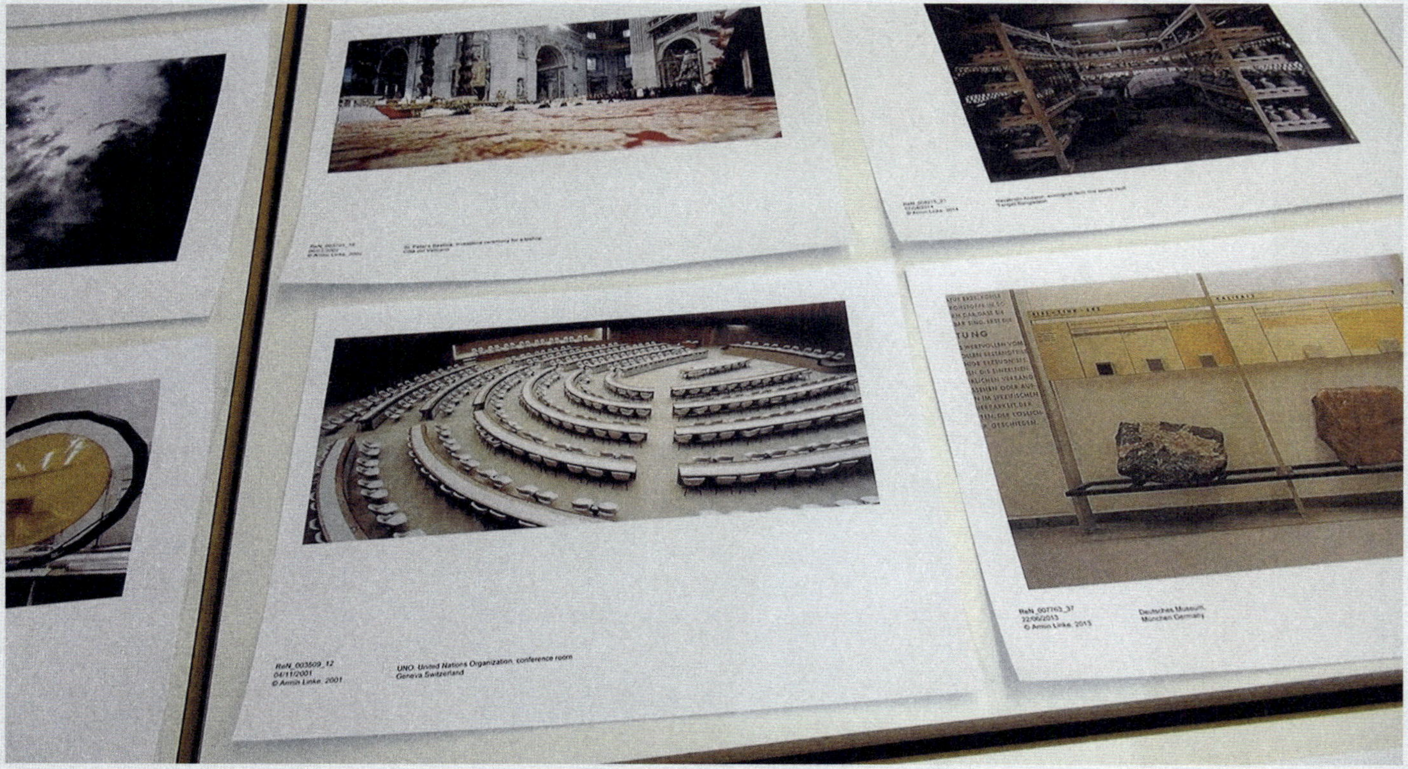

Lorraine Daston and Armin Linke, Goethe Institute, Chicago,
October 2015

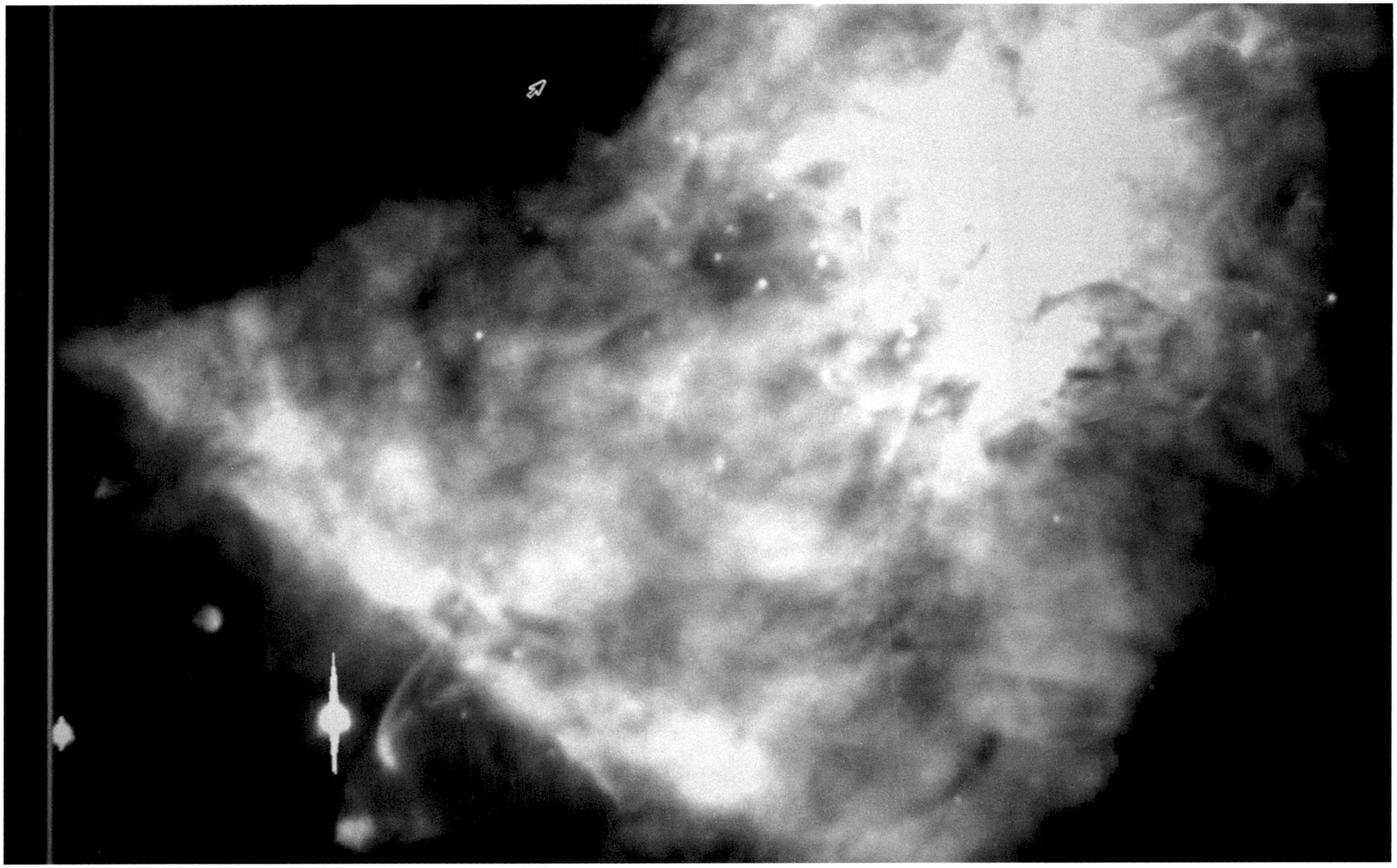

There's almost no system of thought—whether it's mythological or scientific—that does not have a cosmogony. And it's striking that this persists in scientific domains because, as any cosmologist will tell you, theories about how the universe began are wildly underdetermined by the evidence.

ESO VLT, astronomical observatory, Cerro Paranal, Chile, 1999

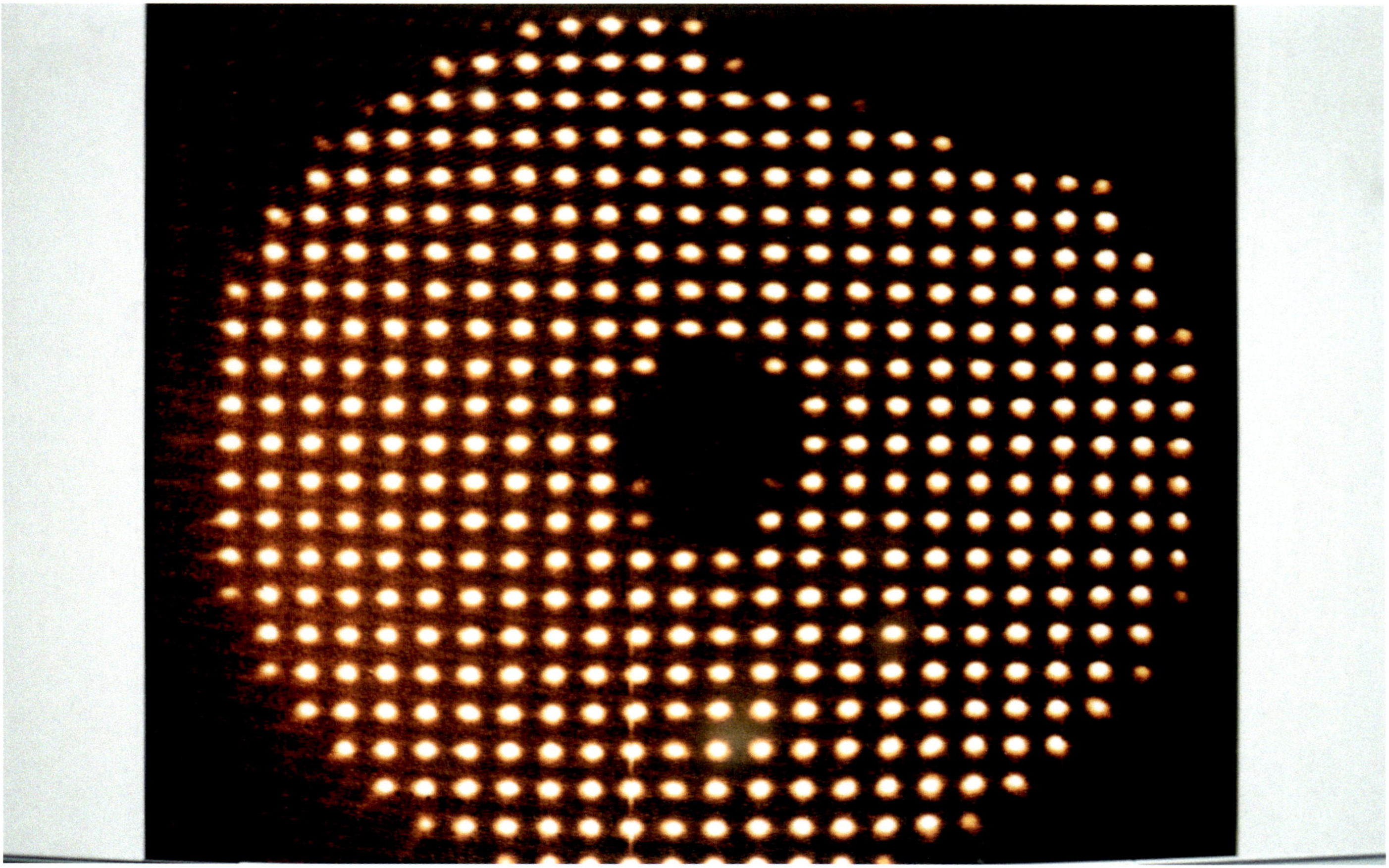

In other words, we don't have enough data to answer the questions that cosmologists ask about the origins of the universe—we're always whistling in the dark. Nonetheless, the question of origins is one that has to be asked, and it's an issue that puts science and religion on a collision course with one another because both of them want to give answers to it. You could imagine a kind of division of labor in which science says, "Religion is responsible for explaining the meaning of life.

ESO VLT, astronomical observatory, Cerro Paranal, Chile, 1999

Science is going to answer other kinds of queries." But in fact, they collide when it comes to cosmogony because it's the ur-question. All this information is coming in, in the form of digital data, and it's going to be ultimately analyzed as digital data. So it's surprising that astronomers interrupt the stream from digital to digital and in the middle of the flow make a picture out of the data. I think that says something about human cognition: we need a picture in order to make sense of the information.

Think about the difference between weather and climate: weather exists right here, right now, but climate can only exist in an archive. It is all about averages of weather, bringing lots and lots of data together to create something called climate. It's like the gross national product. We buy a carton of milk or a computer or a car, but what is measured in terms of the economic productivity of the whole country is a kind of average, a kind of market basket of all those things.

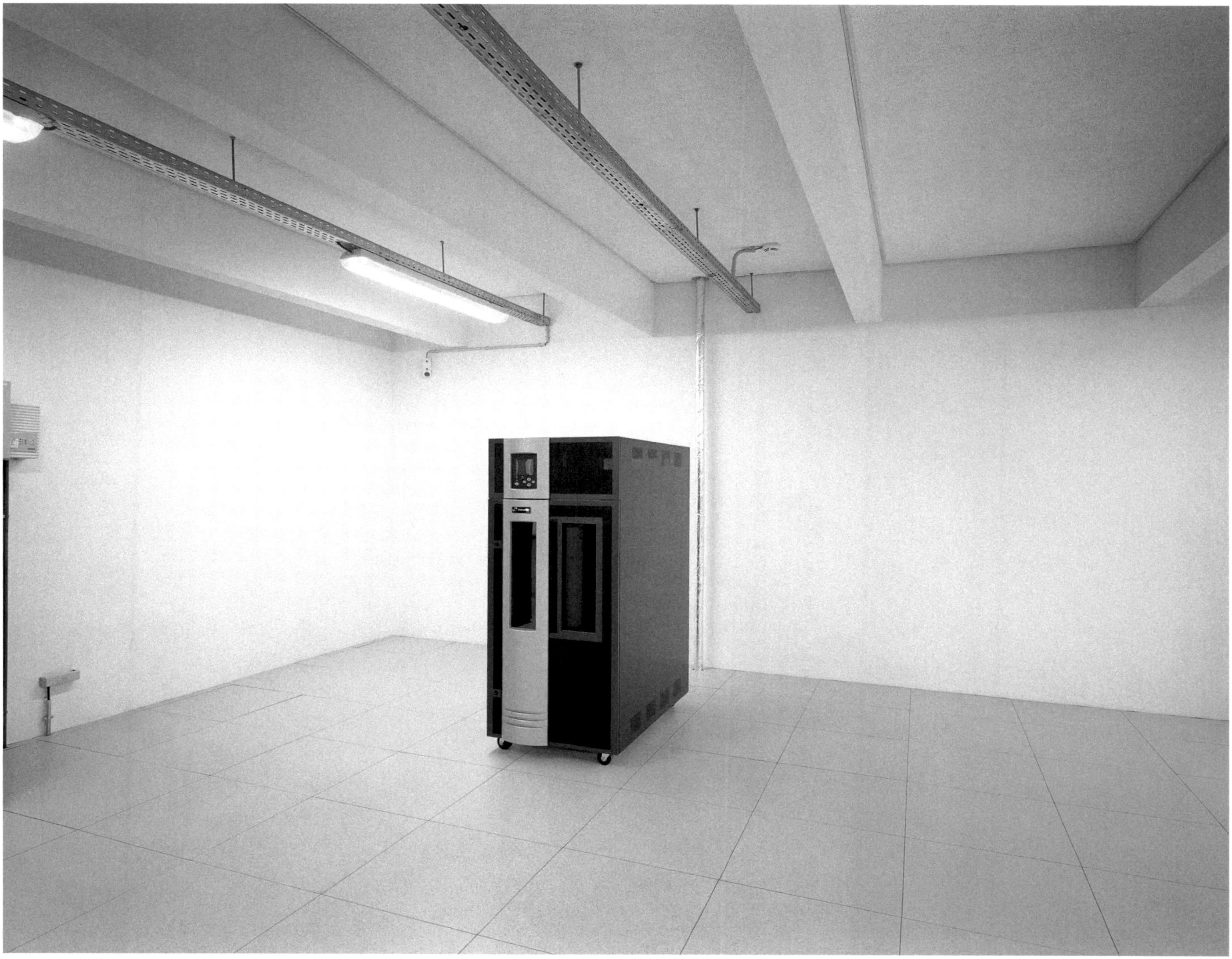

Similarly, the climate is a composite of lots of observations: it's not happening outdoors but in this archive of enormous amounts of data. These images are emblems of the degree to which climate itself is a kind of creation of calculation. That doesn't make it any less real, but it absolutely requires this intermediate step.

DKRZ, German Climate Computing Center, archives, Hamburg, Germany, 2013

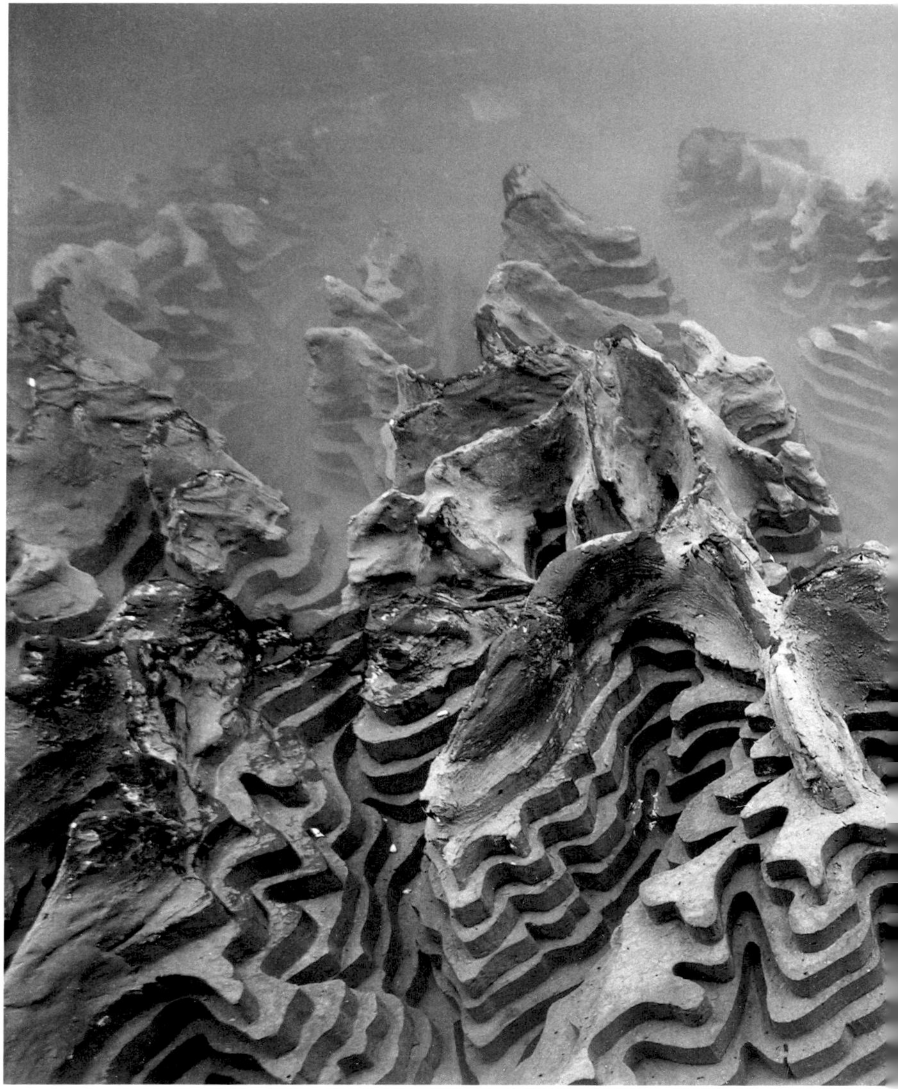

This analogical model has been used since the 1990s at the University of Lausanne to show how clouds move in the area of Mont Blanc and Lake Geneva. Most of these models are now used only as didactical instruments to visualize concepts for students. In research processes they are substituted by digital models.

In a less modern way, this image of the model of the Alps depicts the same idea as the image of the Climate Center in Hamburg: the idea that nature is too complex, too big to be dealt with by human minds.

École polytechnique fédérale de Lausanne (EPFL), Alps model, Lausanne, Switzerland, 2001

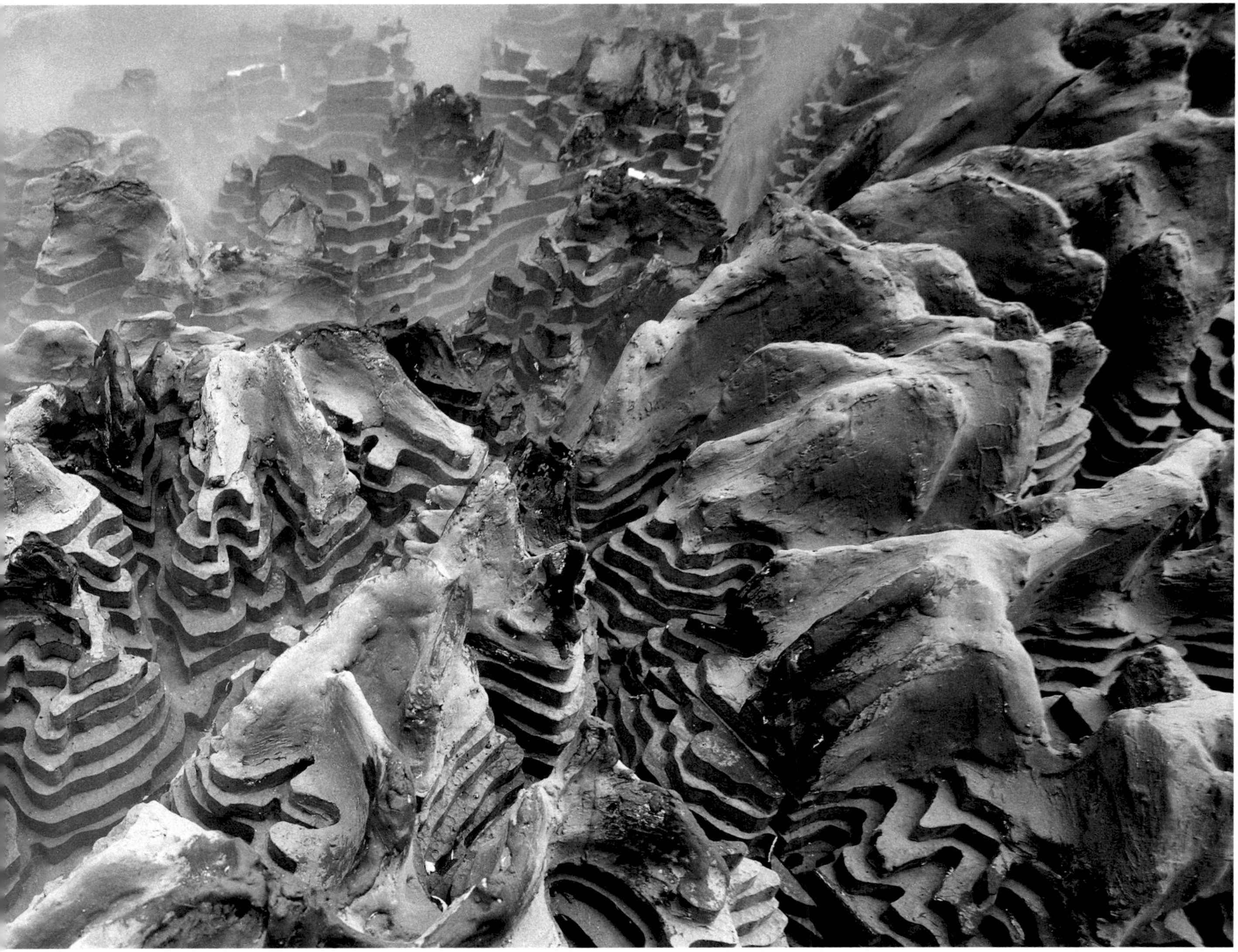

Therefore you've got to shrink and simplify it into a kind of dollhouse version. In this case, the model that tells us nothing about what the Alps look like but a lot about the topography of the Alps. It's like a contour map, another analog model. There's an ancient tradition of making these kinds of models that strip out certain features of the landscape in order to better understand others. All you're basically interested in here is how the crevasses in the Alps can trap the clouds and allow them either to move or not move.

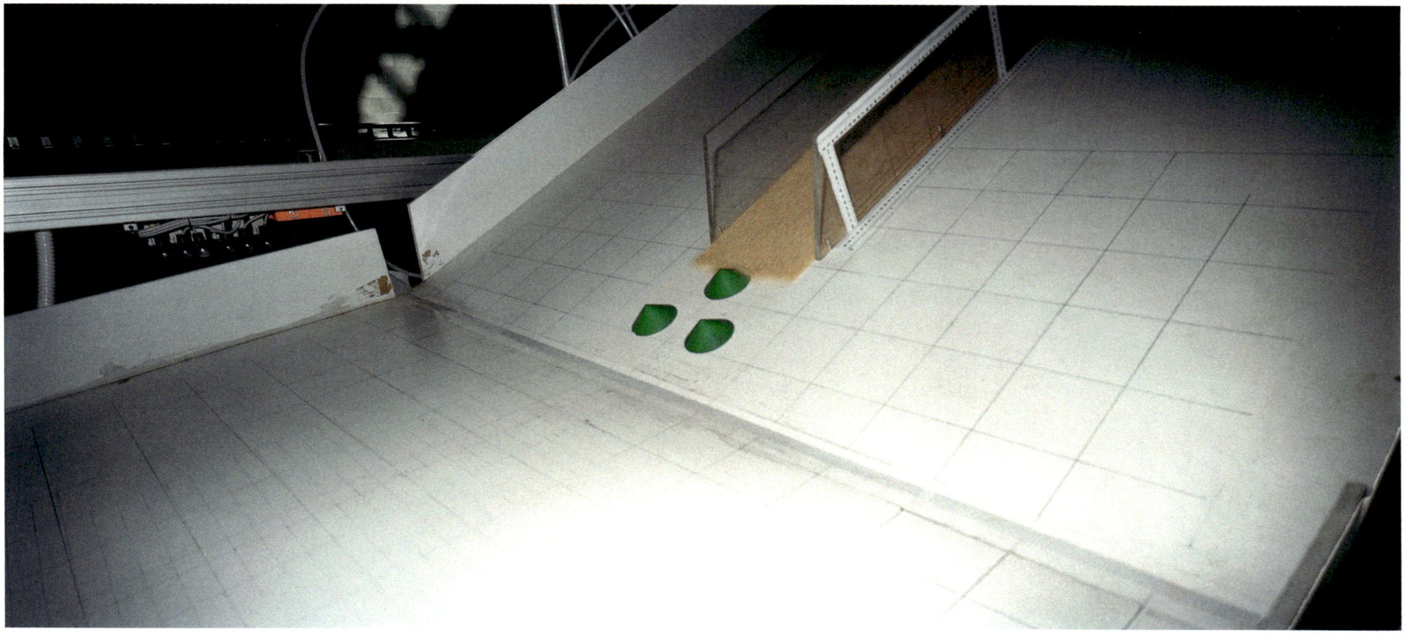

These kinds of models have been used, as I say, for centuries, if not millennia, and every time they have been reinvented, they remake experience. Simulation is a new form of scientific empiricism. There's a big debate going on amongst scientists as to whether or not these simulations can really supplant old-fashioned methods of empiricism, such as observation and experiment, not only in cosmology but also in climatology.

Università di Trento, laboratory experiments on snow avalanches,
Trento, Italy, 2004

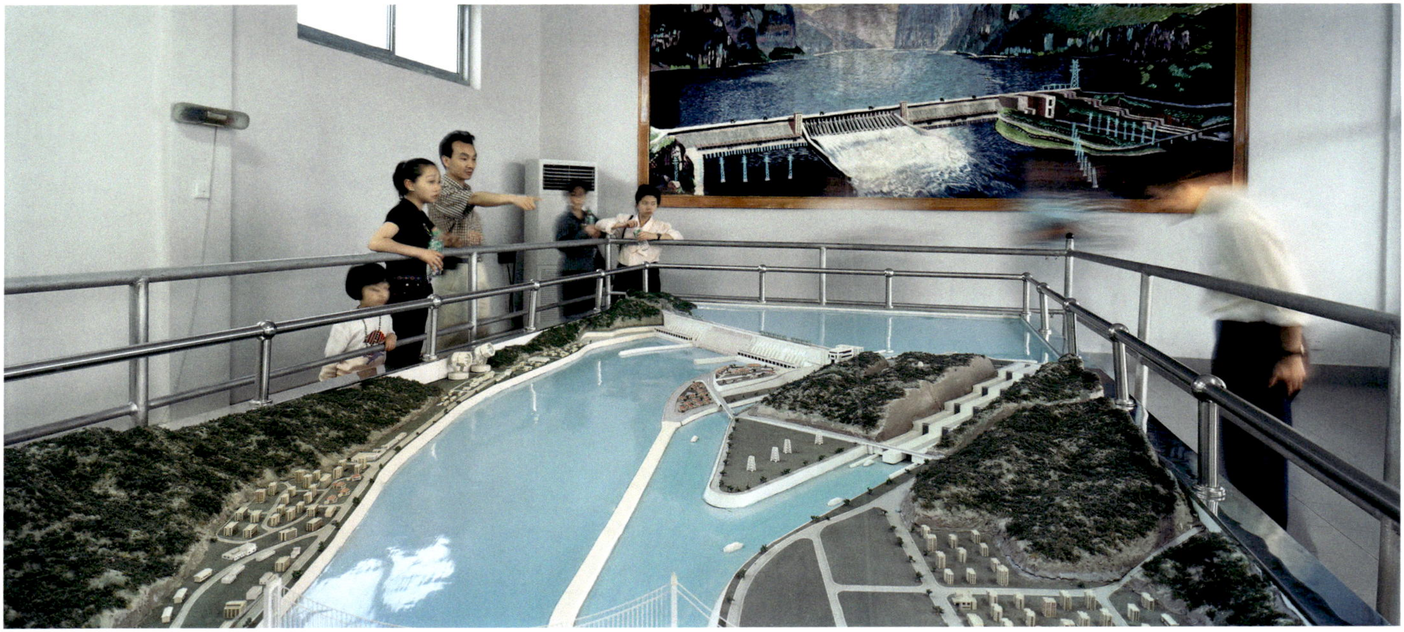

The model of the Three Gorges Dam project depicting the plans for urban development. An area of about 600 km^2 had to be submerged under water, two million people displaced, and all the infrastructure, including houses, schools, and industry, rebuilt.

In most European cities dating back to at least the sixteenth century, tabletop models of the cities were built to give onlookers a bird's-eye view.

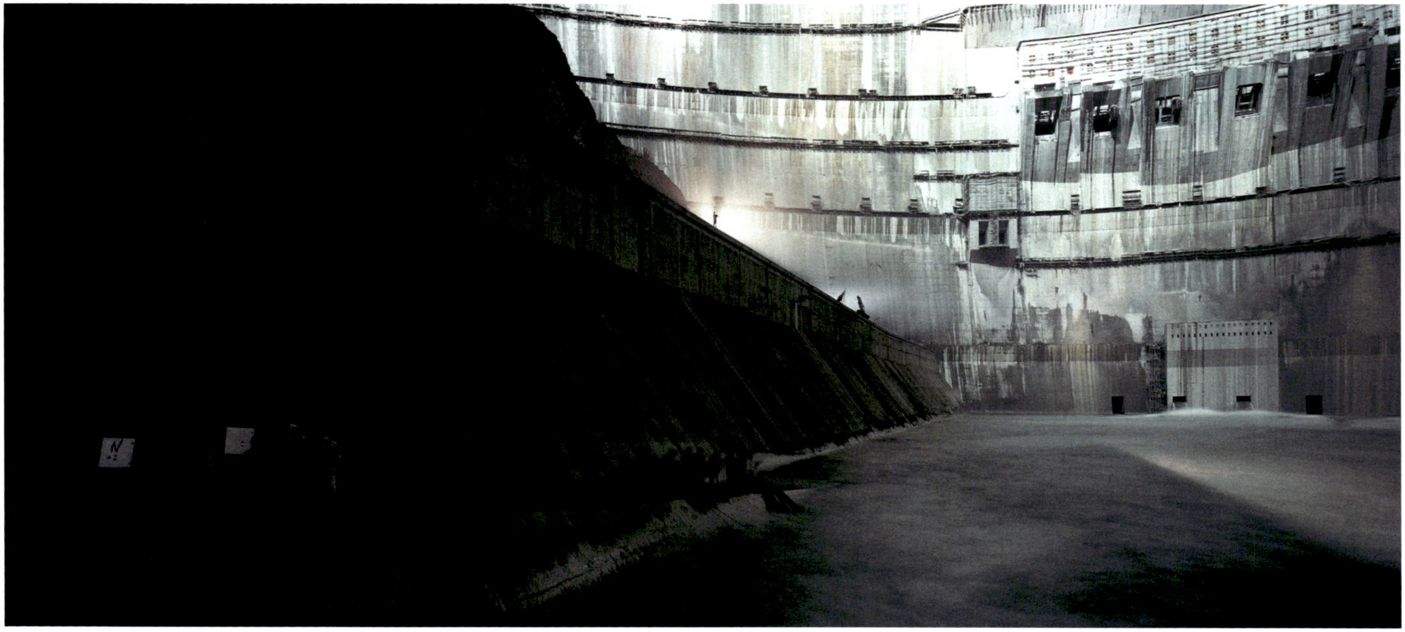

We can't grasp the city as a whole on its own scale, but in this miniature version we can survey it at a glance, a perspective that gives a sense of control. It's really interesting that you see spectators here. There's an element of selling the project to the public and of suggesting that just as the model allows you to survey the entire project in miniature, there's an assurance of perfect control in the project itself. Nothing can go wrong in this dollhouse world. As if to say: Nothing will go wrong when we scale up.

Ertan Dam, downstream side, Panzhihua, Sichuan, China, 1998

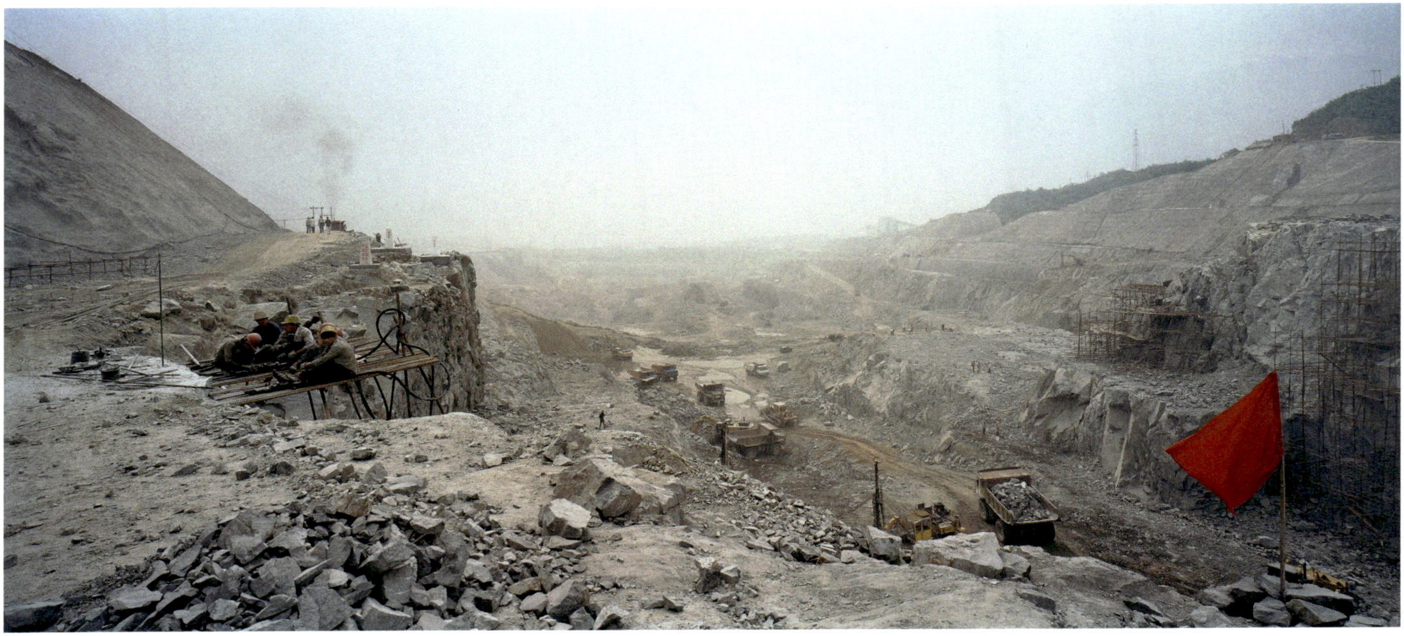

Since the great pyramids of ancient Egypt, architecture has been used as a way of expressing power through sheer enormity of scale. But efforts to attain immortality by leaving a monumental trace behind are always overshadowed by futility. The Three Gorges Dam Project in China has this quality, all the more sobering because it so obviously failed. It was never completed.

Three Gorges Dam, construction of a lift for ships, Yichang (Hubei), China, 1998

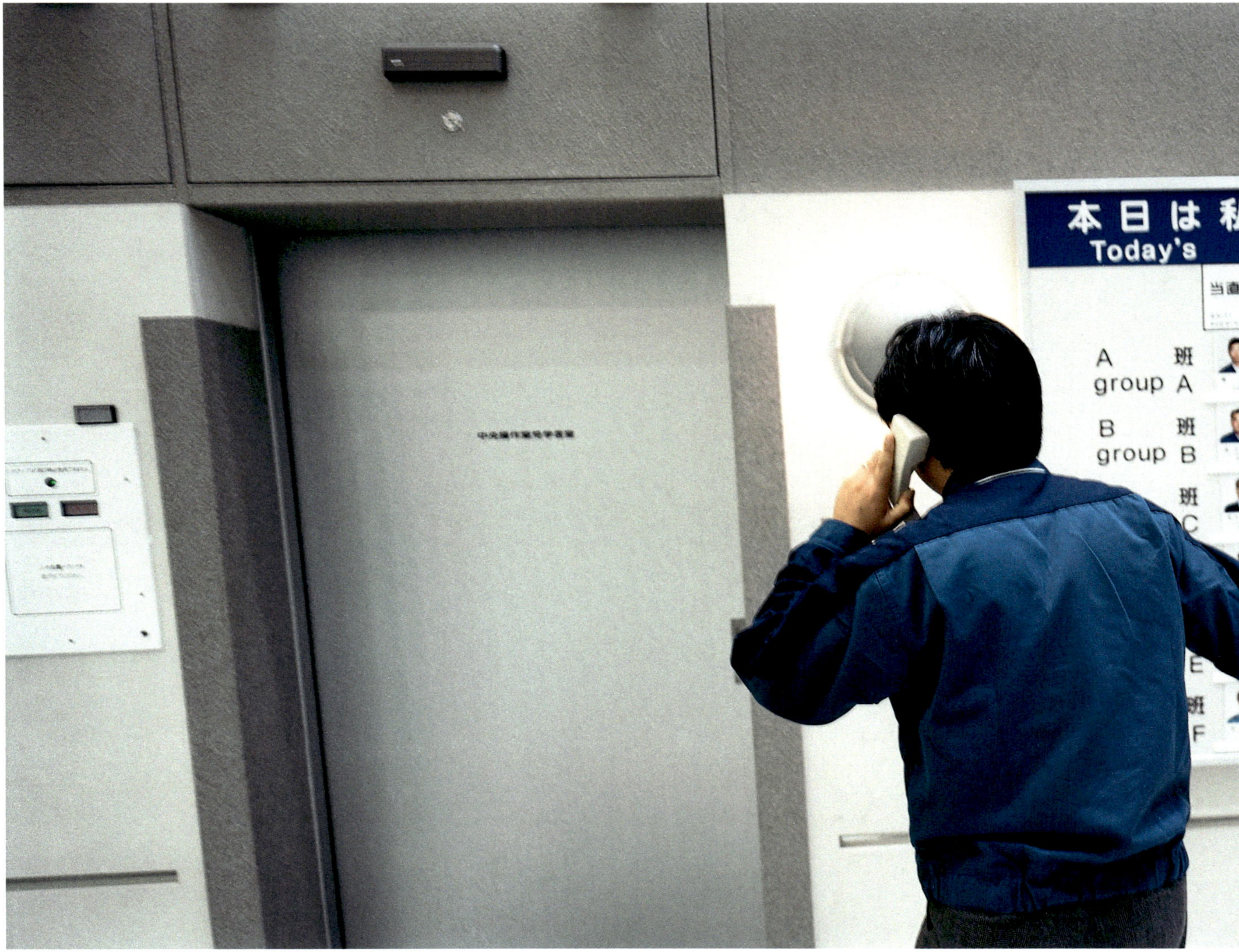

Kashiwazaki-Kariwa is listed as the largest nuclear power plant in the world, with a capacity of 8,212 MW. Following the 2007 Chuetsu offshore earthquake, three of its seven reactor units had to be shut down, with the remaining units rendered non-operational after the 2011 tsunami.

This makes me think of the nuclear accident at Three Mile Island in the United States, which was largely attributed to human error.

Kashiwazaki-Kariwa Nuclear Power Station, entrance to control room, Kashiwazaki, Japan, 1998

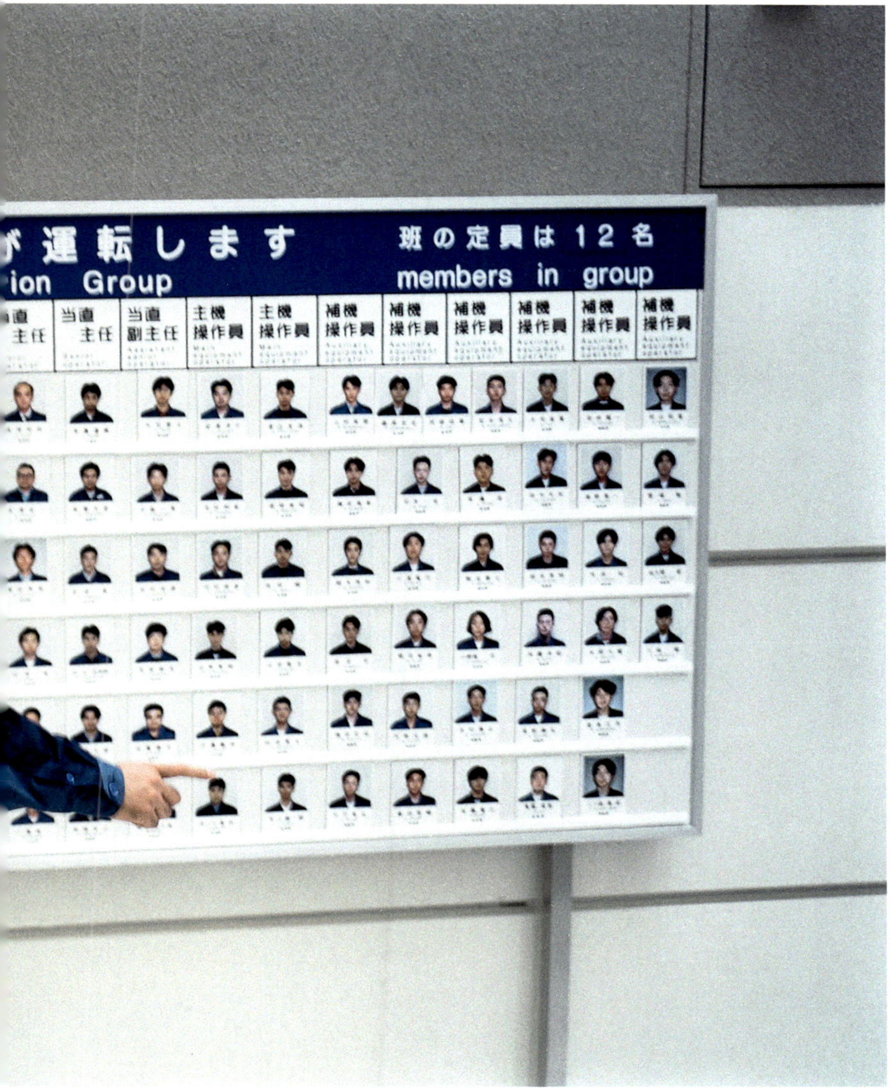

Human error—above all, human boredom—was diagnosed as a major threat to security because much of what the staff of nuclear power plants have to do is just monitor instruments that mostly don't change. That leads to a situation where people increasingly neglect their duties. Ultimately, every work of technology is a kind of centaur. It's a hybrid of the human and the technological. Even if you were to fully automate the workings of the nuclear power plant, there would always be a layer of human surveillance.

The Palm Jumeirah has become a visual cliché of the United Arab Emirates striving for recognition. There's something poignant about it, I must say. If you were to think about this in terms of the politics of global attention, it is a kind of scream of "Pay attention! Pay attention to us!" The idea is to colonize the global imaginary by having an image that is so irresistible in its combination of monumentality and sheer silliness that you can't get it out of your head.

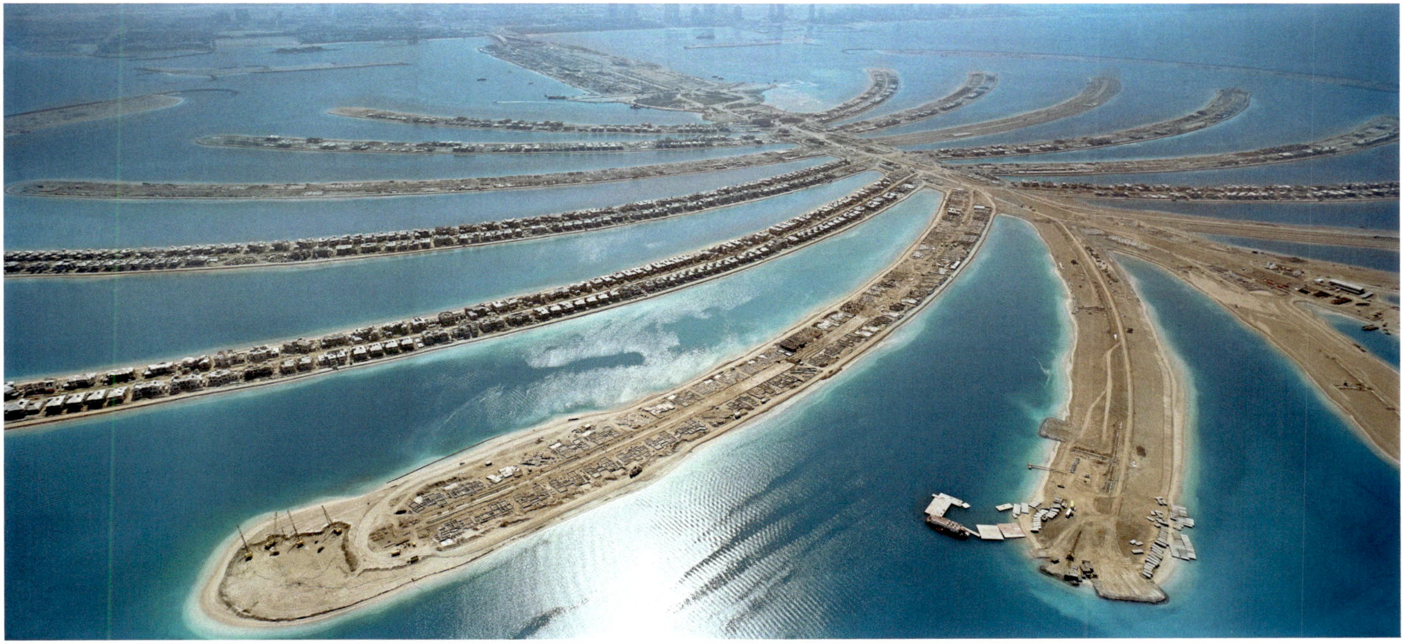

It is an attention-grabbing project, and it makes one think about the economy of global attention, especially in the age of the Internet, which has turned attention into a kind of currency. On a technological and also political level, there's an arms race going on to create ever more spectacular forms of theater on screen.

The Palm Jumeirah, aerial view, Dubai, United Arab Emirates, 2005

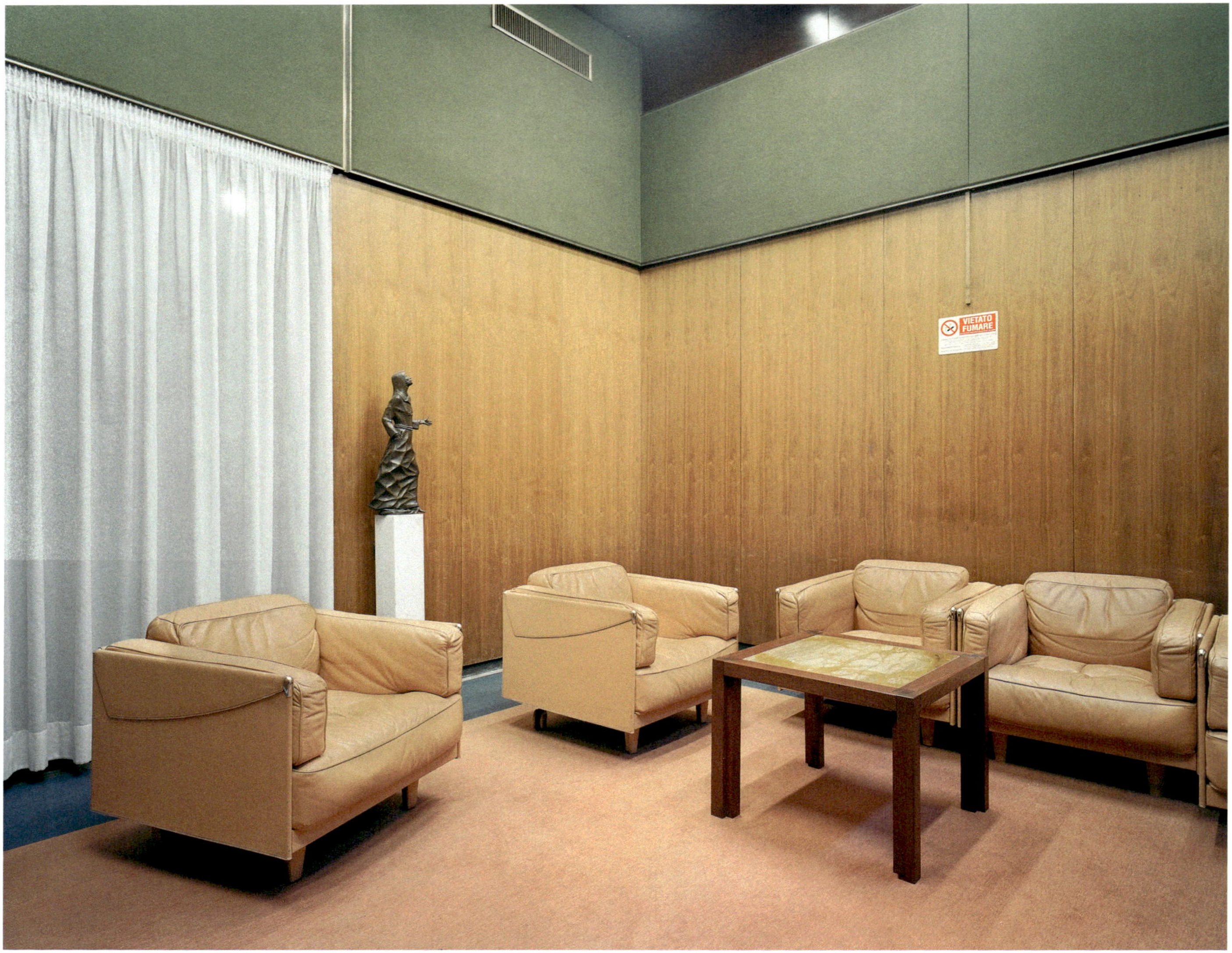

A sculpture of Saint Clare of Assisi, who was canonized in 1255 for her work with Saint Francis of Assisi, graces a RAI building interior. In 1958, Pope Pius XII declared Saint Clare of Assisi the patron saint of television and telecommunications.

Why is Santa Chiara the patron saint of television? I can only guess. She had a reputation for self-promotion. Coming from a wealthy family, she made a huge fuss when her father wanted her to marry and said, “No. I’m going to be married to Jesus.”

RAI, Italian Broadcasting Corporation, Rome, Italy, 2008

All her life, she got what she wanted, apparently from a position of weakness but in fact by steely obstinacy and resolve. She also used her body, especially fasting and other forms of mortification of the flesh, to force the Pope to give her her own order, the Poor Clares. Some witty theologian at the Vatican must have known how impossible she was and decided that this was going to be the saint of self-promotion. What an inspiration. Santa Chiara, of all people.

The idea of the botanical garden was to cultivate plants that were not native to that area; it began in 1506, when the Pisa Physic Garden was founded. New plants were arriving in Europe from the "New World," from far away, from both east and west, and doctors, botanists, and apothecaries hoped to make them grow in a European setting and to use them as medications.

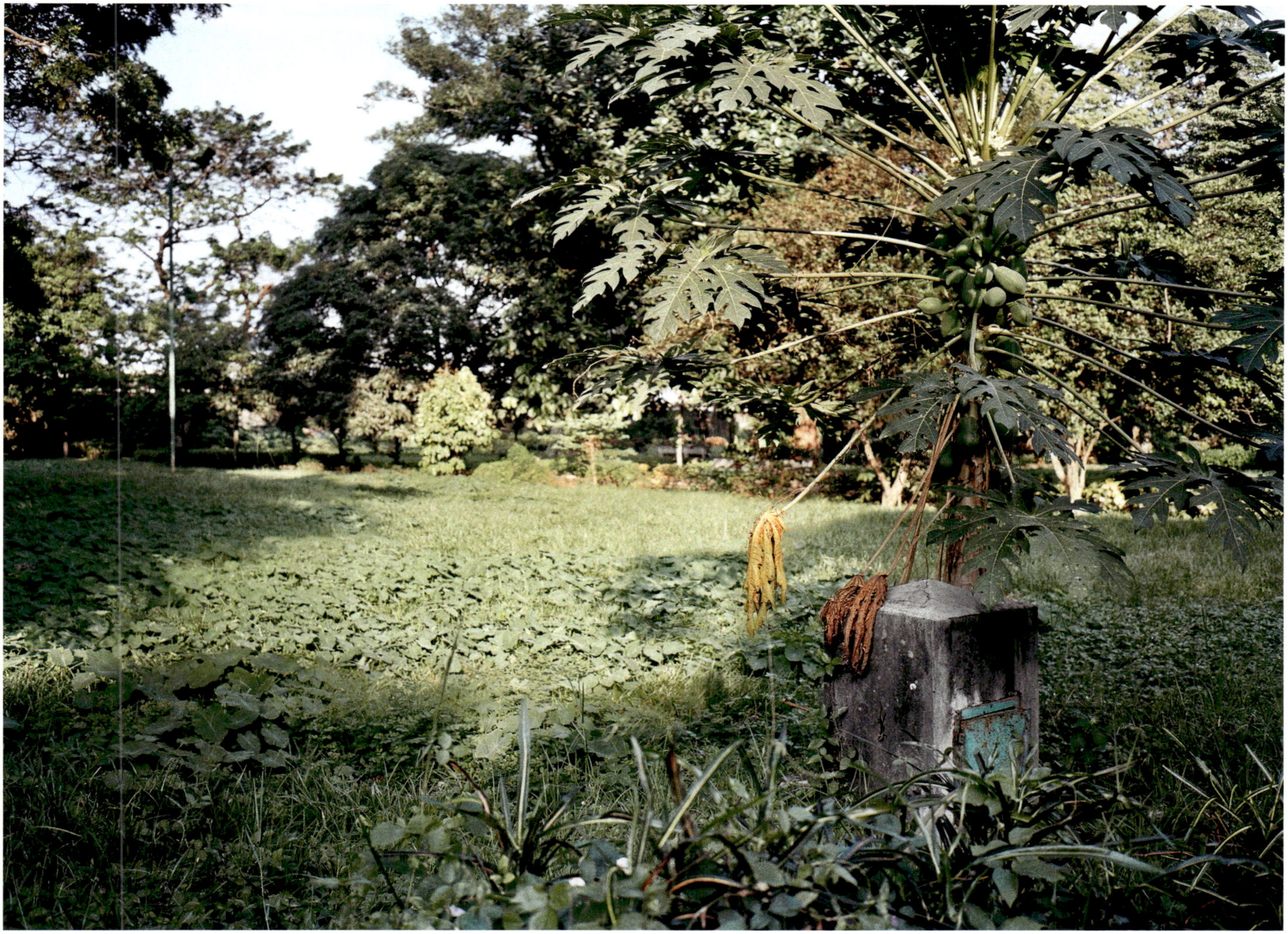

That's why it was called a physic garden, "physic" being the old word for medicine. I suspect that there was a similar idea of bio-prospecting at work here.

Botanical garden, Kinshasa, Democratic Republic of Congo, 2002

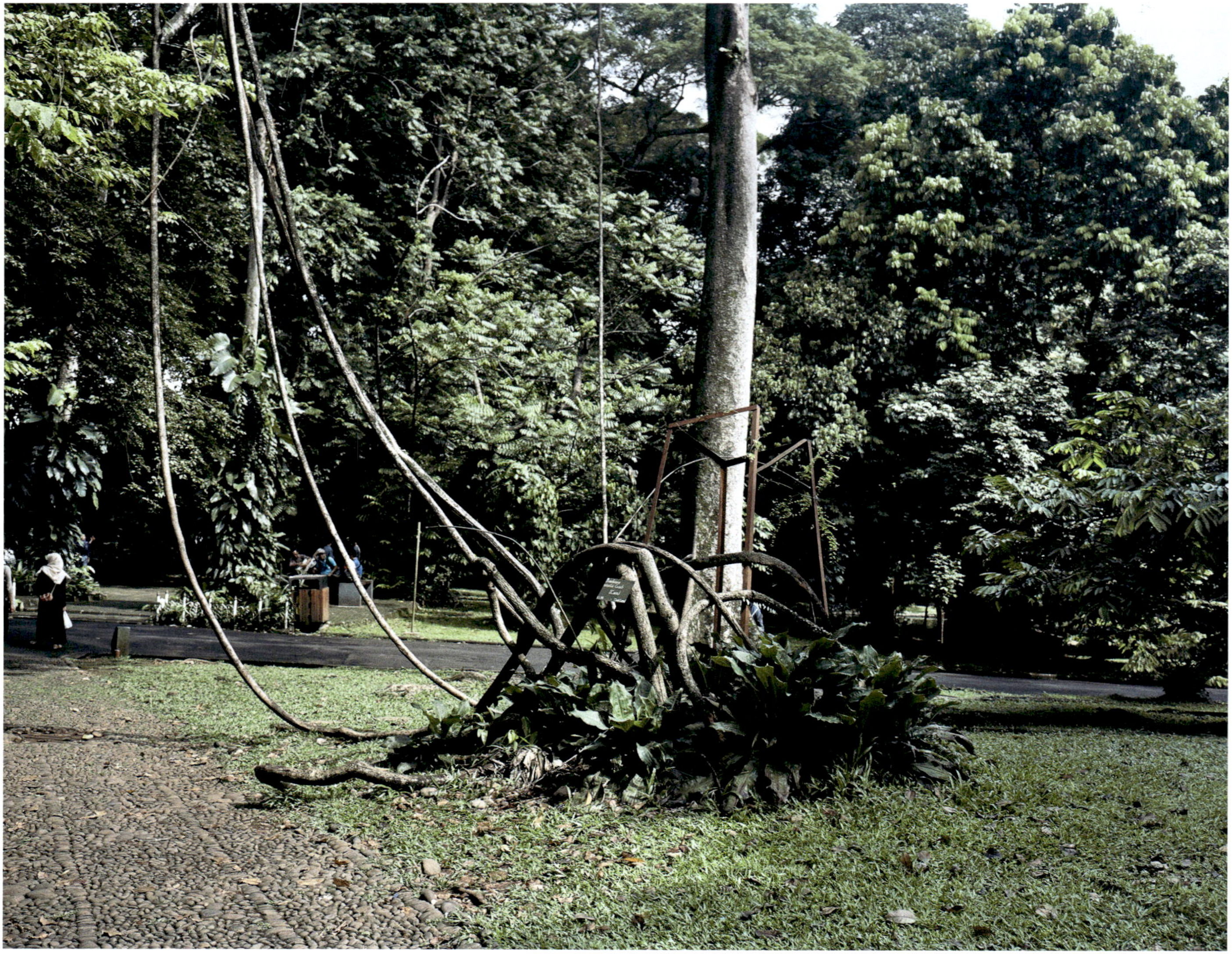

The British biologist and geographer Alfred Russel Wallace investigated the theory of evolution through natural selection. He sold many of the plants grown in Bogor Botanical Gardens to botanical collections in Europe.

Bogor Botanical Gardens, Jakarta, Indonesia, 2016

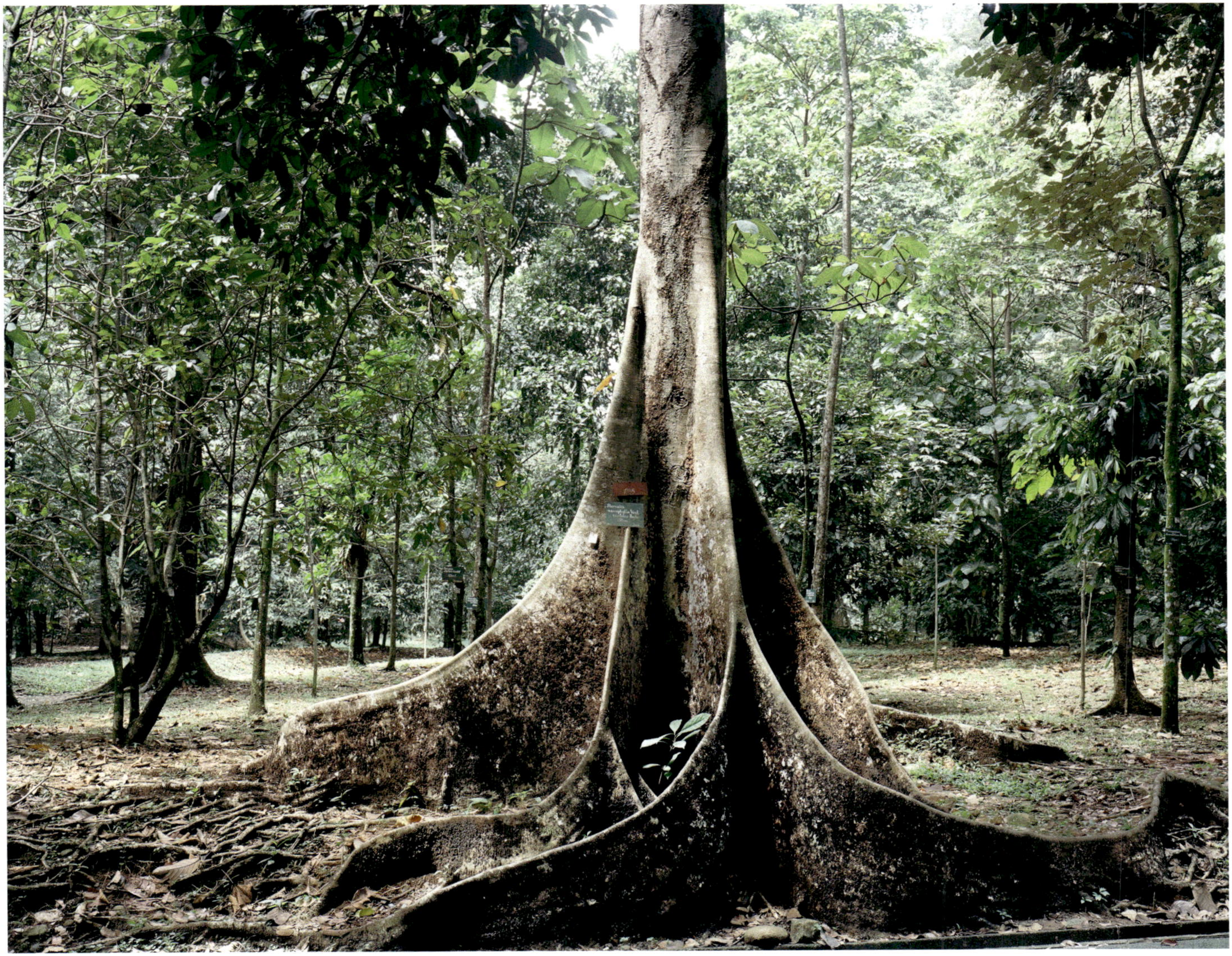

These plants, both native and exotic, were not only cultivated for the purposes of display but also in the hopes of being able to extract some kind of pharmaceutical value from them. Bio-prospecting is still going on, another interesting case of intellectual property rights. What bio-prospectors are doing, as the Spanish were already doing in the sixteenth century, is interviewing the people who live here and asking them about which plants are used for what kind of ailments.

Bogor Botanical Gardens, Jakarta, Indonesia, 2016

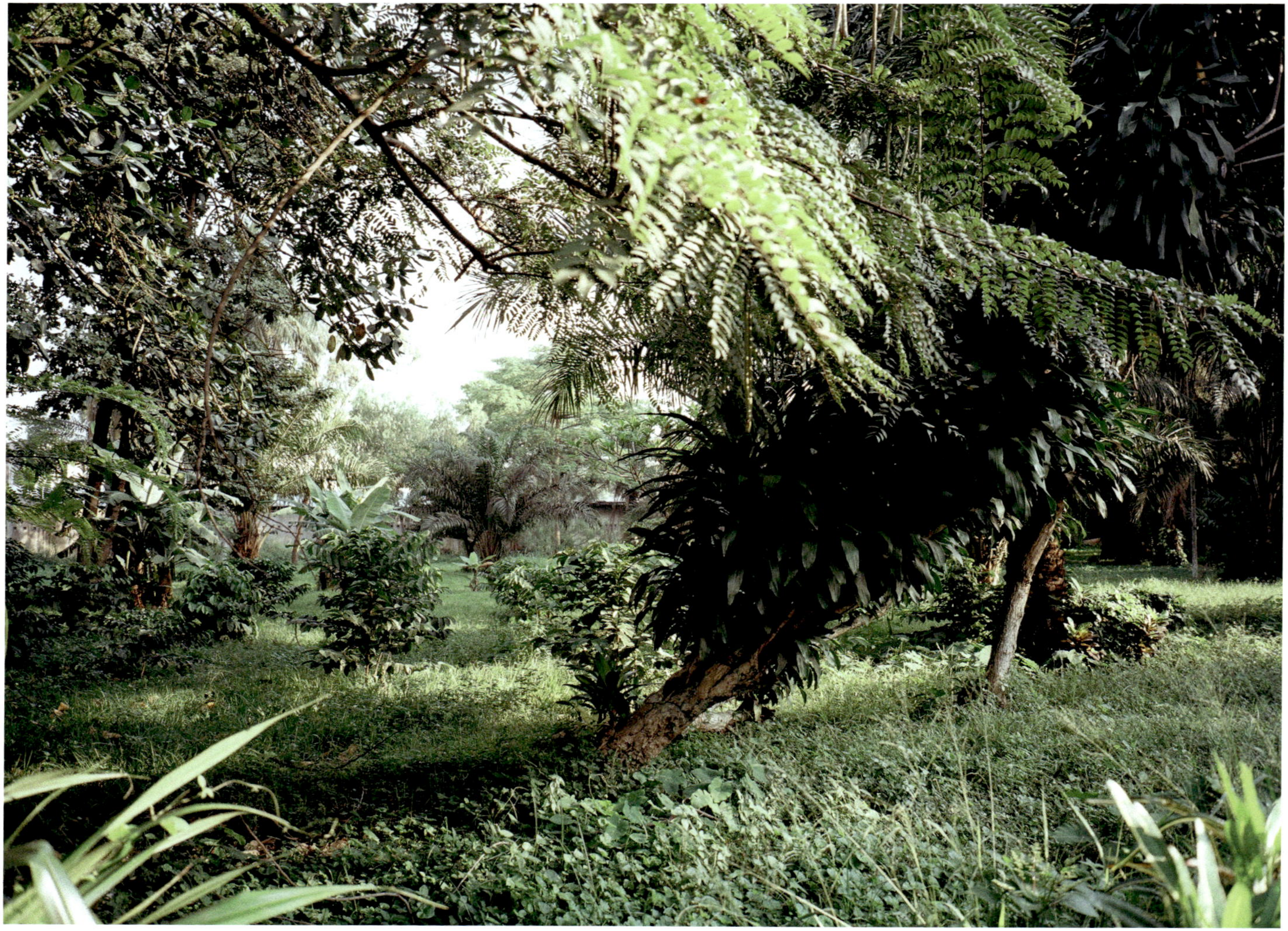

These days, the people who are being interviewed for these purposes wish to assert their rights of ownership to the plants and the active ingredients. So this botanical garden now represents a flashpoint where local knowledge comes into contact and conflict with a global commercial-industrial complex.

Botanical garden, Kinshasa, Democratic Republic of Congo, 2002

In contrast to the periods represented in these murals, science is no longer funded privately by princely patrons. In the days of Galileo, it was the Medici in Florence who were bankrolling him; he named the moons of Jupiter the "Medicean stars" in the hopes of attracting their patronage. And it worked.

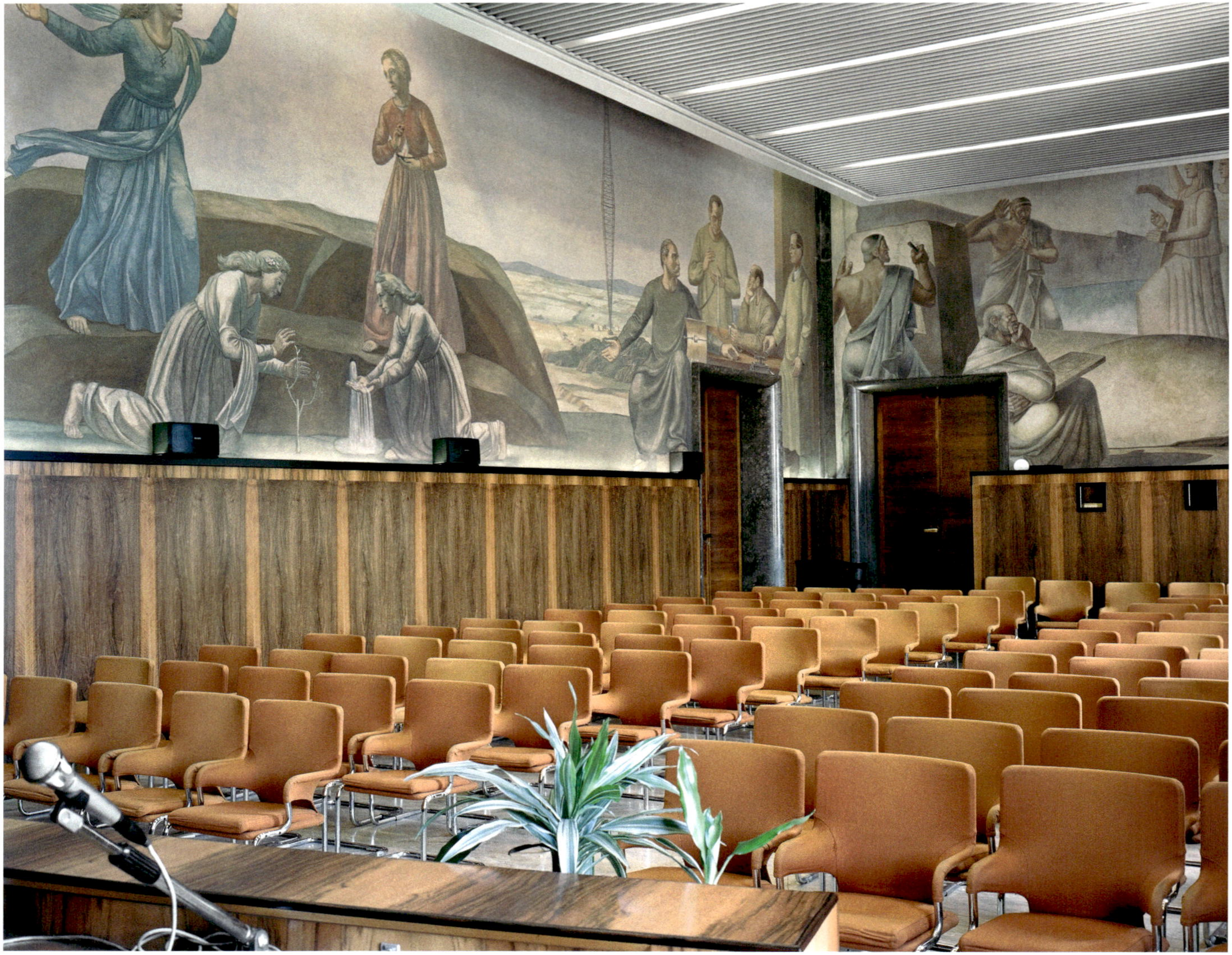

The Fascist-era frescos by Antonio Achilli celebrate Italian scientific achievements through history, from Archimedes to Lucrezio Caro, Galileo Galilei to Christopher Colombus.

CNR, National Science Research Council, Marconi conference hall, Rome, Italy, 2007

He immediately abandoned his job as professor of mathematics at Padua because he got a much fancier job, both better paid and more prestigious, as natural philosopher at the Medici court. But nowadays, a lot of scientific research is financed by the state, unless it's in an area of lucrative applications, such as drug research in the biomedical sciences or resource prospecting in geology.

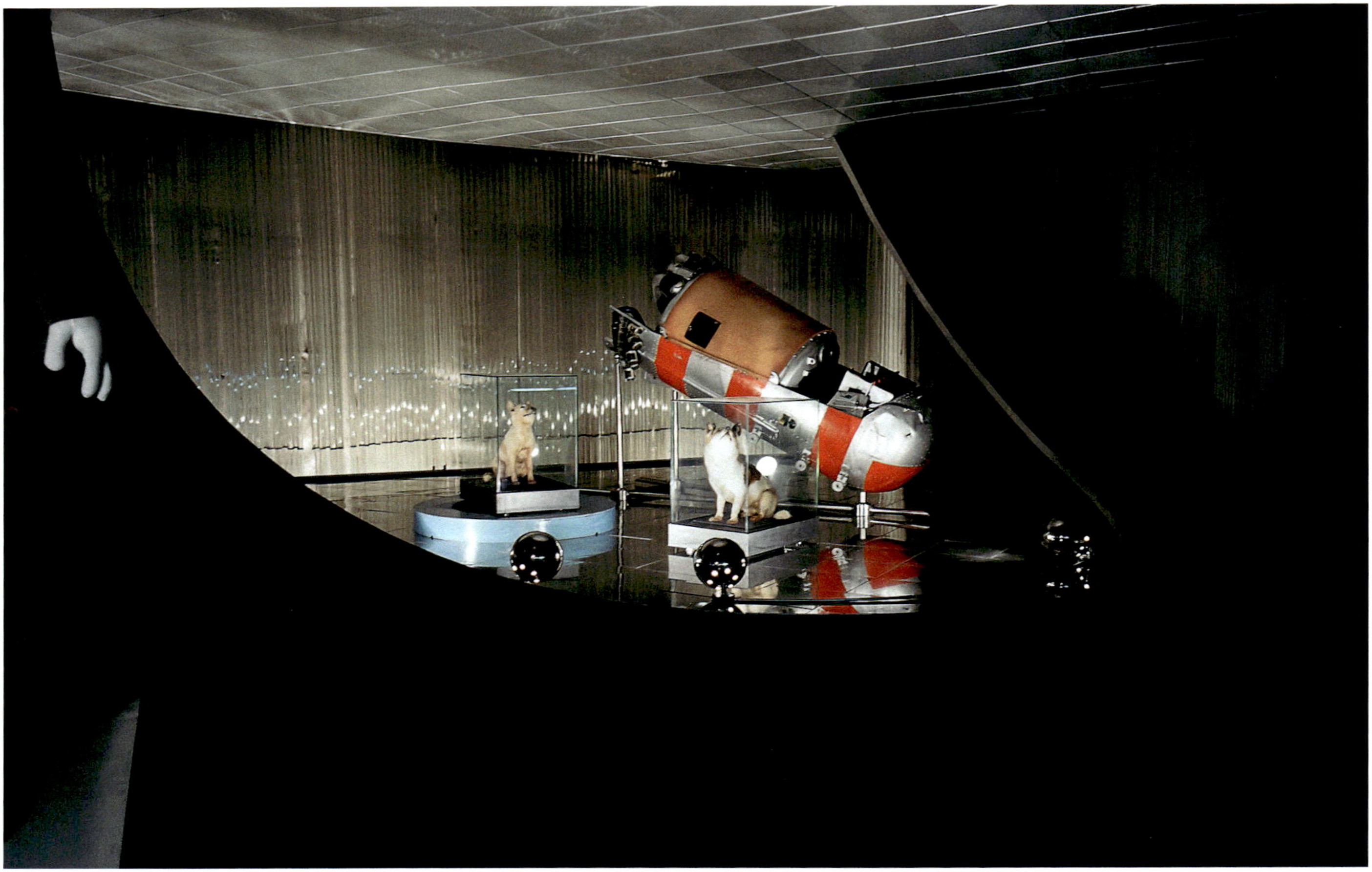

The stuffed dogs on display in the Museum of Cosmonautics are called Laika, Belka, and Strelka. They were the first living beings to be launched into space.

Dogs have a special place in the history of Russian science—think of Pavlov's dogs. But they have also been used for experimental analysis, especially in testing new drugs.

Museum of Cosmonautics, first canine astronauts, Moscow, Russia, 1999

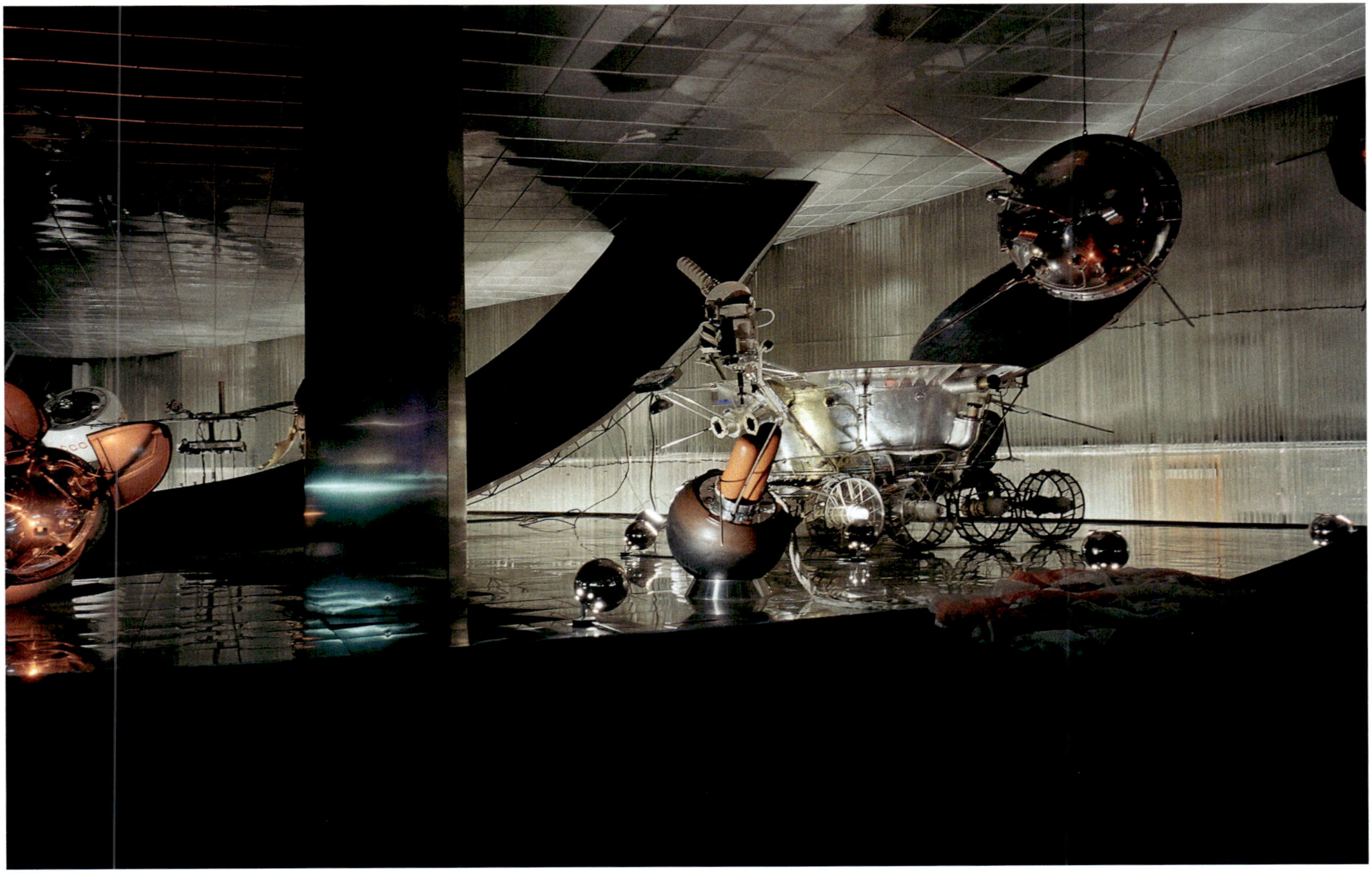

The first dog astronauts are the only example I know of dogs having an individuality and being memorialized. I think that's exactly the right reading here: they are heroic dogs. This is so unusual in the history of experimental animals: think of all the rats that have been sacrificed for medical experiments, and there are surely rats that contributed to lifesaving medicines, but nobody ever thought of stuffing one of those rats and putting it on display as the savior of thousands of patients. "This rat died to cure you."

Museum of Cosmonautics, first canine astronauts, Moscow, Russia, 1999

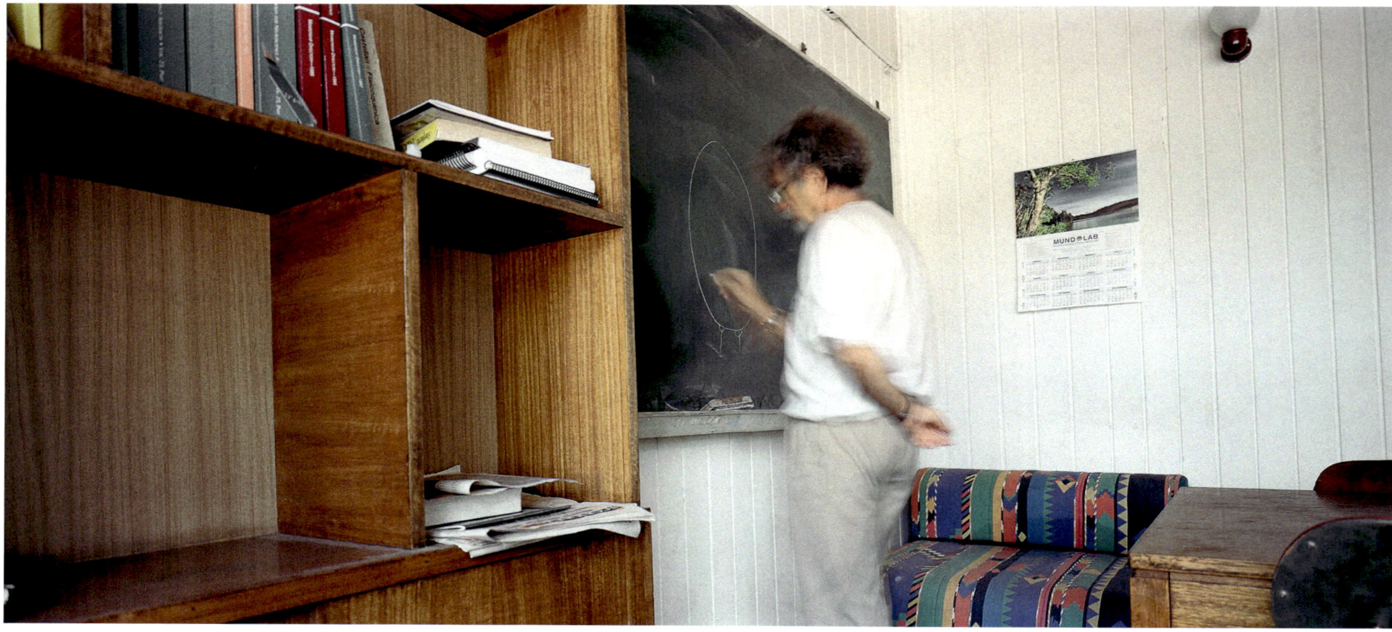

One of Humberto Maturana's best-known books, written together with Francisco Varela, is *The Tree of Knowledge: The Biological Roots of Human Understanding*. It deals with biology, linguistics, and neural programming.

Humberto Maturana, neurophysiology laboratory, University of Chile, Santiago, Chile, 1999

Writing with chalk on a blackboard is a scientific habitus that is now doomed to extinction—except for mathematicians. It's important that in order to teach geometry, in particular, but also almost any other form of mathematics, you've got to have a shared object of attention. The blackboard was used before the invention of projective techniques like the overhead projector. Just like the wax tablet it could be erased and used over and over again, which is emblematic of the nature of science, always generating new images and new objects.

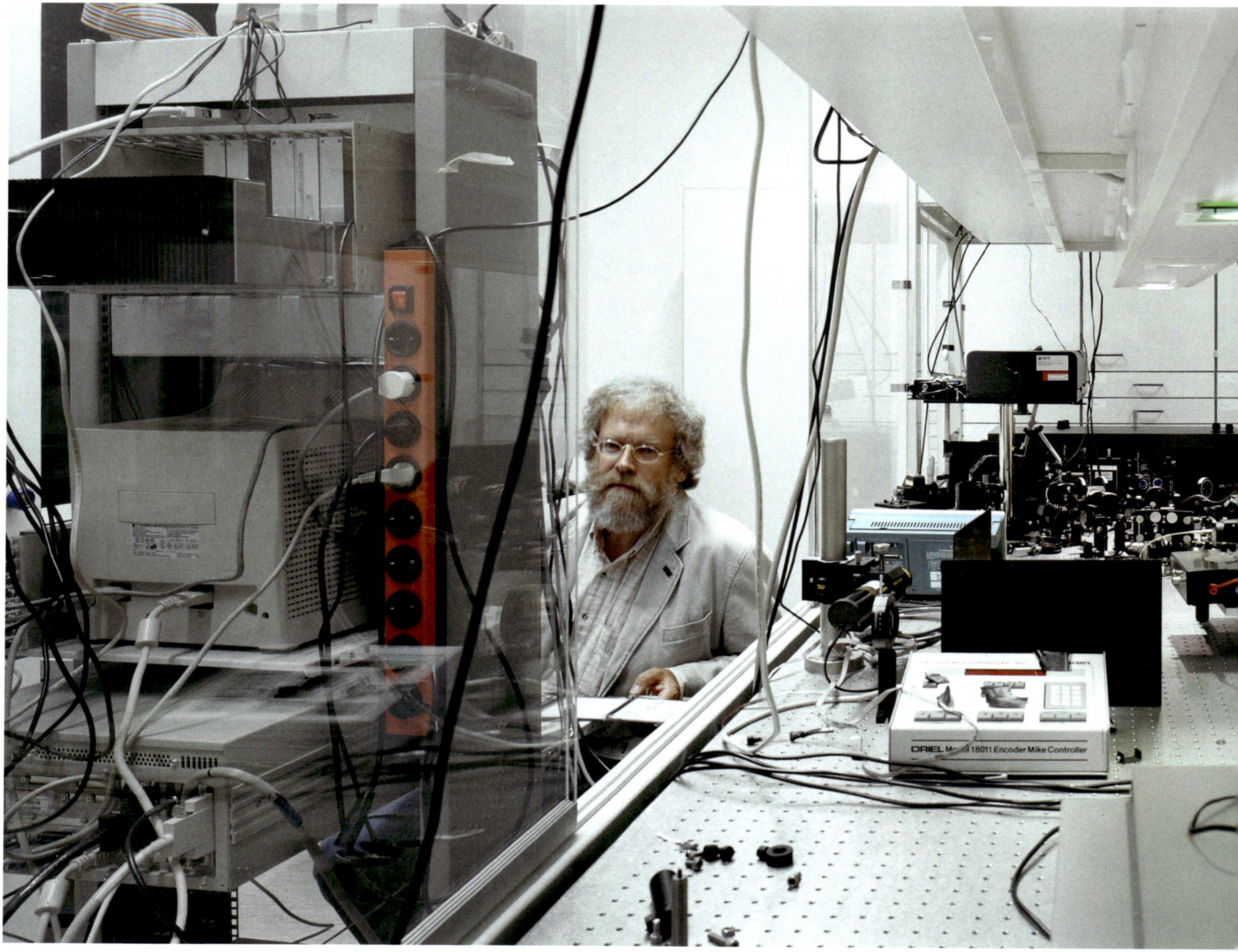

There's something about the dynamic that you can see a lot more easily, I think, with a blackboard or a wax tablet than you can in the image of Anton Zeilinger working in his lab. Whatever screen or dial Zeilinger was looking at, we can't see it. It is not a shared focus of attention. Mathematics depends essentially on the transmission of the tradition. It is not a subject that you can invent all on your own.

Anton Zeilinger, Institute for Quantum Optics and Quantum Information, University of Vienna, experiment, Vienna, Austria, 2001

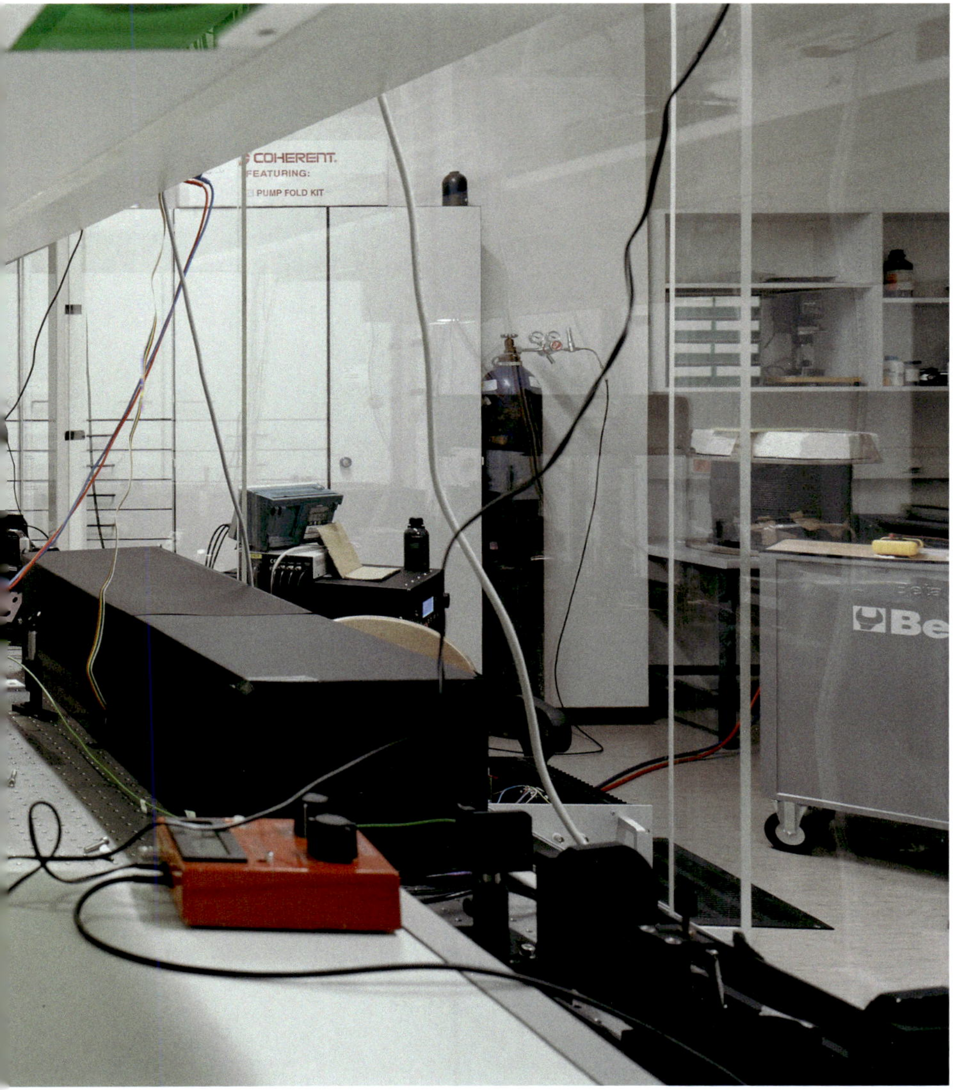

It relies on sustaining a teacher-student relationship over generations, even millennia. In antiquity and long thereafter, transmission took place though the family: we don't have a lot of information, but if you look at generations of mathematicians, there seem to have been a lot of father-child apprenticeships. Just as in other trades, a habitus is being trained that involves not only the mind but also the whole body.

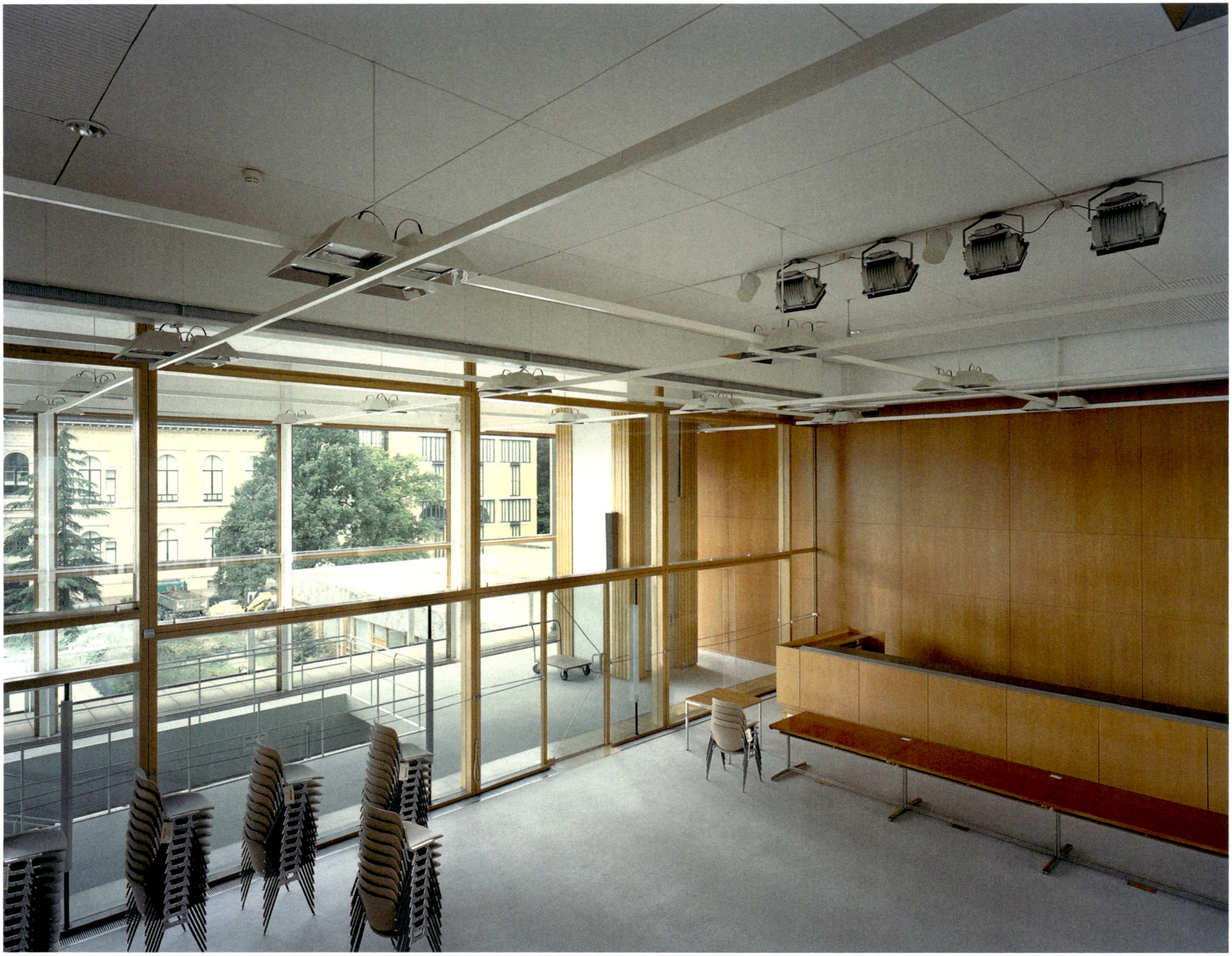

The building of the Constitutional Court building was designed in the 1960s by Paul Baumgarten, who set out to incorporate an impression of transparency and understated power within this piece of modernistic architecture.

Bundesverfassungsgericht (Federal Constitutional Court), Karlsruhe, Germany, 2011

I associate it with a lot of buildings in Bonn, actually, like the headquarters of the Alexander von Humboldt Foundation: very clean lines, a lot of glass, all meant to blend in with the landscape. It is a kind of anti-monumental architecture that is self-effacing rather than self-aggrandizing. It strikes me as very typical of the Bonn Republic, of an insistence upon transparency and a very low tolerance for any kind of flourish or ornament that might be interpreted as pomposity or self-importance.

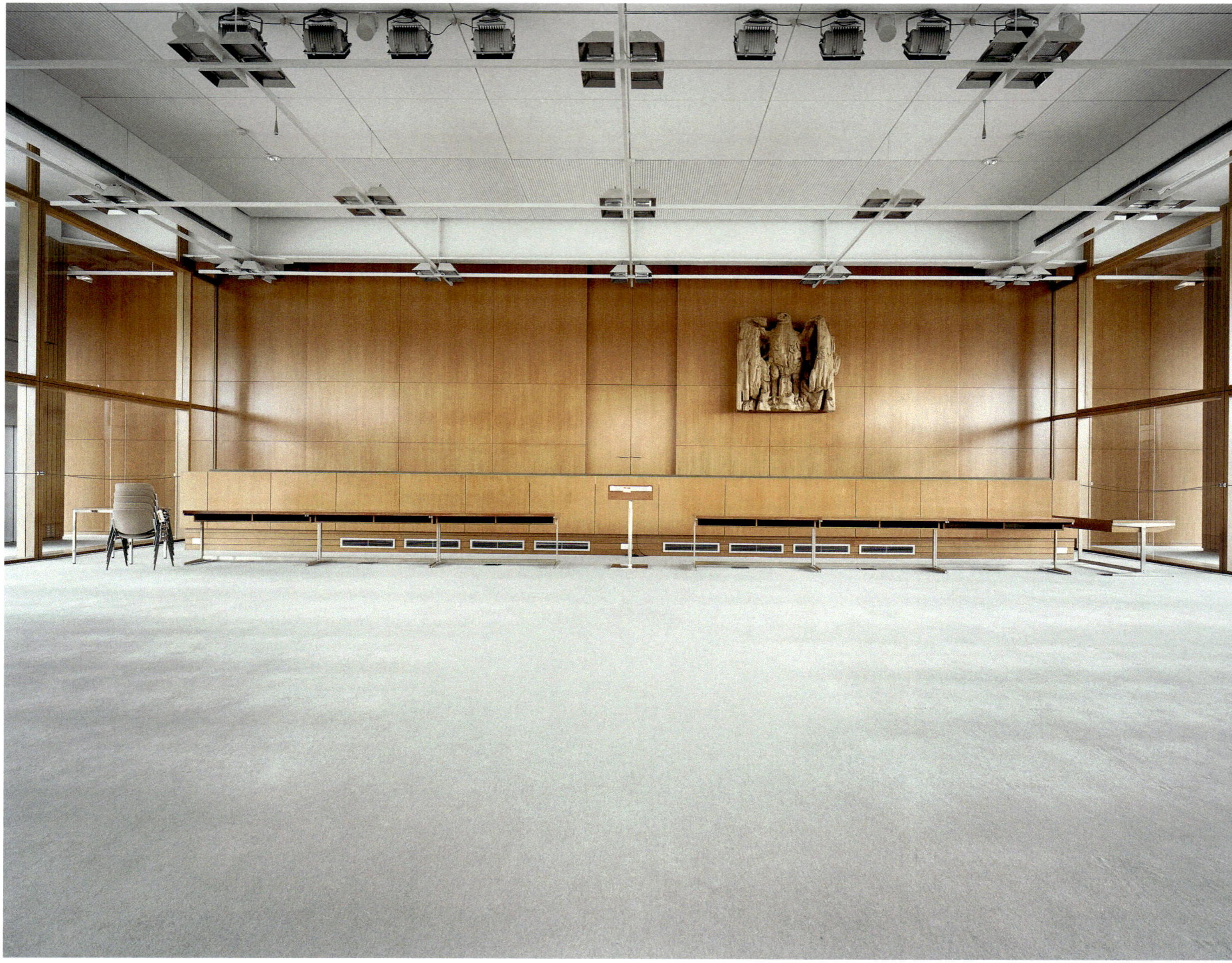

There is a high contrast between the almost dormitory-like simplicity of the wardrobes and the scarlet of the robes—scarlet being a color traditionally associated with emperors. The robes are so outrageously opulent in their color and materials compared to everything else that surrounds them, and yet they're necessary because part of the legitimacy of justice is a legitimacy of tradition.

Bundesverfassungsgericht (Federal Constitutional Court),
Karlsruhe, Germany, 2011

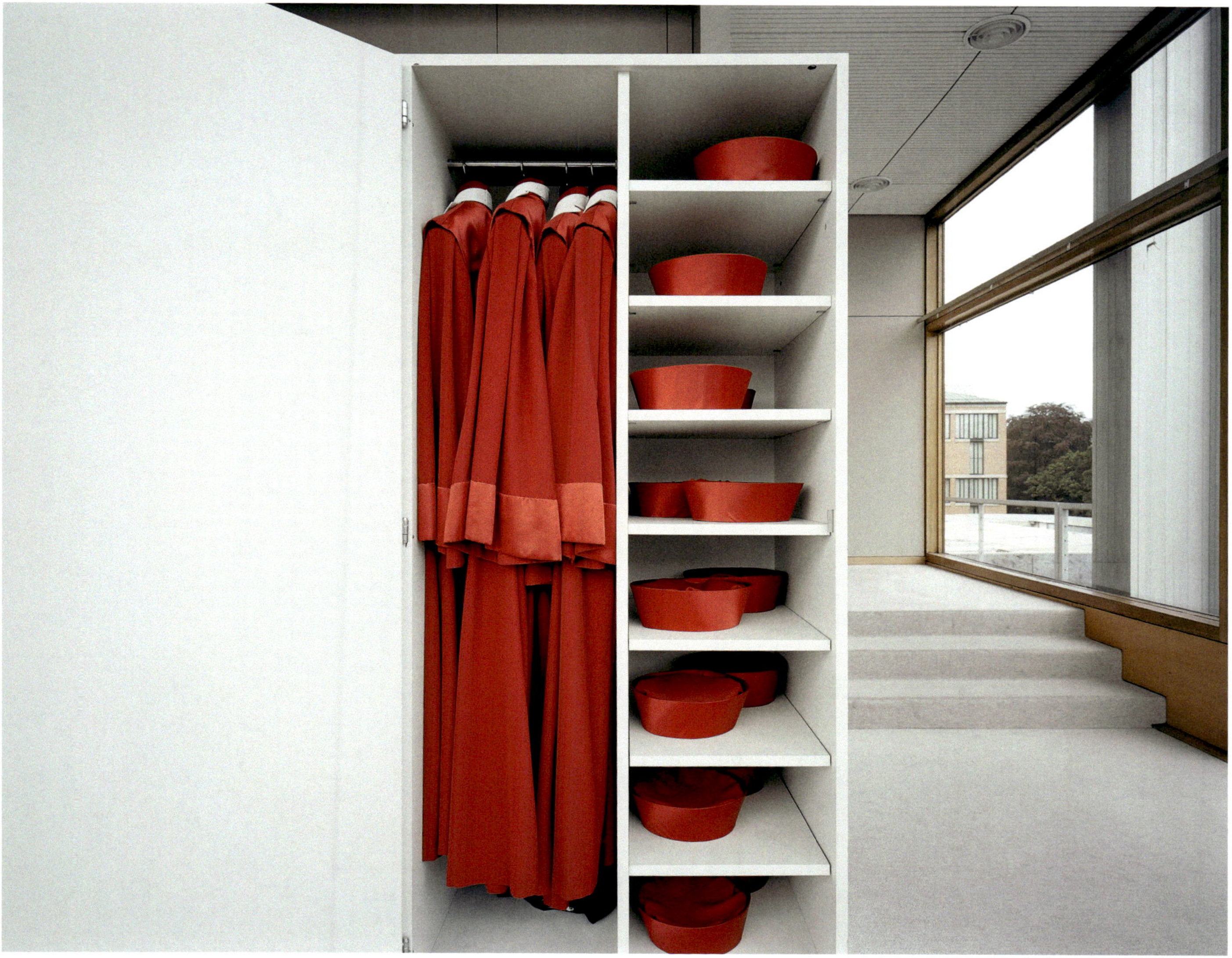

There's something about putting on a scarlet robe. The wearer assumes a different identity, a different persona.

Bundesverfassungsgericht (Federal Constitutional Court), Karlsruhe, Germany, 2011

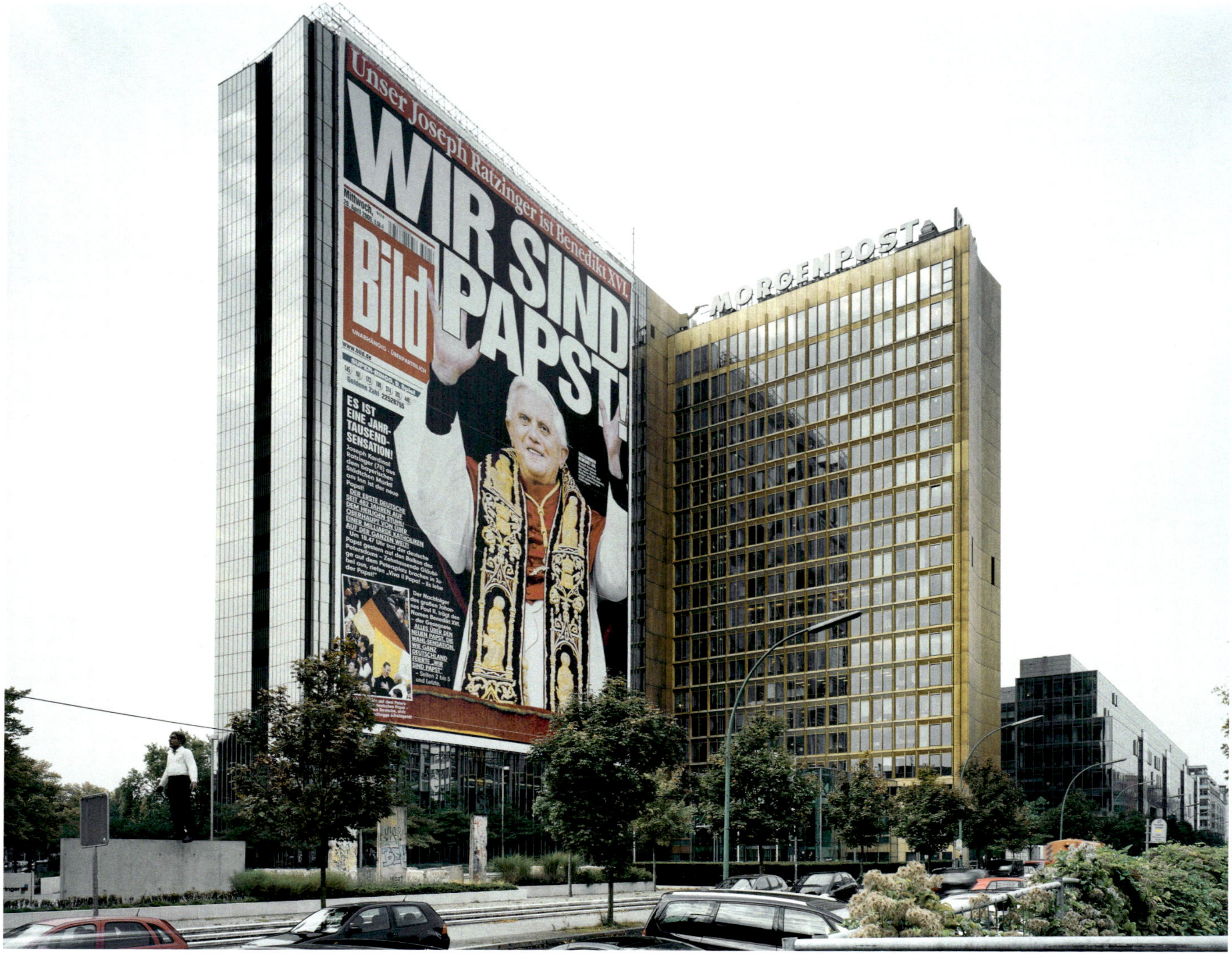

The French anthropologist Marcel Mauss wrote about this moment of symbolic transformation. For example, when a cardinal becomes Pope, he chooses a different name, and he also assumes a different habitus, a different garment. This transforms the person who's wearing these clothes into someone whose own personal interests and biography become irrelevant and disappear into the persona.

Axel-Springer Verlag, Pope Benedict XVI's visit to Berlin,
Berlin, Germany, 2011

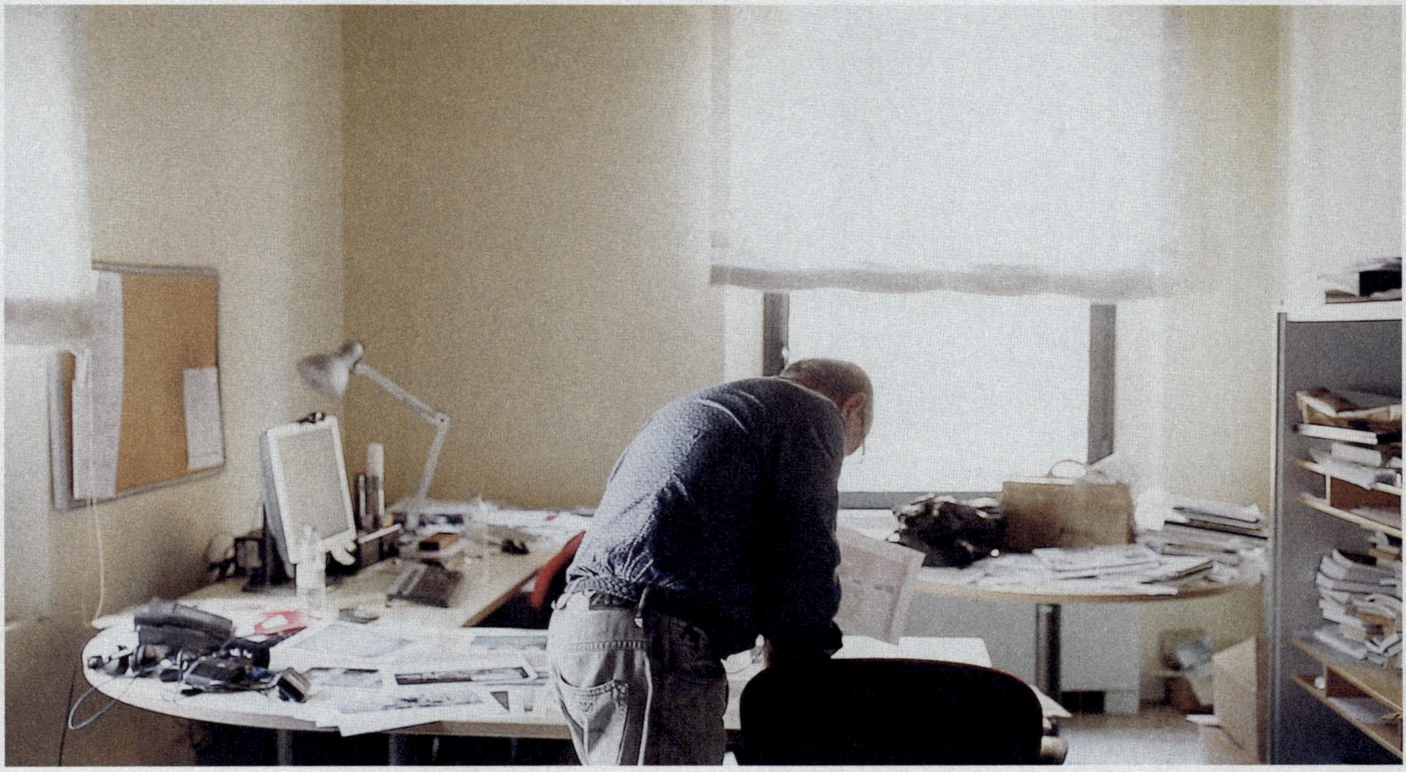

Franco Farinelli

335–372

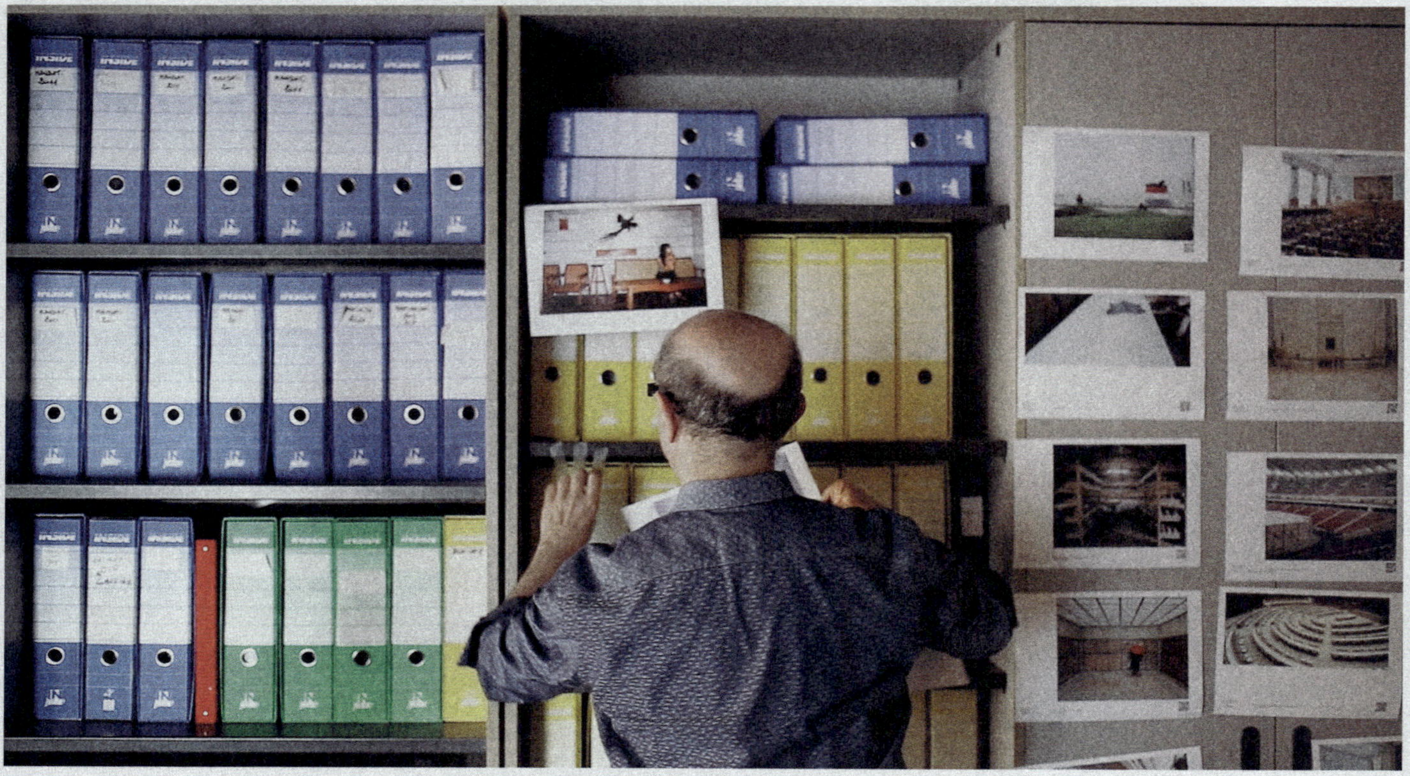

Franco Farinelli and Armin Linke, University of Bologna,
Bologna, May 2016

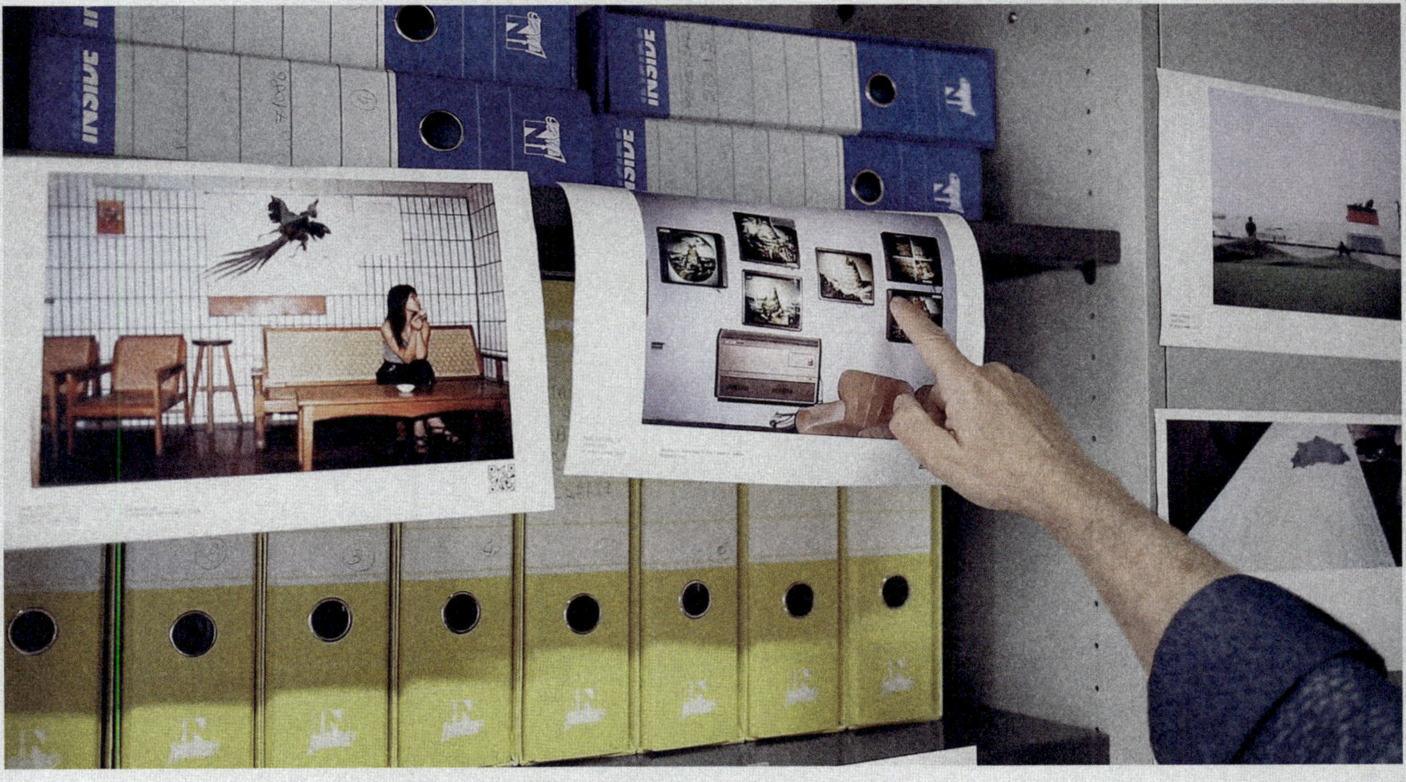

Franco Farinelli and Armin Linke, University of Bologna,
Bologna, May 2016

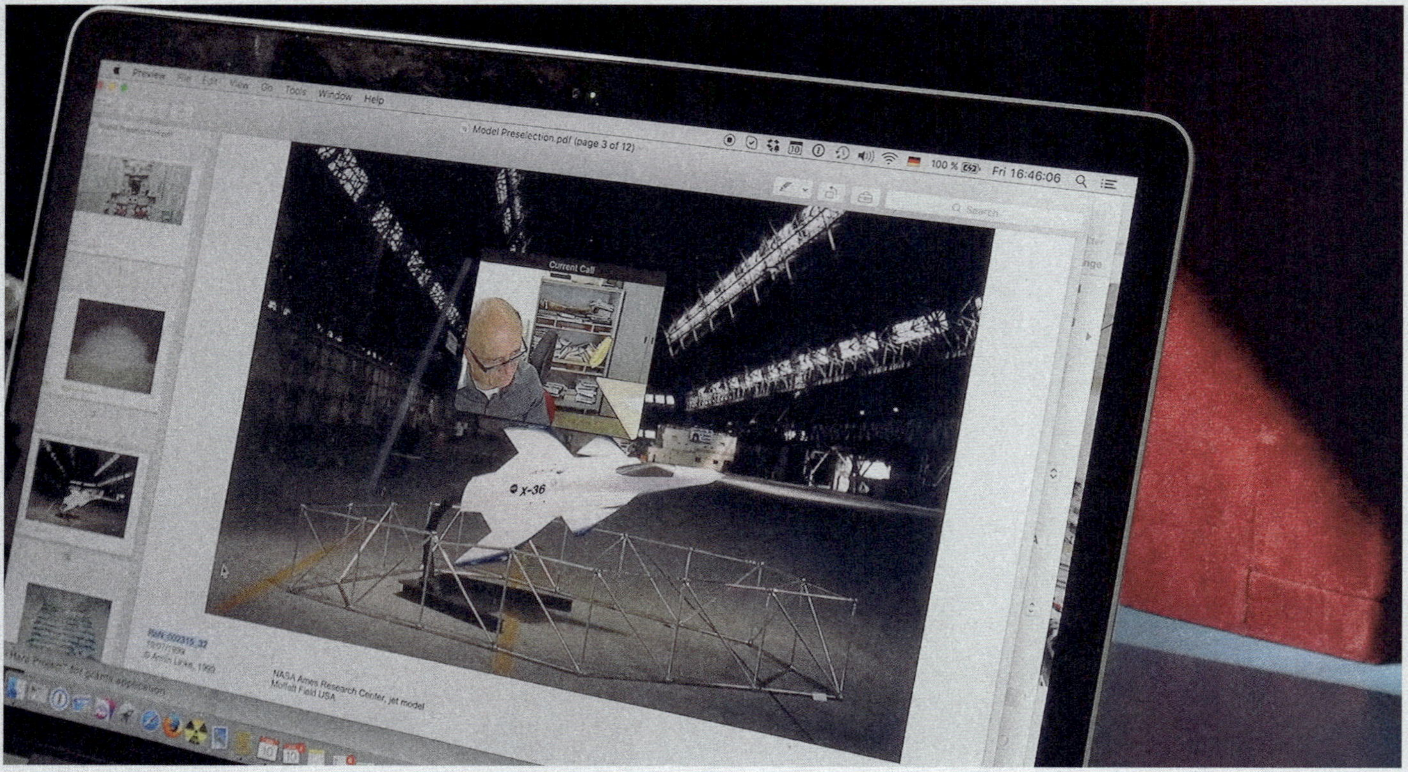

Franco Farinelli and Armin Linke, University of Bologna,
Bologna, June 2016

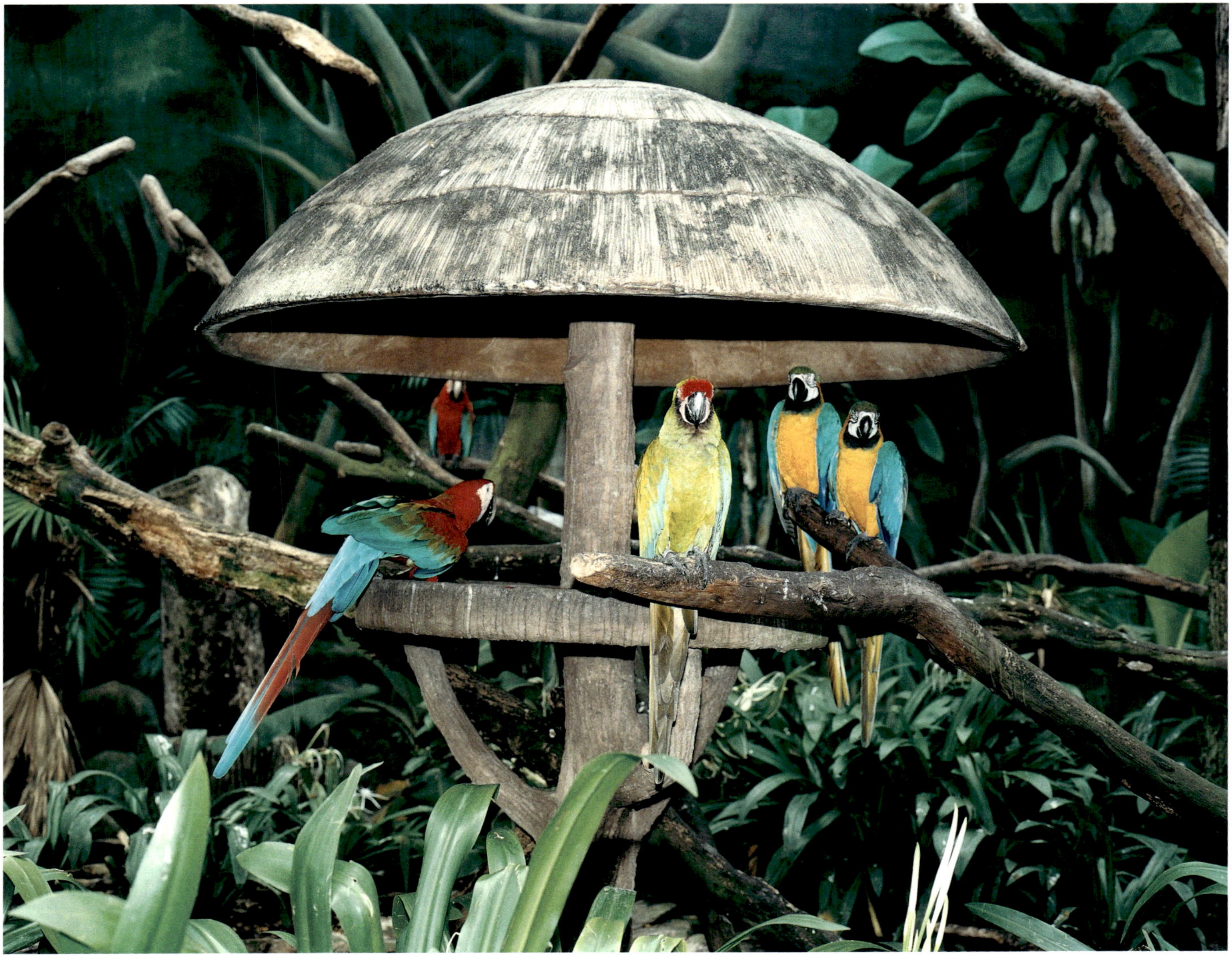

The parrot is an animal that, from a certain mimetic point of view, seems quite similar to humans because it can speak. In the fascinating story of Humboldt's journey to the equinoctial regions—as South America was once called—we are at the very beginning of the nineteenth century. The explorer arrives on a small island at the center of the Orinoco where all the people have been killed by a tribe that came from the sea.

Jurong Bird Park, Singapore, 1999

After witnessing the extraordinary tragic spectacle of skeletons lying in wide hammocks inside spacious caves, Humboldt sees a parrot flying overhead. Humboldt senses that there is something peculiar about that parrot and interviews the indigenous people that are with him. They explain to him that since all the Atures have died, the parrot is the only creature left that carries their language.

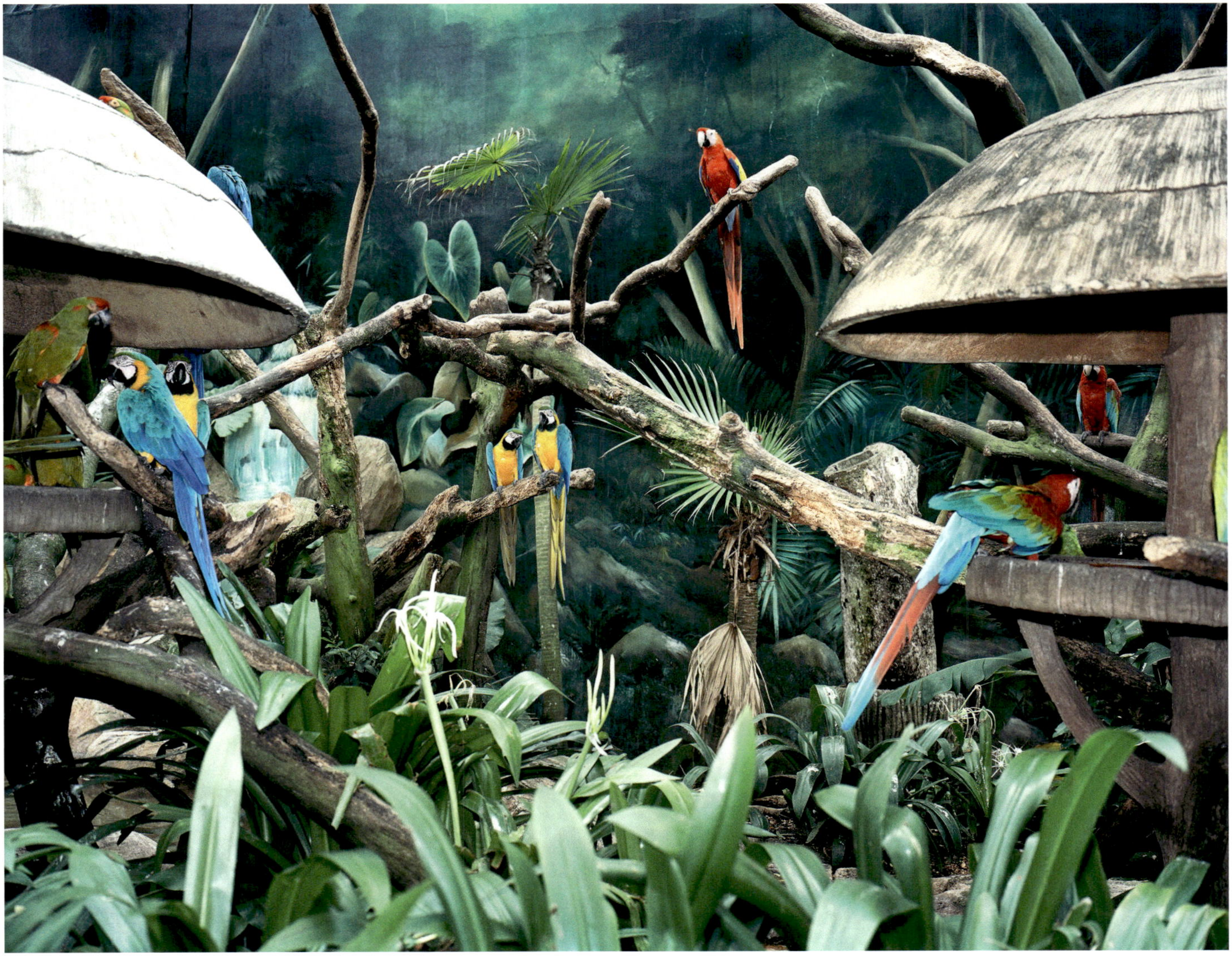

When all the tribe members die, their language dies with them. Culture survives only in the tongue of the parrot. Humboldt evidently remembered this parrot on his deathbed in 1859 because he also believed he was the last survivor to speak a language that belonged to a world and an outdated culture that was about to disappear.

Jurong Bird Park, Singapore, 1999

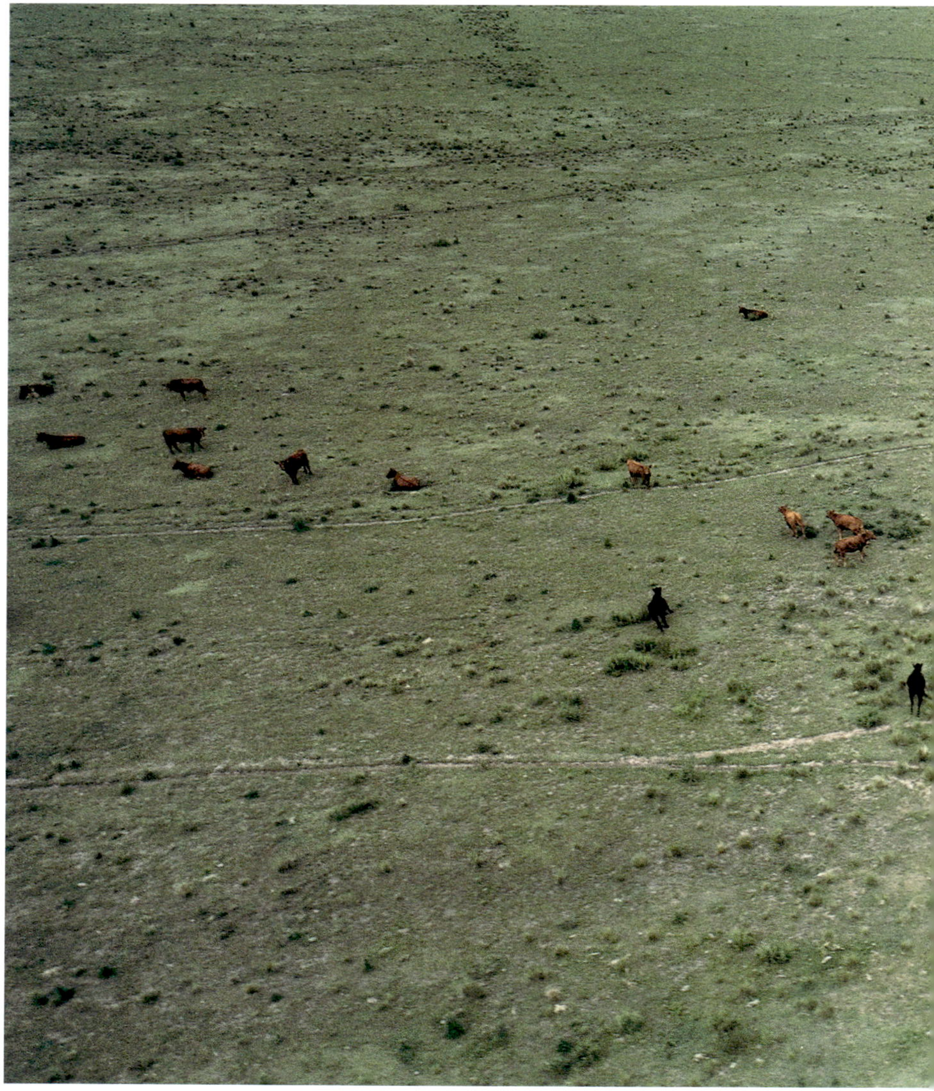

If we knew more about the way a flock usually behaves and the biological and vital relationship between animals and the Earth, we would be able to translate what we see into a geometrical structure. This is a very old issue, an originary one, you might say.

Herd, Cordoba, Argentina, 1999

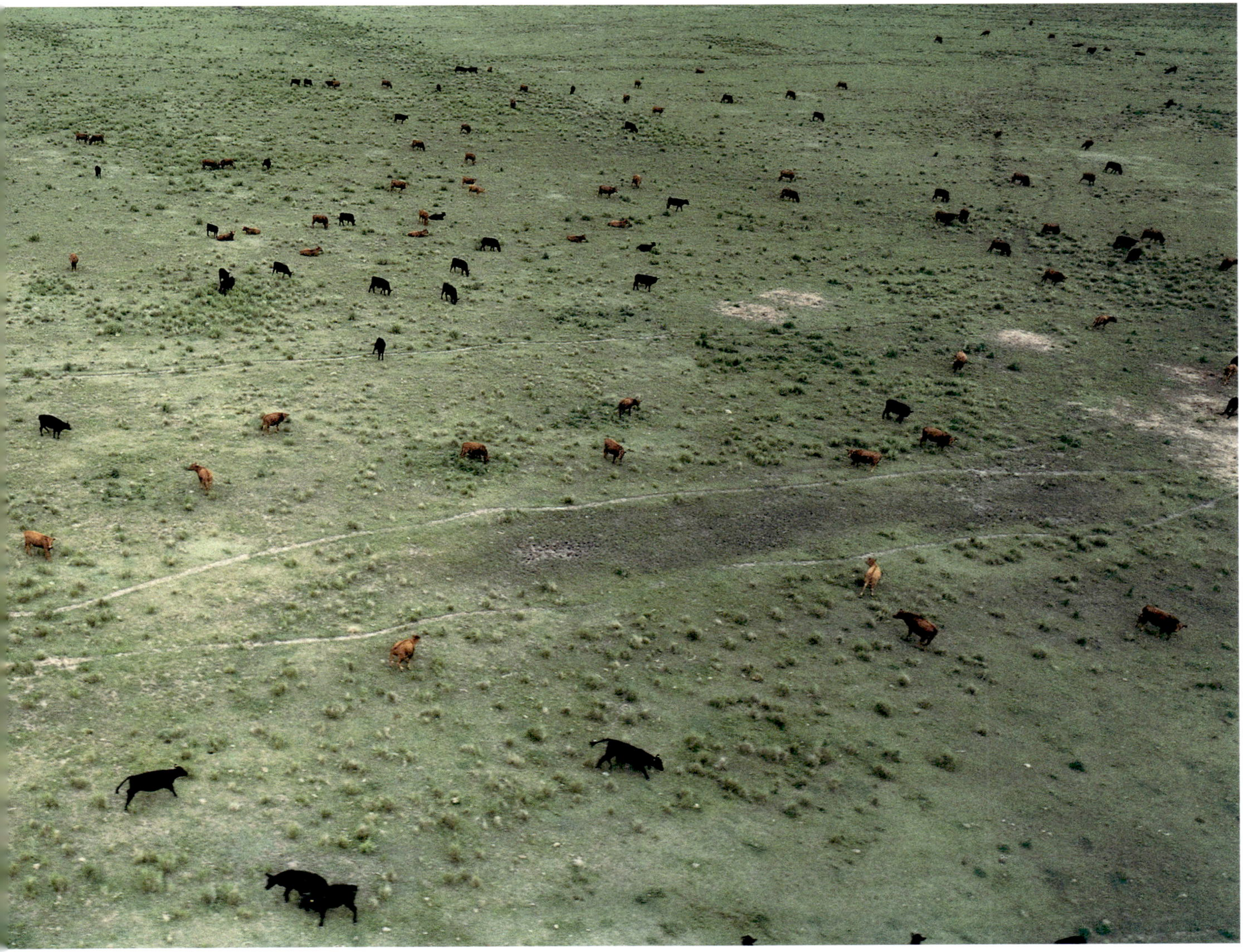

For the ancient Greeks, Nature was not, as it is for us today, an aggregate of things but an aggregate of processes in eternal evolution—in other words, a live entity.

From a topological point of view—that is to say, from a mathematical point of view—a table is the exact opposite of a sphere. Its structural-topological opposition with the sphere or globe is at the root of all epistemological and cognitive issues.

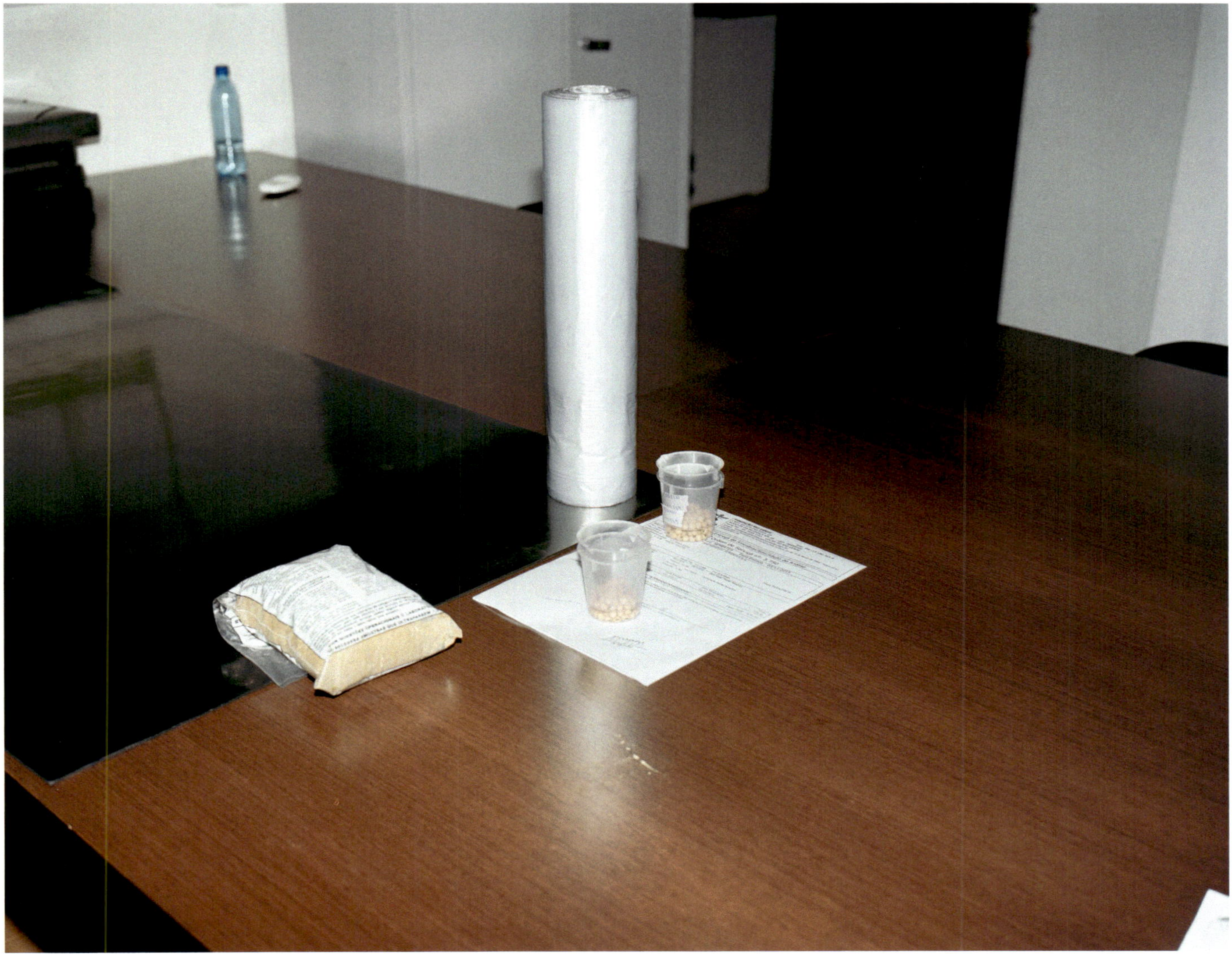

It is also, at the same time, the origin of all the problems and difficulties in understanding what globalization means today; as a matter of fact, the goal of modernity—which has been challenged by the contemporary world order—has been to transform the globe into an infinite series of tables or maps.

Fundação Rio Verde, laboratory for transgenic cultivation and seeds, Lucas do Rio Verde, Brazil, 2015

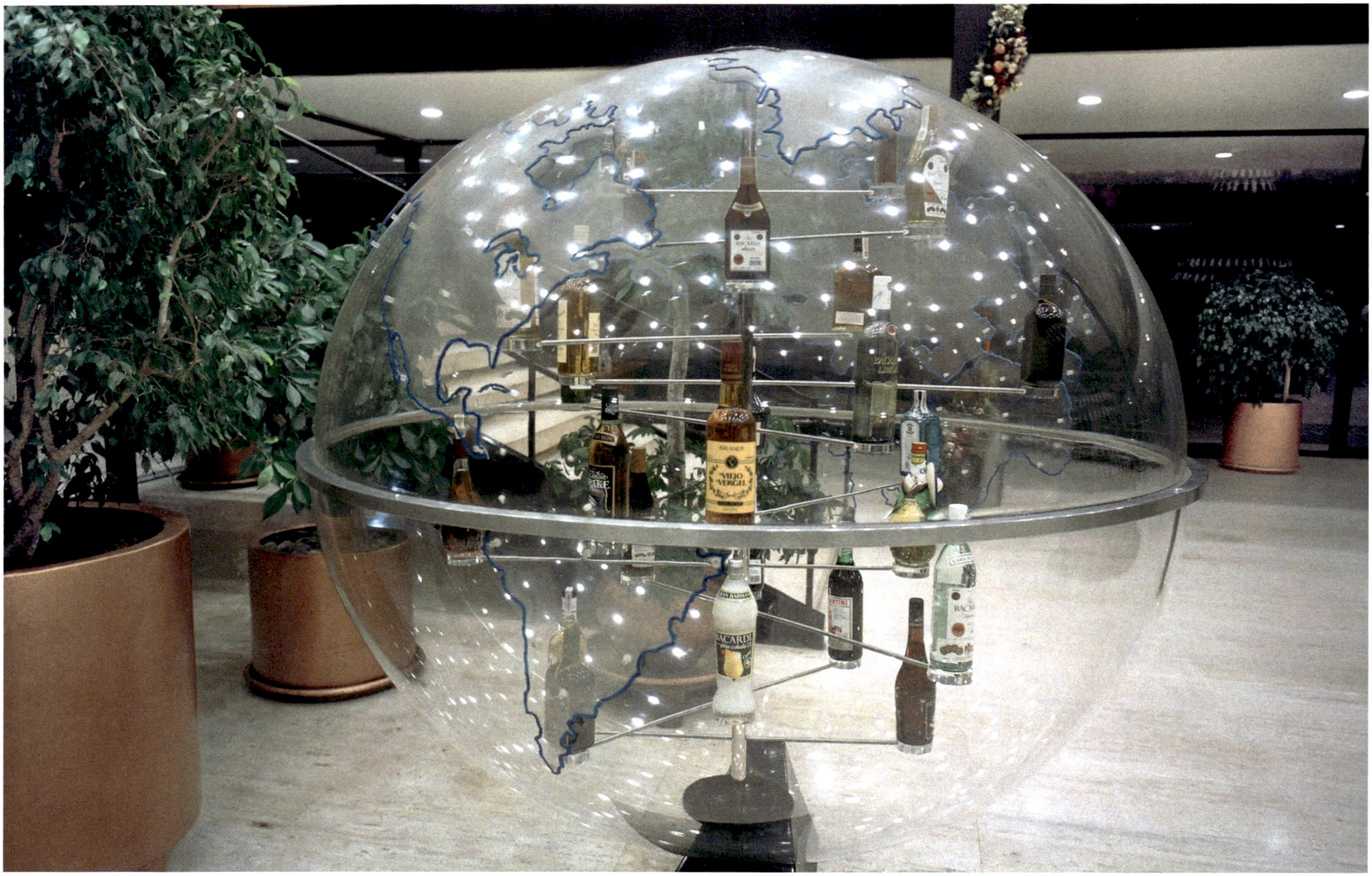

After the revolution in Cuba, Bacardí moved its head office from Havana to Mexico City. Mies van der Rohe designed the modernistic building, which has a structure similar to the New National Gallery in Berlin.

Ludwig Mies van der Rohe, Felix Candela, Bacardí y Compañía, Bacardí World, Mexico City, Mexico, 1999

Every time we look at a globe, we are dumbstruck because, faced with a sphere, we do not know what to say. Initially, we cannot believe our eyes. Even today, we say “è una balla” (that’s a lie) or “non dire balle” (don’t tell lies) in Italian.

The “ball” is nothing more than a sphere. In the Cinquecento, “balla” referred to the idea of the spherical form of the Earth and its alleged advantages. This is striking because, as we know, for ancient cultures to take possession of the sphere, to dominate it, was the equivalent of dominating reality and therefore producing it.

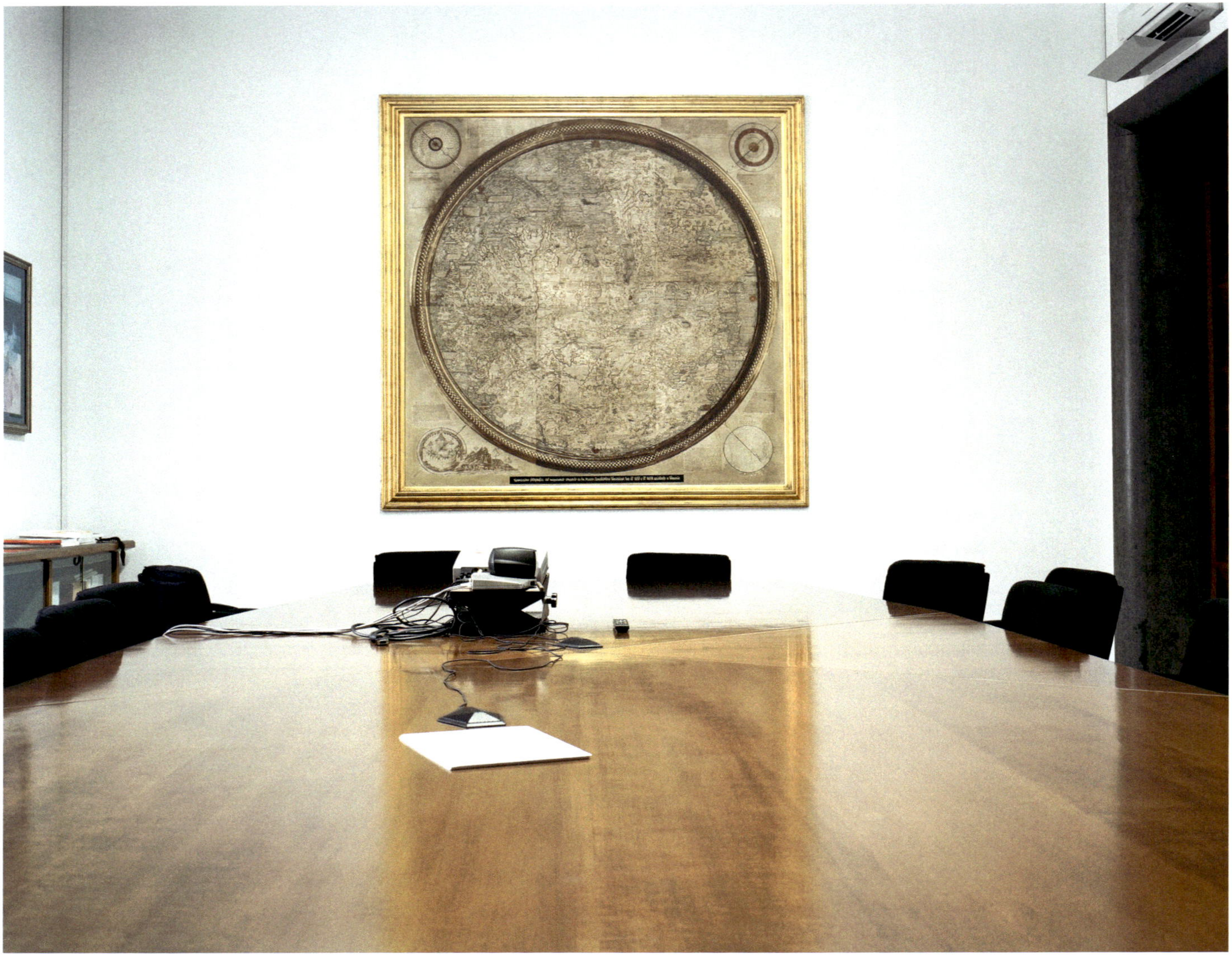

Fra Mauro's world map is the first of its kind, the product of a very self-conscious Venetian culture around the middle of the Quattrocento. While, previously, all medieval mappa mundi had represented paradise as if it were a place on Earth, here paradise is excluded from the representation.

CNR – National Research Council, Fermi conference hall, reproduction of the map made by Fra Mauro in 1460, Rome, Italy, 2007

It is the image with which, at the beginning of modernity, scientific discourse makes its first attempt to free itself from previous models, providing the Earth with the dignity and specific values that it previously lacked. With this image, scientific discourse and the issue of ultimate truth and faith became two different entities.

The word *table*—a synonym for mind—has been used, from Aristotle to the present day, in theories of artificial intelligence, cybernetics, and computation. The mind that traced the signs on the table is not that of an individual called Oscar Niemeyer.

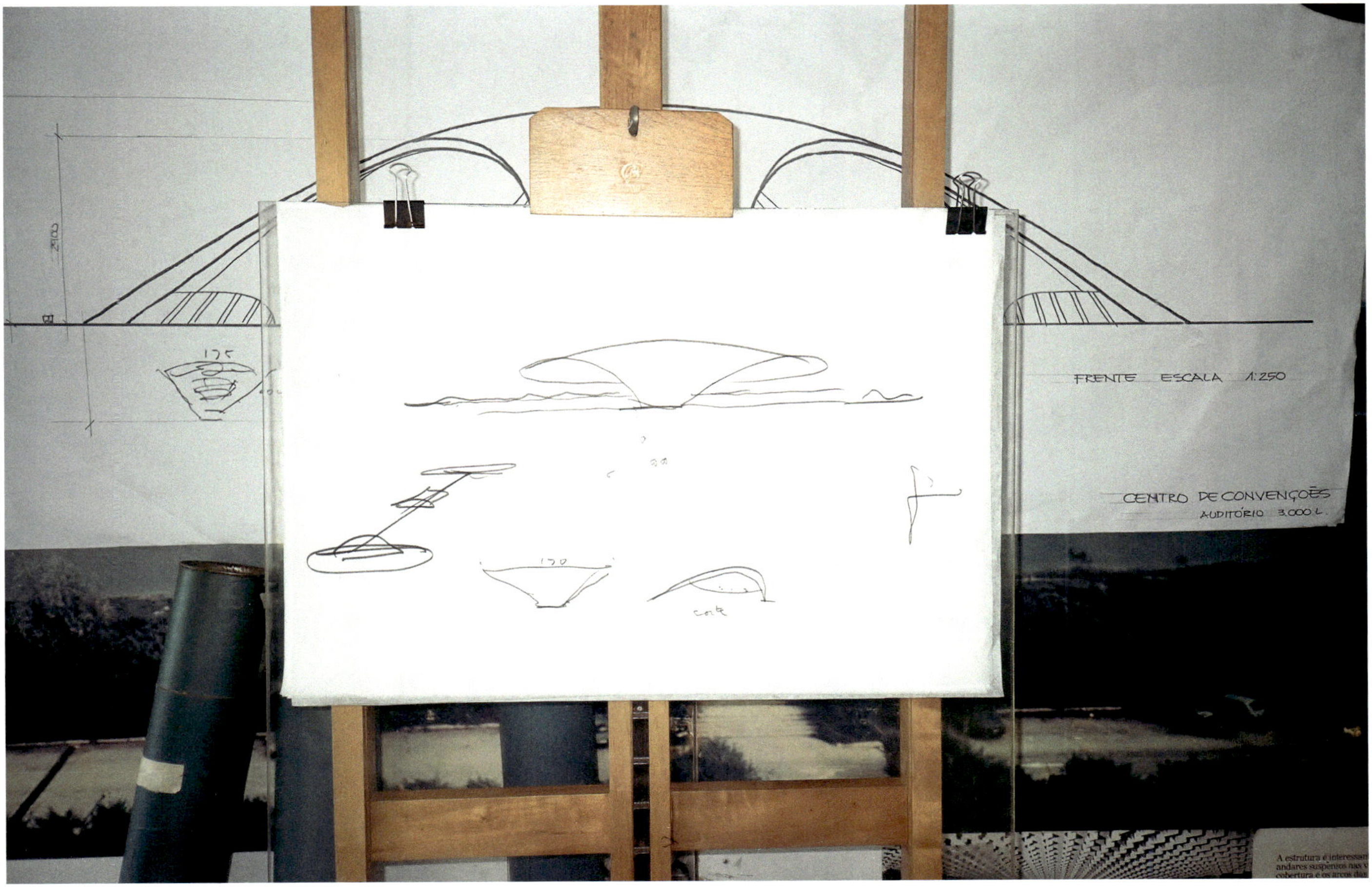

Rather, it is the system—material and, at the same time, immaterial—which formed the mind that produced this image. This is another way of saying that the *table* functions as a fundamental element for any mental operations that can be conceived.

Oscar Niemeyer, drawings, Rio de Janeiro, Brazil, 1999

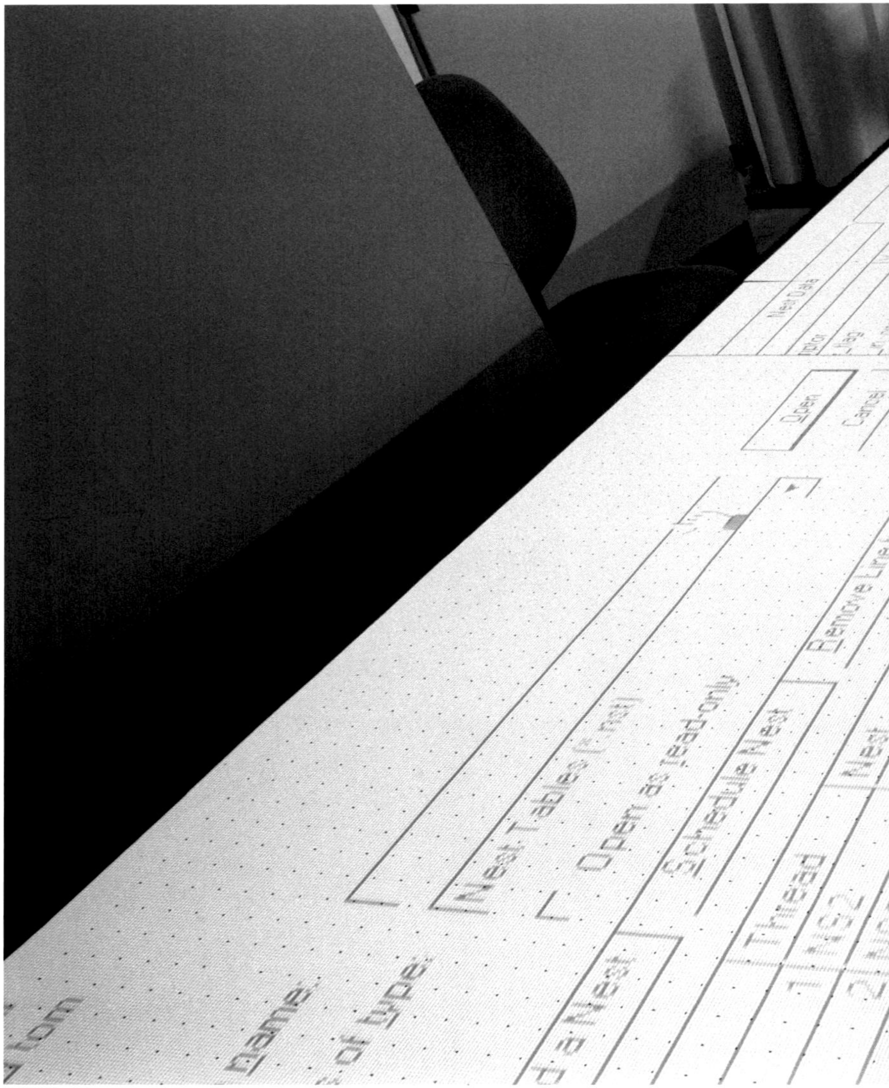

Computer systems analyze rolls of fabric and leather hides in order to plot the optimal distribution of pattern pieces required for daily production. Technology thus maximizes the use of materials.

The assembly line presupposes space, and space presupposes the tabular, as we know from the principles of Florentine perspective. This is the foundation for the principle of transforming reality into a mere abstract tabula.

Lamos Prada, Arezzo, Italy, 2001

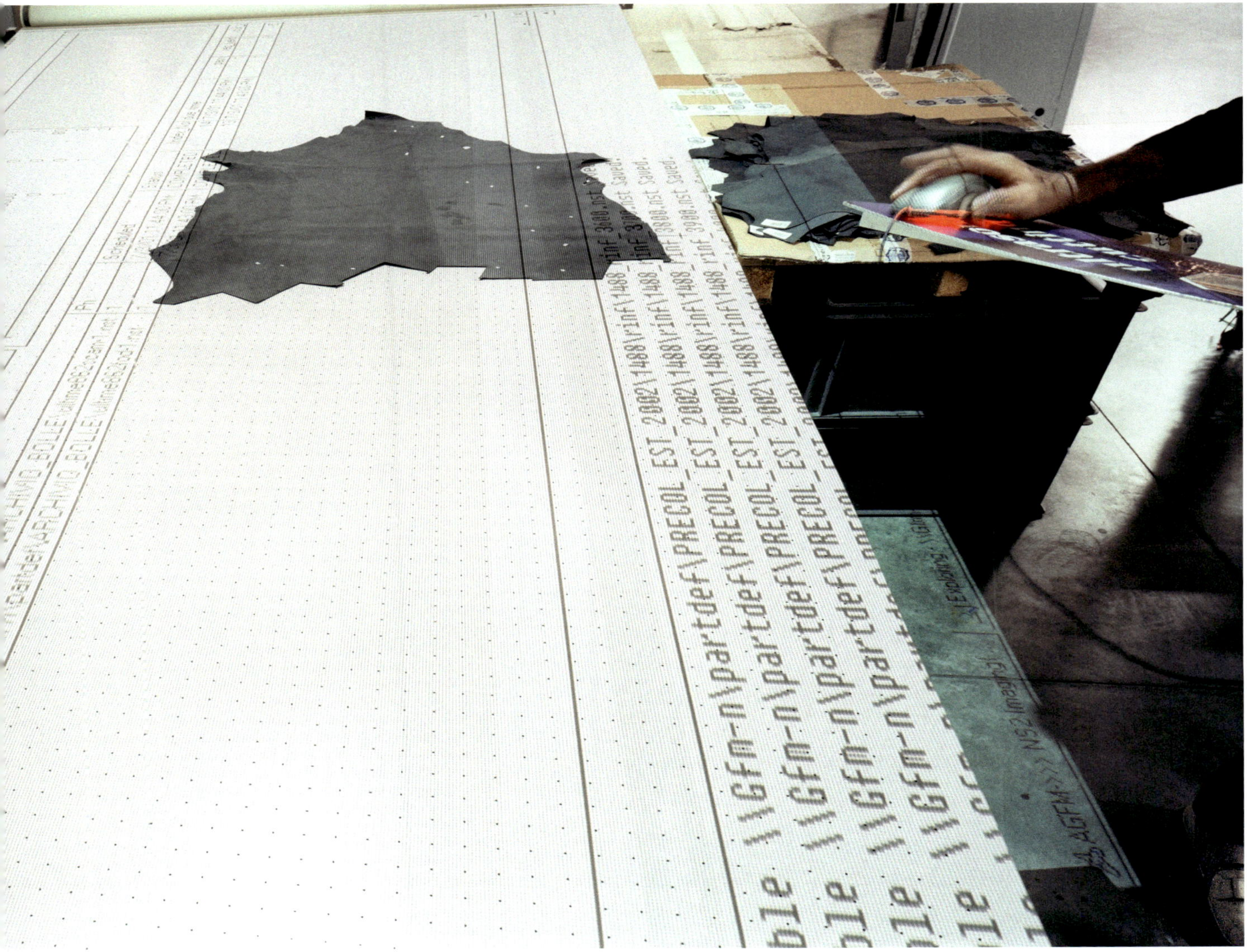

Its logic, as the image shows, has colonized the reproduction of the world. Here, as shown by the long, thin fingers of the worker that can be seen in the upper right corner, human presence risks becoming mere intrusion.

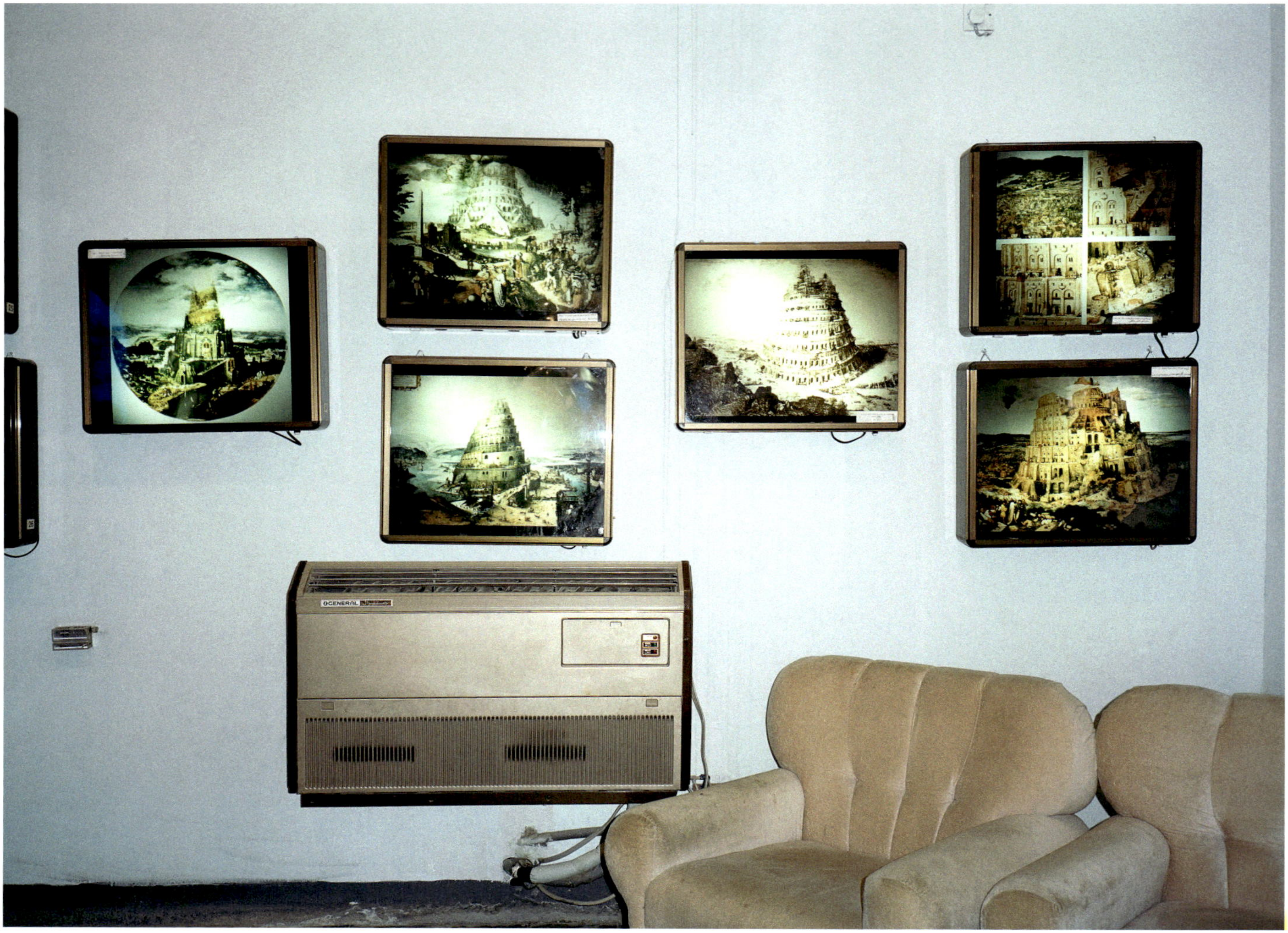

Reproductions of famous artworks depicting the Tower of Babel, displayed in light boxes in the Babylon Museum in Iraq

The structural principle of the Tower of Babel is a hierarchical one, a relational principle based on levels, where what is at the apex has sovereignty and what is below must obey—a series of gradients of authority.

Babylon Museum, Babylon, Iraq, 2002

To imagine something different, you should simply change your point of view and, renouncing the axonometric vision, look at the tower from above. The immediate result is the labyrinth. With this mutation, space also begins to be imagined, and its process of organization can begin.

In his *Communist Manifesto*, Marx refers to Goethe's Faust and writes that modernity is the time in which all that is solid is transformed and vanishes into thin air; it is the time of what Schumpeter has called creative destruction.

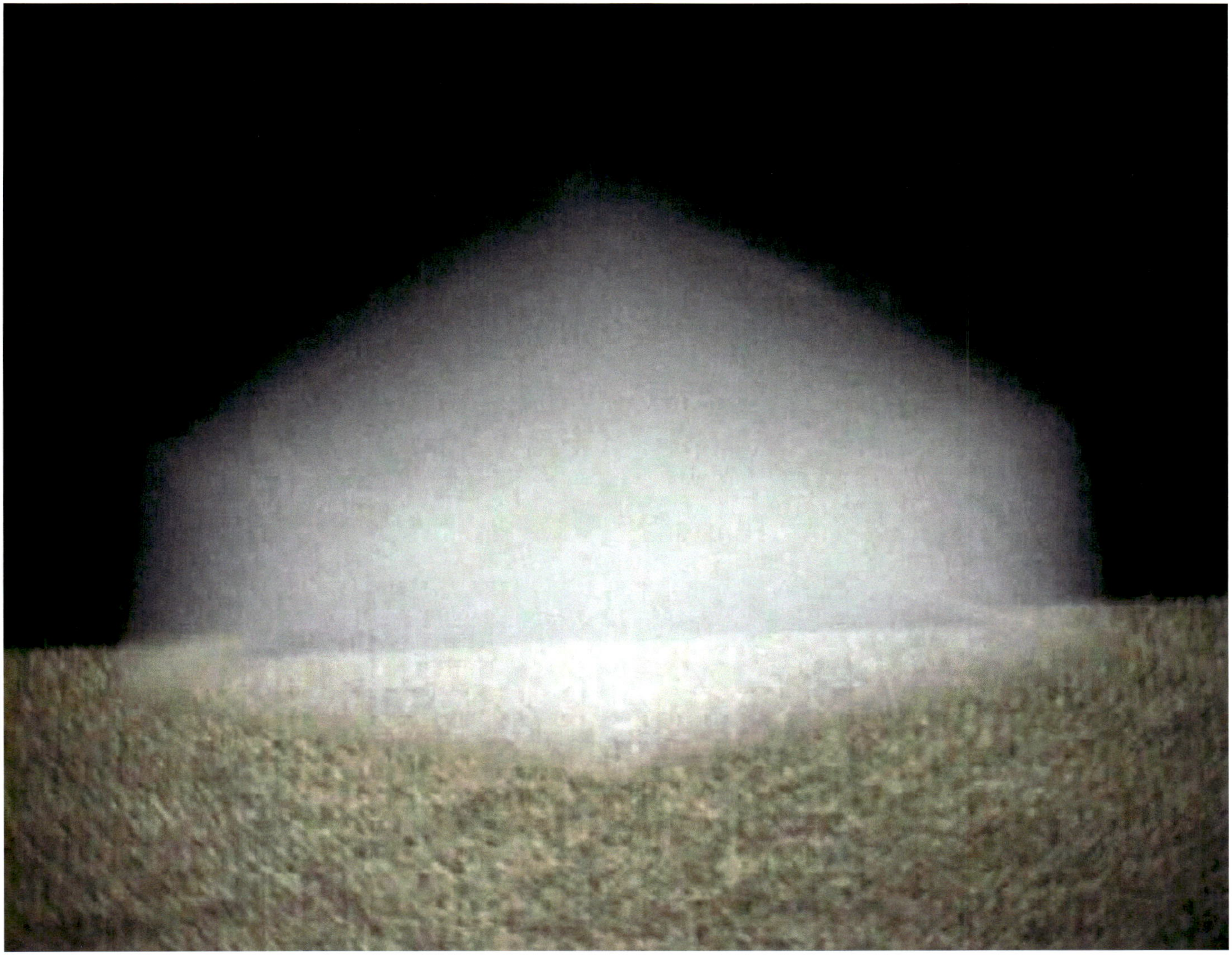

Aerogel is an ultralight nanoporous material: a gel in which the liquid element is replaced with gas. This translucent, extremely low-density substance has the lowest-known heat conductivity in a solid and is used as insulation in space exploration.

Here, the immaterial par excellence—that is to say, air—becomes something material and corporeal. Postmodernity becomes the exact opposite of modernity.

NASA Jet Propulsion Laboratory, Pasadena, USA, 1999

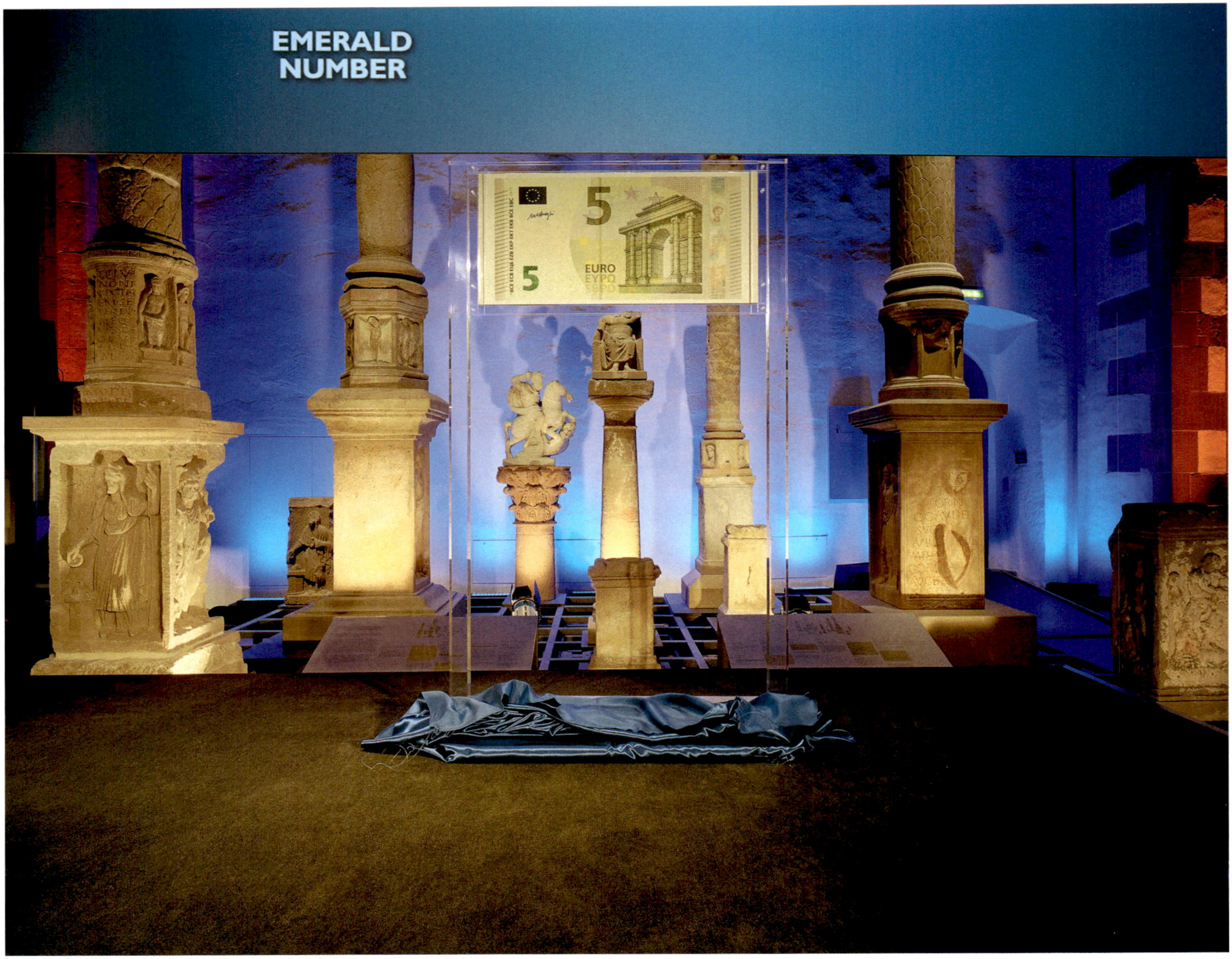

The Europa-series banknotes depict architectural styles from seven periods in Europe's cultural history. The new 5 euro banknote shows Greek archaeological constructions. During the presentation the director of the European Central Bank explains the new anti-copy technologies, like the emerald number and the special UV light-feature on the front of the banknote.

There is a homology between what is represented on the banknote and the group of monuments that surrounds it, as if the banknote were a sort of synthesis able to capture the reality outside it.

Archäologisches Museum, ECB – European Central Bank, presentation of the new 5 euro banknote, Frankfurt am Main, Germany, 2013

When Marx declares in the first book of *Capital* that the market is dominated by the general equivalence principle, we can add that he fails to explain that the general equivalence principle can be found in space, where all parts are equivalent; if these are changed, reality remains unchanged. This constitutes precisely the general meaning of spatial representation. Given all this, what is the meaning of this banknote suspended in the midst of archaeological remains?

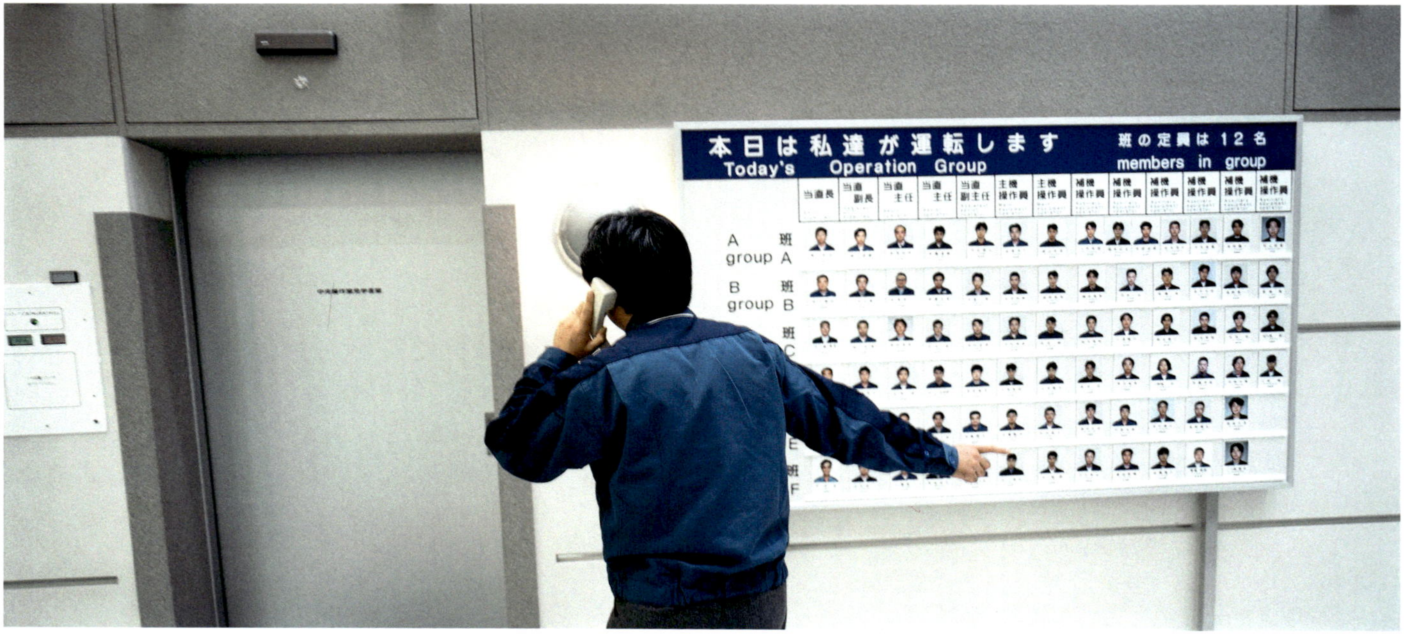

Each figure reproduces a single and distinct person, an individual that is different from all the others. That all portraits seem to be more or less identical here and all images are conflated on a single table inside a single structure refers to an idea, a serial model, a concept that produces interchangeability and replaceability.

Kashiwazaki-Kariwa Nuclear Power Station, entrance to control room,
Kashiwazaki, Japan, 1998

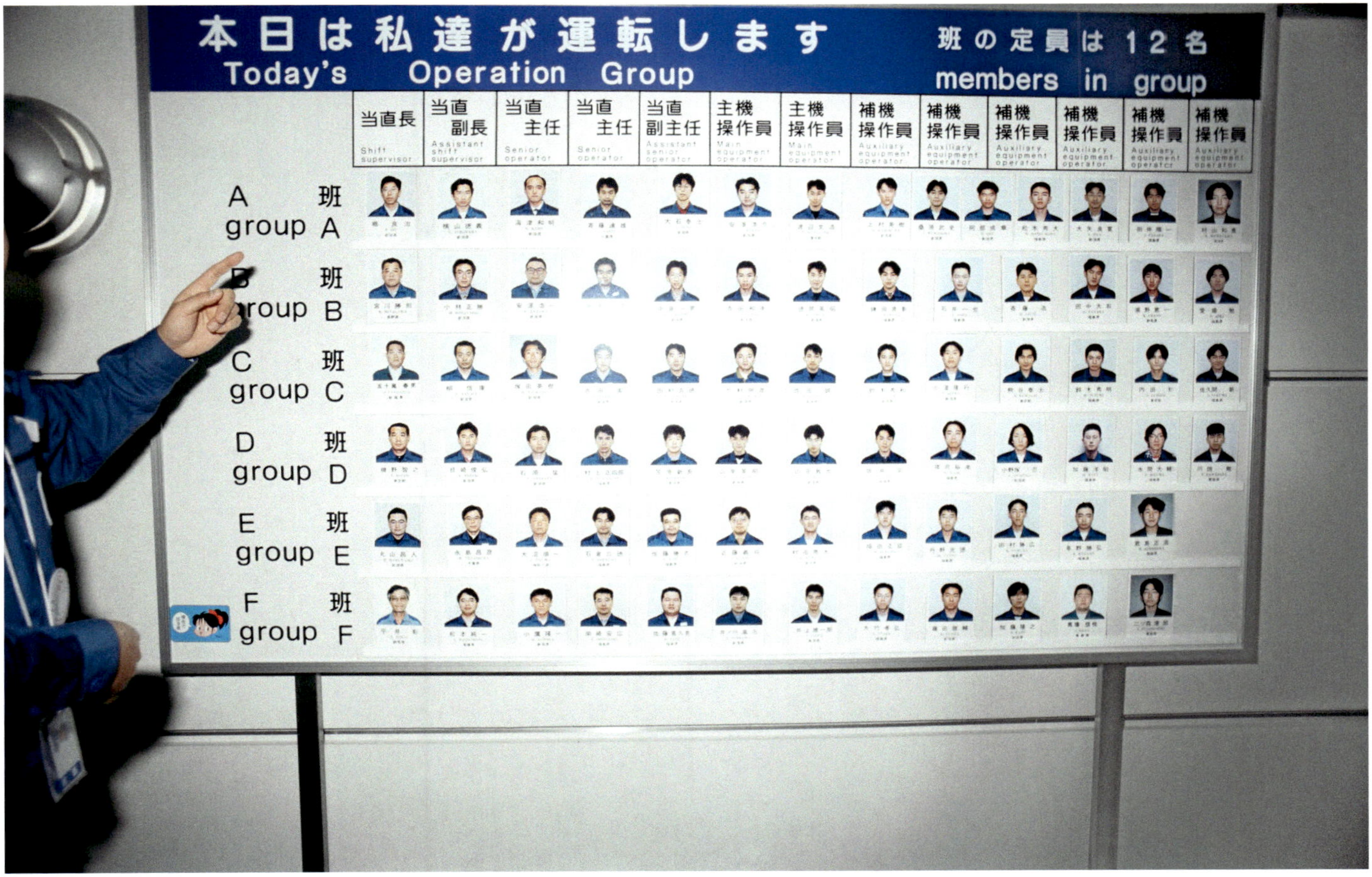

Each supervising team for the seven reactors is shown on the synoptic table in the control room of the Kashiwazaki-Kariwa Nuclear Power Plant. Listed according to their roles and shifts, the workers are identified by the processes and responsibilities they cover. Access to this space is highly restricted.

A finger pointing at the table reintroduces the abstraction of the model. Yet, from the conflation emerges the rupture that leads us to an understanding of realities.

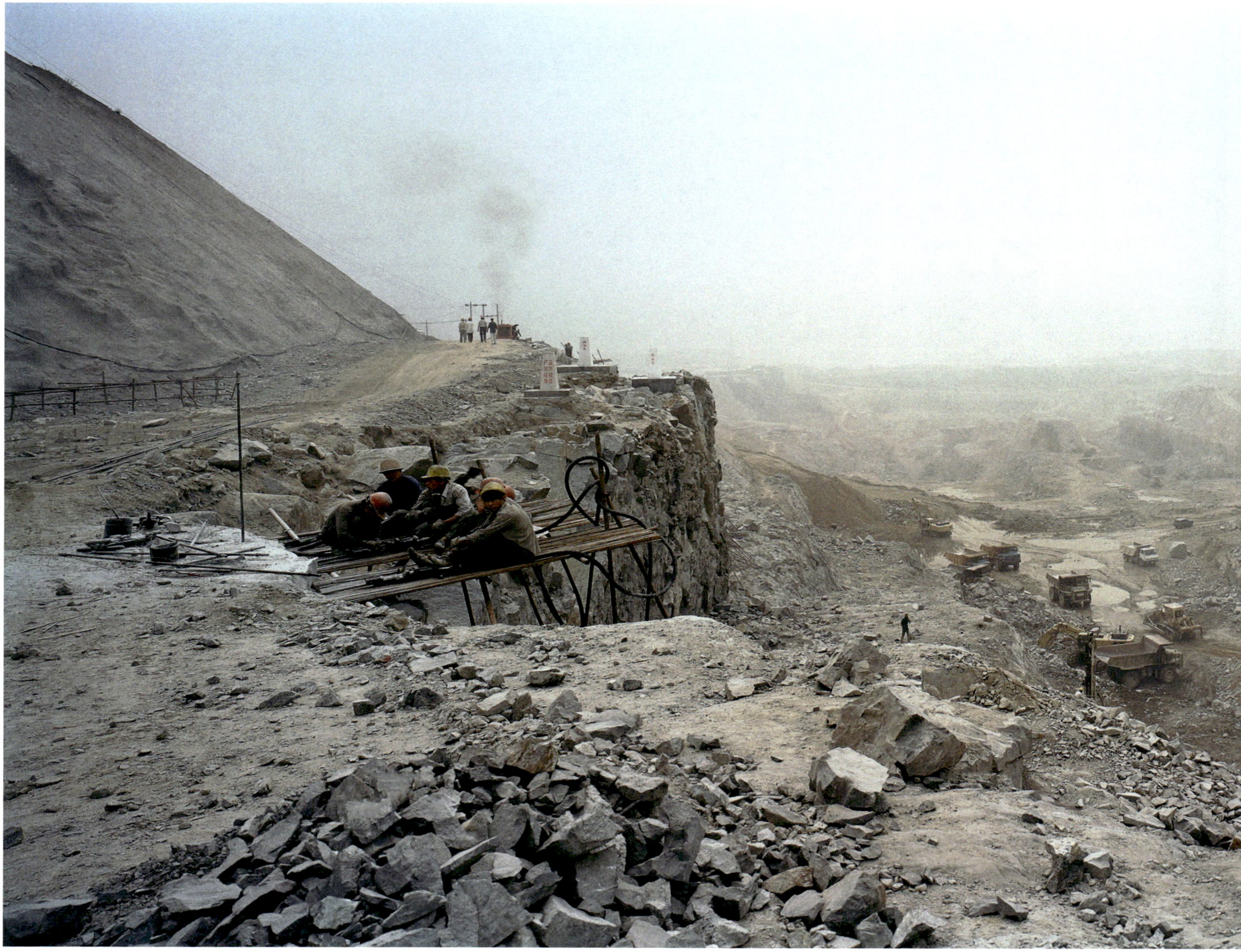

Here the human intervention that artificially corrects the natural datum consists in the transformation of this datum into a table.

Three Gorges Dam, construction of a lift for ships, Yichang (Hubei), China, 1998

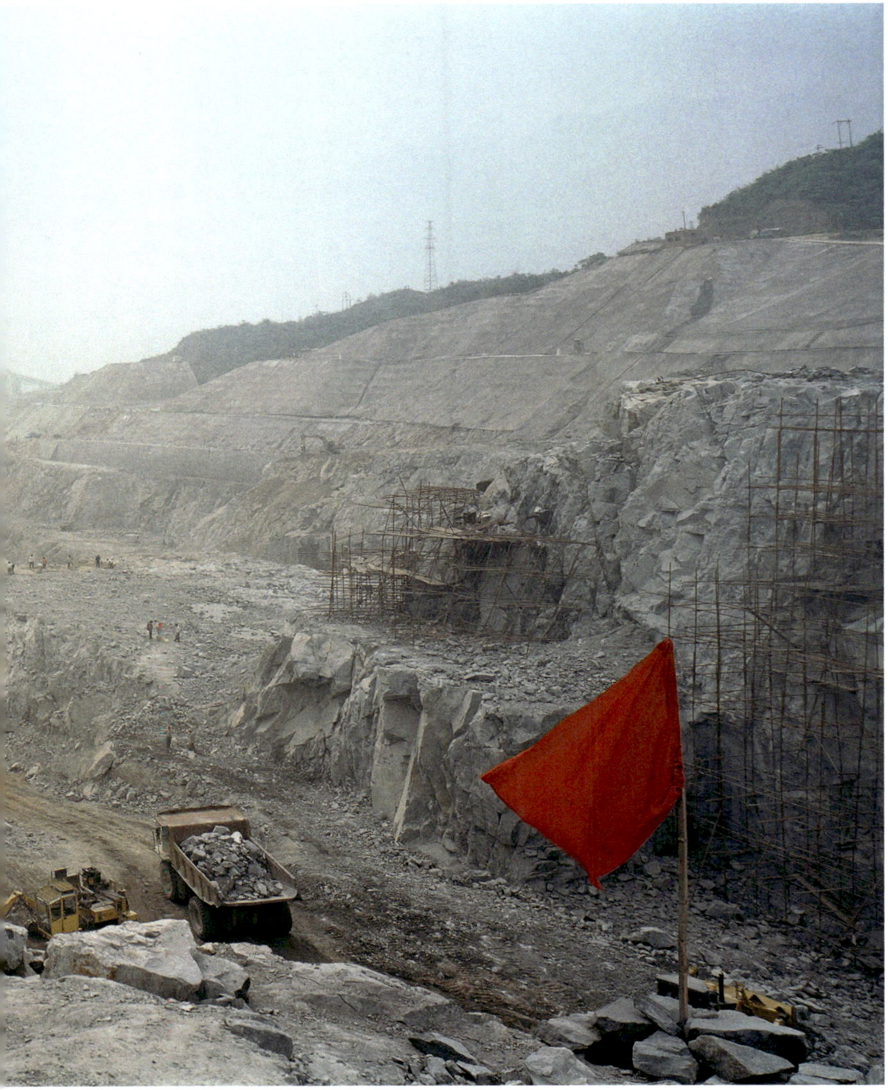

It is well known that the issue of the Three Gorges Dam can be solved only if we transform the landscape's original morphology into a surface with a tabular structure.

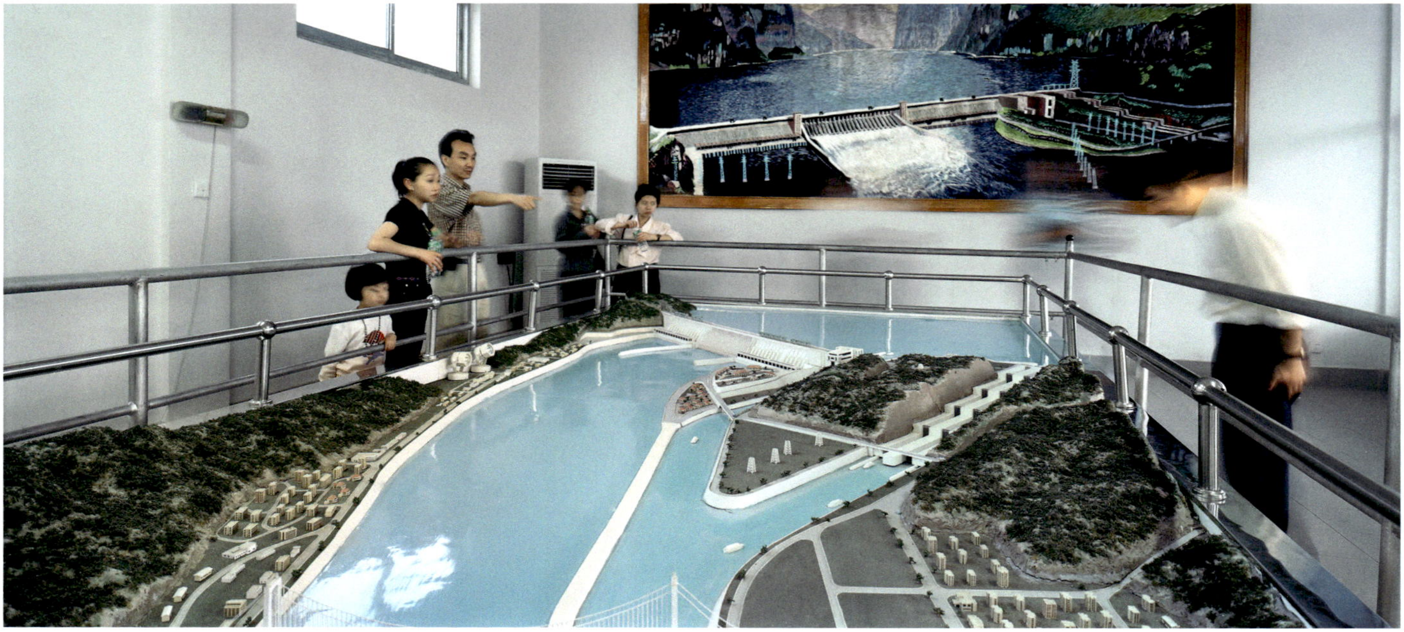

The model of the Three Gorges Dam project depicting the plans for urban development. An area of about 600 km^2 had to be submerged under water, two million people displaced, and all the infrastructure, including houses, schools, and industry, rebuilt.

Compared with the previous image, there is a definite change of scale here, even though the model remains the same.

Three Gorges Dam project, model, Yichang (Hubei), China, 1998

The tabular model imposes a structure that is completely different from reality and as such also presupposes a privileged way of seeing the relationship between the elements or parts that make up reality. This reduces the meaning of the relationship between things to a problem of distance and quantitative metrical data.

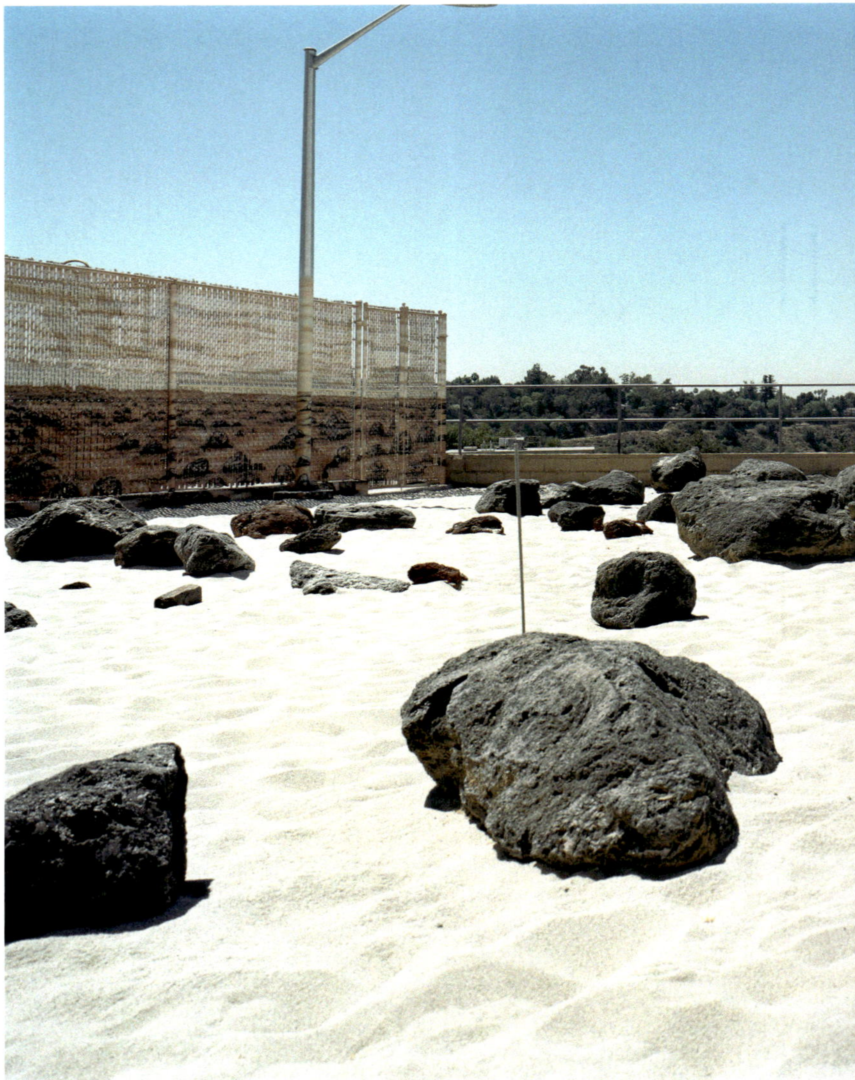

A constructed landscape simulating the surface of Mars. The uneven ground and the obstacles imitate an environment to test the space vehicles in aggravated conditions. Prints on the wall visually expand the testing ground.

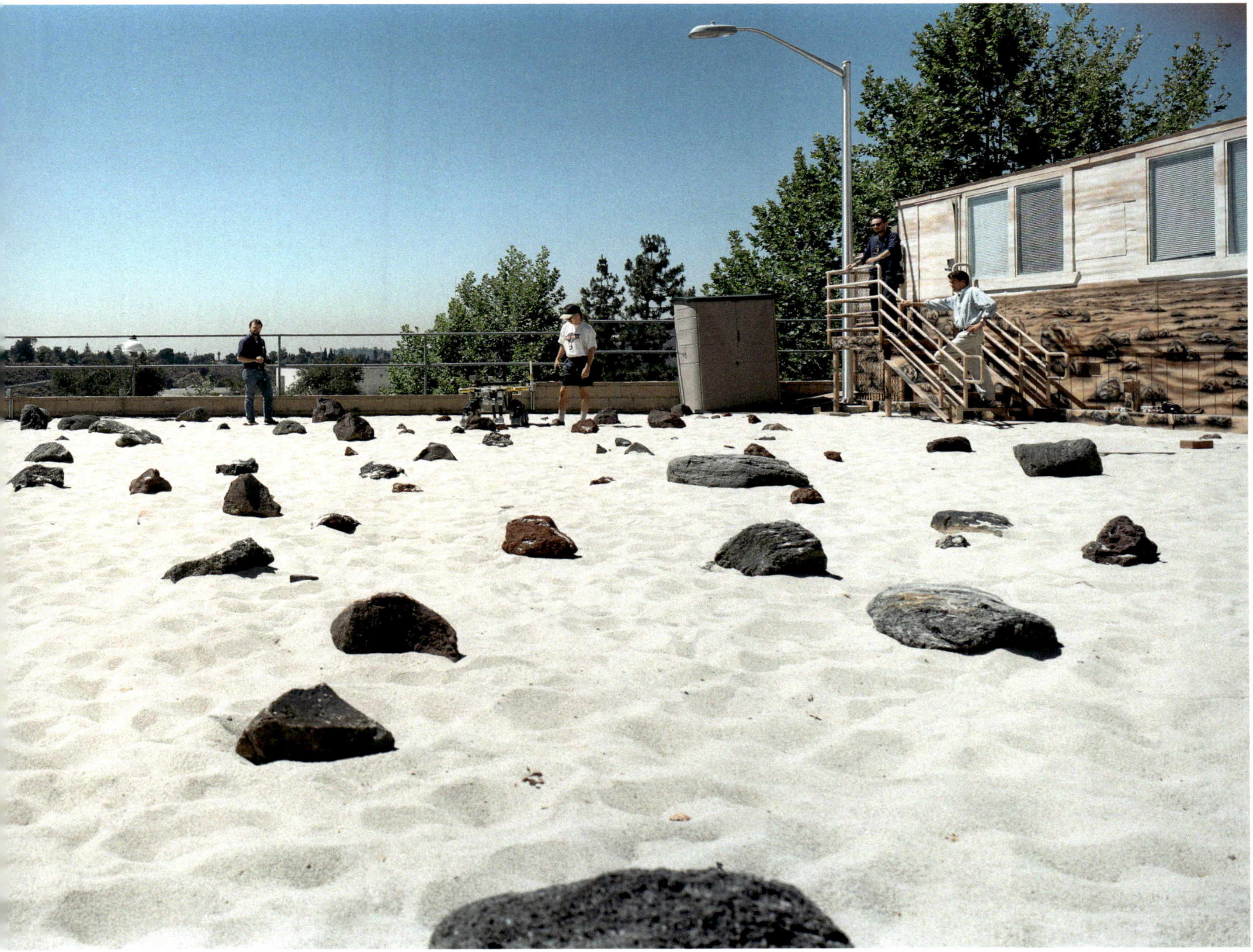

This image of Mars in Pasadena, California, is representative of all we have been talking about: artificiality, domestication, and—within these cognitive and behavioral structures, which correspond to fundamental anthropological needs—the attempt to continue to reduce reality to a flat area. In this case, reality constitutes a very distant planet whose characteristics are reproduced (or at least simulated as far as possible) on the Earth.

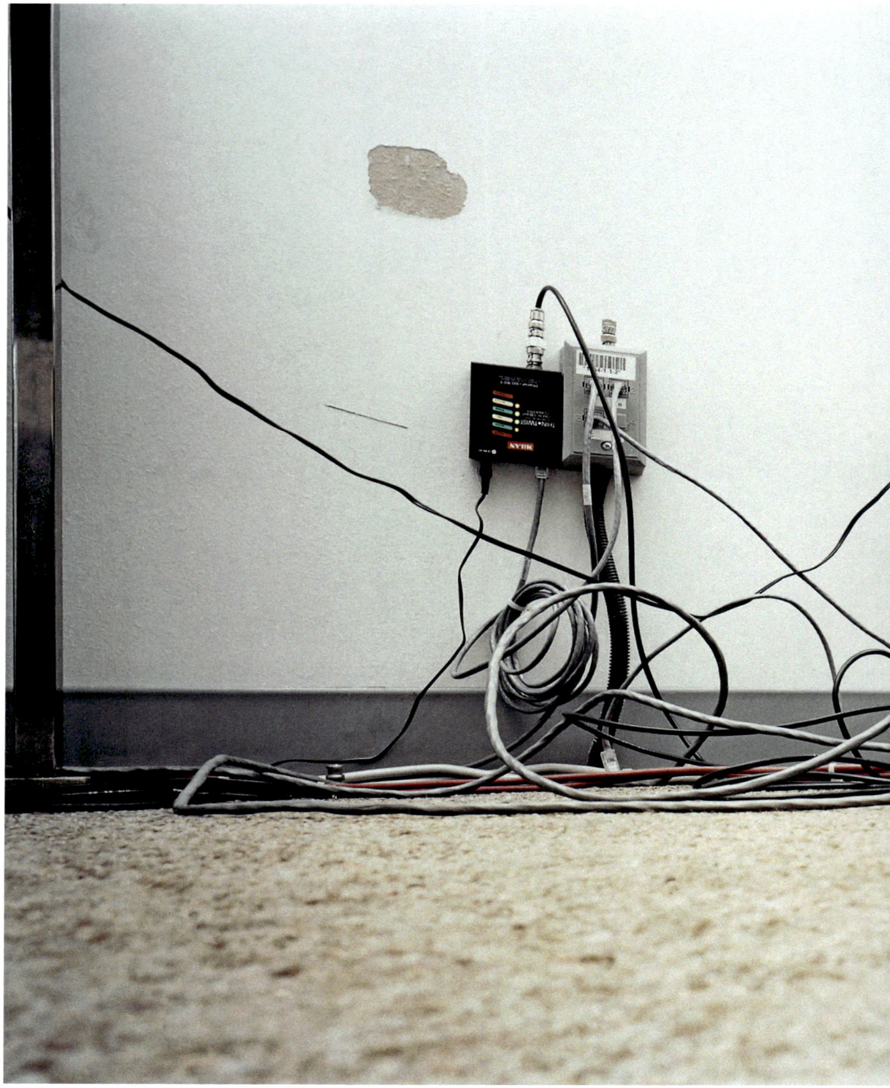

The function of the rocks—that is to say, the volumetric, three-dimensional objects—is defined in relation to a surface that is not wholly flat but nevertheless functions as a base surface. The trajectory of the vehicle is made even more complicated by the presence of these rocks and by the possibility of transforming the surface of its trajectory into a table.

NASA Jet Propulsion Laboratory, Mars Yard, rover recharging batteries, Pasadena, USA, 1999

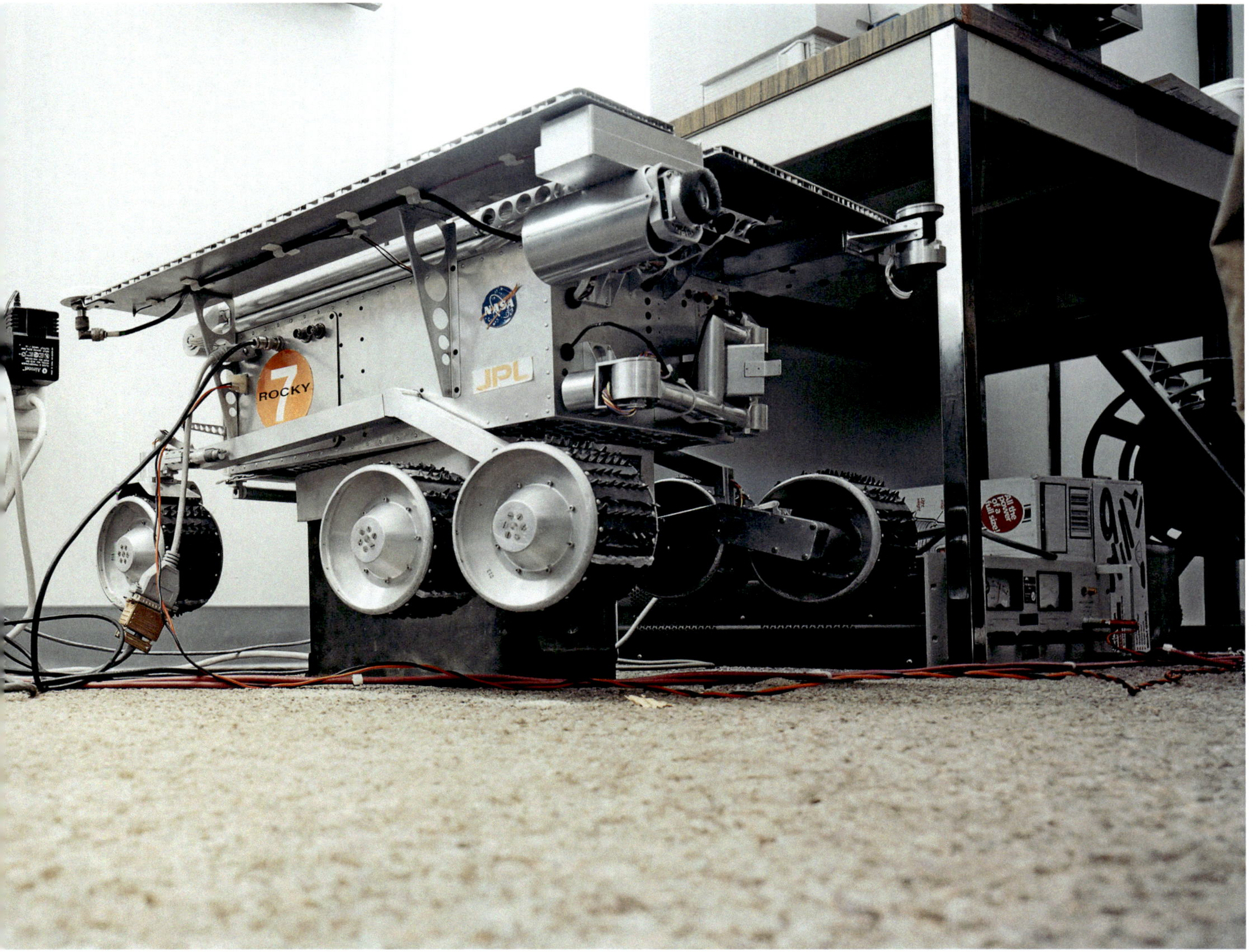

It is as if one was saying that, in abandoning the Earth, one must leave behind any possibility of reducing reality to a tabular structure. The image represents this in a clear and, at the same time, moving way. It shows what is difficult to accept: that outside of the Earth, of the processes of anthropological and historical domestication familiar to everyone, reality is a completely different matter.

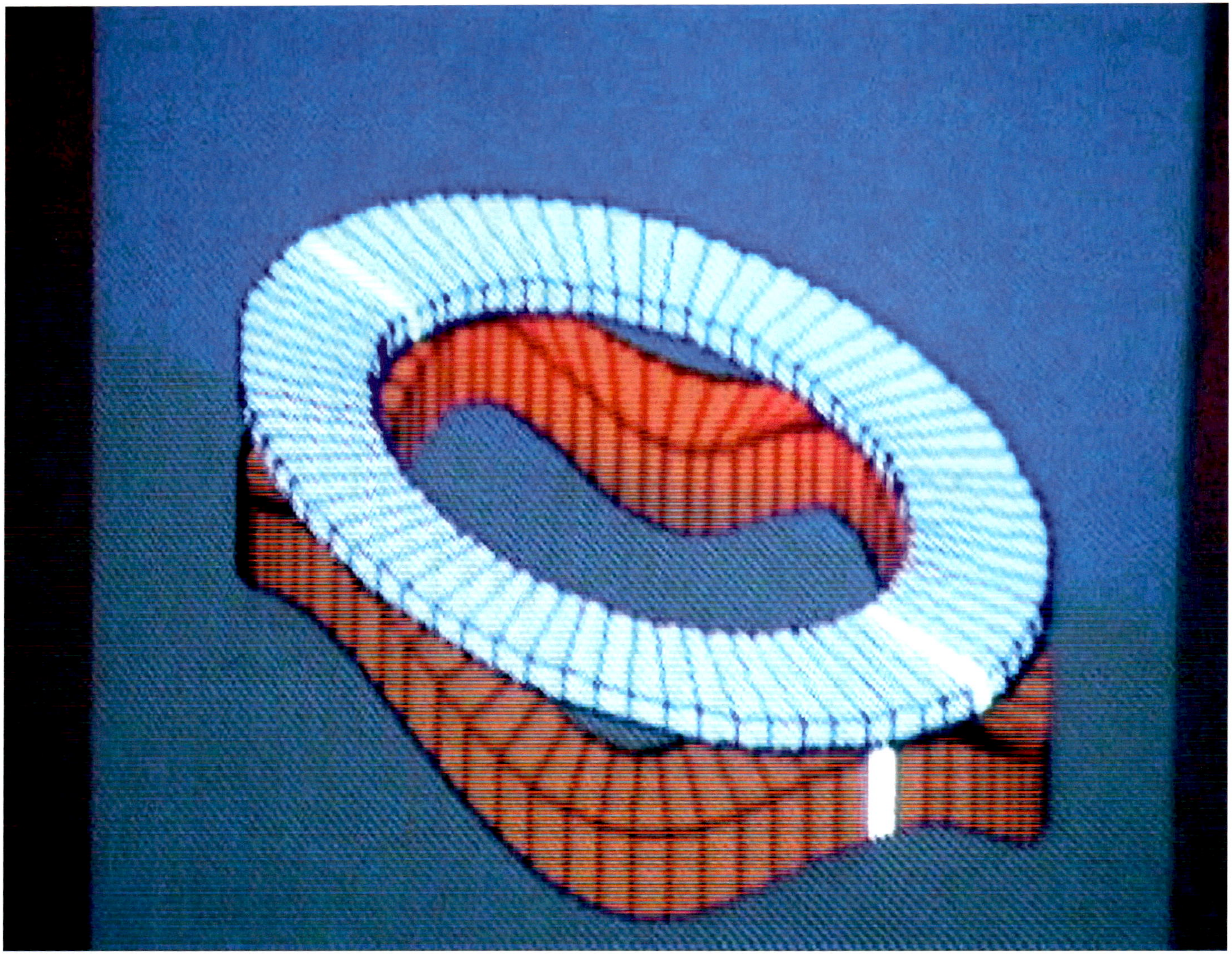

If the upper ring refers to the form of modernity—for example, to the baroque—the lower one refers to something that is older, originary, and archetypal. It is as if underneath modernity, represented by the bifocal ellipse, is hidden the grin of the mask of ancient Greek tragicomedy. And perhaps this is an arresting diagram of our humanity and our Western culture.

NASA Jet Propulsion Laboratory, ultrasonic research laboratory,
Pasadena, USA, 1999

The subtle fascination of the following image depends on the fact that it reverses—and in this way preserves—the logic of what is technically called the "picturesque" image. In the *Encyclopédie*, the picturesque effect is realized when a representation of human beings includes vegetation and natural forms. Here nothing is natural; everything is artificial.

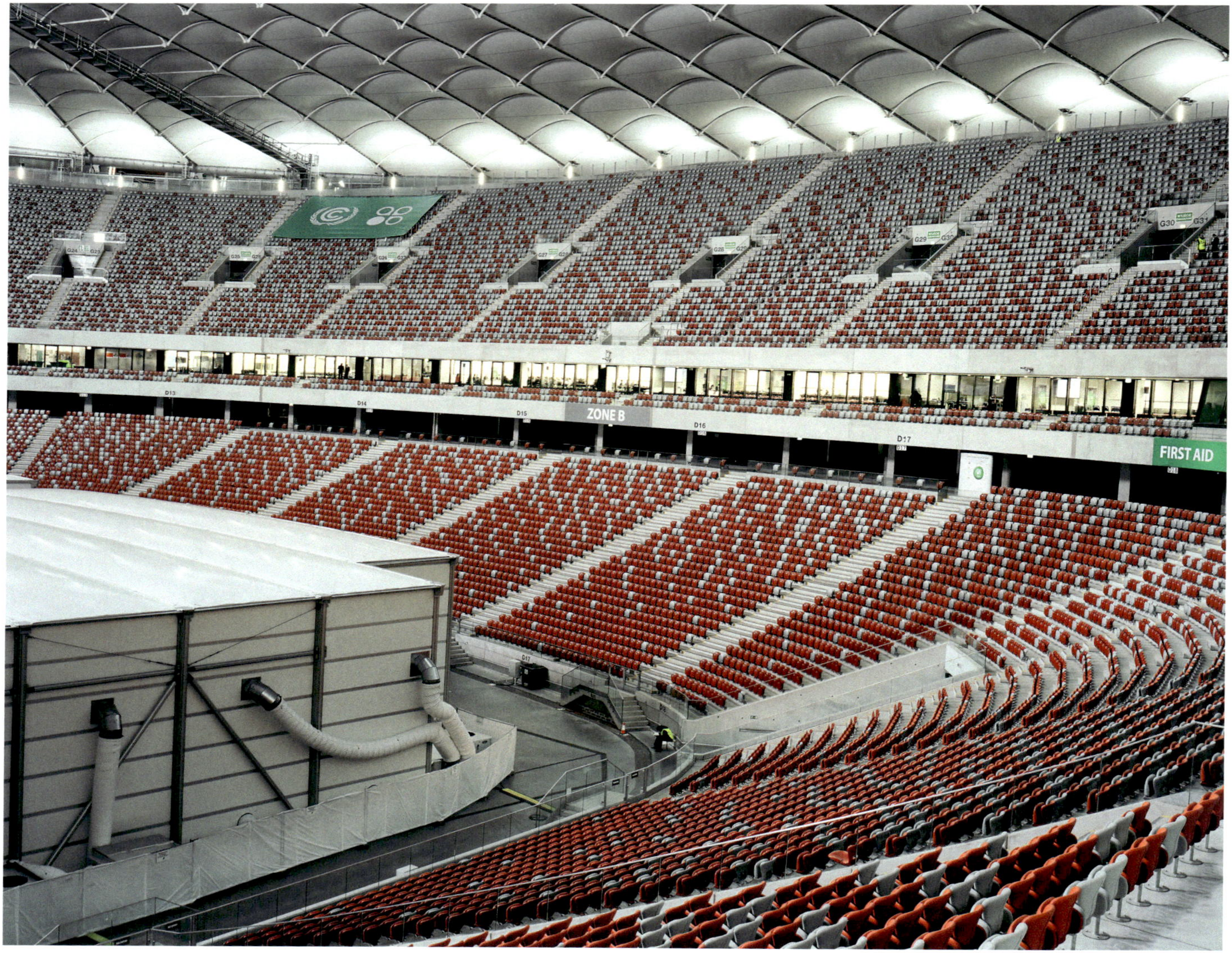

But precisely for this reason, the effect produced is even stronger because it evokes not just the absence of the people that will be crowding the stands but, prior to that, the absence of a code and of a logic that has produced one of the most pervasive images of modernity.

UNFCCC, COP19 Climate Change Conference, Warsaw, Poland, 2013
Photography in collaboration with Giulia Bruno

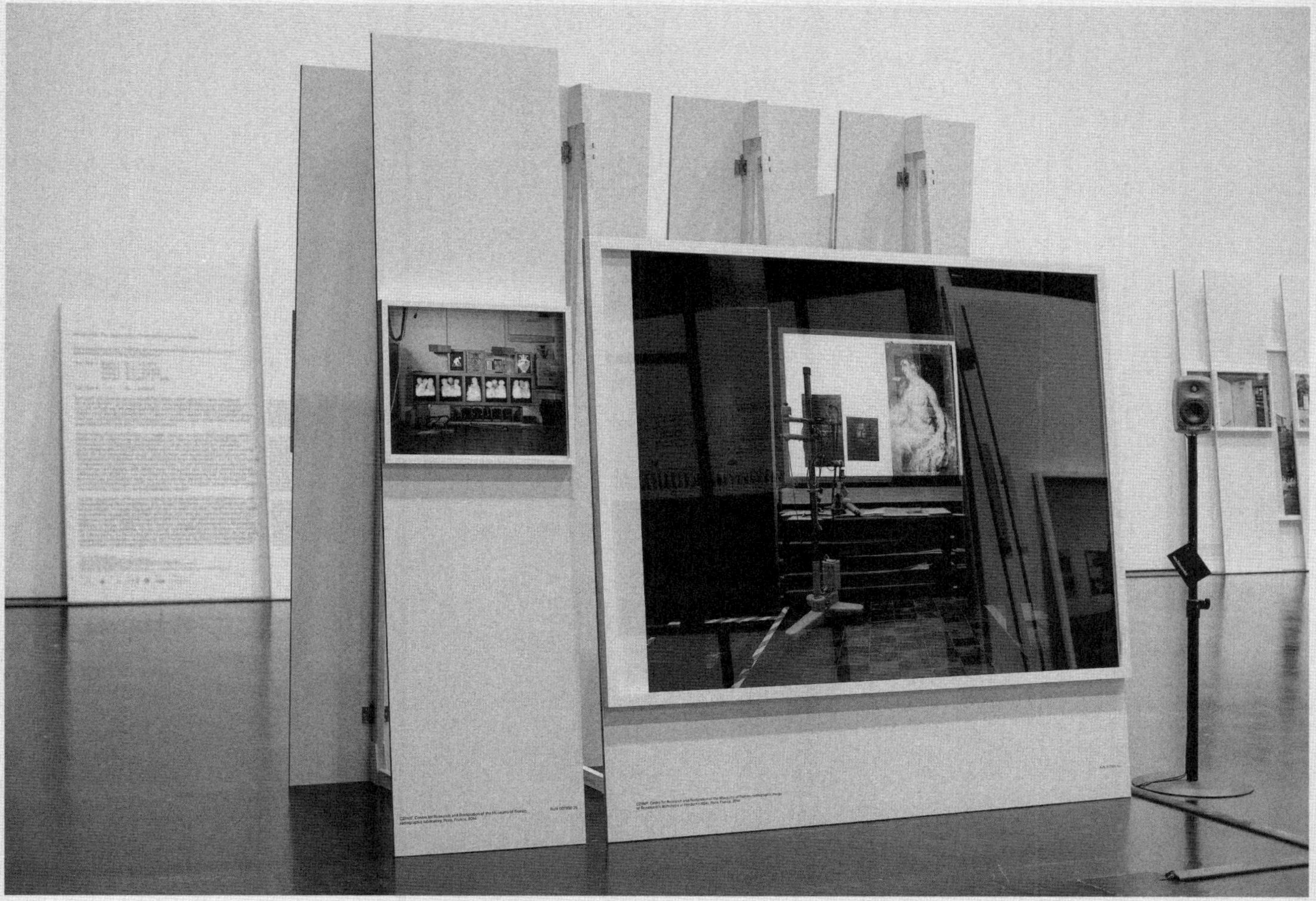

ZKM | Center for Art and Media Karlsruhe, Germany,
September 4 – October 11, 2015, Setting 1

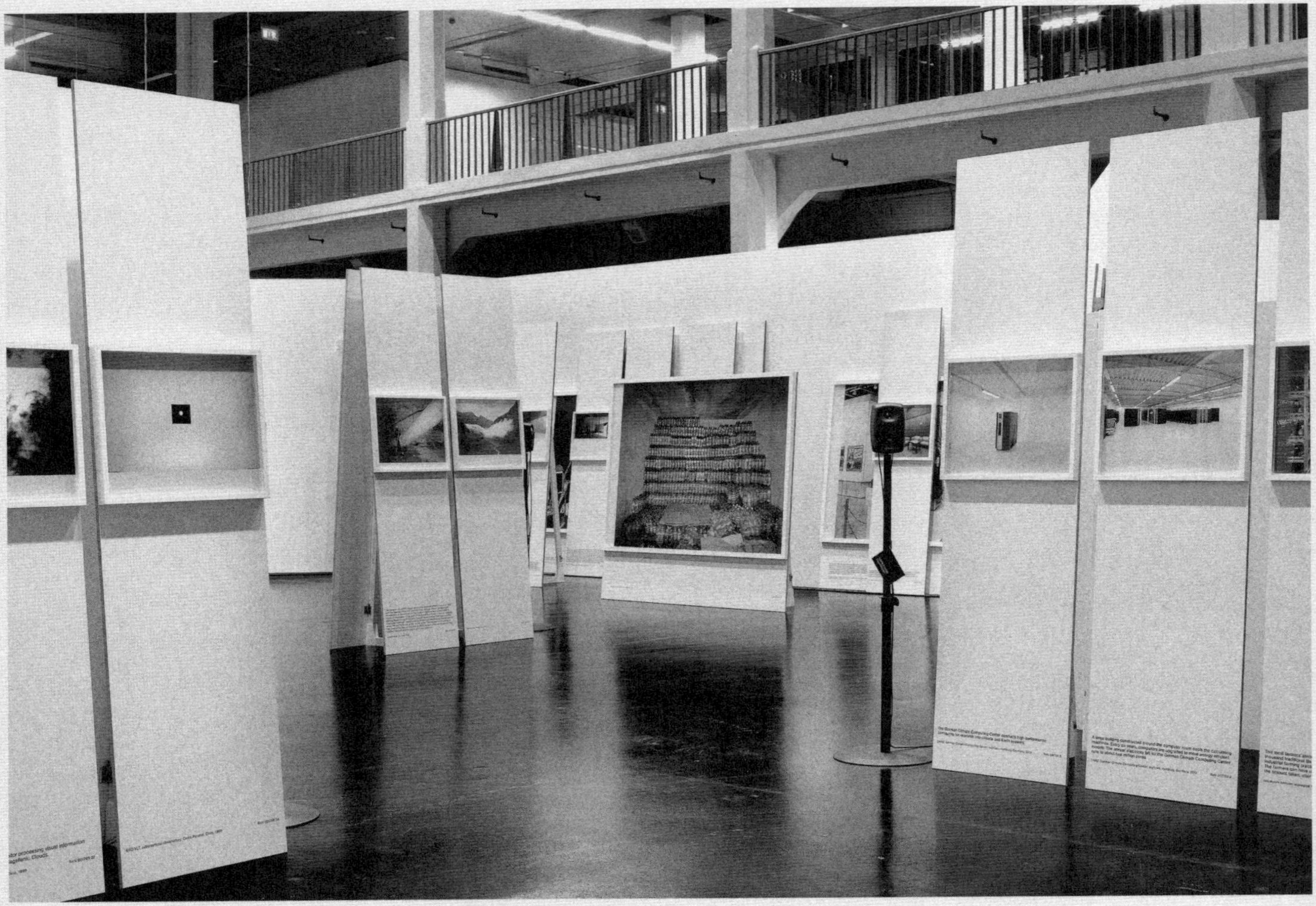

ZKM | Center for Art and Media Karlsruhe, Germany,
September 4 – October 11, 2015, Setting 1

1 From the archive into the book

2 Modern subjectivity shows itself not through the production of things but through their use.

Boris Groys, "Sammeln und gesammelt werden," in *Logik der Sammlung: Am Ende des musealen Zeitalters* (Munich/Vienna, 1997)

3 *Do you regard your archival practice as an act of self-archiving?* – Yes.

4 Does a living room piled up with banana boxes full of exhibition catalogues, invitations, and manuscripts constitute an archive?

5 What distinguishes the real photo archive from art photography? In answering this question, you will almost certainly get involved in questions of authorship and of how the work is understood; more importantly, however, it will be necessary to grapple with the promise or specter of the real. There is something that sets the archive apart from other institutions of cultural remembrance […] and that something is contact to the real.

Knut Ebeling, "Archiv oder Sammlung? Kleine Epistemologie archivarischer Praktiken des fotografischen Bildes," in *Atelier der Erinnerung: Aspekte des Archivarischen als Ausgangspunkt künstlerischer Fotografie* (Ludwigshafen/Essen, 2016)

6 Armin Linke, *Hans Ulrich Obrist, book archive apartment, Berlin, Germany, 2009* → p. 36, p. 52
Armin Linke, *ZKM | Center for Art and Media Karlsruhe, Peter Weibel's back office, Karlsruhe, Germany, 2011* → p. 53, p. 133

7 Georg Friedrich Kersting, *Man at His Desk*, 1811

8 PRODUCTIVITY TURNED FORMLESS – Armin Linke's photographs of Hans Ulrich Obrist's Berlin apartment can be considered part of the "interior" genre. To read them more accurately, it is worth putting these photographs beside reproductions of the paintings of Georg Friedrich Kersting. While the bourgeois interior in the early nineteenth century was organized around the table or desk, from which business dealings were managed, the living room crammed with banana boxes bears witness to another kind of productivity—one that has become formless. The number of accumulated items has become unmanageable here.

9 THE UTOPIA OF THE ARCHIVE – In contemporary art, the archive increasingly became a focus of interest at the point when the number of images produced skyrocketed as a result of digitization. Interest shifted from questions of production to questions of reception. Unlike the museum collection, which aims at stable value—i.e., a kind of timeless static equilibrium—the logic of the archive is based on dynamic properties and permanent reevaluation. Anyone who puts something in an archive is speculating on its future value: that at some point in the future someone will take an interest in it, even if we have no idea as yet what this interest will be; someone will come along for whom all this has meaning. And is this assumption not ultimately the teleological core of all hyper-productivity: the products waiting for their consumers to arrive? The images on the hard drives waiting for someone to look at them. The boxes stuffed with art catalogues waiting for someone to unpack them.

10 Libraries, archives, government offices, all these storage sites. All the rooms in the high rises are crammed with paper and microfilm.

Michel Butor, *Die Stadt als Text* (Graz/Vienna, 1992)

11 Armin Linke: I do not conceive of the archive only as a "together-ing" or as an assemblage of images but also as a test for every single image. As the whole archiving process is very time-consuming, it is also very much a test prior to making an image, before you trigger the shutter or before you position yourself in a space. As you know that it will consume your time, you seriously consider whether the picture you are about to take is worth the "boring" archiving process.

12 *How do you decide what is going to be archived? What are the criteria for archiving something?* – Everything I photograph will be archived: it is a test for my work—if I think it is not worth archiving then it is better not to photograph it.

13 http://www.arminlinke.com (online since 1998)

14 *What do you use your archive for and how?* – To compose a selection of pictures that take on meaning or new layers of significance.

15 By contrast, the idea of accumulating everything, of establishing a sort of general archive, the will to enclose in one place all times, all epochs, all forms, all tastes, the idea of constituting a place of all times that is itself outside of time and inaccessible to its ravages, the project of organizing in this way a sort of perpetual and indefinite accumulation of time in an immobile place, this whole idea belongs to our modernity.

Michel Foucault, *Of Other Spaces: Utopias and Heterotopias* (Cambridge, MA, 1984)

16 Armin Linke: So I'm not so interested in the archive per se but in how the archiving process tests the images, if the singular image can also live in time beyond its first motivation to be taken and if by being preserved in time (and for this you need the archive like you need a cellar for good wine) it can add additional layers of interpretation that you would not have thought about when you took the image.

17 Armin Linke, *DKRZ Deutsches Klimarechenzentrum, archives, Hamburg, Germany, 2013* → p. 82, p. 131, p. 132, p. 167, p. 214, p. 215, p. 303

18 AN INFRASTRUCTURE FOR COOPERATION – Anyone who creates an archive establishes an infrastructure for cooperation; an invitation to reflexive production, a production that draws on what has already been produced, for everything that is put in the archive is waiting for someone else to continue working on it.

19 *How long has your archive existed? Do you think of it as finished and complete?* – Since I was sixteen years old. It is not complete.

20 Armin Linke: Normally you think of an archive as something dusty or old, but I consider my archive, on the contrary, as a system that recontextualizes images, allowing them to be read in contemporary ways, even if they come from other contexts.

21 Armin Linke, *BAPCO Bahrain Petroleum Company, chemical laboratory, Awali, Bahrain, 2014* → p. 76, p. 138

22 THE FORMAL SCHOOL OF APPLICATION – The more natural it becomes to draw on something that has already been produced, the more clearly it emerges that notions like "quoting," "mixing," or "sampling" now fall some way short of the mark. It's necessary to develop a capacity for discernment to describe the different modes of application more precisely. They should be subjected to a stylistic analysis to examine what actually happens there, what content is used where and in what way.

23 *How do you deal with the different aspects of (dis)order?* – I try to order things so that it is then possible to disorder them to create something new.

24 From the garbage into the book

25 I needn't *say* anything. Merely show. I shall purloin no valuables, appropriate no ingenious formulations. But the rags, the refuse—these I will not inventory but allow, in the only way possible, to come into their own: by making use of them.

Walter Benjamin, *The Arcades Project* (New York, 2002)

26 Take me (I'm yours).

27 ACCESS – In 1998 Armin Linke made his photographic archive publicly accessible online. The decision about which images were "valid" was not made by the photographer alone but also by the viewer, who, at Linke's invitation, was to put a selection of "preferred images into a narrative sequence." A division of labor, of the kind that exists in art between artist and curator, or in photojournalism between photographer and photo editor, here became a performative proposition directed at anyone and everyone. The cultural techniques of sharing that we are now all familiar with from social media are road-tested—just as Linke from the start saw the development of technological infrastructures of image archiving and usage as an important aspect of his artistic work.

28 The holdings of photographic archives just need to be there. They are the basis of our cultural visual memory, the stock of images from which a selection can first of all be made. But how does this basis operate if the images it contains lie dormant in the photo archives without ever being looked at? [Michel] Butor makes it clear that the holdings of archives do not decay [...], but rather sleep, that what we are dealing with is a nocturnal store.

Knut Ebeling, "Archiv oder Sammlung?"

29 Every photo that exists leads its own life at night.

Alexander Kluge, *Pluriversum* (Leipzig, 2017)

30 Armin Linke, *Nayakrishi Andalon, ecological farm rice-seed vault, Tangail, Bangladesh, 2014* → p. 213

31 FOR THE ARCHIVE – Build your own archives! Don't wait around until someone comes along who collects what you do! Archive yourself! If you don't have a shelf, use banana boxes! Anything you have to hand will do—anything can become your personal infrastructure! Don't wait, create your ordering systems and find opportunities for others to make use of them too!

32 Armin Linke: My photographic archive has already been presented as part of "Utopia Station" at the Venice Biennale in 2003, where it featured as an interactive Internet project "Book on Demand." It allows you to choose images in the digital environment and receive the results by post as a printed book. When everything was moved from the physical into the digital world, it was important for me to beat a path in the opposite direction, transferring experiences from the digital world into the physical world of the exhibition space.

33 From the archive into the exhibition

34 In an archive, the possibility of meaning is "liberated" from the actual contingencies of use. But this liberation is also a loss, an *abstraction* from the complexity and richness of use, a loss of context. Thus, the specificity of "original" uses and meanings can be avoided and even made invisible, when photographs are selected from an archive and reproduced in a book. (In reverse fashion, photographs can be removed from books and entered into archives, with a similar loss of specificity.) So new meanings come to supplant old ones, with the archive serving as a kind of "clearing house" of meaning.

Allan Sekula, "Reading an Archive: Photography between Labour and Capital," in *The Photography Reader*, ed. Liz Wells (London/New York, 2003)

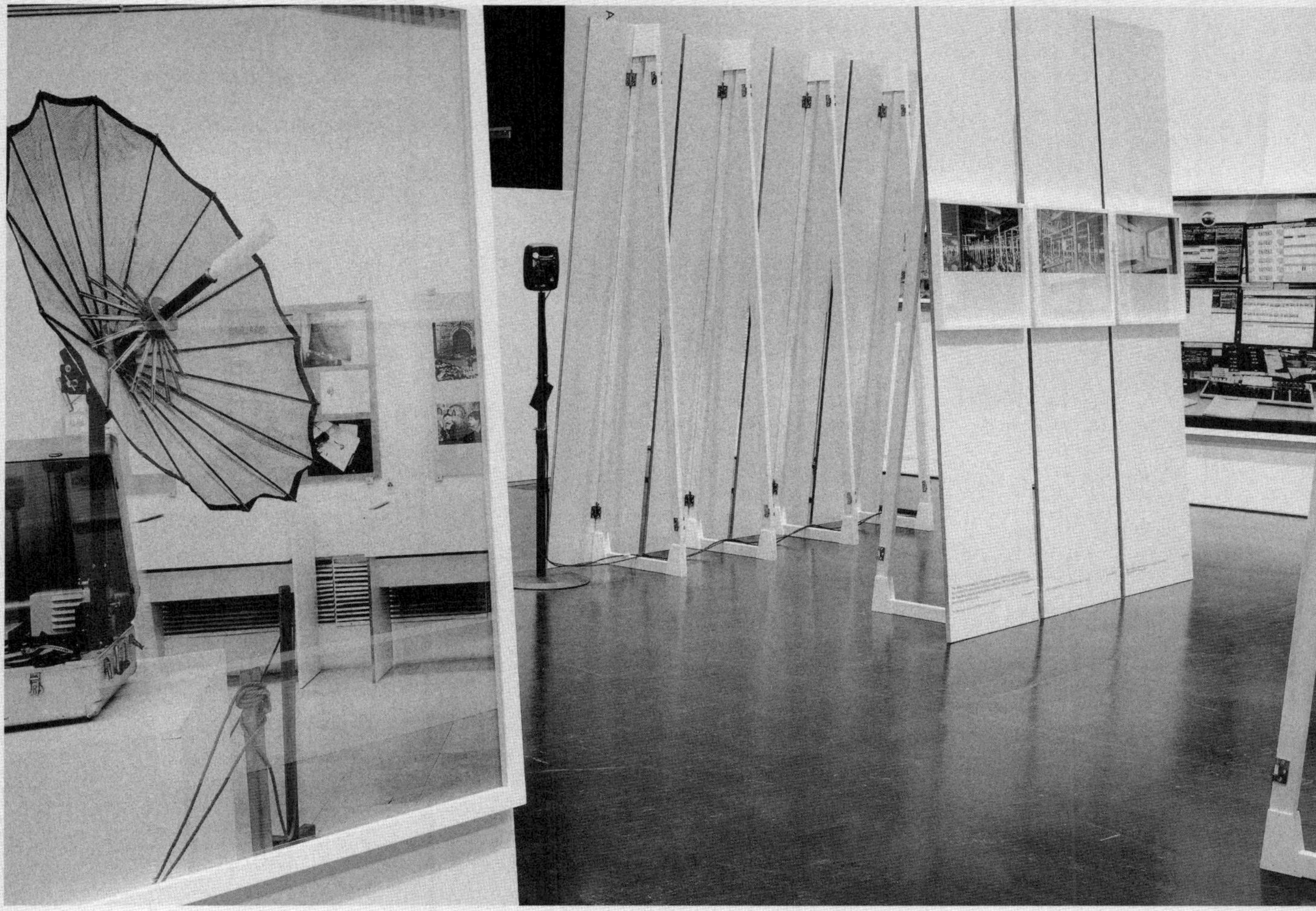

ZKM | Center for Art and Media Karlsruhe, Germany,
October 14 – November 15, 2015, Setting 2

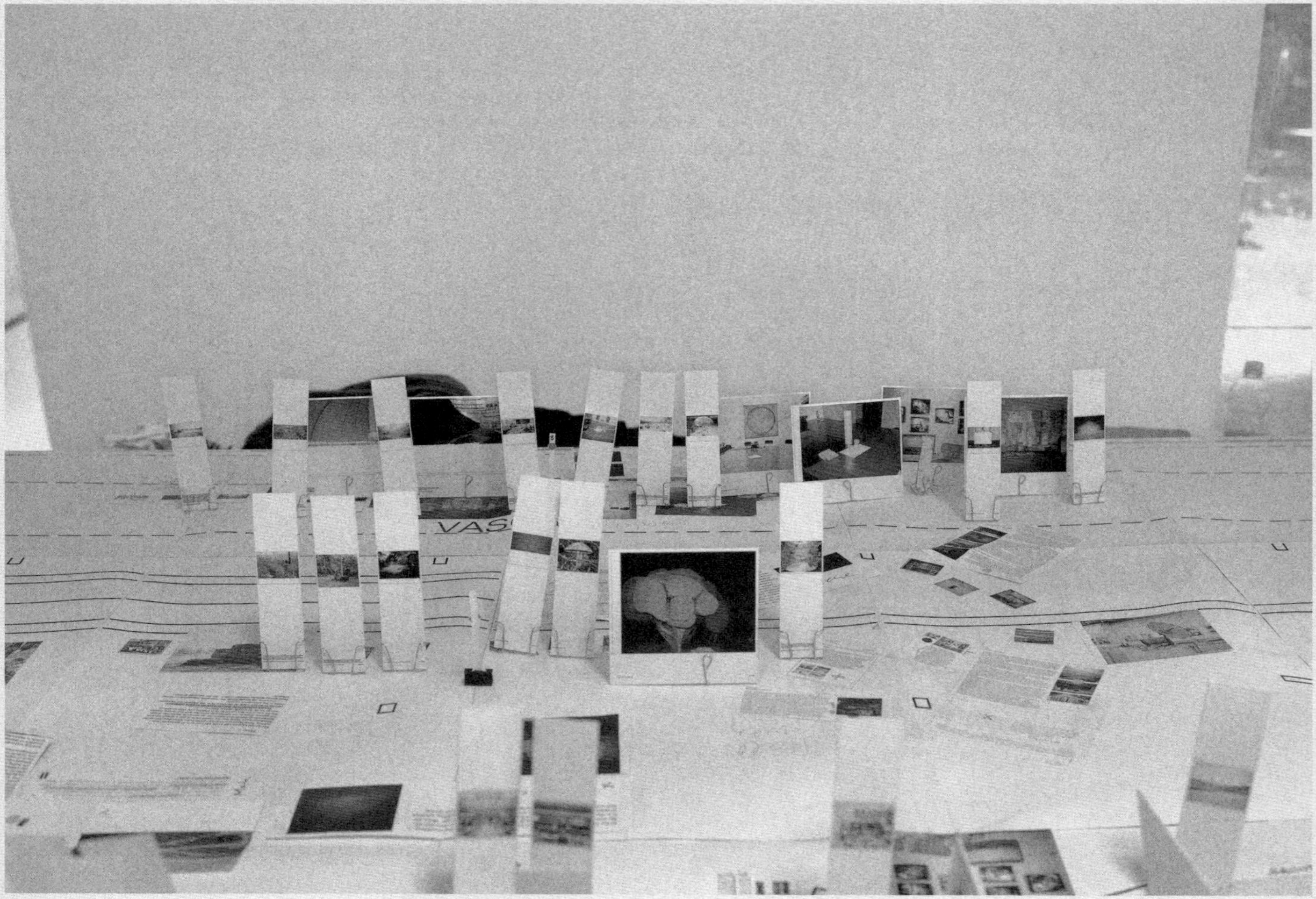

PAC Padiglione d'Arte Contemporanea, Milan, Italy,
October 16, 2016 – January 6, 2017

35 His consumers are they not his producers.
James Joyce, *Finnegans Wake* (New York, 1939)

36 MIGRANT IMAGES – Armin Linke sees photographs not as objects but rather—in a much broader sense—as objects entangled in different interpretational processes. It is not just what a picture shows that is important but also the distribution infrastructures it is incorporated in, the speed with which it is disseminated, where it goes, where it's stored, and who can look at it in situ. And—no less significant—the metamorphoses that the image's materiality undergoes as it travels these ramified pathways: whether it is available as a digital data set, as an exhibition print, or as a double-page spread in a magazine with mass circulation. All of this has an influence on how we view a photograph and how its potential is realized—on the particular aspects of what it shows that come to the fore in each case, the different narratives it is included in, and the agenda it serves.

37 Armin Linke: What interests me is the fact that photography completely changes its meaning depending on how—historically and context-wise—you read it. It's different if you look at a photograph in the context of a magazine, an exhibition, or an essay. The potential of photography actually changes a lot. I am interested in these various potentials.

38 Armin Linke, *Russian State Library, reading hall, Moscow, Russia, 2011* → p. 31, p. 130

39 In order to know, you have to take up a position, which requires you to move and take responsibility for this movement at all times. The movement is both an approach and a distancing: drawing near reservedly, detachment full of desire. It requires contact, but contact that is interrupted, if not disjunct, lost, to the last impossible.
Georges Didi-Huberman, *Wenn die Bilder Position beziehen: Das Auge der Geschichte*, vol. 1 (Munich, 2011)

40 Armin Linke: I began with the project "Book on Demand," which then developed into "Phenotypes Limited Forms," where the idea was to put some of the images on the Internet and give the public the opportunity to select them, curate them, and print their own edition of the book, skipping over all the distribution filters that are typical of publishing. Of course, a project based on this kind of technology will become obsolete in a few years, but it is an interesting attempt to change the classical commercial distribution methods, using a system like a commercial image database for a non-commercial artistic project.

41 TAKE ME (I'M YOURS) – With "Book on Demand" Armin Linke broke new technological ground. He used a digital printing process that had only just come on the market. The firm he worked together with, Graphistudio, produced wedding albums in small quantities; Linke recognized the aesthetic potential of this commercial process. In his 1974 exhibition *Printing Show*, Japanese photographer Daido Moriyama had set out to overcome the distance between photographer and viewer using a similar approach. In those days, he used a photocopier and duplicated the images selected by museumgoers directly in the gallery. The ad hoc photo books produced in this way were bound in situ with a silkscreened cover and then signed. At the time the aesthetic innovation consisted in the combination of a mass-produced item and individual configuration—books normally involve a large print run of identical copies; here, however, the book becomes a medium for recording an individual selection process.

42 CHOOSING MEANS PRODUCING – Like Daido Moriyama, Armin Linke also uses innovative reproduction technology for "Book on Demand" to enable different forms of editing and distribution. While Moriyama's *Printing Show* was inspired by American pop art and the consumerist culture of the 1960s and 1970s, Linke's project reflects new digital production strategies. In the twenty-first century it is not simply that things are produced Just in Time; with digitization it has also become possible to "individualize" industrial mass production. Customers can choose from a number of different versions in order to obtain their personal product. The consumer becomes an actor in the design process, which is now to some extent entirely in the customer's hands.

43 Armin Linke, *Musée du Louvre, Mona Lisa (1503–17) by Leonardo da Vinci, Paris, France, 2013* → p. 40

44 Armin Linke: In 2007 I developed a project at ZKM, "Phenotypes," in which I asked spectators to actively engage with the photographs. I was interested in how my images would be read by other people, and what misunderstandings or different readings there might be that I had not previously considered. After "Phenotypes" it became important for me to keep the reading of my images open, but at the same time to succeed in constructing a specific narrative.

45 Armin Linke: My photo archive has now reached a critical mass. I have traveled round the world several times over, and my previous book publications and exhibitions have only ever shown a fraction of what I photographed. I'm increasingly interested in how other people who are also exploring different forms will read these images. This is, if you like, the second step. First I interpret the world, and then other people interpret my interpretation.

46 How fortunate—being able to choose one's readership.

47 Armin Linke: First there was the French sociologist, anthropologist, and philosopher Bruno Latour. He asked me whether he could select images from my archive for his website

"Modes of Existence." This request was very instructive for me. He made compilations of images that I would never have come up with myself. He also saw connections that only became accessible to me through his approach. In general, then, you could say that my work is about how we can read the world and images of the world, and what technique we can use. We need to learn a grammar of images so that we can read and decipher images, for example, that we get to see over the media. We need to be able to read what is hidden behind the images in order for us to make decisions.

48 It is not the person ignorant of writing but the one ignorant of photography who will be the illiterate of the future.
Lázló Moholy-Nagy, "Die Photographie in der Reklame," *Photographische Korrespondenz* 63, no. 9 (1927)

49 SECOND-ORDER REPORTAGE – Reportage first emerged in the nineteenth century from the pendular movement between mediatized and urban space, from the back-and-forth between the street and the newspaper page. The work of the reporter was, and is, to record spontaneous, fleeting events at the moment they happen, to put unknown aspects of city life in the daily papers as news, and thus to amplify them, to give them resonance. Since the world of the media has become just as vast as the metropolis did in the nineteenth century, it requires a form of second-order reportage.

We must make our way into the media realm, with a mind as inquisitive as any reporter's, and bring something back, observe something, investigate something that finds a place in our own life. Just as the media duplicates the event by producing it in the form of a report, we must give a form to our reading of the news, to our reception of it. We must duplicate the media by showing—reporting—what we pick up from the stream of news, by commenting on it, giving it another spin, another direction. Many posts on social media pursue just this intention—they create a resonance chamber, where the stream of media undergoes multiple refraction.

50 Armin Linke, *National Museum, replica of "Lucy's" remains, Addis Ababa, Ethiopia, 2012* → p. 61, p. 62

51 WE PEDESTRIANS OF THE IMAGES – In his *The Practice of Everyday Life*, Michel de Certeau describes how our daily practices produce statements. It is not only architects that create the city but also pedestrians. It is only through our movements that the city's network of meaning is woven. "Their story begins on ground level, with footsteps. They are myriad, but do not compose a series. They cannot be counted because each unit has a qualitative character: a style of tactile apprehension and kinesthetic appropriation. Their swarming mass is an innumerable collection of singularities. Their intertwining paths give their shape to spaces. They weave places together. In that respect pedestrian movements form one of these 'real systems whose existence in fact makes up the city.' They are not localized, it is rather that they spatialize." In this way, as with de Certeau, walking itself becomes a statement; our movements in the archive—the things we respond to, the things we share and link—are what produce the "real system" of the mediatized space.

52 Armin Linke, *C2RMF, Center for Research and Restoration of the Museums of France, radiographic laboratory, Paris, France, 2014* → p. 64, p. 65, p. 66

53 Armin Linke: The whole "Appearance" project, including our discussions about its installation, was, and still is, a discussion about the question of how to keep the project open, of how, whilst allowing multiple possible readings, to be precise in this openness, achieving a certain narrative, a golden thread in a sense.

54 THE EQUALITY OF IMAGES – Only the conscious renunciation of some of one's own power to make artistic decisions can create this kind of equality amongst the images. Armin Linke's reluctance to evaluate photographs simply on the basis of their aesthetic merit helps maintain a state of equality between them. None of the images in the archive are privileged. Their application, their utility value, the different possible readings of them are what differentiate them. But this process can never be completed—instead it is perpetuated with each new process of selection.

55 Who decides who decides?

56 Armin Linke: It was not so easy. I wanted them to come from different fields. They needed to know my work to some extent, and I needed to know their work. It was crucial that there be some kind of reciprocal trust between the dialogue partners in order to participate in this experiment, knowing that it could also fail. Furthermore, it was important to have the feeling that they would take the time to engage, to "play," and to use my photographs as a tool for their own narration, rather than just commenting on them. So the experts needed to be people whose personal narration I was interested in and who are used in their own practice to dialoguing and asking analytical questions about objects and processes.

57 Naïvety thus has nothing to do with a fatuous simplification of everything and everyone. It is rather a question of a trusting openness to a sensual complexity—of relationships, ramifications, contradictions, contacts—in one's own environment. Naïvety is the gesture of quizzically accepting this kind of complexity. It is the pleasure of wanting to play with it. In this sense, naïvety is both *creative* and *receptive*.
Georges Didi-Huberman, *Wenn die Bilder Position beziehen: Das Auge der Geschichte*, vol. 1 (Munich, 2011)

58 Armin Linke: There are a lot of pieces to this puzzle.

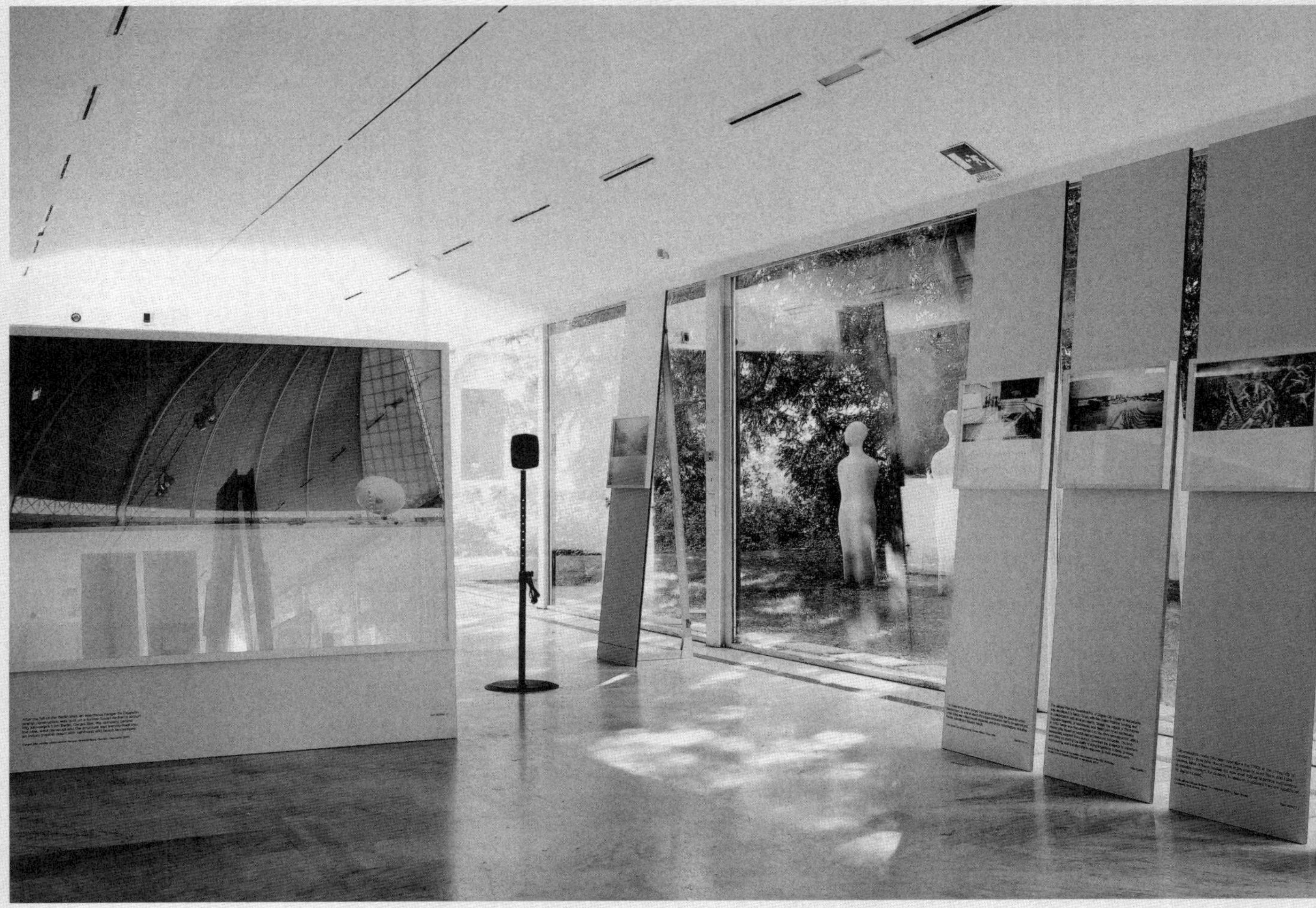

PAC Padiglione d'Arte Contemporanea, Milan, Italy,
October 16, 2016 – January 6, 2017

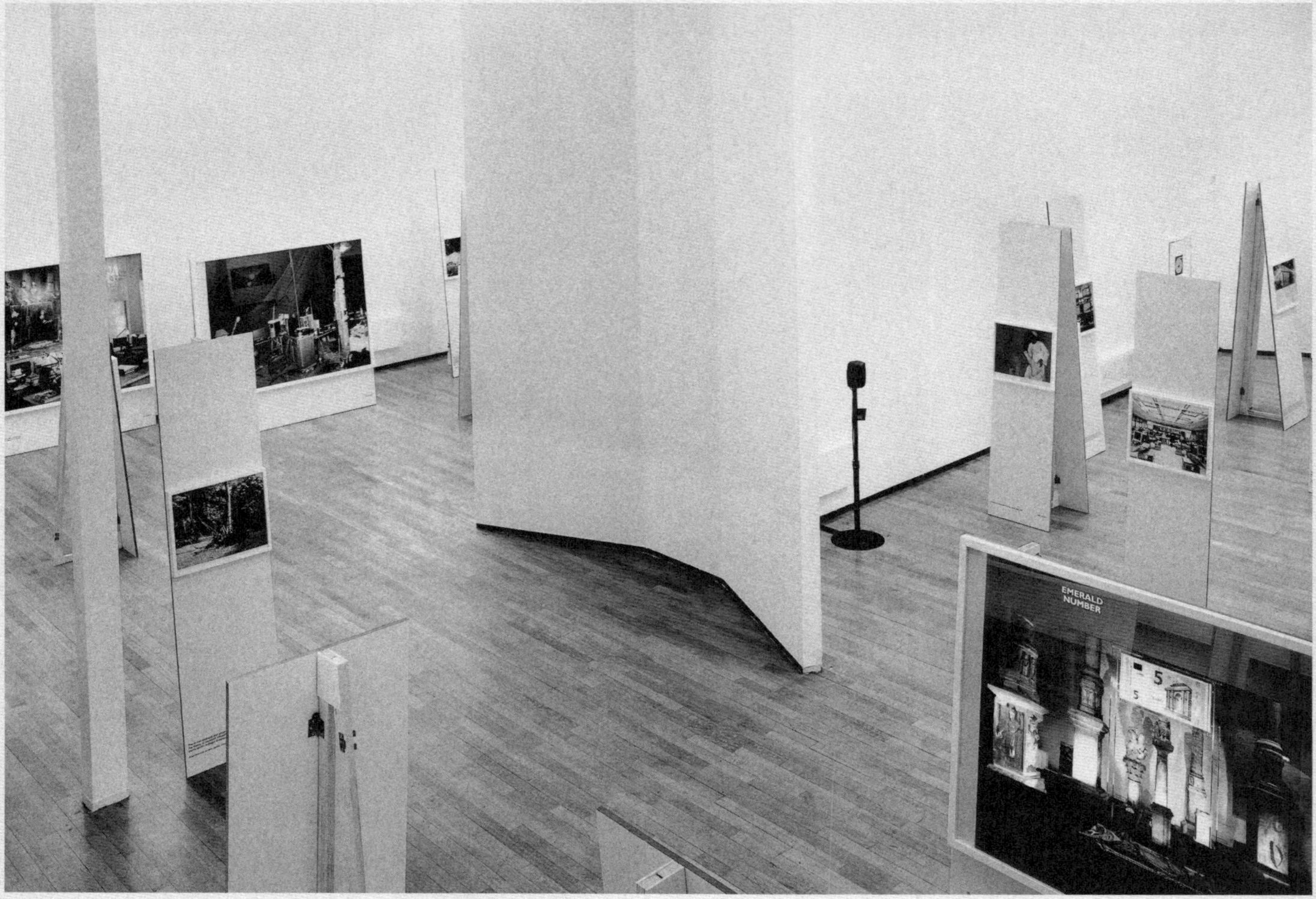

PAC Padiglione d'Arte Contemporanea, Milan, Italy,
October 16, 2016 – January 6, 2017

59 *What can archives ideally achieve?* – They can create surrogates of worlds.

60 Armin Linke: There was a turning point in my photography about eighteen years ago when I read about the construction of the Three Gorges Dam in China. What struck me about this was not only the construction of the dam but the resettling of about two million people living in the area, the fact that houses, schools, hospitals, whole industries, in fact, needed to be reconstructed. The construction of the dam required the flooding of a city with the same population as Milan, the city I was living in at the time. Everything was going to be demolished and had to be reconstructed in a different place. Think of all the financial and psychological consequences!

61 Armin Linke, *Three Gorges Dam project, model, Yichang (Hubei), China, 1998* → p. 307, p. 364
Armin Linke, *Three Gorges Dam, construction of a lift for ships, Yichang (Hubei), China, 1998* → p. 309, p. 362
Armin Linke, *Ertan Dam, downstream side, Panzhihua, Sichuan, China, 1998* → p. 136, p. 308

62 Margaret Bourke-White, *Fort Peck Dam*, Montana, 1937

63 At first glance, Armin Linke's artistic approach resembles that of a photojournalist. Like the classic heroes of the genre, who owed their livelihood to the emergence of large illustrated magazines in the late 1920s, he is constantly on the move. Erich Salomon still traveled by ship and train; Margaret Bourke-White, who journeyed, with her camera in hand, between Magnitogorsk, the Arctic, and the dam on Fort Peck Lake, mostly went by plane.

64 Can the process of globalization be represented photographically?

65 Armin Linke: What also interested me in this context were areas where infrastructural or technological changes would create conflicts or where the conflict was about infrastructure; yet my photographs would focus on the infrastructure and not on the conflict.

66 Finding one's way in the big city, with its uninterrupted succession of impressions, its confusing multiplicity of signals and its fragmented spaces, is an adventure [...]. The big city almost invites exploration; it suggests entry into unknown places. [...] In this context, the reporter functions as a scout [...]. On the readers' behalf, he sets out on a journey into the interior of the metropolis: it is he who reports from the inner world of the sweatshops, the slaughterhouses and the factories; he brings the reader the world of the vaudeville theatres, the great hotels and the department stores; [...] and it is he who embarks on the journey into the "mosaic of the miniature worlds" of metropolis [...]. The big city gives free rein to the art of observation [...]. In however fragmentary a way, the reporter conveys to his readers views from inside unfamiliar worlds.

Rolf Lindner, *The Reportage of Urban Culture: Robert Park and the Chicago School* (Cambridge/New York, 1996)

67 COSMOPOLITANS – R. Buckminster Fuller writes that the Renaissance mariners were the first to merit the title "cosmopolitans," since on their travels, which took them to different countries, they developed a global perspective and "knew, or wanted to learn from experience, 'what it's all about.'"

68 AROUND THE WORLD – Over the last twenty years Armin Linke has taken photographs in countless places around the world: on construction sites, in control centers, at the stock exchange, in laboratories where new technologies are tested, in public squares and in spaces that are difficult to access, in computer centers, banks, courtrooms, at international conferences, in centers of business, politics, science, the media, law, and culture, as well as at the periphery, in the mountains, in the desert, in the rainforest, at sea—in landscapes in which the traces of human activity are inscribed more or less visibly.

69 Armin Linke: I am interested in depicting immaterial structures. The questions for myself are: How can I photograph something that is immaterial or something that is digital? How can I photograph a process instead of an object? How can a process that is at the heart of an institution be visualized through a photograph that is fixed in time and space?

70 Armin Linke, *Axel-Springer Verlag, Pope Benedict XVI's visit to Berlin, Berlin, Germany, 2011* → p. 334

71 Television news producers and newspaper and magazine photo editors make decisions every day which firm up the wavering consensus about the boundaries of public knowledge.

Susan Sontag, *Regarding the Pain of Others* (New York, 2003)

72 Once again: Can the process of globalization be represented photographically?

73 MESSAGES THAT PERSIST – The process of globalization has no center but is rather composed day in, day out of an unimaginable number of parallel activities—commercial contexts, individual decisions, and attempts at political control—which are mutually reinforcing or disruptive and constantly reestablish balance; in the same way a photographic work that seeks to record the process of globalization in pictures is unable to determine any privileged place or event. Signs of this epoch-making process can be found all over the world—only the correlation of a plethora of images can make aspects of this process visible.

74 Armin Linke (photography in collaboration with Giulia Bruno), *UNFCCC, COP19 Climate Change Conference, Warsaw, Poland, 2013* → p. 71, p. 159, p. 213, p. 225, p. 37

75 NEWSPAPERS KNOW ONLY ONE TIME: THE PRESENT – The journalistic image is subordinate to the paradigm of novelty. It has a short period of circulation; after a few days it is already obsolete. Because only what's new is newsworthy. This has an impact on what we see of the world: quick, abrupt change can be turned into a story, but slow processes, humdrum changes escape our attention. You might say that Armin Linke practices anti-journalism, since he photographs situations whose newsworthiness is only apparent years later.

76 Armin Linke: A big part of my practice is about looking at history while it is happening and then seeing in ten or fifteen years if it can be read in a different way. And yet, I do not want to produce journalistic images, because these kinds of images are produced for a specific information industry: an image is produced and distributed immediately, but, in general, its economic potential gets lost within the next days, weeks, or months, depending on the medium it was published in. I want to produce images that might be interesting in ten or twenty years. In other words, I want to depict processes, institutions, or moments that have the potential to be recognized as interesting in twenty years' time. Maybe, at a certain point in time, decades from now, the importance of particular past processes or moments will be realized, but then it is not possible anymore to fix them, or to look at them in order to understand what happened. So, that is what I want to do: fix them upfront, so to say.

77 WHAT IS AN EVENT? – The actuality of world news reports appearing in the media every day is the narrative that shapes our understanding of reality and helps determine what snippets of the world become visible. The mass media define what is perceptible as an event. Mundane occurrences, technological developments, and the history of infrastructures typically escape media attention. In November 1989 the Berlin Wall fell. A few days later a license was issued to the Mannesmann company to construct a digital cellular radio network. The synchronicity of the events is coincidental but it does throw up the question: What is retained as "history" in one's mind? Why is the privatization of telecoms and the thoroughgoing reorganization of social communication that goes along with it less newsworthy than the collapse of a state?

78 In traditional history it was thought that events were what was known, what was visible, what was directly or indirectly identifiable, and the work of the historian was to search for their cause or their meaning. The cause or meaning was essentially hidden. The event, on the other hand, was essentially visible, even if one sometimes lacked the documents to establish it with certainty. Serial history makes it possible to bring out different layers of events as it were, some being visible, even immediately knowable by the contemporaries, and then, beneath these events that form the froth of history, so to speak, there are other events that are invisible, imperceptible for the contemporaries, and are of completely different form. [...] Beneath this layer of events, there exists another type of events that are a bit more diffuse—events that are not perceived exactly in the same way by the contemporaries, but which they have a certain awareness of all the same, for example, a lowering or an increase in prices which will change their economic behavior. And then, beneath these events as well, you have others that are hard to locate, that are often barely perceptible for the contemporaries but nonetheless constitute decisive breaks. Thus the reversal of a trend, the point at which an economic curve that had been increasing levels off or begins to decline, such a point is a very important event in the history of a town, a country, or possibly a civilization, but the people who are its contemporaries are not aware of it. [...] It is history's task to uncover this hidden layer of diffuse, "atmospheric," polycephalic events that determine, finally and profoundly, the history of the world. For it is quite clear to us now that the reversal of an economic trend is much more important than the death of a king.

Michel Foucault, "Return to History," in *Aesthetics, Method, and Epistemology*, ed. James D. Faubion (New York, 1998)

79 Armin Linke: The selection of subjects is part and parcel of an approach that looks at these moments as pivotal points in time. Of course you can also fail with this; there is always the risk that an image is banal. From the very first moment, I told myself not to be afraid of a banal picture. Just do it and see what happens.

80 UNEARTHING NOVELTY – One can only write the history of globalization by drawing on its constituent elements—they are insightful and capable of being represented. On the level of the whole there is in fact no story, no history. For Armin Linke, who sees his photographs as a research tool, the archive provides an appropriate ordering principle for achieving this work. Although what is initially mirrored here is the outcome of a collecting process that it is scarcely possible to make sense of as a whole owing to the huge quantity of photographs, this process can be constantly reexamined, edited, and worked through in the archive.

81 The big decisions in history are not made in the realm what we can experience close at hand. The really big disasters take place in the distance which we cannot experience, for which we don't have the appropriate telescopes (or microscopes) in our senses. The two don't come together.

Alexander Kluge, "The Political as Intensity of Everyday Feelings," trans. Andrew Bowie, *Cultural Critique* 4 (Autumn 1986)

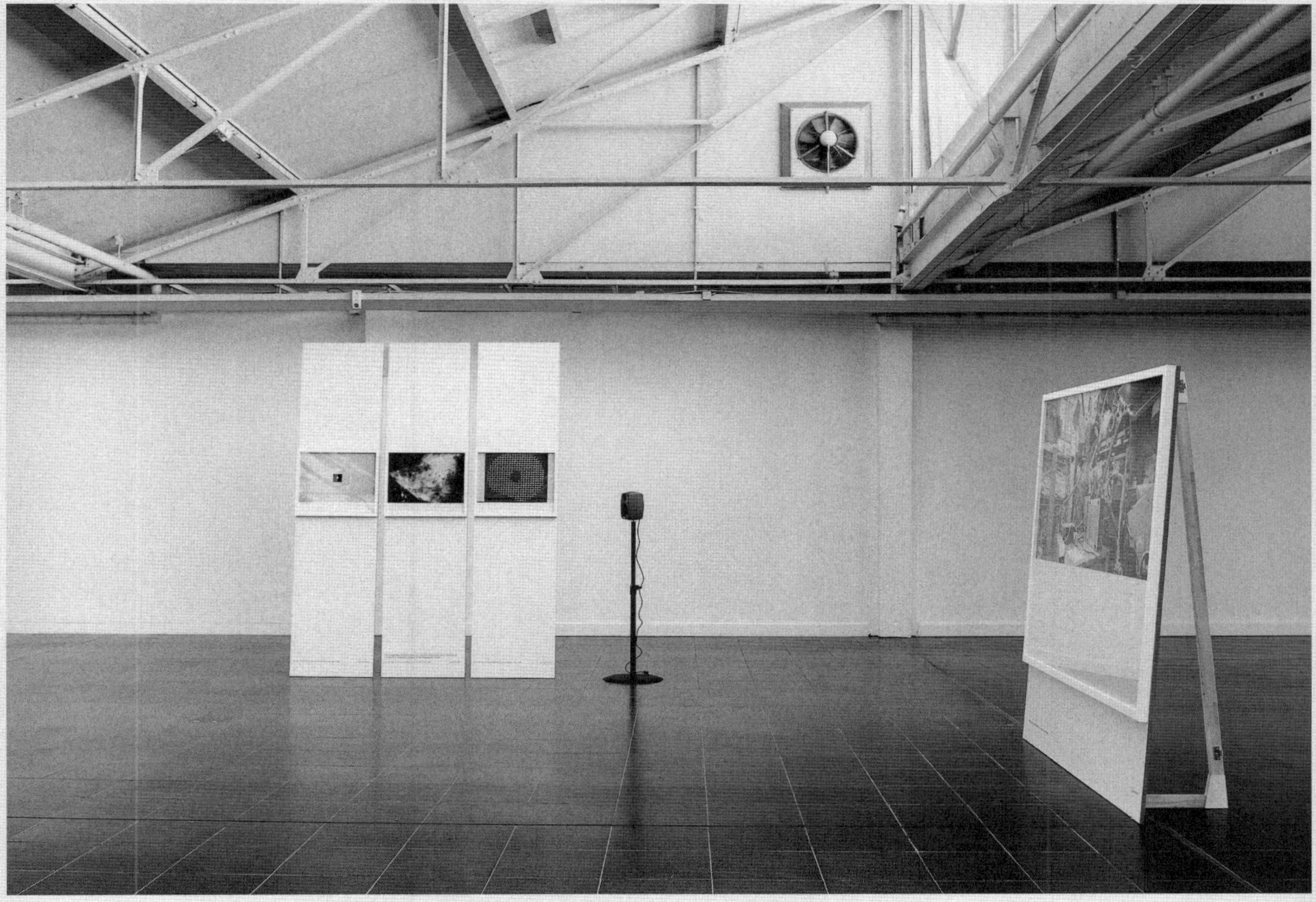

Ludwig Forum for International Art Aachen, Germany,
March 3 – June 18, 2017

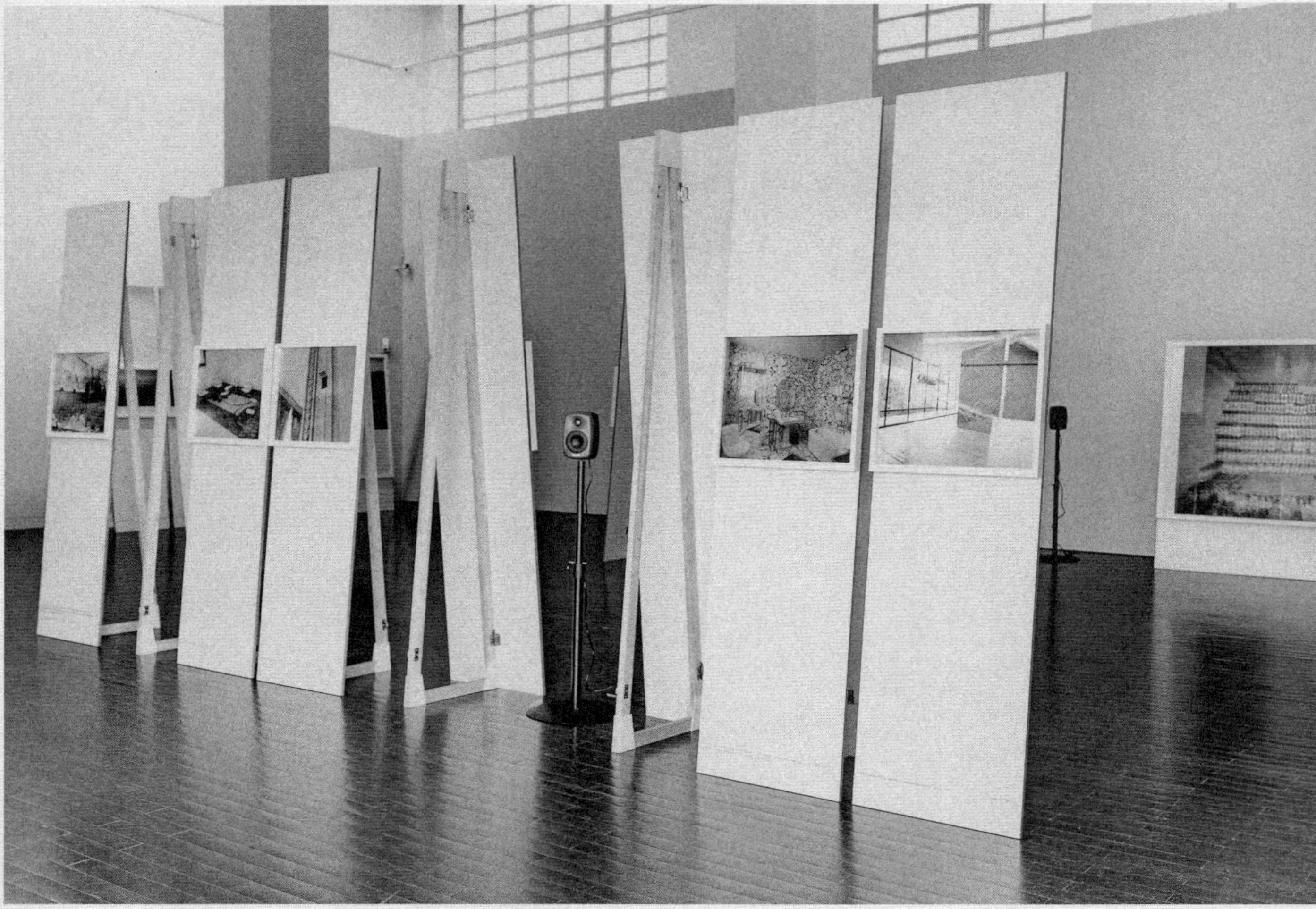

Ludwig Forum for International Art Aachen, Germany,
March 3 – June 18, 2017

82 Who's speaking? Who's acting? Who's watching? And who's validating and authenticating?

83 Armin Linke: No matter where I go, I meet people who, in their local area and in their world, are very, very close to the source of a phenomenon. An environmental problem I photograph may be a long way from Berlin, but for the locals it is always an immediate issue. That's why it's also important for my photographs to have a kind of Virgil constantly at hand—Dante's guide, who escorts you through limbo and can explain each place from a local perspective. Without this Virgil, I would be in danger of seeing what I see from the point of view of a tourist. I need to get someone local to clue me up about the place I find myself in. It requires a kind of inoculation against the superficiality of the picturesque, which always awaits me any place I go. So working with a local guide follows a methodology of a kind.

84 Armin Linke, *TAL Group transalpine pipeline, control room, Trieste, Italy, 2012* → p. 38, p. 118, p. 255

85 The Photograph is never anything but an antiphon of "Look," "See," "Here it is"; it points a finger at certain *vis-à-vis*, and cannot escape this pure deictic language.

Roland Barthes, *Camera Lucida: Reflections on Photography* (New York, 1981)

86 Armin Linke: I've been trying for a long time to express everything with visual means—instead of words. I've always believed in the power of images. But I grant that there was a moment of liberation when I wanted to express something in the new catalogue with captions, which were not like the typical captions used by photo agencies. In conjunction with the remarks of the individual curators, my comments generate a tension between the image in question and the two textual commentaries—opening up a field of interpretation. Text and image attain the same importance.

87 PHOTOGRAPHY IS QUITE GOOD. BUT NOT GOOD ENOUGH – What if photography was not the beginning of a new way of viewing the world but rather the transformation of an older way of seeing? The central perspective, the extension of the Renaissance into the modern age. The translation of the pursuit of rationality and verisimilitude into optical technology, into a form of representation completely focused on earthly things. "What use are all the speculations about Heaven and Earth—let them go—if you could really see a tiny corner of the world," cries Brecht's Galileo. It is this basic trust—that all truth is available to the eye, and seeing, *really seeing*, means understanding—that has given photography its importance.

88 For many decades we have learned to see as though we were a camera. Because we only look at reality with cameras, digital devices, and smartphones, we are beginning to see like a camera. We only see images that look like the pictures we are familiar with from these photographs. With these lighting effects, these shadows, these features. It is my belief that we must relearn how to look, how to see, how reality actually is. We must learn to overcome the SLR in our eyes.

David Hockney, "Die Fotografie ist am Ende," *Spiegel Online*, December 5, 2005

89 Armin Linke: One important experience was a conversation I had with Bruno Latour. He said that he couldn't make a selection of images if he only saw the photos. He needed information from me. I began to explain the images to him as he looked at them in my studio. My whole life I've been shy and reticent when it comes to verbalizing what I photograph, but I understood how important it was for him to hear the things I told him at that moment. The photo on its own was not enough.

90 THAT WHICH IS NOT PHOTOGRAPHED CRITIQUES THAT WHICH IS – Photographs, according to the philosopher Günther Anders, are in constant danger of becoming instruments of stultification, because by their very essence they have not shown any context but are always only ripped-out worlds, at once revealing and shrouding the world.

Since the world of the media has become just as vast as the metropolis did in the nineteenth century, it requires a form of second-order reportage. We must make our way into the media realm, with a mind as inquisitive as any reporter's, and bring something back, observe something, investigate something that finds a place in our own life. Just as the media duplicates the event by producing it in the form of a report, we must give a form to our reading of the news, to our reception of it. We must duplicate the media by showing—reporting—what we pick up from the stream of news, by commenting on it, giving it another spin, another direction.

91 Armin Linke, *Kashiwazaki-Kariwa Nuclear Power Station, control room, Kashiwazaki, Japan, 1998* → p. 179, p. 203
Armin Linke, *Kashiwazaki-Kariwa Nuclear Power Station, entrance to control room, Kashiwazaki, Japan, 1998* → p. 310, p. 360, p. 361

92 VOICES IN THE SEA OF IMAGES – Our trust in photography is receding. This is one reason to add voices to images. Voices that accompany images, that order them. In the project *The Appearance of That Which Cannot Be Seen*, the combination of image and voice creates an essayistic form, in which image and text authenticate one another. This oral turn can be seen as a strategy for working against the dwindling evidential power of the image in photography's current crisis. Perhaps in future we will need voices we can trust in order for an image to have an impact. An advocate will be needed, someone who authenticates the image.

93 Monica Haller, *Riley and His Story: Me and My Outrage; You and Us* (Paris, 2009)

94 This is not a book. This is an invitation, a container for unstable images, a model for further action. Here is the formula: Riley and his story. Me and my outrage. You and us. Riley was a friend in college and later served as a nurse at Abu Ghraib prison. This is a container for Riley's digital pictures and fleeting traumatic memories. Images he could not fully secure or expel and entrusted to me.

Art can be a series of acts and challenges. Currently the artwork is an object in your hand—organized, mobile, tactile—a stable site to see information once elusive. The artist can mobilize information by provoking, listening, imagining, organizing and reorganizing. Right now, I am the artist. I want you to see what this war did to Riley.

Pay attention. This experience happens right in your lap. To make it happen, you must read compassionately, then actively. Then the experience happens wherever you take this container and whenever you respond to my invitation.

You and us, yes. Then you and another. This invitation is a model for veterans, families and friends to speak and share openly with each other. The artwork and artist are adaptable; you, the tactical reader, can use this object for your own device, or you can attend to another archive in need of careful attention. This is not a book. It is an object of deployment.

Monica Haller, *Riley and His Story* (Paris, 2009)

95 Armin Linke, *Babylon Museum, Babylon, Iraq, 2002* → p. 67, p. 69, p. 354

96 SHORTHAND FOR REALITY – It is not enough for the newspapers to produce news. People need to appropriate it, to connect it with what they have already seen and heard. The news must make the rounds, circulate, switch distribution channels; there is no short cut, no straight path. Ultimately, reporting means collectively digesting events.

97 COOPERATION – This book was not authored by Armin Linke or by the seven experts in isolation; rather it is a product of their interaction. Although the photographs can be attributed to Armin Linke, the arrangement of the images and the commentary on them—which is what produces a context in the first place—give rise to a second, independent dynamic core. Brecht's idea that there is no spectator, only fellow actors, holds true well beyond the theater. Something in me must be active, must have the option to respond and create relations.

98 Armin Linke: Working collaboratively in a group, in an open and ongoing dialogue, is kind of a therapy, not for myself but for the project. It gives strength to the project. The dialogue is also a way to search for possible points of weakness, and develop the areas where the project could be more robust.

99 Armin Linke, *Bloemenveiling Aalsmeer, flower auction, Aalsmeer, Netherlands, 1998* → p. 121, p. 144, p. 234

100 For the most important form of human thinking is not reason or analysis, not intuition or feeling, but rather narration. All our experiences, our memories, our goals and aspirations, our rationales, vindications, apologies, and excuses—our whole life is organized into a narrative form.

It is not logic, mathematics, or physics that can resolve the uncertainties to which humans are exposed in a social environment. Only stories can supply any kind of reliable compass in the vague world of togetherness, where coalitions regularly shift. This led the US philosopher Walter Fisher to posit a new name for the human species—not Homo sapiens but rather Homo narrans, a narrative being. [...] Fisher was convinced that humans experience themselves and their surroundings not so much by applying reason or impartial observation as by narrating plausible stories.

Werner Siefer, *Der Erzählinstinkt: Warum das Gehirn in Geschichten denkt* (Munich, 2015)

101 You talk as if you knew me.

102 This is what fools people: a man is always a teller of tales,
he lives surrounded by his stories and the stories of others,
he sees everything that happens to him through them;
and he tries to live his own life as if he were telling a story.

Jean-Paul Satre, *La Nausée* (Paris, 1938)

103 Armin Linke, *BNP Paribas, headquarters, trading floor, Paris, France, 2012* → p. 125, p. 127, p. 182

104 In this sense, aesthetics is not a peripheral sphere or a separate terrain, but a fundamental realm. In aesthetics, we deal with the way in which our experience is organised by our senses, the forms in which we perceive and think (of) ourselves. If aesthetics is a field, where visibility and invisibility are structured, then where aesthetics comes into practice things are not only shown, they are always concealed too. Paradoxically formulated, the sphere of the invisible is also defined. Such a "concealment" is by no means always intentional; it is, rather, particular per se to every articulation because it can only formulate one sentence at a time and therefore no others for precisely this reason.

Olaf Nicolai, "The Communicating Vessels: Aesthetics within Perception, Art, and Politics," *bauhaus – The Bauhaus Dessau Foundation's magazine* 1 (March 2011)

105 Armin Linke: It is also something that you find in this show: the exhibition landscape and the photographic works act like a hypertext so that you can navigate physically in the space, creating relations between images and texts and voices, while giving the public the opportunity to move and decide which narration to relate to.

106 Tell me why.

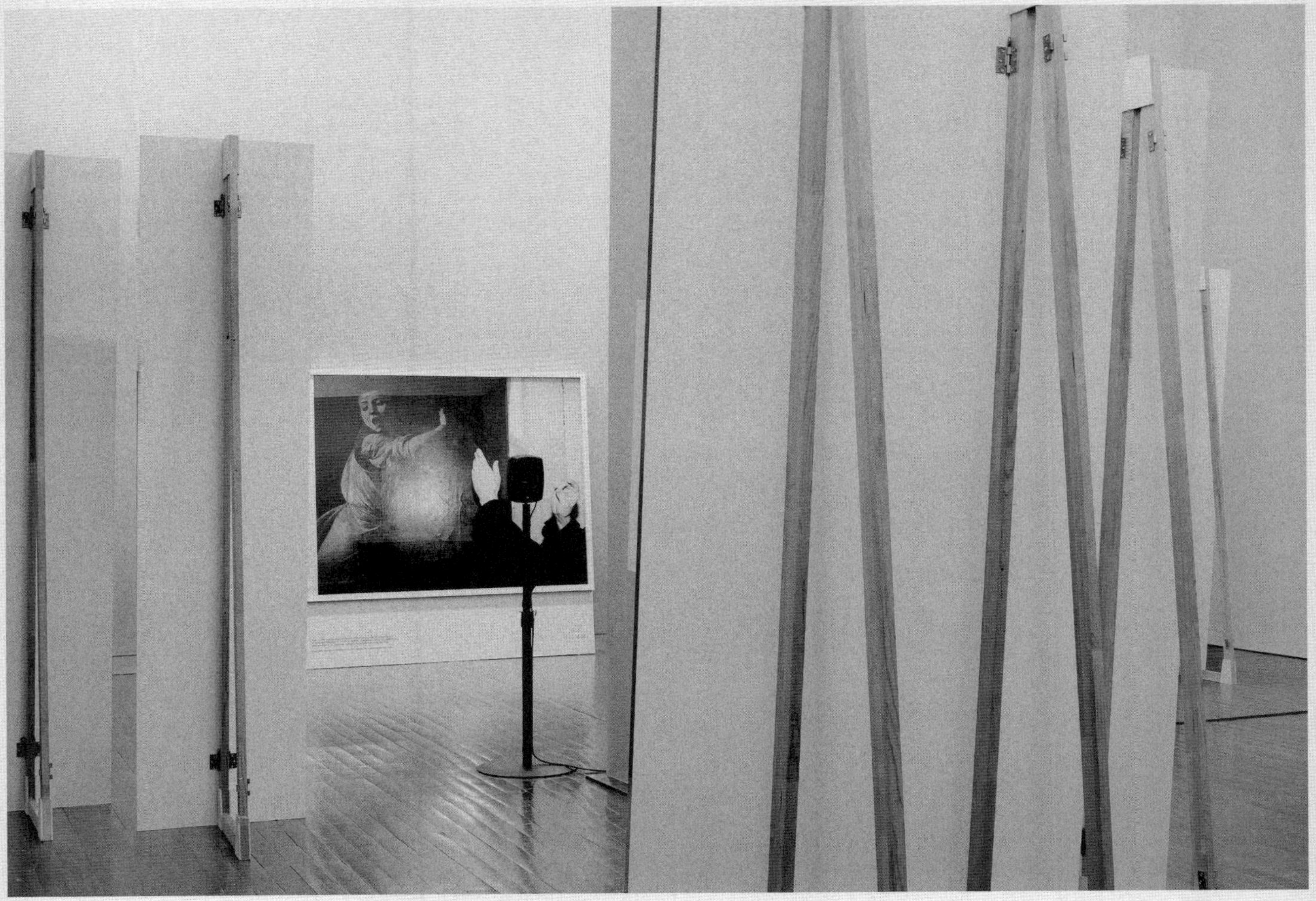

Ludwig Forum for International Art Aachen, Germany,
March 3 – June 18, 2017

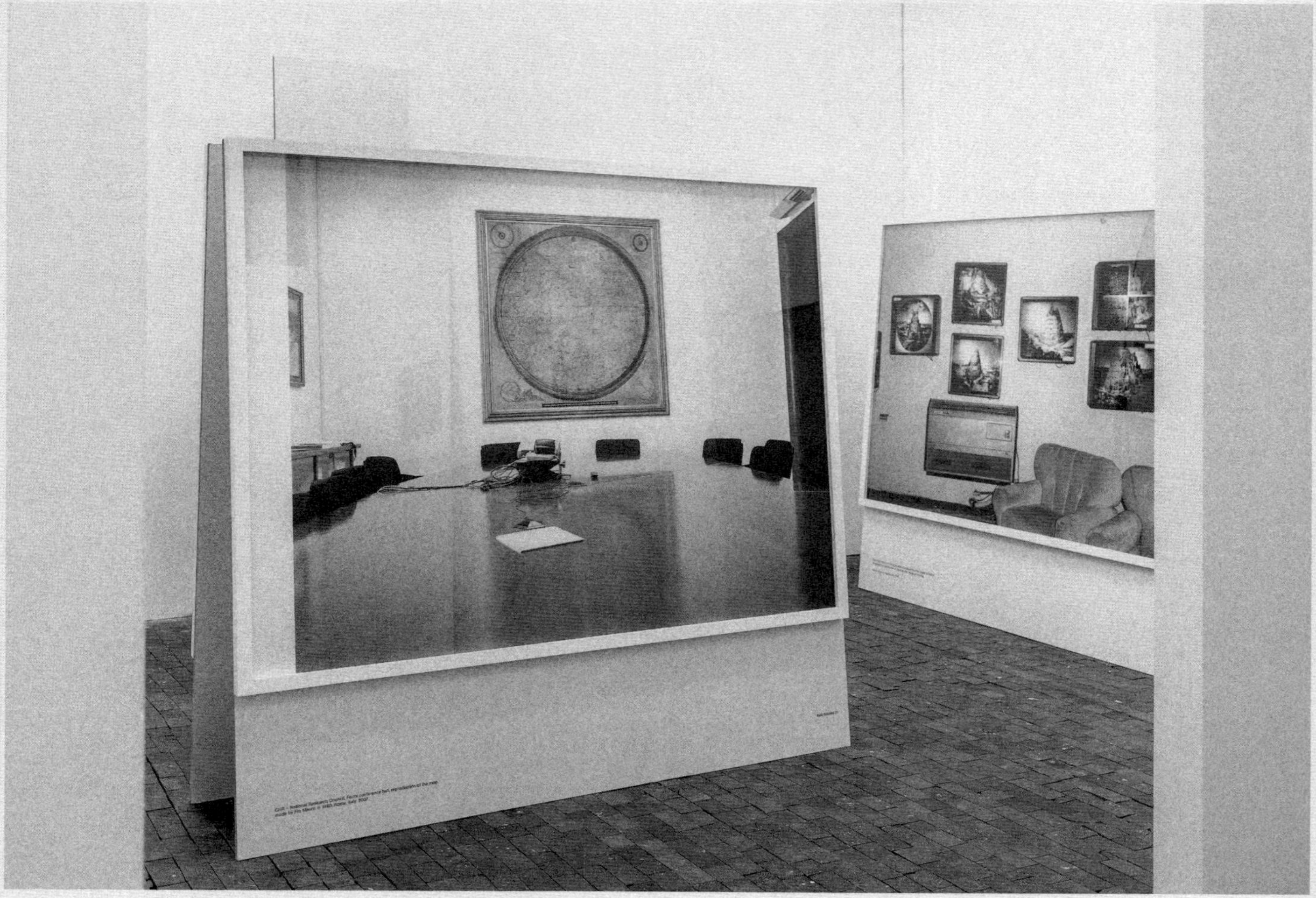

Centre de la photographie Genève, Switzerland,
September 29 – November 1, 2017

107 ARCHIVE PLAY – In the 1920s the writer Gertrude Stein came up with the idea of the "landscape play." Her artistic intention was to imagine theatrical events as a kind of landscape, as a spatial relationship between individual elements, as a constellation that takes on different configurations depending on the viewer's perspective. For Stein it is about defocusing and according equal status to the different parts. In this she was, in principle, merely transferring the artistic logic of her texts to the theater, the principle of the continuous and ongoing present, of syntactic and verbal concatenations that are constantly accentuated in subtle variations and loops. The text that Stein wrote is, in a sense, already a landscape. To an extent that was hitherto unheard of, it liberates the phrase from the sentence, the word from the phrase, and the sound from the contextual meaning. *The Appearance of That Which Cannot Be Seen* is also a form of play, an "archive play," in which the individual photograph is liberated from the context of the exhibition. Here the display, the order of images is not static; it is flexible. Depending on the selection and sequencing of the images, different image landscapes are created, which are constantly rearranged and tested anew at the different exhibition venues.

108 Armin Linke: It was a long process developed with the whole team, as we wanted a system that was as simple as possible that would refer to theater scenography, that could be flexible in designing the space and would not resemble a commercial presentation. We wanted to reduce the display to the simplest structure, incorporating the text and graphic design as part of the installation and not as a comment on the installation.

109 Armin Linke, *Mountain with antennae, Kitakyushu, Japan, 2006* → p. 109, p. 287

110 *vision in motion* is simultaneous grasp. Simultaneous grasp is creative performance—seeing, feeling and thinking in relationship and not as a series of isolated phenomena. It instantaneously integrates and transmutes single elements into a coherent whole. This is valid for physical vision as well as for the abstract.
vision in motion is a synonym for simultaneity and space-time; a means to comprehend the new dimension.
vision in motion is seeing while moving.
vision in motion is seeing moving objects either in reality or in forms of visual representation as in cubism and futurism. In the latter case, the spectator, stimulated by the specific means of rendering, recreates mentally and emotionally the original motion.
vision in motion also signifies planning, the projective dynamics of our visionary faculties.
László Moholy-Nagy, *Vision in Motion* (Chicago, 1947)

111 Armin Linke: I like the reference to theater, as many of the images are somehow a documentary of "real" places, while the structure refers to a temporary and fictional setting; so there is an interesting tension. Many of the subjects of the photos are very large monumental structures, and this creates a nice contrast with the temporality of the display. The exhibition is constructed like a landscape that you can discover and navigate in different ways, or like a hypertext—but instead of moving your eyes over the screen, you use your body in the space to experience the content. If you want to play, you can get lost in it; if you want to study, you can use it as a tool, but it can also be like a radio drama where you just follow the voices.

112 Exhibition play = Landscape in progress

113 Armin Linke: I think that the modular concept of my exhibitions can be directly ascribed to the experience of film editing. The exhibitions in Karlsruhe, in Milan, and thereafter in Aachen and Geneva work with the idea of editing as we know it from film. These exhibitions can be read like storyboards for a film.

114 The more people master and understand this type of "thinking in relationships" the easier it will be to realize social planning and a better living. [...] We are heading toward a kinetic time-spatial existence; toward an awareness of the forces plus their relationships which define all life and of which we had no previous knowledge and for which we have as yet no exact terminology. The affirmation of all these space-time forces involves a reorientation of all our faculties.
László Moholy-Nagy, *Vision in Motion* (Chicago, 1947)

115 Armin Linke, *Occupy Frankfurt, camp in front of the ECB, Frankfurt, Germany, 2012* → p. 113, p. 160, p. 232, p. 233

116 Armin Linke: In general, we are always trying to create different islands of topics, authors, and sound, and we search for the narrative between them. These islands are then the geography of the particular exhibition. The geography changes from venue to venue—each exhibition is unique in that sense. This is the first level of narration. The second level is created by the audience: the spectators move through the space and the different points of attraction that we created, and in this way they can edit their own exhibition through movement. This is what this exhibition is about: we create certain narratives that are precise, but at the same time open.

117 There was a groping for using everything and there was a groping for a continuous present and there was an inevitable beginning of beginning again and again and again. [...]
The only thing that is different from one time to another is what is seen and what is seen depends upon how everybody is doing everything.
Gertrude Stein, *Composition as Explanation* (London, 1926)

118 Armin Linke, *CERN, European Organization for Nuclear Research, computer room, Geneva, Switzerland, 2000* → p. 104

119 Armin Linke: At the beginning of the process, we thought that we would print the pictures directly on the panels. But then we decided on the frames because they also create a kind of aura around the work, and this defines the works not as consumable images or images that are merely informational. It creates a kind of tension, which is really interesting, especially because we show them in art institutions. Maybe if we were to show them in another context, another strategy would be more interesting. We had a lot of discussions about this. Another important point is the temporality of the whole set.

The frame is a kind of module that also permits an involvement with the display. You have this unit that you are able to compose. Then there are, of course, very banal issues. The manual process of printing a photograph is a long one involving a laboratory and a specialist, so you have the frame and the glass to protect this work.

120 Armin Linke, *Sahrawi Republic (SADR Territories), Western Sahara, 2004* → p. 74, p. 75

121 Armin Linke: I use different kinds of cameras, from large-format architecture and landscape cameras to point-and-shoot pocket cameras and also video frames. I have a two-sided format that corresponds to the 50 × 60 cm format (in recent years it was the largest format you could still find industrially cut in a box) and the 150 × 200 cm format, which is more or less the largest format you can print from a photographic paper roll once you cut the border to mount it on aluminum. So the different formats have different diagonals or uses of the frame, and I decided to have these standard frames and adapt the photographs to them, instead of adapting the frame to the photographic dimensions. I treat the photographic paper as a graphic designer would and always push the image to the upper corner or to the right. As I do not cut the white parts that are produced in this practice, I make the image medium, the industrially produced photographic paper, visible. This also creates some disturbance, as sometimes the white area is even larger than the image area, but this effect of *Verfremdung* or distancing is exactly what interests me: I want to show that photography is part of the history of the reproduction technique and has its own industrial history, and that by reading images we do not disconnect them from the history of their production tools and materials.

122 The viewer is seen as a free, responsible being that can move around at will and is simultaneously accompanied by a poetic thought. So the hall is not a dangerous wilderness, but a poetic landscape, where one can move around as one chooses, and yet where one very soon feels that artistic experiences lie in wait everywhere. It generates a sort of counterworld—the pictures we see lead us outside the hall into the spaciousness of the world.

Edgar Reitz, in Michaela Melián, *Rückspiegel* (Leipzig, 2009)

123 The idea now was that one could move around in space, that one could have pictures on all sides, as you might find, for instance, in a Tiepolo church, where there are paintings on the ceiling, the walls, and possibly even the floor. Following this model, entire rooms were to be filled with projected images. [...] Reitz's idea was more of a garden of pictures, where one can walk around and even get lost and then find one's way out again, or like a filmic chamber of mirrors, so that the moment of surprise plays a role spatially. It is an idea he is still thinking about today. These ideas are the starting point for *VariaVision – Unendliche Fahrt*.

Alexander Kluge, in Michaela Melián, *Rückspiegel* (Leipzig, 2009)

124 THE PHOTOGRAPHER AND HIS DOUBLE – In the landscapes and interiors that Armin Linke photographs, we seldom see any human figures. And yet each of his images tells of human activity, of people who are present in these spaces, even when absent. Because the elements of reality are treated as an experimental setup. Like the photographer, we as observers look calmly and with detachment at the activities of a species that we ourselves belong to, a species that has become the most important determinant in our planet's biological, geological, and atmospheric processes—we observe humans in the Anthropocene.

125 Armin Linke: In all of them I tried to look at photography focusing on its anthropological value.

126 Archive play = editing in progress

127 Armin Linke, *Gas pipeline junction, Nadym, Russia, 2011* → p. 221, p. 222, p. 268

128 Armin Linke: I have kind of a continuously updated wish list of subjects, and I will take images as long as I'm curious to learn something. Photography is a great way to have an excuse to enter different worlds and try to experience this world in the field and to interact.

129 The purpose for which a task is done is not identical with the purpose for which it is used. A realization can be used in places other than where it was found.

Bertolt Brecht, "Fatzerdokument" (1929)

Armin Linke's statements are taken from an interview with the curators Ilaria Bonacossa, Philipp Ziegler, and Joerg Bader from summer 2016. It was published in *L'apparenza di ciò che non si vede* (Milan, 2016), the Italian edition of *The Appearance of That Which Cannot Be Seen*. Several passages from an interview that Max Dax conducted with Armin Linke in winter 2017 for *VTph* are also included (83, 86, 89, 113). Jan Wenzel is responsible for the arrangement of the texts and for all unidentified passages.

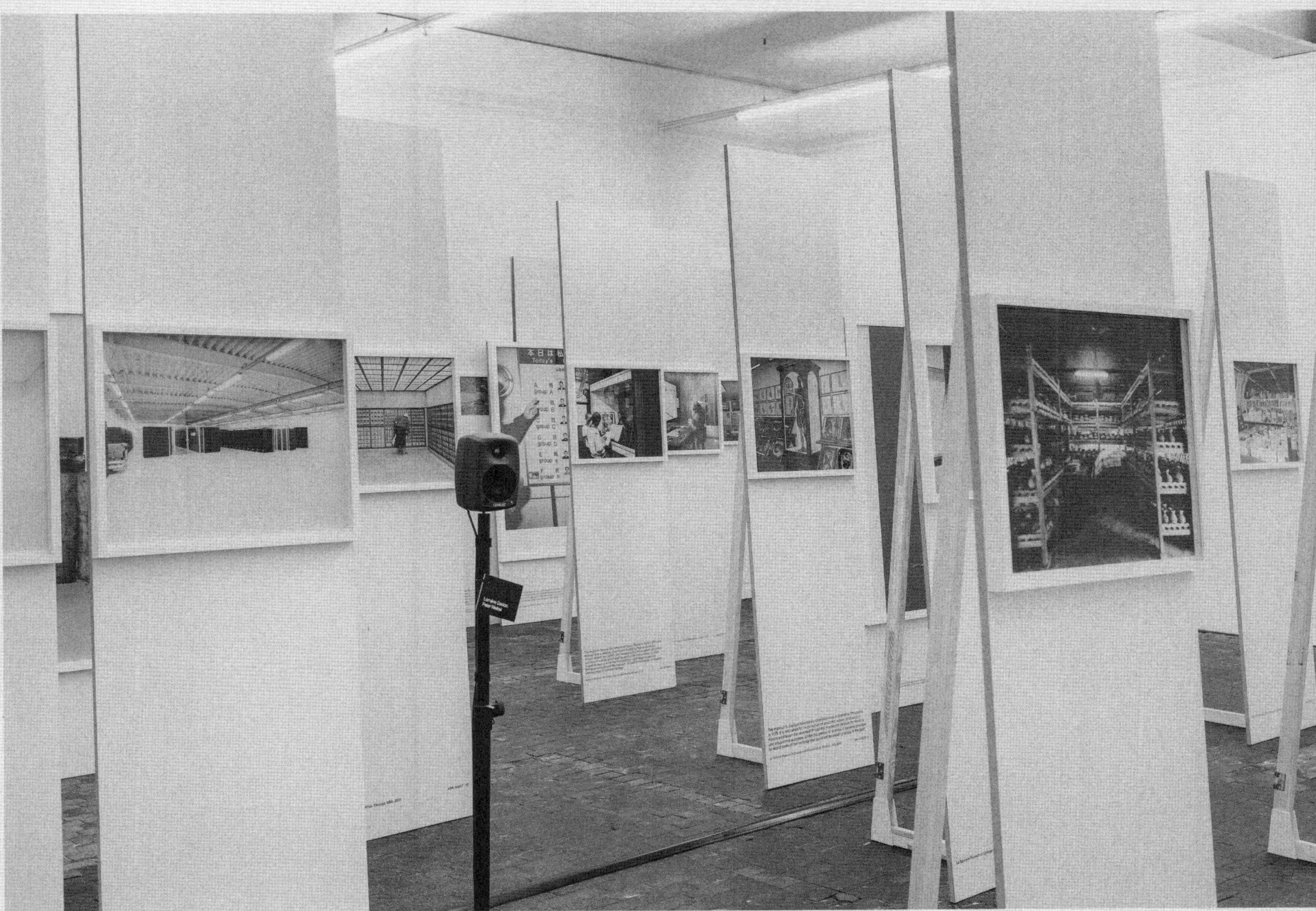

Centre de la photographie Genève, Switzerland,
September 29 – November 1, 2017

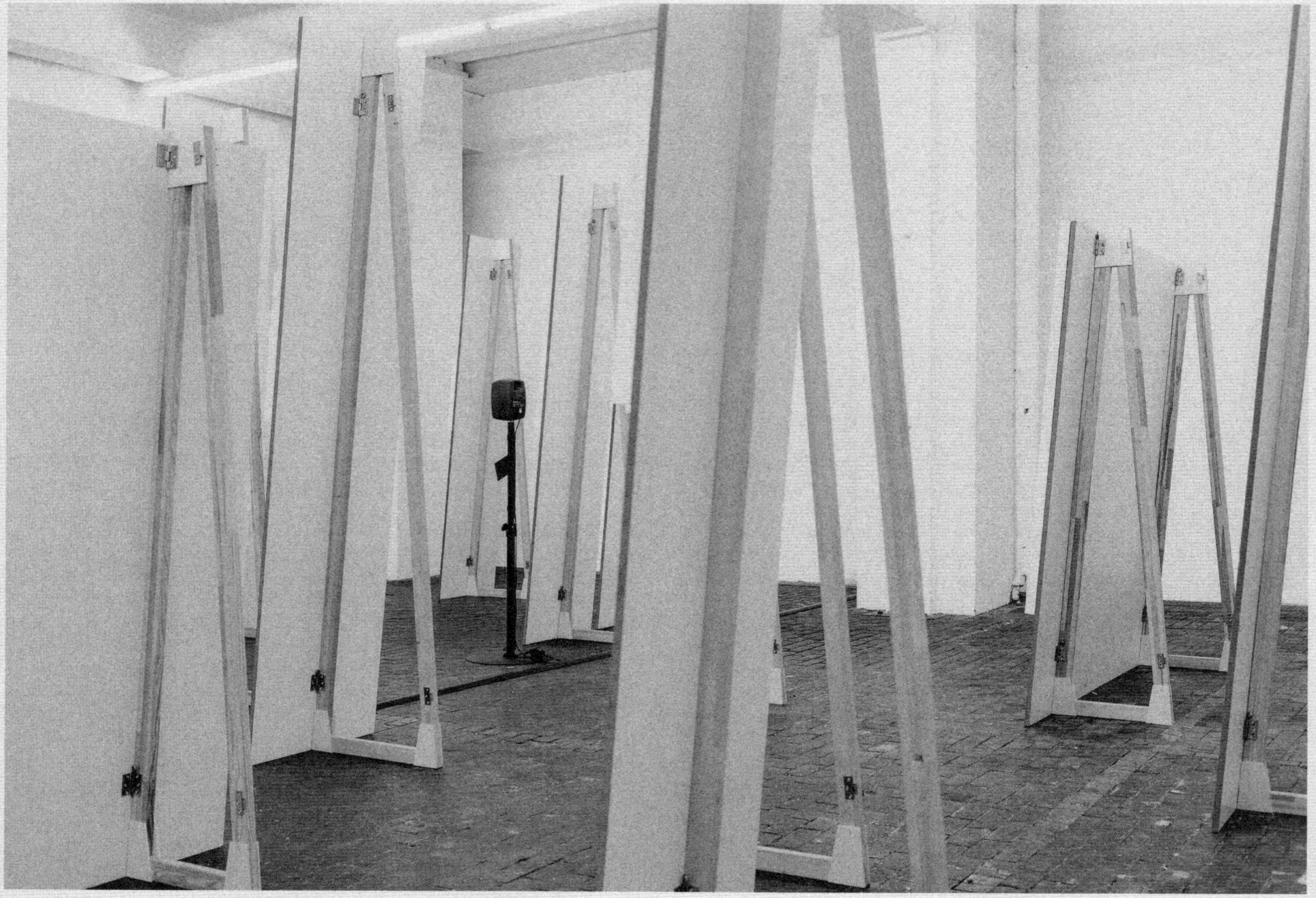

Centre de la photographie Genève, Switzerland,
September 29 – November 1, 2017

Ariella Azoulay (Tel Aviv, 1962) is a professor of modern culture and media at the Department of Comparative Literature, Brown University, independent curator and filmmaker. Her publications include *The Civil Contract of Photography* (2008). Director of documentary films, such as *Civil Alliances, Palestine, 47–48* (2012) and *The Food Chain* (2004).

Lorraine Daston (East Lansing, 1951) is director at the Max Planck Institute for the History of Science, Berlin, Permanent Fellow of the Wissenschaftskolleg zu Berlin, and Visiting Professor in the Committee on Social Thought at the University of Chicago. Her recent publications include *Histories of Scientific Observation* (co-edited with Elizabeth Lunbeck, 2011), and *How Reason Almost Lost Its Mind: The Strange Career of Cold War Rationality* (with Paul Erikson et al., 2014).

Franco Farinelli (Ortona, 1948) is currently head of the Department of Philosophy and Communication Studies of Bologna University, where he teaches geography. Before he taught in Stockholm, Geneva, Los Angeles (UCLA), Berkeley, and in Paris at the Sorbonne and École normale supérieure. His last book is *Blinding Polyphemus: Geography and the Models of the World* (2016).

Bruno Latour (Beaune, 1947) is a French sociologist and philosopher. He is one of the founders of Actor-Network Theory (ANT), former director of the Sciences Po Médialab and professor-at-large at Cornell University. His recent publications include *An Inquiry into Modes of Existence: An Anthropology of the Moderns* (2013), and the accompanying website *modesofexistence.org* as well as *Facing Gaia* (2017).

Peter Weibel (Odessa, 1944) is an Austrian artist, curator, and media theorist. He is Chairman and CEO of ZKM | Center for Art and Media Karlsruhe and professor of media theory at the University of Applied Arts Vienna. He was head of the digital arts laboratory at the Media Department of New York University in Buffalo and founding director of the Institute of New Media at the Städelschule in Frankfurt am Main.

Mark Wigley (Palmerston North, 1956) is an architectural theorist, author, and curator from New Zealand. From 2004 to 2014 he was dean of the Columbia University Graduate School of Architecture, Planning and Preservation, New York.

Jan Zalasiewicz (Manchester, 1954) is professor of palaeobiology at the University of Leicester and chairs the Anthropocene Working Group of the International Commission on Stratigraphy. He studies fossil ecosystems and environments across over half a billion years of geological time. His writings include the books *The Earth After Us* (2008), *The Planet in a Pebble* (2010), *The Goldilocks Planet* (2012), and *Ocean Worlds* (2014).

Armin Linke (Milan, 1966) is a photographer and filmmaker. He combines a range of contemporary image-processing technologies in order to blur the borders between fiction and reality and challenges the conventions of photographic practice, whereby the questions of how photography is installed and displayed become increasingly important. He was Research Affiliate at MIT Visual Arts Program Cambridge, guest professor at the IUAV Arts and Design University in Venice and professor for photography at the University of Arts and Design Karlsruhe (HfG).

Thanks to:
Peter Weibel, Philipp Ziegler, Jens Lutz, Anne Däuper, Anett Holzheid, Marianne Meister – ZKM | Center for Art and Media Karlsruhe; Ilaria Bonacossa, Diego Sileo, Francesca La Placa, Christina Schenk – PAC Padiglione d'Arte Contemporanea, Milan; Andreas Beitin, Annette Lagler – Ludwig Forum for International Art Aachen; Joerg Bader, Alexandra Theiler, Zoé Keller, Carlo Vanni, Vanessa Bianchini, Jérémy Chevalier, Jaime de Oliveira – Centre de la photographie Genève; Jan Wenzel – Spector Books; Benedetta Spalletti – Vistamare, Pescara; BAK, Utrecht; Centre de recherche et de restauration des musées de France (C2RMF); Haus der Kulturen der Welt, Berlin; Karlsruhe University of Arts and Design (HfG); Genelec

Noura Al-Sayeh, Aristeidis Antonas, Rita Antonioli, Elina Axioti, Brada Barassi, Ute Meta Bauer, Estelle Blaschke, Stefano Boeri, Yann Bongiovanni, Ornella Bossi, Laura Bossi, Leo Bossi, Tassilli Calatroni, Clemente Capello, Francisco Careri, Michael Clegg, Paola Clerico, Paolo Daffara, Maria Vittoria Dalla Cia, Max Dax, Chris Dercon, Giulio Di Gropello, Giulia Di Lenarda, Anselm Franke, Jacopo Gardella, Silvia Geronimi, Marco Geronimi, Andrea Ghellere, Irene Giardina, Bruna Ginammi, Gabriele Giussani, Sylvain Gouraud, Stefano Graziani, Joseph Grima, Martin Guinard, Francesca von Habsburg, Clive Hamilton, Dorothea Heinz, Sarah Herda, Sandi Hilal, Adrianne Joergensen, Lena Kiessler, Mikiko Kikuta, Aglaia Konrad, Margret Köll, Wilfried Kühn, Johannes Kühn, Christophe Leclercq, Urs Lehni, Ingeborg Linke, Victoria Linke, Norbert Linke, Luigia Lonardelli, Simona Malvezzi, Amedeo Martegani, Anna Mattirolo, Francesco Mattuzzi, Irmi Maunu-Kocian, Marco Mazzucconi, Doreen Mende, Matteo Mesca, Lara Mikula, Akiko Miyake, Maria Nadotti, Antonio Negri, Hans Ulrich Obrist, Sandra Oehy, Valerie Oleynik, John Palmesino, Alessandro Petti, Cloe Piccoli, Steve Piccolo, Bartolomeo Pietromarchi, Valerie Pihet, Michele Pizzi, Olaf Quantius, Donato Ricci, Francesco Ricci, Anna Rimoldi, Renato Rinaldi, Lorenzo Romito, Margit Rosen, Ann-Sofi Rönnskog, Simone Salvucci, Saskia Sassen, Bernd Scherer, Axel Schöpa, Heike Schuppelius, Giovanna Silva, Faulo Tavares, Philip Ursprung, Ana Vallés Blasco, Vanessa Vasic-Janekovic, Angela Vettese, Eyal Weizman, Rebecca Wilton, Tobias Wootton, Piero Zanini, Paola Zatti, Giulia Zorzi-Micamera

This publication is released in conjunction with the exhibition *Armin Linke. The Appearance of That Which Cannot Be Seen*

Produced by ZKM | Center for Art and Media Karlsruhe and PAC Padiglione d'Arte Contemporanea, Milan

In cooperation with Ludwig Forum for International Art Aachen and Centre de la photographie Genève

zkm karlsruhe

ZKM | Center for Art and Media Karlsruhe, as part of GLOBALE,
Part 1: Sep. 5, 2015 – Jan. 31, 2016
Part 2: Apr. 16 – Aug. 21, 2016
Curated by Philipp Ziegler
Concept GLOBALE: Peter Weibel

PAC Padiglione d'Arte Contemporanea

PAC Padiglione d'Arte Contemporanea, Milan
Oct. 16, 2016 – Jan. 1, 2017
Curated by Ilaria Bonacossa and Philipp Ziegler

Ludwig Forum Aachen

Ludwig Forum for International Art Aachen
Mar. 23 – Jun. 18, 2017
Curated by Andreas Beitin and Annette Lagler

CENTRE DE LA PHOTOGRAPHIE GENÈVE

Centre de la photographie Genève
Sep. 29 – Nov. 1, 2017
Curated by Joerg Bader and Philipp Ziegler

The Centre de la photographie Genève is supported by the Ville de Genève

Exhibition
Photography: Armin Linke
Concept and design: Armin Linke, Jan Kiesswetter, Mevis & van Deursen, Alina Schmuch, exhibition architecture together with Martha Schwindling
Sound design: Giuseppe Ielasi, Nicola Ratti
Woodwork: Thomas Busch, Martha Schwindling
Translations: Martina Kempter, Herwig Engelmann
Photographic prints: Francesco Grandati, Colorzenith srl
Scans: Ulrike Vohrer, Annette Berr, d'mage
Frames: Mauro Telo, Telo Cornici

Studio Armin Linke:
Agostino Artese, Giulia Bruno, Bianca Fasiolo, Laura Fiorio, Ferial Nadja Karrasch, Sarah Poppel, Elisa Scaramuzzino, Katalin Simon, Alberto Stievanin, Arianna Visani
Database programming: Luigi Corte Rappis, Nicholas De Leo

With additional support by

Graham Foundation

GOETHE INSTITUT

The participation of Lorraine Daston was financed with the support of the project *Performing Architecture* by the Goethe-Institut and the Federal Foreign Office Berlin in collaboration with the ETH Zurich.

Publication
Editors: Joerg Bader, Andreas Beitin, Philipp Ziegler
Photography: Armin Linke
Concept, editing and graphic design: Jan Kiesswetter, Mevis & van Deursen, Alina Schmuch
Texts: Ariella Azoulay, Lorraine Daston, Franco Farinelli, Bruno Latour, Peter Weibel, Jan Wenzel, Mark Wigley, Jan Zalasiewicz
Transcription: Hannes Herold
Translations: Jon Kear, Simon Cowper
Copy editing: Simon Cowper
Image editing: Carsten Humme
Printing and binding: DZA Druckerei zu Altenburg

Published by Spector Books, Leipzig 2017
www.spectorbooks.com

First edition
Printed in Gemany
ISBN 978-3-95905-070-8

Distribution
Germany, Austria: GVA, Gemeinsame Verlagsauslieferung Göttingen GmbH & Co. KG, www.gva-verlage.de
Switzerland: AVA Verlagsauslieferung AG, www.ava.ch
France, Belgium: Interart Paris, www.interart.fr
UK: Central Books Ltd, www.centralbooks.com
USA, Canada, Central and South America, Africa, Asia: ARTBOOK | D.A.P., www.artbook.com
South Korea: The Book Society, www.thebooksociety.org
Australia, New Zealand: Perimeter Distribution, www.perimeterdistribution.com

Funded by

STIFTUNG**KUNSTFONDS**